# Sri Lanka at the Crossroads of History

# Sri Lanka at the Crossroads of History

Edited by Zoltán Biedermann and
Alan Strathern

UCLPRESS

First published in 2017 by
UCL Press
University College London
Gower Street
London WC1E 6BT

Available to download free: www.ucl.ac.uk/ucl-press



A CIP catalogue record for this book is available from The British Library.



ISBN: 978-1-911307-83-9 (Hbk.)
ISBN: 978-1-911307-84-6 (Pbk.)
ISBN: 978-1-911307-82-2 (PDF)
ISBN: 978-1-911307-81-5 (epub)
ISBN: 978-1-911307-80-8 (mobi)
ISBN: 978-1-911307-78-5 (html)
DOI: https://doi.org/10.14324/111.9781911307822

# Acknowledgements

The contents of this volume have emerged from a series of meetings, workshops and seminar panels organized by the American Institute of Sri Lankan Studies (AISLS) in Colombo, Madison, Boston and London between 2009 and 2012, and a large conference held at the Centre for Research in the Arts, Social Sciences and Humanities (CRASSH) in Cambridge in June 2011, organized by Sujit Sivasundaram and Alan Strathern with the support of the Trevelyan Fund, AISLS and CRASSH. Other organizations that supported meetings and encounters with the wider public include the London School of Economics, the Portuguese Centre for Global History (CHAM/NOVA) in Lisbon, the International Centre for Ethnic Studies (ICES) in Colombo and the Sri Lanka Foundation Institute. The meetings and workshops included papers from the modern period, but it has been decided to confine this volume to contributions on the period before 1850.

We would like to reserve our biggest thanks for John Rogers, US Director of AISLS. Without his determination to nurture a new generation of scholars of Lankan history, this book simply would not exist. John has acted as a tremendously generous guide and advisor for many younger scholars coming through the ranks. Animating all the initiatives organized through AISLS was an insistence that the island's past be brought into the main currents of the new global history and that foreign and locally based scholarship should be brought into a productive dialogue. Charles Hallisey was president of AISLS for much of this period and has been an important interlocutor, especially since too many of his thoughts resonating throughout this volume are not yet in print. Jonathan Spencer and Dennis McGilvray have given much valued support during their presidential terms at AISLS. Other established scholars whose encouragement has been important include Anne Blackburn, Chandra Richard de Silva and Nira Wickramasinghe. From a distance, Harshana Rambukwella, Jonathan Walters, John Clifford Holt, Jorge Flores, Nirmal Dewasiri, Ronit Ricci and Sandagomi Coperahewa have also all, in one way or another, accompanied the growth of this volume. Some Sri Lanka scholars, including Andrew Jarvis, Anna Winterbottom, Cenan Pirani and Nadeera Senerivatne, while not contributing to this volume, are currently completing projects that have fed into this book in various ways. The volume has benefited greatly from the advice and encouragement of two external readers, as well as the professionalism and support of Lara Speicher and Chris Penfold at UCL Press, and of Sarah Rendell and Victoria Chow on the production team. We would also like to register our gratitude to the Jeffrey Fund at Brasenose College, for providing financial support for the use of images, to Justin Henry, for checking our use of diacritics throughout the volume, and to Deborah Philip for her hard work in compiling the bibliographies.

Alan Strathern would like to thank Samanthi Dissanayake, Aril Strathern and Leela Strathern for their love and forbearance, and Nilmini Dissanayake for her constant help with Sinhala and things Sri Lankan. Zoltán Biedermann would like to thank Eva Nieto McAvoy and Hannah Biedermann Nieto for the many days and weeks of family life sacrificed to the study of a distant island – albeit one populated by elephants, which made the endeavour more appealing. The editors both wish to remember Ira Unamboowe, Executive Director of the Colombo centre of AISLS from 2004 until her untimely death in 2015. Her warmth, intelligence, generosity and fine sense of humour helped countless scholars from around the world through challenging times in Sri Lanka, and shall remain with us for many more years to come.

# Contents

# List of figures

# Notes on contributors

**Stephen C. Berkwitz** is Professor and Department Head of Religious Studies at Missouri State University. He is the author of *Buddhist Poetry and Colonialism: Alagiyavanna and the Portuguese in Sri Lanka* (Oxford University Press, 2013) and other publications on Buddhist literature and culture in Sri Lanka. His current research interests include notions of Buddhist kingship and medieval writings on the Bōdhi tree.

**Zoltán Biedermann** is Head of Spanish, Portuguese and Latin American Studies at University College London. He is the author of *The Portuguese in Sri Lanka and South India* (Harrassowitz, 2014), *Soqotra: Geschichte einer christlichen Insel* (Harrassowitz, 2007), the *Historical Atlas of the Persian Gulf* (Brepols, 2007), and numerous articles and book chapters on the history of European expansion and knowledge exchange in the Indian Ocean region. He is currently finishing a monograph on the Portuguese involvement in Sri Lanka before 1600.

**Robin Coningham** holds the 2014 UNESCO Chair in Archaeological Ethics and Practice in Cultural Heritage at Durham University, UK. Conducting fieldwork across South and Central Asia in Bangladesh, Nepal, Iran and Pakistan, his investigations in Sri Lanka at Trench ASW2 in Anurādhapura have refined early historic chronologies and understandings of the region's second urbanization, the genesis of Indian Ocean trade and the archaeology of early Buddhism. His recent fieldwork in Sri Lanka was as co-Director of the Arts and Humanities Research Council (UK)-funded Anurādhapura Project. He also directs the Polonnaruva Archaeological and Anthropological Research Project with Professor Prishanta Gunawardhana.

**Rebecca R. Darley** is Lecturer in Medieval History at Birkbeck, University of London. She completed her PhD on 'Indo-Byzantine Exchange, 4th–7th Centuries: A Global History' at the University of Birmingham, UK, in 2014 and is currently converting this into a monograph on the role of long-distance trade in the western Indian Ocean in Late Antiquity. She has published articles and book chapters on the discovery and use of Roman and Byzantine coins in South India and the role of money in constructing social and political identity in the early Middle Ages.

**Christopher Davis** is a UNESCO Chair Research Associate in the Department of Archaeology, Durham University, UK. He completed his Arts and Humanities Council (UK)-sponsored PhD at Durham, investigating the economic and social roles of Buddhist monastic institutions in the hinterland of Anurādhapura through an analysis of archaeological, epigraphic and ethnographic evidence. He has participated in archaeological projects in Nepal, Bangladesh, Iran and Cambodia and was a member of the Anurādhapura (Sri Lanka) Project as well as the current Polonnaruva Archaeological and Anthropological Research Project.

**Kate J. Ekama** is a Doctoral Researcher in History at Leiden University within the NWO-funded project 'Challenging Monopolies, Building Global Empires in the Early Modern Period'. She researches slavery under the Dutch East India Company in the Indian Ocean World, focusing on Sri Lanka and the Cape. Her MA thesis was entitled 'Slavery in Dutch Colombo: A Social History' (Leiden University, 2012) and she has published on slave runaways from the VOC Cape. She is currently examining manumission of slaves and related litigation in eighteenth-century Colombo.

**Tilman Frasch** is Reader in Asian History at Manchester Metropolitan University. Specializing in Myanmar history and Theravāda Buddhist Studies, he has published several articles on early Sri Lankan history, the Buddhist chronicles and the Theravāda Buddhist ecumene during the first two millennia of the Buddhist calendar.

**Alastair Gornall** gained his PhD in South Asian Studies from the University of Cambridge in 2012. He is currently an Assistant Professor in the Humanities at the Singapore University of Technology and Design and a Research Associate at SOAS, University of London. His research focuses on the intellectual and cultural history of Buddhism in premodern and modern South and Southeast Asia. He is in the final stages of writing a book on the social history of Pāli literature in late medieval Sri Lanka.

**Prishanta Gunawardhana** is the Director-General of the Central Cultural Fund, Ministry of Education, Government of Sri Lanka, and is Professor of Archaeology at the University of Kelaniya, as well as being a board member of the Sri Lanka Council of Archaeologists. He has written widely on the archaeology of Sri Lanka in more than fifty articles, chapters and books, including *Buddhist Monasteries Towards Urbanism in Southern Sri Lanka* (2009). He was a Co-Director of the Arts and Humanities Research Council (UK)-funded hinterland survey around Anurādhapura, and is Co-Director of the Polonnaruva Archaeological and Anthropological Research Project.

**Justin Henry** is a PhD Candidate in the History of Religions at the University of Chicago Divinity School. He is the recipient of a Robert H. N. Ho Family Foundation Fellowship in Buddhist Studies, and currently teaches in the Department of Theology at Loyola University Chicago. He has spent several years in Sri Lanka studying Pāli, Sinhala and Tamil religious literature, and in 2008–9 was Visiting Research Fellow in the Department of Linguistics at Kelaniya University.

**Mark Manuel** is a UNESCO Chair Research Fellow in the Department of Archaeology, Durham University, UK. He has worked extensively in India, Sri Lanka, Nepal and Bangladesh, as well as in Iran and Egypt. As a landscape archaeologist, he focuses on the relationship between urban and non-urban communities, and how cultural landscapes develop. He has recorded hundreds of new sites and has developed a system of archaeological risk mapping to identify heritage that is at most risk from modern development. He worked extensively on the Anurādhapura (Sri Lanka) Project and is a Field Director on the Polonnaruva Archaeological and Anthropological Research Project.

**Sujatha Arundathi Meegama** is Assistant Professor at the School of Art, Design, and Media, Nanyang Technological University, Singapore. She received her MA in East Asian Studies from Stanford University and her PhD in History of Art from the University of California, Berkeley. She is the author of several forthcoming articles that question the simplistic oppositional binaries of South Indian versus Sri Lankan, Hindu versus Buddhist, and Dravidian versus Sinhalese art. She is currently preparing a book under the working title of *Connected Temples: Patrons, Artisans, and Deities of Buddhist and Hindu Temples in Sri Lanka*.

**Gananath Obeyesekere** is Emeritus Professor of Anthropology at Princeton University. He is the author of eight books and more than a hundred articles, some in Japanese, Turkish, Polish and Sinhala, published during his long intellectual career. Among his many awards is the Thomas Huxley Memorial Medal of the Royal Anthropological Institute (2003) and the Lifetime Achievement Award of the Society for Psychological Anthropology (2011). His most recent published work is entitled *The Awakened Ones: Phenomenology of Visionary Experience* (Columbia University Press, 2012). He is now engaged in a new book on the last king of Sri Lanka deposed by the British in 1815 with the title *The Doomed King: A Requiem for Sri Vikrama Rajasinha*.

**Alicia Schrikker** is Assistant Professor at the Institute for History, Leiden University. She is the author of *Dutch and British Colonial Intervention in Sri Lanka, 1780–1815* (Brill, 2007). Her work focuses on colonial relations in the eighteenth- and nineteenth-century Indian Ocean world. She has published various articles on colonial disaster management in Indonesia and colonial legal practice in Sri Lanka.

**Sujit Sivasundaram** is Reader in World History at the University of Cambridge, Fellow in History at Gonville and Caius College and Co-Editor of *The Historical Journal*. His recent book on Sri Lanka is *Islanded: Britain, Sri Lanka and the Bounds of an Indian Ocean Colony* (University of Chicago Press, 2013). His work on Sri Lanka has appeared in journals including *The American Historical Review* and *Past and Present*, and he is currently working on a book on the age of revolutions in the Indian and Pacific Oceans.

**Alan Strathern** is an Associate Professor of History at the University of Oxford and Tutor and Fellow in History at Brasenose College. He is the author of *Kingship and Conversion in Sixteenth-Century Sri Lanka: Portuguese Imperialism in a Buddhist Land* (Cambridge University Press, 2007), and numerous journal articles and book chapters. He is currently writing a comparative analysis of ruler conversions to monotheism in world history, with case studies including Central Africa, Oceania, Japan and Thailand.

**Fig. 0.1** A Sri Lankan Catholic dressed up as a Roman legionnaire at a Passion Play, Negombo, mid-1980s, photograph by Dominic Sansoni.

# Introduction: Querying the cosmopolitan in Sri Lankan and Indian Ocean history

*Alan Strathern and Zoltán Biedermann*

A young man, proudly dressed up as a Roman legionary, has lowered his gaze to observe us – with a mix of wariness, curiosity and defiance, it seems (Figure 0.1). He is a part of a Catholic Passion play performed in the town of Negombo on Sri Lanka's west coast. The wooden sword in his right hand is raised, the helmet and armour shine assertively even under the cloudy sky. Behind the man is a statue of Christ, hands tied, the symbol of a religion brought to Sri Lanka during one of the many moments of change triggered by more or less violent contacts established across the sea. There is in this single picture a multitude of worlds – an indication of the capability of Lankan society to adopt the foreign, but also to appropriate it, digest it, reinvent it and, if necessary, defy it. To throw light on the deeper history of such ambiguities is the main objective of this book.

The most striking development in history writing of the past decade or two has been the rise of world history, and the most common way of doing world history has been to pursue 'connections' – the more unexpected the better. Societies and regions that were once studied independently are now increasingly being placed within flows of influence and conjunctures that extend across much larger geographies. If all historians write with one eye on the present, then evidently we feel globalization to be the essence of our present condition and the crucible of our history. Global connections are increasingly what we look into the even quite distant past to find.

Perhaps the region of the world in which premodern connectedness has been most gloriously apparent is that delimited by the Indian Ocean. In the port cities that emerged along its coastlines, from Zanzibar to Malacca through Aden, Kochi, Colombo and Kolkata, distant connections and cosmopolitan practices across linguistic and religious barriers were often simply a fact of life. Well before the arrival of the first European interlopers, a multitude of different peoples engaged in exploits of long-distance travel, trade and pilgrimage, and it was not only ports but also vast areas of the Asian mainland that interacted across the waters. Sri Lanka sits exactly at the centre of the Indian Ocean: an excellent laboratory, one might think, in which to test any ideas about the connected and the cosmopolitan. But it has barely been visible in the resurgence of world history. The primary purpose of this book is to begin the process of introducing Lankan material into the mainstream of these recent debates, which shall in turn help to reinvigorate the study of the history of the island itself.

If no man is an island according to the saying, historians are likely to add that no island is an island either. Islands are not by nature condemned to isolation. Before modern technologies suddenly speeded up land-based travel, the seas were often less a barrier to travel and communication than a vehicle for it. This placed many an island in a privileged position, and the navigational routes that connect Sri Lanka with East Africa, the Middle East and Southeast Asia are held to be among the oldest in the world. At the same time, the history of the island is one of continuous dialogue – and sometimes argument – with the mainland it almost touches but for the few miles of the Palk straits. One might say the same for those other large islands or archipelagos moored off the landmass of Eurasia: the British Isles and Japan. Each of these was profoundly shaped by waves of influence and immigration from the mainland and yet each too has a history of genuine insularity and separation from the world.

For interconnectedness and exposure to maritime trade do not in and by themselves produce cosmopolitanism. Long-distance connections may propel the circulation of goods, people and ideas, but they can by no means guarantee that those are absorbed into local cultures without also being detached from the wider world and made into something that is soon perceived as purely local. The possession of foreign artefacts, and even the mimicking of certain imported habits can go hand-in-hand with profoundly parochial attitudes. As Ulf Hannerz put it, cosmopolitanism involves 'an openness toward divergent cultural experiences [...] but not simply as a matter of appreciation'.[1] The tracing of connections may ultimately be a superficial exercise unless we achieve some deeper insights into how societies handle them.

We have therefore invited authors to reflect in detail on the mechanisms by which the supra-local was perceived, received and effected in Sri Lanka. What social and political forces have governed the recognition of the new as 'foreign', and determined whether it faced rejection, addition, adaptation, fusion or complete transformation? How do these logics operate over time (how does the exogenous become the indigenous)? Can objects themselves speak of the cosmopolitan or its opposites? We may know that Roman coins were dropped on Lankan soil 2,000 years ago, or that South Indian elements were present in medieval Buddhist architecture, or that Catholicism struck roots in the southwest of the island in the early modern period, or that Kandyan kingship borrowed artefacts and ideas from various other cultures. But what did – and what do – these things signify? For whose past exactly are they relevant, and in what ways? As Nicholas Thomas has noted about the local appropriation of European objects in the Pacific, 'to say that black bottles were given does not tell us what was received'.[2] It is, then, to further our understanding of how Sri Lanka received and participated in the foreign, and ultimately to identify the local conditions that support or undermine the 'cosmopolitan', that we have put together this book.

## The problem of 'cosmopolitanism'

Most definitions of cosmopolitanism turn on a transcendence of the local and the parochial in preference for overarching entities such as 'humanity' or 'the world'.[3] The cosmopolitan perspective exposes the arbitrariness of political and cultural boundaries, positing that the sole naturally given aspect binding people together is the fact that they are human. From the abundance of recent literature dedicated to it, one is led to conclude that 'cosmopolitanism' usually represents an object of desire, a programmatic viewpoint creating variations on the Kantian theme that postulates the entire human species as the only defensible moral category.[4] In the fields of philosophy, sociology and political science it is often used as an essentially normative term and is rarely held up even by its advocates as a precise concept.[5] Most of us will be sympathetic to Diogenes' much-cited desire to be a 'citizen of the world'.[6] Prasenjit Duara defines cosmopolitanism as 'the idea that all humans belong non-exclusively to a single community', which brings it close to other forms of universalism such as the Kantian or the Christian, but also notes that other theorists regard it as less impositional 'because it is passed on *practices* of common living and belonging in the world'.[7] This tension in the term between a potentially bullying universalism and a habitus of pragmatic tolerance returns repeatedly in attempts to define and use the concept, as we shall see.

Yet for historians the fight will inevitably unfold on two fronts, not just one. On the one hand, we face the danger of Sri Lanka being idealized as a neatly delimited realm of organically grown, unbroken ethnic and religious identity coinciding with Sinhalaness and Theravada Buddhism – a community that sees itself as having survived precisely because it has repelled the forces of the foreign. To resist this is to call upon tendencies that have become common sense in scholarship for some time. Anthropologists have been insisting for generations on the undesirability of approaching any given culture or community as a simple organic whole, and geographers have been equally critical of any aprioristic approaches to naturally distinguishable spatial units such as landscapes, islands or continents. On the other hand, however, there is also a risk of romanticizing Sri Lanka as a wide-open Indian Ocean isle that only stiffened into something more intransigent when it came under the yoke of European imperialism and its heir, global capitalism.[8]

The present volume sits between the two extremes. The series of conferences, lectures and workshops from which it has emerged built emphatically on the perceived necessity of throwing light on the cosmopolitan in Sri Lanka's past. Yet we have also asked our contributors to be alert to what can be at times an excessive tendency to reinvent the premodern past as the perfect reverse of modern discontents: cosmopolitanism instead of nationalism, tolerance instead of bigotry, religious fluidity instead of boundary insistence.

There is, in addition to the problems deriving from the normative nature of many theories of cosmopolitanism, also a more concrete and methodologically vexed issue for historians of the premodern world in particular. The cosmopolitan seems to have acquired significance as a silver lining beneath the dark clouds of modernity: if the latter brought the awful categories of race, ethnicity and nation, it also brought with it melting pots, global communications and expanded horizons. For the term to really make sense it has to shine against the foil of an assumed significance of locality, and easily the most domineering notions of inherently significant locality have been generated by the nation-state.[9] In short, much of what makes the term 'cosmopolitan' meaningful is the promise it holds to liberate from the claims of the nation – but of course the nation itself is a product of a relatively recent past. So, what do we do when it comes to the times preceding the invention of the nation-state? What are the fundamental units against which the cosmopolitan can unfold?

If we wish to use the concept for even the distant past without falling foul of anachronism, it is useful to distinguish between two quite distinct ways of *being cosmopolitan*.[10] The first meaning is perhaps closest to the everyday sense of the word, invoking places and people that somehow contain within them a world of plurality. In essence, we are talking about a way of living or a fact of life, and it may be entirely un-reflected upon as such at the time of its happening. A cosmopolitan city is one in which different tongues may be heard on the streets, and wares from distant parts of the world displayed by its merchants, in which a congeries of peoples has found a way of existing and thriving together. The locus where cosmopolitan attitudes unfold may be a town, a network of towns, or a territory – including perhaps Sri Lanka as a whole – but it will always remain relevant for our analysis to understand what 'local' frame precisely the cosmopolitan transcends, and in what ways it achieves this. This will be different for each and every type of artefact under discussion, be it a certain type of ceramics or coins, an element of literary or artistic style, a religious belief or a political ritual.

The second meaning of 'cosmopolitan' refers to a more profound and consciously cultivated sense of belonging to a world larger than the locality.[11] Sheldon Pollock's definition of cosmopolitanism refers to ways of 'being translocal, of participating – and knowing one was participating – in cultural and political networks that transcended the immediate community'.[12] Strictly speaking, again, cosmopolitanism therefore operates as a relative term, because the nature of the 'immediate community' must shift depending on context. But the challenge here is not only to define what the 'local' may be from which cosmopolitan emerges. The much more difficult question is to what overarching principle or notion the cosmopolitan refers in the premodern period. What 'world' were cosmopolitans to refer to when there was not yet anything like the full picture of the globe as we now know it today? Pollock, again, speaks of a conscious participation of people within a very grand ecumene:[13] the Sanskrit cosmopolis, a swathe of societies from Peshawar to Java that used Sanskrit literature to formulate their vision of the world. For much of Lankan history, its literati did indeed participate in this sphere of the imagination. They also, along with larger sectors of the population to varying degrees, participated in another ecumene of equivalent scale, historically connected with the Sanskrit cosmopolis: the world of Buddhism, or, at a more specific level, what Steven Collins referred to as the Pāli *imaginaire*.[14] In much of the Indian Ocean, the Sanskrit and Buddhist ecumenes were then joined – in some cases, supplanted – by the arrival of an Arabic cosmopolis from 1200 to 1500.[15] Recent work by Tilman Frasch and Anne Blackburn has shown how significant and enduring the interconnections among what Blackburn calls this 'Southern Asian' world were.[16]

Note that this second understanding is not only distinct from the first form but is in some tension with it. For while the first form depends on heterogeneity, even within a rather small space such as a town, the second depends on a certain homogeneity as extending over a vast space. If we grant that, then all kinds of other self-conscious cultural spaces (Christendom, Islam) or political spaces (the Cōḻa Empire, the Portuguese Empire) could be included as cosmopolitan orders. If we resist that conclusion, it may be because we insist that the term must entail the pragmatic toleration of the first definition and somehow avoid the dark side to the universalism lurking in the second.

## Alternative approaches

By now, it should be clear that our focus on the problem of the 'cosmopolitan' is not an unequivocal endorsement of its conceptual utility but rather an invitation to consider it critically and explore alternatives. Scholars of Southeast Asia will quickly perceive that many of the issues raised here have been germane to the debate around what O. W. Wolters called localization.[17] Reacting against the tendency to see the region as a passive recipient of cultural influence from more famous centres of civilization, Wolters was concerned to draw out how powerfully foreign (in this case mostly Indian) ideas were indigenized as they were integrated into Southeast Asian culture. For them to be accepted they 'tended to be fractured and restated and therefore drained of their original significance'. This allowed them to become part, locally, of 'new cultural "wholes"'.[18] Existing power structures could thus benefit from fresh inputs without suffering disruption.

To be sure, localization may, as Pollock and Anthony Milner have alerted, end up transforming the host culture more profoundly and lastingly than Wolters believed.[19] Not all the power is in the hands of those wishing to 'localize' the foreign for their own profit and sometimes the result is new political realities rather than the enhancement of old ones.[20] But all this still clearly indicates that there are manifold mechanisms through which the exogenous may or may not re-configure the indigenous, and that much of this will depend on the agency of various groups locally seeking or resisting change.[21] Recent studies of localization in Southeast Asia have underlined not only how complicated it is to 'distinguish indigenous from foreign elements in the integrated cultures which eventually emerged' as Wang Gungwu put it early on; but also, how much localization depends on a range of complicating factors including 'ecological differences, distance or proximity from a Great Tradition, elite and popular responses to spiritual needs, deeply rooted kinship structures, different uses of rituals and regalia, processes of urbanization and, not least, technology and modes of production'.[22]

In Sri Lankan studies, the work of Gananath Obeyesekere has often touched on issues of what could be described as 'localization', and his analyses of the processes of Sinhalacization and Buddhicization remain touchstones for any further research in this area.[23] Indeed, both he and Stanley Tambiah, two of the most celebrated scholars produced by Sri Lanka, have tended to be concerned with the continuous and peaceful waves of immigration from the mainland and the processes by which they have been accommodated. In scholarship more broadly, recent conceptual preferences indicate a certain distaste for cultural asymmetry. In that vein the imagery of 'centre' and 'periphery' has dropped out of favour in order to acknowledge that cultural transmission tends to be complex and multidirectional. Terms such as 'network' and 'circulation' have therefore become popular instead.[24] Emerging from the same semantic nimbus is the term 'heterarchy', which evokes situations in which diverse polities, often separated by great stretches of land and water, may yet share in some kind of sensation of commonality.[25] These centres may well be jostling among themselves for ways to achieve distinction and superior status, but no one of them has been acknowledged as *the* enduring and undisputed fount of authority and glamour.[26]

Yet in a series of recent articles and conference papers, Marshall Sahlins has been concerned to draw out the exact ways in which communities have indeed been ready to perceive the cultural forms of other societies as worthy of imitation, however uncomfortable it may be for scholars today to follow them. One such process Sahlins refers to as 'galactic mimesis', whereby 'the chiefs of satellite areas assume the political statuses, courtly styles, titles, and even genealogies of their superiors in the regional hierarchy'. This is 'typically motivated by competition with immediate rivals in a given political field, who are thus trumped by the chief who goes beyond the shared structures of authority by adopting a politics of higher order'.[27] Rivals are thus stimulated to draw on both the political and symbolic resources from beyond. One logic animating this process, also explored in the work of the anthropologist Mary W. Helms, is the ubiquitous tendency to attribute abnormal powers to exotic objects and agents.[28]

Some of this is considered further in Strathern's chapter (Chapter 11), which takes it for granted that premodern societies tend to exhibit a certain appetite for the foreign. What he terms the drivers of premodern elite 'extraversion' derived simply from a recognition that the foreign power may be a source of local strength. The most obvious advantages include the riches brought by trade and the military power promised by access to new alliances, mercenaries and weapons. Foreign trade may form a small amount of the overall economic life of the society while bestowing a disproportionate advantage on an elite that is able to funnel, control or even monopolize such activity. There are, however, some less obvious and more interesting aspects to this too, such as the symbolic struggle implicit in status stratification. Both Biedermann and Strathern have emphasized that Sri Lankan kings had been quite ready to signal their vassalage to outside powers before the Portuguese arrived, and that it was therefore no traumatic novelty to extend this to the Portuguese.[29] But nor did this amount to some kind of handing over of sovereignty; it was rather seen as a means of *enhancing* their own internal authority within the island. Even those foreigners resident in the island – and therefore potentially a threat to royal authority – were liable instead to be seen as a counterweight to internal factions and movements that often assailed the kingship. The practice of employing a foreign bodyguard, for example, was in place for a long time before the sixteenth century, for good reason. Foreigners could be a practical necessity for a king, then, but they could also be an adornment of his court. The ideal of kingship in many societies across Asia retained a sort of imperial or quasi-universalist or even cosmopolitan quality insofar as it was considered to be enhanced by the multiplicity of peoples that acknowledged royal authority and majesty. What better way to enhance one's dignity in local eyes than by demonstrating the way in which even foreign peoples clustered to your presence? Thus was domestic authority raised in esteem by a summoning of the exotic.

## Negotiations of power and culture over the long term

If there is a politics of cultural asymmetry to consider, then it also remains to study in more detail the cultural implications of political asymmetry. This is in order to engage properly with the arguments of Sheldon Pollock whose work is among the most important theorizations of premodern South and Southeast Asia to have emerged in recent decades. For Pollock too, the concept of 'cosmopolitanism' promises to convey a sense of community or commonality that is not structured by any particular kinds of power relationship.[30] Indeed, his theoretical instincts are always to problematize any straightforward equation between culture and power. In developing his theoretical reflections on the extraordinary expansion of Sanskrit, therefore, Pollock has been concerned to underline that it was not the by-product of some Sanskrit-peddling empire. It was thus not analogous to the way that Latin carried all before it under the auspices of Rome – and, to some extent, we may add, Portuguese, Dutch and English under the auspices of their respective empires. Pollock points out that adopters of the Sanskrit literary culture used it not to acknowledge the superiority of India as a centre but to reconfigure their own sense of centrality in more impressive terms: thus an endless string of self-conceived centres, each an *axis mundi* replete with its Mount Meru, could unfold.[31] This is a vision of the Sanskrit cosmopolis free not only from empire, but also from the strident universalism of religion: Pollock is concerned with the expansion of a literary culture above all rather than with Hinduism.

And it is free from ethnicity. By means of an unusually sustained comparative project, Pollock sets out to show that the European and the Indic realms embarked on entirely different paths of identity creation. In both regions, a glamorous language of high culture, Latin or Sanskrit, gave way to the increasing use of the vernacular for literary production. However, in the European case this fuelled the rise of ethnic and then national sentiments that had been embedded in the Latin imagination from the start, while the Sanskrit imaginaire allowed no such fantasies to take root. Instead the result was 'vernacular polities' that concerned themselves with dynastic rather than communal politics.

The chapters assembled here tend to suggest that it would be wrong to overlook the strong and obvious associations between the projection of power and the force of cultural attraction more widely – a relationship once encapsulated in the term 'civilization'. In what follows we shall sketch some of the ways that the expansion of external power – either sensed, threatened or actually experienced – may do both at the same time. The case of Sri Lanka is intriguing, in the first place, for how early the vernacular was promoted into a vehicle for literary culture, at a time when the Sanskrit and Pāli cosmopoli continued to exert a profound influence.[32] This fits Victor Lieberman's observation that vernacularization tended to occur first in those regions on the periphery of the older centres from which the universal languages diffused.[33] Sinhala script attained what is essentially its modern form in the eighth century, a development that suggests, according to Charles Hallisey, that 'the recognition of Sinhala as a language capable of literature was markedly new as a social phenomenon'.[34] The crucial aspect here is that we see a vernacular language bound up with a cosmopolitan culture of writing and, vice versa, a cosmopolitan culture of writing appropriated for the consolidation of a vernacular language. The graffiti from the Sigiriya site of that era indicates that a surprising variety of laypeople were making vigorous use of the language's written potential.[35] By the turn of the millennium, literary Sinhala had well and truly arrived.[36]

We find one of the earliest poetic invocations of the island of Lanka in a poem from the tenth century, in which she is personified as a beautiful woman, her blue clothes the surrounding ocean.[37] This poem, embedded within a Pāli commentary, conveys a markedly Sanskrit sensibility and shares with Cōḻa texts a play on the eroticization and feminization of the land.[38] But it was also primarily about Lanka, not the wider world. When King Parākramabāhu II wrote the *Kavsilumina* (the Crest-Gem of Poetry), an epic poem that set the template for the poetic tradition in Sinhala thereafter, he was showing how well Sinhala could exemplify classical Sanskrit aesthetic norms – but of course he was employing the vernacular idiom, and not the one that had formed the cosmopolis.[39] As Charles Hallisey has put it, 'elites in medieval Sri Lanka simultaneously participated in and resisted absorption in "the Sanskrit cosmopolis"'.[40]

This is a good place then to register a simple if vaguely paradoxical point: that vigorous participation – forced or unforced – in wider transregional flows may be precisely what allows a society or polity to fully conceive of its own local identity. To take a better-known and later phenomenon, the briefest consideration of the diffusion of nationalism will indicate how extremely rapid borrowing and imitation often stand in the service of separation, autonomy and hostility.

Indeed, it can be argued that it was the experience of the Cōḻa imperium that helped crystallize certain features of Lankan political ideology, which then endured for most of the second millennium.[41] This was in part simply by providing an external foe against which collective spirits could be mobilized – and the identity-forming power of alterity was to be extensively demonstrated in Sri Lanka throughout the centuries.[42] It has been argued, in this vein, that later Portuguese ideas of nationhood and Christianity came to infiltrate local understandings in the late sixteenth century, stiffening indigenous feelings about their ethnic and religious opposition to the intruders.[43] But more subtly and no less powerfully, Cōḻa visions of what a king should be influenced the Sinhalese reassertion of sovereignty. The dramatic impact of Cōḻa overlordship on Lankan royal culture is obvious to anyone visiting the ruins of Polonnaruva today. We very much regret that it has not been possible to include a chapter on Tamil cosmopolitanism in this volume, although several of our contributors do refer to it. But we can at least acknowledge that the South Indian world also formed a zone of high culture that Lankan elites could aspire to and provided the most significant body of royal peers that Lankan elites sought to emulate and surpass.

When subsequent Lankan kings, for example, referred to themselves as *cakravartis*, they may have been indicating their status as 'supreme overlords' in the Cōḻa manner rather than referring back to its original Pāli Buddhist conception.[44] Incidentally, both the Sanskrit and Pāli concepts of the *cakravartin* appealed to a cosmopolitan vision, a realm of infinite extension, created out of sheer political might but rich in cosmological import. And yet in late medieval Sri Lanka it slipped into usage as a particularly emphatic way of referring to a *bounded* conception: the universe had shrunk to the island itself.[45] To be a *cakravarti* came to mean to have conquered the four quarters of the island, to have captured the most authoritative capital and to be subject to no higher power. This was a mental template for the political unification of a delimited space.[46]

In the sphere of religion, the sense of Lanka's divine specialness, its unique role in the advance of the Buddhist dispensation, is in one sense a profound act of localization. Thus was a universal religion originating thousands of miles to the north rooted in the very soil of Tambapaṇṇi (one can only speculate whether a similar process could have occurred with Islam or Catholicism). That in turn became something that could be adopted by Southeast Asian kings who then became liable to insist on their own special protective relationship to the authentic teachings of Buddha. In other words, extensive participation in the Pāli ecumene hardly stood in the way of the formation of local aggrandizement, while glorifications of the local could themselves be rapidly disseminated in the wider ecumene. Nor should political designs over areas beyond the island be seen as something inherently antagonistic to the development of patriotic or indigenist sentiments. Once again, a quick glance at the better-known history of modern

European imperialism will indicate how sprawling imperial ambitions may easily sit with trenchant domestic patriotism.

The two unifier-hero kings of Lankan history who are such vivid symbols of the nationalist imagination today, Parākramabāhus I (r. 1153–86) and VI (r. circa 1411–67), combined domestic consolidation with an outlook that prized both cosmopolitan pluralism within and a projection of glamour without. What happened to Buddhism is very telling. Both kings were magnificent patrons and promoters of Buddhism, seeking to at once dignify, enhance, control and order the Sangha, which in turn rendered Lanka a magnet for monks and pilgrims from beyond its shores. Yet each reign is notable too for the way in which diverse other cults, gods, ideas and ritual specialists were brought into the embrace of the Buddhist establishment, whether they be Mahāyāna images of the Bōdhisattva, popular forms of astrology, or Brahmanic ritual and dharmaśātric norms. As John Holt has it, Sinhala kingship 'tended to become ever more eclectic in its symbolic expression, more composite or aggregate in its ideology and appeal'.[47] This was at once an opening to the cosmopolitan and a politically interested domestication of it.

By the time of Parākramabāhu VI, the Indian Ocean was witnessing the creation of another vast cultural sphere beyond the Sanskrit and the Pāli: the Arabic or Muslim 'cosmopolis', particularly brought to our attention by Ronit Ricci's recent book.[48] This also was borne not on the back of a single empire but rather seaborne trade – yet it certainly involved the exercise of political and commercial power. Sri Lanka was bound to participate to some extent in the wider Islamic commercial conjuncture because it was the principal source for a world-desired spice, cinnamon, as well as other products such as rubies and elephants.[49] The new importance of seaborne trade certainly had some political repercussions in Sri Lanka as it was partly responsible for the movement of political gravity to the southwest from the thirteenth century. However, unlike in insular Southeast Asia or parts of South India, it did not give rise to essentially independent port cities nor eclipse agrarian-based states.[50] In that sense, Sri Lanka looks more like mainland Southeast Asia, where Theravāda Buddhist polities retained pre-eminence and control of ports. There are only one or two signs that Muslim groups may have been ready to translate commercial into political might in Sri Lanka, as in the seizure of Chilaw by a Muslim chief from Palayakayal at the beginning of the sixteenth century.[51] By this time the Māppiḷas had begun to play an important part in internal politics of the island, as well as in the patterns of its external relations with India, until they were defeated by the Portuguese in the 1530s.[52] It is possible then that the rise of Islam to political pre-eminence in Sri Lanka was curtailed by the rising influence of the Portuguese. But in general, Muslim groups of diverse origin – some of them long settled, some much less integrated – were intent on dominating the seaborne trade that passed through the major ports of Lanka, rather than reaching for power inland.[53] More importantly, the Buddhist and Hindu rulers of Sri Lanka never once indicated that they might countenance conversion to Islam, unlike their counterparts in island Southeast Asia.

What happens, however, if we evoke the language of cosmopolitanism when referring to the cultural and ethnic heritage left by the waves of European colonialism? This deserves to become a topic of wider debate. New connections to Portuguese-speaking, ethnically often quite diverse communities across the Indian Ocean were one of the first things to emerge from the extension of Portuguese interests to the Sea of Ceylon shortly after 1500. On the fringes of the official empire, informal communities of Portuguese merchants established – or reinforced, or reinvented – links between the ports of Sri Lanka and those of the Bay of Bengal and the Arabian Sea. This vast commercial and social network – what Sanjay Subrahmanyam has called the Portuguese 'shadow empire' – was porous and disjointed, and indeed it may well be that in some ways it was no coherent network at all.[54] But it allowed for the ports of Sri Lanka to link up with a wider, global network of Portuguese traders stretching from Bahia to Macao, and even, starting in the late sixteenth century with the Iberian Union of Crowns under Philip II, from the Caribbean to Japan.[55] Escaping as they often did the formal structures of power put in place by the Iberian authorities, the private Portuguese and their descendants exerted their influence in ways that are partly comparable to the practices of other Indian Ocean diasporas. They often practised a pragmatic cosmopolitanism that resonated with three or four interconnected, sometimes conflicting, forms of early modern globalization: the Lusophone (which could include non-Catholics), the Catholic (which could include non-Lusophones), the early capitalist and the Iberian imperial.

It would be all too comfortable to simply dismiss the process by which Sri Lanka became a part of early modern global empires as essentially un-cosmopolitan because the element of power was more directly and formally expressed than in the cultural diffusions theorized by Pollock and Ricci. To be sure, there are evident differences between Catholic universalism and Islamic universalism, the roots of which extend further back than the defeat of Erasmianism in mid-sixteenth-century Iberia. There certainly were very different attitudes towards religious heterogeneity between Islamic and Catholic empires, the latter labouring for mass conversion at an unprecedented scale. But we also need to beware of perpetuating simplistic assertions about early modern European political culture when writing global history. At the very least, imperial formations can, while being deeply repressive on a number of levels, still be conducive to cosmopolitan practices at others. Lisbon and Goa, while irradiating imperial power and hosting such profoundly coercive institutions as the Tribunal of the Inquisition, were also global ports where diverse ethnic and linguistic communities engaged in long-distance trade, intensive cultural exchanges and knowledge transfers. Catholicism indeed constituted a cosmopolitan zone in the second sense as defined above. Conversion entailed not only cultural adaptations that allowed groups and individuals with very diverse backgrounds to participate in global commerce and communication. It also triggered a legal attachment to the empire that allowed converts to make use of its tribunals on a theoretically level, global playing field. The limitations and conditions of conversion in an environment of violent imperial expansion are evident, and there is no reason to downplay them. But to what extent Asians did come to feel a part of a wider Catholic cosmopolis after converting, and how they may have contributed to the way it functioned, is largely to be studied.[56]

Even what we know about the establishment of European colonial rule as such, starting in Sri Lanka in the final decade of the sixteenth century, leaves much space for discussion with regard to the significance of connections and cosmopolitan practices. New institutions such as the Municipal Council of Colombo mimicked similar bodies scattered across the globe from Lisbon and Bahia to Goa and Macao.[57] The people who built them were often only Portuguese in the widest sense of the word. These were instances of participation in an early global cosmopolitan sphere of urban institutions – and it may well be worth emphasizing the importance of cities as forms of political organization in the pre-nation-state world – that remains poorly understood. Other, more overtly coercive imperial organizations set up their quarters in the island and, while often serving the purpose of suppressing resistance to a deeper integration after conquest, also ended up supporting the movement of people and ideas.[58] Similar questions arise, naturally, from the history of the two subsequent colonial invasions, the Dutch and the British.

How we weigh up the global against the local in all this will always depend to some extent on how we feel about associations between culture and political violence in general. Some may feel that the term 'cosmopolitanism' is too innocent for the realities of power and coercion created by seventeenth- to nineteenth-century European imperialism. Walter D. Mignolo has sought, in his studies on Iberian expansion, to place globalization and Christian universalism in a different category to cosmopolitanism, given that 'globalization is a set of designs to manage the world while cosmopolitanism is a set of projects toward planetary conviviality'.[59] But can we really distinguish so clearly between the two? Mignolo's comment is a remarkable reflection of how much the language of cosmopolitanism balks at the reality of power, and how much it retains a normative charge in scholarly discussion.

## Sri Lankan historiography

The present volume brings together the most recent research on premodern Sri Lanka, but it naturally builds on much scholarship from earlier decades. Previous historical writing on Sri Lanka has by no means ignored the manifold ways in which Sri Lanka has been shaped by outside forces over centuries, and in which Lanka left its imprint on Asia in return.[60] The prestigious role played by the Sinhalese in the much larger story of Buddhism, for example, constitutes one instance of cosmopolitan radiation that has never really receded from consciousness in the island. The first volume of Sri Lanka's most 'official' history, *The University of Ceylon History of Ceylon*, published in 1959, had chapters on the development of Buddhism in India and under Aśoka, on the Sangnam age in

Tamilnad, and on the development of Pallavas, Pāṇḍyas and Cōḻas in Southern India. This said, the latter names are also resonant in the Lankan imagination for their violent eruptions. In terms of the dominant form of political history, outsiders have often appeared in the threatening guise of invading elites, as Sri Lanka's 'golden age' of Anurādhapura was disrupted by invasions from the fifth century onwards.[61] From then on Lankan kingdoms were engaged in complex diplomatic and military manoeuvres with the dynasties of Southern India and even became subject to Cōḻa suzerainty in the last years of the first millennium. Military power, it must be added, sometimes flowed the other way, too: when the island was unified under the Sinhalese king Parākramabāhu I, he sent an army to the mainland to assist a Pāṇḍyan ruler against the Cōḻas in 1169. A few years previously, he had sent an invasion force to Burma, which captured two port towns there.

Clearly, invasions, migrations and other incoming and outgoing movements of people and ideas could not be ignored in any discussion of Lanka's past, even in its golden age. However, in general, the historiographical project of the post-independence years was to furnish the new nation-state of Sri Lanka (changing its name from Ceylon in 1972) with its own past as a distinctive entity. This was natural: it was the model for history-writing everywhere and there remains great value in taking the island as the focus for analysis. Over the 1980s, as it became clear that the past was being mobilized to fight political battles amid the strife of the armed ethnic conflict (1983–2009), international academia became more concerned to complicate and undermine its simplistic deployments in the name of ethnic and nationalist projects. The island of Sri Lanka remained the unit of study but what was emphasized was its internal pluralism at any point in time and its discontinuities over time.[62] One principal source of controversy for these debates was the question of the chronology of Sinhala ethnic consciousness.[63] Intent on disrupting the anachronisms inherent in nationalist thinking, and influenced by post-Orientalist interpretations of the power of British colonialism to order local knowledge, it became common for a while, especially among Western historians of Sri Lanka, to argue that Sinhala ethnicity was a modern fabrication, could only ever have been a modern phenomenon.[64] In recent years, however, some scholars have again sought to push the history of Sinhala ethnicity further back in time, while maintaining a distance from the nationalist agenda.[65] This question is germane to the themes of this book, and while readers will find that it is by no means the organizing problem, the interpretive fluctuations it has gone through over the decades are symptomatic of the challenges we attempt to address when engaging with Sri Lanka's connected (or not so connected) history as a whole.

Today, the past continues to be drawn upon in Sri Lanka, as in many other parts of the world, for the purposes of shaping group sentiment and asserting group claims, and these have not ceased with the conclusion of civil war.[66] There remains indeed a general sensitivity towards 'foreign interference' in the past and in the present, whether that is suspected as emanating from the neighbouring behemoth of India or the more distant ex-hegemon of Europe or 'the West'. This is understandable, perhaps, if we appreciate that Sri Lanka has one of the longest histories of subjection to European imperial appetites anywhere in the world, with periods of influence and outright rule by the Portuguese (1506–1656), Dutch (1636–1796) and British (1796–1947).[67] It would be disingenuous to express the hope that this book will be easily received by those who advocate such a position, and that it will not have political resonances. In the current climate, broaching the question of the relationship between Lanka and the wider world cannot but have political implications.

Nevertheless, it is worth underlining that this book is not designed to make a political intervention by assuming that 'cosmopolitanism' is the only appropriate organizing principle for considering the island's past. If Sri Lanka is being dragged into world history, and the history of the wider world pushed into Sri Lanka, that is because such is the direction in which historical writing in general is heading. In Europe itself, 'Eurocentrism' of various sorts has come under sustained attack. Old categories, old problems are dying; new ones are pushing through the cracks. We are not, of course, suggesting that 'Lankocentrism' is in any way equivalent to the centre-periphery bias grounded in Europe's imperial heritage. But the new methodologies of world history deserve to be experimented with for Lanka as for any other place. That is, then, the politics of this book: not to impose 'cosmopolitanism' as the new orthodoxy, but to promote its critical discussion in Sri Lanka and among historians who may wish to engage in genuinely open debate on a wider scale.

## The chapters

In the opening contribution to this volume, Robin Coningham, Mark Manuel, Christopher Davis and Prishanta Gunawardhana look for clues to the cosmopolitan in the material evidence from ancient Lanka. In doing so they provide us with an up-to-date assessment of the latest archaeological findings. After an overview of how issues of identity, ethnicity and migration have been treated in archaeological writing, the chapter explores the themes of Indian Ocean trade, pilgrimage, religious patronage and urbanism, in each case setting the broad lines of narrative from the textual sources alongside what excavations have revealed. As well as drawing out Lanka's connectivity to the wider world, the authors are concerned to show the extent of internal heterogeneity (particularly in social and religious terms). Among the conventional narratives that are questioned along the way is a depiction of a comparatively 'pure' Buddhist culture in the Anurādhapura period that was subject to Indian and 'Hindu' influences in the Polonnaruva period. Nevertheless, the great importance of Buddhism as an institutional presence outside the towns in the first millennium CE is heavily underlined.

Rebecca Darley's chapter provides a critique of a tendency in the literature on the ancient and early medieval periods of Lankan history towards 'implicit cosmopolitanism', that is, a celebration of far-reaching connectivity as a self-evident sign of cosmopolitan practices. Darley offers a forensic examination of coinage evidence in particular, but also a critical reading of the much-cited *Christian Topography*, a sixth-century anonymous text often attributed to Kosmas Indikopleustes, and a reassessment of the findings of port archaeology. In this area, where there are so few scholars with relevant expertise, it is easy for conclusions to circulate unexamined. The central issue here is just how extensive and far-reaching Lanka's participation in seaborne trade was in this early period. New thinking on this question will have implications for many further areas of enquiry, such as whether the rise of Anurādhapura was propelled by seaborne trade or the harnessing of agrarian resources. While Darley questions the grand narrative of connectivity in many ways, she does find that there was a well attested upsurge in connections to the West in the mid-fifth to sixth centuries CE.

Tilman Frasch's contribution allows us to see Sri Lanka not as a receptacle for influences washing up on its shores but as the transmitter of a Pāli worldview that would come to form a cosmopolis stretching across to mainland Southeast Asia. At the same time, it is concerned to decentre Lanka somewhat by showing how for a time Bagan established itself as the most secure and fruitful centre of the Theravāda world, and to pluralize Lankan Buddhism, by showing how the Mahāvihāra version struggled against and sometimes lost out to other monastic centres in the first millennium. Unlike Pollock's presentation of the Sanskrit cosmopolis, however, this was an ecumene explicitly founded upon the importance of the preservation and expansion of a religious tradition. This meant that Lankan Buddhists participated in a religious culture that stretched across the Bay of Bengal and beyond, swept by common currents of millenarian anxiety, and united by the transference of ordination lineages and even the occasional council, such as the convergence of monks on Lanka in the 1420s. This was, in fact a brief flowering, for political fragmentation after Parākramabāhu VI and the arrival of the Portuguese in 1506 led to a precipitous decline in Lanka's centrality within the Theravāda world. This chapter thus also underlines how closely the cultural primacy of any one polity was associated with the political strength of its kings.

Alastair Gornall and Justin Henry explore the tensions that issued from the reception of Sanskrit literary theory by Lankan scholar monks working in Pāli in the early second millennium. They show how the tremendous prestige of Sanskrit high culture and its insistence on the moral significance of the aesthetic sphere becomes evident in works on Pāli poetics that were written from the twelfth century. To judge by the anxious note sounded in some of the Pāli texts, this was felt as a real intellectual challenge. The same texts indicate that the Sanskritic vision was, in another sense, profoundly resisted and transformed: the Pāli Buddhist ethical framework remained dominant, most visibly in its deprecation of eroticism. And yet there was another discourse, which breaks out in Pāli *kāvya*, in which not only the erotic, but also the martial and royal were unproblematically glamourized. Dealing carefully with difficult issues of reception, the authors finish by comparing the Pāli ecumene and the Sanskrit cosmopolis.

Stephen Berkwitz's analysis of the genre of Sinhala *sandēśa* poetry from the twelfth to the sixteenth century provides us with an apposite case study of how to think about the relationship between the local and the cosmopolitan. His analysis of how local authors sought to 'adopt the prestige of a cosmopolitan cultural order while asserting the distinctive value of an indigenous one' could stand as a literary equivalent to the way that Indic deities were both localized and Buddhicized. In some ways, the chapter serves as an illustration of Pollock's vernacularization thesis, although Berkwitz draws out some distinctive ways in which Sinhala poets shaped the genre in a way that rejected – perhaps even consciously – aspects of the Sanskrit model. Most interestingly, the Sinhala *sandēśa* poems were very explicitly concerned with the themes of kingship and religion: their function is the glamorization of royal power and its territorial expression, and they take the form of appeals to the gods for the protections of kings and the Buddhist *sāsana*. Berkwitz's emphasis on the erotic quality of the poems – in which the evocation of female bodies is not a function of the romantic gaze but the natural accompaniment to virile royal power – presents an intriguing counterpoint to Gornall and Henry's arguments. Different genres allow the expression of different sensibilities, we may conclude: a principle that could equally be extended to contrasting the lack of interest in xenophobic and ethnic sensations in the *sandēśa* with their appearance in the *haṭanas*.

Sujatha Arundathi Meegama presents an innovative art historical approach to Sri Lanka's convoluted sixteenth-century transition to early colonial rule. Bridging a deeply rooted gap in the study of different artistic genres, Meegama brings together the architectural remains of early modern buildings in Sri Lanka (most of which are in ruins) with the ivory caskets produced in the island during that same period (most of which are now in European and American collections). She argues that, while the participation of Lankan artists including masons, carvers and architects in a wider South Asian sphere of visual culture cannot be denied, the notion of 'influence' is in urgent need of replacement by a more inclusive concept such as 'appropriation'. As she shows in her compelling analysis of certain visual elements of the caskets traditionally disregarded by European art historians as merely decorative, Lankan artists and patrons made highly elaborate, consciously construed and persuasive choices to convey complex messages about the relationship between Lanka and the outer world. Such choices call, as Meegama argues, to be read in a wider context of global artistic transfers.

Zoltán Biedermann explores the largely overlooked movement of Lankans who, from the medieval through the early modern period, took strategic refuge overseas, generally in order to escape from unfavourable political conditions in the island and obtain support for their own power building projects. The history of these exiles, resonances of which can be found in the chapters by Gananath Obeyesekere and Sujit Sivasundaram, is traceable through the classic Lankan chronicles, but only becomes fully discernible after the appearance of the Portuguese in the early sixteenth century with their abundant production of written sources. From the 1540s, Biedermann shows, exile in the Portuguese outposts of South India became gradually associated for Lankan princes with conversion to Catholicism. From the turn of the seventeenth century, when the Iberian authorities engaged in the full military conquest of the island, the exile of Lankan throne pretenders in the Portuguese Empire became increasingly definitive. The stories of the men and women who spent the rest of their lives in Goa or Lisbon have rarely been told, but deserve to be reintegrated into the fabric of Sri Lankan history as a whole. They also provide ample ground for discussions about the possibilities of being cosmopolitan in repressive imperial contexts.

Gananath Obeyesekere will remain an inspiration to future generations working not only on Sri Lankan anthropology and history but on many of the themes of this volume more generally. Among the abiding themes of his work have been the vexed nature of identity construction, the cultural construal of the foreigner, and the relationship between the universal and the local in interpreting human behaviour.[68] In many ways, his career has been marked by the spirit of global history *avant la lettre*. This is not just because his work has ranged widely in geographical terms, but because a profound comparative sensibility has underpinned his reflections.[69] Moreover, Lanka's relationship with the mainland has also been a longstanding concern of his, which means that he has long been pursuing a form of connected history too. He returns to this theme in his chapter for this volume, which explores the cosmopolitan culture of the Kandyan court during the seventeenth and eighteenth centuries, with an emphasis on the complex politics around the adoption of foreign practices. This chapter demonstrates the intensity of Kandyan–South Indian relations and reveals the quasi-pendular movement, in the mountain kingdom, between the habitus of embracing and rejecting the foreign.

Alicia Schrikker and Kate Ekama offer a novel insight into the world of slavery in eighteenth-century Sri Lanka. On the basis of Dutch court records, they throw light on the cosmopolitan cultural and social practices of slaves brought from the Malay world to coastal ports such as Colombo, Galle and Jaffna. The authors discuss, on the one hand, how such sources can enrich our understanding of the various existing practices of bonded labour in Sri Lanka. On the other hand, they suggest that the Dutch legal sphere – including texts, tribunals and intensive negotiations at the local level regarding the application of Dutch VOC laws – can be understood as a cosmopolis in its own right. Schrikker and Ekama explore the clash between rigid Dutch notions of slavery as the complete opposite of freedom, on the one hand, and longstanding notions of caste, hierarchy and unfree labour in Jaffna society, on the other. They thus offer a promising window into the early modern history of Jaffna, a region that has been suffering from historiographical neglect in recent decades.

Sujit Sivasundaram engages with the complex transition to British rule. He explores archival, in part unpublished, materials from the four crucial years of 1815–18 to ask questions about continuity and change. As he shows, no clear lines can be drawn, and the picture as we have known it so far requires substantial qualifications. Above all, a clear-cut contrast between cosmopolitanism and ethnicity can be ruled out. Any consideration of the conquest of the Kandyan highlands and their integration into British imperial structures and discourses will necessarily have to take into account the way British observers reacted to what Sivasundaram calls 'local cosmopolitanism', and local elites responded to the supra-local realities of empire. In the jigsaw puzzle of Lankan politics at the transition to the modern period, the process of imperial 'islanding' played as crucial a role as indigenous notions of ethnicity and cosmopolitan diversity.

In the last chapter, Alan Strathern sets out to provide a panoramic perspective on the development of 'ethnic' group emotion and its relationship with dynastic rule over the long term of Lankan history. He does so through three distinct parts, which all have some comparative element. The first and longest part offers an examination of how the case of Sri Lanka obstructs Sheldon Pollock's theorization of the contrasting politics of ethnic and religious identity in premodern South Asia and Europe. Medieval Europe is thus the reference point here, implicitly or explicitly. Strathern argues that Lanka shows signs of both ethnic feeling and 'Providentialist' forms of political legitimation, in ways that are comparable to European developments. The second part explores the paradoxical manner in which ethnic emotion may coincide with 'stranger kingship' or an insistence on the non-domestic qualities of the ruling dynasty. At issue here is what he refers to as 'elite extraversion' rather than 'cosmopolitanism'. The final part is chronologically comparative, and explores the ways in which Lankan society responded to the imperial presence in the Portuguese and early British periods, focusing on a grammar of rebellion that is evident in both 1590–1650 and 1815–18.

1

# Archaeology and cosmopolitanism in early historic and medieval Sri Lanka

*Robin Coningham, Mark Manuel, Christopher Davis and Prishanta Gunawardhana*

## Introduction

This chapter will examine the applicability of the concept of cosmopolitanism in Sri Lanka during the early historic and the medieval period across a timespan of between c. 500 BCE and 1200 CE, utilizing archaeological evidence augmented by epigraphic and textual sources. It will focus on north central Sri Lanka and Anurādhapura but draw on wider references, comparisons and analogies where appropriate. Within an archaeological context, cosmopolitanism is a relatively underexplored phenomenon. While some volumes have addressed issues of identity and cosmopolitanism,[1] they have been more concerned with how this may have been represented in the present (largely through cultural heritage), as opposed to exploring the nature of its ancient manifestations. Philosophically, cosmopolitanism may be taken to refer to the concept that all humans belong to a single community with shared moral codes and philosophies, and that such a concept should be nurtured.[2] However, to a wider public, cosmopolitanism has often been used to reflect multiculturalism, sophistication and a general worldliness. In an archaeological context, the former definition is inherently problematic and challenging; however, the latter set of definitions is more achievable to identify, but to varying degrees as will become apparent.

How archaeologists commence the process of defining and identifying cosmopolitanism within archaeological communities is, in itself, a challenge although one may simply acknowledge the presence of multiple communities in the past. On a more ambitious level, archaeologists may investigate the relationships between such communities more deeply and the influences they may have had on each other. In such a way, the concept of cosmopolitanism may assist the development of a greater understanding of the complex and multifaceted identities of individuals and communities in the past. For instance, individuals may have had allegiances to multiple communities, may have spoken numerous languages and may have participated in various religious, ritual and belief systems. However positive an ambition, the inclusive and integrating nature of cosmopolitanism makes it difficult to define and even more difficult to identify within the ephemeral material remains with which archaeologists have to contend.

The focus of this discussion must also acknowledge the underlying and underpinning concepts of identity. Early archaeologists, such as Gustaf Kossinna (1858–1931), linked material archaeological remains with cultures, and variations within these cultural groups were attributed to ethnic diversity. Each clearly defined cultural province was thus correlated with an ethnic group and, simultaneously, also linked to contemporary nationalist concerns.[3] Although in opposition to this political agenda, pioneering archaeologists, such as Vere Gordon Childe and Stuart Piggott,[4] continued to identify and map cultural provinces across time and space in Europe and South Asia through differences and distributions of material culture, maintaining the assumption that cultural groups correlated with ethnic and linguistic groups. In Western Europe and, by imperial proxy, in South Asia, archaeologists utilized concepts of diffusion and migration to explain cultural and linguistic variations, for example in the debate over the development and spread of Indo-Aryan languages, linked with the ubiquitous Aryan invasion theory.[5]

Sri Lanka may be perceived as representing a microcosm of this latter Aryan question. Indeed, Tamil and Sinhalese ethnic identities have been created and curated on the basis of relatively modern distributions of Indo-European and proto-Dravidian linguistic communities, combined with references to oral and literary traditions relating to the Vijayan colonization of the island.[6] Despite this long scholarly tradition, there has been a more recent and rigorous examination of concepts of ethnicity within archaeology, leading some scholars to reject the notion that ethnic identity was ever concrete or could be traceable to a definable point. Jones has suggested that 'ethnic identity is based on shifting, situational, subjective identifications of self and others, which are rooted in ongoing daily practice and historical experience, but also subject to transformation and discontinuity'.[7] Archaeologists have also focused on issues of identity within the archaeological record, challenging preconceptions relating to age, gender, ethnicity and religion, and recognizing that 'identity… is not a static thing, but a continual process… Identities are constructed through interaction between people and the process by which we acquire and maintain our identities requires choice and agency'.[8]

Crucial within this quote is the recognition that identity is not singular but a plural concept. Individuals may hold many different identities simultaneously and this is something that becomes increasingly evident when examining the complex Sri Lankan past. This is equally true of the challenge of trying to discern religious identities from archaeological remains, individual objects or artefactual corpora. For instance, many monuments and motifs were commonly shared by a number of major religious traditions,[9] making it difficult to offer firm affiliations. With regard to Sri Lanka, a number of deities, such as Ganesh, Viṣṇu and Kubera, continued to be venerated after the advent of Buddhism but their positions were reconstituted within a cosmography that placed the Buddha centrally.

The survival of old beliefs and the appropriation of new traditions can be traced throughout the island's archaeological sequence, ranging from the introduction of the Buddha image in the first half of the first millennium CE to the emergence of traditions associated with the terracotta artefacts of the so-called 'Tabbova-Maradanmaduva Culture' at the beginning of the second millennium CE.[10] In order to investigate cosmopolitanism in ancient Sri Lanka and evaluate the appropriateness of the concept itself, this chapter will examine a series of case studies. These range from the role of pilgrimage, in particular Buddhist, to and from the island; local and global trade networks and the impact these have had on the island's inhabitants; patronage within the island and Sri Lankan patronage elsewhere in South Asia; and the religious and economic landscapes of Anurādhapura and its surrounding hinterland. This study will focus on archaeological data but will introduce textual and epigraphic evidence where appropriate, and will begin by examining these sources and critically discussing how modern ethnic constructs in Sri Lanka have been intrinsically linked to the island's past.

## Textual narratives and the linking of archaeology to ethnicity

The precolonial history of Sri Lanka has been constructed from a variety of textual sources, in particular the *Dīpavaṃsa*, *Mahāvaṃsa* and *Cūḷavaṃsa*. Wilhelm Geiger argued that the *Dīpavaṃsa*'s contents relied upon an earlier chronicle known as the *Aṭṭhakathā-Mahāvaṃsa*,[11] and that while the *Dīpavaṃsa* is viewed as a first attempt at collating Pāli verses, the *Mahāvaṃsa* can be seen as a younger, more elaborate, treatment of the same material. Geiger even went as far as to suggest that the *Mahāvaṃsa* represents 'a conscious and intentional rearrangement of the *Dīpavaṃsa*'.[12] Although its authorship is unknown, the *Dīpavaṃsa* is believed to have been compiled in the fourth century CE, while the *Mahāvaṃsa* has been argued to have been written by various monks of the *Mahāvihāra* and compiled into a single document by the Buddhist monk Mahānāma in the fifth to sixth century CE.[13] It narrates the history of the island from its colonization by Prince Vijaya through to the reign of King Mahāsena (r. 275–301 CE).[14] The *Cūḷavaṃsa* was a continuation of this narrative, detailing the island's history up to the eighteenth century CE.[15] Initially scholars believed these narratives to be legends, but the rediscovery of palm leaf manuscripts by George Turnour at Mullgiri-galla near Tangalle[16] led to the serious reconsideration of their contents as historical. Sir James Emerson Tennent, Colonial Secretary of Ceylon between 1845 and 1850 CE, stated that this 'long lost chronicle… thus vindicated the claim of Ceylon to the possession of an authentic and unrivalled record of its national history'.[17]

This rediscovery led to an increase in Western studies of the island's history,[18] paralleled by significant research undertaken by members of the Sangha whose translations of Pāli works into Sinhalese and correspondence with European academics facilitated the development of 'Oriental' scholarship.[19]

Unique across South Asia, the chronicles provided a historical framework for the island from before the Mauryan Empire through to British rule and, with colonial endorsement, the chronicles became the privileged source of evidence for scholars studying Sri Lanka's past. This focus has produced what has been termed by Seneviratne as the '*Mahāvaṃsa* view',[20] reflecting the fact that ever since the rediscovery of the chronicles, the disciplines of Sri Lankan history and archaeology have been largely influenced by as the *Mahāvaṃsa*'s narrative.[21] It has also been suggested that archaeological evidence from excavations in Anurādhapura, while often referring to 'popular' culture and history, has been used to reinforce academic narratives derived from the chronicles.[22]

The narrative itself details, as is widely known, the arrival of Prince Vijaya, the exiled heir to a kingdom in northern India, with his 700 followers on the uninhabited island of Lanka in the middle of the first millennium BCE. On arrival, Vijaya slays the demonic *yakkhas* who reside on the island, while at the same time having two children by the *yakkhiṇī*, Kuveṇī. Descended from a lion, Vijaya refers to his followers as Sinhala, or 'people of the lion'. However, having borne his children, Prince Vijaya spurns Kuveṇī in favour of an Indian princess, and Kuveṇī and their children retreat to the jungle, forming the Pulinda people.[23] After the conversion of the Sinhalese to Buddhism in the third century BCE as a result of Aśōka's proselytizing (see p. 29), the *Mahāvaṃsa* makes its first reference to differentiated communities by mentioning Demaḷas, a term often associated with Tamils, although this is contested.[24] With the exception of those Tamil-speakers brought across as indentured labour for the colonial tea plantations, the Tamil communities of present-day Sri Lanka have often been directly linked with the invading South Indian Pāṇḍyas and Cōḷas during the later phases of the Sinhalese rule from Anurādhapura.[25] The chronicles thus seem to establish within their narratives three distinct communities that have often been perceived to have been at odds with one another, rather than recognizing a framework for a multicultural island with a shared history. Frequently, the underlying question here has been to do with who the rightful autochthons were.

This link of past to present has often been translated into the notion of the Sinhalese as rightful 'heirs' to the island,[26] while Tamils were portrayed as latecomers or outsiders. The reasoning behind this partially originates from colonial interpretations of Sri Lankan history. As well as endorsing the *Mahāvaṃsa* as history, Tennent equated the Pulinda with the modern communities of hunter-gatherers or väddās, often described as the aboriginal inhabitants of the island; the Sinhalese as the civilized creators of the architectural and engineering masterpieces of the northern plains or the Rajarata; and finally, the Tamils as the 'debased' destroyers of that civilization.[27] These views became mainstream historical opinion, although other scholars sought to attribute a much deeper antiquity to the Tamil communities of the island,[28] with some suggesting that sites such as Mantai were part of a separate early Tamil trading civilization,[29] or that an early Dravidian population was already present on the island at the time of the Vijayan colonization.[30] However, these latter views never garnered broader acceptance.

Central to colonial interpretation was the concept that Indo-European-speaking people had invaded South Asia from the north and west around the first millennium BCE, bringing with them a cultural package that included writing, iron, horse-riding and advanced social institutions.[31] Within South Asia, the Indo-Aryan invasion was portrayed as part of a long pageant of historical precedents that helped to legitimate British control of the region as the latest wave of conquest elites following Aryans, Greeks, Persians and Turks.[32] The civil servant and historian, H. W. Codrington, pursued these legitimacies in his *Short History of Ceylon*, when he reminded readers that the British invasion of Kandy and exile of the last king, Śrī Vikrama Rājasiṃha (r. 1798–1815 CE) was to deliver 'the Kandyans from their oppressors and the subversion of the Malabar dominion', Rājasiṃha being a South Indian Tamil by birth.[33]

Episodes and events of oppression were also portrayed within the chronicles and they frequently referenced the destruction of Buddhist heritage by South Indian aggressors. For instance, during the reign of Mahinda V (r. 982–1029 CE) the chronicles recorded that Anurādhapura was abandoned, leaving the capital open to plunder by the South Indian Cōḻa polity:

> Thereupon they sent the Monarch and all the treasures which had fallen into their hands at once to the Cōḻa Monarch. In the three fraternities and in all Lanka (breaking open) the relic chambers, (they carried away) many costly images of gold etc., and while they violently destroyed here and there all the monasteries, like blood-sucking *yakkhas* they took all the treasures of Lanka for themselves.[34]

These descriptions were also used during the anti-colonial Buddhist revival by leaders of that movement, such as Angarika Dharmapala (1864–1933 CE), who identified modern Europeans and ancient Tamils as 'barbaric vandals' of Sinhalese culture.[35] This fitted a framework promoting Sinhalese and Buddhist concerns while noting European interference. However, colonial archaeologists also laid the blame for the destruction of monuments in antiquity at the hands of Tamils, utilizing similar narratives.[36] Early archaeological interpretations drew from such descriptions and H. C. P. Bell, the archaeological commissioner for Ceylon between 1890 and 1912, described the stone Buddhist railing at the Jetavana monastery of Anurādhapura as damaged by an aggressor:

> The indescribable confusion in which the fragments were found heaped one upon another, and the almost entire wreck of the railing, leave little room for doubt that this unique relic of Ceylon Buddhist architecture must have perished under the ruthless destruction of those invaders from South India at whose door lies the mutilation and ruin of the best works of the sculptor's art in Anurādhapura.[37]

Such interpretations were not rare, as illustrated by the discovery of fractured Buddha sculptures in Jaffna recorded by Sir Paul Pieris. He noted that earlier scholars, such as Sir William Twynam, the government agent for Jaffna, had suggested that Buddhist sculptures found in the north 'have been similarly mutilated – an undoubted sign, he thinks, of Dravidian invasion'.[38] Such viewpoints were not restricted to the infancy of archaeological enquiry but continued through the twentieth century. For example, excavations at Abhayagiri in Anurādhapura in the 1980s revealed Buddha statues lying flat with their heads removed and this was cited as evidence of the Cōḻa destruction as narrated in the *Cūḷavaṃsa*.[39] The latter findings were recovered from excavations conducted as part of Sri Lanka's major heritage programme, the UNESCO Central Cultural Fund, established by president J. R. Jayewardene in 1980. Tasked with excavating, conserving and presenting the ancient cities and Buddhist monuments of Sri Lanka, the sites of Anurādhapura, Polonnaruva and Sigiriya were inscribed on the UNESCO World Heritage list in 1982, followed by Kandy in 1988 and Dambulla in 1991.[40] Although colonial Galle was inscribed in 1988, the focus on Buddhist sites was pointed out by Tambiah, who stated that while there should be no barriers to the sponsorship of the restoration of Buddhist monuments, '[i]t would also behove a Sri Lankan government to recognize at the same time that there are monuments, archaeological remains, and literary and cultural treasures that are neither Sinhalese nor Buddhist as these labels are understood today'.[41]

One of the unintended consequences of the increasing alignment of the state-sponsored promotion of Buddhist heritage with the *Mahāvaṃsa*'s narrative was to focus the attention of the separatist Liberation Tigers of Tamil Eelam (LTTE) on the symbolic importance of such monuments.[42] Indeed, the early methods of the Central Cultural Fund were also queried by one of its own directors-general, Professor Seneviratne, who observed that 'interpretative studies were mainly commissioned to strengthen the Buddhist history of Anurādhapura and to authenticate the *Mahāvaṃsa* narration'.[43] Reflecting the new post-conflict era across the island, and the Central Cultural Fund Act, which states that the Fund was established 'for the development of cultural and religious monuments in Sri Lanka',[44] project offices have now been opened in Jaffna, Batticaloa, Trincomalee and Ampara, with recently inaugurated conservation programmes at the Sivan Kōvil at Trincomalee, the Yonakapura mosque in Dickwella and the Roman Catholic church at Duwa in Negombo, as well as the promotion of the intangible heritage of väddā, African and Malay communities. Furthermore, the Fund is sponsoring more inclusive research, such as the current investigations at Siva Devale No. 2 at Polonnaruva, which involves participants from across Sri Lanka including Sri Jayewardhanapura, Rajarata, Kelaniya and Jaffna Universities as well as international partners from Nepal, India, Australia and the UK.

On reflection, the character of the ancient heritage of Sri Lanka was far more complex, diverse and fluid than recently constructed identities and representations suggest. For example, although Sinhalese monarchs were guardians of Buddhism within the island, close marriage ties with non-Buddhist South Indian dynasties were formed, culminating in the accession of the Nāyaka dynasty to the Kandyan throne in the eighteenth century.[45] The current Temple of the Tooth in Kandy was partly constructed by a Nāyaka, Śrī Vikrama Rājasiṃha II

(r. 1798–1815 CE), a Tamil/Telugu-speaker from a Hindu dynasty of South Asian origin. The attack on the Temple of Tooth by the LTTE in 1998 therefore not only resulted in damage to a monument constructed by a South Indian dynastic king from the Nāyaka dynasty, but also damaged adjacent shrines to Pattini and Viṣṇu,[46] important to both Buddhist and Hindu communities. The patronage and protection afforded by 'non-Buddhists' is further reinforced by a Tamil inscription on a stone slab beside the Tooth Relic Temple in Polonnaruva. Known as the Aṭadāgē, this structure was built under the patronage of Vijayabāhu I (r. 1055–1110 CE) and the epigraph instructs guards from South India, Vēlaikkāras, to protect the Buddha's Tooth Relic within[47] (Figure 1.1). Part of a long tradition of 'Sinhala'

**Fig. 1.1** Tamil inscription at the Atadage, Sacred Quadrangle, Polonnaruva, authors' photograph.

states employing South Indian guards, the Vēlaikkāras are stated to be adherents of the *Mahātantra*, and this further highlights the diversity and complexity of identity, religiosity and the construction of royal legitimacy within medieval Sri Lanka. All these complexities are crucial for the consideration of evidence for potential signs of cosmopolitan practices in the archaeological record.

## Indian Ocean trade

Although Anurādhapura has been investigated for more than one hundred years, intensive stratigraphic archaeological analysis only commenced through the instigation of fieldwork programmes by Dr Siran Deraniyagala in the 1990s. One associated investigation was the excavation at trench Salgha Watta (ASW2), directed by one of the authors, which began in 1989 and continued into the 1990s. The trench measured ten by ten metres and was excavated to a depth of ten metres.[48] While trench ASW2 identified and dated a sequence with more than 1,000 years of occupation, rebuilding and eventual abandonment at the site, it was also designed to develop a typological sequence for the island and, in so doing, allowed the identification of trade networks. Many early studies of the island's archaeology have attributed Sri Lanka's apparent peripheral position to its seemingly marginal geographical location, off India's southern tip.[49] As a result, the island was assumed to have adopted a number of innovations, such as writing and urbanization, later than North India.[50]

On a broader scale, this interpretation reflected a deeply rooted colonial concept, namely that contact with the Roman world was the catalyst for the beginnings of Indian Ocean trade. In line with his tradition of linking South Asian archaeology with established Western chronologies, Mortimer Wheeler presented the early, pre-Roman levels of his excavations at the port of Arikamedu in South India as populated by 'simple fisher-folk' living in 'a leisurely and enterprising fashion just above subsistence level'.[51] An adherent of the theory of cultural change through invasion, diffusion or trade, Wheeler believed that Roman traders provided the stimulus for the settlement to develop into an international hub.[52] He felt supported by the presence of finds of Arretine Ware and other Roman goods. While he focused on the sequence from a single trade entrepôt, the ideas and concepts that he developed were transposed to Sri Lanka and into narratives of the island's development. Yet Begley's re-excavations at Arikamedu[53] and Coningham's trench ASW2 at Anurādhapura demonstrated the weakness of these models, the latter confirming the presence of well-developed trade networks across South Asia before contact with the Roman world.[54]

Archaeologists now recognize the highly diverse character of the wider region's trading communities. For example, the Italian excavations at Khor Rohri on the Omani coast have provided evidence of South Asian wares[55] and the presence of sherds with inscriptions in Early Brahmi, the *lingua franca* of early historic trade, at Myos Hormos and Berenike in the Red Sea suggest strong contact with – and possible residence of – South Asian traders there in the first century CE.[56] The excavations at trench ASW2 also provide evidence of a diverse repertoire, indicating links across the early historic and medieval Indian Ocean. Objects demonstrate links with Afghanistan and Gujarat, with finds of lapis lazuli and carnelian in the first millennium BCE, but later expanded to include glazed ceramics from the Persian and Islamic worlds and Eastern Asia with delicate monochrome lustre ware bowls and Changsha stone wares in the first millennium CE. While some objects, such as the Egyptian glass kohl sticks, were already well-known artefact categories, other objects represented the introduction of new tastes. For example, during Period F (300–600 CE), 'torpedo' jars were imported from Sasanian and Early Islamic regions. Lined with bitumen to make them watertight, they were used to transport liquids. Gas chromatography–mass spectrometry and stable isotope analysis of torpedo jars from trench ASW2 identified that the bitumen was derived from Susa in Iran,[57] and while it was not possible to determine what liquids were transported within the Anurādhapura torpedo jars, it is likely that one of the commodities was wine.[58] Torpedo jars have also been found at Mantai,[59] Sigiriya[60] and Tissamaharama[61] and undoubtedly represent a broadening of such consumption habits.

A more utilitarian development was also recognized within the sequence of trench ASW2 in the form of sherds with inscriptions. Predating Aśōkan contact, the presence of Early Brahmi script in levels dating to c. 400 BCE raised questions as to its presence within the island.[62] North Indian Prakrit, the direct ancestor of Sinhalese, may have been adopted as a trade language at that time. The communities using it at Anurādhapura may have been bilingual and gradually replaced their own language in favour of Prakrit – a process that resulted in Sinhala.[63] The striking nature of its presence within the city has been further stressed by the fact that only a single inscribed sherd was identified outside the walls during a major campaign of survey – restricting the cosmopolitan nature of its use to the capital and differentiating this settlement from its rural hinterland, where evidence of writing was again restricted to inscriptions at monastic sites.[64] The presence of early trade links at Anurādhapura and Mantai also demonstrate that distant connections existed long before scholars had suggested. Indeed, the excavations across the ramparts at Anurādhapura demonstrated that the urban nature of the site was defined long before contact with Aśōka in the third century BCE[65] and the supposed 'Mauryanization' of the island, while the earliest levels of the site (c. 800 BCE) also detail an extensive intra-island network of trade and exchange.

Although this evidence of trade goods in Anurādhapura may have informed us of the extensive trade networks flowing through the site, it still remains to be seen how these systems were organized. Were international merchants and traders residing within the city itself or was the port of Mantai established as a trading entrepôt with goods shipped to Anurādhapura by local traders?[66] Were Sri Lankan traders setting forth to procure goods from around the world to bring home for local markets? The recent discovery of the Godavaya shipwreck off the southern coast of Sri Lanka promises to shed more light on the identities of the sailors and their cargos.[67] As is often the case in archaeology, it is difficult to be absolutely certain and the answers are likely to be a combination of all of the above. The later travel itineraries of the Chinese pilgrim Faxian, for example, noted the presence of 'The houses of Sa-pho (Sabaean) merchants' within Anurādhapura,[68] but scholars differ in their identification of the ethnicities involved. Note must also be made of the discovery of a Nestorian Cross at Anurādhapura. This was interpreted by early archaeologists as marking the presence of a church,[69] but also recently reassessed by Prabo Mihindukulasuriya, who linked the find with records by the historian Cosmas and the presence of a Nestorian bulla from Mantai to suggest that Anurādhapura hosted a thriving Christian community.[70] Although the presence of isolated artefacts may not necessarily equate to the permanent presence of particular groups, they do certainly call for a reassessment of the record.[71]

## Pilgrimage

The earliest contact between Sri Lanka and northern India recorded in the *Mahāvaṃsa*'s narrative was the Vijayan colonization. The second notable contact was between Devānaṃpiyatissa's (r. 250–210 BCE) kingdom and the Mauryan Empire, which had emerged in the mid-fourth century BCE from the internecine warfare between the various *mahajanapadas* of South Asia.[72] After his conversion to Buddhism, it is recorded that the Mauryan emperor Aśōka (272–235 BCE) sent missionaries to neighbouring states to spread the Dharma.[73] Aśōka's son Mahinda was sent to Sri Lanka and, after converting Devānaṃpiyatissa, supported spreading Buddhism throughout the island.[74] Later, Aśōka's daughter Saṅghamittā brought a branch of the Bōdhi tree from Bodhgaya, under which the Buddha gained enlightenment, to Sri Lanka[75] forming a centrepiece that is still venerated at the Śrī Mahā Bōdhi in Anurādhapura. Further relics were brought to Sri Lanka, such as the Buddha's alms bowl, while his collarbone was enshrined within the Thūpārāmaya in Anurādhapura.[76] Although the archaeological evidence cannot confirm these textual claims in detail, it can support the broader point that relics were moving across South Asia as diplomatic and religious gifts. There is a close parallel between the recorded arrival of the Bōdhi tree and the advent of tree and swastika coinage in the third century BCE. The presence of Northern Black Polished Ware at Anurādhapura also constitutes 'physical evidence of links between the core of the Mauryan culture sphere and Sri Lanka'.[77] Although a link can be identified, its exact nature is less certain, as the ware predates the rule of Aśōka and may represent down-the-line trade rather than courtly exchange.

Once Buddhism was established, the monasteries of Anurādhapura gained an international reputation and links throughout Asia continued to expand. In the late fourth and early fifth century CE, the Chinese pilgrim Faxian journeyed to Sri Lanka during his travels around South Asia visiting sites associated with the life of the Buddha and major Buddhist centres. In addition to describing

Anurādhapura and the religious ceremonies that occurred within the citadel, he described the wealth of the monasteries of the Sacred City. Here, Faxian reported that more than 10,000 monks and nuns resided, with the Abhayagiri Vihāra housing 5,000 and the Mahāvihāra 3,000 monks.[78] The treasury of Abhayagiri was said to contain jewels and gems of incalculable value, garnered from patronage.[79] The Sangha's networks continued into the medieval period but, after the purported damage to the Sangha caused by Cōḻa incursions in the eleventh century CE, as recorded in the chronicles, it was reported that no ordination had been conducted in Sri Lanka for many decades. These networks were called upon to assist the restoration of the Sangha, and Vijayabāhu I was aided by King Anuruddha of Rāmañña, whose realm coincided with modern Burma/Myanmar, to bring monks to Sri Lanka to fulfil these duties.[80] In later periods, after the decline of Polonnaruva, a major mission of monks from Chiangmai and Pegu came to Sri Lanka in the 1420s CE to worship the Tooth Relic and receive higher ordination.[81] The Indian Ocean-wide Buddhist worldview illustrated by these examples may have been encapsulated symbolically not only in textual sources, but also architecturally, with Tilman Frasch suggesting recently that the layout and structures of the twelfth-century Sacred Quadrangle at Polonnaruva represented a cosmogram of international Buddhist contacts.[82]

This is not to suggest that Sri Lanka acted solely as a receptacle for external impulses as there is also evidence for Sri Lankan communities influencing distant partners. For example, Pliny noted that a Sinhalese monarch sent an embassy to Rome in the second century CE[83] and an inscription on the Aśōkan period stone railing at the Mahabodhi Temple in northern India was translated by Sir Alexander Cunningham as the 'Gift of Bodhi-rakshita of Tambaparna (Ceylon)'.[84] References to Sri Lanka have also been identified at other sites in India. At Nagarjunakonda in Andhra Pradesh, an inscription recorded the Sīhala-Vihāra and the dedication of a shrine to the fraternities of Tambapaṇṇi.[85] A decorated moonstone discovered at one apsidal temple, unlike other examples at Nagarjunakonda, resembles the ornately carved moonstones of Anurādhapura, decorated with elephants, lions, deer, horse, bull and buffalo, which may be connected to Buddhist communities from Sri Lanka.[86]

Later contact is confirmed by an inscription dating to 792 CE, found at a monastic site in the Ratubaka plateaux of Java, commemorating the founding of a branch of the Abhayagiri Vihāra of Sri Lanka in this locale.[87] Sundberg has argued that the *pendopo* architectural unit at Ratubaka has similarities with the layout of Padhānaghara Pirivena, or double-platform monasteries, that have been identified on the western outskirts at Anurādhapura and at Ritigala. These sites have been linked to the fraternity of monks known as the *paṃsukūlika* or 'those clothed in rags from dustheaps',[88] who rose to prominence from the eighth century CE onwards. The architecture of a Padhānaghara Pirivena is usually characterized by two quadrangular units connected by a stone bridge. These platforms are surrounded by an enclosing wall, occasionally a moat, as well as cisterns and ponds. Padhānaghara parivena do not possess typical Buddhist structures or iconography such as *stūpas*, but are often associated with meditational pathways.[89] Sundberg has suggested that the Javanese *pendopo* shares these features such as a lack of ornamentation, cardinally oriented double-platforms, artificial rock-cut ponds and the presence of a compound wall.[90] Although it is not clear whether the *paṃsukūlika* associated with the Padhānaghara Pirivena of Sri Lanka were present in Java, or vice versa, it is clear that there was communication and that shared architectural concepts existed across the Indian Ocean region.

Furthermore, inscriptions in Sri Lanka, such as two twelfth-century CE inscriptions from Polonnaruva, record the construction of a temple in South India[91] and the construction of alms-houses abroad.[92] Artefactual evidence is also suggestive of international Buddhist contacts, and it has been argued that a tenth-century CE bronze Buddha figure found in Thailand originated in Anurādhapura.[93] Textual sources also illustrate the influence of Sri Lankan monarchs overseas not just in religious matters. For example, Parākramabāhu I (r. 1153–86 CE) is recorded as instigating military campaigns against Southeast Asian polities as well as sending an army to South India to assist a Pāṇḍyan ruler against the Cōḻas in 1169 CE.[94]

Finally, it is worth noting that not all pilgrims to Sri Lanka came for 'Buddhist' monuments or 'Buddhist' relics. It has been hypothesized that the site of Sigiriya, a creation of Kassapa I (r. 473–91 CE) and historically a site that attracted large numbers of visitors and pilgrims, was constructed symbolically to recreate the city of Āḷakamandā, the celestial home of Kubera, god of wealth.[95] Inscription 28 of the Sigiriya graffiti records: 'The resplendent rock named Sighigiri captivates the minds of those who have seen [it] as if [the mountain] Mundalind, which was adorned by the King of Sages, had descended to the earth.'[96] Mundalind has been equated with Mount Meru and, continuing this symbolism, Paranavitana suggested that the lake at Sigiriya represented the celestial lake Anotatta, the white-washed boulders before the outcrop stood for the snow-clad Himalayas, and the royal palace pointed to the abode of Kubera on the summit of Meru. The famous Sigiriya frescoes have also been interpreted in various ways, one being that they are depictions of divine cloud damsels representing cloud and lightning, reaffirming Kassapa's ability to control the elements.[97] If indeed viewed as the creation of Kassapa, the graffiti and cosmological symbolism of Sigiriya produced what is argued to be the clearest example of an urban microcosm in early Sri Lanka.[98]

This symbolism suggests the physical modelling of South Asian-wide concepts, such as Mount Meru at the centre of a cosmic universe, were already present previously in Anurādhapura[99] and continued into the medieval and post-medieval periods at the urban forms of Polonnaruva and Kandy.[100] The Sigiriya graffiti also demonstrate that individuals from various communities travelled from all over Sri Lanka to visit the site,[101] and not always for religious reasons. However, it has also been argued that Sigiriya was in fact not an urban centre, but rather a vast Mahāyāna-Theravāda Buddhist monastic complex,[102] and if this view held by Raja de Silva is correct, then another intriguing explanation for Sigiriya's design may exist. Rather than depicting cloud damsels surrounding the summit of Meru, de Silva argues that the paintings of female figures were representations of the

Bōdhisattva Tara.[103] There is also the possibility that these two interpretations were both held side-by-side, again highlighting the diversity in symbolic meaning that could be attached to physical remains in the Sri Lankan past.

## Patronage

While evidence from Sri Lanka's monumental centres demonstrates the breadth of connections throughout the Indian Ocean region, until recently the extra-urban networks around those hubs have been neglected. New fieldwork in the hinterland of Anurādhapura has begun to redress this imbalance, providing an archaeological dataset that has been combined with geoarchaeological, epigraphic and textual studies in order to understand the development of the city in relation to its wider landscape context.[104] One of the key findings of this fieldwork is the central role of Buddhist monasteries in the administration of landscape,[105] a state of affairs that had already been suggested from archaeological landscape surveys in Sri Lanka[106] and India.[107]

The two major site categories identified during six years of field survey in Anurādhapura's hinterland were Buddhist monasteries and small-sized ceramic scatters. These sites presented deep occupation sequences at monasteries as opposed to shallow ephemeral traces at ceramic scatter sites. Artefacts such as coins, precious and semi-precious stones, fine ware ceramics, as well as monumental architecture and, as stated previously, writing, were restricted to monastic sites, and these sites appear to have acted as both religious and secular administrators with jurisdiction over large temporalities in the hinterland.[108] This pattern reached its climax in the early medieval period when the most dominant form of Buddhist patronage in the hinterland was through immunity grants, recorded in inscriptions on stone pillars, rather than the direct construction or maintenance of religious structures. Accounting for almost half of all donations and found across Anurādhapura's hinterland for this period,[109] these immunities alienated vast tracts of land and transferred authority from the Crown and local officials to the Sangha.[110] Creating an integrated landscape administered by monastic institutions, inscriptions found throughout Sri Lanka from the early historic period onwards corroborate the links between monasteries of the hinterland and urban monasteries of the Sacred City, recording the affiliation of monasteries to the Mahāvihāra, Abhayagiri Vihāra and Jetavana Vihāra.[111] However, the growing diversity and division within Buddhist sects ensured some heterogeneity to the hinterland in addition to the diversity of other religious practices present in the landscape, such as those indicated by the presence of terracotta figurines.[112]

The fact that three distinct monasteries are referred to in the chronicles indicates in itself that the Buddhist Sangha at Anurādhapura was not monolithic. The chronicles state that the Mahāvihāra was founded in the reign of Devānaṃpiyatissa with the arrival of Mahinda's mission and incorporated the Bōdhi tree and the Ruwanwelisaya stūpa.[113] The first major recorded schism occurred during the reign of Vattagamani (r. 89–77 BCE) and led to the founding of Abhayagiri

Vihāra,[114] often cited as a centre of Mahāyānist doctrines. Mahasena (r. 275–301 CE) not only founded the Jetavana *Vihāra* at Anurādhapura, but also, under the influence of a 'lawless bhikkhu',[115] withdrew support from the Mahāvihāra. This led to the abandonment of the Mahāvihāra for nine years, with the monks leaving for Malaya and Rohana. Construction materials were then taken from the complex and brought to Abhayagiri, which became wealthy under state support.[116] Later under the rule of Mahasena's son Sirimeghavaṇṇa (r. 301–328 CE) the Mahāvihāra was reconciled,[117] but all three major fraternities continued to receive state patronage.

Different sects of monastic orders have been identified architecturally within Anurādhapura. In addition to *lena*, natural rock-shelters with Early Brahmi inscriptions engraved along drip ledges, which represent the earliest extant category of monastic establishment known at present in Sri Lanka,[118] Bandaranayake identified three categories of monastic complex. The first was the organic or centric monastery, dating from the first century CE onwards. Termed 'organic' due to associations with locales with pre-existing traditions,[119] they are also designated as centric due to a layout focused around a colossal *stūpa*, and in this regard, the Mahāvihāra, Jetavana, Abhayagiri, Vessagiriya in Anurādhapura, as well as Mihintale fit this model.[120] These monasteries were often later elaborated by the construction of a focal-type *stūpa*, with such modifications dating to the early medieval period (600–1200 CE).[121] The second was the Padhānaghara Pirivena, also known as double-platform monasteries, mentioned in the previous section, and thought to be associated with the *paṃsukūlika* fraternity. As stated above, these sites were built from plain ashlar blocks and did not possess typical Buddhist structures or iconography, the only decorated features there being the urinal slabs that seemingly depict images of 'orthodox' ornate vihāras (Figure 1.2). Such iconography can be interpreted as a visible, physical representation and reaction against the wealth and grandiose nature of the ornate monasteries of Anurādhapura.[122] Decorated urinal slabs, meditational pathways and the architectural style suggest that the Padhānaghara Pirivena represented a contestatory discourse from the other monastic categories of Anurādhapura.[123]

Third, the *Pabbata vihāra* is a monastic form thought to date from between 700 to 1200 CE.[124] Believed to be a royal foundation, its architecture shows evidence of a preplanned scheme with a core monument zone of *stūpa*, image house, Bōdhi tree shrine and chapter house surrounded by individual residential structures within a major moated enclosure.[125] They have also been tentatively identified as having Mahāyāna affinities due to their resemblance to prescriptions outlined in the Mahāyāna architectural treatise *Mañjuśrī Vastuvidyāśāstra*.[126] This Mahāyāna influence has been illustrated at these sites through the recovery of copper plaques and plates inscribed with text from the *Pabbata Vihāra* of Vijayārāma,[127] as well as from stūpas at Mihintale and Jetavana Vihāra. This suggests evidence of the Mahāyāna practice of *Dharma-dhātu*, or venerating the word of the Buddha,[128] at monasteries with Mahāyāna leanings.[129] Bronze figures depicting Mahāyāna deities have also been excavated in *pabbata vihāras*

**Fig. 1.2** Urinal stone at one of the Western Monasteries, Anurādhapura, authors' photograph.

within Anurādhapura.[130] Mahāyāna traditions have also been recorded in textual sources. For instance, the first recorded Bōdhisattva image is attributed to the reign of King Mahasena (r. 275–301 CE) and was produced on his request at the Abhayagiri Vihāra.[131] Other Mahāyāna practices, such as *Dharma-dhātu* mentioned above, are attributed in the chronicles to the sixth century CE,[132] and a group of Sanskrit inscriptions provides evidence of Mahāyāna traditions referencing concepts such as *Trikaya*.[133]

The cosmopolitan aspect of Buddhism is further demonstrated in the *Cūḷavaṃsa*, in a passage narrating how the queen of Udaya I (797–801 CE) donated a monastery to a 'Demaḷa bhikkhu community'.[134] Although the meaning of the term 'Demaḷa' is contested,[135] the fact that a distinction was drawn suggests a group with possible differing practices. As well as being identified in textual sources and in the architecture of monumental sites, such a pattern of architectural monastic variation was also apparent in the early medieval (600–1200 CE) hinterland of Anurādhapura.[136] A *pabbata vihāra* site was identified at Parthigala (Z001) in the vicinity of the Nachchaduwawewa, located 4.8 kilometres away from a Padhānaghara Pirivena site at Marathamadama (C112). Although both sites appear to have belonged to different Buddhist traditions, they also appear to have been occupied contemporaneously. Furthermore, 'orthodox' monasteries of the focal type were also widespread at the same time.[137]

At an individual level of analysis, scholars have also been able to identify significant areas of differentiation within chronologically contemporary schools of sculpture and image-making. In a study of six sculptures, based on lead isotope and trace element scatter plots, Arjuna Thantilage identified two distinct groups and interpreted them as representing two separate schools of image production within the Anurādhapura period, possibly representing different Mahāyāna fraternities.[138] There are also architectural differences in *stūpa* construction across the island. While perhaps reflecting differences in patronage or access to distinct building materials, the brick and stone constructions of Anurādhapura and Polonnaruva, particularly the examples of 'Buddhist giganticism',[139] are in stark contrast to the coral and limestone *stūpas* in the Jaffna peninsula, as in the monastic complexes of Delft and Kantarodai[140] (Figures 1.3 and 1.4).

**Fig. 1.3** Stūpas at Delft, authors' photograph.

**Fig. 1.4** Stūpas at Kantarodai, authors' photograph.

That such diversity existed elsewhere within the island is illustrated by the presence of the free-standing crystalline limestone Avalokiteśvara statues, ten metres tall and dating to the seventh century CE, close to a free-standing 14.5-metre high Buddha statue at Maligawila. Furthermore, at Buduruwagala a large rock carved image of the Buddha, dating to the ninth–tenth century CE stands alongside possible depictions of Tara, Avalokiteśvara, Vajrapāṇi holding a thunderbolt, Maitreya and either Viṣṇu or Sahāmpati Brahmā (Figure 1.5). Again, their co-existence demonstrates the variability and diversity of Buddhism and religious practice, as reflected though worship, patronage and architecture, within Sri Lanka.[141]

The population of Rajarata was also anything but homogenous in terms of rank. Early Brahmi inscriptions dating to between the third century BCE and first century CE document a broad spectrum of patrons of early Buddhism, highlighting the diverse society at this period.[142] In an analysis of the 458 inscriptions dating to the early historic period (340–200 BCE) within a fifty-kilometre radius of Anurādhapura, donations mentioning monarchs only accounted for 20.22 per cent of the corpus. Parumakas, identified as representing local chiefs, were the most prevalent at 25.22 per cent, while those where no definitive rank could be assigned accounted for 24.35 per cent. The role of those thought to represent monks was also important in the early patronage of Buddhism, providing 18.91 per cent of donations; with other ranks such as Gamikas (6.09 per cent), Gapatis (3.70 per cent) and Brahmans (1.52 per cent) contributing, as well as those where the donor was unknown (5 per cent).[143] When analysed island-wide, the

**Fig. 1.5** Rock carved images at Buduruwagala, Monaragala District, authors' photograph.

prevalence of donations by monarchs drops to only 6.4 per cent.[144] While the high frequency of donations by monarchs around Anurādhapura could be anticipated, the overall picture is in stark contrast to the *Mahāvaṃsa*'s narrative, whereby rather than an expected elite-driven process of conversion, under the patronage of Devānaṃpiyatissa, leading to the majority of donations being royal in origin, a broader swathe of segments of society contributed to the establishment and growth of Buddhism.

The disparity between the donations mentioned in the chronicles and those in the epigraphic record may be due to the rise of the Mahāvihāra and its capacity to shape memory. It has been suggested that the chronicles 'may represent a contrived ecclesiastical tradition legitimizing the contemporaneous status quo by awarding a central position to the successful kings of Anurādhapura and ignoring the contributions of the failed kings',[145] as well as other segments of society. Indeed, it has previously been noted that in the Early Brahmi epigraphic corpus of Sri Lanka, only ten kings mentioned in the chronicles have been found.[146] Senarat Paranavitana reported failing to identify a single inscription relating to a donation by Devānaṃpiyatissa.[147] Moreover, the corpus of inscriptions reveals genealogies of previously unknown royal lineages, and lineages that have been either ignored by or edited out from the *Mahāvaṃsa*'s narrative.[148]

While the epigraphic corpus illustrates that many different communities and segments of society were patrons of Buddhism, there is also evidence that the Sangha was not the sole recipient. Indeed, pre-Buddhist beliefs are attested to in the chronicles in connection with the presence of Yakkhas. Yakkhas are also recorded in the Vijayan narrative[149] and in the narrative of the laying-out of Anurādhapura by King Paṇḍukābhaya in the fourth century BCE.[150] In this description, additional religious groups, such as 'ascetics', 'heretical sects' and 'Brahmans' were alluded to but were located outside the city.[151] Many of these orders are recorded as having received state patronage, with Paṇḍukābhaya building 'a monastery for wandering mendicant monks, and a dwelling for the Ājīvakas, and a residence for the Brahmans'.[152] Brahmans were recorded as undertaking important religious roles prior to the arrival of Buddhism, and it is noted that during the reign of one of Sri Lanka's first monarchs, King Paṇḍuvāsudeva, the wisdom of 'Brahmans skilled in sacred texts'[153] was called upon for important matters. This importance continued after the arrival and adoption of Buddhism in Sri Lanka, as shown by the twenty-two Early Brahmi inscriptions that mention Brahmans. While there is a possibility that the title 'Brahman' may have continued to be applied after changes in religious affiliation, there is also a possibility that Brahmanism continued alongside early Buddhism in early historic Sri Lanka.[154]

This suggests that the historical developments of the later Anurādhapura period and the shift of the capital to Polonnaruva, traditionally associated with the emergence of a polyvocality of religions and an increased South Indian influence, was not completely novel. In the chronicles, there are records of Anurādhapura's kings supporting non-Buddhist institutions, although for other reigns the only recorded events are the destruction of such institutions, such as Mahasena's demolition of the temples of Brahmanical gods.[155] Later, the chronicles recorded that Mahinda II (r. 777–797 CE) 'restored many decayed temples of the gods here and there and had costly images of the gods fashioned'.[156] Sena II (r. 853–887 CE) was recorded as supporting Brahman rituals.[157] Conversely, Pathmanathan has also drawn attention to the Tamil inscription recording the establishment of a Buddhist monastery in the new Cōḻa capital by a South Indian mercantile group, the *Aiññūṟṟuvar*.[158] As stated above, the transfer of the capital to Polonnaruva has been portrayed as connected with a religious shift towards a more pluralistic and eclectic patronage at state-level, incorporating Buddhist, Brahmanical and Saivite practices.[159] Indrapala has suggested that in tandem with the widespread appearance of tenth-century Tamil inscriptions dated to the regal years of Cōḻa rulers, there was also an increase in Saiva temples.[160] In the chronicles, it is also stated that Parākramabāhu I (r. 1153–86 CE) constructed twenty-four temples to the gods, and Pathmanathan has recorded the presence of at least fourteen temples within Polonnaruva.[161] In support of this plurality, archaeological investigations at Polonnaruva have identified Saiva and Vaisnava shrines with bronze Nataraja, Śiva and Parvati images.[162] A twelfth-century inscription of Niśśaṅkamalla (r. 1187–96 CE) at Dambulla recorded the construction of a Hindu temple as well as the restoration and construction of Buddhist temples.[163] In Anurādhapura itself, structures north of Abhayagiri dating to the later phases of the city's occupation were identified as 'Hindu ruins' on the basis of their architectural layout and the recovery of several lingams,[164] although this identification has been contested.[165]

Artefactual evidence from Anurādhapura's hinterland also illustrates additional 'non-Buddhist' religious and ritual practices about which the *Mahāvaṃsa*'s

**Fig. 1.6** Terracotta figurine fragments from the site of Nikawewa (D339), including a depiction of a human face (right) and an anthropomorphic phallus (left), authors' photograph.

narrative appears silent. From a hinterland survey around Anurādhapura, a total of 489 terracotta artefacts from eight sites, the majority excavated at Nikawewa (D339), were recorded.[166] Dating to between 900 and 1300 CE,[167] these artefacts include human and animal figurines as well as anthropomorphic phalli (Figure 1.6). They were deliberately broken and may reflect a practice not far from that described in studies of the *Gammaduva* ceremony.[168] Deposited in caches across the Dry Zone and known from more than twenty sites, they display a distinct uniformity of design and were clearly restricted to non-monastic and non-urban sites. Traditionally categorized as 'folk' art, they have nevertheless been found associated with a monumental structure at Nikawewa. We have thus reinterpreted them as representing a powerful shared and formalized corpus of ritual practice parallel to Buddhism.[169] This example highlights the ability of archaeology to recognize groups operating outside official state or elite circles. It further suggests that early medieval Anurādhapura was capable of incorporating multiple religious and ritual networks.[170]

## Urbanism

Nestled within the diverse monastic landscape of Anurādhapura was the citadel, measuring one kilometre square, and defined by a ditch and rampart. This has been subject to more than a century of excavations.[171] Early historic treatises, such as the *Arthaśāstra*, contain details of how urban forms should be planned; quadrangular, surrounded by three moats and a rampart,[172] and internally structured by cardinally orientated roads and gateways.[173] Within the city, the *Arthaśāstra* advises that the inhabitants should be separated along *varna* and occupational lines, with heretics and *caṇḍālas* (outcastes) banished outside the city walls.[174] Furthermore, as outlined in the previous section, the description in the *Mahāvaṃsa* of the laying-out of Anurādhapura in the fourth century BCE by Paṇḍukābhaya records that the city was divided into four quarters, and that separate areas of the city were allocated for different social groups.[175] Such textual descriptions have been linked to the archaeological evidence[176] and, architecturally, Anurādhapura appears to match these descriptions as its moat, rampart and cardinally orientated structures seem to conform to the *Arthaśāstra*'s precepts and the description of Paṇḍukābhaya's city. It has been argued that Anurādhapura's layout 'was no casual cluster of buildings but a cosmography that reflected the universe'.[177] This follows the argument of Hocart, who suggested that during the early historic period 'the doctrine of the four quarters [...] had a considerable influence on the planning of cities'.[178] As stated above, other Sri Lankan urban forms correspond to cosmological symbolism, with their plans recreating the universe in microcosm.[179]

However, much evidence from Anurādhapura now suggests that such plans were idealizations. Working on the premise that distinct social groups may be identifiable through artefactual variability across a site, Coningham and Young analysed craft waste and faunal remains from different areas across the citadel.[180] They found no distinct areas associated with specific crafts. The faunal record is particularly interesting in that species forbidden and permitted by the laws of Manu were found together throughout the city.[181] Following suggestions by anthropologists and historians that caste rigidity may be a recent phenomenon,[182] this analysis reinforces the notion that social divisions based on material differentiation were not present in early historic Anurādhapura – or may require more refined archaeological methodologies than those at our disposal in order to be identified.[183] This is not to say that Anurādhapura did not host various differentiated communities, as outlined above. It rather suggests that while there is abundant evidence for plurality, there were *also* widely shared practices. Cosmopolitan practices were compatible with both differentiation and unifying concepts and lifestyle choices.

## Studying the cosmopolitan through archaeology in Sri Lanka

It is clear that Sri Lanka was not a uniquely Buddhist island but had strong Hindu influences as well as more localized traditions, as evidenced by the emergent terracotta cults in the hinterland of Anurādhapura. Rather than focusing on the religious and spiritual aspects of Buddhism, archaeological evidence suggests that the monastic institutions of Anurādhapura seemed to have played a dominant material role in the colonization, management and development of the wider landscape surrounding the city. Monasteries remained the only viable long-term structures within the hinterland, as attempts to secularize the management of the landscape faded. The epigraphic record reveals how land was donated by kings and other elites to these monasteries, to the degree of completely alienating it from state control. Sri Lankan scholars have long hypothesized about this, with Leslie Gunawardana stating in 1979 that 'considerable powers were transferred to the monastic administration by withholding the authority of government officials to intervene in their affairs',[184] Even more starkly, Dias wrote that 'lands and villages beyond the control of the central authority were given to the monasteries to bring some control over them [...] This way the monastic institutions became the landed intermediary between the central political authority and the people.'[185]

The recent research-oriented fieldwork developed in the hinterland of Anurādhapura has demonstrated the existence of a complex patchwork, itself consisting of intricate networks of religious and secular cooperation and communication. As noted above, six years of field research have allowed us to identify more than 750 archaeological sites, ranging from small scatters of eroded ceramics, through rock-cut caves, stone bridges over the Malvatu Oya, metal-working sites and a corpus of sites containing terracotta figurines, to monastic complexes several hectares in size.[186] The ceramic scatters can be interpreted as short-term villages linked to slash-and-burn (*chena*) agriculture. Monastic sites, in contrast, ranging from rock-cut shelters to large complexes, reflect a much more permanent and highly visible presence. This contrast led us initially to theorize about a 'Theocratic Landscape' in which monasteries functioned as centres of economic and political control (in lieu of towns), while villages kept shifting around them.[187] Since then, we have developed a more complex model of 'Buddhist Temporalities' and low-density urbanism, reflecting our growing awareness of multiple heterarchies in the Anurādhapura hinterland. Our Buddhist Temporality model reflects the complex relationship between monastic institutions and secular authority, contending that 'the city's surrounding landscape of villages and rural communities was not centrally regulated by the state through higher-order settlements and royal officials but through a network of *Vihāras*, closely linked to the great monasteries of the city rather than the throne'.[188]

Certainly, the critical reappraisal of archaeological evidence allows us to narrow the gap between Anurādhapura and Polonnaruva. While the latter has long been archaeologically interpreted as a cosmopolitan urban centre, similar evidence from Anurādhapura has been largely undervalued but is now overwhelming. The remains of Polonnaruva, traditionally dated to between 1017 and 1293 CE, have revealed Buddhist monasteries *and* Hindu temples with bronze sculptures of Hindu deities. This has led some scholars, rightly in our opinion, to speak of religious plurality and harmony.[189] Excavations within the Alahana Pirivena in Polonnaruva uncovered quantities of pottery with appliqué designs, including swastika, *śrīvasta* and *vajra* or *triśūla*,[190] which have now also been identified in the city's hinterland (Figure 1.7). Bronze figurines excavated at Polonnaruva and representing deities such as Śiva and Parvati have been put forward as evidence of the presence of Hinduism in the city.[191] And yet such evidence was not restricted to Polonnaruva. For example, figures of Śiva, Parvati,

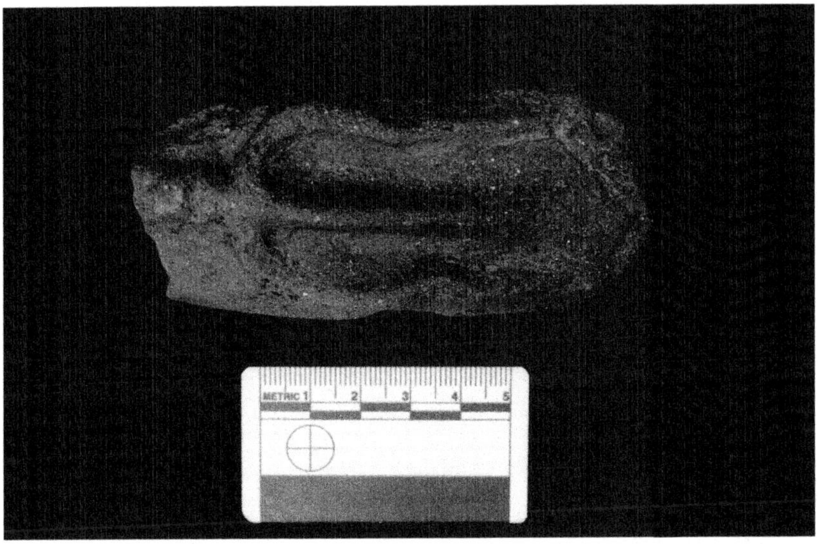

**Fig. 1.7** Appliqué *triśūla* on a pottery rim sherd from site Kalahagala (S360) in the hinterland of Polonnaruva, found during the 2016 field season of the Polonnaruva Archaeological and Anthropological Research Project, authors' photograph.

Kevalamūrti and Nṛtyamūrti, and potentially Ardhanarīśvara, were recovered from a pillar foundation at Jetavana in the 1980s.[192] Furthermore, three appliqué ceramic sherds with symbols similar to those from the Alahana Pirivena were discovered in the later sequence of trench ASW2 at Anurādhapura,[193] as well as in the vicinity of Jetavana.[194] The later evidence at Anurādhapura is striking in its similarity to the evidence usually given for plurality of belief in Polonnaruva, and yet Anurādhapura, persistently presented as an essentially Buddhist capital, is generally not advanced as a similar example of religious plurality. The transmission of the capital from Anurādhapura to Polonnaruva has been projected as an abrupt and singular event, yet recent research has shown the abandonment of Anurādhapura and its hinterland to have been a slow process that happened over several centuries.[195] We would argue that around Polonnaruva there is likely to be evidence of much earlier settlements and communities that would shed more light on the nature of early medieval Sri Lanka. To this end, the Central Cultural Fund and British Academy have sponsored successful pilot hinterland surveys around Polonnaruva, as well as excavations at Śiva Devale No.2 and the citadel's northern wall.

We are, of course, far from constructing a clear narrative and it remains problematic to assign certain artefactual forms to particular groups. Widely shared symbols, such as the swastika and vajra / triśūla, highlight the difficulties inherent to South Asian archaeology. Indeed, they lead to questions about the

**Fig. 1.8** Head from a Buddha image rededicated as an image of Ayanayake, Anurādhapura hinterland, authors' photograph.

extent to which artefacts can be defined as Buddhist, Hindu or Jain. The fluid identity of artefacts has recently been noted at a modern shrine to Ayanayake, lord of the jungle, in the Anurādhapura hinterland. The shrine was constructed using reclaimed pillars from nearby monastic structures damaged during road construction but was also equipped with an eroded Buddha head, which was painted with the trunk of Ayanayake, as the focus of the shrine[196] (Figure 1.8). While objects may be used in more than one context with changed meanings, the opposite may also occur, with similar architectural motifs being part of several traditions. Stūpas and vihāras share many traits with Jain and Hindu architecture.[197] A further challenge that needs addressing is the archaeological visibility of women within early Sri Lanka's history and archaeology. Indeed, Faxian noted the presence of nuns within the Sacred City of Anurādhapura[198] and inscriptions record donations by female devotees throughout Sri Lanka.[199] Furthermore, communities of Buddhist nuns from Sri Lanka are recorded in an inscription at Nagarjunakonda in India[200] but, in spite of this, there has been little discussion of this challenge within both archaeological interpretations and Buddhist discourse.[201] Gender is notoriously difficult to identify within the archaeological record, especially when dealing with the ephemeral remains of a subtropical landscape. However, if we want to truly understand the cosmopolitan nature of early historic and early medieval Sri Lanka, such challenges have to be acknowledged and then addressed.

The landscape we have been studying was highly contested, closely integrated into the secular and monastic core, yet at the same time divorced from the networks and linkages enjoyed by the urban elite. Tensions prevailed between the pressing need to participate in larger networks of exchange, patronage and religious merit through the royal centre and major monastic institutions of Anurādhapura, on the one hand, and the practice of non-Buddhist rituals, on the other. Such diversity continued into the late medieval period, as attested by the fifteenth-century trilingual inscription of Admiral Zheng He in Galle. The inscription in Tamil, Chinese and Persian records the veneration of an incarnation of Viṣṇu, of the Buddha, and of a Muslim saint, providing evidence for the continued, diverse and dynamic linguistic and religious framework of the island.[202] Taking all this together, we find evidence of what can be interpreted as a highly cosmopolitan society with broad international links and outlooks and considerable internal diversity. This society participated in an ever-expanding network of religious and economic exchange and patronage. Yet, at the same time, there were also distinctly pervasive traditions – subsistence, ceramic forms, craft manufacturing and patterns of low density urbanism. This apparently contradictory stance reflects the many possible facets of community identity, ranging in scale from the local to the regional and the global. The degree to which different communities had access to opportunities probably changed over time but the archaeological record overall strongly suggests that Sri Lanka, far from being a peripheral island, was at the very heart of many social, economic and religious developments of the Indian Ocean World.[203]

# 2

# 'Implicit cosmopolitanism' and the commercial role of ancient Lanka

*Rebecca R. Darley*[1]

> *2250 years of Sri Lanka's history is dominated by a complexity of religious, political and above all commercial relations that the island had maintained with the outside world throughout many centuries.*[2]

This comment on the history of the island and the continuity of its ancient and modern engagement with the wider world reflects a perception of ancient Lanka that is deeply invested in what may be termed 'implicit cosmopolitanism'.[3] While the term 'cosmopolitan' is rarely applied directly to the island's history from c. 600 BCE to c. 650 CE, a collection of themes – of connectedness, transregional significance, and religious and social pluralism – are repeatedly invoked.[4] At their heart lies the contention that due to its pre-eminent role in Indian Ocean trade networks, ancient Lanka played a leading role in long-term, largely cooperative contact with all of the major cultures surrounding it, from Rome (later Byzantium) in the west to China in the east and India in the north.[5]

In this respect, the cosmopolitanism of ancient Lanka may be perceived (and, indeed, on occasion has explicitly been evoked) in contrast to the early modern cosmopolitanism enforced on the island by the expansion of European imperialism.[6] Just as the 1977 Bandaranayake government of Sri Lanka inaugurated a continuation of the chronicle of the island as an assertion of continuity of community and purpose and thus absorbed the period of European domination into a longer narrative, which itself contained periods of foreign rule and military conflict, so has modern scholarship on the commercial relations of ancient Lanka provided fertile ground for constructing a cultural and economic identity for modern Sri Lanka, which situates the present in the past and claims continuity and peace rather than disjuncture and conflict as the nation's core values.[7]

Such a vision of the island's past connects closely with a common historiographical representation of ancient Lankan history, when Anurādhapura functioned as the island's capital, as a 'golden age'.[8] This golden age is characterized, however, by a cosmopolitanism that emphasizes Lanka's relationship to the wider – and, above all, Western – world rather than the internal relationships that constituted the island. Such an outward-looking cosmopolitanism on the one hand reinforces a perception of the ancient period as one of grandeur and influence that implicitly accepts modern associations of commercial success, power and positivity, and on the other does not challenge homogeneous nationalist visions of the island as Buddhist and Sinhala.[9] It is a cosmopolitanism situated in numerous imagined encounters between a prosperous, peaceful, powerful and culturally unitary Buddhist Lanka and a dazzling, diverse and delighted array of foreigners, whose visits to the island were too brief and too limited to coastal regions to impact on Lankan culture but that nevertheless demonstrated the island's significance far beyond its shores.

The purpose of this chapter is not completely to disavow ancient Lanka's commercial role in the Indian Ocean. It is, however, to demonstrate that assertions about the nature of its ancient commercial role have in places outstripped or distorted the available evidence. Numismatic evidence has been central to many of the claims made about ancient 'cosmopolitan' Lanka, making it first necessary to unpick a narrative constructed from evidence that is often represented as 'objective' because it is tangible. Following a rereading of published coin evidence from the island, this chapter presents five previously unpublished, or only partially published, Byzantine coins of the fifth to sixth centuries CE, which purport to have a Sri Lankan provenance, demonstrating the difficulty of imposing a simple, linear narrative onto ancient evidence. Coin evidence, moreover, has consistently been interpreted in light of, inserted into and used to strengthen and modify conclusions derived from textual and archaeological sources, where a similar impulse towards a preordained conclusion can be identified. Finally, this chapter offers a new synthesis of ancient Lanka's commercial and cultural connections, pointing to developing areas of research and suggesting new ways of understanding the island's growth as an interface between the western and eastern Indian Ocean regions from the late fifth and early sixth centuries.

## Unpicking 'implicit cosmopolitanism': the case of the coins

Coins datable to the ancient period and found in Sri Lanka often appear to provide external corroboration of textual sources that refer to foreign connections, discussed later in this chapter, and thus form the backbone of a narrative of cosmopolitanism.[10] A sampling of publications discussing ancient Lanka and particularly its connections with other regions, its pluralism and its implicit cosmopolitanism yields multiple cases, among which the following 2005 publication by Boulnois is a typical example of a widespread strategy of using numismatic evidence to support wider arguments about Lanka's extensive trade relations:[11]

> In the first centuries of the Christian era, Ceylon seems to have been a sort of huge cash-register, a treasury of coinage and money from various countries which indicates the multiplicity and importance of its trade. Tens of thousands of coins – Indian, Roman, Kushan, Sassanian Persian and Chinese – have been unearthed there. In the first three centuries AD, the island had active commercial relations with northern India and with Western states, either directly or through the intermediary of Indian sailors. Silver *denarii* of nine Roman emperors have been found, as well as a few copper coins from Alexandria, and silver coins from northern India and from the Kushan Empire. From the 4th century on, with growing economic crises in the Roman Empire and in Egyptian commerce, Sri Lanka became the largest maritime trade centre of the Indian Ocean. Tens of thousands of bronze and copper Roman coins (no longer silver ones) have been discovered there dating to the 4th and 5th centuries, issued in the mints of Rome, Alexandria, Carthage, Antioch, Constantinople and other Mediterranean cities. The numerous Sassanian and Byzantine coins date from the 6th and 7th centuries, while Arab coinage marks the period when sailors from the caliphates visited Serendib, as Ceylon was also known.[12]

The picture presented here is powerful but quickly begins to fray under close analysis. The first problem concerns chronology. 'In the first centuries of the Christian era' provides only a broad anchor, but it also encompasses and therefore implies the contemporaneity of everything that follows, i.e., Indian, Roman, Kushan, Sasanian Persian and Chinese coin finds. While the first four categories are broadly contemporaneous, the same cannot be said of the Chinese coins, which only seem to have arrived on the island later, from the tenth century onwards.[13] Subsequently, the citation purports to chart a series of shifts in trade relations. The first to third centuries are characterized by trade with India and 'Western states' (Rome). The fourth and fifth centuries represent, on the basis of 'tens of thousands' of coins from the mints of the eastern Mediterranean, the high point of Lanka's trade with the Roman Empire; the sixth and seventh centuries are epitomized by Byzantine and Sasanian coin finds (with the continued and implicit connection between coin finds and commercial contact). Finally, Arab coinage, although not dated specifically, appears to mark a move, presumably in the late seventh or eighth century, towards Muslim trade with the island. It is a narrative of continuous, evolving and exotic interconnections between ancient Lanka and the eastern, but above all, western edges of the Indian Ocean.

Such a narrative cannot withstand close scrutiny. Taking only the coin varieties mentioned, not a single seventh-century Sasanian coin from the island has been identified. Moreover, the transition in trading relationships with the island from either Roman/Byzantine or Sasanian to Arab/Muslim is marked not by the gradually shifting identity of coin finds implied by Boulnois' account but rather by a gap of around five centuries in the coin record; the earliest documented Arabic coins in the island date from the twelfth century.[14] Furthermore, few indications of the quantity or significance of coin finds are provided. This is important since coins may offer evidence for communication, contact and economic and social systems but they are also small, mobile, durable objects that historically might travel great distances without carrying any significant meaning for the reconstruction of economic networks or historic 'cosmopolitanism'. The famous case of a coin of Kanishka I discovered in Wales, for example, is remarkable but as an isolated find does not indicate ancient connections between northern India and northern Wales.[15]

In the case of ancient Lanka, quantity is highly relevant to the conclusions drawn from coin finds and Boulnois' language is misleadingly ambiguous. 'Silver *denarii* of nine emperors', for example, implies chronological and numerical breadth. Equally true, but perhaps more relevant, is that fewer than twenty imperial *denarii* in total have ever been found on the island, and some of these may have reached the island as curios in the modern period.[16] As the coins from the de Saram collection (below) demonstrate, modern collecting habits are disregarded at the peril of any reconstruction of ancient patterns. The same numerical paucity is true of the disputed total numbers of Kushan coins (either one or around twenty-four specimens).[17]

Boulnois then refers to Byzantine and Sasanian coins. The copper-alloy examples, treated separately by Boulnois, are also given separate consideration in this chapter. Beyond them, the record is thin indeed. Codrington recorded a handful of finds of Byzantine precious metal coins (six in total, including one imitation probably produced on the island).[18] Walburg's work to catalogue new material and re-evaluate older notices of coin finds reduces this list to three Byzantine gold examples with a certain island provenance.[19] In addition, a total of twenty Byzantine coins (eighteen gold, one copper-alloy and one silver) are listed from private collections but were probably not found on the island.[20] Additionally cited as evidence of Byzantine coins on the island is a hoard described thus by Codrington:[21]

> [E]arly in the nineteenth century a pot of gold coins inscribed in 'ancient Greek characters, *konob-obryza*' was found in the north of Ceylon, apparently in the Jaffna peninsula (J. Roberts, *Oriental Illustrations of the Sacred Scriptures*, 1844, p. 531): these in all probability were solidi, possibly of the Byzantine period.[22]

This description recalls Byzantine *solidi* but no specimen from the hoard was recorded in detail or preserved. Moreover, the description provided by Roberts *evokes* a Byzantine *solidus* but could not have *been* a description of one. The account refers to the mint mark (*konob-obryza*) as being in 'ancient Greek characters'. This refers to and is instantly recognizable to anyone familiar with Byzantine coinage as the mint or quality mark, CONOB. This, however, was always abbreviated to CONOB, not *konob-obryza*, and given in Latin rather than Greek characters (hence, C rather than K). This is significant because it indicates that Roberts either did not describe the coins exactly as he saw them or he did not see them but heard a description from a third party, determined their likely identity and filled in the blanks from his general numismatic knowledge, in either case expanding and translating the mint mark. There is, furthermore, no indication of the size of the pot or the number of coins. While interesting, therefore, as the foundation of weighty historical conclusions, this account is open to serious question.

Application of the term 'numerous' to Sasanian coins is even more dubious. Codrington recorded three Sasanian silver *drachms* and to these O. Bopearachchi added five more (recorded with images, but no weights or details of find location or provenance), all eight dating from the fourth to sixth centuries.[23] Bopearachchi has subsequently noted four additional fourth- to sixth-century finds.[24] Walburg, by contrast, lists seven Sasanian coins, all described as of doubtful Lankan origin, and one Lankan imitation of a Sasanian copper-alloy type.[25] In other words, numismatic evidence for Sasanian contact, direct or indirect, with ancient Lanka consists, generously, of ten partially documented examples. Conservatively, the evidence dwindles to three genuine coins found in fairly securely documented hoards and one local copper-alloy imitation. Given the quite large-scale manufacture of imitation Roman copper-alloy coins, one Sasanian imitation does not mean that large numbers of prototypes reached the island. It only proves that metalworkers, already accustomed to cutting die imitations of small, foreign copper-alloy coins, came across an example.

The description of early Arab coins also elides small numbers of total finds into a language that implies significance. As already noted, the start date of Arab coins on the island is not as early as Boulnois' description implies, but the quantities of those that remain are also extremely small and spread over a very long time span.[26] For almost all categories of coin mentioned by Boulnois the evidence falls catastrophically short of 'tens of thousands' of examples.[27] Boulnois' book, like many other works where similar claims can be found, is not primarily numismatic nor focused on Lanka and thus relies on specialist publications to enable the creation of new perspectives and approaches. This is not inherently a problem, and underpins all transregional and multidisciplinary work. Nonetheless, given the widespread perception of numismatics as esoteric or obscure, it demonstrates the ease with which erroneous or misleading data and ideas may proliferate rapidly through secondary scholarship if scholars too easily accept and combine synthetic conclusions without at least surveying the underlying evidence and methodologies being used.

This presentation of far-reaching conclusions from quite limited evidence also demonstrates a tendency to present numismatic data in a way that strongly supports a more general impression of ancient cosmopolitanism. This is undoubtedly partly a consequence of the easily exportable summaries with which some coin publications conclude, often constructing dramatic soundbites from very small amounts of data.[28] At times, however, it is possible to see a more insistent interpretative bias towards a narrative of connectivity. One study devoted to the question of the circulation of Roman/Byzantine and Sasanian precious-metal coinage on the island concludes that, since Sri Lanka lacks natural gold sources, incoming Roman gold coins must have been melted down to create the Lankan gold types that are known from the eighth century, and that bear some resemblance in their weights to the Byzantine *solidus* or fractions thereof.[29] Thus, '[t]here can be no doubt that Persian silver coins and Byzantine solidi reached the island in quantities during the fifth and sixth centuries and perhaps even later'.[30] This is an argument based primarily on the lack of surviving material. It fails to explain why gold coins entering the island up to, at the latest, the first half of the seventh century should not have inspired a local gold coinage until the eighth and it does not address in any way the possible fate of the Sasanian coins whose presence on the island is, by the logic of the argument, indicated by an equally striking scarcity. There was no silver Lankan coinage into which they could have been transformed and no alternative explanation is offered for why a lack of finds must indicate a circulating presence.

While finds of precious metal coins feature prominently in numismatic literature, however, the numismatic narrative of 'cosmopolitan' Lanka stems above all from publication of the 'tens of thousands' of Roman copper-alloy coins found on the island.[31] It is these coins and their startling number that underpin hypotheses about ancient Lankan commercial ties to the Mediterranean. These are also the coins that have the most problematic history of modern publication. The figure of 'tens of thousands' (and even hundreds of thousands) of late Roman copper-alloy coins derives from a tendency to publish notices of discoveries that are variable in their enumeration but consistent in the deployment of large numbers (or simply invocations of quantity) and few details, for example, '[a]ccording to my estimation, the number of published and unpublished Roman "third brass" and their so-called "Indo-Roman" imitations found in the island comes to more than 200,000'.[32]

In addition to a vagueness about quantity, the mention of 'Indo-Roman imitations' – also referred to as Roman 'third brass' or 'Naimana' for one of the locations at which they were first discovered in large quantities – is significant. These terms all refer to locally made imitations of Roman copper-alloy coins, which are found, as well as original Roman copper-alloy coins, on the island. They display designs clearly based on Roman models and are frequently found, like original Roman examples, in hoards.[33] They are unique to Lanka. Although Roman copper-alloy coins are found in South India in significant quantities, there is no evidence that they were routinely imitated there.[34] Given that references to huge hoards of copper-alloy coins on the island frequently present the volume of finds as in some capacity correlative with the volume or commercial significance of Roman contact with ancient Lanka, it is problematic that such imitations are often included under the umbrella of 'Roman' coinage, and that secondary literature concerning ancient Lanka so often depends on precisely these publications.[35]

Walburg's *Coins and Tokens from Ancient Ceylon* has offered some important correctives to this numismatic picture. Walburg estimates the number of Roman and imitation Roman coins found in Sri Lanka at 30,000 to 40,000.[36] This figure is derived from the coins Walburg was able to see and a conservative estimate of the quantity of other finds that might reside in private collections.[37] His presentation also makes it possible to assess roughly the relative quantities of genuine Roman and imitation Roman coins from Lanka. He cites the only documented hoards of Naimana, listed as containing roughly 4,350 specimens.[38] This should be compared in particular to the 5,000 Roman coins Walburg regards as very certainly attested from the island. Since Walburg's catalogue includes reference to hoards now lost for which exact numbers are not recorded or for which descriptions are suspect, these figures (suggesting similar orders of magnitude for original and imitation coins) remain approximate, but are based in analysis of identified sources.

Walburg's examination of the Naimana has also revealed various features of their production and deposition that suggest that they should not be regarded primarily as indicators of long-distance maritime trade. For example, the lead content in these coins is as high as 30 per cent, making the metal very brittle. Striking Naimana was, therefore, a complex and delicate procedure and the coins that resulted were not very robust.[39] The gentle handling required to prevent these coins from cracking during the minting process also invalidates earlier interpretations of them as being worn by long use, further suggesting that they did not circulate as regular coinage.

Imitations were also probably struck over a fairly short period in the southern region of the island and those found in hoards were deposited at around the same time. They do not appear to have been hoarded with, and therefore to have circulated alongside, Roman coins as a functioning currency.[40] Instead, in the case of both original and imitation Roman coins Walburg proposes that they were used as 'special purpose money', mainly serving the needs of ritual depositions and limited transactions among elites, with the imitations made when the Roman pieces ran out as a consequence of this hoarding practice.[41] Walburg's analysis of the chronology of the original Roman copper-alloy finds, moreover, causes him to reject completely the hypothesis that Roman coins on ancient Lanka necessarily indicate direct contact with Romans. Walburg argues that the coins were shipped as a single hoard or small number of cargoes in the second quarter of the fifth century to South India, whence some filtered to Lanka, with the production of imitations beginning around the middle of the fifth century.[42]

Although Walburg's treatment of this evidence is well-documented and most thorough, it has not succeeded in displacing the traditional narrative. One reason is that the myth of an ancient cosmopolitan Lanka appeals to a particular vision of the island's past, which combines global significance, ancient glory and an uncomplicated view of maritime interconnections.[43] It is also likely, however, that the account of 'tens of thousands' of Roman coins and 'numerous' Sasanian, Byzantine and Arab coins from ancient Lanka has permeated the secondary literature of the island because it is easy. The alternative is less straightforward, with no easily exportable icon to project into larger accounts. Its presentation demands a degree of engagement with the raw data even by scholars who are interested mainly in the end product.[44] Above all, using numismatic data requires reflection on its limitations. Coin finds (along with excavations) are the most common source of new data for ancient Lankan history, but new data cannot be expected to provide a new linear narrative, especially one constructed in terms of continuities with later evidence and modern prerogatives, as demonstrated by coin finds recently rediscovered in the UK.[45]

## Coins from the Leslie de Saram collection

On 1 October 1955, a Saturday, British coin collector, Philip D. Whitting purchased five gold *solidi*. A high purity gold coin usually weighing around 4.5 grams, the *solidus* served as the core denomination of the Byzantine monetary system from the fourth century until the eleventh.[46] Whitting bought the coins at a total cost of around £19 from A. H. Baldwin, one of Britain's leading coin dealers and now auction houses.[47] The coins had come from the collection of Leslie William Frederick de Saram, a solicitor, heir to one of Colombo's oldest and most respected law firms, and for most of his life a resident of Colombo.[48] De Saram was also a collector of antiquities, including coins, and travelled widely. He was born in 1877 and died in 1961, leaving most of his collection to the University of Peradeniya.[49] De Saram's choice prior to this bequest to sell some of his coins to a London-based dealer demonstrates the international networks within which he participated.[50]

While de Saram's reasons for selling are unknown, Whitting's taste for buying Eastern coinage is eloquently illustrated by the Barber Institute collection.[51] Whether knowing Whitting's interests or as a matter of standard practice, it seems clear that Baldwin conveyed some of the provenance of de Saram's coins to Whitting. Closer examination of Whitting's records in the Barber Institute cannot, however, add precision to the cryptic note 'found in Ceylon'. It is unclear who was responsible for the label, whether de Saram himself from his own or his dealer's information, Baldwin, assuming island provenance from the seller, or Whitting, assuming it from Baldwin's information about the seller. It is possible, however, to link these coins partially to earlier notifications about the de Saram collection, and so situate them within larger debates about the meaning of ancient coins in modern Sri Lanka, and to offer some tentative suggestions as to their likely (or unlikely) island provenance.

Two of the most influential writers on the subject of ancient foreign coin finds in Sri Lanka – Codrington in 1924 and Walburg in 2008 – have discussed the de Saram collection. It is also clear, from the notes of Walter Howard Biddell, an irrigation engineer and amateur numismatist collecting on the island in the first half of the twentieth century, whose notes have been extensively mined by Walburg and who knew de Saram personally, that de Saram purchased many of his coins (including *solidi*) in London.[52] Either without knowing this or without acknowledging it, Codrington provided a list of the Roman and Byzantine coins in de Saram's collection, probably based on inspection prior to 1921 (when Codrington's acknowledgements, thanking de Saram for access to his collection, are dated), implying – although not stating – that the coins had been found on the island.[53] These were, in chronological order: an *aureus* of Tiberius (r. 14–37 CE), four *solidi* of Constantius II (r. 337–61), two of Valentinian I (r. 364–75), three of Valens (364–78), three of Honorius (r. 393–423), one of Theodosius II (r. 408–50), one of Anastasius I (r. 495–518) and one of Maurice (r. 582–602), plus a *semissis* and a *tremissis* (one half and one third of a *solidus*, respectively) of Justinian I (r. 527–65). The collection represented the mints of Constantinople, Antioch, Nicomedia, Rome, Treveri and Milan.[54] The Barber Institute finds make it clear that de Saram continued collecting Byzantine material after the publication of *Ceylon Coins and Currency*, since not all of the items match this list, but do not make it easier to identify whether the coins were found on the island.

Walburg, in part relying on Biddell's insights into de Saram's purchasing habits, speculated that the majority of the coins listed by Codrington, and especially the earlier coins from Tiberius to Honorius, were unlikely to have been found on the island.[55] In addition to Biddell's information, Walburg's reasons for doubting the island provenance of most of de Saram's coins seem to be cautious but sensible: namely that three come from mints in the western Mediterranean or Northern Europe, rather than the east Mediterranean and that the earlier examples date to reigns from which few examples of coins are attested in either India or the island. This is not a watertight argument, especially for Sri Lanka where the total number of securely provenanced finds, discussed in this chapter, is so small as to make any argument from absence extremely fragile. Nevertheless, in conjunction with the textual and archaeological evidence also examined here for Lanka not having been a significant player in western Indian Ocean networks until at least the fifth century, it seems prudent to treat the earlier examples with great scepticism.

Of the five coins identified in the Barber Institute collection by Walburg as possibly genuine island finds (which all come from the later period), two examples apparently from Italian mints and an overall spread from Theodosius II to Maurice make the probability of this group having been a single hoard extremely low. The profile is suggestive of a collection constructed for chronological, iconographic and minting breadth. Three of the Barber coins are probably identical with examples recorded by Codrington: specifically, the *solidi* of Theodosius II from Constantinople (Figure 2.1), of Anastasius recorded by Codrington as Constantinopolitan (Figure 2.2), and of Maurice (Figure 2.3).

Coins of Theodosius II are attested both on the island and in South India.[57] This example (LR489, Figure 2.1) parallels a type found in the Akki Alur hoard in South India, and may be an imitation rather than a genuine Byzantine issue, suggested by its light weight – 3.8 grams.[58] Nevertheless, it seems far more likely to be an imitation produced in or near the Byzantine Empire and purchased by de Saram in London for his collection than one made in India or Lanka. The weights of the coins in the Akki Alur hoard are not known for comparison

**Fig. 2.1** Gold *solidus* of Theodosius II, minted in Constantinople, Barber Institute of Fine Arts, LR489 (Whitting No. G522), 3.82 grams, die axis 6 o'clock, *RIC* X, 202.[56]

**Fig. 2.2** Gold *solidus* of Theoderic I of Italy, struck in the name of Anastasius, probably in Italy, Barber Institute of Fine Arts, VV07 (Whitting No. G520), 4.28 grams, die axis 6 o'clock, Hahn *MIB* 9.[61]

but most Indian imitations mirror the weight of official *solidi* suggesting that this was important for their acceptability in the East.[59] Furthermore, Ratto, a European collector with no known connection to the Indian Ocean, in the 1930 sale catalogue of his own collection, recorded an example of such a lightweight *solidus* of Theodosius II, noting that it was 'de poids réduit... Très rare. Très beau.'[60] If this were an Indian Ocean imitation, it would be highly unlikely for a collector in Europe to have come across an identical specimen. It therefore seems likely that de Saram purchased this coin in Europe precisely because of its rarity and fine condition.

**Fig. 2.3** Gold *solidus* of Maurice Tiberius, struck in Constantinople, Barber Institute of Fine Arts, B1767 (Whitting No. 518), 4.49 grams, die axis 7 o'clock, *MIB* 6E.[64]

VV07 (Figure 2.2) may be the same *solidus* of Anastasius recorded by Codrington as having been part of the de Saram collection. It is indeed struck in the name of Anastasius, and in 1924 Codrington's attribution of the coin to the mint of Constantinople on the basis of its mint mark, COMOB, may have accorded with his knowledge and observations. By 1955, when Whitting recorded the coin, however, he listed it, as current scholarly consensus holds, as a *solidus* of the Ostrogothic king of Italy, Theoderic I, minted in the name of Anastasius. Sixth-century gold coins struck anywhere in the Byzantine Empire usually carried the CONOB mark, standing for *Constantinopoli obryziacus* or 'fine gold of Constantinople', apparently as a guarantee of purity rather than location of minting. The COMOB variant has been linked to Italy.[62] This coin should, therefore, be considered a probable Italian issue, but it could have travelled from Italy to the eastern Mediterranean and thence to India or Sri Lanka, and coins of Anastasius are also known in South India, although none have yet been identified there with the COMOB mint mark.[63] It could, however, also have been bought by de Saram because of the interest value to a collector of its Italian connection. There is no way to determine the likelihood of this find having come from European purchase or South Asian discovery.

Finally, the *solidus* of Maurice (B1767, Figure 2.3) seems to be a genuine, Constantinopolitan issue. Coins of Maurice are not attested in India, but chronologically they would fit the extremely sparse but visible picture of later Byzantine coin finds from Sri Lanka.[65] It is therefore plausibly an island find, but only plausibly, and could just as easily have been a fine example bought by de Saram to expand the range of his collection.

Apart from these three coins, possibly already identified by Codrington, two Barber Institute specimens testify to de Saram's continued collecting beyond the

**Fig. 2.4** Gold *solidus* of Valentinian III, struck in Ravenna, Barber Institute of Fine Arts, LR540 (Whitting No. G521), 4.36 grams, die axis 7 o'clock, *RIC* X, 202.[66]

early 1920s. They are both atypical for Byzantine coins found in India, but cannot on that basis be excluded from a Sri Lankan provenance, since finds from the island are too few to make such generalizations. The first (Figure 2.4) is a *solidus* of Valentinian III (r. 425–55) from Ravenna.

The Ravenna origin of this coin is indicated by the letters R and V in the reverse field. Legally, gold coins of good weight and issued in the name of the emperor could circulate anywhere in the Roman and Byzantine Empire, making it possible for this coin, like the Anastasian issue from Italy, to have reached Lanka in antiquity.[67] In addition, Krishnamurthy records an Indian imitation of a Byzantine *solidus*, found in Tamil Nadu, which uses the reverse design of a type of Valentinian III, providing a chronological link.[68] On the other hand, a fine specimen of a type that testifies eloquently to a tense political moment in the western Roman Empire, making it an attractive piece for a collector, may suggest a European purchase. Again, it is not possible to determine likely provenance.

Finally, a *solidus* of Theodosius II from the mint of Thessaloniki presents the most challenging case to assess (Figure 2.5). If an Indian Ocean find, it would be the first Thessalonikan gold coin to appear so far east along maritime routes, although the same type but issued by the mint at Constantinople has a parallel in the Akki Alur hoard.[69] Crucially, this coin appears to be an imitation, and quite a crude one in comparison with official issues. It is also quite damaged, with two deep gouges on the reverse and some evidence for bending, possibly as a result of ploughing. The damage makes it less likely that de Saram would have bought this specimen in Europe simply to enhance his collection. The accurate but distinctive style of imitation, which preserves even minor details of the type and legend, but which is nevertheless differentiated by its execution and, at times, legibility, from genuine issues also conforms well with imitations of Byzantine coins found in India, although this does not distinguish it with certainty from imitations produced

**Fig. 2.5** Gold *solidus* of Theodosius II, struck in Thessaloniki, Barber Institute of Fine Arts, LR482 (Whitting No. G519), 4.42 grams, die axis 6 o'clock, *RIC* X, 361.[70]

further west. Of all of the coins found in the Barber collection, therefore, this one, despite the Thessalonikan mint signature, seems the most likely to have a historical Lankan provenance.

These coins offer a kaleidoscopic view of the interaction of ancient and modern ideas and realities of cosmopolitanism on Sri Lanka. Leslie de Saram was a man who lived his life in the conflicted but undoubtedly interconnected world of Sri Lanka's transition from colony to independent nation-state. He travelled extensively and had numismatic contacts in London. He probably read, or at least had access to, books that celebrated, publicized and sometimes overstated the connections of the Roman world with the Indian Ocean, and he collected Roman and Byzantine coins.[71] It is impossible to interpret newly identified survivals from his collection within these multiple contexts and reach any certain judgement as to their origin. Each of them could have represented to de Saram either finds from the island collected as evidence for ancient trade, purchases at foreign auctions chosen for fineness, breadth of coverage and rarity, or a combination of local and foreign acquisitions put together for entirely personal and ad hoc reasons. They all form part of a material and cultural tapestry of modern interactions, which directly shape visions of the past. Some, especially the Thessalonikan coin of Theodosius II, and the *solidi* of Valentinian III and Maurice, may speculatively contribute to the handful of Byzantine coin finds connected to ancient Lanka. None provides unequivocal evidence of ancient Lanka's supposed connection with the west, but it seems that this possibility appealed to Whitting, as it had to Codrington and as the interpretation of coin finds from the island often does today. It is a possibility that has been constructed in careful combination with both textual and archaeological sources pertaining to ancient Lanka.

## Pliny's *Natural History* and the *Christian Topography*: text and intertextuality

If coins, already considered, and archaeological material, discussed later in this chapter, represent the expanding frontier in evidence for ancient Lanka, the framework they are fitted into continues to derive primarily from textual sources, at least with respect to long-distance contact, and here too a tendency to see cosmopolitanism is striking. Ancient Lanka is better served than any other region of South or Southeast Asia by textual sources, including two chronicles compiled probably in the fourth and sixth centuries CE (the *Dīpavaṃsa* and *Mahāvaṃsa*), the latter of which was maintained thereafter throughout and beyond the period under discussion.[72] Thousands of inscriptions from the island have also been studied, transcribed, translated and published.[73] The island was also the subject of numerous ancient notices by foreign writers, including pilgrims from China.[74] Greek and Latin sources, however, have been most significant in creating a narrative of ancient commercial Lanka, of which the most commonly cited are the accounts of Pliny in the first century and the anonymous *Christian Topography*.[75] The latter is examined here first because of its remarkable level of detail and consequent prominence in literature on ancient Lanka.

The *Christian Topography* is a multi-chaptered work in Greek, datable by internal references to the middle of the sixth century.[76] Of the author nothing is known outside the clues within the text.[77] The name usually given, 'Kosmas Indikopleustes' (Latinized, Cosmas Indicopleustes = 'Kosmas, sailor to India'), is most likely a later addition and the text should be considered anonymous, although the attribution has become somewhat entrenched.[78] The main purpose of the *Christian Topography*, as the author explains in detail, is to propose a Christian cosmology, in which the Earth, contrary to 'pagan' Greek notions of a spherical body, is flat and shaped like the biblical tabernacle. The earliest copies of the work are preserved in three manuscripts, dating from the ninth to the eleventh centuries. The ninth-century copy contains ten books of cosmological argumentation.[79] The eleventh-century copies both contain an additional two books: Book Eleven on the plants and animals of India and the island of Taprobanê and Book Twelve, summarizing the conclusions of the preceding chapters.[80] It seems, however, that multiple copies of the work, including the twelve-book version, were already extant by the ninth century.[81]

Book Eleven is widely known and cited in almost all studies of pre-Muslim trade between the Mediterranean and the Indian Ocean, but in a manner that shears it of all but a perfunctory mention of the whole work.[82] It is rarely considered as a work of literature, with its own stylistic and rhetorical aims, but rather as a first-hand account of the island, to be mined for information. This is apparent from the use of a particular passage describing the visit of an acquaintance of the author, named Sopatros, to the island. This passage is sufficiently important and famous within studies of classical Lankan commerce and transregional connections to be worth quoting at length:

Anyway, one of the business people from here, named Sopatros, who has been dead for the past 35 years to my knowledge, once reached the island of Taprobanê on a business venture, when a ship from Persia had just cast anchor... Then, as was the custom, the local magistrates and the tax collectors welcomed them and took them off to the king. The king welcomed them, received their salutations, and told them to sit down, and then he asked, 'How are your countries, and how are things getting on there?' 'Nicely', they replied. Then, in the general conversation, the king put the question, 'Which of your kings is the greater and more powerful?'

The Persian got his word in first and said 'Our king is the more powerful and greater and richer, and he is the king of kings. And whatever he wills he is able to put into effect.' Sopatros kept quiet; and then the king said, 'What about you, Roman? Haven't you anything to say?' And Sopatros replied, 'What can I say, after these statements of his? If you want to know the truth, you have got both kings here. Have a look at each of them; and you can see which is the more glorious and powerful.' In hearing this, he [the king] was astonished and said, 'How have I got both kings here?' He [Sopatros] replied, 'You have the coins of both, the *nomismata* of the one, and the *drachm* (i.e. the *miliaresion*) of the other.[83] Look at the image on each of them; and you will see the truth.'

The king praised and commended the idea and ordered both coins to be produced. Well, the *nomisma* was of gold, brilliant and of fine shape, for the coins which are exported there are specially selected, whereas the *miliaresion,* to put it in a nutshell, was of silver, and that is enough to rule out any comparison with the gold coin. The king turned both coins over and over, and inspected them, and full of praise for the *nomisma*, he said, 'Truly, the Romans are glorious, powerful and wise.' So he ordered Sopatros to be highly honoured, and mounted him on an elephant, and to the beating of drums paraded him round the town in great honour.[84]

The narrative has been used to argue forcefully for the importance of Lanka in trade networks by the sixth century and for the circulation of Roman and Persian currency on the island.[85] It is, however, intriguing to note, as Weerakkody does in his collation of such foreign notices, that the narrative shows similarities with the first-century *Natural History* of Pliny in which Roman coins also impress the king of the island: in this case, a shipwrecked Roman freedman is stranded on the island long enough to learn the language, which enables him to discourse with the king about the Roman Empire. The king listens to him but above all is struck by the equal weight and appearance of continuity he observes when handling *denarii,* declaring the Romans to be particularly honest.[86] An initial suggestion of a literary connection between these two stories was made by Tennent in the 1860s but in subsequent analyses of ancient Lanka it has consistently been ignored or rejected without explanation in favour of interpretations that preserve both texts as objective sources for economic reality rather than reflections of a shared literary culture, even suggesting that the stories are similar because they must have described a commonly occurring scenario.[87]

It has been established that the author of the *Topography* was widely read in the classical works of geography and natural science he sought to repudiate, and it is thus possible – indeed likely – that he had read Pliny. It is also possible that he was thereby inspired during his excursus on the island of Taprobanê to modify an existing tale to contemporary circumstances.[88] While the details of the accounts show marked differences, including the shifting mores of 'Romanness', their central narrative (a Roman at the court of the king of Lanka using the contemporary standard precious-metal unit of account – the silver *denarius* of the first century, the gold *solidus* of the sixth – as material evidence for the effective governance of the Roman state) is strikingly similar.

The possibility of links between the *Christian Topography* and Pliny (indeed, specifically Pliny's account of Taprobanê) is further suggested by the description found in both authors' works of 'silent trade'.[89] This practice, attributed by Pliny to Lanka, supposedly entailed traders and local indigenous groups bringing products of value to a known location. These local groups being unfamiliar or uncomfortable with direct commerce, the traders would leave their goods (in Pliny, beside a river, in the *Topography* in the branches of thorn bushes) and withdraw. The locals would approach and inspect the goods and if they were satisfied take them and leave behind their own trade items. The author of the *Topography* places his account of 'silent trade' in east Africa, and, as in the case of Sopatros at the court of the Lankan king, produces a longer and more detailed story than Pliny, but the central narratives remain identical.

It seems a distinct possibility, therefore, that the *Topography* made use of elements of the *Natural History* (or both authors drew on existing tropes concerning 'other' places) to furnish his exotic and faraway places (whether Africa or Lanka). Reflections on foreign places in both texts also share an emphasis on Roman values and political circumstances: Pliny's claim that the king of Lanka recognized the honesty and stability of the Roman state echoes the values espoused (including numismatically) by the contemporary Flavian dynasty.[90] Similarly, the emphasis in the *Topography* on Roman superiority over Persia may reflect the increasing challenge posed by the Sasanian state by the sixth century, such that elsewhere in the text the author explicitly refers to the widespread acceptance of the Byzantine gold *solidus* in contrast to the Persian *drachm* as a mark of God's preference.[91] This hypothesis is supported by the dramatic device of the king of Lanka asking to see the coins of both empires. In a text suffused with biblical allusion, this seems to evoke the account, undoubtedly familiar to the Christian author and his intended audience, in the Gospel of Matthew (22:19–20), in which Christ asks for a coin of Caesar to be brought forth and examined, culminating in the injunction to 'render unto Caesar that which is Caesar's'. This allusion, like the author's correlation of monetary success with divine favour, associates the sixth-century empire with the continued unfolding of biblical destiny and, like his cosmology itself, asserts the ultimately eschatological meaning of all aspects of reality, from the religious to the apparently mundane and secular.

These sources do not, therefore, any more than foreign coins found in Sri Lanka, support a simple reading, which takes them as 'eye-witness accounts' or 'windows' into history. They reveal far more about the rhetorical role of faraway places in the Roman and Byzantine mind than about volume of trade, and should be viewed extremely sceptically as sources for understanding the significance of commercial connections to the attitudes, policies and practices of Lankan actors. Lankan figures, when they play a part in these narratives, do so as canvases for the projection of Mediterranean ideas about power and influence, not as speakers on their own behalf. But that does not mean that investigation is futile. The use of literary motifs does not prevent them from suggesting something of the structures and changing shape of trade over time.[92]

Behind the stories lies a variety of details suggestive of possible changes in Lanka's engagement with the West. When Pliny wrote his account, contact with the island appears to have been situated in the realm of accident. Later references and accounts reinforce this impression, highlighting natural wonders or the strange habits of the islanders, but giving little impression of contact or of the island as being connected with wider worlds.[93] By the late fifth or early sixth century, Sopatros' journey to the island, whether the named character was real or a narrative device, is portrayed as intentional and related to trading journeys by other merchants, Roman and foreign. This is perhaps most clearly arguable from another passage in the description of Taprobanê, which states explicitly that '[f]rom the whole of India, Persia and Ethiopia, the island acting as intermediary, welcomes many ships and likewise dispatches them' and describes in addition the links between Lanka, the Arabian kingdom of Himyar and various parts of the Indian subcontinent.[94] It is the most explicit surviving description in support of the traditional narrative of ancient Lanka's commercial role and is unparalleled in earlier sources. Read in light of this description, Sopatros' royal audience may simply be a narrative vehicle but the peripheral details of revenue collectors at the port, and of a Persian Christian community, suggest a fairly regularized communication with the island, in which travellers from the west could be fitted into a (theoretically) managed commercial system, and contextualized in relation to residents on the island of the same religious identity, language or origin. It is a more structured vision of contact than that of Pliny's shipwrecked freedman. The lack in the *Topography* of any explanation of the way the various characters communicated with one another may also imply increased familiarity though it may simply reflect the preoccupation of the author with Roman affairs in which the foreign characters become simply exotic extras.

The Greek-speaking identity of Sopatros and the anonymous author of the *Topography* suggest a Near Eastern emphasis in trade that emanated from the Roman Empire as a legal entity, but which was dominated by personnel from its eastern regions, passing through Alexandria to the Red Sea.[95] The text cannot, however, provide a basis for judging the volume of trade or contact with the island, or the relative roles of groups from the Roman or Sasanian Empires. In particular, its reference to a Persian Christian group on the island has been used to argue for a significant Sasanian mercantile diaspora in the Indian Ocean.[96] It is entirely unclear, however, that the spread of Christianity can be used in the ancient period as a proxy for the make-up of Indian Ocean trade.[97] Furthermore, the emphasis of the *Christian Topography* on Christian geography makes reference to churches at the far reaches of the world a difficult foundation for arguments about scale or significance. For the author of the text, there was benefit to be gained simply from demonstrating the expansion of Christianity as far as possible into the known world. Like the indications provided by numismatic evidence, re-examination of these two sources complicates a simple narrative of cosmopolitanism, but likewise suggests a change, however imprecisely reflected in our sources, between the first century and the late fifth or sixth. It is a picture that finds tentative support in archaeological finds from the island, but only once the superstructures of the traditional narrative have been dismantled from around it.

## Godavaya, Mantai and the archaeology of port sites

In recent decades, an explosion of archaeological excavations and publications has contributed enormously to available evidence concerning ancient Lanka.[98] Among these is a shipwreck discovered in 2003 off the Sri Lankan coast near the site of Godavaya. By 2012, initial Carbon-14 dates had demonstrated that, with a first- or second-century BCE date, at least for some of the timbers, it is the oldest known wreck in the Indian Ocean and the only wreck datable to the ancient period of Lankan history. Excavation and publication of the site by an international team, including the Institute of Nautical Archaeology (US), the Sri Lankan Department of Archaeology and the Maritime Archaeology Unit of the Central Cultural Fund, will hopefully prove extremely significant for the study of ancient Lankan commerce and maritime history. Meanwhile, preliminary notifications, including on scholarly and scientific blog sites, demonstrate the potential advantages of modern technology for the speedy integration of archaeological discoveries into historical research but also demonstrate the tenacity of traditional explanatory paradigms.[99]

The Godavaya wreck certainly suggests strongly that Sri Lanka was in regular commercial contact with India in the ancient period. Beads from Mantai appear similar to types produced at Arikamedu in Tamil Nadu, and the shipwreck has yielded finds of large glass ingots,[100] which may have been part of an Indian Ocean bead trade.[101] Ceramics from the wreck include some apparently Indian wares, suggesting that 'the origin of the ship may be traced regionally (in broader sense [to] the Indian subcontinent)'.[102] Godavaya is, therefore, an exciting site for local maritime commercial history, the history of ancient boat-building technologies and the development of marine archaeology in the Indian Ocean.[103] It is unclear, however, why a wreck that has not revealed a single published artefact with any link to Rome or the Mediterranean should have been heralded as '[giving] us a look at a ship and its cargo from the era of the Roman Republic'.[104] The most recent official publications on the wreck have not continued to invoke a Roman connection,[105] but as recently as 2014 the interpretative shadow of ancient Lanka's implicit cosmopolitanism was still visible in the following interview with one of the lead excavators:

> Carlson said they likely won't find a "smoking gun" that definitively proves the doomed ship was headed for Rome... But discoveries at the sunken ship might at least help illustrate that Sri Lanka was a 'linchpin' in this trade, as so many of the goods that passed through the island reached the Mediterranean.[106]

The long-awaited publication of the excavation report of the site of Mantai, often described as the port of Anurādhapura, also highlights the ways in which archaeological data has been forced into a narrative it cannot sustain.[107] Despite a series of excavations between 1886 and 1984, the last interrupted by the outbreak of civil war and consequent hasty evacuation, the publication in 2013 of *Mantai: City by the Sea* represents the first compilation of results from previous excavations and the publication of full catalogues from the 1980s excavations.[108] The evidence from Mantai is thus inextricably bound up with the difficulties of analysing a site that has been disturbed on numerous occasions and has sometimes been inadequately documented.[109]

The 'Historical Sources' chapters of the publication give an account of the ancient port city of Mantai in Indian Ocean trade typical of many of the themes already highlighted in this chapter. These include an invocation of the island's position as a basis for its commercial history, and the assertion that 'archaeologically... it seems to have been the most frequented and the most important port of the Anuradhapura Kingdom'. It also asserts that '[t]he rise of Mahatittha [Mantai] was a direct response to the growth of Western trade in the Indian Ocean' and comments that '[t]he increasing tempo of the trade with the west is indicated in the large quantities of Roman coins of the fourth and fifth centuries CE found in various parts of the country'.[110] A further chapter explores Western sources dealing with the island, concluding that:

> We are now in a position to suggest that Mantai housed a colony of Roman traders recognized as an emporium by the time Ptolemy wrote *Geographia* [i.e. second century CE] ... Roman finds at Mantai include ceramics which can be dated from the late first or early second century.[111]

Individual reports on various ceramic types and artefacts and a series of appendices provided on disc with the publication, including more than 2,700 photographs of finds from the site, however, provide a crucial counterbalance to this synthetic historical narrative that at times directly contradicts the testimony of the artefact catalogues.[112] Roman ceramics from the site are referred to three times in the introductory material, but always pointing to earlier publications.[113] These publications do record a handful of sherds of probably Mediterranean origin, but not in quantities that could support the contention that the site housed a colony of Romans, nor even that it traded substantially in goods from the Mediterranean (whether directly or via, for example, Indian intermediaries).[114] *Mantai: City by the Sea* itself significantly does not have a chapter for Roman or Western ceramics. Nor, indeed, does it mention Roman/Mediterranean ceramics excavated either from a stratified context, or even from disturbed fill levels anywhere on the site. The sum of diagnostically Roman finds in the catalogue is two beads[115] and three copper-alloy coins, plus two additional coins confusingly described as probably being 'Indo-Roman imitations' (presumably Lankan imitations).[116] Even the assumption, made forcefully in the introductory chapters, that Mantai was a (major) port in the ancient period cannot be maintained from close analysis of the evidence. Only two trenches datable to the ancient period were excavated and these produced no evidence plausibly representing port structures or other evidence of maritime activity.[117] These trenches revealed some Indian wares, suggesting contact with the subcontinent, further supported by the testimony of the Godavaya wreck, but overwhelmingly the ceramics were local. Neither structures nor objects suggest the site to be distinctively a 'port' rather than any other type of settlement.[118]

Identifying Mantai as a port is, in any case, complicated by the lack of clearly articulated criteria for recognizing a port site archaeologically. Port remains may be extremely ephemeral owing to major changes in water courses, industrial land use and the lack of built port structures to begin with.[119] Even in the case of a documented commercial site near to the coast, such as that of Godavaya, evidence of port infrastructure remains elusive and difficult to understand in the absence of comparative models.[120] Certainly, there were sites on ancient Lanka that served as marketplaces and at which revenue was collected in some official capacity. For example, in the oft-cited inscription at Godavaya, most likely of the second century CE, the king awards the revenue of the emporium to a third party, although it is not clear that this refers to external rather than internal trade.[121] The account of the *Christian Topography* also refers to revenue collectors.[122]

Beyond the correlation of textual and archaeological material, coin finds have also been used as a basis for arguing for extensive networks of ports, vital to long-distance maritime trade and extant much earlier than the first historical records of them (which are mostly medieval), along rivers and the coasts of southern and western Sri Lanka.[123] With some exceptions, the use of these ports (and indeed their existence) in the ancient period remains a speculation based on the convenience of their position for routes documented in later periods, extrapolation from later sources[124] and the evidence of coin finds nearby.[125] Such an approach to site identification (local surface finds, topography and later documentary references) is not invalid but here poses two distinct problems. First, identifying sites with coin finds as ports assumes too simple a connection between coins and long-distance maritime commerce, ignoring other possible uses for coins.[126] Second, while correlations of multiple, tentative clues may suggest locations of certain types of site, such a hypothesis ought to be supported by the discovery, at least at one such location, of such a site type. In the absence of an excavated ancient port site anywhere on the island (identified by whatever means), it is problematic to navigate a literature that argues that port sites can be identified because of the high incidence of coin finds at them and that coin finds can be interpreted as evidence for commercial activity because of their high incidence at port sites.[127] This is a circularity that exemplifies the quest for a particular vision of the Lankan past, in which data is decorative rather than structural, and which produces summaries such as: 'The major ports were cosmopolitan in character with resident communities of various nationalities, so that, in addition to the collection of duties, the officers may have been entrusted with the welfare of foreign merchants at the port.'[128] Although it is a vision of the past that remains attractive to scholars working with a range of evidence types an alternative can be dimly discerned in the material examined here.

## Conclusion: Lanka at the sixth-century interface

If read within a context that does not privilege commercial cosmopolitanism or Western connections as the dominating structure of a narrative of ancient Lanka, the numismatic, textual and archaeological sources potentially come into clearer focus. None of the available evidence suggests that in the first to third centuries Sri Lanka was significantly connected to either the eastern or the western Indian Ocean regions. There is no physical or textual evidence for regular contact with China or Southeast Asia, and while Roman trade with India appears to have been comparatively buoyant on the basis of ceramic and numismatic evidence there is no sign of any direct contact with Sri Lanka.[129] Occasional finds of Roman coins, probably from India, supplement the discovery of Indian finds on coastal sites to suggest that external commercial relations extended no further on a regular basis than South India, as also supported by the evidence of the Godavaya shipwreck.

By the fourth century, as increasing focus in Southeast Asian studies on the maritime routes of Buddhist pilgrimage and movement of ideas is highlighting, it was not primarily Western or commercial connections that began to link the island into wider networks. Rather, the increased interest by Buddhists further east in the teachings as preserved and practised on Lanka seems to have linked the island to China and the coasts and archipelagos of Indo-China.[130] Pilgrim accounts and inscriptions discovered elsewhere in the eastern Indian Ocean testify to the movement of these Buddhist travellers around the Indian Ocean and to Lanka specifically, even if physical remains on the island, such as Chinese coins or ceramics, are extremely uncommon prior to the tenth century.[131] Studies of this Buddhist network have emphasized, as on the northern land routes between China and India, the close although not always uncomplicated relationship between traders and religious travellers in the Buddhist world in this period; there is no argument here against increasing commercial interactions between Lanka and areas further east, but the close connection between travel, trade and Buddhist and Hindu activity is subtler than the commercial cosmopolitanism of the classic narrative of ancient Lanka. These are not necessarily new narratives in the context of Indian activity in the first millennium CE, but their implications for ancient Lanka are still to be fully explored.[132]

Finally, between the middle of the fifth and the middle of the sixth centuries, Lanka's role in networks of connectivity seems to have shifted. The finds of Roman copper-alloy coins, probably arriving from India, and their imitation on the island, may suggest either growing monetization or growing interest in Western aspects of commercial or material culture (or both), and in the sixth century, at around the time that finds of Byzantine coins in South India cease, the *Christian Topography* gives a graphic but unique account of an island poised between two networks: the eastern and western Indian Ocean regions. The few finds of Byzantine and Sasanian coins documented from the island give some support to this picture, although also serve as a reminder of how ephemeral these networks probably still were in comparison to local exchange within the island and with the nearby coast of India. It is difficult to assess what may have caused this change, and the tendency where it has been identified to attribute it to political changes in the Mediterranean world or to changes in Byzantine and Sasanian demand seems to derive more from the persistent narrative structures highlighted throughout this chapter than from the surviving historical evidence.[133]

Walburg points to the period of Pandyan dominance over Lanka as a turning point, highlighting the regular communication between Lanka and China up to the early fifth century, and citing the end of Pandyan rule as cause for the resurgence of trade in the sixth century.[134] This focus on events internal to Lanka seems appropriate to the evidence as it stands, which does not suggest that ancient Lanka was ever dependent on trade to the extent that inter-regional connections would be determined by commercial dynamics, rather than commercial networks responding to social and political forces. Nevertheless, this thesis does not fully explain why a break in Lanka's engagement with long-distance networks should cause not just a revival at a later date, but simultaneously an increased, although never exclusive, focusing of that revival westwards. Agency remains crucial and it is a feature not fully recognized in accounts of Western textual sources that from the fifth century Mediterranean commentators speak of trade with India and Lanka as being driven primarily by actors from India and Lanka.[135]

Only by turning away from arguments of geographical inevitability or explanations focused on Western connections and demand and examining far more closely Lanka's own internal resource management strategies, and its more immediate communications with India, will ancient Lanka's commercial role in the Indian Ocean become clearer. Arguments built on a vision of 'implicit cosmopolitanism', by rendering connectivity an inevitable fundament of the island's character, are structurally unable to explain Lanka's transition from predominantly self-reliant networks, and short- to medium-distance links with India, to an island that by the late sixth century stood at a largely new interface between eastern and western Indian Ocean regions.

# 3
# A Pāli cosmopolis? Sri Lanka and the Theravāda Buddhist ecumene, c. 500–1500

*Tilman Frasch*

If nothing else, Pollock's concept of a Sanskrit cosmopolis has provided a useful prism through which to observe and analyse the interactions between states, societies and cultures, which complements other analytical tools such as 'transculturalism', 'ecumene' or even 'empire'.[1] While Pollock offered a welcome framework, his approach has been and still is open to criticism, notably for the way he has tried to separate the aesthetics of the Sanskrit language from its potential to become politically powerful, as well as his indifference to the Brahmans as the ones who control it.[2] Ultimately, if reduced to its very core, the concept of the Sanskrit cosmopolis appears to be an updated and modified version of the old theory of an 'Indianization' (or 'Hinduization') of Southeast Asia with all its open or hidden forms of Indian cultural dominance.

This hierarchy – or rather its deconstruction – forms the starting point for the reflections presented here. Instead of being subsumed by and subjected to a Sanskrit cosmopolis, Sri Lankans might prefer to locate themselves within (and possibly at the heart of) an alternative cultural system, which can be termed a Theravāda or Pāli cosmopolis.[3] In fact, many Sri Lankans, from the ancient chroniclers to modern scholars, have done exactly that. Noticing that the Theravāda canon and, more importantly, the Pāli language, both originated on the island before moving across the Bay of Bengal to make Theravāda the mass religion of mainland Southeast Asia, they perceived and portrayed the island as the fountain and centre of a transnational cultural system. This notion was informed by the belief in Lanka being the 'chosen land of Buddhism' (*dhammadīpa*), which was based on the claim that the Pāli canon, compiled on the island, preserved the Buddha's teachings (*dhamma*) better than any other Buddhist tradition. Over the centuries, interaction within this Theravāda cosmopolis loosened and intensified over time and eventually provided a backbone for the pan-Asian cooperations of the nineteenth and twentieth centuries[4] – in fact until the present day, when the Buddhist nationalists of the Sinhale Urumaya and the 696 movement in Myanmar announced their plan to work together.[5]

Focusing on the period before c. 1500 CE, this chapter will reinvestigate Sri Lanka's position in the Pāli-Theravāda cosmopolis from its inception on the island around the first centuries CE, when possibly both the Pāli language and a standardized, exclusive Theravāda canon took shape. This chapter will identify the factors that may have contributed to this process, the ways in which the Theravāda 'school' was transmitted to areas outside Lanka, and how Lanka acquired and retained a central position within this cosmopolis. It will be argued that Lanka's pre-eminence was not a given, as by the early thirteenth century, the religious and intellectual centre began to shift towards Bagan in Myanmar. But the sudden decline of Bagan after the Mongol conquest at the end of the thirteenth century prevented the completion of Theravāda's 'great translocation' to Southeast Asia.[6] The forming Theravāda communities at Sukhodaya or Chiang Mai turned to Sri Lanka and not to Myanmar for valid ordinations lineages, scriptures and other material sources such as relics or images. As a result, Sri Lanka's position as the bedrock of Theravāda, which had been effectively challenged since the end of the first millennium CE, was reconfirmed and revalidated.

There is, however, a second aspect to be considered here, which has a more immediate consequence for the concept of Theravādin cosmopolitanism. It refers to the transmission and preservation of textual traditions. As has been argued here, Theravāda Buddhism owed its existence to a set of scriptures – the Buddha's teachings, mnemonic and other learning aids, grammars and commentaries – all written in a specific language, Pāli. The transmission and preservation of these texts had been entrusted to the order of monks (Sangha). As Buddhism spread across the Indian subcontinent and beyond, this task of preserving the precise wording and meaning of the Buddha's teachings (which were transmitted orally anyway) became increasingly difficult, and inevitably schools of interpretation began to form, one of which emerged in Sri Lanka. But even there, in a relatively small Buddhist community (if compared to India), the preservation of the true texts became problematic, not only because of factionalism within the Sangha, but more so because of the frequent disruptions and destruction caused by foreign invaders (notably from South India). Spreading the *dhamma* beyond the island, as described below, not only created the Pāli cosmopolis explored here, but also a common textual archive that supported and complemented the individual traditions of each of its parts. On several occasions down to the eighteenth century, canonical and collateral scriptures were reimported to the island from Buddhist communities in India and Southeast Asia. In this respect, the Pāli cosmopolis can be compared to an extended memory board, which provided backups in case of a loss of data.[7]

## The making of the Pāli cosmopolis

A persistent bias that has dominated both the self-perception of the Theravādins (and the view of many scholars of Theravāda Buddhism) is that their lineage and textual tradition can be referred back to Gautama Buddha himself, and that they succeeded to preserve his teachings with so much accuracy to make it the most reliable of all Buddhist canonical collections.[8] A collateral of this view is the belief that Pāli – now seen as a language rather than as a set of texts – was similar or at least closely related to the language in which the Buddha had preached.

However, since the publication of works by scholars such as Steven Collins, this traditionalist view of Theravāda and Pāli can hardly be repeated any longer. Collins has convincingly argued that the Theravāda 'school' has not existed from the time of the Buddha but formed in a certain political and intellectual environment in third–fifth-century Sri Lanka. Part of this formative process was the canonization of their collection of scriptures.[9] The context Collins refers to was the competition between two major monasteries at Anurādhapura, the Mahāvihāra and the Abhayagirivihāra, and the standing they enjoyed under various kings.[10] For Collins, the conflict came to a head in the mid-fifth century under king Mahānāma, through whose support the pendulum seemed to swing in favour of the Abhayagirivihāra, but whose reign was also marked by the arrival of Buddhaghosa and the revival of the Mahāvihāra.

Collins is certainly correct in placing the formation of the Mahāvihāra-Theravāda tradition in the context of the sectarian struggle between the Mahāvihāra and the Abhayagirivihāra. However, his reference to king Mahānāma is unconvincing as the conflict had entered its most intensive phase already a century earlier, under King Mahāsena, who attempted to close down and destroy the Mahāvihāra altogether by preventing potential supporters to make donations to it.[11] He also violated the monastery's boundary (*sīmā*) by removing building materials and establishing a new monastery, the Jetavanavihāra, inside the boundaries of the Mahāvihāra.[12] The monastery survived because (as its chronicler claimed) some of the Mahāvihārins had hidden in an underground chamber for nine years. The price of survival was the loss of religious and ritual pre-eminence, as the Tooth Relic and its procession were controlled by the kings and became associated with the Abhayagirivihāra.[13] It was only another fifty years later that the Mahāvihāra regained some of its former glory when it provided a home and study for Buddhaghosa. Yet even this regaining of scholarly importance did not seem to increase its attractiveness, as the Chinese visitor Fa Hsien (Fa Xian) noted in the late sixth century. He counted 5,000 monks dwelling at the Abhayagiri monastery and only 3,000 at the Mahāvihāra.[14]

Still, the survival of the Mahāvihāra cannot gloss over the fact that the crisis of the monastery during the reign of King Mahāsena had been existential, bringing the royal embargo, the destruction of its buildings and finally the infringement of its *sīmā*. The chronicler of the Mahāvihāra is suspiciously curt about the reasons for the king's assault, merely hinting at a dispute concerning the monastic code of conduct (Vinaya).[15] Given the seriousness and size of the royal response, this justification sounds rather thin, the more so since Vinaya rules regulate individual behaviour but can hardly be applied to a whole chapter (*gaṇa*), unless all of its monks are found guilty of one of the four grave offences (*pārājika*) – stealing, lying, intercourse with women and doing magic. As a group, a chapter would have to cause the split of the order (*saṅghabheda*) to warrant excommunication.

Accusing the Mahāvihārins of the first two *parajikas* is obviously unsubstantiated. Having intercourse with women could have been closer to the point as fully ordained nuns still existed at the time and moreover had residences inside the Mahāvihāra compound.[16] Their very existence or their cohabitation with male monks inside the Mahāvihāra may have become an issue then, as illustrated by the Buddha's famous (although possibly later added) remark, which held nuns responsible for a quicker decline of the *sāsanā*. In the preparations for the end of the first millennium of the Buddhist Era in 456 CE and the decline this event would herald, such misogyny would have made sense.[17] But this is no more than a speculation.

This also holds for the last of the *pārājikas*, the pretension of possessing supernatural power, which can potentially include occultism and the possession of secret texts or teachings. At first glance, accusing the Mahāvihārins of owning non-standard texts would seem far-fetched, not least because they themselves insisted on having preserved and transmitted the scriptures better than any of the other Buddhist 'schools' existing at the time. But crucially, if the version of the scriptures kept at the Mahāvihāra had become 'canonized' in the sense of becoming an exclusive, closed set of texts,[18] they had also been recorded in a language only the few monks of the Mahāvihāra were conversant in. Although the origins of Pāli are still a contentious matter, it seems certain that the language was widely used in the Mahāvihāra and received its final recognition as a canonical language through Buddhaghosa, who used Pāli for his works throughout.[19]

The imminent destruction and eventual survival of their monastery must have welded the Mahāvihārins together and reinforced their belief in their own righteousness and exclusiveness. Their obstinacy in keeping separate from the other fraternities, which also meant carrying on as a minority, their 'scripturalist' insistence on a defined set of texts that was not to be altered, and their resorting to an artificial language incomprehensible to outsiders bear all the hallmarks of a fundamentalist movement.[20] In addition to this, the Mahāvihārins displayed a certain missionary zeal through attempts to disseminate the 'canonized' version of the scriptures in order to find allies for moral and perhaps material support.[21] Extracts from the Pāli canon written on gold foils and encased in the stūpas of Sri Ksetra (Myanmar) have been dated to the fifth–sixth century CE,[22] and roughly contemporary to these are the earliest short Pāli inscriptions coming from the Dvarāvatī kingdom in what is now Thailand.[23] Given the proximity of and close interaction with South India, Pāli texts will also have been spread in South India, mainly in Andhra Pradesh and Tamil Nadu.[24] It must be added, however, that this dissemination was neither a given nor a straightforward triumphal march as the Mahāvihārins remained a numerically small group while at the same time their opponents, the monks from the Abhayagirivihāra and other Mahāyānists,[25] apparently spread their texts in Southeast Asia with similar success. Around 1000 CE, Theravāda and Mahāyāna Buddhists lived side-by-side in various Southeast

Asian regions.[26] The eventual rise of the Theravāda tradition there was less due to the missionary efforts of Mahāvihāra monks than to a coincidence, which provided the ongoing translocation of Buddhism from South to Southeast Asia with a fresh momentum.

## The 'great translocation' and the Theravāda cosmopolis in the eleventh–thirteenth centuries

By the time the Mahāvihārins struggled to maintain what they regarded as the true words of the Buddha, Buddhism entered a slow but steady decline in its Indian homeland; a process that would eventually see it disappear almost completely from its place of origin. This process – the outcome of which was by no means predetermined – was complex, drawn out, and affected various regions of India to a differing degree. Its major component was the revival of Hinduism through individual devotion to a Hindu god (*bhakti*). The *bhakti* movement started around the seventh century in South India, from where it expanded across the subcontinent.[27] As the people and more so the ruling families of India opted for this new form of Hinduism, support for Buddhist monasteries and monks waned, leading to their gradual disappearance. By 1200 CE, Buddhist communities and institutions in India either existed as pockets within a predominantly Hinduist environment or had been pushed into peripheral regions of India such as Ladakh or East Bengal. The latter region suffered further from the Islamic conquerors who invaded the Ganges valley and established the sultanates of Delhi.

Around 1000 CE, the future of Buddhism in Sri Lanka came into danger as well, as the South Indian Cōḻas under the kings Rājarāja and Rājendra set out to not only conquer the island and its capital Anurādhapura, but also made it a province of the Cōḻa Empire for most of the eleventh century. Despite being separated from the mainland, the Anurādhapura kingdom had always been part of the political structure of South India and had experienced invasions from the mainland on several occasions. The latest Cōḻa conquest was a particular disaster, as it first resulted in the plunder and destruction of the capital and then the integration of the island into the Cōḻa empire, with Poḷonnaruva becoming the capital of the new province.[28] More importantly, the destruction and plundering of the capital terminated the hitherto uninterrupted lineage of the Mahāvihāra. Never again mentioned in the chronicles, it continued to exist only as a notion, while relics (and especially the Tooth Relic) took the monastery's place as a central religious site.[29] The relics were salvaged by monks, who had managed to escape to Rohana, the island's southern region.[30] It also was in Rohana that a resistance movement formed under Vijaya Bāhu I, which eventually succeeded to restore the former Sinhala kingdom in the north and push the Cōḻas back to India. But before this, by the mid-eleventh century, Theravāda Buddhism seemed set to become extinguished on the island.

At that moment, the Burmese ruler Anawrahta (Aniruddha) unintentionally saved the Theravāda tradition by making it the 'state religion' of the nascent

Bagan kingdom. The reason for this royal measure is anything but clear as the available evidence comes from Burmese chronicles and records written long after the actual event.[31] According to them, the king carried out the reform in two steps, the first being his conquest of the city of Thaton in Lower Burma, from where he abducted the royal family and the leading members of the Sangha headed by Shin Arahan. With the help of that monk, the king then purged the Sangha at Bagan of monks who disobeyed the Vinaya, notably the Aris.[32] The royal purification of the Sangha cemented the leading role of the Theravāda tradition over all competing Buddhist (and other religious) groups and set Bagan on the path to become its foremost intellectual and ceremonial centre.

This new status became manifest soon after, when the Sinhalese king Vijaya Bāhu I (r. 1070–1112), the liberator of the island, required the help of monks from Bagan to restore the Sangha of Lanka.[33] This event initiated a series of encounters between the Buddhists of Lanka and Burma, which comprised royal missions and individual pilgrimages and included the exchange of canonical texts and relics as well as holding joint recitations (*saṅgīti*) and ordination ceremonies.[34] The encounters at Bagan intensified after 1200, when the Buddhist institutions and sites of India were overrun by the troops of the sultan of Delhi and Sri Lanka entered another phase of civil war and outside invasions.[35] Poḷonnaruva, which had replaced Anurādhapura as capital, had to be evacuated twice and was ultimately abandoned in favour of Gampola in the 1270s.[36] Amid this overall political instability, however, Buddhism continued to flourish on the island, as attested by both a substantial number of religious treatises,[37] although frequent religious convocations resulting in royal edicts to regulate the behaviour of monks also illustrate a degree of decay affecting the Sangha.[38]

In the light of all this, Poḷonnaruva fell back behind Bagan, which at the same time attracted Buddhist scholars from all over Asia. This can be seen in the city's composite settlement pattern and population as well as the widespread use of Pāli as a *lingua franca*. As mentioned, numerous Mons from Lower Burma had been resettled there in the mid-eleventh century, and thereafter Bagan provided a safe haven for Bengali artists and Sinhalese monks who fled the turmoil of their respective countries. Recent research has also shown that the presence of Cambodians at the city increased markedly after around 1230. A Cambodian monk even participated in a purification of the Sangha (*saṅghavisuddhi*) held around 1248.[39] The various foreign communities at Bagan seem to have preferred to stay together in clusters sometimes centred on a Buddhist temple or monastery. The Mons brought in from Lower Burma were apparently resettled in the Myinkaba village south of the citadel of Bagan, where a temple still bears the name of their ruler, Manuha. The village may also have catered for the small South Indian community, as the only Tamil/Sanskrit inscription of the period was found there,[40] and more recently an inscription mentioning a 'headman of the *kaliññ*', probably Kalingans, has been retrieved from a mound south of the village.[41] Further south towards the Dhammayazika stūpa were the monasteries of the Sinhalese, of which the Tamani complex was the most important. Its image house – a temple curiously shaped like a stūpa – houses a statue of the seated Buddha in the meditation gesture (*dhyāna mudra*), which is very common for images from the island but exceptional at Bagan.[42] Although the outer enclosure of the Tamani complex cannot be established precisely any more, it appears to have been an extensive institution, including several monastic dwellings, buildings for the study and a tank, providing space for a sizeable number of monks.[43] Still further south, now in the middle of New Bagan Town, is another small compound where Bodhiramsi Thera 'from Sinhala' resided with his two disciples.[44] This set of monasteries with links to Lanka may have stretched as far south as the Setana stūpa, one of the largest stūpas at Bagan with unmistakeably Sinhalese features such as a semi-global dome and a square *harmika* above it. Sculpted elephants in frontal view bear the platform on which the stūpa is erected.[45]

This cosmopolitan cohabitation and interaction of monks whose mother tongues included Burmese, Mon, Sinhala, Bengali (or others of the emerging regional languages of India), Cambodian and perhaps even Chinese or Tibetan required a *lingua franca* to communicate in. That this language was in all likelihood Pāli becomes clear from the numerous Pāli inscriptions that record donations made to or involving foreign monks as well as events important for the Bagan Sangha as a whole. Bagan has produced a relatively large number of Pāli inscriptions ranging from brief prayers scribbled on the back of a clay votive tablet to at least twelve stone inscriptions of ten or more lines. The use of Pāli began under king Anawrahta (Aniruddha), who signed the tables he left at Buddhist sites across the country with the declaration that he had made the image with his own hands,[46] while the writing of long inscriptions in Pāli began in the early twelfth century. These include Prince Rājakumār's Myazedi inscription (which is written in Pyu, Mon and Burmese as well as Pāli), King Alaungsithu's poetic Shwegugyi inscription, and a fragmentary record possibly attributable to King Saw Lu.[47]

More importantly, there is now a set of three inscriptions (two of them discovered quite recently), which sheds further light on the cooperation of the monks staying at the Pāli cosmopolis of Bagan. Around 1248, they assembled for a joint ceremony which resulted in a 'purification' (*saṅgham visodhayi*). The leading monk on that occasion was Subhuticanda, who had Cambodian roots.[48] One of the newly found inscriptions, probably dating from the 1270s, singles out the monk Ananda, who had been to Cambodia and northern Malaya before coming to Bagan.[49] He was very likely the same person who was praised in a Pāli verse as the thera 'who had sprung from the line of Mahinda and constantly strove to stay true to it'.[50] The donor of the former record was a certain Amaṅga – clearly not a Burmese name – who also gave a bronze bell to the monk Tamalinda, the monk from whom the Tamani monastery derived its name.[51] This brief selection of examples shows that Pāli was used at Bagan whenever non-Burmese-speaking monks were concerned or involved in donations and religious activities. Turned the other way, we may also assume that whenever Pāli was used for an inscription (which sometimes was only a short passage), the record was addressed to a monk from outside the Burmese heartland.

What this brief survey of religious activities and exchanges at Bagan also illustrates is that the intellectual and ceremonial centre of Theravāda Buddhism was gradually shifting towards Southeast Asia, particularly to Bagan. This does not mean that the earlier centres in Lanka (which in the twelfth–thirteenth centuries would have been at Poḷonnaruva and probably in the region of Rohana) ceased to function entirely: the leading chronicle, the *Cūḷavaṃsa*, notes that in the thirteenth-century kings sponsored the copying of the Pāli canon and oversaw purifications of the Sangha,[52] and the literary production of the period was still impressive.[53] But Bagan was catching up, notably in the area of Pāli studies and literary production. Obviously, many of the works produced at the Bagan period were grammatical studies and aids, which helped monks to solidify their knowledge of the Pāli language as a prerequisite for further studies and compositions.[54] But at the same time, full sets of the Tipitaka were frequently listed in donative inscriptions,[55] and some monasteries had substantial holdings. One of the largest libraries on record was given in 1223 and consisted of more than 30 volumes of grammatical works, chronicles and of course canonical works.[56] These comprehensive literary activities illustrate that the Buddhists at Bagan were increasingly able to reproduce, comment on and interpret the Buddha's teachings without external input. Rather than their reconfirming the accuracy of their versions of the canon by obtaining 'approved' texts from Lanka, they attracted monks from the island and other parts of the Theravāda ecumene to come to Bagan and share their knowledge there. The perception of Sinhalese monks being the ultimate authority for the correct wording of the canon and therefore dominating the activities within the Theravāda cosmopolis, which is still current in the works of scholars representing a Sinhala nationalist school of interpretation,[57] will have to be replaced with a notion of Sri Lankan monks playing a less dominant and prominent role.[58]

However, this shift of the centre from South to Southeast Asia, from Poḷonnaruva to Bagan, remained unfinished, as the invasion of the Mongols and their occupation of Bagan at the end of the thirteenth century brought the transition to an abrupt halt. The royal court and many monks fled the city, and when the Mongols withdrew, both its political status and its sanctity had gone. In fact, some of the larger monastic complexes at Bagan continued to exist and receive donations well into the fourteenth century,[59] but the city's outreach and attractiveness had decreased in dramatic fashion. When the polities of the Mon and Thai rulers of modern-day Thailand began to establish themselves, they also adhered to Theravāda Buddhism but validated their ordination lineages through missions sent to Lanka rather than to Bagan.

## The reconfiguration of the Pāli cosmopolis

Although the decline of Bagan as a political capital was not accompanied by a similar decline as a religious centre, the city had to compete with other Buddhist places of learning emerging elsewhere on the Southeast Asian mainland. In Upper Burma, those new centres developed in the vicinity of Pinya and Ava (which became the new capital in 1364) on the one hand, and in the lower Chindwin region – then known as Aneint and Amyint – on the other. This latter region, which had been associated with the movement of the forest monks (*araññavāsi*) since the Bagan period,[60] served as the single most important centre of traditional Buddhist scholarship and education in Burma until the nineteenth century.[61] But even though Bagan lost its former importance and fell behind these new local and regional centres, the city did not disappear completely from the mental map of the Theravādins in Southeast Asia, as it was occasionally visited during the fourteenth century by Buddhists from elsewhere on the mainland.[62] They were driven by curiosity and, in the case of King Indrāditya, by the hope of gaining skilled craftsmen and their know-how, but apparently not by an interest in acquiring religious scriptures, let alone ordination lineages. For these, the Buddhists of the upcoming polities turned to Sri Lanka instead. This contact had had a double outcome: while introducing the oldest and purest ordination lineage to their respective realms, it re-established and reconfirmed the position of Sri Lanka as a Therāvada mainstay that it had seemed to have lost to Bagan.

The inclination towards Lanka is most obvious in the cases of the Mon and Thai polities of Sukhodaya, Chiang Mai and Lamphun, and to a degree in the 'Mon-land' of Lower Burma as well. The latter area was a peculiar case as much of the overseas traffic to and from Sri Lanka went through its ports, for instance Bassein (Kusumiya) or Martaban (Muttama). This may date as far back as the fourth–fifth centuries, when (as argued above) the Pāli canon was transmitted, and persisted throughout the Bagan period. Unsurprisingly, this transit left a kind of trail in the form of Pāli inscriptions, two of which dating from the Bagan period have been found there.[63] Opening into the Bay of Bengal but still being accessible from the central mainland, these ports subsequently served Buddhist travellers as gateways for Lanka, who preferred them over the long and potentially dangerous journey around the Malayan peninsula.

But it was the rulers of Sukhodaya who played a crucial role in linking their monastic institutions and lineages to the perceived Mahāvihāra tradition of Sri Lanka. A series of missions between the 1330s and the 1360s, often with royal support, resulted in the transfer of a Sinhalese ordination lineage, the *araññavāsi* tradition, and of course tangible items such as texts and a branch of the Bōdhi tree.[64] A Pāli eulogy from 1361, written by a mahāthera in praise of the ruler of Sukhodaya is usually seen as proof for the presence (if not dominance) of the Theravāda tradition, but even before that record, Pāli had been used for recording passages from the scriptures (including the '*ye dhamma*...' formula).[65] The contacts between Sukhodaya and Lanka by and large coincided with the rise of Ayudhya, whose rulers established their own link with the island.

All these efforts culminated in the 1420s, when a large delegation of monks from various Southeast Asian regions travelled to Lanka to receive higher ordination according to the Sinhalese tradition.[66] This convention, reports of which had a sedimentation in several historiographic traditions of Southeast Asia, will have to be seen in the light of the imminent end of the second Buddhist millennium in 1456.[67] As predicted by the Buddha and explained by Buddhaghosa, the first signs of the decline of the *sāsanā* were becoming visible, but by then Theravāda Buddhists had realized that the decline could be prevented through a set of measures, which aimed first and foremost at the purification of the Sangha, the spread of the scriptures, and the conservation of its sacred places. All through the fifteenth century, Buddhist rulers and communities of Southeast Asia copied the buildings (notably the Mahābodhi temple) and texts that monks sent to Lanka and India had brought back, held recitations and ordination ceremonies, sent monks to frontier districts, adopted the Buddhist calendar and wrote histories to link their own local branch of Theravāda to the broader stream modelled by the Lankan chronicles. Once again, it was a Pāli cosmopolis: it was informed by the belief in the decline of the *sāsanā* and the advent of a future Buddha Metteyya, built on a shared, canonized set of scriptures and their interpretations written in Pāli, and united in the ceremonies and activities that promised to avert decline and preserve the canon in its pristine form. This Pāli cosmopolis of the fifteenth century was both a perceived community comprising all Buddhists who shared that textual foundation (and probably beyond, given that the scriptures were copied on several occasions and spread further across Asia)[68] as well as a place, when it brought Buddhists together at Kōṭṭe, Chiang Mai, Pegu and elsewhere. This also makes clear that it became only temporarily manifest, while at other times the Buddhists who belonged to it were at war with each other.

## Conclusion

This chapter has attempted to draw an outline of the Pāli cosmopolis during the second millennium of the Buddhist Era and determine the position of Sri Lanka/Sri Lankan Theravāda in it. It has been argued that the language that lent its name to the cosmopolis appears to have taken its final shape in the Mahāvihāra of Anurādhapura in the context of both millennial expectations (the advent of the future Buddha Metteyya) and a struggle for spiritual superiority, which in the case of the Mahāvihāra followed attempts to abolish the monastery completely. At that point, the Mahāvihārins went for a canonized version of the canon written in a language mostly incomprehensible to outsiders, to underpin their claim of being the true keepers of the *dhamma*. Missionary efforts to find allies outside the island seem to have become part of this project, as the earliest quotes from the Pāli canon found in central Burma suggest. At any rate, this dissemination of the scriptures abroad laid the foundations for the Pāli cosmopolis.

The further fate of the cosmopolis depended on the one hand on a general trend in India after c. 700 CE, which saw a revival of Hindu ritual and devotion at the cost of other belief systems, mainly Buddhism and Jainism, and on the other hand on political events affecting Sri Lanka and its Sinhalese-Buddhist polity

Anurādhapura. Successive invasions and conquests eventually resulted in the destruction of the Mahāvihāra and the interruption of its monastic lineage. That the Sangha on the island could only be restored with the help of Burmese monks illustrates that the centre of the Pāli cosmopolis was shifting towards Southeast Asia – Theravāda's 'great translocation' was well underway. This process continued in the thirteenth century, as Sri Lanka struggled to regain political stability, while Bagan emerged as Theravāda's foremost intellectual and ceremonial centre. Monks from all over the Buddhist realm flocked to the city, studied texts and performed monastic acts (*Sanghakamma*). Pāli was central for this mixed transnational community, providing the foundation for both study and communication, as the numerous short and long Pāli inscriptions from Bagan demonstrate. However, the 'great translocation' was never completed due to another political incident, this time the Mongols raiding Bagan. The city was abandoned as a political capital, and even though some of its larger monastic estates continued to exist until the fifteenth century, fostering religious studies and the production of texts throughout, it could not preserve its former status as a central place for Buddhists.

The Buddhist communities and rulers at the new centres that emerged elsewhere on the Southeast Asian mainland from the late thirteenth century sought to found and validate their monastic lineages on texts and higher ordinations obtained from Sri Lanka again. These contacts had effects at both ends as the demand for Theravāda 'made in Lanka' acknowledged the superiority of the Sinhalese tradition preserved by the Mahāvihāra – no matter whether this lineage still existed or not – over those traditions that had formed in Southeast Asia. The various traditions forming on the mainland were temporarily found together once more in connection with the advent of the third millennium of the Buddhist Era in 1456. Instead of accepting the inevitability of decline, they attempted to preserve the purity of both the order and the canon through a set of measures that had developed over the past centuries. The first moment the Pāli cosmopolis of the fifteenth century reconvened was at Kōṭṭe in the 1420s, and from there it flowed, back and forth, through the Southeast Asian mainland. By then, Sri Lanka had regained its former status as champion of the Theravāda regardless of the periods of turmoil the island and its Sangha had been thrown into during the preceding five centuries.

4

# Beautifully moral: cosmopolitan issues in medieval Pāli literary theory

*Alastair Gornall and Justin Henry*

This chapter explores the extent to which we can speak of medieval Pāli literary culture as a cosmopolitan formation, with particular focus on its moral and political dimensions.[1] As an ecclesiastical koiné – a monastic language used to compose literature addressing exclusively Buddhist concerns – at first glance, medieval Pāli would seem to have little to do with cosmopolitanism. The model of literary cosmopolitanism in premodern Southern Asia was supplied originally by Sanskrit, the inscriptional discourse, grammar, lexicography and poetry of which articulated a 'Sanskrit cosmopolis' – a community of literary producers and consumers united not by any single geography or polity but through what Sheldon Pollock identifies as a 'self-assumed cultural universalism', supra-regional in its extent, and close in its political associations.[2] The Sanskrit cosmopolis was further characterized by a shared 'care for language', wherein literature and literary theory were imagined as recapitulating the social and political orders. Well-composed literature was a reflection of good governance and ultimately of the rectitude of society in general. Thus according to Sheldon Pollock, the premodern Indian court's care for language was a genuine moral one, 'not a sham or a show but a core value of what it meant to be just and good'.[3] Later Sanskrit literary theorists advocated that literary education facilitated the moral education of the individual, thus assigning an essential place in social life to the sophisticated use of language.[4]

After 'more than a millennium of what seems to have been stubborn and self-conscious resistance to Sanskrit's cultural project' (to quote Pollock), Pāli scholar-monks became increasingly affected by cosmopolitan Sanskrit. Monastic literati writing at the end of the first millennium embraced Sanskrit literary forms, in particular *kāvya* – Sanskrit court poetry and its accompanying philological toolkit (poetics, grammar, metrics and lexicography) – despite the fact that Sanskrit was never a dominant literary or inscriptional language in Sri Lanka.[5] Monastic authors became increasingly self-aware of their participation in a broader, transregional, multilingual literary milieu, and grew sensitive to the possibility that their work would be evaluated by Sanskritic literary standards (by those within their own monastic circles at home or by critics, sectarian and otherwise, abroad). Pāli literary culture at this time also became increasingly widespread, culminating in the rapid diffusion at the beginning of the second millennium of Sri Lankan Buddhist ordination lineages into Southeast Asia.[6] For these reasons, in terms of its geographical reach and literary style, medieval Pāli literature shares some important features with cosmopolitan Sanskrit. What is less clear is whether the introduction of cosmopolitan literary style into Pāli necessitated the adoption of a Sanskritic 'care for language' too. In this chapter we argue that this was indeed the case, and we examine the anxieties, compromises and innovations of Lankan Buddhist authors as they – along with the Pāli language – navigated their way into the literary world of their age.

The first half of this chapter explores the transmission of Sanskrit literary theory into Lankan Pāli Buddhist monastic discourse, with special attention given to Saṅgharakkhita's thirteenth-century *Subodhālaṅkāra* (*Lucid Poetics*), the first manual of Pāli poetics. In this connection, we argue that Lankan authors also articulated their care for language in socio-moral terms, relying partially on antecedent Sanskrit śāstric conceptions of aesthetic acumen, and partially recasting Brahmanical vocabulary to better suit a Buddhist framework. The second half of the chapter addresses the function of Pāli in late medieval Sri Lankan courtly culture, exploring tensions between the often erotic and militaristic content of Sanskrit *kāvya* and the monkish concerns of Sri Lankan Buddhist literati. We conclude by speculating more generally on Pāli's relationship with the royal court, arguing that the unique status of Pāli as an ecclesiastical language affected its application as a cosmopolitan language on analogy with Sanskrit.

## The Sanskrit cosmopolis and the *Kāvyādarśa* in Sri Lanka

Beginning in the fifth century but intensifying in the first centuries of the second millennium, Pāli[7] underwent a process of 'literarization' in which in terms of style and vocabulary it became increasingly influenced by Sanskrit. Treatises on Pāli grammar, lexicography, prosody and poetic composition modelled on older Sanskrit works circulated in abundance in Sri Lanka during this period, culminating in the scholastic achievements of the thirteenth century. In Sri Lanka, educational complexes administered by Buddhist clergy (*pariveṇa*-s) were centres of training in Sanskrit, prosody, rhetoric, history, logic and medicine.[8] Monks were then by necessity in touch with the cosmopolitan world of broader South Asia.[9] It is this milieu that gave birth to that which Steven Collins calls 'later Pali *kāvya*',[10] or, as we might simply call it, Pāli *kāvya*. It is true that verse compositions in Pāli date far back, the *Thera*- and *Therīgathā*-s, for instance, probably predate the Common Era. Two significant histories of Sri Lanka, the *Dīpavaṃsa* (third or fourth century CE) and *Mahāvaṃsa* (the earliest portion of which dates to perhaps the sixth century), are also composed in verse.[11] One should note, however, that these works do not contain in abundance the rhetorical figures (pun, simile, alliteration, etc.) nor the chapter divisions or content that have come to characterize *kāvya*, and that make up the concerns of Sanskrit composition manuals on poetry.[12] It is not until the very end of the first millennium that Pāli *kāvya* – a poetic style imitative of Sanskrit antecedents – comes into being in its own right.[13]

One of the pivotal events in the development of second-millennium Pāli *kāvya* was the composition in the thirteenth century of the first work on Pāli poetics, the *Subodhālaṅkāra* of Saṅgharakkhita Mahāsāmi. Its main Sanskrit source was Daṇḍin's *Kāvyādarśa*, a work that had a large influence on poetics in medieval Sri Lanka in general.[14] This seventh-century manual of Sanskrit poetics has long been recognized as playing a pivotal role in the theorization of vernacular poetry in South Asia.[15] Its influence has been acknowledged in the production of poetry and poetical treatises in Sinhala, Tamil, Kannada and also Tibetan, among others.[16] In Sri Lanka, the work had a direct influence on the creation in the tenth century of the first poetical treatise in Sinhala, the *Siyabaslakara*.[17] Ratnaśrījñāna, a Sri Lankan monk, also wrote a highly influential Sanskrit commentary on Daṇḍin's work, the so-called *Ratnaśrīṭīkā*, while living in northeast India.[18] This transmission of Sanskrit poetical knowledge into the curricula of the Buddhist monastic literati not only formally codified new conventions of literary beauty, but also brought the Sanskrit attitudes to language into Pāli literary culture, in particular the idea that literature was a reflection of the social order.

In an early articulation of this connection between language and society, Daṇḍin in the *Kāvyādarśa* provides two verses (vv. 3–4) at the outset of his work expressing the eternal significance of language for the continuation of knowledge and the normative social order. Language is praised as the means by which society functions[19] and is likened to a light that ensures that the three worlds are not plunged into ignorant darkness.[20] After a famous verse glorifying the immortalization of kings in literature,[21] Daṇḍin creates a dichotomy between the proper and improper use of language and likens those who use language incorrectly to beasts: 'According to the wise, a correctly used word (*gauḥ*) is a wish-fulfilling cow. But when it is incorrectly used, the speaker reveals his own bovine nature (*gotva*).'[22] Daṇḍin wittily exploits the dual sense of the word *go* (cow/word) here to make a broad point about the correlation of verbal eloquence and social status: the cultured aesthete actualizes his or her humanity through the use of correct language. Similar physiognomic metaphors are also used by Daṇḍin to describe the quality of literature. He relates the beauty of poetry to the attractiveness of the human body by likening poetic defects to spots of leprosy, for instance.[23] Daṇḍin then turns in verse eight to the socio-moral importance of the rules that underpin beautiful literature – that is, the importance of literary theory (*kāvya-śāstra*) – and asks: 'How can people who do not know *śāstra* distinguish between qualities and faults? How does a blind man have the authority to discriminate between different colours?'[24]

In these opening verses on the purposes of literature and literary theory, Daṇḍin blurs the boundaries between the literary, ethical and social orders. By not being able to distinguish between right and wrong as defined in the *śāstras*, one identifies oneself as an outsider to Brahmanical courtly society. The incompetent poet acquires a marginal social position, as a beast (v. 6) or blind man (v. 8), and his poems are viewed as bodies spotted with leprosy (v. 7). Daṇḍin ends his introductory section by stating that it is for the above reasons that the sages (*sūrayaḥ*) – and we must include Daṇḍin here by way of his emulation of their practices – sought to educate the people (*prajā*) in the ways of language.[25]

Writing in the tenth century, the Sri Lankan monk Ratnaśrījñāna elaborated on Daṇḍin's nascent socio-moral vision of literary appreciation, although he did so in terms that were not recognizably Buddhist, and in fact more germane to courtly life. Ratnaśrījñāna was active in northeast India during his early scholarly career and wrote his commentary on the *Kāvyādarśa*, the *Ratnaśrīṭīkā*,[26] under the patronage of a certain king Tuṅga, a scion of the Rāṣṭrakūṭas and feudatory of the Pāla king Rājyapāla (r. 929–960s).[27] Commenting on verse three of the *Kāvyādarśa*, Ratnaśrījñāna argues that literature (*kāvya*), like society (*loka*) as a whole, needs theory or rules (*śāstra*) to keep it in tune with the aims of society; that is, the life-goals (*puruṣārtha*-s), namely, *artha* (material wealth), *kāma* (physical pleasure) and *dharma* (duty, personal responsibility with respect to one's station in life), to which is sometimes added a fourth, *mokṣa* (liberation, i.e., emancipation from rebirth).[28] Elsewhere Ratnaśrījñāna elaborates on the idea that the ability to use language correctly distinguishes humans from beasts and states, for instance, that 'one who is ignorant of *śāstra* lapses into nonsense and, as such, is declared by the wise to be a beast in human form'.[29] He continues to remark on the fact that knowledge of literary theory elevates one to divine status and brings about the life-goals:

> Even if there is no distinction in the matter of being a human, one who knows the *śāstras* is worshipped as a god by those attracted to good qualities (*guṇa*), though the other [i.e. the one who does not know the *śāstras*] is regarded as a beast, since everywhere the discrimination between merits (*guṇa*) and faults (*doṣa*) is only due to *śāstra*. And a merit connects one to the life-goals (*puruṣārtha*), whereas a fault joins one to the opposite (*itareṇa*). By relying on *śāstra*, therefore, a *kāvya* with good qualities is exclusively a fulfiller of the life-goals. But a fault, even if very small, is to be removed only with the help of *śāstra*.[30]

The merging of socio-moral and literary value systems implicit in Daṇḍin's opening verses is thus made explicit by Ratnaśrījñāna: being a connoisseur of literature and literary theory is a mark of one's own moral standing – the merits (*guṇa*) of literature join one to moral goals and the faults (*doṣa*) of literature separate one from them. Ratnaśrī summarizes his position well at the end of his commentary on Daṇḍin's introduction, stating: 'One should recognise all merits and faults everywhere, for in reality [literary] merits are simply constitutive of the life-goals/ends of man (*puruṣārtha*).'[31] Although Ratnaśrī was a Sri Lankan Buddhist monk, his work displays few indications of his monastic background, reflecting instead his courtly associations and the concerns of his royal patron. Yet it was this work that stimulated the study of Sanskrit poetics in late medieval Sri Lanka and introduced Sanskritic notions of the interconnection between literary and moral sensibilities.

## The cosmopolitan care for language and the *Subodhālaṅkāra*

In the Sri Lankan poetical works that followed the *Ratnaśrīṭīkā*, the most elaborate and creative discussion of these ideas can be found in Saṅgharakkhita's *Subodhālaṅkāra* and his autocommentary, the so-called *mahāsāmi-ṭīkā*. Saṅgharakkhita's writings reveal that the acceptance of Sanskrit aesthetic theory within Buddhist monastic culture included its socio-moral ideas too. At the beginning of his work, Saṅgharakkhita devotes two verses in praise of śāstric learning, remarking first that 'those who have not amassed wisdom found in the various different *śāstras* are afflicted by a cloud of ignorance and do not understand anything'.[32] He continues by stressing the importance of a teacher when learning the *śāstras*: 'What is the use in this world of those who do not desire to listen at the feet of teachers? It is those who are covered with the dust of [their teacher's] feet who are good and discerning.'[33]

It is in his commentary on these verses that Saṅgharakkhita reproduces the social message of the *Kāvyādarśa* and the *Ratnaśrīṭīkā*, adopting the conception of the bestial person ignorant of literary theory found in verse six of the *Kāvyādarśa*. He remarks for instance that 'only those who know *śāstra* have what is called the [ability] to discriminate between the different merits and faults. Those who do not know *śāstras* – the beast-like men (*purisapasu*) – do not'.[34] Echoing the sentiments of Ratnaśrī's commentary on verse eight of the *Kāvyādarśa*, Saṅgharakkhita elsewhere writes (regarding a man educated in the *śāstras*) that

> such is the wise [one] who has the authority here (*ettha*) to discriminate between the different merits and faults. The other who is the opposite of this, a beast-like human,[35] is not [entitled to discriminate between merits and faults].[36]

It is significant too that Saṅgharakkhita very rarely refers to the *puruṣārtha*-s (life-goals) in his discussions. Instead he replaces the term with the more general ethical expression: 'what is to be rejected and what is to be accepted' (*heyyopādeyya*). This decision to omit the term *puruṣārtha* and to define the life-goals in a more capacious way has precedents in earlier Sanskrit Buddhist interpretive schematics. Dharmottara, for instance, also defines *puruṣārtha* in the more general sense of 'what is to be rejected and accepted' when commenting on the use of the term in Dharmakīrti's first *sūtra* of the *Nyāyabindu*.[37] It is possible that some Buddhist authors looked towards a more general interpretation of the *puruṣārtha*-s, one that sought to establish meaningful 'ends of man' disentangled from equivalent Brahmanical Hindu terms.

Unlike Ratnaśrī, who makes no real attempt to integrate the socio-moral vision of Sanskrit poetics within either the Buddhist or Sri Lankan literary tradition, Saṅgharakkhita occasionally recasts the vocabulary of the Sanskrit tradition in a Buddhist light and makes allusions to well-known Pāli scripture to support his views. When commenting on the word 'wisdom' in verse four, Saṅgharakkhita defines it in terms of the ability to discriminate between 'what is to be rejected and what is to be accepted' and states that such wisdom is found in the *śāstras*. He continues by delineating śāstric knowledge as that which is contained in 'the *tipiṭaka*, philosophy (*takka*), grammar and poetics'.[38] Saṅgharakkhita takes the moral goal that he had previously introduced in relation to the study of literature, ('knowing what is to be rejected and what is to be accepted'), and establishes it as the goal of all *śāstra*, within which he innovatively includes the *tipiṭaka* (the canonical Pāli Buddhist textual corpus).[39] Nothing is said here about the *content* of the *tipiṭaka* in relation to other pan-Indic sciences, and we are left with only the neutral assertion that all are equally valuable in directing one to moral ends.

Another area in which Saṅgharakkhita shows sensitivity to his Lankan Buddhist audience concerns the relationship between guru and pupil in a śāstric education. Commenting on verse four, Saṅgharakkhita writes that the wisdom gained from the *śāstras* is 'received from the refuge that is worshipping at the feet of such a teacher (*guru*) who does not direct one to useless ends (*aṭṭānāniyojakatā*), etc'.[40] As noted by its late commentary, the *abhinava-ṭīkā*,[41] the description of the teacher as someone 'who does not direct one to useless ends' is in fact a canonical reference to a verse found in the *Dutiyamitta Sutta* in which the ideal *kalyāṇamitta* (a good friend) is described as one who 'is loveable, esteemed, respectable, speaks sensibly (*vattā*), listens patiently, is able to have serious conversations, and does not direct one to useless ends'.[42] Within the Pāli canon, a *kalyāṇamitta* is a soteriological helper who assists another on the Buddhist path. The use of this canonical passage to describe the qualities of the guru – even though that teacher may be imparting the knowledge of literary theory rather than knowledge from the *tipiṭaka* – serves to assimilate the function and role of the śāstric guru within the locally accepted model of the *kalyāṇamitta*.

When commenting on verse five, Saṅgharakkhita addresses the hierarchical and devotional nature of this relationship specifically. He defines the good (*sādhu*) pupil who is distinguished by wisdom as one: 'strewn, [i.e.] covered and furnished, with the pollen, [i.e.] the dirt, of their teachers' feet', maintaining that only such 'good, discerning people who are complete with the attainment of wisdom – which differentiates the different merits and faults that are to be rejected and to be accepted – can discriminate between merits and faults'.[43] For Saṅgharakkhita then the prestige of studying literary theory is equated here with the honour of covering oneself in the dirt of the teacher's feet and it is this educational rite that qualifies one as an expert in moral and literary matters. Elsewhere Saṅgharakkhita cites a canonical verse from the *Sevitabba Sutta* to support his emphasis on devotional pupillage and the resulting hierarchy between śāstric guru and student:

> A man who associates (*sev*) with a lower descends,
> And [a man] who associates with an equal never fails.
> The wise one who attends upon (*upa-nam*) a superior rises,
> Therefore revere one who is superior to yourself![44]

This verse is used to support the śāstric intellectual hierarchy and to defend the reliance on a guru as a teacher, since 'the wise one who attends upon a superior rises'. Saṅgharakkhita connects the lesser man in the canonical verse with the idea of the beast-like human (*purisapasu*), unable to discriminate between merits and faults. In its canonical context, however, this verse is used to support a slightly different form of social order. The verse in the *Sevitabba Sutta* does not delineate an intellectual hierarchy but concerns a hierarchy of morality, meditative concentration and wisdom. The goal of esteeming and worshipping those of higher morality, concentration and wisdom is connected to one's interest in developing these three Buddhist virtues rather than out of a desire to separate oneself socially and morally from bestial people.[45]

While reproducing much of the socio-moral rhetoric of the *Kāvyādarśa*, Saṅgharakkhita along with other Buddhist theoreticians also recasts certain ideas of the Sanskrit poetic tradition in a Buddhist light. While Ratnaśrījñāna replicates the normative ideal of the Sanskrit care for language in emphasizing the link between *śāstra* and *kāvya* with the four classes (*varga*-s) and the four life-goals, Sangharakkhita supplants the *puruṣārtha*-s with more general (and less worldly) admonitions for the aspiring poet. Familiar notions of literary-moral excellence, wisdom gained from the study of systematic knowledge, and the ultimate objectives of human endeavour are subtly co-presented with, and made to allude to, well-known Pāli scripture and Buddhist religious tenets. Yet fundamentally, it seems Saṅgharakkhita accepts the view of one's *literary aptitude* as an index to one's *moral aptitude* derived from the Sanskrit poetic tradition.

## Audience, anxiety and envy

At roughly the same time that Saṅgharakkhita was active in Sri Lanka, the Burmese Saṅgha also began to adopt Sanskrit literary practices and inherited many of the new śāstric intellectual lineages flourishing in Sri Lanka at the beginning of the second millennium. Perhaps the most iconic example of the Burmese Saṅgha's participation in this engagement with the Sanskrit cosmopolis is the *Saddanīti*, a twelfth-century encyclopaedia of literary sciences that was composed a little earlier than the *Subodhālaṅkāra* by a certain Aggavaṃsa. A late Burmese tradition has it that upon its completion the work was brought to Sri Lanka and was praised by the monks there as unlike anything they had produced.[46] Of particular relevance to the reception of Sanskrit poetics within the Saṅgha is a passage in the *Saddanīti* that defends the fact that the older Pāli canonical literature does not conform to the standards of Sanskrit literary theory:

> The Buddha, furthermore, does not take into account the heaviness and lightness (i.e. the metrical weight) of his speech. He constructs his teaching according to the dispositions of those capable of enlightenment, without obscuring the essence of the Dhamma. The length or shortness of sounds is not to be criticised at all.
>
> Even so, why do previous teachers state here and there that: 'There is an elision of a syllable in the verses for the sake of guarding the metre,' 'also there is metathesis for the purpose of guarding the pronunciation,' and 'for the purpose of guarding the metre and for pleasant pronunciation'? [...]
>
> This is true but where the metre and pronunciation are to be guarded, the Buddha has guarded the metre and pronunciation. Where both are not to be guarded, however, the Buddha has not guarded the metre and pronunciation. It is in this connection that it is said: 'The Buddha, furthermore, does not take into account the heaviness and lightness (i.e. the metrical weight) of his speech,' etc. Moreover, the Buddha does not guard metre and pronunciation like the poets who do it as part of their profession. Rather, those words – that have been perfected by his expertise in literary science (*akkhara-samaya*) from time immemorial, for countless, hundred thousands of births, when he was a Buddha-to-be – fall from his propitious, lotus-like mouth. Some of them have a form as if [they were intended] to guard metre and pronunciation and some do not. In connection with those that have a form as if [they were intended] to guard metre and pronunciation, it could be said that 'the Buddha guards metre and pronunciation.' In connection with those that do not, it could be said that 'the Buddha does not guard metre and pronunciation.' It should be understood that the Buddha is not anxious or fearful on account of the criticism of others and that he does not guard metre and pronunciation out of anxiety or fear.[47]

In this fascinating discussion, the author is clearly concerned that Pāli literature will be judged on the basis of śāstric literary theory and takes great pains to explain that, while the Buddha has mastered literary science for countless eons, he does as he pleases. His intention is the liberation of sentient beings and he is not concerned with the aesthetic preoccupations of poets. The unease of the author concerning the seeming incompatibility of śāstric literary theory and the Pāli canon is made clear in his final lines. He states that the Buddha does not adhere to literary beauty out of an anxiety or fear of others. This statement intimates that some Buddhist authors at the time were fearful of the scrutiny of the śāstrins of the Sanskrit cosmopolis.

When presented with a discourse that regards those who are ignorant of Sanskrit aesthetics as animals, it is easy to see why these monks reimagined the Buddha as a perfectly accomplished aesthete who simply chose not to use his skills. The personal responsibility the monks felt for their irregular Pāli is made explicit in a variant of this passage found in R. C. Childers' notes to his translation of the *Khuddakapāṭha*. In Childers' manuscript of the *Saddanīti*, the author continues that 'in this work, with its confused syllables, [we] write in accordance with the tradition of the Pāli texts. We are not to be blamed (*dosa*) for this'.[48] The author of this interpolation makes it explicit that he is not to be held morally responsible for the 'irregularities' of Pāli literature. It is not his fault (*dosa*).[49] His use of the word *dosa* intimates that the merits and faults of literature were viewed not just as a matter of literary acumen but also one of moral aptitude for the Buddhist Saṅgha. The passage makes it clear furthermore that Buddhist monks felt compelled to conform to the standards of Sanskrit literary theory. The adoption of Sanskrit aesthetics into Pāli literature was, then, perhaps not simply a choice based on aesthetic attraction but was part of a wider concern or fear for the moral status of their intellectuals and literature.

In the *Subodhālaṅkāra* and other thirteenth-century Sri Lankan literature there is also an acute awareness of the scrutiny and critical gaze of other intellectuals. The mention of such an audience is important as it shows that there was a broader intellectual community (or at the very least the *perception of* a broader intellectual community) evaluating Pāli literary production on the basis of trans-regional, trans-linguistic aesthetic criteria. Verse eleven of the *Subodhālaṅkāra* offers another hint to that effect, when Saṅgharakkhita warns that a fool who attempts to use literary embellishments without the instruction of a teacher will face the mirth (*hāsabhāva*) of the wise.[50] A similar concern for censorship is expressed by Anomadassi at the beginning of the *Daivajñakāmadhenu*, his manual of court astrology written during the reign of Parākramabāhu II (r. 1234–69), wherein he boldly announces that he 'does not care about those envious demons who binge on quivering souls and cast scorn'.[51]

Such outbursts indicate the sensitivity in thirteenth-century Sri Lanka to the scrutiny of other intellectuals in Sri Lanka and possibly in other parts of the Sanskrit cosmopolis. The ethics of aesthetics that were brought into the Pāli tradition through the commentaries on the *Kāvyādarśa* were not simply reinforced according to the conscience of the individual author. Rather, fear of opprobrium from a broader intellectual community would ensure correct (e.g. normative from the point of view of the *Kāvyādarśa*) reproduction of literature and literary theory. What we have then is evidence not just of the spread of Sanskrit literary theory but more importantly of the acceptance of its socio-moral worldview, one that ensures the reproduction of its literary aesthetic.

## Eroticism, kings and the Buddhist social aesthetic

While some monastics expressed anxiety over their foray into the cosmopolitan literary world, others denied that *kāvya* was a suitable medium of expression for Buddhists altogether. Monastic reluctance towards poetry is attested early on in Pāli Buddhist literature,[52] manifesting itself in medieval Sri Lanka as well. The *Daṁbadeṇi Katikāvata*, a thirteenth-century monastic encyclical, decrees that 'verses, etc., should be neither recited nor composed for laypeople'.[53] The document warns furthermore that, 'the despicable arts such as poetry and drama should neither be studied nor taught to others'.[54] The criticisms of the *Daṁbadeṇi Katikāvata* are all the more significant in light of the fact that Saṅgharakkhita himself was a leading figure in the reforms that brought about the composition of this edict.[55] Despite any such rhetorical opposition, the abundance of *kāvya* composed by Sri Lankan Buddhist authors indicates that, if these cautions were not entirely ignored, at least some efforts were made to accommodate Buddhist poetry within the cosmopolitan expectations established by Sanskrit authors.

*Prima facie* we can grasp some reasons as to why monastics would be anxious over the embrace of Sanskrit literary norms. Beyond defining literary education as a component in the fulfilment of *kāma* (physical pleasure in the broad sense), Sanskrit theorists in addition upheld the 'erotic mood', *sṛṅgāra rasa*, as the most appropriate thematic sentiment for a poetic work. In the *Nāṭyaśāstra* we are told: 'Generally, all emotions come from sexual love.'[56] Bhoja goes so far as to say: 'Passion alone is *rasa*, [and] the sole means of fulfilling the four life-goals.'[57] Thus the motivation to render the *puruṣārtha*-s within a Buddhist vocabulary (as do Saṅgharakkhita and Dharmottara) is perceptible: *kāma* and *artha* – the attainment of physical pleasure and material wealth – are both fundamentally anathema to the Pāli Buddhist monastic ideal. The sex act, *methunadhamma*, is reviled in the Pāli Vinaya and elsewhere in the canon as the greatest obstacle to the ascetic lifestyle (*brahmacariya*).[58] In order to abate male lust, Pāli works offer practitioners tools to grasp the ephemeral nature of physical beauty, and to perceive what is in reality the disgusting condition of the female body.[59]

The sensualism of Sanskrit poetic imagery is furthermore in tension with Buddhist monastic sensibilities. In early Buddhist literature, sexual imagery was often invoked with the expressed purpose of showcasing the futility of a life directed towards *kāma*. The scene of the night of Siddhartha's renunciation (ubiquitous in Pāli Buddhist literature and art) depicts him waking up amid his voluptuous servants and entertainers after an evening of feasting and presumed debauchery. The women are now asleep in contorted, unflattering poses – drooling and dishevelled. In the Pāli Nikāyas and Vinaya, they are explicitly likened to corpses, with Siddhartha's boudoir appearing 'like a cremation ground before the eyes'. In a similar fashion, early Buddhist poetry inverts the function of the 'erotic sentiment' to serve its own soteriological ends. Johannes Bronkhorst suggests that the Sanskrit works of the Buddhist poet Aśvaghoṣa (mid-late first or second century CE) represent something of a 'Trojan horse', designed to weaken

Brahmanical religion from within.[60] In his *Buddhacarita* and *Saundarānanda* (in fact two of the earliest Sanskrit *kāvya*-s), Aśvaghoṣa uses erotic imagery not to excite the reader but as an instrument to make a point about impermanence.[61] The *Saundarānanda* is particularly arresting in that the Buddha actually uses Nanda's predilection for beautiful women to commit him to a life of religious practice. The Buddha transports Nanda to the enchanted land of the Himalayas, where he shows him divine young women of superlative beauty. Nanda entreats the Buddha to tell him how to attain these women, and the Buddha tells him that they can be won by practising the highest asceticism. Nanda eagerly assents, and in the course of his subsequent practice realizes that beautiful women are only a temporary pleasure, soon after which he attains *nirvāṇa*.[62]

That eroticism was one concern common to early second-millennium Lankan Buddhist authors is detectable in places. The *Subodhālaṅkāra* replaces most of the explicitly erotic verses of the *Kāvyādarśa* with devotional ones to the Buddha and treats the erotic sentiment in a cursory manner, briefly reviewing this *rasa* in its fifth and final section.[63] The *Siyabaslakara* attempts to redirect poetic enthusiasm towards worthwhile ends, stating that poetry should be used to narrate the lives of the Buddha.[64] Many Pāli poetic works do nonetheless contain stock sensual imagery of Sanskrit *kāvya*. The *Jinacarita*, a thirteenth-century Sri Lankan Pāli poem, describes the Bōdhisattva's mother with conventional *kāvya* tactile eloquence:

> Queen Māyā, whose lips were as red as the *bimba* fruit, whose eyes were like blossoming lotus flowers, with eyebrows curving like a creeper (*or, arched like Śakra's bow*) and conducive to the increase of passion (*rativaḍḍhana*); whose noble face was like the pure and splendid full moon, and whose charming breasts were like two golden swans.[65]

This verse does not attempt to reverse the reader's first cognitive impulse from sensuality to aversion (as does Aśvaghoṣa in his poetry). It is essentially ornamental, supplementing a biography of the Buddha with pleasant imagery along with pun (*śleṣa*) and simile (*upamā*). In reference to early Pāli literature, Steven Collins makes the distinction between images of beautiful women as merely 'aesthetic' as opposed to 'erotic'.[66] There is an argument to be made that it is possible for a poet to make use of sensual imagery without endorsing *śṛṅgāra rasa* or the pursuit of sense pleasure, with the *Jinacarita* as testament to such an intention on the part of its author.

There is one further aspect of the content of Sanskrit *kāvya* that may have given Buddhist authors pause. Pāli monastic regulations censure interaction with royalty and martial affairs quite severely,[67] and yet royal eulogy and descriptions of military conquest are often central themes in Sanskrit *kāvya* (indeed they are the thematic content from which Sanskrit *kāvya* derived its political significance and popularity in the first place, Pollock argues). Interaction with royalty is a longstanding theme in the Pāli Buddhist tradition. Gotama Buddha himself in the

Pāli Nikāyas is depicted receiving alms and places of residence for the Bhikkhu Saṅgha from kings, giving them a personal audience often in return. This reflects a fundamental empirical reality and tension: while the ideal of the monk involves a detachment from society, the reality was and is that large monastic corporations (in the case of Sri Lanka, with large landholdings and a complicated bureaucracy of their own) required extended interaction with governing bodies.[68] Most importantly, monastics needed to secure for themselves a steady supply of food and, to maintain the institution, a continuous supply of new initiates. The Pāli textual tradition portrays kings as central suppliers of the Buddhist Saṅgha in these respects.

Although Sri Lankan monks were custodians of a textual tradition mandating that a perfectly righteous king never exercise violence (the *Temiya Jātaka* goes so far as to portray kingship as criminal[69]), they are the authors of poetic texts (or at least in some instances historical texts containing poetic elements) sanctioning – in places we might even say celebrating – military force and royal prowess.[70] An inordinate portion of the *Mahāvaṃsa*, for instance, is devoted to the victory of King Duṭṭhagāmaṇi over the Tamil usurper Eḷāra, a triumphalist theme that grew even more pronounced in Pāli Buddhist historical works over time. The thirteenth-century *Thūpavaṃsa* devotes an entire chapter to Duṭṭhagāmaṇi's campaign against the Tamils, weaving in verses from the *Mahāvaṃsa* while offering exciting visual detail reminiscent of the battle scenes of Sanskrit epics. At the final battle of Anurādhapura, the great Sinhala and Tamil warriors engage one another:

> Sūranimmala, as he beheld [the Tamil warrior Dīghajantu] soaring into the sky over the King [Duṭṭhagāmaṇi], announced his own name and shouted it to him abusively. When Sūranimmala saw Dīghajantu, overcome with rage and leaping into the sky, intending to kill him first he descended upon him, holding out his shield. His opponent attacked, thinking to cut him down together with his shield, at which point [Sūranimmala] released his shield. Cutting it Dīghajantu fell to the ground, whereby Sūranimmala attacked him with his spear. At that instant Phussadeva blew his conch shell, which was like the roar of thunder, and the people seemed to become mad (with jubilation).[71] The Damiḷa army was routed and Eḷāra fled. At that time too they slew many Damiḷas.[72]

Amusingly, prior to this battle, unable to do for long without the recreation befitting a person of his social class, the Buddhist prince takes a holiday from vanquishing Tamils, excavating a pond at Kāsapabbata in order to indulge in water sports (*udakakīḷa*) for one month. It is noteworthy that the *Siyabaslakara* permits the composition of epic poetry (*mahākāvya*), insisting, however, that the protagonist be the Buddha in his final or previous incarnations (as Bōdhisattva or 'Buddha aspirant'). Duṭṭhagāmaṇi of course does not meet this qualification (he is not the Buddha), although he does represent in Jayawickrama's words 'the ideal hero and the ideal lay disciple'.[73]

By the second millennium, Pāli poetry furthermore celebrated royal power in the manner of Sanskrit court poetry by embedding *praśasti* (royal encomium). After three verses of invocation to the Buddha, Dhamma and Saṅgha, the *Dāṭhāvaṃsa* (late twelfth or early thirteenth century) extols General Parākrama (not to be confused with Parākramabāhu I), Queen Līlāvatī (the author's sponsor), along with the Pāṇḍava prince appointed by General Parākrama to succeed Līlāvatī:

> The army commander Parākrama, compassionate and an ornament upon the lineage of Kālakanāgara, who steeps himself in the dispensation of the Buddha and who desires after the advancement and welfare of the people,
>
> Who placed on the consolidated throne of Laṅkā Queen Līlāvatī – she having been born of the pure, resplendent, stainless Paṇḍu lineage – highly devoted to the Buddha's dispensation, pleasant in speech, one who follows the path of good conduct,[74] like a mother to the people at all times, loving queen to King Parākramabāhu, possessed of discriminating intelligence and sought after,
>
> [Parākrama] appointed [as Līlāvatī's successor] the prince who is loved by councillors, kind-hearted, born of the lineage of Paṇḍu kings, faithful, named Madhurinda, well-learned in religious matters and worldly arts,
>
> [Parākrama] dispelled the disgrace of Tisīhaḷaṃ,[75] which was kingless for so long, and made the well-disciplined Saṅgha pleased with good meals, robes and other requisites.[76]

The twelfth-century extension of the *Mahāvaṃsa* also famously celebrates posthumously the accomplishments of Parākramabāhu I in highly poetic style.[77] Ironically, the Sinhala *Daṁbadeṇi Katikāvata* – the very same thirteenth-century document prohibiting monks from composing poetry – offers a verse of praise for its royal sponsor in the classical mode of Sanskrit *praśasti*, replete with simile and other conspicuously *kāvya*-esque motifs:

> The noble son of Vijayabāhu, the great king Parākramabāhu, who, like the autumn sun which dries up mud completely destroys his enemies, and who possessed abundant strength as does the full moon in illuminating the milky ocean of Buddha-sāsana, brought the entire surface of Laṅkā under his domination, having settled the various disturbances of the Draviḍas, Keraḷas and Yāvakas through the splendour of his meritorious accomplishments.[78]

Although the tone of Pāli and Sinhala poetic manuals and monastic guidelines is cautionary with respect to *kāvya*, in practice Pāli poetry and history finds room to celebrate royal prowess, violence and recreation. This seems to be admissible, however, only if it is portrayed to be ultimately for the benefit of the Buddhist religion, the *buddha-sāsana*. Such a caveat was easily enough accomplished as the subject matter of stand-alone Pāli poems is exclusively Buddhist, and the kings recorded in Pāli chronicles were generally patrons of Buddhist institutions (conspicuously remembered as having not been when they were not).

One might perceive the celebration of monarchy and warrior culture as a tacit endorsement of the Brahmanical caste system, or the portrayal of courtly recreation as an allowance for the pursuit of *kāma*. Although royal eulogy and descriptions of battle might be regarded as a concession to the Brahmanical, monarchical status quo of Sanskrit *kāvya*, as noted throughout this section, Lankan Pāli authors were keen to maintain a Buddhist frame of reference in their work. Eroticism is at no point the *telos* or governing sentiment of poetry. The *puruṣārtha*-s are redefined in a more capacious light or ignored altogether in favour of the narration of the Buddha's life, his asseverations to Buddhahood in former lives, and the religious history of Sri Lanka.

## The Pāli cosmopolis?

Can we speak of a 'Pāli cosmopolis' – of a transregional community of literary producers and consumers valuing Pāli literature for its ability to ennoble social and political life – on analogy with Sanskrit? Certainly, as the previous section of this chapter highlights, Lankan Buddhist monastic authors were not exempted from interactions with royal courts (they depended on royal patronage, supplied and updated dynastic chronicles, and composed secular *praśasti*). Steven Collins submits, for instance, that sophisticated Pāli Buddhist authors and their literary products were intimately connected with political power, helping to solidify rule by conferring prestige on kings and courtly elite:

> Monks and their texts, as also their relics and images, are prestige objects, circulating in an exchange system of precious goods: law-texts, for example could be and were put together with other power-objects by kings in impressive displays. In the perspective of socio-historical analysis it is an element in the rhetorical, theatrical constitution of civilization-bearing state-systems: symbolic capital contributing to the prestige of both the *maṇḍala*-organizing king and his clients [...] Premodern literati, like virtuoso musicians, were embodiments and indices of high culture.[79]

Yet while *kāvya* and other elite Sanskrit literature circulated largely within learned audiences associated with royal courts, Pāli literary activity was limited almost exclusively to Buddhist religieux. Collins' proposal necessitates a basic inquiry into the question of audience: if Pāli was a literary language known only to Buddhist monks, how could royal patrons be sure that they were getting their money's worth? In other words, how would they ever be able to judge the quality of the contents of literary works, or show them off to their competitors for symbolic capital?

There is the possibility that any sponsor who knew Sanskrit could have understood Pāli with ease, and could have listened to or read the works for themselves. King Parākramabāhu II was himself, for instance, a Pāli scholar, to whom is attributed a Sinhala commentary (*sannaya*) on Buddhaghosa's *Visuddhimagga* as well as a translation of the *Vinaya-vinicchaya* of Buddhadatta.[80] At present however there is little evidence that Lankan kings commonly knew Pāli, although further research on this issue is a desideratum. Another possibility is that the prestige conferred to court sponsors (to 'the *maṇḍala*-organizing king and his clients') from sophisticated Pāli literature was only epiphenomenal in relation to prestige earned between competing monastic institutions, examples of which may be found in the work of Alastair Gornall and Anne Blackburn.[81] Gornall shows that debates over the intricacies of Pāli phonology among Buddhist grammarians in the twelfth century were one manifestation of competition for ritual authority between South Indian and Lankan monastic orders. Blackburn draws on twelfth- and thirteenth-century documents to demonstrate how Lankan monks able to present themselves as forest-dwellers (members of an *araññavāsi* lineage) consistently benefited from royal patrons during a time of political uncertainty and monastic reorganization.

A third hypothesis (not incommensurate with the previous two) is that Sri Lankan lay Buddhist sponsors may have had a chance to enjoy the fruits of monastic labour when works were written in Sinhala, or translated into it from Pāli. From the twelfth century – coincident with the development of highly literate Pāli – Sinhala texts were for the first time composed with a general lay audience in mind. Many *baṇa pot* ('preaching texts'),[82] like contemporary Pāli poems and works of history, copiously incorporated *kāvya* conventions and tropes, as well as a heavily Sanskritized vocabulary. While *baṇa pot* were written with the explicit purpose of public recitation, there is epigraphic and internal textual evidence that Sinhala historical works were read aloud to lay audiences as well.[83] In fact, works of history seem to have been imbricated in a complex and ongoing project of translation, elaboration and oral performance between Sinhala and Pāli.[84] The *Mahāvaṃsa* claims to be a reworking of earlier Sinhala historical material (its *ṭīkā* lists a now lost *Sīhala Mahāvaṃsatthakathā* as one of these). Later, heavily *kāvya* influenced Pāli *vaṃsas* – the *Mahābodhivaṃsa* (tenth century), *Dāṭhāvaṃsa* (late twelfth or early thirteenth century) and *Thūpavaṃsa* (thirteenth century) – say the same thing with respect to themselves.[85]

While the Sinhala source materials for these Pāli works are now lost, new Sinhala versions were created in the thirteenth century and first half of the fourteenth century.[86] Following the *Sinhala Thūpavaṃsaya* and *Daḷadā Sirita*, the *Mahābodhivaṃsa* was enlarged and re-translated into Sinhala as the *Elu Bodhivaṃsa*. Pāli and Sinhala *vaṃsas* had different authors, but were produced within the same literary milieu (the Pāli and Sinhala *Thūpavaṃsa*-s most likely even at the same court).[87] There is a sense that court-sponsored, monastic intellectual production in the Poḷonnaruva and Daṁbadeṇiya periods (including *kāvya* quite centrally) was on display to broader lay audiences in one form or another, whether merely in Sinhala, or in Pāli and Sinhala both.

We can imagine then regents and other wealthy patrons in literate circles (such as the sponsor of the original Sinhala *Thūpavaṃsa*) investing in a literary work as a source of personal prestige, anticipating its recitation as a public event. So as not to reduce the entirety of medieval textual production to the material-political, we should qualify that such motivation could have been one among a host of others: a moral care for language, genuine devotional feeling, efforts to accrue merit (*pin*, *puñña*), appreciation and personal respect for a given monastic intellectual. That is, for much the same reasons that a Buddhist today might donate a *tipiṭaka* to a monastery, hold a large almsgiving with friends and family invited, or pay to have their name recited by a monk leading a pilgrimage at Bodh Gaya.

While Sinhala could have provided monastic authors with a means of showcasing their work within Sri Lanka, this situation was possible only within the island's shores. Regionally, Pāli texts circulated within the restricted sphere of the Buddhist monastery. To what extent *praśastis* of Sinhalese kings embedded in Pāli poems would have impressed foreign readers or found their way to the attention of the rulers of distant lands must remain within the realm of speculation, although there is some evidence that learned monks themselves were highly prized. *Araññavāsi* monks were sought from Sri Lanka by Thai monastic leaders in the fourteenth and fifteenth century for their erudition and literary ability, for instance.[88]

Discussing the extent of a Pāli cosmopolis becomes then a complicated affair. Its contours appear differently depending on the degree of geographical magnification. One might preferably view Pāli poetry as one facet of a broader emerging cosmopolitan literary culture in late medieval Sri Lanka – as one literary language and one form of literary expression among others. Sinhala, as discussed briefly above, underwent a similar process of literarization at approximately the same time as Pāli. Sanskrit learning and literary production continued from the first millennium,[89] and even Tamil works were sometimes financed by Sinhalese kings. In addition to Sinhala, Pāli and Sanskrit, the *Daṁbadeṇi Asna* records that Parākramabāhu II was also accomplished in Tamil.[90] The *Caracōtimālai*, a Tamil astrological text, was completed and recited in the court of Parākramabāhu III (grandson of the aforementioned) in 1310.[91]

## Conclusion

In his own theorization of the 'poetry of polity', Sheldon Pollock stresses the voluntary nature of the adoption of Sanskrit literary practices within the Sanskrit cosmopolis, emphasizing that 'literarization' was a process that did not involve political coercion.[92] Certainly in the case of the transfer of Sanskrit aesthetics to Pāli we can agree that this was true (Pāli literary production was diffuse, temporally and geographically, and no single political formation was responsible for 'imposing' Sanskrit literary standards on Buddhist monastic authors, if indeed such a thing ever occurred at all). Sanskritic literary discourse held a more subtle allure for Lankan monastic authors. Pāli Buddhist authors felt a twofold anxiety over the reception of their literary products: at the most elementary level, they were concerned simply that their work conform to cosmopolitan literary standards so as to avoid derision at the hands of religious and/or intellectual competitors; at a deeper level, as we have endeavoured to show, monastic authors worked to render assumptions regarding the *moral* stature of effective authors and aesthetes in the Sanskrit *alaṅkāra-śāstra* tradition in line with those of Pāli Buddhist canonical literature.

Armed with their own treatises such as the *Subodhalaṅkāra* and *Siyabaslaraka*, no longer could anyone say that a monk writing in Pāli or Sinhala was a 'beast' rather than a 'god' (like a rival steeped in Sanskrit learning). The shared aesthetic of Sanskrit court poetry and late medieval Pāli poetry reflected a common moral vision. The choice to retain the vocabulary of Daṇḍin's *Kāvyādarśa* and its commentary in terms of the correlation of *moral* and *aesthetic* aptitude signals that the attraction of Sanskrit aesthetics was not merely a matter of fashion, but rather indicative of a wider concern for the moral status of Lankan monastic intellectuals and their literature. This moral care for language was cosmopolitan insofar as it transcended religious and linguistic boundaries, though importantly it only allowed a privileged and elite few to be called true human beings.

Sanskritized Pāli prose and poetry in Sri Lanka was also employed in the service of political discourse, amplifying and expanding upon the role of Pāli in statecraft (which prior to that point had come principally in the form of the Lankan Buddhist chronicles (*vaṃsa*-s)). In this way, despite its limited readership, Pāli *kāvya* was employed in a similar capacity as Sanskrit and other vernacular literatures in a 'workly' fashion – eulogizing Lankan rulers and their ancestors, 'enhancing reality' through figures of speech (*alaṅkāra*-s) 'by coding reality in the apparent impossibilities of poetic configuration'.[93] Yet participation in the Sanskrit literary cosmopolis was at once a magnetic and repellent notion for late medieval Lankan Buddhist monastic authors. Sanskrit itself, as the ecclesiastical and academic language of Hindu competitors and continental Buddhist sectarian rivals, had to be treated with caution. Lankan Buddhist authors felt anxiety over acculturation – both with the very notion that Pāli should be expected to conform to Sanskrit literary norms, and with respect to the content of Pāli *kāvya*. The erotic and martial aspects of Sanskrit *kāvya* were also mitigated in Pāli (and, while not dealt with in any detail in this chapter, also Sinhala) *kāvya* in order to serve religious, historical and political purposes, sometimes simultaneously.

Does it make sense then to speak of a Pāli cosmopolis in the same way as we speak of a Sanskrit cosmopolis? Medieval Pāli literary culture shared many features with the Sanskrit cosmopolis, in terms of its style, geographical reach, common socio-moral literary sensibility and its political associations. Unlike Sanskrit, however, Pāli could never truly separate itself from its ecclesiastical functions. Its most salient role continued to be as a language of the Buddhist monastery rather than the royal court. As such, medieval Pāli literary culture can be viewed as a form of qualified cosmopolitanism, one that advanced many of the cosmopolitan literary ideals of its time but also staunchly protected its exclusively Buddhist identity.

# 5
# Sinhala *sandēśa* poetry in a cosmopolitan context

*Stephen C. Berkwitz*

The genre of messenger poetry in Sinhala literature represents a derivative, yet distinctive, form of poetic composition, which one may use to reflect upon the concepts of 'cosmopolitan' and 'local' as signifiers in premodern literary cultures. A consideration of this genre reveals a strategy by Sri Lankan authors to imitate and transform literary forms from outside Sri Lanka into vehicles for expressing and praising local forms of power and culture. As noted by Sheldon Pollock, Sinhala may be counted among those South Asian vernaculars that developed in royal courts in response to, and in imitation of, the values and forms of Sanskrit literature. According to this theory, the use of Sanskrit in poetry and royal inscriptions produced the forms of cultural and political expression upon which a cosmopolitan order of cultural power was formed across Southern Asia.[1] The production of Sanskrit texts endowed various polities with a self-styled pretence to universal fame and power, although such pretensions rarely if ever achieved their grandiose claims in actuality. Nevertheless, following Pollock, Sanskrit court poetry (*kāvya*) and royal panegyric (*praśasti*) were jointly responsible for producing and popularizing certain assumptions about elements of power that aspired to universality but, falling short of that, were replicated in more localized contexts through the development of regional polities and vernacular forms of literature. This too was the case in Sri Lanka. Although there are some extant examples of Sinhala poetry in inscriptions from as early as the sixth century CE in Sri Lanka, the development of a vernacular poetic literature with extant works and modelled after Sanskrit norms dates from around the eleventh century.[2]

The development of Sinhala poetry and the deployment of the distinctive poetic dialect called *eḷu* took place mainly in proximity to Sinhala kings and courts. There are hints in such texts that they were often recited aloud before royal assemblies, although there are other poetic works in Sinhala that address broad religious and ethical concerns, which may have been directed to broader segments of the general public. The development of this literature, and the dating thereof, is consistent with Pollock's model of the 'vernacular millennium', and yet it also serves to complicate the idea of Sri Lankan 'cosmopolitanism'. In Sri Lanka, literary cultures came to embrace the vernacular and to put it to work in the creation of regional polities with claims to widespread fame and influence. Such works appear to have been often deployed for the sake of generating certain impressions and expressions of political power.[3] The Sinhala *sandēśas*, for their part, are literary works that locate power in the intersection between local and translocal spheres. These texts evoke a sense of both the local and the cosmopolitan, utilizing features of both while being limited to neither. In other words, the use of the term 'local' for premodern Sinhala poetic works should not be understood as exclusive of cosmopolitan, translocal forms and features. We would do well to contest the implication that texts composed in local languages can only result in 'local texts' with greatly diminished horizons. Sinhala poets, as we shall see, employed their native language to extend the fame and influence of their kings and their works of literature.

Emerging out of the interplay of poetry (*kāvya*) and power (*rājya*) in Sinhala courts beginning around the eleventh century, Sinhala *sandēśa* poetry became especially popular in the literary culture of fifteenth-century Sri Lanka. This culture emphasized the composition and enjoyment of fine poetic works to distinguish the aesthetic skills of poets and kings, while imagining the court as a centre of power and refinement. South Asian courtly culture was, in general, held to be the home of the noble and the good, populated by those who have cultivated superior moral and aesthetic characteristics.[4] Employing such models of political and social power that emanated from the literature of Indic courts, Sinhala poets between the twelfth and sixteenth centuries sought to replicate these models in Sri Lanka.

One common way for doing so was to imitate the *sandeśakāvya* genre that was widespread across the Indic subcontinent. Such works belong specifically to a distinctive genre of poetry that emulates Kālidāsa's *Meghadūta* (*Cloud-messenger*) poem. Kālidāsa's classic sixth-century Sanskrit work, in which a *yakṣa* petitions a cloud to carry a message of love to his wife from whom he has been separated, helps to frame the broader context for the composition of *sandeśakāvyas* throughout the Indic world. The popularity of the *Meghadūta* is illustrated through some references to other such Sanskrit *sandeśas* or *dūtakāvyas* ('messenger poems') in the early eighth century, the large number of commentators on this work, and translations of it into languages such as Sinhala by the twelfth century.[5] There is ample evidence of *sandeśakāvyas* composed in Sanskrit, Tamil and other Indic languages that dwell on the love and longing of separated lovers for whom the delivery of a message – often by a bird, a bee or some other natural phenomenon – promises to ease the grief of separation.[6] These works customarily follow a two-part structure, comprising a detailed description of landscape for a messenger to travel, followed by the specific message to be delivered upon arrival.[7] The very existence of such works throughout South India and Sri Lanka remind us of the fact that local literary cultures such as those involving Sinhala, Tamil, Telugu and Malayalam were informed by and connected with each other.[8]

Poetic accounts of a message carried by some non-human messenger comprise one of the pre-eminent cosmopolitan genres of South Asian literature. Steven Hopkins has rightly described the *sandeśakāvya* as a 'transregional and multireligious poetic genre' that is found in most South Asian languages and across religious traditions.[9] One finds numerous works in which messages are carried by various flying creatures or atmospheric phenomena (such as clouds or wind) from one individual to another. Certain ancient works in Sanskrit and Pāli contain narratives that foreshadow the development of this genre. Rāma sends a message to his kidnapped wife through the monkey Hanumān in the *Rāmāyaṇa*, a swan carries a message from King Nāla to Damayantī in the *Mahābhārata*, and a crow is called upon by a dying man to carry a message to his wife in the Pāli 'Kāma Vilāpa Jātaka'.[10] In time, entire works become devoted to the subject of messages of love being carried by third parties. The Sinhala *sandēśas* may thus be located within this broader South Asian literary genre.

Upon closer inspection, however, one finds certain distinctive features in Sinhala works that deviate from their Indic prototypes. Messenger poetry in India typically revolves around themes of love and longing experienced by separated lovers, in which even the conventional descriptions of landscapes serve to evoke the feelings of absence and eventual reunion found in the main characters of the work.[11] In most cases, a lover persuades some kind of messenger to deliver a long, lyrical exposition and then describes a detailed route to convey the messenger to the absent lover, who is often portrayed in a state of acute lovesickness.[12] The messages sent are thus poetic expressions of love that convey desire for one's lover and grief from being apart from her or him. For example, many such works employed the pretence of having the *gopī* maidens employ some sort of messenger to send word of their longing for their beloved Kṛṣṇa.[13] A further characteristic of this genre includes pairing the messenger with its own mate, which helps it to sympathize with the miserable, lovesick state of the recipient to whom they deliver the message.[14] However, Sinhala *sandēśas*, as we will see below, show little interest in love as the motive behind sending messages. This striking departure from one of the definitive characteristics of the genre deserves more consideration, as it suggests that Sinhala poets chose not to imitate Indic *sandeśakāvyas* too closely.

More questions arise concerning the specificity of local landscapes in messenger poems. In works such as the Tamil *Haṃsasandeśa* (*Message of the Goose*), written by the thirteenth–fourteenth-century author Vedāntadeśika, the messenger's journey is dotted by familiar cities, hills, rivers, forests and temples within a particular region. The locations referenced in such works are found scattered throughout the Indic subcontinent and occasionally even cross over to the island of Sri Lanka. The particular geographic details found in messenger poems speak to the genre's capacity to identify and valorize certain locations. This literary mapping of landscapes may also promote what Hopkins calls a particular 'religio-geocultural *imaginaire*' that is amenable to the royal or sectarian patron of the work.[15] A related argument about Sinhala *sandēśas* has been made by Anoma

Pieris, who argues that these works 'stressed the importance of *geographic* belonging' that fostered the development of 'place-based and politically-constructed ethno-cultural loyalties'.[16] The literary conceptualization of territory is a key feature of Sinhala *sandēśas*, and this subject will be taken up in more detail below.

To this end, closer attention to the fifteenth-century *Kōkilasandēśaya* (*Message of the Cuckoo*) and the sixteenth-century *Sävulsandēśaya* (*Message of the Cock*) will facilitate a critical assessment of the aims and places found in Sinhala messenger poetry and, in turn, the manner in which this genre illustrates the complex and sometimes contradictory interests in cosmopolitan affiliations in premodern Sri Lanka. *Kōkilasandēśaya* and *Sävulsandēśaya* have been chosen in part because they appeared more than a century apart and thus together indicate some degree of continuity in the genre's poetic style and interests. They are also works of substantial length and depth, and they are neither well-known nor accessible to many scholars since they have not been translated into a western language.

## Indigenizing Sinhala *Sandēśas*

Since the genre of messenger poetry was nearly ubiquitous throughout South Asia, Sinhala poets had numerous examples from which to model their own compositions. The writing and reciting of Sinhala *sandēśas* enabled writers, readers and listeners to participate in a cosmopolitan literary culture. Nevertheless, it would be misleading to assume that Sinhala *sandēśas* lacked originality. Even the repeated takes on poetic elements supplied by Kālidāsa can, as shown by Yigal Bronner, be rearranged, revalorized, or relocated to create something novel in Sanskrit messenger poems.[17] The will to innovate in this genre, however, appears even stronger in Sinhala works. While evoking translocal images and ideas connected to the circulation of Sanskrit literary culture, Sinhala *sandēśas* asserted particularly local visions in the forms and contents of their poetry. It has been noted that as many as 114 *sandēśas* were composed in Sinhala between the fourteenth and nineteenth centuries.[18] The proliferation of such works speaks to their value and role in the vernacularization of literature in Sri Lanka, particularly in terms of poetry.[19] The high point for Sinhala *sandēśa* literature appears during the fifteenth century when King Parākramabāhu VI (r. 1411–66) ruled over a united island from his court in Koṭṭe. In this period, many classical bird-messenger poems were composed in Sinhala, including the *Parevisandēśaya* (*Message of the Dove*) and *Sälaḷihiṇisandeśaya* (*Message of the Mynah*), written by the renowned monastic author Śrī Rāhula, along with the *Haṃsasandēśaya* (*Message of the Goose*) and *Girāsandēśaya* (*Message of the Parrot*), whose authors are not definitively known. The *Kōkilasandēśaya* appears later in the fifteenth century by a monk from a family called Irugalkula. Around a century later, a lay poet named Alagiyavanna composed the *Sävulsandēśaya* in the early 1580s under King Rājasiṃha I (r. 1581–93).

Although the use of birds to carry poetic messages was not new, the rendering of this genre into the Sinhala poetic language introduced several distinctive features. By virtue of their composition in *eḷu*, the literary dialect of Sinhala poetry, all of these works display a commitment to the local language and its particular use of rhyme and metre. Like other South Asian vernaculars, Sinhala *kavi* employed a vision of literature that could transcend time and place, giving rise to a literary culture that imagined itself as utilizing a language equal to Sanskrit in terms of power and beauty.[20] And yet the adoption of norms and forms from Sanskrit *kāvya* into Sinhala *kavi* entailed distinctive efforts to superpose local Sinhala features on to their Sanskrit paradigms. Charles Hallisey has argued that the Sinhala literary culture from the tenth to fifteenth centuries self-consciously adapted what counted as literature in Sanskrit, but also distanced itself from the prototype by rejecting Sanskrit loanwords (*tatsamas*) and incorporating some new phonemes such as the nasalized 'ä' vowel and half-nasal consonants.[21] This ambivalent stance of modelling a local literary culture after a cosmopolitan Sanskritic one, while insisting upon several distinctive features to mark its separation from Indic literary cultures, speaks to the ability of Sinhala literature at once to evoke universality while reasserting locality. The authors of Sinhala *sandēśas* participated in this textual juxtaposition of near and far, local and cosmopolitan, by employing Sinhala poetic forms and metres to recast an otherwise transregional genre in indigenous terms. Their engagement with and transformation of Sanskrit messenger poetry, rather than Pāli *sandesas*, offers more evidence of the Indic orientation of this genre.[22]

The *Kōkila-* and *Sävulsandēśas* make use of the distinctive alphabet and vocabulary of Sinhala *eḷu*, as well as the *sivupada* style where, in a given quatrain, four lines of verse each end with the same letter – vowel, consonant or combination of both. The rhyming scheme of this type of Sinhala poetry may also incorporate forms of internal rhymes repeated in each line to add aesthetic richness. Further, such Sinhala *kavi* employed the restrictive *eḷu* alphabet that reduced the number of permitted letters from fifty-seven in prose to thirty-six in poetry, doing away with aspirated consonants and the palatal and retroflex sibilants written in Roman letters as 'ś' and 'ṣ'.[23] The smaller alphabet prevented the use of Sanskrit loanwords and led to a reliance on shorter words that were often homonyms, which could be used poetically to generate complexity as a sign of poetic virtuosity. For instance, the Sinhala word *sam̆da* could be derived from the Sanskrit *candra* ('moon' or 'eminent'), *saṃdhi* ('connection'), *chanda* ('desire'), *candana* ('sandalwood'), *chandas* ('prosody') or *saṃdhyā* ('evening') and refer to any of those meanings depending on context. Learned connoisseurs could be expected to distinguish and identify the correct meaning of a homonym in a line of verse. The plurality of meanings found in a single word could dignify the talents of Sinhala poets and confirm the sophistication of their local audiences.

One finds further evidence of the localization of the *sandeśa* genre in the narrative themes that appear in its Sinhala variants. As noted above, one typically finds *sandeśakāvyas* throughout South Asia that transport messages sent from an exiled lover to a distant beloved.[24] Most works in the genre mimic and evoke the *Meghadūta*'s focus on love in separation, where the message that is carried by a bird or some other messenger expresses strong feelings of affection and attachment to someone far away. And yet, contrary to this custom, classical Sinhala *sandēśas* do not deal with separated lovers who long to be reunited. The messages that are carried by birds in Sri Lanka usually concern or address a deity, who is petitioned to grant a blessing or a boon resulting in some form of worldly success related to the protection and prosperity of a king. Having the protection of others (and in later centuries, oneself) as the primary aim for the authors of the Sinhala *sandēśas*, such works distinguished themselves from the messenger poems from the subcontinent.[25] For instance, the *Sälaḷihiṇisandēśaya* carries a message to the god Vibhīṣaṇa from King Parākramabāhu VI's son-in-law beseeching the deity to grant his wife a son and heir to the throne. The *Parevisandēśaya* addresses the god Upulvan in Devinuvara, asking for his help to find a good husband for the king's daughter and, eventually, a son and heir to the throne. The *Haṃsasandēśaya* contains a message for a leading monk instead of a god, but still aims at protecting the king and extending his reign. As for the works under consideration here, the *Kōkilasandēśaya* conveys a message of reassurance to Prince Sapumal in Yāpāpaṭuna (Jaffna) to confirm that the monastic author has been praying to the god Upulvan for the prince's prosperity and protection in the land that he has recently conquered.[26] The author of *Sävulsandēśaya* beseeches the god Saman to protect the Buddha's Dispensation, the beings of the world and particularly King Rājasiṃha I, his ministers and his fourfold army.[27] In the fifteenth and sixteenth centuries, Sinhala *sandēśa* poems recount journeys but reference no separated lovers or anticipated blissful reunions in their verses.

Instead, these Sinhala works adapt the conventions of the Sanskrit *sandeśakāvya* genre to celebrate and enhance the power of local kings. Conspicuous, political interests lie behind the poems, as reflected by the respective paths that are described to the bird-messengers. The sphere of the political here is no afterthought lying behind a romantic storyline. Instead, birds are dispatched to carry messages that seek divine blessings for kings and their progeny, as well as the religious institutions attributed to the Buddha in his Dispensation (*śāsana/sāsana*). Emotional expressions of love and longing are nowhere to be found in the Sinhala *sandēśas* at the height of their popularity in the fifteenth and sixteenth centuries. If anything, romantic love is displaced by lust, as numerous Sinhala *sandēśa* poems include erotically charged descriptions of female bathers and dancing girls whose physical charms are conventionally described to indicate the power of kings and the talent of poets. Such erotic verses, as we shall see below, are neither incidental nor merely ornamental to a story about separated lovers.[28] They are instead integral pieces for depictions of royal power and majesty. In this sense, attractive female bodies mimic attractive landscapes as indices to a beautiful, bountiful kingdom ruled at the centre by a strong monarch.

In addition to local variations of poetic language and themes, Sinhala *sandēśas* are also distinguished by their abundant references to local places. The cities and shrines to be visited by the bird-messengers are found exclusively in the island of Sri Lanka, and no bird is ever sent across the Palk Strait to visit India. The cuckoo in *Kōkilasandēśaya* makes a lengthy journey starting in Devinuvara on the southern coast, travels up to Väligama, the monastery at Toṭagamuva, Kalutara, the monastery at Päpiliyāna, the royal palace at Koṭṭe, up through Kontagantoṭa, Mīgamuva and further up the western coast to Jaffna in the far north.[29] Throughout the cuckoo's thirteen-day journey, he is told to rest in various small villages and to observe the local shrines, landscapes and women at each spot. For instance, in the village of Mātara on the south coast, the bird is told to gaze at the women with moonlike faces and bodies like gold creepers, then he is to observe the flowers and peacocks in Polvattē, before proceeding to the Mahaväli village with market stalls of gems and women who rub sandalwood and saffron paste on their breasts.[30] Likewise, the cock in *Sävulsandēśaya* begins his journey in the capital city of Sītāvaka, stops at the Bhairava Kovil, goes by the rest house in Vasuvilviṭa and the guardpost at Gaṭasätta, proceeds through various other villages until arriving at Delgamuva to worship the Tooth Relic and spend the night, and then journeys on through Kuruviṭa to admire the river and jungle, passing by other villages where peacocks and women wander about, before arriving at the city of Saparagamuva, home to beautiful city-women and the shrine of the god Saman.

Both works describe local landscapes with great specificity and elaborate details. In addition to religious shrines both large and small, one comes across ponds, forests, rest houses, guard posts, paddy fields and other sites that collectively serve to construct a detailed local geography wholly within the island of Sri Lanka. In doing so, these Sinhala *sandēśas* formally resemble the messenger poems from Tamilnadu and Kerala, among other South Asian regions, that similarly mark out and valorize specific places such as temples, mountains, fields and cities.[31] Of course, each messenger poem reconstructs a particular journey and distinctive geographical vision, which in turn represent a strong commitment to endowing local settings with the honour of being described in poetic verse. The routes taken by the bird-messengers are full of realistic details of one-time roads and places in the island.[32] Such details help to produce a sense of local landscapes that in Sinhala *sandēśas* are roughly coterminous with the geographic spread of the reigns of kings, who often were the patrons of such poems.[33] Each stop along a bird-messenger's journey thus becomes a symbol of the extension of royal power, territory that falls within the sphere of control and vision of the king and his court. This is seen most strikingly in the long northerly journey of the cuckoo, who is sent to inform Prince Sapumal of the divine blessings that will help him to stabilize his recent conquest over the region of Jaffna, where he acts as the king's regent. The text effectively serves to demarcate and confirm the newly enlarged extent of King Parākramabāhu's reign.

While Sinhala authors located their narrative journeys in specific places, they also recognized local figures that resided therein. Local elites in the form of ministers, monks and ritual officiants are often named in these works, serving to locate these texts in nearby space and time, and endowing their narrative representations with what Stephen Greenblatt calls the 'touch of the real', where 'elements of lived experience enter into literature'.[34] The *Kōkilasandēśaya* mentions numerous local personages aside from the king. One learns of chieftains such as Virabāhu and ministers such as Devādhikārī who built a city and a monastery respectively.[35] Renowned monks are also mentioned, such as Vijayabāhu Thera at Toṭagamuva and the chief monk named Dharmakīrti in Jayavaddanapura, along with other monks linked to particular temples on the route.[36] Similarly, the *Sävulsandēśaya* mentions two monks by name in its verses – Mihiňdulakara at the Delgamuwa Temple and Dahaṁlakara in Saparagamuva, both of whom are praised for being excellent poets.[37] The narrator also praises the ritual officiant at the shrine dedicated to Saman, a man named Nānambi Kuruppu, who was installed in this position by King Rājasiṃha I. Such references underscore the authors' careful attention to local details and networks of power and patronage. Inclusion in *sandēśas* suggests that such personages enjoyed royal favour and support, while playing key roles in the king's realm.

Sinhala *sandēśas* take on additional indigenous characteristics by emphasizing certain gods located at particular shrines within the island's territory. Although the poets remain aware of Indic deities and their mythological features that permeate Sanskrit poetry, the bird-messengers address local gods that reside at shrines in the island rather than universal ones such as Kṛṣṇa or Śiva. For instance, several poems petition Upulvan in the southern city of Devinuvara, or Vibhīṣaṇa in Kälaṇiya, or even Skanda at his shrine in Kataragama, a favourite of *sandēśa* poets in later centuries.[38] The *Kōkilasandēśaya* praises Upulvan and describes the might and physical splendour he exudes in his shrine at Devinuvara, which is the cuckoo's starting point on his journey. The cuckoo is told to 'honor with devotion the lotus-feet of the beautiful king of the gods, Upulvan, who is well adorned' and who appears in a local shrine to be worshipped.[39] In one verse, the author compares the appearance of Upulvan to a heavenly tree, which signifies both the god's beauty and generosity.

> The noble, heavenly tree of this king of the gods [Upulvan], presents the highest splendor,
> Adorned with the bees of his garland made of pleasing blue sapphire gems,
> And heaps of the flowers of pearls, made heavy with the fruits of great gifts,
> Being decorated with the branches of his hands and the luminous shoots of his very red fingers.[40]

This same deity is praised in several other verses to make clear how others who listen to this work should venerate him. The poet praises his beauty by mentioning how goddesses gaze upon his dazzling body, and likewise praises his courage by stating that Upulvan alone did not desert the Bodhisattva when Māra, the God of Death, sought to prevent him from attaining Buddhahood.[41] It is Upulvan who at the end of the work is petitioned for protection, to dispel calamities and to bestow prosperity upon the king, the chief ministers and the army.[42]

In *Sävulsandēśaya*, the poet Alagiyavanna chose a different local god as the focus of his work. The cock-messenger is sent on a journey that ends in Saparagamuva, where the god Saman resides in a shrine not far from the site of the Buddha's footprint relic on top of Śrī Pāda or 'Adam's Peak'.[43] This local guardian deity is also called the 'king of the gods' and is extensively praised by the poet. The bird is told to worship Saman, gaze upon his beautiful appearance and convey the message with which he was dispatched. The description of Saman in *Sävulsandēśaya* is extended and elaborate, with the god's physical charms being related from head to toe. One verse describing his arms by comparing them to the heavenly tree adopts much of the imagery and language of the verse from *Kōkilasandēśaya* quoted above.[44]

> The arms of the lord of the gods display the appearance of branches on the heavenly tree,
> Always bestowing all forms of wealth, pleasing gods and humans,
> Upon which the bumblebees of delightful ornaments of blue sapphire gems reside,
> With heaps of the flowers of fingernails and the shoots of very long, very red fingers.[45]

The description of Saman's eyes, ears, arms, chest, thighs and feet, among other parts of his body, serve to vividly recreate his physical presence in his shrine. The eyes of goddesses are drawn to this divine body, giving further proof to his splendid beauty. The poet praises not only Saman's appearance, but also his compassion, generosity, and devotion to the Buddha.[46] Finally, the cock is told to petition Saman to protect the Dispensation of the Buddha, King Rājasiṃha I, his ministers and the fourfold army. Thus, in both of these *sandēśas*, requests are made to gods associated with local shrines on behalf of those who rule righteously and protect bravely the kingdoms in which the poets reside. As a rule, the people, places and deities highlighted in these Sinhala works all exist in local settings.

## Cosmopolitan frames

The conspicuous efforts of Sinhala *sandēśa* poems to map and celebrate the local cannot, however, mask the cosmopolitan imagery and ideals that shaped such texts. Despite their distinctive use of the vernacular language and local referents, these works remain beholden to a translocal literary genre in terms of form and inspiration. They are, after all, called '*sandēśas*', and they employ the literary convention common throughout the Indic world of sending a bird on a journey across a particular landscape to deliver an important message. For all of their attempts to invest this genre with local significance, the Sinhala *sandēśas* gesture to a wider body of South

Asian literature. It is in this sense that authors such as Śrī Rāhula, Irugalkula Thera and Alagiyavanna consciously composed messenger poems in a literary form of the vernacular in order to exalt both their works and themselves. Like other poets who contributed to the vernacularization of literature in South Asia, Sinhala authors of *sandēśa* poetry could claim to belong to a cosmopolitan cultural order while still proclaiming local cultural affiliations that enabled their texts to compete for fame and recognition with those after which they were modelled.[47] Such works, in other words, were invested with both local and cosmopolitan significance at the same time. Their attention to that which is both near and far is reflected in the praise of their royal subjects and the elaborate descriptions of the settings for their rule.

The localizing practices found in works such as *Kōkilasandēśaya* and *Sävulsandēśaya* always implied a cosmopolitan frame and were frequently written as such. For every local site or personage mentioned in a text, there are other references to translocal concepts. Sites and figures associated with Indic mythology, such as Mount Meru and Mount Kailaśa, or Viṣṇu and Śrī, occupy prominent places in Sinhala *sandēśa* literature. For instance, in one verse of Alagiyavanna's work, King Rājasiṃha is praised by the goddesses on top of Mount Meru and the *siddhas*, *vidyadhāras* and *kinnaras* that reside in the Himalaya Mountains.[48] He is compared to gods such as Anaṅga in terms of his beauty and Rāma in terms of his military prowess.[49] Meanwhile, in *Kōkilasandēśaya*, Prince Sapumal is likened to the god Śakra in terms of wealth and his devotion to the Buddha, while the ministers in his court stand around him like divine subjects.[50] Even the merchants in Mahaväli are compared to the gods Kuvera in terms of splendour, Skandakumara in terms of strength and Bṛhaspati in terms of eloquence and wisdom.[51] Clearly, images and ideas derived from texts based in the Indic subcontinent find their way into these Sinhala narratives, enhancing the power of the local in the same way that allusions to cosmopolitan forms of Sanskrit literature could enhance their vernacular counterparts. This process could work so well as to obscure the 'foreignness' of those elements that came from outside of the island. The local relies on the translocal for its identity and its ability to transcend its immediate surroundings. Meanwhile the translocal could also begin to lose its identity as something distinctive and foreign. Although the composition of Sinhala *sandēśas* supplied the means for employing translocal forms to map and celebrate local instantiations of culture and power, the cosmopolitan features of these works are never wholly subsumed under the local. Instead, they persist as layers in Sinhala works that lend such poems a measure of status and complexity, enabling them to be associated with wider literary and cultural spheres.

A closer examination of Sinhala *sandēśas* reveals that even in their descriptions of particular sites across the Sri Lankan countryside, they often reflect more generic, conventional locations than uniquely specific places. Local landscapes are in this way transformed to resemble idealized places found in other poetic works. The manners in which cities are described appear almost interchangeable among various *sandēśas*. The city of Devinuvara, from where the cuckoo is dispatched in *Kōkilasandēśaya*, is thus described as a heavenly abode.

Look at the city of glorious Viṣṇu, overspread with the sounds of instruments,
Having fully blossomed flowers in the house gardens that shine continuously,
Having great halls filled with gems and coral on both sides of the main road,
And radiance like the King of Mountains that spreads many colors.

This beautiful city, always bearing the crown of the King of the Gods,
Having a pair of ear-ornaments of the moon and sun, shining with rays,
Having a large neck of the city gate, made tall and decorated well,
Whose ramparts appear as a girdle of gems, and whose anklet is the water-filled moat.

Since the beautiful faces of women within the window terraces of the mansions,
Which are overspread with blue sapphire gems, are like numerous moons,
The ruddy shelduck birds that amble about continuously, entering large house ponds,
Suffering from confusion, abandon them and go away.

Friend, the banners affixed to the tops of the large, crystal mansions in this city,
Fluttering rapidly in the wind,
Support the splendor of one hundred waterfalls that pour down continuously,
From the beautiful, celestial river off the head of Lord Śiva.[52]

Such poetic accounts of that city seem curiously detached from any of its actual identifiable features. Similar verses are found in Alagiyavanna's description of the sixteenth-century capital Sītāvaka, whose beauty and majesty likewise symbolize the character of its ruling monarch, King Rājasiṃha, who is directly compared to Viṣṇu:

The high, solid ramparts that shine with crystal rays,
Being equal to the beautiful light of the moon that spreads to the ends of all directions,
Are like the coils of the Lord of Cobras, Ananta, that are laid all around,
The Milky Ocean of this city, which shines with the Narāyaṇa of the king.

The manner in which the water of the moat rippled and spread out in rows of waves,
Near the high, expansive, white ramparts that shine with light,
Is like the well-decorated, celestial river that falls around the Kailāśa Mountain,
When Iśvara resolutely begins to dance with the strength and speed of his body.

There the rutting elephants, looking at the splendor of the faces of the
beautiful, adorned women,
Who have come to the window terraces of the spotless jeweled mansions,
Thinking, "It is a beautiful, fully bloomed lotus",
Extend their trunks and wander around with puzzled minds.

When the blue sapphire gems on the banners that flutter on the roofs of
tall, great mansions,
Shine and reflect on the ground in this illustrious city,
It displays the splendor of the various kinds of fish that glisten and shine,
Sporting continually in the beautiful Kaliňdu River.[53]

Even though such verses purport to describe particular places in premodern Sri Lanka, they actually express idealized visions of a city that exists both nowhere and everywhere. Sinhala *sandēśas* depict cities in perfect splendour and without adversity, places where masculine heroes reside amid countless attractive women with faces like moons, eyes like blue water lilies and breasts like swans.[54] In such texts, local cities are recast in terms of poetic ideals of beauty and prosperity. They possess local names but universal features. Meanwhile, forests are invariably decorated with sweet-smelling trees and flowers, and rivers always contain cool water and playful, topless bathers. Although the names are distinctive to the local settings mentioned in the text, their actual depictions are almost wholly conventional and interchangeable.

Sinhala poets relied on the poetic imagery of cosmopolitan literature for more than just their descriptions of local sites through which their birds pass or stop to rest. They also drew liberally from Indic mythological symbolism to glorify local kings in the manner of the *praśasti* genre of praise-poetry. King Parākramabāhu VI and King Rājasiṃha I, the royal heroes of *Kōkilasandēśaya* and *Sävulsandēśaya* respectively, are consistently portrayed in superlative terms, even on a par with Indic gods whose spheres of influence transcend the island of Sri Lanka. Parākramabāhu VI was celebrated for bringing the island under his sovereign rule, having built a capital in Koṭṭe, subduing the Uḍaraṭa district in the central highlands, repelling an attack by the forces of the Vijayanagara Empire and overseeing the conquest of the Jaffna kingdom in the north by his son Prince Sapumal.[55] Eulogized during his long reign in several fifteenth-century *sandēśas*, Parākramabāhu VI could be compared to any number of magnificent objects of praise.

Like the Lord of the Gods, who is the chief of the north, with his splendor
and strong arms,
Like the Lord of Mountains that delights the mind, shining with noble
ornaments,
Like the Lord of the Stars and the disk of the sun in terms of his extensive
fame and glory,
The Lord of Men, Śrī Parākramabāhu, resides in that city [of Koṭṭe].[56]

The king's power and glory, compared here to Kuvera, the god of wealth, together with Mount Meru and the moon, transcend the sphere of the local and thus require universal symbols to convey their expansive nature. The monastic author of *Kōkilasandēśaya* goes further to praise his king by drawing upon other divine symbols to demonstrate how he excels all other rulers.

> Just as there is no tree in the great forest that is equal to the Heavenly Tree,
> There is no king in this age that has power and glory that is equal,
> To this Lord of Men, who is of the Solar Dynasty, and whose ancestral home is the Goddess Śrī's,
> And who is the disk of the sun that causes the lotuses in the pond of the community of poets to bloom.[57]

Depicted as the divine, wish-fulfilling tree of Indic mythology and a ruler whose prosperity is associated with that of Śrī, the goddess of wealth, Parākramabāhu VI emerges in this poem as a king of incomparable magnificence. Both his descent from a legendary royal lineage and his patronage of poets point to his identity as a majestic ruler.

Similarly, the *Sävulsandēśaya* lavishes poetic praise upon King Rājasiṃha I, the implacable foe of the Portuguese, who drove them out of Koṭṭe into an isolated coastal fort, and who subdued the mountain kingdom of Kandy in 1582.[58] The poet Alagiyavanna eulogized his king's power and glory in numerous verses that compared him to universal symbols of divine majesty. Indeed, *praśasti* works characteristically stress the paradigmatic qualities of kings over their particular features in order to enhance their fame.[59]

> This renowned Lord, who is like the Lord of the Gods in majesty,
> Who adorns the necks of the noble women of all directions with the pearl necklace of fame,
> Always guards the attachment to his own life fourthly,
> After his firm power, generosity, and true speech.[60]

The comparison drawn with the majesty of a divine ruler serves to elevate Rājasiṃha into a praiseworthy king whose extensive fame is matched by his great virtue. The poet's ornate description of his majesty elevates his stature to that of a universal deity. Among the many other verses used to praise the king – thirty-nine in all, which exceed any other Sinhala *sandēśa* composed earlier – one finds abundant, conventional descriptions of Rājasiṃha's majesty, prowess and virtue.[61]

> Because of this Lord of Men's great and pure heap of fame,
> Having the shining body of Viṣṇu and the appearance of Iśvara,
> He dwells comfortably, dispelling the doubt,
> From the faultless, long, wide, and brilliant eyes of Śrī.[62]

Such comparisons to Indic deities signal how the king of Sri Lanka is attributed with divine qualities that represent the apparently boundless measure of his fame and power. From the poem's perspective, Rājasiṃha is known and revered by all in much the same manner as deities who are worshipped by devotees in many different lands. Poetry magnifies the king's qualities as he is shown to embody universal characteristics that surpass local frames of reference.

In another gesture to the cosmopolitan origins of messenger poetry, both the *Kōkila-* and *Sävulsandēśas* contain erotic imagery of nameless women depicted in titillating, albeit formulaic ways. Whether these women are portrayed as bathing in rivers, strolling around capital cities, or dancing in shrines or royal courts, their portrayals are designed to elicit the erotic sentiments (*śṛṇgāra rasa*) of an audience that imaginatively gazes upon their attractive bodies. By comparison, most examples of messenger poetry composed in Sanskrit also emphasize the erotic sentiment, although usually in the context of the theme of love in separation.[63] The descriptions in Sinhala *sandēśas* of women dancing and sporting in water are also more extensive than in comparable messenger poems from the subcontinent.[64] The women described in the Sinhala *sandēśas* typically lack speech or emotion, as they appear chiefly to embellish the narrative as background characters rather than protagonists in their own right. For instance, the monastic author of the *Kōkilasandēśaya* uses several verses to describe the physical charms of the city-women who surround King Parākramabāhu VI in Koṭṭe and the dancing women near Prince Sapumal at his royal court in Jaffna. The narrator tells the cuckoo that while in the king's capital,

> Look at the women, who stand, appearing in each doorway,
> Giving slight smiles with their mouths that are worth this whole world,
> Bending every direction with their thin waists that can be grasped with one's hand,
> And adorned with the weight of their pairs of firm breasts.[65]

Later, once the bird has arrived in Jaffna, he is told to gaze upon the dancing women that excite and entertain the people in the prince's court. The dancing women are said to have tied strings of pearls on their foreheads, which are made to resemble the new moon moistened with rays, while jiggling their breasts that are covered in unguents and shaking the jewelled girdles around their waists.[66] Such descriptions of women may illustrate longing and attachment, but these feelings are felt independently of separated lovers, who are altogether absent in these works. Great kings are apparently signified not only by their majesty, but also by the female beauty that surrounds them.

Alagiyavanna's *Sävulsandēśaya* also highlights the physical charms of women in proximity to the Lord of Men, Rājasiṃha I, in his court at Sītāvaka, as well as those women who bathe or dance around the environs of the shrine in Saparagamuva where Saman, the 'Lord of the Gods', resides. Indeed, the juxtaposition of these two lords who attract beautiful females and are entertained by them must surely be intentional. The powerful figures of the king and the deity are also said to be beautiful, and thus they draw other beautiful bodies to them. In Sītāvaka, where Rājasiṃha dwells, attractive city-women play on the balconies of mansions, captivating the young men with their eyes like blue lotuses and their faces like the full moon.[67] Later, when the cock reaches the city of Saparagamuva, the poem describes the enchanting beauty of the women who bathe in the river there.

> The breasts of the noble women that please the mind,
> Remaining above the surface of the water that spills over and strikes the front of their chests,
> Appear like luminous, very splendid golden swans,
> Grasping and pulling the lotus stalks with the tips of their beaks.[68]

The erotically charged descriptions of women serve not only to indicate the presence of a powerful, masculine king or deity, but they also evoke the style of messenger poetry composed outside of the island. These efforts to arouse the erotic sentiment are wholly consistent with the cosmopolitan form of Sanskrit *sandeśakāvya* or *dūtakāvya*. The inclusion of such female figures, even by a monastic author, satisfies at least in part the standards established for poetic excellence, bringing as much fame to the poets as to the kings and other celebrated characters who are objectified in verse. The assimilation of cosmopolitan features associated with messenger poetry connects local Sinhala works with their Indic prototypes, evoking yet also rivalling their referents in Sanskrit and other languages.

## Paying tribute to kings and poets

The very existence of Sinhala *sandēśas* is a testimony of the degree to which poets writing between the fourteenth and sixteenth centuries imagined themselves as belonging to a wider literary world. These authors were, of course, not the first Sri Lankans to engage the literary forms and values of texts composed in other lands. The sixth-century *Jānakīharaṇa*, a Sanskrit *mahākāvya* composed by a poet named Kumāradāsa, shows that Sri Lankans had adopted literary forms developed outside of the island much earlier.[69] And yet the ways in which poets like Irugalkula Thera and Alagiyavanna composed *sandēśas* in the poetic *eḷu* dialect of Sinhala reveal complicated ties between local and translocal literary forms. There is no question that works such as *Kōkilasandēśaya* and *Sävulsandēśaya* are the products of conspicuous efforts to effect the vernacularization of a cosmopolitan literature composed primarily in the Sanskrit language. In both name and form, these *sandēśa* texts work to evoke much of the style and prestige of texts celebrated in other lands.

And yet, one may ask if the composition of bird-messenger poems in Sinhala is simply a straightforward example of poetic borrowing, whereupon the forms and values of a cosmopolitan Sanskrit genre were adopted in full to compete with it on the universalist terms it had set.[70] Sinhala *sandēśas* adapted and subverted their Indic models by recasting them according to indigenous tastes and interests. The Sinhala authors of *Kōkilasandēśaya* and *Sävulsandēśaya* composed works that borrowed heavily from older Sinhala texts, while deviating in important ways from their counterparts in the Indic subcontinent. As noted above, Sinhala *sandēśas* dispensed with the romantic overtones of most other messenger poems, replacing the pathetic pleas of absent lovers with petitions to deities or monks in order to obtain blessings for the kingdom and the Sangha. Political interests appear foremost in such works, and they adopt the style of *praśasti* poetry with eulogies of contemporary kings to a greater extent than typically appears in the Sanskrit *sandeśakāvyas* and *dūtakāvyas*. This would indicate that in addition to the pursuit of poetic renown, the Sinhala authors of messenger poetry were more concerned with enhancing the fame of their rulers than celebrating love. This subversion of certain aspects of cosmopolitan literary norms suggests that the poets' interests had shifted away from simply mimicking Sanskrit *kāvya* and its universalist aspirations.

In other words, the Sinhala *sandēśas* addressed a number of specifically local interests within the cosmopolitan genre of messenger poetry. One such motive is seen in the notable innovations that the authors of *sandēśas* contributed to the development of Sinhala literature. Whereas earlier Sinhala verse works tended to focus on stories of the Bodhisattva in the non-rhyming couplet style of *gī* verse, the *sandēśas* composed in the late fourteenth century and later emphasize worldly topics, including praise for contemporary kings and monks, in the rhyming quatrain style of *sivupada* verse.[71] This change in the composition of Sinhala poetry coincided with an increase in poetic writing during the period when King Parākramabāhu VI was ruling in Koṭṭe. For kings who styled themselves after powerful Indic rulers, there was a strong impetus to combine adherence to the Buddha's Dharma with the enjoyment of aesthetic and other pleasures.[72] As this interest gained prominence, the Sinhala *sandēśas* began to take on more of the qualities of *praśasti* poetry, with the glorification of powerful rulers replacing the celebration of romantic love and devotion to Indic deities in the messenger poems from the subcontinent. What appears striking when reading select Sinhala *sandēśas* next to messenger poems in Sanskrit, Tamil, Malayalam and other languages is the degree to which a cosmopolitan literary genre is appropriated to signal the distinctiveness of its Sinhala variants. There is abundant evidence for literary and cultural exchanges between Sri Lanka and various South Indian regions during the fifteenth century.[73] These relations facilitated the adoption of some of the formal characteristics of messenger poetry, while also giving cultural salience to the Sinhala transformation of the genre.

This pattern of adapting from a cosmopolitan literary world while simultaneously distancing oneself from it mirrors what Hallisey has noted in his consideration of the development of Sinhala literary culture between the tenth and fifteenth centuries. Referencing Sri Lanka's 'constant struggle for autonomy' while in proximity to large-scale imperial formations in medieval South Asia, Hallisey observes that the position of Sinhala authors towards Sanskrit literature involved both participation in a cosmopolitan world and the attempt to mark distinctions through the creation of an autonomous literary space.[74] The suggestion that premodern Sinhala authors balanced adaptation with innovation speaks to a general ambivalence felt towards belonging to a wider cosmopolitan sphere rooted in the subcontinent. Works such as *Kōkilasandēśaya* and *Sävulsandēśaya* participated in the appropriation of Sanskrit literary forms, but without employing mimicry to such a degree that their distinctive features would be lost. The local appropriation of *sandeśakāvya* could enhance the reputations of indigenous poets and elites by imitating the cultural transactions of the larger Indic world, while at the same time reasserting the validity and vibrancy of Sinhala literary culture.[75] The distinctive emphasis on the fame and power of contemporary kings in Sinhala *sandēśas* resonates with broader efforts to protect their kingdoms from being overrun by foreign armies and foreign texts.

This wary stance towards the appropriation of a cosmopolitan literary genre resembles efforts by other vernacular literatures to conform to cosmopolitan literary conventions while still creating difference from them in order to rival and displace them at the local level.[76] One finds the ambition to replicate cosmopolitan images of power and fame. Yet the focus of Sinhala poets in the fifteenth and sixteenth centuries remained squarely on the island of Sri Lanka. Although appropriating certain features of Sanskrit poetry, the Sinhala authors under study here were careful to distinguish their works from messenger poems composed in the subcontinent. Nor should we assume that these works reflect political processes to shape discrete ethnicities and contrive a corresponding sense of geographical belonging, whereby Sinhala authors could have claimed the island for themselves.[77] The politics in premodern Sinhala *sandēśas* are instead concerned with enhancing the reigns and reputations of kings and the literary cultures that they were expected to support. Any indication of the salience of ethnic identities appears too faintly to register in these works. The routes travelled by the cuckoo and the cock map the spheres of royal power, not the territories belonging to distinct ethnic communities. Sinhala *sandēśas* from the fifteenth and sixteenth centuries evince premodern concerns about the reigns and patronage of kings but do not anticipate or intervene in modern debates over races and nations.

Insofar as the *Kōkilasandēśaya* and *Sävulsandēśaya* represent the broader genre of Sinhala messenger poems in premodern Sri Lanka, one may deduce that these works exemplify how people in the island negotiated their place within a wider politico-cultural order. The idealized locales in the island, conventionally described but particularly identified in these texts, serve as a kind of pivot, whereby familiar settings take on the trappings of the universal through the use of familiar poetic tropes. Sinhala *sandēśas* enabled local kings and poets to appear to rival those on the Indian mainland, as their respective reigns and writings were attributed with far-reaching influence. As noted above, the author of

*Kōkilasandēśaya* asserts that Parākramabāhu is without equal in power and glory among all other kings of his age.[78] Whereas, in *Sävulsandēśaya*, Rājasiṃha is celebrated as the 'the Lord of the Four Directions' (*satara digata hiṁ himi*), whose glory obscures the fame of enemy kings.[79] Sinhala poets similarly appropriated the cosmopolitan order by composing works in the messenger-poet genre, but they distinguished their works by their use of language, their eulogies of living kings and the descriptions of local routes and places in the island. They praised themselves as great poets who produce fine literary works that are second to none. The monastic author of *Kōkilasandēśaya* refers to himself as the 'noble, spotless lord of the Tilaka Monastic Collage' (*piruvan*) who increases the fame and splendour of his lineage.[80] At the conclusion of *Sävulsandēśaya*, the poet Alagiyavanna praises his own reputation by claiming to have immersed himself in the poetry and drama of Sanskrit and Pāli, and to have destroyed the other 'elephants of poets' like a lion.[81] These poets' imitation of Indic messenger poetry was the sincerest form of self-flattery, offering the means to enhance the fame of local kings and authors. Both figures emerge from the *sandēśas* as individuals who act on a cosmopolitan scale and who rival – if not defeat – their counterparts in the subcontinent.

One way to understand Sinhala *sandēśas* within the larger Indic genre of messenger poetry is to compare how they appropriate the cosmopolitan and exalt the local with descriptions of tributary relations between kings. Tribute paid to other kings had been an age-old tradition both in Sri Lanka and throughout the region, serving to maintain diplomatic relations while asserting one's power as an overlord, even when done to honour others.[82] The idea of tribute is a common element in both *Kōkilasandēśaya* and *Sävulsandēśaya*, figuring as a characteristic of the kings that are eulogized therein. In the former text, King Parākramabāhu VI is described as having 'the great and noble kings of the Coḷas, Pāṇḍyas, and Kēraḷas' offering the 'flowers of the shining gems on their crowns to the soles of [his] feet'.[83] This image of having foreign kings prostrating before one's own king is extended in the next verse of the work:

> Taking camphor, sandalwood, and musk that have lovely fragrances,
> And various cloths together with beautiful, delicate silk,
> The kings of various countries, giving these [to him] continuously like a flood of water,
> Stand there while venerating again and again without interruption.[84]

The *Kōkilasandēśaya* serves in this way to glorify the local king by illustrating how neighbouring kings do obeisance and offer precious gifts from their respective kingdoms. Likewise, in *Sävulsandēśaya*, King Rājasiṃha I is extolled for the honour and recognition that he receives from other kings. He is compared to the 'beautiful king of swans' that takes 'the nectar of tribute (*paňḍuru*) from the lotuses of the hands from the kings of various countries'.[85] And like those before him, he too is said to be honoured by Indic kings in person.

The collection of delightful Coḷa, Pāṇḍya, and Kēraḷa kings,
Who have become caught in the fire of his faultless glory, which is like the sun,
Submerging themselves in the great river of the rays of the toenails of the Lord's feet,
Stand offering their lotus hands on the top of their heads, venerating [him] again and again.[86]

The similarities in these descriptions of the two kings in these *sandēśas* is noteworthy in itself. However, it is the image of Sri Lankan kings receiving gifts from subservient Indic kings that is pertinent for our analysis of Sinhala *sandēśas*. The portrayals of Parākramabāhu and Rājasiṃha receiving tribute and honour from countries in the Indic subcontinent do more than simply enhance their royal statures. They also reflect how Irugalkula Thera and Alagiyavanna envision their own relations to the authors of *sandeśakāvyas* composed elsewhere. Like Sri Lankan kings who accept tribute from Indic kingdoms as a way to assert their superiority, the authors of Sinhala *sandēśas* accept the riches of Indic poets and yet improve upon them with their own compositions that effectively transform the genre. They receive gifts from other lands but are neither defined nor constrained by them. These poets rather are like kings who enjoy and use foreign wealth for their own ends. Their imitation of cosmopolitan literary culture serves the purpose of dignifying their own poetry, making a compelling case for their own skill and fame. In this way, the development of Sinhala *sandēśa* poetry, including the innovations made by local authors, represents a way to adopt the prestige of a cosmopolitan cultural order while asserting the distinctive value of an indigenous one.

6

# The local and the global: the multiple visual worlds of ivory carvers in early modern Sri Lanka

*Sujatha Arundathi Meegama*

In contrast to South Asian ivory carvers, European ivory carvers in the late medieval and early modern period are generally not anonymous – their identities are known by their precise locations and names: for example, we know that in the fourteenth century, the Embriachi workshop in Venice made polygonal ivory caskets as marriage gifts; while in the 1600s, Nikolaus Pfaff created beautiful ivory statuettes for Emperor Rudolf II.[1] But while contemporary Sri Lankan ivory carvers produced objects of comparable quality, most notably for the Portuguese court, we struggle to identify where exactly these were created, by whom and for whom; and we know almost nothing about how they functioned in their first context in Sri Lanka.[2]

Sixteenth-century Sri Lankan ivory carvers created the now-famous ivory caskets scattered in public and private collections throughout the world, as well as a number of fans and combs, and also religious representations, including images of the Virgin Mary and Jesus.[3] These artists' visual world was destroyed by Portuguese plundering missions[4] and the subsequent occupation of the kingdom of Kōṭṭe and its environs.[5] In fact, not much sixteenth-century art survives today in Sri Lanka itself. Writing the history of the country's art between the 1400s and the 1700s is challenging because much of what is left consists of ruins, scattered pillars, doorways and basement mouldings, or monuments that underwent later reconstruction. Yet the visual world of sixteenth-century Sri Lanka partially survives precisely because artefacts from this complex encounter were scattered across the globe as a consequence of the Portuguese presence in the region. Thus, even if we cannot retrieve the names of the carvers or their workshops,[6] some aspects of their identities and their visual worlds have withstood the passage of time. The traces these carvers left behind on the thirteen surviving ivory caskets[7] currently datable to the sixteenth century may help us not only retrieve some aspects of the art of ivory carving and architecture in Sri Lanka, but also reveal a deeply connected global visual world in the early modern period.[8]

Several of the caskets can be categorized as diplomatic gifts or exotic luxury goods, created with the Lisbon court or European patrons in mind.[9] The Sri Lankan ivory caskets are modelled on the form of sixteenth-century European leather caskets adorned with metal handles.[10] But, in contrast to those, they are covered with floral designs, animal motifs and human figures. Some caskets illustrate historical scenes, while others show local ideals of kingship. Depictions of Sri Lankan rulers, seated on thrones at court like Bōdhisattvas, are placed opposite portrayals of kings riding elephants to battle. The niches of some caskets feature scenes from the Rāmāyaṇa, a narrative that has received little attention in Sri Lanka, but that became popular in the sixteenth century.[11] Others depict Christian imagery, with stories from the Life of the Virgin and the Life of Christ. A few caskets depict elaborate fauna and flora, with hardly any negative space left on the surfaces.

Previous scholarship has emphasized the subject matter – historical, mythological, Christian – of these ivory caskets, and linked it to the caskets' specific functions as diplomatic gifts,[12] luxury curiosities[13] or export art.[14] Yet while we have learned much about the place of such objects in Renaissance curiosity collections[15] as well as about their famous collectors,[16] these kinds of frameworks, despite their merits, have limited our understanding of the makers of these objects and their multiple visual worlds.

That European prints were used by the carvers is no secret: the presence of European motifs on the caskets has received attention for more than eighty years now.[17] Most scholars, however, have focused on the 'European-ness' of these complex objects of encounter – or to put it more mildly, the European aspects that were introduced and hence brought about change in what has been perceived as the comparatively static art worlds of South Asia. Thus the Portuguese art historian Nuno Vassallo e Silva has noted that 'it is relatively easy to identify European prints as the *sources* used for the decorative motifs on Sinhalese ivory during this period'.[18] More recently, Annemarie Jordan Gschwend's extensive exhibition catalogue on ivories from Ceylon has also highlighted, very convincingly, the use of European prints in Sri Lankan ivories.[19] However, such an emphasis implies that Sri Lankan artists copied European models with assiduity but little originality, as passive subjects of a new, global market growing beyond their reach. In other words, these objects are ascribed a derivative nature even when their genesis is seen as part of an encounter.

When non-European aspects of the caskets are commented on, the picture tends to be schematic. Amin Jaffer and Melanie Anne Schwabe, the authors of the most frequently cited article on the subject, acknowledge the importance of local motifs and emphasize the intertwinement of the *two* striking visual traditions in these caskets. But they also argue that the caskets can be 'differentiated according to the degree of European influence found in their decoration'.[20] Implicit in the latter statement is a problematic preconception: that all South Asian art looks similar, so that only by studying the degree of European influence can one differentiate between artworks, not by examining the South Asian characteristics at play.[21]

In reality, however, the ivory caskets have much more to tell us if we are willing to study the hybrid logic of their ornamentation – the use and the placement of South Asian motifs, and the way European motifs have been appropriated rather than simply 'copied' to become a part of the island's visual world. Although the makers of these caskets put much effort into carving traditional South Asian motifs, their visual responses to European prints indicate that they were also quite clearly part of a larger connected world. I therefore propose that we situate these ivory caskets primarily within the context of the Sri Lankan and South Asian art worlds where they materialized in the first place. I suggest that the local motifs themselves, and their location on the caskets, illustrate the similarities between various local artistic mediums, including ivory carving and temple architecture. This chapter will show, through a close visual analysis of a group of motifs on the caskets, that these can be observed in connection with significant features on temples. I shall then place the ivory caskets back in the wider visual traditions of the early modern world, but maintain an emphasis on the agency of Sri Lankan artists, arguing that it is at least as important as the agency usually ascribed to the European models that circulated throughout the continents.

Read in such a light, the materials show that the Sri Lankan ivory carvers were as inventive and innovative as painters in the Mughal Empire and Japan, ivory carvers in Africa and the Philippines, and other artists from China to Latin America, in appropriating and transforming European motifs and forms. The visual complexity of these ivory caskets needs to be located in the visual traditions of a connected early modern world, in which sometimes the same European print was appropriated in different ways by artists in the Americas, Africa and Asia. The emphasis on the act of appropriation and transformation – something that might be termed 'visual response'[22] – not only helps in retrieving traces of the historical identities of the carvers and their visual surroundings, but also brings attention to the importance of local agency in the transfer of artistic knowledge across early modern art worlds.

## Revisiting the 'local': ivory caskets and temple architecture

Although the comparison of ivory caskets and temple architecture may seem peculiar, scholars have adopted a similar framework, bridging genres and materials, to understand the origins of a particular group of ivories produced during Portugal's encounter with various African kingdoms.[23] In the early 1460s, when the Portuguese started to interact with what is now called Sierra Leone, ivory objects such as saltcellars, spoons, forks, knife handles, hunting horns and pyxes began to be imported to Portugal.[24] A term coined by William Fagg, 'Afro-Portuguese' ivories,[25] refers to ivories from first Sierra Leone, then Benin,[26] and lastly the Kingdom of Kongo. Scholars propose that such ivories were carved as 'gifts for the patrons of the Portuguese voyages',[27] and were also 'made for sale to Portuguese elites, missionaries, and traders'.[28] Although their origins were generally forgotten in *Kunstkammers* and in other Western collections, Afro-Portuguese ivories clearly contain both African and Renaissance components.[29] Recent scholarship suggests that the ivories from Sierra Leone may be related to the local carving tradition of small stone figures (*nomoli*).[30] William Fagg and Ezio Bassani have pointed out the similarities in the treatment of the faces, the scarification marks on the upper bodies, and the objects or themes depicted on the local stone figures to those on the exported ivories.[31] Similarly, the geometric patterns that adorn Kongo 'oliphants' (carved elephant tusks) reflect the designs on Kongo textiles.[32] In other words, artists working in a particular medium can be inspired by designs common in other mediums. This may help us to think about artistic practice, repositories of artistic knowledge and the ways in which ideas cross material and visual boundaries, not only in Africa but also in Sri Lanka from stone architecture to ivory and prints to ivory.

At first glance, all thirteen ivory caskets from sixteenth-century Sri Lanka create an impression of similarity due to their material, shape and pervasive ornamentation. Although they come in different sizes, they are all formed as rectangular boxes, presenting a rectangular front and a back with arched sides and a pitched lid.[33] All five rectangular faces of the ivory caskets are generally divided into three panels each.[34] The method of construction is also shared; 'the front, back and side are dovetailed to each other and the bottom fashioned in panel-and groove construction'.[35] The similarities continue with the carvings, showing Sri Lankan or European mythological stories, historical events, religious narratives and figures, and motifs that include fauna and flora, as well as geometrical patterns.

Jaffer and Schwabe have argued that the 'ornament on the caskets can be related to the changing socio-political situation in Ceylon, that is to say, that those caskets worked exclusively with indigenous ornament pre-date those worked with European motifs'.[36] Most often, the ornamentation does indeed correspond to the socio-political context, but my intention is not to question this chronological approach. Instead, I suggest that we look at the ornamentation itself – the motifs, the figures and their placement – to locate these objects in many visual contexts. This should allow us to turn to the multiple visual traditions that these objects are in conversation with, and understand the complexity of such hybrid objects in the early modern period.

The similarities in the ornamentation extend not only to the subjects depicted but also, at a more fundamental level, to the placement of particular motifs. Their arrangement reflects, crucially, the visual organization of the substructures of South Asian temples. Initially made with a flat bottom surface,[37] the ivory caskets are generally adorned with a row of lotus petals on all four sides at the very bottom; this can be seen in the Rāmāyaṇa casket in the Kunsthistorisches Museum in Vienna (Figure 6.1) and the second ivory casket in the same collection. The so-called Robinson casket at the Victoria and Albert Museum has two rows of lotus petals facing each other (Figure 6.2). The most elaborate petals are found on

**Fig. 6.1** 'Rāmāyaṇa casket', front panel, Sri Lanka, mid-sixteenth century, KHM-Museumsverband, Wien, Inventory no. KK 4743.

**Fig. 6.2** 'Robinson casket', Sri Lanka, probably Kōṭṭe, mid-sixteenth century, © Victoria and Albert Museum, London, Inventory no. IS.41–1980.

**Fig. 6.3** 'Coronation casket', Kōṭṭe, c.1541, Schatzkammer der Residenz, Munich, Inventory no. 1241.

the bottom of the so-called coronation casket at the Residenzmuseum in Munich (Figure 6.3). Caskets that do not have the row of lotus petals instead have a less elaborate arrangement, again resembling the basement mouldings of some South Asian temples: the ivory casket at the Boston Museum of Fine Arts thus sits on a plinth, which in turn supports the S-shaped *cyma recta* topped by a small fillet (Figure 6.4); a similar plinth, further ornamented with gold and rubies, can be seen in a casket kept in an undisclosed private collection.[38] Such features ornamenting basements, especially lotus petals, are often found in Sri Lankan temple architecture from the Anurādhapura period (c. 250 BCE–982 CE) onwards.[39]

This is where the issue of whether or not a distinct local style exists comes into the picture. Senake Bandaranayake's extensive studies on the basement mouldings of temples in Anurādhapura indicate a particular pattern of mouldings that consist of rectilinear and curvilinear mouldings.[40] The curvilinear mouldings include the plain S-shaped *cyma recta*, which at times is adorned by lotus petals – as seen above, some of the ivory caskets follow curvilinear mouldings that have lotus petals carved on them. Much closer in time to the ivory caskets, we have the Bäräṇḍi Kōvil of Sītāvaka (Figure 6.5), a rare example of a sixteenth-century temple that has not been completely rebuilt since its destruction at the hands of the Portuguese. The basement moulding of this Hindu temple is quite complex, given that it sits on a particularly large plinth on which devotees may have circumambulated. The basement moulding of the temple proper consists of a plinth,

**Fig. 6.4** Casket, front panel, Sri Lanka, mid- to late sixteenth century, Photograph © 2017 Museum of Fine Arts, Boston, Bequest of William A. Coolidge, Accession no. 1993.29.

**Fig. 6.5** Basement moulding, Bäränḍi Kōvil, Sītāvaka, mid-sixteenth century, author's photograph.

two fillets, a *cyma recta* adorned with lotus petals, followed by a fillet-dado-fillet, then a carved rectilinear torus (tripaṭṭa kumuda), with again the standard fillet-dado-fillet, followed by a *cyma recta* with elaborate lotus petals, and finally ending with the cornice. Like the earlier Sri Lankan temple mouldings and the Sri Lankan ivory caskets, the Bäränḍi Kōvil has the S-curved *cyma recta* adorned with lotus petals. But, the latter also includes the moulding tripaṭṭa kumuda, which is a feature associated with South Indian temples built in the subcontinent.[41] The presence of the architectural feature, the tripaṭṭa kumuda, indicates that this temple was built by a South Indian rather than a local workshop – as were in fact a number of earlier, Hindu *and* Buddhist temples in Anurādhapura, Polonnaruva, Yāpahuva, Gampola and Kandy.

But what exactly do we mean by 'South Indian' in a Sri Lankan context; on what grounds can we distinguish 'South Indian' or 'Sri Lankan'? In general, specific motifs or features and their combinations are taken as strong indicators of whether a monument was built by a local or a South Indian workshop. Thus, for example, in describing a group of ivory panels containing numerous representations of the dancing Śiva, Ananda Coomaraswamy identifies a motif of 'horned and bird-headed "lions"' and notes that such a feature points to a South Indian origin.[42] Under such a lens, the casket in the Távora Sequeira Pinto Collection, with its filigree-like surface ornamentation and the dynamic horned and bird-headed lion motif, may well turn out to be from South India.[43] But apart from divulging the possible geographical association of creation, what else might such motifs or architectural features tell us of relevance to Sri Lankan and South Indian art histories? That such practitioners were born abroad? That they were trained overseas? That they followed imported models? That they migrated for work? That local and South Indian practitioners worked side-by-side?

If we entertain such questions, then what exactly does an architectural element that originated outside of Sri Lanka mean for our quest of a potentially cosmopolitan artistic culture on the island? The presence of the tripaṭṭa kumuda alone certainly does not mean that a building is automatically a South Indian Hindu temple. This feature, for example, can also be found on the basement mouldings of Buddhist temples (the Temple of the Tooth at Yāpahuva and the Gaḍalādeṇiya Rājamahā Vihāraya). One must underline that this architectural element appears in various types of religious structures in Sri Lanka, including Hindu kōvils, Buddhist vihāras and the hybrid devāles (temples to pan-Indic and local deities) – indicating that perhaps South Indian workshops were responsible for more than just the construction of Hindu kōvils in Sri Lanka. In other words, an architectural feature alone can hardly be associated with a particular religion or a bounded region.[44] Motifs and forms circulated between India and Sri Lanka, and between various religious traditions; practitioners travelled across the Palk straits, perhaps to find new patrons and work. To separate the exogenous from the endogenous thus requires more study, and yet at the same time we must remember that South Indian workshops may have worked alongside local workshops; after all, there are no exact replicas of South Indian temples in premodern Sri Lanka.

The Sri Lankan ivory caskets do not display such complicated basement mouldings as temples do, and the mouldings on the ivories do not indicate as clearly as those on temples whether South Indian workshops played a role or not; however, certain features found on the bottom layer of the caskets in London, Munich, Vienna and Boston are clearly inspired by this architectural tradition, which is seen in both Buddhist and Hindu temples.

A few of the ivory caskets also share the symbol of a lion: a lively row of lions runs along the bottom of all four sides of the so-called coronation casket in Munich (Figure 6.3), the casket that depicts certain scenes from the Rāmāyaṇa in Vienna (Figure 6.1), and the casket with more Rāmāyaṇa scenes on it at the Teaching and Research Museum of the University of Peradeniya in Sri Lanka (Figure 6.6). The motif of lions, here seemingly moving towards each other from both directions, or moving away from each other in opposite directions, is generally associated with royalty.[45] The ivory carver(s) of the second casket in Munich chose to use the motif only on the two side-end scenes (Figure 6.7), which are related directly to Sri Lankan kingship: these lions are more robust and are compressed together, seemingly lacking space as they stride towards the middle. The casket in Boston, too, has lions only on its two shorter sides (Figure 6.8). The fact that the lion motif is not used on all thirteen caskets seems to suggest that at least five caskets came out of possibly royal workshops – although perhaps not from the hand of the same carver, since the lotus petals mentioned above are different in each casket, and the lion motif itself appears similarly differentiated through number, placement, direction and style.

Like the lotus petals, rows of lions appear on the basement mouldings of certain medieval monuments. At Polonnaruva (1017–1215 CE), this motif is found

**Fig. 6.6** 'Peradeniya casket', back panel, Sri Lanka, mid-sixteenth century, The Senarat Paranavitana Teaching and Research Museum, Department of Archaeology, University of Peradeniya, author's photograph.

**Fig. 6.7** Casket, lateral panel (left), Kōṭṭe, 1540s, Schatzkammer der Residenz, Munich, Inventory no. 1242.

on the basement mouldings of the audience halls of King Parākramabāhu I and King Niśśaṅkamalla, as well as at the Buddhist structures of Manik Vehera (*stupa*) and Hāṭadāgē (image house). From the fourteenth-century Gampola kingdom, we see lions carved in various postures on the stone basement mouldings of the entrance pavilion to Niyamgampāya Rājamahā Vihāra. At Gaḍalādeṇiya Rājamahā Vihāraya, a row of lions adorns the stone steps leading up to the temple

**Fig. 6.8** Casket, lateral panel (left), Sri Lanka, mid- to late sixteenth century, Photograph © 2017 Museum of Fine Arts, Boston, Bequest of William A. Coolidge, Accession no. 1993.29.

(Figure 6.9). This motif and its location echo the vyāla, or mythical-lion motif, found especially on the basement mouldings of Hindu temples in South India, as well as in those built in Sri Lanka. The basement mouldings of Śiva Devale No. 1 in Polonnaruva, an eleventh- or twelfth-century stone Hindu temple in Sri Lanka (Figure 6.10) built by a South Indian workshop, provide an excellent example of the historical visual complexity of the lion motif and its placement at the bottom

**Fig. 6.9** Gaḍalādeṇiya Rājamahā Vihāraya, 1344 CE, author's photograph.

**Fig. 6.10** Śiva Devāle No. 1, Polonnaruva, eleventh or twelfth century, author's photograph.

of these ivory caskets. It is associated not only with kingship, but also with South Indian temples and workshops.

This analysis suggests that the carvers did not refrain from using motifs and structural features from temple architecture, and also reveals that at times such features were taken originally from the South Indian architectural tradition.[46] A number of architectural features – such as the lion motif on the basement mouldings – were introduced to the island at various moments of engagement with South Indian architectural traditions. They were then adopted by ivory carvers, whose works eventually gained a better chance of survival than the temples because they were exported to Europe. So were the ivory carvers aware of the origins of these architectural features? Or does their engagement with such elements of the architectural tradition indicate that those features were long localized? It is difficult to give a clear answer at this point.

However, it is certainly useful to remind ourselves that not all South Indian architectural features were adopted wholesale: various imported elements were appropriated, transformed or rejected by local workshops creating localized architectural formulas. The ivory carvers, in turn, chose only certain architectural features for their ivory caskets; and even then, each casket differs in its use of mouldings and the lion motif, indicating perhaps different hands or workshops. The architectural references found in the caskets clearly allude to shared visual heritages between Sri Lanka and South India. While colonial and postcolonial scholarly constructions of national boundaries and art historical canons have led to an emphasis on the separateness between Sri Lankan and Indian art, it seems necessary to reconsider the connectedness of the art histories of the region as a whole. Clearly, the local is not so local after all – it, too, is part of larger, connecting art histories.

## Reconnecting with the 'global': ivory caskets and European prints

The presence of European motifs on Sri Lankan ivory caskets indicates that carvers in the island turned to a visual world extending well beyond the limits of South Asia. But what exactly was the gesture underlying such an operation? Were Sri Lankans copying European motifs? Were they doing something more complex? Is there a fundamental novelty to bringing elements of European, rather than 'just' South Indian art, into Sri Lankan objects? In this section, I focus on the appropriation of European prints in the so-called Robinson Casket (Figure 6.2) at the Victoria and Albert Museum in London.[47]

Nuno Vassallo e Silva declares that the Robinson Casket 'is a noteworthy example of the use of European prints in a Sinhalese work, demonstrating how the two influences mixed in *random fashion* with *no coherent discourse*'[48] – a statement that is indicative of how poorly understood the history of the ivory caskets remains. Asian artists, like artists in Europe – or for that matter, most artists anywhere in the world, whether anonymous or not – had intentions behind their creations. There is rarely such a thing as a completely random artistic act. It thus makes sense to search for the rationale underlying the visual programme of the caskets.

In fact, Amin Jaffer and Melanie Schwabe have examined the Robinson Casket in great detail, bringing attention to the socio-historical context of its production.[49] They suggest that this is the first casket to include Christian subject matter, and so date it to 1557, the year of the conversion of King Dharmapāla. They also argue that 'the iconography of the casket [...] develops the themes of birth and re-birth in both Christian and Sinhalese motifs',[50] and therefore celebrates the birth of a Portuguese heir, Sebastian, the grandson of John III.[51] The concerns of the two royal houses are thus brought together in one object. To further their argument, Jaffer and Schwabe examine in detail the foreign and the local subject matter depicted. They turn first to the depiction of two events that are seminal in the Life of Christ: on the back of the casket, the left niche features an image of Mary and Joseph, while the right panel shows them resting during their escape to Egypt (Figure 6.11); Vassallo e Silva argues that these two scenes show the Visitation and the Nativity.[52] On the right end of the casket, the genealogy of Christ is depicted through the Tree of Jesse, a common representation of the ancestors of Christ (Figure 6.12); this imagery has been traced to a Book of Hours

**Fig. 6.11** 'Robinson casket', back panel, Sri Lanka, probably Kōṭṭe, mid-sixteenth century, © Victoria and Albert Museum, London, Inventory no. IS.41–1980.

**Fig. 6.12** Tree of Jesse on the 'Robinson casket', lateral panel (right), Sri Lanka, probably Kōṭṭe, mid-sixteenth century, © Victoria and Albert Museum, London, Inventory no. IS.41–1980.

printed by Thielman Kerver as early as 1499 (Figure 6.13), and reprinted repeatedly at least until 1546.[53] Apart from these depictions, Jaffer and Schwabe point to the reproduction of a print by Albrecht Dürer from 1514 on the front of the casket, which appears twice, in the right and left niches (Figure 6.2). They also point to two other scenes on the uppermost portion of the lid of this casket that were inspired by European prints.[54]

After this exhaustive account of the presence of European prints, Jaffer and Schwabe turn their attention to the local motifs on the Robinson Casket that are associated with birth and rebirth or creation,[55] especially the 'cord of life' that

**Fig. 6.13** Tree of Jesse from the Book of Hours of Thielmann Kerver, Paris, c. 1507, Collection Paulus Swaen Auctions.

**Fig. 6.14** *Kalpavrksha/Kalpalata* (auspicious vines) on the 'Robinson casket', lateral panel (left), Sri Lanka, probably Kōṭṭe, mid-sixteenth century, © Victoria and Albert Museum, London, Inventory no. IS.41–1980.

emerges out of the tails of the half-man, half-bird creatures (Figure 6.11) as well as from the mouths of two *makara*-headed lions on the left end (Figure 6.14). Based on the unusual combination of the *makara* and the lion, they suggest that 'here the artist may have sought to emphasize the role of kingship (represented by the lion) in creation, as represented by the *makara* and cord of life'.[56] Jaffer and

Schwabe conclude that the combination of these various motifs, both local and foreign, 'join to convey the message of creation, rebirth and renewal of life in the Christian faith and tradition'.[57]

Despite all this perspicacious reasoning, there is no concrete visual or textual evidence that this casket was sent as a gift for John III from Kōṭṭe to Lisbon in 1557. At most, we may say that it was likely made after the arrival of the Franciscans at King Bhuvanekabāhu's court in 1543; for the Franciscans surely brought gifts and teaching materials, including European prints, to present to Bhuvanekabāhu.[58] While the casket has been interpreted as a diplomatic gift, it could be pointed out that a comparable display of scenes from the Life of the Virgin appears in 'Afro-Portuguese' pyxes from Sierra Leone, produced for liturgical purposes.[59] The casket and the pyxes share similar European print sources,[60] but could they also share similar patrons? In other words, was this casket produced for a missionary, or perhaps as a gift to a church official in Lisbon?

Rather than venturing any further into who the patrons of such objects may have been and what functions the caskets may have been meant to perform, I suggest that we shift our attention to the act of appropriation of European prints by Sri Lankan ivory carvers, and engage with the idea of recovering the traces of an anonymous subject in an early colonial context in Asia. This approach should allow us to highlight the connected nature of the ivory carvers' visual world, and the active agency performed by them as they appropriated foreign motifs. 'Appropriation' as a process has been explored by the art historian Robert Nelson with reference to the discipline of art history;[61] in particular, Nelson notes the inadequacy of terms such as 'borrowings' and 'influence', which have been used by scholars in the discipline when referring to artworks adopting 'pre-existing elements'.[62] His insightful observations bring attention not only to the agency of 'the maker or receiver',[63] but also to the production of meaning. Each time a sign is appropriated, the agent builds on the meaning of the previous sign to generate a new significance.[64]

With this theoretical framework in mind, let us return to the Robinson Casket, shifting our attention to the ways in which the agent – the Sri Lankan ivory carver – appropriated a European print.[65] As we have seen, in the large panel on the left end of the casket, the carver has carved the Tree of Jesse, which follows a pre-existing model from a European print (Figure 6.13). Looking back through a long history in the West,[66] one can see that this motif was appropriated not only by Sri Lankan, but also by South Indian, African and Latin American artists around the same period. Unlike the versions in Sierra Leone,[67] Colonial Mexico,[68] or South India,[69] the version by the Sri Lankan ivory carver faithfully reproduces the subject matter and the composition of the print – the tree, the framing pillars, the floral motifs that create a bower at the top, the number of figures and their location, the hand gestures and body postures of all the figures, their head-dresses and clothing, and the cartouches.

There are, of course, some subtle differences between the print and the ivory version,[70] the most obvious being the twelve empty cartouches and the addition of two 'floating flowers' – the latter a distinct mark of Sri Lankan ivory carvers and painters.[71] Perhaps it was not important for the carver to copy faithfully the writing on the twelve cartouches: the initial patron of the casket may have felt that the writing did not matter as much as the image. In fact, the cartouches do not even appear in all European versions of the Tree of Jesse,[72] indicating that the image can function without the textual notation providing the names of the twelve figures. Scholars who have examined this casket so far have not only ignored these slight changes the carver made; more importantly, they have not paid adequate attention to the carver's visual response to the Tree of Jesse in a different panel on the same casket.[73] Based on the representation of the Tree of Jesse along with other events from the Life of Christ, scholars have argued that the casket represents Dharmapāla's conversion – the rupture between Buddhist and Christian beliefs. However, the visual response to the Tree of Jesse in another niche on the same casket reveals a more complex relationship between Western colonial culture and a soon-to-be Asian colony. Rather than being merely a straightforward narrative of rupture, the visual response of the ivory carver also indicates a narrative of recognition, familiarity and continuity. The imagery is about not only Western, but also South Asian notions of kingship, creation, auspiciousness and prosperity. This act of appropriation, I suggest, responds both to the global visual world and to the local South Asian context.[74]

How is the ivory carver's visual response a narrative about kingship, creation, auspiciousness and prosperity? On the large panel forming the opposite end of the casket (Figure 6.14), two vines emerge out of the mouth of two *makara*-headed lions, placed on either side at the bottom of the panel. Like Jesse, the ancestor of Christ, the lion is the ancestor of Sri Lankan kings: Vijaya, the first king of the island, is believed to have descended from the union of a lion and a human princess.[75] Apart from its royal connotations, the lion is also a motif associated with the Buddha, one of whose epithets is 'Shakya Simha'.[76] The mythical *makara*, associated with water and consisting of an elephant's head and a lion's body, brings together two important and auspicious animals associated with kingship.[77]

As for the branches of this 'tree', the carver has placed animals on them instead of kings, and some of these carry strong auspicious associations. Encircled within beaded vines, some are placed frontally, while most others are in profile: at the very centre, in the first circle from the bottom, is a frontally seated lion; above him is a peacock displaying his fan; further above is a lion in profile; on top of that is a deer; next comes what is perhaps a lamb; and finally, at the very top, is a frontally positioned bird. This vertical sequence of animals functions visually in correspondence with the strong central trunk of the Tree of Jesse. Moving downwards from left to right, more vines with various creatures emerge out of this central trunk-like motif: the carver has placed a pair of similar birds or animals extending across horizontally; some are encircled by the beaded vines, while others seem to roam the 'tree' free of any vines, in-between the stems, leaves and flowers.

As can be seen, there is a striking similarity between the compositions of the Tree of Jesse and the ivory carver's visual response: the bottom row of three leonine creatures functions as the basis of this tree, very much like Jesse himself in the European tradition; the central row of animals mimics the latter's strong vertical branch; the different levels of animals encircled by vines correspond to the various branches in which figures sit on the Tree of Jesse; and at the pinnacle of this 'tree' a bird is placed in a circle that corresponds to the final figures in the Tree of Jesse: Mary with the infant Jesus, placed within a circle of sacred light.

The ivory carver could have chosen to depict various kings from the local chronicles,[78] but chose instead to use the motif of a creeper encircling animals, which are traditionally found on pillars and doorways of South Asian monuments as an auspicious motif. The *kalpavrksa* or 'wishing tree' motif, and the *kalpalata* or 'wishing creeper motif', are seen on pillars in Anurādhapura as early as the first century CE.[79] This, it may be noted, is not exclusively a Sri Lankan visual resource: auspicious animals emerging out of the wishing tree or creeper are common across South Asia. The *Jātakas* have the Buddha being born in previous lives as an animal (such as a hare, elephant, monkey, etc.), while the vāhanas, or vehicles, of Hindu deities and Bōdhisattvas are equally held to be animals (such as a bull, lion, tiger, peacock, mouse, elephant, etc.). All this reinforces the impression that the local vine-with-animals is placed in dialogue with the Tree of Jesse, not only in its formal composition, but also in its iconography.

In fact, the vine-with-animals motif populates nearly every remaining niche of this ivory casket,[80] even one of the niches that depicts scenes from the Life of the Virgin. Thus, on the back of the body of the casket (Figure 6.11), in the central niche, two vines emerge out of the tails of half-human half-bird creatures called *kinnaras*. Placed in-between these mythical creatures is a peacock, with animals encircled by beaded creepers, and animals outside and in-between the beaded vines. Adjacent to this central niche, Mary, cradling the baby Jesus, sits under a tree populated by birds and monkeys, while Joseph looks on. A deer standing on its hind legs looks at the baby, while a parrot, just above Mary's right shoulder, peers down. Unlike in typical vines-with-animals seen in these caskets, the animals are not placed within circular vines; but the tree is similar to the vines in that it has beaded branches. It is clearly visually connected to the theme of the wishing creeper, while also dialoguing with the Christian elements that it embraces.[81]

Apart from these two scenes on the reverse side of the casket, the lid has various niches carrying the same motif: of a vine populated by auspicious animals. On the reverse side of the pitched lid (Figure 6.11), all three niches have animals contained within five circular beaded vines. The carver placed other animals in-between these vines and around the edges of the niches. Initially, although the niches may seem similar, the combination of animals and the directions in which they look are different. The centre niche stands out, as pairs of animals are carved inside the circular vines except for the centre one; however, the overall composition of the three niches is the same. On the front of the pitched lid (Figure 6.2), the carver has again placed three niches, filled with similar vines and animals. The centre niche follows the same configuration of encircled vines as all three niches on the back: animals are placed within the vines as well as in-between vines and along the edges of the niches. The niches on either side take on a different composition from the centre niche as well as from the niches on the reverse side of the casket. Animals are still encircled within beaded vines, but the configuration of the circles differs.

This close – and deliberately long and detailed – visual analysis of the niches may in itself be sufficient to suggest that *randomness* is not a term appropriate to the labour of the carver(s) responsible for this casket. There was certainly some degree of freedom in the application of motifs: the carver could depict the wish-fulfilling creeper in many different ways, using different combinations of animals and circles, and placing them differently to create a variety of compositions. Exact symmetry was not a concern; and perhaps the differences in the niches also indicate that more than one carver was involved. But, more importantly, the composition and iconography of the wish-fulfilling tree opposite the Tree of Jesse on the side panel is not replicated elsewhere on this ivory casket. In fact, the visual response, through a variety of wish-fulfilling vines containing animals instead of men, indicates a complex response to the Tree of Jesse by the anonymous ivory carver. He – assuming that carvers were mostly men – understood it and engaged with it within a vibrant visual tradition of depicting auspicious vines of fertility that goes back very far in South Asian art history.

Ananda Coomaraswamy has brought attention to an old Indian parallel to the Tree of Jesse: the birth of Brahma. In one of the earliest stone temples in Deogarh, dating from the Gupta period (c.320–647 CE), Brahma is depicted seated on a lotus that emerges from a reclining Viṣṇu.[82] Citing various literary sources, Coomaraswamy connects the image of the 'tree rooted in the navel' to an old 'iconography of water cosmology'.[83] He notes that this iconography typically consists of a stem of a lotus framing animals or human beings, and emerges from a pot or the mouth of the mythical-water creature, the *makara*, or a dwarf *yaksa*, a vegetation spirit.[84] And indeed, our casket depicts vines emerging out of the mouths of two *makara*-headed lions and framing multiple animals with their stems. Rather than using a *makara* or a *yaksa*, the ivory carver chose a *makara*-headed lion: Jesse is thus echoed by one animal aspect associated with water, and by another associated with the Sri Lankan royal lineage. What was initially assumed to be a 'randomness' in the inclusion of a European print along with local motifs, thus gives way to a remarkably rich and coherent discourse about fertility, auspiciousness and a genealogy tracing the ancestry of the Sri Lankan kings to a lion.

Crucially, too, the Robinson casket does not stand alone in this regard. This type of vine replete with birds and animals also appears in the two caskets in Munich, the two caskets in Vienna, the caskets in Boston, Paris and Peradeniya,

**Fig. 6.15** Casket, lid, Sri Lanka, mid- to late sixteenth century, Photograph © 2017 Museum of Fine Arts, Boston, Bequest of William A. Coolidge, Accession no. 1993.29.

and a casket in a European private collection. In the last, as well as in one of the caskets in Vienna, this motif dominates every single panel.[85] The carver of the casket in Boston, too, chose to use the motif on three faces of the lid (Figure 6.15) and on the main body (Figure 6.4 and Figure 6.16); however, in this case, the carver also decided not to use it in the large side niches at each end of the casket (Figure 6.8). In the other caskets, the motif is mostly visible on the lid: in the 'coronation casket' it appears on the topmost section of the lid (Figure 6.17); in the second casket in Munich the vine is also seen on the topmost portion of the lid; and similarly in the 'Rāmāyaṇa casket' in Vienna and in the Peradeniya casket the motif is seen only in the uppermost portion of the lid. Using this motif to adorn the upper portions of caskets seems to have become a standard manner of ornamenting ivory caskets: by the fourteenth century, if not earlier, such auspicious vines with animal and human figures entwined within creepers appear on stone doorways of medieval temples (Figure 6.18); and indeed, the choice of ornamenting a lid with an auspicious motif does not seem surprising, as its function corresponds to that of a doorway.

If the Robinson casket stands out, along with the casket in Vienna, for the way in which the vine motif dominates the side panels, it is also important to point out that the caskets present substantial differences between them. In the Robinson casket, the wish-fulfilling tree composition clearly corresponds to that of the Tree of Jesse. In the large side panels of the Vienna casket, the Tree of Jesse as such is

**Fig. 6.16** Casket, back panel, Sri Lanka, mid- to late sixteenth century, Photograph © 2017 Museum of Fine Arts, Boston, Bequest of William A. Coolidge, Accession no. 1993.29.

**Fig. 6.17** 'Coronation casket', lid, Kōṭṭe, c.1541, Schatzkammer der Residenz, Munich, Inventory no. 1241.

absent: the panels are completely ornamented with vines full of birds and animals, the latter encompassed by six circles of vines; and in-between the vines and at their edges are birds. The composition is similar to that of the vines full of animals and birds that are found on the lids of most of these caskets: rather than from an

**Fig. 6.18** Galapatha Rājamahā Vihāra, Bentota, fourteenth or fifteenth century, author's photograph.

animal, the vine emerges from a potted plant in the centre – perhaps a pot of plenty, yet another local motif of fertility. Various types of animals are placed within circular vines as well as outside the vines. The panel at the left end consistently depicts animals being attacked at every level; in fact, this casket is full of animals attacking one another – a motif and an aesthetic that are not seen in the Robinson casket. The composition and iconography of these two side panels in the second casket in

Vienna show that although sixteenth-century ivory caskets may seem to contain similar motifs, each casket is different, leaving much work for art historians willing to engage with and learn from such iconographic programmes. More importantly, none of the other caskets that contain various versions of the wish-fulfilling tree or vine replicate the tree-like vine found on the Robinson Casket.

The Tree of Jesse itself travelled around the world as a motif during the sixteenth century. In each instance, it was appropriated differently by artists in Sierra Leone, Mexico, South India[86] and Sri Lanka. In Sierra Leone – as Sri Lanka before the end of the sixteenth century, a region outside of Portugal's growing empire – the Tree of Jesse was deployed to adorn the body of an ivory pyx, a container used for carrying the Eucharist.[87] The three extant pyxes are cylindrical in shape, presenting a form similar to that of the European liturgical vessels used in this period. Two have lids and are supported by small figures of four lions.[88] As in the Sri Lankan ivories, the surfaces of these pyxes are completely covered in carvings. The three pyxes are adorned with scenes from the Life of the Virgin and the Passion of Christ, again modelled after illustrations in printed European Books of Hours.[89] In one pyx, the Tree of Jesse is combined with numerous other scenes inspired by various illustrations from a Book of Hours printed by Philippe Pigouchet, namely the Annunciation, the Visitation, the Birth of Jesus, the Annunciation to the Shepherds and the Adoration of the Magi.[90] The African carver has chosen six scenes out of the twenty-one coloured illustrations about the Life of the Virgin and the Life of Christ given by Pigouchet, if indeed he saw the Book of Hours published in 1498.[91] Each scene is separated by a pillar-like form with a twisted ribbed effect and a knob in the middle. The Tree of Jesse is clearly the central image on the body of the pyx because, as with most ivories made in Sierra Leone, the lid or the uppermost portion of this container includes a three-dimensional figure as well: the figure of Mary cradling the baby Jesus, facing in the same direction as the Tree of Jesse. Jesse lies at the bottom of the niche with the tree emerging out of his navel. His right arm is placed by his side, while he raises his left to his face.[92]

The configuration of figures is different from the European print: rather than twelve kings, the carver chose to depict seven; and rather than six branches, the carver chose to depict four. The goal seems to have been not to render faithfully each figure but to depict the gist of the story. In the centre, Mary holds the baby Jesus as she emerges out of a halo of flames. The ultimate flowering of the tree in the form of Mary and Jesus is replicated beyond the two-dimensional surface of the pyx: in a sensitive portrayal, Mary emerges carrying Jesus. Mary is portrayed in a more humble manner, without a crown but wearing a cross at her neck – she is covered from head to toe in cloth that has a distinct pattern of a series of dots within lines,[93] a pattern seen again and again on these Afro-Portuguese ivories to depict the clothing of Western figures. The replication of the Virgin Mary with her son in a two-dimensional as well as a three-dimensional form in the same object indicates not only the importance of this figure for the Catholic Church, but also the carver's ingenuity.[94]

In colonial Mexico, the Tree of Jesse was used multiple times by different artists, possibly for different reasons; and unlike in the African and South Asian cases, the subject's use in Mexico has been studied extensively. Recently, Angelica J. Afanador-Pujol has noted that the motif first appears in an open-air chapel in Central Mexico.[95] Around 1540, local artists adorned two bishop's mitres with this motif,[96] and between 1539 and 1541 it was also deployed in a manuscript now called the 'Relación de Michoacán', which records the customs in the state of Michoacán, Mexico. Although the manuscript was commissioned by the Spanish viceroy of Mexico, the text and the accompanying illustrations represent the indigenous voices of the local nobility as well as the native artists.[97] One of the anonymous artists of this project appropriated the motif of the Tree of Jesse and replaced the lineage of Christ with that of the Uanacaze family, who were ruling this region when the Spanish arrived.[98] Afanador-Pujol argues that the purpose of this 'visual mimicry [...] was to help the Uanacaze overcome the claims of competing indigenous pretenders, [...] as well as to challenge contending claims by Spanish colonizers'.[99]

As with the Tree of Jesse, the Uanacaze family tree also begins with a reclining figure, this one being named Thicatame. His eighteen descendants occupy the branches that spread across a whole page. As with the print, they hold cartouches containing their names,[100] but their clothing, accoutrements and posture differ, and they sit on little stools that perch on the branches; many are also depicted with wounds. At the very top of the Uanacaze family tree are three figures dressed in white baptismal tunics: Zinzicha Tangaxuan is in the centre, with his two sons, Don Francisco and Don Antonio, on either side.[101] If the artist had followed the Tree of Jesse more passively, the two sons would have been placed in the centre as the final descendants of this family tree. However, Afanador-Pujol argues that Tangaxuan is placed at the centre because his death at the hands of the Spanish was embroiled in debate, and also affected the political and economic inheritance of his sons.[102] On the grounds of these many alterations, Afanador-Pujol suggests that the visual mimicry was not motivated by European interests; instead, it was a unique response to the local colonial situation: 'a tree that reveals a more complex relationship between colonizers and colonized'.[103]

What can we learn from Afanador-Pujol's careful study of the use of the Tree of Jesse in colonial Mexico? This use of the tree is best understood not as a passive act of rendering (in the sense of simply copying an alien original), but as an active appropriation that 'builds on a previous meaning of a sign to create yet a new sign'.[104] Using a motif familiar to a European audience and transforming it, the anonymous artist depicted a local genealogy and a complex political history. The choice, and the development of a motif that the local audience could relate to, also reflected indigenous beliefs about trees, especially oaks.[105] Drawing attention to the actions of this anonymous painter, Afanador-Pujol shows how he responded to a completely different visual tradition, and effectively communicated with *multiple* audiences. Likewise, the Sri Lankan ivory carver chose, as a response – and indeed, as an element in a proper dialogue – a motif he was familiar with, and one that his local audience would immediately recognize: his response to the Tree of Jesse builds on an old South Asian motif of the wish-fulfilling tree or creeper. His choices of location, composition and iconography further cement the notion that he construed, consciously and intentionally, a visual response well beyond the randomness suggested by other art historians.

Examining the use of the same European print across three vastly different visual traditions and colonial contexts highlights the possibilities of appropriation in the early modern world, at a moment when Sri Lanka was connecting with distant realities through the Portuguese. At times, the artists' (and certainly their patrons') choices responded to Western visual traditions and complex political histories, but above all they were anchored in local or regional visual traditions and belief systems. These visual responses are not passive copies, but active appropriations in which colonized artists – or, in the case of mid-sixteenth-century Sri Lanka, ivory carvers producing objects for a diplomatic exchange in which Europeans were slowly gaining the upper hand over Sri Lankans – left their traces. Each time the Tree of Jesse was appropriated, it was reborn with a new meaning. Whatever the exact processes by which caskets were produced in Sri Lankan workshops, the approach I propose also throws light on the complex visual worlds, beliefs and identities of non-elite subjects, who are often overshadowed by the voices of monarchs, ministers, missionaries and merchants in the written records of the early colonial encounters.[106]

## Conclusion

The two contrasting but intertwined narratives in this essay suggest that these complex objects of encounter must be situated simultaneously within both local and global visual traditions. Even if we cannot retrieve the names of the carvers or workshops that produced these objects, we can, using visual analysis, uncover the agencies and art worlds that inform them. This chapter illustrates how their makers were engaged in dialogue not just with European prints but also with South Asian architecture. Both these art worlds and the various agencies in them are equally important in the process of their creation.

What this analysis then suggests is that it may be worthwhile for art historians to take up the challenge posed by Claire Farago: to write art histories from many points of view, or from many sides of an encounter. As Farago suggests, this intervention is about replacing the 'binary model of centre and periphery implied in constructs that privilege European civilization'[107] with a more genuinely 'dialogical model'[108] – one in which the voices of the local artists from the peripheries can be heard. The varied responses in Sierra Leone, Mexico and Sri Lanka to a single European print show that these new versions are best understood not as copies that simply privilege the European print, but as responses, allowing us to locate them in a global dialogue with European prints. It is then important to underline that the appreciation of ivory caskets as dialogic objects adds to, rather than detracts from, their importance to our understanding of premodern Sri Lankan visual culture. Hence, my project does not deny the European-ness of sixteenth-century Sri Lankan ivory caskets in comparison with earlier scholarship: it acknowledges it, and at the same time places the local visual world on an equal footing with the visual traditions of European prints from the Renaissance.

# 7
# Cosmopolitan converts: the politics of Lankan exile in the Portuguese Empire

*Zoltán Biedermann*

This chapter explores one of the least studied aspects of Sri Lankan history: the lives of Lankans who left the island and spent time abroad before the modern period.[1] There is a long precolonial history of elite movements between Sri Lanka and South India, and possibly other parts of Asia, deserving in principle to be explored, as a brief overview in the first section of this chapter suggests. It is only from the so-called Portuguese period onwards, however, that the written record allows us to retrace some of those itineraries in detail. This is in line with the wider realities of exile in Asia, which are far better documented in the context of European expansion than before.[2] From the mid-1500s, numerous Lankan nobles, often of royal lineage, crossed the border into the Portuguese realm and left traces in the imperial archives. Some kept going back and forth, as the second section of this chapter illustrates. Others remained in exile for the rest of their lives, as I explore in the subsequent sections.

The principal questions to be asked are why and how Lankans travelled abroad, what assumptions governed their political and cultural behaviour, and how they combined the cosmopolitan impulses of early modern globalization and imperial integration with Lankan political projects. Certainly the cases explored in this chapter suggest that the relationship between Lankan politics, exile culture and European imperial expansion is more complex than has been assumed. The similarities and continuities with some of the stories presented in this volume by Gananath Obeyesekere and Sujit Sivasundaram (Chapters 8 and 10) are also a sign that explorations in the *longue durée* – as proposed in Alan Strathern's chapter (Chapter 11) – may significantly enrich our understanding of Lankan history.

## Lankan refugees in India before 1500

The practice of leaving Lanka to court rulers overseas constituted no novelty to the Lankan power elite when the Portuguese arrived in the early 1500s. The ease with which influential and ambitious individuals left the island for South Indian shores during the sixteenth century suggests that they were following an established practice that resulted from the often very complex negotiations surrounding the access to Lankan thrones. Even a superficial reading of the Lankan chronicles suggests that it was common for royal candidates and their followers to look for support outside the island if necessary. Princes, often accompanied by substantial retinues of relatives and faithful nobles, regularly took refuge in South India. They often resurfaced, sometimes years later, with foreign troops, intent on conquering their ambitioned positions in the island.

From the long list of such cases, a few examples may here suffice to illustrate the matter. In the early sixth century, a rival of King Kassapa known as Silākāla fled to India. He was a member of a clan with a distant connection to the Lankan royal family and was reluctant to give in to the ruling monarch. In India, Silākāla was ordained as a monk at Bodh Gaya, took the name of Ambasāmaṇera, and returned to Lanka in possession of the Hair Relic of the Buddha after Kassapa was overthrown by Moggallāna. He became a key political leader and, some years later in 518, successfully launched his own bid for the throne at Anurādhapura.[3] Shortly after the beginning of his reign in 628, King Aggabodhi III (or Siri Saṅgha Bodhi) was challenged by Jeṭṭhatissa and defeated. Having fled to India, he soon returned with Tamil troops and took the throne back – upon which his rival turned to South India himself, suggesting that exilic movements often alternated between rival factions of the Lankan elite.[4] In fact, Indian princes also occasionally took refuge in Sri Lanka.[5]

Towards the end of the first millennium, the increasing Lankan involvement in South Indian politics, which saw the growth of the Sinhala-Pāṇḍya alliance against the Cōḻas, eventually triggering the invasion of the island by the latter, can only have brought about a further intensification of the movement of diplomats and ambitious princes.[6] This is not the place to go into the complex ramifications of Lankan dynastic history, which connected the various branches of the ruling elite in the island to various royal houses in the subcontinent.[7] Given the complicated legacy of Lankan-Indian royal intermarriage, the circulation across the region of individuals seeking power must have been fairly intense even in periods for which the written record is scant.[8] But it is important to note how the Cōḻas, among others, played a strong role as king-makers in Lanka well after they had to retreat from the island. In the centres of Cōḻa power, disgruntled princes from Lanka must have been observed keenly as a means of maintaining an influence across the straits.

Closer to the period that concerns us, Parākramabāhu III, the son of Vijayabāhu IV, gained power in Sri Lanka after seeking in person the support of the Pāṇḍyas in the late 1280s.[9] Strategic exile could also occur within the island itself. The demise of Parākramabāhu V, who ruled over parts of the south of the island, and the subsequent rise of Vikramabāhu III in the late 1350s, involving the Āryacakravarti of Jaffna, bear all signs of having been supported by various disgruntled nobles from the south who had joined the Jaffna court years earlier.[10] In 1391, Vīra Alakeśvara, a member of the Alagakkonara family that held *de facto* power in Kōṭṭe during much of the second half of the fourteenth century, was ousted, only to return from South India – where the family itself had originated – four years later with a powerful army. He then ruled for another twelve years.[11] There is a possibility that Parākramabāhu VI himself, who controlled large parts of the island from c. 1411 to 1467, was placed on the throne with the support of the Chinese admiral Zheng He after spending time abroad.[12]

## Border crossings and religious conversion in the 'Portuguese period'

There are striking similarities between these early instances of elite mobility and comparable practices described by Gananath Obeyesekere in the present volume for the later Kandyan period (Chapter 8). The South Indian links remained important for the management of power relations in most Lankan kingdoms even after the Portuguese became involved in Lankan politics – in fact, the Portuguese *Estado* itself, with its key positions in Goa, Kochi and numerous other outposts, was an Indian polity of sorts. Such continuities aside, however, it is also important to point out a key difference: from the 1540s, border crossings by elite factions looking for support in the expanding Portuguese Empire became associated, in Sri Lanka as in other parts, with religious conversion. This is necessarily a key aspect to take into account for any discussion of the 'cosmopolitan' in contexts of imperial expansion. To what extent does the imposition of a new religion infringe the unfolding of cosmopolitan practices in other areas of daily life and hence the workings of the cosmopolis to which individuals attach themselves in their quest for power or refuge?

From the early 1540s onwards, policy discussions between Goa and Lisbon gained an increasingly confessional tone. If military resources were to be deployed in Lanka, the reasoning now went, there needed to be a religious incentive to legitimize action. From the Lankan perspective, the full cultural consequences of such a change may not have been grasped immediately. A Portuguese royal decree passed in 1542 gave subject status to Catholic converts in Goa, establishing a clear connection between political vassalage and conversion as a means of expressing it. While Lanka was not a Portuguese possession,[13] conversion gave members of the Lankan elite a means of expressing their political allegiance to the Portuguese Crown. The transition was gradual and is well illustrated by the earliest documented travels of Lankans through the Portuguese Empire. In 1541, Bhuvanekabāhu VII, King of Kōṭṭe (r. 1521–51) and formally a vassal of John III (r. 1521–57), decided to send an ambassador to Portugal. The *purōhita* Śrī Rāmarakṣa spent several months at the royal court in Lisbon and nearby Almeirim in 1542. His mission consolidated the alliance of Kōṭṭe with the Portuguese Crown for decades to come.[14] Śrī Rāmarakṣa later entertained epistolary relations with John III, the monarch's younger brother Dom Luís, and Queen Catherine of

Habsburg,[15] and organized the supply of luxury goods such as high-end ivories for the latter.[16]

Śrī Rāmarakṣa played an active role as mediator not only between Kōṭṭe and Lisbon, but also with Goa, especially in the turmoil surrounding the end of Bhuvanekabāhu's reign in 1551. He led Bhuvanekabāhu's last embassy to Goa offering a large sum of money to the viceroyalty[17] in order to counter a diplomatic offensive by Māyādunnē, the king of Sītāvaka, who also sought Portuguese support.[18] After Bhuvanekabāhu's death, Śrī Rāmarakṣa actively attempted to limit the disruptive impact caused by the new viceroy Dom Afonso de Noronha, a hardliner not inclined to maintain Kōṭṭe's status quo.[19] Noronha felt sufficiently threatened by the energetic *purōhita* to attempt taking him as a hostage to Goa. The subsequent agreement also shows how influential Śrī Rāmarakṣa remained: it was decided that a four-year old son of Bhuvanekabāhu should be taken instead. It seems that the viceroy failed to realize how this would be precisely to the advantage of Śrī Rāmarakṣa and his faction at the Kōṭṭe court. The late king himself had had little interest in seeing this boy compete with his own chosen successor, Dharmapāla (r. 1551–97).[20] It was only in 1552, when Kōṭṭe was left exposed to the full brunt of Māyādunnē's military power, that Śrī Rāmarakṣa decided to take baptism.[21] In his gradual approximation to Catholicism, he was accompanied by a towering figure of the old Kōṭṭe elite, Tammiṭa Sūirya Baṇḍāra (himself a man of royal lineage and known to the Portuguese as the 'chamberlain major').[22] On a diplomatic mission in Goa, Tammiṭa Sūirya Baṇḍāra converted. He returned to Kōṭṭe as 'Dom Francisco Barreto' in 1555.[23]

Another early example of border crossing that gradually involved pressures for conversion comes from Jaffna. This is particularly interesting as the local power struggles were here more closely intertwined with South Indian politics than anywhere else in the island. Claims by Vijayanagara and Travancore to overlordship over Jaffna in the early years of the sixteenth century sustained a continuous movement of diplomatic agents and throne candidates across the straits.[24] Like the rulers of Kōṭṭe, those of Jaffna were used to paying tribute to Indian overlords in return for military support. King Çankili (r. 1519–61) relied on Telugu-speaking warriors settling in the island in exchange for military services. His main source of concern was an older brother who had been the chosen successor to the throne until the assassination of the king, Pararājasēkaran, in 1519.[25] This brother, who can probably be identified as Varothaya Śrī Pandaram, spent much of his life in exile in the Kayalpatanam area, aspiring to regain power.[26] His name surfaces in the Portuguese written record in the early 1540s, when he seems to have attempted to convince the viceroy Dom Garcia de Noronha (gv. 1538–40) to consider his claims to kingship and issue orders for an expedition to place him on the Jaffna throne. The planned campaign did not materialize, but Varothaya Śrī Pandaram persevered. He offered the new Portuguese governor Martim Afonso de Sousa (gv. 1543–5) the sizeable sum of 4,000 *pardaus* to help finance a military expedition to Jaffna.[27]

As Sousa accepted a tributary payment of 5,000 *pardaus* from the reigning king, however, Varothaya understood that he needed to up his bid.[28] In 1544 he proposed to be baptized. When he encountered the Jesuit missionary Francis Xavier in South India in January 1545,[29] he prompted the latter to report back to Europe how he was the 'true heir of the kingdom' and how he would help Jaffna become Catholic.[30] The Jaffna question remained open.[31] In early 1546, the new governor Dom João de Castro (gv. 1545–48) asked for Varothaya Śrī Pandaram to be contacted again. He was found residing three leagues from Kayalpatnam on the Indian side of the Strait, with 'his son, his grandchildren and many of his relatives and friends',[32] still hoping to regain the Jaffna throne. An expedition was planned once more, but then the archival evidence thins out again and we lose track of the ambitious exile. His attachment to the Portuguese power structures remained sporadic, his commitment to Catholicism probably pragmatic, but there is no doubt that he managed to make skilful use of Portugal's imperial channels of communication to further his own cause. Others soon followed and went further in their endeavours.

Lankans coming to the field of diplomatic negotiations with the Portuguese after 1543 (the year the first Franciscans settled in the kingdom of Kōṭṭe) felt the pressure to convert almost immediately. In 1544, three potential heirs to the throne of Kōṭṭe sought alliances with the Portuguese *Estado* and proposed to convert. As the official policy in Lisbon was still to support Bhuvanekabāhu VII, theirs was not a straightforward project. But taking baptism proved an effective means of giving weight to their otherwise feeble political claims. The first of the Kōṭṭe neophytes was Jugo Baṇḍāra, a son of Bhuvanekabāhu who, after enjoying his father's support until 1539, had lost out to Dharmapāla, the king's grandson. There can be little doubt that Jugo was encouraged to convert by Portuguese intermediaries, including the entrepreneur André de Sousa and the Franciscan friars who also tried in vain to persuade Bhuvanekabāhu to be baptized.[33] Jugo, who had the support of a powerful courtly faction, was eventually murdered following orders from Bhuvanekabāhu towards the end of 1544.[34]

Jugo's death was followed immediately by the baptism of two other disgruntled princes.[35] Much to the distress of Bhuvanekabāhu, these young men soon escaped to India and began to lobby for an expedition against Kōṭṭe.[36] Dom João – the prince took his name from John III – arrived with his entourage in Kochi in January 1545. There he dispatched a letter to Queen Catherine explaining his plight.[37] He also met (as his distant relative Varothaya Śrī Pandaram did around the same time) with the Jesuit Francis Xavier, who described the encounter in a letter to Rome and offered support.[38] From Kochi, the prince moved to Goa where he and his younger brother, who had taken the name of Dom Luís in honour of the Portuguese monarch's younger sibling, set up quarters in a property owned by André de Sousa. They were accompanied by 'many honoured [i.e. noble] people' from Sri Lanka.[39] Sousa covered food and clothing expenses (quite possibly a sign that wearing an appropriate attire compatible with that of other Catholics in Goa was important), and kept an eye on the education and public relations of the princes. The future of a Lankan political faction hostile to Bhuvanekabāhu VII began to take shape between the house of a private individual involved in Lankan affairs and a governor, Martim Afonso de Sousa, increasingly interested in South

Indian matters. Sousa received the princes well and, although he had no official mandate from Lisbon to do so, promised Dom João the ownership of lands that had previously belonged to Jugo Baṇḍāra in Lanka.[40]

The timing for all this was perfect because any campaign in the region could be styled as retaliation for king Çankili's massacre of the Christians of Mannar in 1544. In an interesting twist, an embassy of Jaffna nobles soon arrived in Goa to express how they too supported Dom João and Dom Luís in their bid to take Kōṭṭe.[41] The governor ordered a fleet to be put together, and the initiative only came to a halt due to the arrival of a new governor, Dom João de Castro, in September 1545.[42] Soon prince Dom João was writing to Queen Catherine that his mother was awaiting him impatiently in Kōṭṭe, and that 'the entire island of *Ceilão* will become Christian'.[43] The project only collapsed because Dom João and Dom Luís died in Goa of an infectious fever. Once the exiled princes were dead, the Goan authorities saw no reason to proceed with the planned campaign.

## From border crossing to long-term exile

Another life story from the mid-sixteenth century appears less well-documented in its Asian dimension, but very significant with regard to the receptivity of the Portuguese court to Lankan exiles. The four-year-old boy deported from Kōṭṭe at the suggestion of Śrī Rāmarakṣa in 1551–2, also baptized as Dom João, underwent a Christian education in the household of viceroy Dom Afonso de Noronha in Goa.[44] He then accompanied Noronha to Portugal, where he was further educated by the Jesuits and received an annual grant of 600,000 *réis* from John III. According to the chronicler Diogo do Couto, who must have gleaned the story in Goa, the prince spent 'many years' at the royal court, where 'the king honoured him, and had him sit on a chair like a Count when he spoke to him'. Later on, Dom João returned to India and married a Portuguese woman in Goa. He seems to have been in the right place to launch a bid for a return to his homeland, but perhaps at the wrong time. Dom João never made it back to Ceylon, and his remains were deposited in the church of St Francis in Old Goa.[45]

Another, more copiously documented case appears in the 1580s, at a time when the Portuguese Crown, now in the hands of Philip II of Spain, began to pay increasing attention to the possibilities of military intervention in Sri Lanka. When Karaliyaddē, king of Kandy, was toppled in 1582 by Rājasiṃha, king of Sītāvaka, he managed to escape to Trincomalee with his retinue and, before he died, had his nephew Yamasiṃha Baṇḍāra married to his daughter Kusumāsana Dēvi and acclaimed as the rightful heir to the Kandyan throne.[46] Yamasiṃha left his young wife in Jaffna and, from there, travelled to Goa. In the capital of the *Estado*, he converted and took the name of the head of the new global monarchy that he was attaching himself to: Dom Filipe.[47] He then began to lobby the authorities to obtain support for a military expedition to Kandy, in terms that were very similar to those of the Kōṭṭe princes in the 1540s. In fact, the parallel was not lost on the

Portuguese authorities, who commented on the connection between Dom Filipe, Dom João and Dom Luís.[48]

Dom Filipe was ready to go global not only in his symbolic gestures. He requested permission to travel to Europe and present his political project to the monarch in person.[49] Although this was not granted, Dom Filipe was finally dispatched from India to Mannar in 1588. When about a year later a revolt broke out in Kandy against Rājasiṃha, the young pretender to the throne obtained an expeditionary force in Mannar to march to Kandy. The expedition was successful, and Dom Filipe ascended to the throne.[50] Clearly, there was a predisposition among the notoriously unruly elite of the mountain kingdom to call in a man who had little experience of governing but good pedigree and a privileged access to Portuguese resources. It was eventually another exile who put an end to Dom Filipe's rule in 1591.[51] Konappu Baṇḍāra also known as Dom João before he apostatized and became Vimaladharmasūriya, had spent time with Dom Filipe abroad, although he himself was attached to a rival faction of the Kandyan nobility. He eventually founded, as Alan Strathern has explored in detail, the dynasty that most staunchly resisted Portuguese expansion during the seventeenth century – although remaining attached to a court culture often described as cosmopolitan by foreign travellers.[52]

For some time in the 1590s, everything seemed possible in Sri Lanka as Sītāvaka imploded, Kōṭṭe rebounded with Portuguese assistance, and Kandy reinvented its place in the new political landscape. A letter written by Dharmapāla requesting grants for some of his subjects throws light on how an increasing number of Lankan nobles chose to seek an attachment to the Portuguese Crown even without fostering higher ambitions. The document includes a petition formulated by the Sinhalese king for a man called Dom João, a nephew of a queen consort identified as Dona Isabel. This young man, who was to be given 'many privileges and honours',[53] was a grandson of Dom Francisco Barreto, originally known as Tammiṭa Sūriya Baṇḍara – the above-mentioned 'chamberlain' who had worked with Śrī Rāmarakṣa through the transition following Bhuvanekabāhu's death. Mention was also made, in the same letter, of a brother of Dona Isabel known as Dom Antão, a military leader assumed to deserve Portuguese Crown support. A letter of Dom Antão himself has, incidentally, survived in the Spanish state archive, corroborating the picture conveyed by Dharmapāla. In this document, the Sinhalese noble attempted to persuade the new imperial authorities that his services as a military leader had been to the benefit of the Portuguese Crown now held by Philip II.[54] These were high-ranking personalities of the Kōṭṭe elite seeking potential safe havens in a time of rapid political change.

After the death of Dharmapāla in 1597, attachment to the Catholic Monarchy became not just an option, but a necessity for many Lankans wishing to maintain their status and fortune. During the second half of the sixteenth century, the political and military framework of Lankan-Portuguese interactions had changed significantly. In 1551, Bhuvanekabāhu VII was assassinated and the Temple of the Tooth looted. During the 1550s to the 1580s Kōṭṭe was very much on the defensive, the royal court ending up transferring to Colombo in 1565, and the new capital was repeatedly besieged by the forces of Sītāvaka. In 1580, Dharmapāla signed away the right of succession to the throne – in case he died without heirs – to the Portuguese monarchs. When he died in 1597, the military conquest of Sri Lanka, initiated locally in the context of the implosion of Sītāvaka after Rājasiṃha's death in 1593 but soon embraced most brutally by the new imperial authorities in Lisbon and Madrid, was an inescapable reality.[55] The early 1600s and especially the 1610s brought an increasing pressure on Lankan nobles in the southwest to adapt and to convert.

At the same time, the circulation of Lankan princes through the Catholic Monarchy also became a matter of political concern for the new imperial authorities. Philip II and his successor Philip III (r. 1598–1621) saw themselves as rightful successors to Dharmapāla and began to consider any Lankan throne candidates as potential competitors, not allies.[56] A particularly telling case originated precisely in the context just explored. By the time Dom Filipe Yamasiṃha had been murdered in Kandy in 1591, he had produced an heir old enough to attempt to rule for a few weeks before being forced to flee.[57] This young man, known to us only by his Christian name, Dom João, moved first to Mannar and then to Colombo where, spending some time at the court of Dharmapāla, he was joined by another disinherited prince, Dom Filipe, formerly known as Nikaepiṭiya Baṇḍāra, a pretender to the throne of Sītāvaka.[58]

Sometime after Dharmapāla's death in 1597, both men were forced to leave the island. Their presence in Colombo had been deemed problematic by the Goan authorities for some time.[59] With Dharmapāla dead and Philip II acclaimed as his successor, it seemed of the essence to handle any Lankan pretenders to the throne with caution. In 1598, orders arrived from Portugal for the young men to be taken to Goa as it was reckoned that their mother might challenge the donation of Kōṭṭe.[60] In Goa, Dom João and Dom Filipe spent almost a decade at the *Colégio dos Reis Magos*, a Franciscan college at some distance from the city. They were finally allowed to leave for Lisbon in 1608.[61] This, it seems, had been what they were asking for since at least 1606,[62] possibly in connection with the death of Vimaladharmasūriya in Kandy in May 1604 and the difficulties experienced by Senarat in establishing his rule.[63] For the princes, lobbying the court in Lisbon for an expedition to conquer Kandy was as logical as it had been for many other Lankan royals to seek support in South India before. In fact, a decade or two earlier, the princes' strategy might well have prevailed.

By now, however, the Habsburg administration was not interested in the establishment of vassal rulers anymore. Philip II sought full sovereignty over Sri Lanka as a whole, and the authorization granted to the princes for a trip to Lisbon served, from the monarch's perspective, essentially to keep them under control. While religious conversions as they occurred in earlier decades among royal pretenders and exiles were often guided by a pragmatic spirit and left considerable space for agency in the pursuit of Lankan political projects, the picture here becomes more sombre. The power structures that now funnelled Lankan political energies were more restrictive than before, raising very serious doubts about whether 'cosmopolitanism' as a term can be appropriately used. Surely we are now at a considerable distance from the world described – but also, to some extent, idealized – by Sheldon Pollock in his exploration of the Sanskrit cosmopolis.[64] The power to uproot and move individuals through forced exile to the centres of the monarchy, to control their whereabouts and to make sure they could not return to the Lankan theatres of war, reduced drastically the element of choice in these trajectories. However, it is equally important not to overestimate the monarchy's capacity to regulate the lives of their subjects in Lisbon and Goa. While control was tight in key moments of the trajectories of exiles under the new seventeenth-century regime, there remained, as we shall observe in the following section, long periods of time during which individuals could explore multiple relatively open social and cultural spaces in the empire.

## Being a royal convert in exile: the 'Black Prince' of Telheiras

The two princes arrived in Lisbon around 1610,[65] where the ex-governor of India Dom Francisco da Gama officially received them. From their temporary lodgings at the main Franciscan convent of the Portuguese capital, it was attempted to transfer them to Coimbra where, the authorities suggested, they might further their education. Dom Filipe accepted, but passed away upon arriving at his destination. Dom João, in contrast, refused to leave for the small university town north of Lisbon.[66] His wished to live in the capital and he demanded to be treated in accordance with his royal status, as had been the case half a century earlier with the homonymous prince exiled by Bhuvanekabāhu VII and Śrī Rāmarakṣa. It seems that Dom João may soon have travelled to Madrid to negotiate the renunciation to the Kandyan throne. He certainly felt entitled 'to claim the right he had to the kingdom of Kandy and the states of Vellasa and Seven Kōraḷēs, which belonged to him by inheritance from his father'.[67] As such claims were taken seriously from a legal point of view and could indeed be seen as an embarrassment to Philip III, the prince had some leverage. He ended up renouncing his rights and taking Franciscan vows, but in return a royal decree passed in November 1611 conceded him a sizeable grant of 4,000 *cruzados* per year.[68] Apparently, the prince petitioned for further privileges and, as this went ignored, travelled to Madrid again. In 1626 he was finally granted a very substantial annual pension totalling 8,000 *cruzados*, along with the honour of being made a grandee (*Grande*) and various other aristocratic privileges.[69]

We shall never know how willingly this Kandyan prince accepted the deal, and it is certainly reasonable to argue that he may have seen no alternative to giving in, exiled as he was thousands of miles from his country of birth and with no other allies than a handful of friars. But Dom João spent the rest of his life as an aristocrat in Lisbon, where he died a wealthy and well-considered man in 1642, widely known for the largesse of his charitable acts and the amplitude of his property portfolio.[70] Despite having taken Franciscan vows, he fathered a child around 1634, whose fate had to be monitored tightly by the authorities until she passed away in 1708. This legitimate daughter, named Dona Maria de São João, was mentioned in Dom João's testament as living in the well-known convent of Vialonga, not far from Lisbon.[71] She had been known in her secular life as Dona Maria de Cândia, in reference to her Kandyan ancestry. Her mother was a certain Susana de Abreu.[72] Dom João's testament also mentions another young woman, a novice called Simoa Batista. She was in all likelihood an illegitimate daughter and had to be equally kept under control in a convent.[73]

The prince's residence in the Mouraria district of central Lisbon was filled with the usual luxuries of a typical noble household – tapestries, silverware and other valuables dispersed after his death.[74] Dom João kept a sizeable number of servants and slaves.[75] There is even a record signalling the death of a man in 1640 who had been the prince's trumpeter.[76] His entourage included other Lankans who had most probably come with him through Goa. One of the executors of the prince's will was a certain Dom Jaime de Ceilão. Here again, the title *Dom* indicates a high social rank, even though we know nothing else about this individual. To Dom Jaime, Dom João left a golden necklace worn to his last day, described as a *cadeia de cordão* – quite possibly a final surviving piece of Lankan royal paraphernalia.[77]

Dom João's tomb is in the Franciscan convent of Telheiras, an institution that he himself founded in the suburbs of Lisbon in 1625.[78] That he did what he could to pass as an Iberian Catholic aristocrat – albeit of an exotic origin – is evident. He adopted the lifestyle of a high-ranking noble, bought up numerous properties in Lisbon and other parts of the country, and lived with a permanent entourage including at least two Catholic clerics. According to the Franciscan chronicler friar Manuel da Esperança, a portrait of Dom João, today lost, existed in the convent. Displaying what the friar perceived as a tall, well-proportioned body and the gravity proper to his princely nature, the picture was seen as mirroring João's status to perfection. He was, as Esperança added, *pardo* of colour; that is, of a dark skin 'like all the people of Ceylon'. Yet his face and his hair, the friar wrote, 'were no different from [those of] a European'.[79]

To say that Dom João went entirely native in Portugal would not be correct, as we shall see. But the lengths to which he went in his quest to live as a Lankan Catholic royal in the capital of the empire are remarkable. In founding a Franciscan convent at Telheiras, he was doing what the wealthiest Portuguese aristocrats practised at the time *and* emulating the traditions of patronage of the Lankan royalty. The statutes of his pious act show very clearly that he remained fully in charge of his foundation. The Franciscans were granted an annual income of 100,000 *réis* originating from one of the prince's properties in the south of the country.[80] The chapel at Telheiras would serve the purpose not only of cementing Dom João's standing as a grandee, but also of receiving his bones along with those

**Fig. 7.1** Royal escutcheon of Prince Dom João of Kandy, Museu Arqueológico do Carmo, Lisbon, Inventory no. ESC221, author's photograph.

of his cousin Dom Filipe, which, it seems, were brought back from Coimbra.[81] On a wall of the chapel, an escutcheon carved in stone showed a shield not only bordered by the seven castles of Portugal's coat of arms, but also with, at its centre, the Sinhalese lion rampant (Figure 7.1). Next to it stood a tower-like object crowned with the cross of Avis in reference to the dynasty named in the testament of Dharmapāla. Above the lion and the tower, the escutcheon showed a resplendent sun in reference to Dom João's descent from the solar dynasty, the *suriya-vamsa*. Returning to a more assumedly Iberian register, the shield also supported an open crown, the proud symbol of all grandees.[82]

This escutcheon proclaims with clarity and confidence who Dom João considered himself to be: a man of royal extraction and the legitimate heir to the throne of Kandy and various other lordships in Sri Lanka. While we are yet to find the paperwork documenting his renunciation of the Kandyan throne in Madrid, it is very likely that the act itself was surrounded by a discourse of merging the ancestral Lankan royal lineage with the fate of a new global polity known as the Catholic Monarchy. If there ever had been any doubts about the purity of his blood as someone not born a Christian, then the high rank grounded in a long pre-Christian tradition of royalty would trump those.[83] Note how the construction of such a hybrid coat of arms was no complete novelty in the Luso-Lankan context: a comparable combination can be found on an ivory casket believed to have been made in Kōṭṭe around 1580 to celebrate the proximity of king Dom João Dharmapāla to the Portuguese monarchy. In the latter case, the lion rampant and the Sinhalese power vase were placed around the royal Lusitanian coat of arms.[84]

Incidentally, it may well be that behind the façade created by all this Catholic paraphernalia, Dom João and his other companions never fully surrendered to post-Tridentine orthodoxy – or rather, that they developed their own understanding of the latter in connection with their status as exiles in the host society, thus maintaining some control over their spiritual life. What follows is more speculative than anything discussed so far, but may help us think about how to study the spiritual world of exiles. Three years after the death of the prince, a friar at the Telheiras convent called Manuel da Madre de Deus was denounced to the Inquisition. His nickname, *o negro*, suggests in this particular context that he may well have been of Lankan extraction; that is, a surviving member of the late prince's entourage.[85] The charge was spectacular: he had, in the presence of an illustrious audience of Portuguese nobles, professed that of all the sacraments of the Church, the least valuable was the Eucharist itself.[86] Frei Manuel thought that this point was simple to prove: a Muslim (*mouro*) who had committed many sins would still go to Heaven if only he was baptized. In contrast, a Catholic priest who had committed a single mortal sin would, despite performing the Eucharist time and again, still be stained. To be sure, the fact that such claims ended up with the Inquisition tells us much about the power relations at play. Had the process not been archived for reasons so far unknown, it could well have ended in a very heavy-handed sentence. But the ideas as such voiced by the friar regarding baptism may be of significance.

The openness of friar Manuel's statements about salvation was certainly in tune with the relatively widespread popular belief, deeply rooted in Iberian culture, that 'all could be saved' – a tradition of thought that the Church battled ferociously during the seventeenth century.[87] It may also have had Asian roots, as Manuel noted that 'he had heard the greatest preachers of all religions' pronounce themselves on the matter of salvation.[88] The issue addressed by the 'black' friar regarded not only the existence of a divinity transversal to various religions, but also the comparative value of being a Christian by late baptism as opposed to being a Christian by birth (or, to be precise, by early baptism as a consequence of having been born to Christian parents). This was a matter of great importance to converts in the empire from the mid-1500s. The above-mentioned royal decree of 1542, reissued repeatedly over the following decades, had established that converts in Goa had the same rights as others who had been born to Christian parents. Legally, then, being a subject of the Portuguese Crown by conversion (conceived of as an act of rebirth or *regeneratio*) became equivalent to being a subject by birth (*generatio* or *natio*). As the historian Ângela Xavier has shown, the Goan elites were quick to interiorize the language, the religion and the laws of the new empire they were part of in order to pursue very successfully their own local interests, often in ways that had not been expected by the authorities in Lisbon.[89] A comparable process occurred, partially at least, in Sri Lanka. Even before the kingdom of Kōṭṭe became a Portuguese possession, the baptism of Dharmapāla in 1557 prompted the production of an ivory casket celebrating the transition. As has been demonstrated by art historians, the Christian notion of *regeneration* through baptism was here closely intertwined with Lankan symbols of renewal such as *kinnaras*, *makaras* and beaded ropes, signalling how the central themes of Christianity were present already in the Lankan visual and religious tradition.[90]

While the evidence may be thin so far regarding the continuity of such preoccupations, it is plausible to assume that seventeenth-century Lankan exiles were still making the same point about the high value of their recent baptism in comparison to the repetitious acts of worship performed by Old Christians. It was certainly in their interest to emphasize the infinite divine grace bestowed upon individuals when they converted in the face of a society where prejudice against anyone born in Asia was widespread. In fact, a closer reading of the name chosen by Dom João for the church he founded further corroborates this working hypothesis. The chapel in Telheiras was dedicated to Our Lady of the Door of Heaven (*Nossa Senhora da Porta do Céu*) and to St John the Baptist.[91] The latter invocation requires few explanations: *São João Baptista* served as a stark reminder to everyone that Christ himself had been baptized as an adult man. The 'Door of Heaven', in contrast, was a highly unusual invocation that must have intrigued the public at the time. Dom João's was the first church in Portugal ever to receive this name. The choice makes most sense in relation with the primacy, in the worldview of recent Asian converts, of baptism or *regeneratio* over other aspects of the Catholic religion.

The most specific indication that these ideas are connected comes from the Roman missal, where the chapter titled 'In Dedicatione Ecclesiae' refers to the words *porta coeli* (door of heaven, *porta do céu*) originally given in Genesis 28:17. The Missal, a key tool for the consolidation of Tridentine orthodoxy at the time, here reminded all Catholics that the utterance of the words of Consecration required the utmost humility.[92] The building in which mass was celebrated should inspire even the most seasoned priests – proud guardians of a sacrament that Asian converts were allowed to perform in theory, but rarely in practice – to self-effacement. The church was to be seen as a place of awe by all, not just new converts: 'Terribilis est locus iste: hic domus Dei est, et porta coeli; et vocabitur aula Dei', the Missal proclaimed ('Awesome is this place: it is the house of God, and the gate of Heaven; and it shall be called the court of God'). In the sacred hall where baptism and mass were celebrated, and through which access could be gained to eternal life, all men stood equally in awe before God.

This connection gains plausibility if we look into the history of the motif of a heavenly door. The Missal's reference to the *porta coeli* originates, as mentioned, from the Book of Genesis. Here Jacob – himself a wanderer sent away from Canaan by his parents to find a wife elsewhere and soon to be given by God the name of Israel – has a dream vision of a ladder connecting the earth with the door of heaven. Dom João, a man trained over many years in Catholic theology, made a well-informed choice to assert his own dignity as a convert in Lisbon. The ladder as such, leading up to the *porta coeli*, was widely seen in the Christian tradition as a metaphor for the ascent of the soul, an interpretation that must have seemed most plausible to Dom João as a Catholic. It may also have resonated with ideas of spiritual progress coming from the South Asian tradition. One connection could have been through the motif of *Tāvatiṃṃsa* (Pāli) or *Trāyastriṃśa* (Sanskrit), a level of heaven in Buddhist cosmology that was the only one to present a direct connection to the earth (the Buddha was said to have ascended to this level to visit his late mother Māyā and bring her the Buddhist teachings of the Abhidhamma). While we have no explicit textual evidence to support such connections in this concrete context, the similarities in general between Māyā and Mary as motherly figures at the heart of Buddhism and Christianity are well-known, and it is difficult to imagine converts from Buddhism not reflecting about possible parallels between the Buddha and Christ as well.[93] Naturally, echoes would also have appeared in the way converts saw the spatial structures of the spiritual world.

To the verticality inherent to such interpretations of the ladder to heaven, one may add another, more horizontal, dimension as it came attached to the notion of wandering. To Jacob, God declares, also in the Book of Genesis:

> I am the Lord God of Abraham thy father, and the God of Isaac: the land whereon thou liest, to thee will I give it, and to thy seed. And thy seed shall be as the dust of the earth, and thou shalt spread abroad to the west, and to the east, and to the north, and to the south: and in thee and in thy seed shall all the families of the earth be blessed. And, behold, I am with thee, and will keep thee in all places whither thou goest.[94]

In Telheiras, less than a mile from the church of Nossa Senhora da Luz founded in 1575 by the royal princess Dona Maria – *Luz* also being, remarkably, the original name of Bethel, where Jacob had his dream[95] – Dom João found the perfect place to erect a monument to his own salvation. A place proclaiming that the doors of heaven stood open to him, the converted exile, as much as (or even more than) to anyone else around him. Exile is often a place of deep ambiguity, an experience marked as much by the hope of finding a new home as it is by the hope of someday going back to one's place of birth. Jacob himself was, when he awoke from his dream and understood how close he had come to God, still hopeful of returning to Canaan someday; 'if God will be with me [...] so that

I come again to my father's house in peace; then shall the Lord be my God'. How could such emotionally intense passages from the Old Testament not resonate with the mental world of an educated exile settling thousands of miles away from his Asian home?

## Prince Vijayapāla in Goa: exile at a global crossroads

Dom João was neither the first nor the last Lankan prince to have lived through a prolonged period of displacement in the Portuguese Empire. Kandy was not conquered, and the war of attrition between the Portuguese in the southwest and the kingdom in the central highlands continued throughout the entire first half of the seventeenth century, perpetuating instability. This also meant that Kandy did remain an open challenge to the Catholic Monarchy, and that the potential role of local royal pretenders could not be ignored by Iberian strategists after all. Dom João was soon followed by Prince Vijayapāla, one of three heirs of king Senarat of Kandy.[96] In 1628, Senarat divided his realm into three parts, entrusting each of his three sons with one of them: Kumārasiṃha received Uva, Vijayapāla Matale, and Maha Astana – the youngest of the three – the heartlands of Kanda Uda Rata. When Kumārasiṃha died in 1634, tensions arose between the two surviving brothers over who should control Ūva. Vijayapāla, already experienced in dealing with the Portuguese, turned to Goa for assistance. Although he soon reached an agreement again with Maha Astana, by then known as Rājasiṃha II, the two were never fully reconciled. It appears that Vijayapāla maintained communications with the Portuguese, eventually coming to their rescue against the Dutch at Colombo in 1641 in the hope of obtaining assistance for the conquest of Kandy. When this assistance failed to materialize, Śrī Rāmarakṣa confronted the captain-general of Ceylon, Dom Filipe de Mascarenhas. The latter jailed him, and soon decided to have him removed to Goa. There the prince arrived in March 1643.

What ensued is, again, revelatory of how Lankan princes made the best of apparently desperate situations far from their homeland. It also helps us appreciate the cultural practices in the contact zone of Lankan royalty with the Portuguese Empire. P. E. Pieris summarized Vijayapāla's stance rather pointedly as follows: in writing to the viceroy, the prince 'set out his claims, his grievance at the treatment he had received from Mascarenhas, and his decision to accept Christianity under certain conditions'.[97] Vijayapāla's principal ambition was to be treated in accordance to his rank, receive compensation for fortune lost during his time in Colombo, and obtain the means to march to Kandy and seize the throne. When he failed to obtain a positive response in Goa, he turned to Europe: first to the Portuguese King John IV (r. 1640–56) and soon to Pope Urban VIII (1623–44). It was the latter who reacted more favourably, certainly pressed by other ecclesiastics embracing Vijayapāla's cause. Having obtained a congratulatory letter from Urban VIII in 1644, the prince set out to undergo baptism – and asked no one less than John IV, the king who had ousted the Habsburgs from Portugal, to be his godfather.

The ceremony took place in Goa in 1646, although both the outgoing and the incoming viceroys remained sceptical about Vijayapāla's motifs. The prince appeared unbroken despite his financially and morally precarious situation. Having taken the name of Dom Teodósio (in reference to the late Duke of Braganza, the father of John IV), he surrounded himself with an embryonic court including another Sinhalese prince known as Dom Duarte de Bragança, confidently styled as 'great chamberlain'. Dom Teodósio requested permission again to travel to Portugal, but met with the staunch opposition of the secular authorities in Goa. Only ecclesiastic figures such as the Portuguese patriarch of Ethiopia supported him. In 1650, sometime after rumours had begun to circulate that the Dutch were interested in Vijayapāla, the prince's monthly allowance was suddenly raised from 250 *xerafins* to an unspecified sum. Finally, permission was also granted for a trip to Portugal, in 1652. It was only Dom Teodósio's death in 1654 that prevented him from following the footsteps of Dom João. Given the rise of the Dutch East India Company (VOC) in the region and their capabilities to interfere with Portuguese navigation, it is little wonder that the authorities wished to prevent any ties from developing with the Dutch. What we do know, however, is that throughout his exile the Kandyan prince also remained in contact, through letters, with his rival Rājasiṃha II in the Lankan highlands.

Two centuries and a half after Vijayapāla's demise, P.E. Pieris stated with the confidence of a Sinhalese patriot who had made his career in the British Empire that 'European ideas, badly digested, denationalized this well-meaning but shallow man, and ruined his life'.[98] These may seem to be universal truths regarding exilic displacement. In fact, Pieris was quite incisive with regard to his own contemporaries, stating that for Vijayapāla 'resounding honorifics were to him as acceptable a compensation for the loss of the reality of power, as they are to-day among his countrymen'.[99] Such statements resonate naturally with nationalist historiography today. Yet as Pieris himself admitted, Vijayapāla never ceased to be a Sinhala prince. In a somewhat odd epilogue to his own harsh judgement, Pieris listed a number of princely qualities that – one is inclined to argue today – are much better understood as a function of Vijayapāla's status as an exile, rather than in contradiction to it.

Despite what appears to have been an overall precarious situation, Vijayapāla maintained what any observer at the time – Portuguese or Lankan, or both – would have identified as a posture indicative of his royal status. In Goa he was remembered for being 'dignified, modest, courteous, and of a stately bearing'.[100] He maintained an entourage of Lankan nobles, kept the royal insignia he had been able to bring with him to Goa, and surrounded himself with as much pomp and music as was affordable.[101] Pieris himself felt inclined to speculate that, beneath the Baroque folds of this stately apparatus, the principles of *dasarājadhamma*, the Ten Precepts for the Guidance of Princes, survived. When Vijapayāla wrote about 'keeping his word', he was 'speaking the truth' in the Indic tradition; when he gave generously to widows, orphans and the Goan poor, he was 'taking under his protection those who seek his aid'.[102] We need to be careful here not to overstretch the argument. Pieris goes as far as stating that Vijapayāla was religiously tolerant in a manner that could only be rooted in the Buddhist tradition.[103] This is not the point, however. We cannot, on grounds of the evidence found so far, establish whether the prince *was* more or less tolerant than others to cultural difference, and whether this had anything to do with his original religious affiliation. What we are reminded of is that certain generic virtues could be evoked across religious boundaries, especially with regard to transcendental aspects shared by Buddhism and Christianism.

Pieris' stance is, of course, that of a nationalist projecting the values of a presumably cosmopolitan Lankan culture into the past and, through it, across the sea onto the dark canvas of an intolerant Catholic empire. The historiographical problem of Catholic cosmopolitanism is a matter too complex to be resolved here, although the trajectories discussed in this chapter offer valuable clues about the complicated realities of global circulation in the Habsburg monarchy. But it does seem rather striking how many norms in the early modern period transcended cultural boundaries, allowing for the transversal deployment of notions such as 'nobility', 'truthfulness' and 'charity'. Some of these values have been shown to be grounded in a shared courtly culture binding together the elites of Europe and Asia.[104] Others seem to have gone well beyond the realm of courtly commensurateness, apparently supported by religious discourses – although here the risks for misunderstandings and mutual rejection were also greater than anywhere else, as the accusations wielded against the 'black' friar of Telheiras indicate. It seems important, in any case, not to dismiss the gestures of Vijayapāla as empty *Ersatz* mechanisms deployed by an uprooted exile to deceive himself while he was being stripped of layer after layer of his dignity. Like Dom João in Lisbon, Vijayapāla in Goa carried the signs of Lankan royalty as more than just a piece of exotic disguise. He rather affirmed, vociferously and ostentatiously, a condition that constituted the foundation of his creditworthiness, and also of his growing political significance against a backdrop of the *Estado*'s gradual demise at the hands of the Dutch in Ceylon. Any political exile with a minimum of diplomatic skill would have grasped the opportunities arising from such a situation, where the pressure was significant on the Portuguese authorities not to lose an ally to the VOC. We can only speculate what Dom Teodósio would have done, had he been able to travel to Lisbon as promised – or escape to a Dutch ship, of which there were many in South Indian waters during the 1650s.

There are numerous contradictions at play in these biographies, and it would be unwise to attempt to iron them out. On the one hand, we have stories of uprooting and humiliation. The first of the Lankan princes to be sent to Portugal was merely a boy. He had been shuffled around as a potentially valuable piece on a chequer board, and was not able to inscribe his name in the history of his country beyond a brief reference in a Portuguese chronicle. Yet he also spent years at the royal court in Portugal, treated as other aristocrats by the monarch before returning to India.[105] These are certainly stories with a tragic undertone, involving difficult personal experiences, years of struggle in unfamiliar environments, and the constant threat of death in exile. It could be argued that the matrimony of Dom João, the 'Black Prince of Telheiras', with Susana Abreu, a woman who seems to have been a commoner and even possibly of Jewish background, further points to an embattled social status. But between the lines it is hard not to also see the eagerness of these men to be treated as aristocrats and their capacity to look after themselves. They were more than simply helpless victims tossed into exile by *vis maior*. Vijayapāla insisted on his status as a descendant of Dharmapāla, whom he designated as *emperor* of Ceylon in the Kōṭṭe tradition that, after all, had been the anchor for the Portuguese project of conquest in the island. It was Dharmapāla who had bequeathed the throne of Kōṭṭe to the kings of Portugal, and it was thus quite right for Vijayapāla to insist on being treated by John IV as a 'brother'.

The escutcheon of Dom João in Telheiras expressed to perfection the complex image cultivated by the prince at the intersection of two royal traditions. Ever since the beginning of Luso-Lankan relations, an assumption had been at work that the two traditions of kingship and empire were to some extent commensurable, their terms translatable into each other's language, basic notions of dignity and authority transversal to both cultures. The dignity of any prince is by definition hard to efface. These members of the Lankan royalty in particular remained historical agents in control, to some extent at least, of their own destinies. While they were much more restricted in their agency than exiles in earlier periods seem to have been (note, however, that we know nothing at all about the practicalities of Lankan exile in South Indian polities), Vijayapāla maintained a vivid correspondence with his rival Rājasiṃha II at the same time as he attempted to mobilize the Goan authorities against him. In the murky field of mid-seventeenth-century Portuguese-Dutch-Kandyan rivalry, the prince remained a player to be reckoned with precisely because of his ability to talk and move across borders.

Seen under such a light, Vijayapāla's gesture of handing over his Lankan eagle penchant – purportedly the last piece of Lankan *regalia* he carried with him – during his baptism in Goa may be submitted to a less pessimistic reading than that proposed by Pieris. Leaving the church of São Francisco in Old Goa with a golden crown on his head as the crowds cheered on was certainly more than just a hollow act of symbolic compensation. It was an affirmation that his aspirations to the Kandyan throne remained alive, and that he could serve as a token in further negotiations involving two global empires, the Portuguese and the Dutch. As he was readying himself to travel to Lisbon, he kept styling himself as a Lankan 'emperor'.[106] Nor did John IV, who himself could not officially carry such a title, deny him the honours: the Portuguese king addressed Vijayapāla as 'Emperador de Candia' ('emperor of Kandy')[107] – probably much to the chagrin of the viceroy, who insisted on designating him only as 'rei' ('king').[108]

## Conclusion: exile as cosmopolitan practice

In one of his letters, Vijayapāla wrote, 'though I am a Chingala by blood I am a Portuguese in my ways and affections'.[109] This was, of course, in a note to the viceroy in Goa. What the prince would have put in his letters to Rājasiṃha II, we can only guess – but it might well have been a similar phrase with an inverted order of words; 'though I am a Portuguese in my ways and affections I am a Chingala by blood'. There was, to be sure, nothing unusual about adopting foreign 'ways and affections' in an increasingly interconnected world. 'Denationalization', perceived by Pieris in the early twentieth century as the worst of all conditions, is evidently not only less dramatic today, but also an anachronistic term in this historical context. Vijayapāla lived and went through acculturation far from Lanka, but this did not make him the equivalent of a stateless pariah. At a time when Polish nobles wore Turkish attires, Goan merchants invented fashions combining garments and styles from all over Asia, Kandyan kings fused Lankan and European material culture at their court, and even a minor ruler in Vellassa requested foreign-bred hunting dogs from the Portuguese,[110] there was no fundamental contradiction between the adoption of exogenous signifiers of identity and the pursuit of locally rooted political projects. Certain cultural practices that are strikingly global in scope were perfectly compatible with the pursuit of local political agendas – and vice versa.

Before the nation-state transformed exile into the radical experience of statelessness it is today, transcontinental mobility was a natural ally in the quest of Lankan princes for power. That asylum and exile came with certain conditions attached, the most important of which was the obligation to convert, is a potent reminder of how the global balance of powers was tilting. But taken one by one, the stories gathered here also read as signs of a notable predisposition of Lankans to participate in wider political and cultural realities across the early modern world. The ease with which this happened suggests that the continuities with earlier exilic practices in India were substantial.

In one way, this may be a matter of 'elite extraversion' by which, as Strathern argues, 'the supra-local (its commercial fecundity, modes of civility, technology, potential allies, spiritual force) is seen as a source of local power'.[111] There are also signs, to be sure, that even in their willingness to go global and carry themselves and their retinues across the oceans, exiled Lankan princes still remained attached to the single desire of one day returning to their island, re-localizing themselves, and becoming Lankan kings. But in the process, participation in the supra-local was intense and prolonged. As for the intertwinement of such practices with matters of power, it may still seem tempting to assume that Iberian imperialism, with its crushing pressure on others to convert, is fundamentally incompatible with the notion of the cosmopolitan. Yet it is important that we embrace the fact, of which Gananath Obeyesekere's contribution in this volume (Chapter 8) is a strong reminder, that any process of cultural change, from religious conversion through the adoption of poetic forms to the appropriation of new ways of dressing, cooking or drinking, always occurs in a field of power. Cultural contact and acculturation, however detached they may seem at times from the harsh realities of power-building, never happen in a power vacuum.[112] Cosmopolitan practices can be as tough a business as any other.

Like most exiles, Lankans negotiated their way through a complicated labyrinth of cultural and political practices imbued with complex, often contradictory symbolic meanings. Perhaps they became not so much 'strangers nowhere in the world' – an idealized notion springing specifically from the French Enlightenment – as 'strangers everywhere they went'. Most probably, they were a little of both, and the latter may well be as valid a description of cosmopolitan realities as the former. If the cosmopolitan is to remain with historians as a meaningful category, it ought to carry the full set of contradictions that exposure to cultural difference implies. For Pollock, the genuine cosmopolis – the Indic, as opposed to the Latin – appears to be a reality unfolding without the interference of political power. As early modernists confronted with a much wider range of cases and sources, we are compelled to wonder whether the opposite may not be the case: any manifestation of a belonging to the supra-local is always inevitably also a part of the wider, often violent political transformations that shape the world. The establishment of global networks of communication was and still is deeply intertwined with that of global structures of power. And while we are far from proving the existence of a clearly and fully formed cosmopolitan mindset – be it Lankan, South Asian, Portuguese or Catholic – in the early modern period, there are strong signs indicating the ample relevance of cosmopolitan impulses traversing Sri Lanka and the Portuguese Empire at the same time.

# 8

# Between the Portuguese and the Nāyakas: the many faces of the Kandyan Kingdom, 1591–1765

*Gananath Obeyesekere*

This chapter explores the signs of a cosmopolitan court culture that flourished in the kingdom of Kandy, and in particular at the royal court of its capital Senkadagala, from the late sixteenth to the mid-seventeenth centuries.[1] The Kandyan kingdom resulted from a secession led by Sēnasammata Vikramabāhu (r. 1469–1511), the 'founder ruler' of the *kande uḍa pas raṭa* ('the five regions of the hill country') from the realm of Kōṭṭe. For much of the sixteenth century, Kandy stood in a field of tension between Kōṭṭe, Sītāvaka and the Portuguese, taking part in numerous alliances and often unpredictable diplomatic games.[2] Catholicism was brought into the kingdom by its rulers as part of their strategy to gain full independence from the lowland kings. Under Jayavīra Banḍāra (r. 1511–52) Catholic friars appeared at court and some conversions took place. Karalliyadde Banḍāra (r. 1552–82) publicly embraced Catholicism, but ended up fleeing the kingdom with, among others, his infant daughter Kusumāsana Devi in his retinue. The princess was soon baptized by the Portuguese and called Dona Catarina. After a period of great political turmoil involving a Portuguese-supported military campaign in the Kandyan highlands, Dona Catarina was captured by the forces of Vimaladharmasūriya I (r. 1590–1604) in 1594 and the king espoused her as his chief queen. Vimaladharmasūriya, originally known as Konappu Banḍāra, was the son of a distinguished aristocrat from the province known as *hatara kōrale* ('four districts', roughly equivalent to today's Kegalla District) who was cruelly murdered by Rājasiṃha I of Sītāvaka. Consequently Konappu had to flee to Portuguese Goa where he became a Catholic convert as Dom João de Áustria.[3] Such conversions were quite common in the Kōṭṭe kingdom and also among the rulers of Kandy prior to Vimaladharmasūriya. Consequently there is no way in which one could in hindsight decide their 'sincerity'. *Vimaladharma* means 'of the pure doctrine', apparently a name bestowed on him by monks possibly unsure of his previous antecedents while *sūriya* refers to the 'dynasty of the Sun'.

A profound yet creative contradiction was at the heart of Vimaladharmasūriya's reign as the first consecrated king of Kandy. As a Buddhist ruler resisting Portuguese attacks, and also attempting to cement his position against the traditionally unruly elite of Kandy, Vimaladharmasūriya sought the recovery of the Tooth Relic and, to house it, had a 'two-storeyed, superb relic temple [i.e. relic house] erected on an exquisitely beautiful piece of ground in the neighborhood of the royal palace'.[4] Following the example of previous kings, he publicly demonstrated his faith by going on pilgrimage to Śri Pāda, the holy footprint of the Buddha. He also sent a delegation to Rakkhanga (Arakan in Burma) to bring monks to Sri Lanka to revitalize Buddhism, owing to a lapse in the higher ordination (*upasampadā*). When they arrived within the *sīma* or ordination boundary, the king himself 'led the bhikkhus [and] had the ceremony of admission to the Order performed in this Great bhikkhu [monk] community on many of the sons of good family and thus protected the Order of the Enlightened One'.[5]

However, quite unlike what later historians have come to see as Lankan patriotism, Vimaladharmasūriya's reign was also culturally and politically very complex. Kandyan society in the early seventeenth century reflects a modernity that was not permitted to fully develop in later times. Dona Catarina herself, although usually listed by Sri Lankan historians as Kusumāsana Devi, never gave up her Catholic faith when serving as queen consort. According to an early Dutch source, she 'visit[ed] no pagodas' at all, a potential sign of Catholic intransigence, while her prolonged presence at the heart of the Kandyan court certainly alerts us to the complexity of the situation.[6] From a Buddhist perspective, Catholicism could be treated as an addition to the existing religious landscape. The openness in principle and in practice of many Buddhists to the adoption of new religious faiths is well-known. As Kitsiri Malagoda pointed out in respect of conversions in the early British period, one could become a Christian nominally but remain at heart a Buddhist.[7] Jesus can be easily absorbed into Lankan culture as Viṣṇu, Saman or any other of the adopted Hindu gods; and the Virgin Mary easily became one of the many mother goddesses adored by Lankans, often identified by Sinhala Catholics with the goddess Pattini. The missionaries were aware of these overlaps and, while hoping that in the next generation or two the descendants of the first converts would become 'genuine' Christians, they also learned to live with such dilemmas on the ground, especially where they lacked military backing by the empire. The very word used to designate what we now call 'conversion' – *kulavädī* – is polysemic. It certainly refers to the act of being baptized, but implies more generally the joining of a new group, caste or faith.[8]

Differences in religion aside, Dona Catarina and Vimaladharmasūriya were familiar with Portuguese customs, to which they had both been exposed during their time away from Kandy. And yet Vimaladharmasūriya's openness to Western ways of living is something that we would hardly know of if we had to rely exclusively on Pāli and Sinhala sources. It is the Dutch accounts of the time that offer the most remarkably cosmopolitan panorama of Kandy. According to Phillippus Baldeaus, the Lankan king 'ridiculed the idea of all religious tenets, permitting everyone a free exercise of it according to their own will and pleasure'.[9] The Dutch envoy Sebald de Weert famously mentions how he saw the king holding 'a gold cup full of wine made from the grapes that grow in his house'.[10] The Spilbergen embassy of 1602 on visiting the court recorded the presence of 'many Spanish chairs [and] a table on which all was arranged in the Christian manner'. It further noted that Vimaladharmasūriya had 'all new buildings constructed according to the Christian style'. The king himself took some of the Dutchmen into his courtly service and 'even began to learn to play several instruments'.[11] Spilbergen was brought into the 'chamber of the Queen where she sat with her children, the Prince and the Princess, who were all dressed in the Christian manner'.[12] This of course was in part to please the guests, but it is likely to reflect broader changes in the material and visual culture of the Kandyan court. As Paul E. Pieris summed it up, 'for a century Portuguese ideas molded the fashions of the Court at Senkaḍagala'.[13] In fact, the preference for certain elements of Western fashions remained evident under Narēndrasinha, the last of the patrilineal line of Vimaladharmasūriya I, who 'used to wear white wigs [...] with the necessary powder and pomade the Dutch sent him'.[14]

In contrast with some of the later Nāyaka rulers, Vimaladharmasūriya cultivated a remarkably open attitude towards foreign envoys at court. Distinguished guests were permitted into the inner chamber of the palace to meet the royal family. Of course ambassadors had to pay homage to the king, but not in the abject ceremonial style that the British and Dutch ambassadors had to endure especially during and after the reign of the great Nāyaka king Kīrti Śri Rājasiṃha in the mid-eighteenth century.[15] As the Dutchman Sebald De Weert noted, he greeted Vimaladharmasūriya 'in the manner of *our* country, with one knee on the ground', and was then permitted to see his children.[16] There is a beautiful picture of the king shaking hands in Western style with Spilbergen.[17] And De Weert, the next Dutch envoy says that when the king was with some of his counsellors he tried to kiss the king's hand as a token of honour but the king 'took me in his arms and squeezed me heartily, so that he made my ribs crack'.[18] One of his reputed actions surely anticipates our own time when he informed De Weert 'that he was prepared to send his own son, when of suitable age, to Europe, to be trained under Prince Mauritz [Prince of Orange]'.[19] According to Phillippus Baldaeus, the king was 'in every sense of the word a finished courtier'.[20]

When the Spilbergen account places emphasis on the fashionable outfits of the men and women of Kandy,[21] this naturally refers to the elite of the capital in the first place, rather than the general population as it was described by the English captive Robert Knox.[22] Even so, village women dressed in style when visiting family and friends. Wine and foreign foods may have been served at court, but ordinary people, like all Sinhalas of the time, were 'not allowed to eat bull's or cow's or buffalo meat nor can they drink any wine'.[23] What we do not know is whether court culture had an influence in other important cities, especially Bintänna-Alutnuvara, the alternative residence of the Kandyan kings, and the location of the great pilgrimage centre at Mahiyangana.[24] In these urban centres, house and dress fashions were certainly at a premium, following not only Western but also other Asian models. Much of this had to do with the growth of international trade, which was in the hands of South Indian Muslim merchants beginning to establish communities in the Kandyan area. This in turn had linguistic consequences, because no trade or businesses could be conducted without the knowledge of Tamil and, to some extent, Portuguese – two widely diffused *linguae francae* across much of South and Southeast Asia. Even those who did not wear expensive foreign clothes would thus have come into contact with the wider flow of cultural goods.

The Kandyan policy of toleration and cultural cosmopolitanism was fraught, tense, and perhaps even paradoxical for a kingdom struggling so fiercely against the Portuguese. It was nevertheless a thriving reality and continued by Senarat (r. 1604–35). This former Buddhist monk in fact married the widowed Dona Catarina.[25] Both he and his son Rājasiṃha II (r. 1635–87), in spite of their political hostility to the Portuguese, continued a policy of religious toleration.[26] Senarat gave shelter to about 4,000 Muslims expelled from various parts of the coastal lowlands by the Portuguese, allowing them to settle on the East Coast.[27] His successor, in turn, took in Catholic refugees persecuted in the lowlands by the Dutch.[28]

It should be remembered that, under the influence of his mother, Rājasiṃha II was educated in his early childhood by Christian friars. He 'could read, write and speak Portuguese fluently, and was familiar with the manners and customs of many European peoples'.[29] It seems that a clear distinction must be made again, in this specific context, between Catholic friars serving as the king's teachers and the Portuguese colonials fighting Kandy from the lowlands. Unlike in the Portuguese territories, friars in Kandy began to recognize that the dominant religion was Buddhism and that, beyond the boundaries of the *Estado da Índia* – the Portuguese Empire in the East – they lacked political clout. Further, we must remember that the Catholic Church was not in practice a unitary organization. While some priests carried the full set of colonial prejudices, others could act more diplomatically even without abandoning in principle an exclusivist notion of religion. It is thus logical that, while Vimaladharmasūriya I, Senerat and Rājasiṃha II were unrelenting in their hatred of Portuguese rule, this attitude did not necessarily extend to Catholicism as such; that is, to Catholicism as an intellectually provocative religious culture introduced by educated priests.

It is, again, the European sources that give us the most vivid depictions of religious and ethnic diversity in mid- to late seventeenth-century Kandy. Spilbergen says that, 'among these *Singales* there live many *Moors*, *Turks* and other heathens, who all have special laws. *Brahmos* [Brahmins] are there in large numbers, who are very superstitious and respected by the other nations'.[30] Numerous Hindu ascetic wanderers such as *āṇḍis* and *paṇṭārams* carried their own brands of faith throughout the country. Spilbergen mentions how he 'was received [in] the city of *Candy* by some thousand armed soldiers of all nationalities, such as *Turcken* (Turks), *Mooren* (Moors), *Singales*, *Cafferos* (Kaffirs) and renegade Portuguese'.[31]

Knox tells us that many Englishmen captured during the reign of Rājasiṃha II were kept as 'prisoners' in the villages close to the city, naturally failing to mention that they, like a number of Frenchmen and perhaps some Danes, enjoyed substantial liberties.[32] Rājasiṃha II was especially keen to have foreigners in his kingdom for a variety of reasons: as servants, as interpreters, craftsmen, soldiers, mechanics and gunners. He also seems to have appreciated – like many other Asian rulers – the variety of humanity in his domain, just as he loved to have a good stable and many animals and birds in his menagerie.[33] As H. W. Codrington nicely put it, 'luckless Europeans as fell into his hands [were treated] as curiosities, much in the same way as the lion and other animals sent him by the Dutch'.[34]

After Rājasiṃha II, there are some signs of a regime shift under his son Vimaladharmasūriya II (r. 1687–1707) and his grandson Narēndrasinha (r. 1707–39), but no straightforward rupture. The developments are best understood against the backdrop of Dutch conquest in the lowlands formerly held by the Portuguese, including almost all of the island's ports (the last Portuguese ports to fall were Colombo in 1656, and Jaffna and Mannar in 1658). The Dutch might have been religious liberals in Holland, but not in Sri Lanka.[35] Here, the Dutch conquest suffocated Catholicism in the low country, generating a remarkable clandestine revival under Father Joseph Vaz, a Catholic Brahmin from Goa, and his Oratorian mission.[36] Kandyan attitudes towards Catholicism after Vimaladharmasūriya II cannot be understood without taking into account this key development, including the enormously successful apostolic mission of Vaz. Father Vaz's missionary outreach embraced a vast area, and there is little doubt that today's Catholic population in the Kandyan kingdom and much of the low country owe considerably to the toleration of this apostolic work by the Kandyan kings.[37] Vimaladharmasūriya II apparently ignored the treaty of 1638 between the Dutch and his father Rājasiṃha II that stated that the monarch 'should not allow Roman Catholic monks and priests and other ecclesiastics to domicile themselves in his dominions'.[38] When one of the missionaries died, Vimaladharmasūriya II permitted him to be buried in Christian style in the church in Kandy, within the city limits itself, an action that certainly upset the Dutch and might have been considered outrageous in later Nāyaka times. But it is also telling that, along with his support of Catholicism and the many Indian ascetic sects, Vimaladharmasūriya II remained concerned with the welfare of the *sāsana* or the Buddhist dispensation and civilizational order. A splendid account of his Buddhist activities is found in chapter 97 of the *Cūḷavaṃsa*, the overall content of which is confirmed by a Catholic report from 1701.[39]

More than Vimaladharmasūriya, it has been his son Narēndrasinha who has received a particularly bad press regarding his Buddhist credentials. Lorna Dewaraja, for example, has it that there was public discontent about this ruler's 'inadequate support of Buddhism'. The distinguished historian adds that although he did 'at times show a superficial interest in Buddhist art and literature [...] no whole-hearted attempt was made to resuscitate the most vital organization, the Sangha'.[40] The historiographical problem at stake is, however, not so much the connection of discontent with a lack of Buddhist patronage. The main issue is how resentment against the king is naturally assumed to have been 'caused' by the latter's 'partiality' for Catholics and the alien Nāyakas. The fact of the matter is that resentment against kings by rival factions at court is hardly exceptional. I would say that tolerance for another religion ought to be considered a compliment to Narēndrasinha as an expression of his Buddhist and cosmopolitan values that commenced with the reign of Vimaladharmasūriya I.

As so many other Lankan rulers did, Narēndrasinha supported the presence of various religions in his realm. He does indeed seem to have known Father Joseph Vaz since childhood and regarded him with some veneration.[41] He also conversed with his disciple Father Jacome Gonçalves, admittedly a much more problematic figure.[42] Yet like other Kandyan kings he was highly educated and must have had regular conversations with the *sāmaneras* he housed in his palace premises, as well as with his teachers who were educated, albeit not fully ordained monks. As a monarch he could hardly have avoided consulting his Brahmin *purōhitas* (counsellors) at court. However, it is time to move beyond such categories as 'patriotic' versus 'unpatriotic', or 'Buddhist' versus 'non-Buddhist' in such complex settings. Let us revive, for the sake of a nuanced picture, Narēndrasinha's Buddhist persona as expressed in the *Cūḷavaṃsa*. If this monarch was a crypto-Catholic, he would hardly have provided accommodation to Buddhist novices in his palace premises in Kuṇḍasāle and performed so many other acts of Buddhist merit-making. He continued the grand tradition of giving alms to monks and had religious texts copied for their benefit. 'His heart was grieved' when he noted that the Palace of the Tooth Relic his father had erected in the capital had fallen into disrepair, and set about rebuilding it into a beautiful two-storey structure 'resplendent with all kinds of brilliant ornaments'.[43]

Narēndrasinha's artistic patronage included support for a graceful roof and the depiction of thirty-two jatakas, actually listed in the *Cūḷavaṃsa*.[44] Earlier in his reign we are told that he went to Mahiyangana-Bintänna (i.e., Alutnuvara), where his grandfather Rājasiṃha was born, and offered several *pūjas*. Mahiyangana was one of the great pilgrimage centres and palace complexes and according to Buddhist myth it was here that the Buddha banished the demons and cleared a space for Buddhism. It was such an important place that Narēndrasinha went twice again to Mahiyangana at the head of a great army (or following) where he 'celebrated a great sacrificial festival'.[45] He went on pilgrimage to Śri Pada and also once to Anurādhapura.[46] He supported Viṣṇu by endowing the god's shrine in Kandy with extensive maintenance villages, just as he might have supported Christ as a kind of Viṣṇu. He constructed a rampart or wall to enclose the Bōdhi tree, the Buddhist temples and the shrine for the god Nātha, the future Buddha Maitreya in the city.[47] According to Codrington, the king also built the Mahā Dēvāle for Viṣṇu in Kandy in 1731 but if this author is right, this might mean that either he did extensive reconstruction of the already existent Viṣṇu shrine or that the present Mahā Dēvāle is the work of his later years.[48]

Religious patronage in Kandy was not a matter of either supporting Buddhism or going against it. Rather, it involved a skilful combination of patronage extended to many different currents of thought and groups, as indeed was the case at many other South Asian courts. To understand this complexity, it is crucial that we further observe the connection with the Nāyakas of Madurai and its impact on Kandyan kingship.[49] In her important chapter on the Nāyakkar dynasty and its origin, Dewaraja sums up what many historians think:

> Śri Vīra Pārakrama Narendrasiṃha, known to his subjects as Kuṇḍasāle *deyyo*, the last of the royal Sinhalese line of Sēnasammata Vikramabāhu, died in the year 1739. His brother-in-law who hailed from the outskirts of Madura in South India ascended the throne of Kandy as Śri Vijaya Rājasiṃha (1739–1747). He and the three kings who ruled after him until 1815, constitute the Nāyakkar dynasty, so called because of their association with the Nāyaks of Madura. *In Kandy they were aliens, not only in race but in language, religion and culture as well.*[50]

Sri Lankan historians often assume that the presence of the Nāyaka dynasty resulted in the 'Dravidianization' of Sri Lankan Buddhist culture. This is Dewaraja's position, too, although she recognizes that the *Cūḷavaṃsa* unreservedly praises the Nāyaka kings. As Dewaraja further admits, there were only a few rebellions, and 'we also have the unanimous verdict of all our sources that all the Nāyakkar rulers except the last were popular with their subjects'.[51] But if the Nāyakas were 'aliens' in respect of race, language, religion and culture, why their remarkable popularity? To deal with this issue we must move away from observing the Nāyaka kings as simple foreigners, to exploring the impact of the Nāyakas on Kandyan society against the background of what we have observed already.

Long before Nāyaka rule began in Sri Lanka, the Kandyan kings had political and marital relations with the Nāyakas. Evidence in this regard is abundant for the reigns of Rājasiṃha II, his son Vimaladharmasūriya II and his grandson Narēndrasinha.[52] Military cooperation may have been an early trigger, although a longer tradition of Lankan rulers seeking support in the Madurai-Tanjore region against Kōṭṭe and the Portuguese has been pointed out.[53] Dewaraja notes that 'no less than a thousand men from Madura fought for Rājasiṃha [the second of that name] in the victorious battle of Gannōruva [against the Portuguese] in 1638'.[54] Some of these would have married Sinhala women, just as other immigrants and foreign settlers did. It should be remembered, incidentally, that the Nāyakas were not Tamils but Telugu speakers, *vaḍuga* (northerners) originally from Andhra Pradesh and Karnataka. Madurai itself had important historical connotations for the Sinhalas, whose ancestral hero and founder, Vijaya, having discarded his demon-wife Kuveṇī, espoused a princess from Madurai as his *mahēsi* along with other Madurai women as wives for his followers. Both in mythic and practical terms, the Nāyakas of Madurai were hardly aliens and therefore marital alliances with them could be seen as a further cementing of political and mythic relations with Madurai.

The first marital alliance recorded in the *Cūḷavaṃsa* happened under king Rājasiṃha II, who 'brought royal maidens [*kaññā*] from the city of Madhurā'.[55] What is striking is that this marriage alliance must have occurred when the notable king Tirumala (r. 1623–59) reigned in Madurai. The overlap with Rājasiṃha's reign gave the two plenty of time to contract an alliance against the Portuguese, who were a potential threat to Madurai's integrity on grounds of their proselytism among the Paravas and other castes of the 'Fishery Coast'. It is thus likely that Rājasiṃha obtained one or more of Tirumala's daughters as his own *mahēsi* or *mahēsi*s. Alternatively, the *Cūḷavaṃsa* statement that Rājasiṃha married royal maidens could be interpreted to mean that he might have brought home daughters of Madurai *rājas* and married some of them as secondary queens known as *yakaḍa dōliya* in Kandyan kingship, in contrast with *ran dōliya*, the chief queen or queens, a metaphorical distinction between palanquins (*dōliya*) of gold (*ran*) and iron (*yakaḍa*). Multiple chief queens or *mahēsi*s (*ran dōliya*) were an acceptable Sri Lankan royal custom.

Rājasiṃha's son Vimaladharmasūriya II (1687–1707) continued the Madurai connection in respect of marriage. The *Cūḷavaṃsa* states that he 'took to wife the daughter of the queen who was brought from Madhura, and made her his chief queen', implying that the king married his father's *mahēsi*'s daughter.[56] As for Vimaladharmasūriya's son Narēndrasinha, Dewaraja is right to point to the official negotiations conducted in the Madurai kingdom by Lankan emissaries, as described in the Dutch sources.[57] After a first unsuccessful mission around 1706 (when the powerful Madurai regent Mangammal was about to relinquish her rule to her grandson, the impetuous Chokkanātha), a second mission succeeded: the Kandyan side 'fetched princesses from the town of Madura and made them first mahēsis'.[58] Intriguingly the *Cūḷavaṃsa* wording implies that Narēndrasinha may have married 'princesses' belonging not necessarily to the ruling family *sensu stricto*. They may have been from a lateral line or even an unrelated, yet politically influential, family of the complex Madurai polity. What we do know for certain is that the princesses came with their own retinues of male and female relations, and that the impact of all these individuals at the court in Kandy must have been substantial, both 'biologically' and culturally. South Indian connections were, in essence, an integral part of the life of the Kandyan rulers through much of the seventeenth century already.

Virtually every Sri Lankan historian refers to Narēndrasinha, the son of Vimaladharmasūriya II, as the 'last Sinhala king'. It may thus be no surprise that Lorna Dewaraja should point, as we have seen already, to his 'inadequate support of Buddhism'. The reality, however, is much more complex, and best understood if we observe religious matters as a part of the wider power struggles in the kingdom. Take the much-touted issue of an absence of fully ordained (*upasampadā*) monks. The first king to bring in monks to renew the ordination had been, as mentioned above, Vimaladharmasūriya I. Vimaladharmasūriya II again sent, in 1697 and with Dutch assistance, an embassy 'to the country of Rakkhanga [Arakan] and invited the bhikkhu community with the thera [monk] Santana at the head'.[59] Thirty-three monks arrived from Burma who, on the king's orders, conferred the higher ordination on thirty-three 'sons of good family', and initiated as novices (*sāmanera*) another 120 men.[60]

By contrast, Rājasiṃha II and Narēndrasinha allowed full ordination to lapse again and made no moves to renew it. Difficulties in dispatching ships across a Dutch-dominated Bay of Bengal may have played a role, but certainly more significant was the dependence of both kings on powerful non-ordained monks known as *ganinnānses*, those who did not wear the yellow robe but instead wore white or some other sartorial marker. Many belonged to the aristocracy and owned large estates, some served in the courts and as diplomats (for example, a certain Kobbäkaḍuve Ganebanḍāra served repeatedly in negotiations with the Dutch), and a few even contracted marriages.[61] Their knowledge of the doctrine was variable, although in theory they were supposed to be proficient in the Ten Precepts (*uposatha*) obligatory for novices, know the basics of Buddhist ethics and the main *jātakas*, and perform Buddhist rituals for lay folk. If the *Cūḷavaṃsa* categorically states that Narēndrasinha, at the start of his reign, 'showed care for the bhikkhus who had been admitted to the Order during his father's life' and also 'had many sons of good family submitted in faith to the ceremony of world-renunciation',[62] then we have to ask ourselves why, if not for political reasons, he should have allowed ordination to lapse again by around 1714. In my view the young king, in order to consolidate his position, was forced to compromise with the established *ganinnānses*. This is the best possible explanation for an otherwise inexplicable action of the king in 1715, when he ordered the execution of an important monk, Sūriyagoḍa Rājasundara, for treason. The venerable Sūriyagoḍa had been ordained by the Arakanese delegation in 1697, and he must have got involved in some resistance against the young Narēndrasinha and the *ganinnānses*. The latter clearly won the war, at least for the time being.

Again, once we question the supposedly natural connection between 'the foreign' and local discontent, and identify such conflicts as primarily political, the religious panorama appears much more fluid and complex in early eighteenth-century Kandy than is usually said. Kandyans, as we have seen, were not only familiar with the presence of outsiders and their religious beliefs, but clearly open to engaging with them without necessarily undermining their traditional faith in Buddhism. The Nāyaka migrants, in their turn, were particularly prone to eclectic combinations, worshipping Viṣṇu along with Śiva, the powerful goddess Mīnaskṣī and many others. In Kandy they found shrines or *dēvāles* where they could easily worship Viṣṇu and Skanda (aka Murugan or Kataragama). As for Buddhism, from the view point of early Nāyaka immigrants, the Buddha was the ninth avatar of Viṣṇu and hence neither they (nor other Hindus until very recently) had any problem worshipping him. Gradually some of the Nāyakas would become more and more Buddhist, further encouraged by the inclusive practices of Rājasiṃha II, Vimaladharmasūriya II and Narēndrasinha.

As we now approach the reign of the first Nāyaka king of Kandy, Śri Vijaya Rājasiṃha (r. 1739–47), we ought to recognize how difficult it is to draw the dividing lines. Having grown up in Kandy from his very birth Śri Vijaya was surely acquainted with Buddhism, knew his Sinhala, and was familiar with the politics and culture of the court and society at large, including those of his Telegu kinfolk.[63] He contracted a marriage (or marriages) with an influential royal family from Madurai, and his father-in-law Nārenappa Nāyaka later became one of the most powerful persons at court. It is impressive that Śri Vijaya's queens soon became 'good Buddhists'. According to the *Cūḷavaṃsa* 'they gave up the false faiths to which they had long been attached and adopted in the best manner possible the true [Buddhist] faith', worshipping the Tooth Relic day by day with many offerings. Most strikingly, 'they kept constantly the five moral commandments and the *uposatha* vows [the ten precepts] even on days that were not *uposathas*'. Among their acts of piety described in great detail, they also 'had sacred books copied'. Naturally 'they were highly regarded in the whole of island of Lanka'.[64] This account of the Nāyaka queens is the longest description of any instance of female Buddhist piety in the whole *Mahāvaṃsa/Cūḷavaṃsa*. It was as easy for the Nāyakas to slip from Vaishnavism to Buddhism as it is for anyone to slip from seeing the Buddha as the ninth avatar of Viṣṇu to seeing Viṣṇu as a kind of avatar of the Buddha.

But could we see all this as just an attempt by a foreign-minded king to be more Buddhist than the Buddhists? Certainly not, albeit the picture is again rather complex. Śri Vijaya Rājasiṃha combined two religious strategies that had not quite gone together so closely before. On the one hand, he attempted to reintroduce the *upasampadā* ordination that Narēndrasinha had neglected. On the other hand, and more disturbingly, he persecuted the Catholics. On the first front, it seems clear that the king felt strong enough to defy the power of the *ganinnānses* and the entrenched aristocratic class. But this task could not succeed without the cooperation of the Dutch. While the king's first attempt was to restore the ordination through Pegu in Burma, failure on this front forced him to contact Ayutthaya in Thailand with Dutch help. Although the death of the Kandyan king in 1747 resulted in a cancellation of this endeavour, the dynamic was not broken, and the ordination went ahead in the reign of Kīrti Śri Rājasiṃha (r. 1747–82). This indicates quite clearly, in my view, the growing power and confidence of the Nāyakas in Kandy and their sustained power struggle against established interests, but also their ability to play successfully on the international field.[65]

It would make sense to assume that Śri Vijaya Rājasiṃha's persecution of the 'Portuguese' and other Catholics may have had to do both with this confidence and the Dutch factor. According to the *Cūḷavaṃsa*:

> The infamous Parangis, the infidels, the impious ones who at the time of King Rajasiha [Rājasiṃha II] had still remained behind in the town and now dwelling here and there, rich in cunning, endeavored by gifts of money and the like to get their creed adopted by others, lead a life without reverence

> for the doctrine (of the Buddha). When the king heard thereof he became vehemently indignant, issued commands to the dignitaries, had their houses and their books destroyed and banished from the country those who did not give up their faith.[66]

However, a third condition needs to be taken into account. I believe that the hostility to Catholics developed in Kandy only during the second phase of Oratorian proselytism, after the death of Joseph Vaz in 1711. This phase was dominated by the work of Jacome Gonçalvez, another Konkani Brahmin who arrived in the kingdom in 1706 and stayed until his death in 1742. Narēndrasinha was well-disposed in principle to Gonçalvez, but Gonçalvez was quite unlike Vaz. He was a militant type of missionary in the spirit of Francis Xavier. He was openly hostile to Buddhism and to Dutch Protestantism, using his thorough familiarity with idiomatic Sinhala and Tamil, not so much to build bridges but rather to tear them down.[67] His enormous theological and polemic output began with *Upadesa* ('advice' or 'instructions') in Sinhala and Tamil and a catechism of Catholic doctrine, followed by a mass of popular and theological work in Sinhala (and Tamil) that made him the leading exponent of Sinhala Catholicism. According to Father S. G. Perera, 'perhaps his greatest achievement was that he enriched the Sinhalese language', replacing the stilted terminology operative at that time with idiomatic Sinhala 'to convey the essentially Christian ideas of the one true God, Church, Sacrament, Eucharist, Gospel, Confession and the like'.[68] Consequently, 'for the first time in the history of Ceylon, Catholics were able to read explanations and vindication of their faith in their mother tongue, in compositions that vied with the Buddhist classics in elegance and purity of language'.[69] Among Gonçalvez's many works listed by Don Peter is *Vēda Kāvyaya* in 528 stanzas on the life of Christ and his teachings and modelled apparently on the great Sinhala Buddhist classic of Vīdāgama, the Buduguṇālaṅkāraya dealing with the life of the Buddha.

These are no doubt remarkable achievements but it is hard to believe that they did not produce negative reactions and hostility among Buddhists, who were now being empowered by their own remarkable resurgence of faith under Saranaṃkara and his sophisticated novice followers popularly known as the *silvat samāgama*, 'the pious community'. Gonçalvez tried to influence Śri Vijaya Rājasiṃha while he was still a 'crown prince' (Prince Asthāna), presenting him in 1737 a copy of the *Budumula* (*The Root of Buddhism*), a refutation of Buddhism. But, as one might expect, 'it failed to convert him'.[70] Śri Vijaya, owing to the serious illness of Narēndrasinha, was the *de facto* ruler already, and chose to maintain an image of a good Buddhist under the influence of Saranaṃkara. Gonçalvez was also an unrelenting anti-Calvinist polemicist, confronting in one of his most famous debates Nauclairs de la Nerolle, a French Calvinist active at the Kandyan court. Defending the worshipping of images as an aspect binding Catholics and Buddhists together, one might have expected the Oratorian's stance to be successful. But Gonçalvez's venture backfired on both fronts, providing ammunition to his Buddhists and also Dutch opponents.

The complexity of the situation comes out beautifully in a Catholic report from 1746.[71] From the viewpoint of the Portuguese, the villains were the heretical Dutch who were supported by Saranaṃkara and a couple of the ministers of the court and especially the governor (*disāva*) of the Four Korales, an area that already had seen considerable proselytization during Portuguese times. According to the 'report', the Dutch failed to incite the king, but stirred up 'commotion among the *sangatares*, or priests of the Budun, and the *Chingala* common people'.[72] They threatened Śri Vijaya with revolt if he favoured the Christian community, namely the Catholics, and tried to win '*Ganne* Villivata' [Valivita Saranaṃkara] with 'a good deal of money'.

> Thus, the *Chingalas*, allied with the heretics [Dutch], demanded that as our Fathers were the authors of these books [that were] contrary to the doctrine of the Budum which they follow, the king should give a command to arrest them, confiscate their properties, have them brought before him, and destroy the churches they had built in his kingdom.[73]

The ministers, whether or not with the king's permission, did what the Dutch requested and what their own passions dictated. Thus 'each *dissava* sent order to his province where there were Christians, to seize the missionaries, bring them to the capital, confiscate their property and destroy the churches'.[74] One of the influential ministers (*Adikārama* or *Adigar* in popular usage) 'ordered the church of Candia to be surrounded', and had Father Mathias Rodrigues taken and all church property confiscated on 17 March 1744.[75] In effect, wherever possible missionaries were pushed out of the areas under Kandyan and Dutch control. According to this report, the Dutch ambassador ('the deadliest enemy') instigated Saranaṃkara to threaten the king, and said that his monks would 'either kill themselves or quit the country of Ceylao if the king and his councilors allowed the missionaries to remain in the realms'.[76] The king then ordered the expulsion of the missions.[77] According to another Catholic report, the king was sympathetic to Catholicism and so was another influential minister but both were compelled to withdraw their support of the missions. Needless to say, this was not primarily a matter of doctrine, and the king acted under heavy political pressure.[78] Although the persecution was a reality, the missionaries found support in the vast and relatively uncharted area of the Vanni. When exactly things went back to normal is not clear, but there is no evidence that the Nāyaka kings who followed Śri Vijaya evinced a comparable hostility to Catholicism. Consequently, it is likely that Catholics continued as an important presence in the Kandyan kingdom.[79] The Dutch, by contrast, fell out with Kīrti Śri very early in the latter's reign, seeking alliances with local chiefs against him well before military confrontations began in 1762. They thus created the conditions for the more radical demonization of Śri Vikrama during early British times, in substantial measure propelled by the spy John D'Oyly – an issue to be explored in a forthcoming work.[80]

Let us stay with the Dutch then, but only insofar as they can throw additional light on some changes in Kandyan court culture during the late eighteenth century. It is in Narēndrasinha's reign and in connection with the VOC's diplomatic and military strategies that we have the first clear example of Madurai ceremonialism in Sri Lanka, along with a version of cosmic kingship that began to radically change the norms governing the earlier traditions of Kandyan kingship. A key event may have been the visit of the Dutch governor Joan Wilhelm Schnee to Kandy in 1732, recorded in detail by a prominent Sinhala interpreter from the low country.[81] I shall focus here on the style in which the Dutch ambassador was received in Narēndrasinha's court. Let us start with the embassy arriving in the proximity to the city where it was met by four major Kandyan chiefs and thereupon it 'moved on through two rows of armed lascorins [lascars] with a line of tusked elephants on one side amidst the whirling of lighted flambeaux' until it reached the first gate of the palace (*vāhalkaḍa*). There the embassy officials were met by still higher echelons of the bureaucracy, the second adigar (one of two chief ministers) and the disāvas of three of the most powerful districts, namely, Sabaragamuva, the Seven Kōrales and Four Kōrales. The adigar on the king's orders informed the ambassador to bring with him the letter of authorization while his secretary and interpreter would wait in the neighbourhood of the king's Audience Hall (*dakina sālāva*). After some time the ambassador received the letter from the hands of several lesser officials (*appuhāmis*), who then placed the letter on his head and climbed up the stone steps to the audience hall. The interpreter took his position on the ambassador's right, while the two adigars and the disāvas grouped themselves on either side as the following events unfolded:

> After a short pause the seven curtains were drawn aside and revealed His Gracious Majesty seated on his throne. Immediately the Ambassador sank on his knee, while the rest of the chiefs and I [the interpreter] prostrated ourselves six times; we then entered the Hall of Audience repeating the same salutation at three places. On reaching the edge of the carpet which was spread in front of the Throne, His Majesty commanded that the letter should be presented [...]. Thereupon the rest of the chiefs advanced with the Ambassador, and as he knelt on one of the steps leading to the throne, His Majesty took the letter in his own royal hand and commanded the chiefs to place it with its wrappings and the silver tray on his right, which they immediately did. The Ambassador them immediately removed his hat and saluted according to custom, and moved backwards with the chiefs till he reached the middle of the carpet, where he remained kneeling on one knee.[82]

Much of this ceremonialism could be read simply as an exaggeration of the existing Kandyan ritualism, where the king is often enough treated and addressed as a god (*deviyo*). Narēndrasinha himself was known as 'Kunḍasāle Deviyo', the god of Kunḍasāle. Yet, the grand development of 'abjection', and especially the emergence of the king from behind seven curtains, are signs that a more radical concept of divine kingship was at play. This does not necessarily indicate an instance of direct South Indian 'influence', because ritual ceremonialism had been developing in the Kandyan court for some time before Narēndrasinha. Thus Rājasiṃha II was known as 'Rāsin Deviyo', the god Rājasiṃha, but there is no evidence that he adopted the extreme ceremonialism that we have associated with the Nāyakas. But we have to ask why this sudden stepping up in diplomatic ceremonials occurred, at a time when Narēndrasinha was forty-two years old and had been suffering from various illnesses since the early 1730s.[83] It seems that the king's illness had begun to take its political toll, leaving important matters of state in the hands of the designated successor, the future Śri Vijaya Rājasiṃha. And it would not be surprising if we found that state ceremonialism was by this time under the control of the king's Nāyaka relatives, especially Śri Vijaya Rājasiṃha's powerful father-in-law. The *full* development of this form of ceremonialism occurred in the reign of Kīrti Śri Rājasiṃha, the successor of Śri Vijaya, and afterwards.

In any case, we need to handle this period with as much caution as the previous one. Historians have paid a heavy toll for seeing the later Nāyaka kings simply as 'foreigners' in a static political landscape dominated by tensions between the 'indigenous' and the 'exogenous' or the 'foreign'. As we have seen, the Nāyakas in Kandy were a little of both, allowing for polemics to crystalize around their perceived alien-ness in certain moments and contexts, but by no means as a fixed condition and an inevitable necessity. Kīrti Śri Rājasiṃha's was certainly more vulnerable than others to being picked out as a foreigner because he did not succeed Śri Vijaya in direct line (he was in fact the brother of the late king's wife).[84] It seems that the sense of Nāyaka foreignness began to be developed as a matter of public discourse *during* his regime when a few influential aristocrats and monks grew increasingly hostile to him and decided to label him as an alien Tamil. This was encouraged by deliberate misinformation on the part of the Dutch who feared his ambitions in the Maritime Provinces and resisted his indigenization by labelling him a 'Malabar', a synonym for 'Tamil'. Are there 'signs' that might allow us to 'test' the ruler's sense of identity because historians are anything but straightforward in their representations of this king? John Holt has pointed out that Kīrti Śri Rājasiṃha had strong Śaivite beliefs and that these were part of his own inherited tradition.[85] One hostile account written in the late nineteenth century says that he daubed himself in sacred ash.[86] Even if this late rumour were true, we know that the same practice was rather common for ordinary persons, especially when they worshipped at Skanda shrines. The accusation thus only made sense in connection with a wider discourse of exclusion directed against the king on grounds that he was an outsider who became king by default. It is possible that Kīrti Śri Rājasiṃha knew little or no Sinhala when he was selected to be king at age sixteen, but it is certain that he picked it up later. He gave his own strong signs of Buddhist piety, which cannot be reduced to a simple façade. Remember it was Kīrti Śri Rājasiṃha who helped institute the Siamese fraternity, today's dominant order of Buddhist monks. Although Kīrti Śri Rājasiṃha supported Saranaṃkara as the head of the newly instituted Siamese fraternity, the latter in conjunction with a few influential monks and aristocratic officials attempted – unsuccessfully – to assassinate him in 1759. It is to Kīrti Śri Rājasiṃha's credit that although he executed some of the conspirators, he did not exact revenge on Saranaṃkara, who under Kandyan law could have suffered the death penalty. Thanks to his sustained commitment to Buddhist orthodoxy he ended as a popular king for the generality of the Sinhala public, as did his Nāyaka successors Rājādhi Rājasiṃha (1782–98) and Śri Vikrama Rājasiṃha (1798–1815) both born and raised in Sri Lanka. The former was a good Buddhist extolled in *Cūḷavaṃsa* and a pundit who rendered a well-known text, *Asadruśa Jātaka*, in 598 stanzas, a remarkable achievement by any standard. A strange Nāyaka indeed![87] Yet in the historiographical tradition, Nāyakas have all been subjected to exclusion again and again.

Nevertheless, it was during the Nāyaka reigns that the model of sacred kingship we first encountered in the 1730s fully unfolded wherein the divinity of the king was emphasized as never before. I believe that when any Sinhala king is consecrated he becomes a divine being but how that sense of the divine is expressed in courtly life is another issue. With the Nāyakas the divinity of the king and the ceremonialism associated with it developed to a degree unthinkable earlier, even in the case of the powerful Rājasiṃha II (Rāsin Deviyo). The public prostrated before the Kandyan kings because they too were 'gods' and thus their 'abjects'. Nonetheless, these ideas were carried to an extreme degree in Nāyaka kingship. With that came a series of rules on public life designed to keep the king away from the public gaze and enhance his exceptional status, very likely based on the conventions of Madurai of that time. Consider the following episode from the reign of King Ranga Krisna Muttu Vīrappa (r. 1682–89), illustrating the Nāyaka ruler's attempt to humiliate the representatives of a Muslim ruler:

> When they were ushered into the presence of the King, after some little delay and with an absence of deference on the part of the gentlemen ushers which astonished and angered them not a little; the Nabobs found the King seated on a gorgeous throne, splendidly arrayed and resplendent with jewels; and surrounded by a brilliant staff of ministers and courtiers skillfully grouped together with a view to scenic effect, whilst the hall of audience had been magnificently furnished and decorated for the occasion.[88]

With Nāyaka kingship in India in steep decline precisely at the time of its Sri Lankan ascendancy, it was in Kandy that this cultural practice was fully formed, intensified to impress not only foreign envoys but also the Sri Lankan public and the Nāyakas themselves. This comes out very vividly in the report of the British embassy of John Pybus in 1762. As the envoy attempted to approach Kīrti Śri, he had to put up with humiliating ceremonials unthinkable among earlier Kandyan kings.[89] Three decades later, the British representative Robert Andrews experienced the same sort of ceremonials and gave a graphic account of them in 1795–6. Andrews tells us that when he visited the palace of Rajadhi Rājasiṃha, Kīrti Śri Rājasiṃha's successor, seven curtains were drawn, finally allowing him to see:

> the Sovereign of Candia arrived in all his glory seated on a Throne of solid Gold studded with precious Stones of various Colors [A] Crown of Massy Gold adorned his brows and enriched with valuable and shining Gems the product of his native Sovereignty [T]he moment he blazed upon our sight Lieutenant Kingston and myself (with the salver on my head) were directed to kneel while Native Courtiers who attended us prostrated themselves on the ground.[90]

The Dutch ambassadors even at the time of Narēndrasinha used to only bend on one knee before the king but by the time of Rājādhi Rājasiṃha in 1782 they were forced to perform complicated ceremonials of abjection, which they thoroughly resented.[91] During the later Nāyaka reign, says Lorna Dewaraja, only the king could build a two-storey house and 'in the vicinity of Kandy the use of tiles and lime was prohibited except in the temples'.[92] In the capital city, adds Dewaraja, only the king and the gods could be accompanied with drums and within the larger city the use of palanquins, horse or elephant or use of footwear were prohibited (although Kandyans did not wear footwear and even kings for the most part abstained using them). John Pybus had to get off his palanquin and 'trudge ankle deep in mud through the miry paths of Kandy'.[93] There is no gainsaying the fact that such prohibitions had been for the most part alien to the earlier Kandyan kings. It would have been impossible for Vimaladharmasūriya II and Narēndrasinha to converse and entertain Catholic priests in such a stultifying atmosphere. Nevertheless, once outside the capital, the kings visited the provinces and went on pilgrimages to Buddhist sacred sites. This means that the Kandyan cosmopolitan ethos came under siege but did not succumb. Nāyakas after Kīrti Śri continued to be open to persons of different nationalities and were not hostile to the many Catholics domiciled in the Kandyan territories or for that matter to Brahmins and wandering ascetics from the neighbouring subcontinent. Perhaps part of the resentment of the Nāyakas by monks and the aristocracy was not to their being 'too foreign' but, ironically, to their excessive imitation of divinity. These, however, are issues that need further exploration.

Note, again, how none of this happened against a backdrop of the ruler challenging Buddhism, but rather of enriching it. Kīrti Śri, although a staunch Hindu, was *also* staunchly Buddhist and more so surely after he engaged in the construction of a large number of temples and engaged in Buddhist practices. As Dewaraja herself acknowledges, one of the first acts of his reign was to 'reclaim the Peak from the Śaivites (who had occupied it in the time of Rajasimha I) revive its rites and ceremonies, endow it with valuable lands and restore it to its pristine sanctity'.[94] True, he made some important changes in the annual procession associated with the Tooth Relic during the month of *äsela*, generally in July or August – but certainly not to undermine it. Kīrti Śri Rājasiṃha incorporated the popular Hindu gods Viṣṇu, Skanda, Nātha and the goddess Pattini into the public ritual associated with the processional events at the Palace of the Tooth Relic. By doing this, he created one of the most popular spectacles that the Sri Lankan public enjoys to this very day. The blend is so enticing that, ironically, these rituals with their displays of music and dance are now regarded by many as part of an ancient Sinhala tradition. In this sense Kīrti Śri was a great inventor of tradition – but even he knew exactly where to draw the line, and refrained from introducing the Hindu gods anywhere near the inner sanctum of the Palace of the Tooth Relic. Viṣṇu or Skanda could not be allowed to compete, as gods and as kings, with the Buddha as the 'god among gods' (*devāti deva*).

The Tooth Relic was inextricably tied with Lankan kingship, and all Nāyaka kings not only respected and worshipped it but also saw to its safe upkeep and maintenance. Lankan kings may contract all sorts of rituals of consecration, but none could replace the need to possess the sacred Tooth Relic. Parākramabāhu I (r. 1153–86), for example, could only assume full kingship when he obtained the relic formerly in possession of the ruler of Ruhuna, the southern division of the Tri Sinhala.[95] The same ambitions guided Parākramabāhu II and Parākramabāhu IV.[96] The king as *rājā* is empty of significance unless his capital contains the Tooth Relic. Incidentally, the king's palace is in general small in comparison with the 'palace' housing the relic, as are the shrines of even major gods such as Viṣṇu, Skanda, Vibhīṣaṇa, Saman, Nātha and Pattini – a marked contrast with Indian kingship, including Madurai, where palaces *and* temples were of magnificent proportions.[97] It is the British who produced a radical change in the cosmic significance of the Tooth Relic when they appropriated it and later redefined the office of the Diyavaḍana Nilame ('the water bearer') as the guardian and custodian of the Palace of the Tooth Relic. That is an innovation without precedent in the history of Sri Lanka.

There can be little doubt that tensions existed during the Kandyan period between different religious communities. But one must recognize that when we speak of a religious culture we also concomitantly speak of the political. Much of what I have emphasized in this chapter pertains to the domain of the political that then is seen or rationalized in terms of the religious. In Kandy, as with the world in general, the political and the religious are in intimate relation with one another, although for analytical purposes we might want to disaggregate them as separable entities.

It seems from our account that the cosmopolitan discourse has stood in a field of tension between those who wished to resolve inter-religious issues and those who wished to perpetuate them. Cosmopolitanism is never a fixed entity, it is a matter of constant negotiation, at the mercy of different ways of interpreting and appropriating the 'foreign'. The foreign can, without losing its supra-local connections, be a valuable addition to whatever constitutes the local. The interplay between the local and the foreign is not simply a phenomenon of Nāyaka rule but existed in different shapes and forms in Lankan history and, one might even add, in the history of other nations. But then: this is not a matter of kingship alone because the indigenization of 'foreigners' and 'outsiders' has been a historical phenomenon the world over, a larger issue that I cannot deal with here.

9

# Through the lens of slavery: Dutch Sri Lanka in the eighteenth century[1]

*Alicia Schrikker and Kate J. Ekama*

This chapter engages with the theme of cosmopolitanism in Sri Lanka through the lens of slavery in the eighteenth century. Slaves were, during this period, one of the largest, culturally pluriform groups in the island. We do not have clear figures of how many slaves lived in the Dutch forts, but through occasional censuses and other statistical records, it is possible to estimate that at least half the population in Colombo consisted of slaves, most of whom would have had roots outside the island. The majority of these people were privately owned by Dutch and Lankan individuals. A minority was direct property of the Dutch East India Company (VOC). Adding to this the number of manumitted slaves who continued to live in the same areas, it becomes clear that slavery and its legacy form important aspects of Sri Lanka's urban history.[2] Because the majority of the slaves in these towns originated from various regions in the Indian Ocean, a large share of the underclass of the island's coastal ports carried with them experiences from and ties with a world beyond Sri Lanka's shores. Rather than labelling them *a priori* as cosmopolitan, however, we propose to assess to what extent they inhabited and perhaps constituted a world of cosmopolitan cultural practices. To what extent were they in a position to treasure the ties and memories of their distant place of birth? And in what ways did local notions and practices of bondage interact with Dutch conceptions of slavery?

By singling out slaves, this chapter consciously inverts the elite approach to cosmopolitanism. The introduction to this volume raises the question of whether cosmopolitanism can be conceived of as a product or even a constitutive part of European colonialism, given the coercive nature of the latter. It brings up the example of the Portuguese Empire, but clearly the Dutch colonial enterprise is equally relevant. The Dutch period in Sri Lanka has for a long time been studied in isolation from the broader Sri Lankan historiography, but also from the emerging Indian Ocean World studies that highlight connections and interactions in the region.[3] For many years, the Dutch period was framed mainly in terms of

Dutch-Kandyan political-diplomatic history, or as the study of commercial and economic relations on the coast. The main antecedents for our focus on slave experiences are to be found in the work of Lodewijk Wagenaar and Remco Raben on cultural interaction in the towns of Galle and Colombo. Slaves, manumitted slaves and slave-owners feature extensively in Wagenaar's rich analysis of the ups and downs of Galle town society in the years 1758–60.[4] The legal approach is inspired by the work of Nadeera Rupesinghe, whose recent PhD dissertation presents an in-depth analysis of the practices of the rural court set up by the Dutch in the Galle district, pointing to the high degree to which the rural population acted as stakeholders in court. The Dutch rural civil courts, Rupesinghe shows, were a place where Dutch rule was imposed, while simultaneously being negotiated.[5] Both Wagenaar and Rupesinghe have revealed the depth of interaction between foreign and local norms in eighteenth-century Sri Lanka. These are exactly the themes upon which this chapter will further expand.

It is plausible to conceive of the Dutch Empire as a network regulating, forcing and facilitating flows of peoples, goods and ideas. Recent studies by Kerry Ward and Ronit Ricci on Javanese exiles in the Cape colony and Sri Lanka have placed the Dutch Empire more firmly than before in Indian Ocean studies. They both reveal how various Dutch outposts in the Indian Ocean region were connected through the peculiar punishment and labour regimes of the VOC, and how this resulted in the movement of Asian princes, convicts, soldiers, sailors and slaves across the sea. They also show how these exiles continued to foster spiritual and social ties with their places of origin, albeit not without interacting with their host societies. Through the presence of these people, Sri Lanka became more tightly connected to island Southeast Asia during the Dutch period than it had ever been before.[6] Because of the coercive nature of the regime facilitating these connections, however, the problem of using 'cosmopolitanism' as an analytical term in this context is particularly complex.

The first two parts of this chapter discuss the prominence of slavery in Sri Lanka and the experiences of slaves who entered Sri Lanka via Dutch importation. Through a number of compelling examples from eighteenth-century criminal cases in Colombo we will show the degree to which this diverse group of forced migrants were localized through economic and social relations that they forged with other people in the Lankan coastal areas. Furthermore, an episode recounted here raises the possibility that some slaves imagined themselves to be part of supra-local, transoceanic spiritual worlds. The third and fourth parts of this chapter then discuss the implications of imported slaves for Sri Lankan society beyond the personal connections forged in the coastal ports. In the third section we will discuss the interface between Dutch and indigenous norms and show how in practice Sri Lankan coastal society was drawn into a Dutch world of entangled institutions, rules and regulations. These represent more than a mere paper world and bear traces of actual interaction and negotiation. Fourth, we will look at the practice of law-making and focus on the codification of customary law in Jaffna in 1707. Here, as we shall see, slavery was instrumental in the way in which Jaffna elites and Dutch administrators jointly came to describe and act upon Jaffna society.

Following the editors' thoughts on the cosmopolitan in the introduction to this volume, we have chosen to integrate three questions into our analysis: 1) To what extent can we observe a sense of belonging among the enslaved that transcends the immediate community? 2) Did the slaves contain 'a world of plurality' within them? If so, was this transferred through interaction with Lankans? 3) Did foreignness, in this case Dutch norms and practices of slavery, become localized in any way? These questions provide us with important and fruitful new inroads into the history of coastal Sri Lanka in the eighteenth century and lay bare unexpected global connections. They are particularly helpful in understanding the history of Sri Lanka's underclasses during the Dutch period. Furthermore, we will argue that the Dutch Empire can be conceived of as a legal cosmopolis, in which Lankans participated willy-nilly.

## Slavery in Sri Lanka

Slavery is a little-studied subject in Sri Lankan history for the simple reason that slaves and slavery do not immediately surface in Sri Lankan memory, nor in colonial and indigenous texts. Instead the literature focuses on caste-based service labour especially from the seventeenth and eighteenth centuries onwards, and how the Dutch appropriated that system to meet their labour demand.[7]

One key historical text that deals explicitly with slavery is the description of rules and regulations regarding slavery in the Kandyan kingdom, drawn up by Simon Sawers at the request of the Commissioners of Enquiry in 1828.[8] This text suggests that debt slavery and the selling and pawning of children in times of duress was practised in the region. In their seminal introduction to slavery in South Asia, Chatterjee and Eaton point at the variety of forms of bondage and dependency that existed side-by-side in the wider region, arguing that war, debt and duress were the main reasons for enslavement in South Asia.[9] There is thus no reason to reject Sawers' interpretation of Kandyan society, even if it may have been influenced by the abolitionist context in which the author operated. At the same time, slavery also seems to have remained a marginal feature in Kandyan society in comparison with other forms of bondage dominating social relations.

The socio-legal landscape of Sri Lanka was diverse, with possible contrasts between the various regions along the coast and inland. Unfortunately we know very little about the actual practice of slavery in Kandy and of the background of the enslaved at the court. More is known about practices of bondage in Jaffna, where it seems the situation differed somewhat from that in the rest of the island. According to some colonial officials, ethnographers and later anthropologists, caste-based chattel slavery was common in this region. The landless people of the Naḷava and Paḷḷar castes were identified by such officials and scholars as chattel-slaves.[10] Other scholars preferred to describe their situation as one of hereditary serfdom.[11] For this chapter, it is imperative that Dutch administrators in Jaffna identified particular castes as slave-castes and acted upon it. It will be argued below that in Jaffna they sanctioned and tapped into this perceived local practice of slavery rather than limiting it as they proclaimed to be doing elsewhere.

That the Dutch applied different standards regarding slavery and freedom in various parts of the island is characteristic of the way the Dutch acted in the Indian Ocean as a whole. The VOC operated in an Indian Ocean world in which various forms of slavery and trade in enslaved persons were common. In regions such as Burma, South India and eastern Indonesia, the slave trade became a lucrative side-business for the VOC and its officials. Jim Warren's study of the Sulu archipelago shows how in the course of the eighteenth century a growing Dutch and Chinese demand for slaves influenced and boosted the existing practices of slave-trading and raiding in the region.[12] A similar argument can be made for Burma in the middle of the seventeenth century, where the Dutch demand for slaves fuelled local conflicts.[13] Curiously, the Dutch influence on local patterns of slavery seems to have been strongest in areas that were peripheral to overall Dutch trade interests. In other areas, the Dutch response was more situational, such as during the famines in South India in the years around 1660, when the VOC transported more than 10,000 Indian slaves to Ceylon and Batavia.[14] Richard Allen recently estimated that the Dutch were involved in the transport of between 67,000 and 91,000 people across the Indian Ocean during the seventeenth and eighteenth centuries, with the larger share of this trade having taken place in the seventeenth century.[15]

In administrative centres of the VOC, such as Batavia or Colombo, imported slaves were one of the most important sources of labour for the Company and for private individuals. Along with convict labour, and in some cases service labour, the enslaved were used for construction work on the fortifications, roads, rural exploitation and in the households of private individuals.[16] It was not uncommon for wealthy families to own up to twenty slaves, or even more. Slave orchestras were an asset and gave status to some European families.[17] When in 1808 three ships carried Dutch families from Colombo to Batavia, Dutchmen were outnumbered by their slaves, even after having been forced to leave the majority of the slaves they owned behind. With the advent of British abolitionism it became difficult to sell slaves, and they were presumably absorbed into the urban underclasses as many manumitted individuals had been over the previous centuries.[18]

## Constituting a world of plurality: the lived experience of slavery

Incidental European descriptions and drawings give glimpses of the lives of the enslaved, mainly mediated through their relationships with their masters and the duties they performed.[19] Criminal proceedings before the Council of Justice in Colombo provide deeper insight into the lived experience of slaves as, in some cases, the enslaved themselves revealed details of their daily lives. While historians of the Cape and Batavia have made excellent use of such sources, much is still to be done for Sri Lanka.[20] Here, court cases and emancipation deeds are the starting points for teasing out the ties that connected slaves to the cosmopolitan spheres of Colombo and other ports.

Cases heard before the Dutch Council of Justice in Colombo involved slaves as victims, witnesses and perpetrators of criminal activity. Some of the court cases illuminate the violence of relations between slaves and the slave-owning class such as when the slave woman Tamar accused Pierre Laborde of rape in 1791. Other cases point to the emotional dishonour experienced by slaves such as the Javanese Itam, leading to an intense, violent outburst against his master Captain Johan Christiaan Emanuel Berski in 1774. Other cases relate specific life stories of slave-suspects and give us impressions of daily contacts and connections beyond the relationship with the master. For example, we encounter slaves like Floris, who ran away from his master three times, and each time found refuge with the Chetty Mannan Dias.[21] The 1794 case of Amber, Truna de Wangso and Andries brings cross-cultural connections and relationships that crossed the slave–free legal divide sharply into focus. Furthermore, the case gives an indication of where such ties were forged. The three men were accused of theft, having allegedly stolen a copper bowl. Amber was a slave of unknown origin, owned by the vice-*mudaliyar* of the Attepattu, Christoffel de Saram; Truna de Wangso was a Muslim convict from Demak, on Java, who arrived in Sri Lanka in 1784 and was set to work in the *materiaalhuis* (workhouse); Andries was noted down in the records as being Sinhalese but he did not appear in court because he had run away. The statements of the accused and witnesses were complicated, contradictory and confusing. Such a case reveals the wide-ranging local social connections forged by the men and women involved; it touches on the forced movement of people – slaves and convicts to Sri Lanka – through the broader Asian ties of the VOC; and it provides an indication of the sites of interaction, in this case the lively markets in the streets of Colombo.[22]

That slaves interacted and forged connections with different groups in Colombo also becomes clear from the emancipation deeds. The legal requirement for emancipation was that one or two individuals promised financial support for the manumitted slave for a period of six years. A cursory glance at the signatures provided by the guarantors reveals numerous Sinhalese and Tamil signatures, along with Xs indicating that the guarantor was illiterate. When the slave woman Cleopatra was freed in 1781, two sailors – Pieter Post and Jan Paulus – took on the responsibility of guarantors. In numerous cases free Sinhalese took on the responsibility, for example Daniel and Joan Fernando who signed as guarantors for three of the sixteen slaves emancipated by Anna Maria Giethoorn in August 1784. In three deeds signed in 1784, Philipie Pieris and Louis Gomes stood as guarantors for four slaves – Apollo, Juliaan, Christina and her child Agida. Philipie Pieris and Louis Gomes were described as *vissers* (fishermen) indicating they were of the Karava caste. The diversity of guarantors and manumitted individuals is striking. If the assumption of a relationship – emotional or pecuniary – between slave and guarantor is correct, it leads to the conclusion that slaves' contacts and connections were ample and integral to their lives both in bondage and in freedom.[23]

Cosmopolitanism in Biedermann and Strathern's first sense – that being cosmopolitan involves containing 'a world of plurality' within – was thrust upon slaves by their forced migration to the island; once there, slaves not only inhabited but also constituted and cultivated a 'world of plurality'. Slaves who were transported to the island from across the Indian Ocean were simultaneously thrust into and constitutive of the world of religious and ethnic diversity that was Colombo.[24] The above cases demonstrate the ways in which slaves lived out that cosmopolitanism, actively entering into relationships with others across lines of ethnicity, religion and legal status. Court cases and emancipation deeds reveal the variety of those relationships, from familial ties to criminal collusion. We should not lose sight of the fact that it was precisely the creation and maintenance of these connections that embedded slaves in their locality. We are left to wonder what the effect of these connections was – finding evidence to support the idea that interaction with the heterogeneous slave population expanded the horizons of the rest of society is almost impossible. Be that as it may, it is not hard to imagine that the worlds the enslaved remembered – religious, cultural, material, linguistic – were introduced in the market, in the streets of Colombo, and in the relationships that developed between slaves and free people of diverse backgrounds, including Sinhalese.[25]

A 1781 case of murder against a Malay slave woman named Deidamie suggests that the connections sketched out above were not the only ways in which slaves experienced or effected cosmopolitanism. Deidamie was accused of murdering her youngest child, a young boy named Filareuse. The company authorities were less interested in the murder per se than in the small letter that Deidamie was found to be carrying. Tracing Deidamie's connections, and thus following the route by which she came to be in possession of the 'letter', brings into view a world beyond her master's household, Colombo, and even the island. This points to the idea that, for some slaves at least, there were opportunities to cultivate connections beyond their locality.[26] The enslaved woman was denoted in the court documents only by her slave name, Deidamie, with no toponym. The only indication of her background is that she was described as Malay, likely an indication that she herself or her parents originated from Southeast Asia, possibly traded via Batavia.[27] During the murder case it came to light that Deidamie had been in possession of a small piece of paper inscribed with *maleijdse karacters* (Arabic letters). The attribution of protective powers and the suggestion that the text was a prayer from the Qur'an indicate that it was a talisman. Deidamie revealed that she received it from a Malay slave named Ontong. He had received the talisman from a Malay soldier named Draman, who, although from Java, resided in Colombo. This again reinforces our impression of the interaction among the town's underclass. The man from Java, Draman, had not made the talisman himself; he received it from a 'priest' in Batavia, presumably referring to a Muslim religious leader. Thus, over and above the social connections between slave and free within Colombo, we see the connections forged between three Malay individuals in the city, and through those connections a link to the Muslim community of Batavia.

While we cannot be sure of the significance Deidamie attached to the talisman in terms of how she identified herself religiously, we should be aware of the risk that carrying such a talisman might have constituted for the enslaved woman. She surely would not have concealed it in her hair as she did if she did not attach some power to being in possession of it; nor would she have hidden its origins from the court when investigated, if it were not a risk. The VOC authorities were certainly very concerned about the talisman and expended much energy on determining its origins. They also had it translated by a Malay sergeant, thus coming to the conclusion that it was a prayer. Perhaps Deidamie was merely 'talisman-shopping'; nor can we discount the possibility that it was a signifier of belonging to a spiritual world that, although facilitated by the Dutch imperial web in the Indian Ocean, extended beyond that Dutch world. This case shows just how difficult it is to draw conclusions about belonging in the absence of sources such as memoirs or personal letters in which individuals themselves express or reflect upon identity. This is surely not only true of the enslaved, but extends to all social strata. What we can say is that Deidamie's actions raise the possibility that she herself chose to cultivate a sense of belonging in this wider spiritual world, which not only connected her to slaves and non-slaves in her immediate surroundings but linked her to co-religionists in the Indonesian archipelago. Perhaps this is an example of an enslaved woman taking part in what Ronit Ricci has called the 'Arabic Cosmopolis'.[28] Deidamie may have been cosmopolitan both in the sense that she inhabited and constituted a 'world of plurality' and that she sought to be a part of a world beyond that locality, albeit one marked by a single religion.

This section on slave experiences in Colombo is a snapshot of daily aspects of the lives of Colombo slaves. From these cases, a somewhat veiled picture emerges of the Dutch period, during which Sri Lankan society connected to new regions and peoples from the Indian Ocean world even at the lowest level of society, or perhaps we should say in particular at that level. This added yet another layer to the existing political, mercantile and religious networks of which, over time, the island had become a part. Slaves from around the Indian Ocean who were transported to Colombo became embedded in Lankan society through the creation and maintenance of connections to people across ethnic, religious and legal-status lines. Deidamie's relationships point to the supra-local quality that such connections could take on. Slavery in Sri Lanka is not a neat story, but rather one of contradictions of security and of violence, pressures and dependency, a type of duress that these people shared with many others across the Indian Ocean who got entangled in the Dutch world.

## Who were they to judge? Slavery in a European legal cosmopolis

Even if borders between Kandy and Dutch Sri Lanka had been formally drawn, in practice the inland and coastal areas of Sri Lanka were never completely separated from each other.[29] In fact, in some instances records from the coast allow us insights into deeper connections between the two areas and practices that are otherwise difficult to document for Kandy. In 1780, a Sinhalese woman from the Kandyan kingdom was tried in Colombo by the Dutch because she had sold her child there as a slave. What happened to the child we do not know, but the Sinhalese woman was sentenced to corporal punishment and to work for five years in chains.[30] Yet, who were the Dutch to judge? If slavery was part and parcel of Dutch activities in Sri Lanka and beyond, this judgment seems quite out of place. It signposts the emergence of a legal or normative world – a cosmopolis, in Biedermann and Strathern's second sense of the term cosmopolitan, perhaps? – where Dutch or European conceptions of slavery and freedom were imposed on existing structures and practices. Through the lens of slavery we very clearly observe what the implications of these legal entanglements were.

Living with the Dutch implied an imposition of the Dutch legal apparatus, but at the same time the institutional and procedural set-up that came along with it opened up possibilities for negotiation as we see in the case of yet another woman, named Helena. In the early 1790s Helena accused her so-called master of claiming her as his property, while she insisted on being a free woman. She disagreed with the verdict of the court, which was in favour of the Chetty master, and appealed to Batavia for redress.[31] Helena or her parents might have come from Batavia, but in any case, seeking redress in the distant regional headquarters of the VOC reflects a consciousness, or at least an imagination, of being part of a world of Dutch institutions and norms that stretched beyond Sri Lanka. The Dutch world of institutions and regulations had become a reality for inhabitants of Sri Lanka like Helena and the Kandyan woman who had tried to sell her child. Their cases were judged by the Council of Justice in Colombo, the highest court on the island. It was presided over by Dutchmen only, who in theory adjudicated cases according to Dutch regulations. In practice, most of these men spent the larger part of their careers in Asia if they weren't born there themselves, and may well have been influenced by local customs.

This section sets out to describe the Dutch institutional set-up with which Lankans actively engaged. The institutions themselves were more dependent on negotiations than their typical Dutch names may lead us to believe. Legal institutions formed clusters in the three main towns, each of which had its court for civil cases (*Civiele Stadsraad*) and a Council of Justice (*Raad van Justitie*) for criminal cases and those civil cases with large sums of money at stake. Beyond Colombo, Galle and Jaffna, *Landraden*, or rural courts, were set up to adjudicate in civil disputes in those inland parts where the Dutch claimed territorial rule. Over time the number of these courts increased to eleven. As was common in Europe at the time, there was no division of powers and so the VOC's main administrators were also involved in the courts. In each town a public prosecutor (*fiscaal*) was appointed who also held police powers for the town and its direct surroundings.[32] The ties between the legal institutions in the island were hierarchical and in turn connected to the Council of Justice in Batavia, which functioned as a supreme court in the VOC world. Within the island, it was possible to appeal to Colombo's Council of Justice from the other towns; beyond that – as we have seen in Helena's case – one could appeal to the Council of Justice in Batavia, where the legal circuit ended.

Courtrooms like the *Landraad* or the Council of Justice may have had a very Dutch outlook on paper, but as Rupesinghe shows, they functioned as arenas of cross-cultural encounters that featured victims, perpetrators and witnesses from all segments of society, with Dutch and indigenous elites functioning as judges and with local advisors and translators at work. As early as 1619 the board of directors of the VOC in the Netherlands, the Gentlemen Seventeen, had announced that Batavia should adopt the laws and practices of the provinces of Holland, while specific local issues were to be dealt with in an ad hoc manner via ordinances (*plakkaten*) following customary and Roman law.[33] This left space for local negotiation and response, and the performance of the courts in practice was highly dependent on location and the specific issues at stake.

Legally and officially, slavery did not exist in the Dutch Republic, but was practised nonetheless in all Company settlements and factories. In 1642 the numerous ordinances that had already been issued in Batavia were gathered together and printed as the Statutes of Batavia, and henceforth adopted as the basis for government in all company settlements. The statutes included a slave code that had developed through years of practice in Batavia and was inspired by a Roman, or Justinian, conception of slavery as an absolute state.[34] In places like Ceylon, the Statutes of Batavia, including the slave code, were important as guidelines for the administration of justice. The slave code regulated, among other things, slave-ownership, the public behaviour of slaves and master–slave relations.

The legal system that the Dutch created across the Indian Ocean carried a sense of unity through the Statutes of Batavia, while in the different settlements the Statutes were amplified in response to specific local or supra-local issues throughout the period. This 'on the spot law-making' was situational and should be understood as responsive rather than pre-emptive. As a consequence, the ordinances have to be understood in the specific context in which they were proclaimed. These contexts could be local, or could relate to interests elsewhere in the VOC world. An example of such a responsive local ordinance that relates to very specific circumstances is the Colombo ordinance of 1660 that forbade all slave trade within and from the island. Some historians have anachronistically labelled this ordinance as humanitarian.[35] However, to properly understand the function of this ordinance, one needs to evaluate the immediate context in which it was issued. The war with the Portuguese had only recently come to an end and had left the countryside in ruins. The Dutch aimed at restoring social order and settlement and this regulation was part of that project. It should not be misunderstood as a general humanitarian attitude to slavery. It was in this same period that the Dutch exported more than 10,000 slaves from South India, of whom a share ended up in Colombo and Galle presumably to work on the fortifications and restore infrastructure after the war, while the rest were transported to Batavia.[36]

The argument of local order and efficiency is repeated a year later in the 1661 instructions for the dessave in Matara. They mention the practice of people selling themselves and their families into slavery to local chiefs. It is explicitly stated that this practice, if continued, would lead to a depopulation of the land and hence a decrease in revenue. The prohibition of selling free people here is further motivated by a strangely misplaced enthusiastic expression of the respect of freedom: 'een yders vrijheid is 't kostelijke goed des aardbodems' ('everyone's freedom is the greatest good on earth'). Surely, it reveals some rhetoric of 'liberty' and humanitarianism at work, but this was fundamentally secondary to pragmatic and strategic objectives.[37]

Another example of an ordinance that can easily be misunderstood is one from 1685 that forbade the import of slaves from South India into the Ceylon ports.[38] Again, pragmatism ruled: the document itself explains that the Company dearly needed the slaves on the spot. Rules and regulations about slave trade and imports always have to be understood in the light of interrelated stakes at the various VOC strongholds in the Indian Ocean. About ten years later the issue was no longer considered pressing; in 1695 around 3,500 slaves were imported into Jaffna by local traders, as evidenced by the import duties paid.[39]

Overall, the Batavia and Colombo ordinances that dealt with slavery can be divided into those regulating 1) slave ownership (who owned slaves, and which religions the latter practised; legal proof of ownership required); 2) trade and transportation of enslaved persons; 3) punitive measures against slaves; 4) sexual, social and commercial relations of slaves (concubinage, gambling and entering contracts prohibited); and 5) public behaviour of slaves, in particular in relations to dress and religion (no hats, no shoes, no conversion or baptism allowed).[40] Court cases dealing with extremely violent masters, questionable proof of ownership or manumission, and slaves involved in illicit trade indeed appeared before the criminal and civil courts. Helena essentially disputed the legality of her slave status. Her disputed master was a local Chetty, which reminds us that the Dutch ordinances were not merely regulating the relationship between Europeans and their slaves, but also among other social groups.[41]

Slave owners included Dutch men and women, Chetties, 'Moors', Sinhalese and Tamil *mudaliyars* and lower chiefs, and other Europeans. While slaves could have a great variety of backgrounds, from Madagascar to Manila, they or their parents were most likely to come from around the Bay of Bengal, Malabar or Eastern Indonesia. Although the norms of all these groups regarding important issues of bondage and freedom, and status and social relations, would have differed, the ordinances reveal the attempts made by the Dutch to create some sort of unity to keep control over the communities of slaves and masters within their jurisdiction. Locally created ordinances were communicated through translation into Sinhala and Tamil, and they were presumably read aloud and stuck on walls of important buildings and trees. People like Helena, who were aware of this and tried to use it to their own benefit, had the chance to become agents in the legal cosmopolis.

The extent to which the Dutch regulations were applied literally in court is difficult to establish. The Kandyan woman mentioned above did not receive the death penalty, even though that was the legally established punishment for her misdeed. In the case of Ali van Makassar, who appeared before the court around the same time, no capital punishment was given for his second offence of house-breaking because, as the governor argued, he was unfamiliar with the stipulated punishment for his crime.[42] Ordinances were responsive, and so was the actual application of these rules in court. The ordinances represent an attempt at merging various legal traditions and experiences into one normative order, which the Dutch administrators in turn inconsistently imposed on local inhabitants and which some local inhabitants tried to use to their own benefit. This adaptive practice has made the Dutch presence on the island appear so elusive. Ordinances and court cases can be studied as expressions of Dutch rule, but through the lens of slavery we see very clearly how general Dutch norms, local considerations and supra-local stakes played out in practice. It shows that the everyday interaction between society and the state was much more complex and had much deeper local implications – which in turn reflected transoceanic connections – precisely because so many different groups participated.

## The slippery grounds of codification: social hierarchies, freedom and bondage in Jaffna

Along with their slaves, the Dutch brought a Justinian conception of slavery as the complete opposite of freedom. For slaves, the business of achieving freedom was regulated through notarial deeds. Considering the repetition of ordinances on this matter we can assume, however, that this was not always acted upon. Moreover, manumission could also be used by the Company as a tool for social engineering. In the late 1760s, the Dutch transported a number of 'slave' families from Jaffna to Puliyanthivu, in Batticaloa, to work in freedom as toddy tappers. These families were actually of the landless Naḷava caste, whom the Dutch labelled as a slave caste in an act of bold ethnographic-legal interpretation, applying their rigid notions to the way the Naḷava were treated by their Vellala or high-caste masters. In 1771, the VOC published a reminder that the Naḷavas of Batticaloa were to be considered free.[43] Apparently this was to no avail, as twenty years later, the Dutch administrator of Batticaloa complained that despite the granted freedom, wealthy Vellalas continued to lay claim to these families.[44] The tension we observe here may be generated by the fact that local conceptions of freedom were much more complicated than the Dutch imagined. In fact, one may wonder whether there was an indigenous legal concept of freedom comparable to that of Roman law, or rather a complex hierarchy of social obligations.

Everywhere on the island, caste served as the basis of local labour extraction and the VOC always found ways of appropriating service labour. Only in Jaffna, however, did slavery and caste-base service labour become closely intertwined. The Company identified four castes as slave castes: the Chandios,[45] Koviyar ('Cowias'), Naḷava ('Nalluas') and Paḷḷar ('Palluas'). In fact, the VOC kept a number of people of the Naḷava and Paḷḷar castes as slaves within the workhouse in the Jaffna fort, where a total of about eighty slaves were kept, and demanded service labour or remuneration (*chikos*) from those living under their masters in the countryside.

The tension between the Dutch absolute definition of slavery, as promulgated in the general ordinances from Colombo and Batavia, and the local definition of slavery is clearly visible in the Thesawalamai, or the Jaffna customary law, drawn up by a Dutch administrator in 1707, in consultation with 12 *mudaliyars*. The curious history and legacy of the Thesawalamai has been studied before.[46] The text was produced in 1707 in response to a request by the rural court for better knowledge of local customs. The task was assigned to the Dutch *dessave* Isaac Isaaksz. He used his thirty-seven years of experience in court as a basis for a report that he had translated into Tamil and read and commented upon by the twelve major chiefs in the region. While we do not know exactly how the code was used in court, it remained an important text for the Tamil population in the British period and beyond.[47] The text has been analysed by legal scholars, and some have pointed out the influence of Roman-Dutch and Portuguese law on issues such as property.[48] When read closely, these rules and regulations also offer vivid insight into aspects of daily life in Jaffna. The Thesawalamai is an early example of Europeans fixing and appropriating indigenous customary laws through close cooperation with local elites, a theme that has been studied for Bengal through the activities of William Jones and others. In Jaffna, it was the Vellala chiefs who were involved in the production of the text, and who most likely benefited from it.[49] They certainly had a stake in labelling certain groups in society as slaves and in defining the rights of masters over these people.

We encounter slaves and slave trade throughout the code, such as in the sections on inheritance, pawning and transfer of property. References made to slaves in these instances resonate with those of the ordinances, in the sense that slaves are referred to as a homogeneous legal category. Slaves formed transferable property and could be bought and sold, inherited and manumitted at the will of the owner. Usufruct of cows, sheep and slave women are dealt with in the same section.[50] No mention is made here of the legal proof of slavery necessary in these transactions, such as that demanded elsewhere in the island according to the ordinances. Ownership of slaves, their children and their property must have given rise to much conflict, as the numerous stipulations in this respect suggest. The final paragraph in the section on transfer of property deals with the practice of selling children in times of duress. Here the general rule applied, according to which free persons could not be sold into slavery. Yet the regulation refers to the practices nonetheless, narrating how people from Matara sometimes sold their children in Jaffna and pointing out that these parents had always had the right to buy back their children at a reasonable price as soon as their situation allowed it.[51]

Apart from these brief references made to various practices, a whole separate section of the text was devoted to the legal situation of slaves. This section covers about 10 per cent of the total text, indicating the importance of the issue to Jaffna society.[52] Here the group of slaves discussed turns out to be heterogeneous, with different historic foundations and different rights and obligations. The Chandios and the Koviyar were called 'slave castes', although it is mentioned that in practice not many slaves were found among the Chandios anymore. Apparently Koviyars, upon achieving freedom, would often have themselves registered as Chandios, inadvertently indicating a degree of inter-caste mobility. The Chandios and Koviyar were presumed to have entered slavery in the recent past, although it is not said how exactly this happened. As with the children from Matara sold by their parents, the history of having once been free but subsequently enslaved through misfortune provided them with a distinct legal status. One could say that they were better off in comparison to the Naḷavas and Paḷḷars to whom the Dutch referred as '*erfslaven*', that is, hereditary slaves. The Chandios and Koviyar could rely on more privileges and protection from their masters than the Naḷavas and Paḷḷars. For example, when a child was born, the master would have to send Chandios and Koviyar mothers a larger sum of money as a gift than to a new mother of the Naḷava or Paḷḷar caste.

The Naḷavas and Paḷḷars came closest to the Dutch concept of absolute slaves. Enslaved individuals from these groups were owned by the Dutch along with the slaves who originated from elsewhere in the Indian Ocean. The entitlement to ownership over these people claimed by the Dutch went further than simply appropriating service labour. How this worked is made explicit in the first paragraph of the slavery section: the Company would by custom be entitled to one out of five or six children – boys and girls – born of the marriage between a Naḷava or Paḷḷar slave owned by the Company and a slave woman from the countryside. While presumably these Company Naḷavas and Paḷḷars lived in circumstances similar to other slaves kept by the VOC in the island, the situation differed for those in the countryside. The latter lived separate from their masters, and made their living out of agriculture. Masters did not impose a continuous demand on their labour, even though they were in control. Young boys could be taken out of the household to perform long-term duties for the masters, such as keeping herds.[53]

The Dutch had no interest in prohibiting indigenous slavery in Jaffna as they did in the southwest, because it provided them with a regular source of labour. And so the Dutch adapted their norms to the local practices, while simultaneously imposing their own. That the Dutch saw the Naḷavas and Paḷḷars as equal to slaves brought from overseas is clear from the section that discusses the right of masters to punish manumitted slaves if they publicly insulted their former master. Despite explicit petitioning by the twelve *mudaliyars* in this respect, the

Dutch decided that such cases were to fall under the provisions (slave code) of the Batavian Statutes.[54] This illustrates how Dutch conceptions of authority and norms regarding punishments were imposed upon local customary traditions. Overall, the Thesawalamai leaves us with a complex panorama of local and supra-local concepts, laws and practices and their negotiation between the VOC and the Jaffna elites.

The Dutch sanctioned indigenous practices of slavery through their legal codification and at the same time some of their own norms regarding slavery crept into their codification of these practices. So far, we know little of how the local traditions and Dutch norms played out in court.[55] What we do know is that the Dutch appropriated the labour of Naḷavas and Paḷḷars, but to what extent the Dutch were involved in the making and unmaking of slaves is unclear. Yet the scattered sources provide us with some hints. The story of the eighty or so Naḷavas living in freedom under the Company's protection in Batticaloa suggests that manumission occurred: the Company had taken the liberty to free them from what it considered to be their slave status. The Company officials presumably followed the reasoning that if these people were legally slaves, they could also be legally free. The opposite occurred as well: we know that by the late eighteenth century, the local *Commandeur* appropriated around 140 Naḷava and Paḷḷarr slaves from the chiefs in lieu of tax arrears. These people were then sold on the market as regular slaves, to the outrage of the local chiefs and probably themselves.[56]

The complex story of slavery and customary law in Jaffna further illustrates the tension between Dutch norms and local practices. The Dutch recognized the need to create security and order through legal fora and legislation. Through the lens of slavery we see how the Dutch kept local rules in practice, while intervening when they sensed that their authority was threatened. The fact that they considered aspects of the Batavian Slave Code applicable to indigenous 'slave-castes' underlines how, from a legal point of view, the Dutch framed Jaffna slaves in absolute terms, just as they did in other parts of the Indian Ocean. But in practice, the use of the Naḷavas and Paḷḷars as transferable property turned out to be problematic when the Dutch unilaterally freed these people from their hereditary bondage. It was regarding freedom, rather than over bondage, that the Dutch clashed with the Vellalar elites. The Thesawalamai as a product of Vellalar–Dutch synergy and competition signals a process whereby the lower strata of Jaffna society became more rigidly controlled. A question that remains to be answered is how people responded to the classification and what the long-term impact was: did it result in more rigid social relations and hence a society less open to external influences and contact?[57]

## Conclusion

The Dutch, who brought slaves to an island where various forms of social bondage comparable to, but not always identical with, slavery existed, also brought with them conceptions and norms about what slavery and freedom entailed. These were grounded in Roman law and in the Dutch experience in Batavia. Rules and regulations regarding slaves and slavery were then shaped over time through an engagement with Lankan practices of bondage and slavery. As we saw, the various conceptions played out in codification practices and in court and as such are exemplary of hybrid practices of socio-legal negotiation during the Dutch period.

Slavery as such was not new to Sri Lanka, and at least from the Portuguese period onwards, slaves had been actively imported into the island. According to late seventeenth-century censuses, slaves formed the larger part of the urban inhabitants in the coastal port cities. Their backgrounds varied greatly, encompassing provenance zones from Africa to Southeast Asia. Slaves were thus part of a connected world of forced migration that also included convicts and exiles. Furthermore, they inhabited towns and cities that were diverse in ethnicity, religion and language. In this way, slaves were both constituents and inhabitants of cosmopolitan spaces. However, slavery and cosmopolitanism are an uncomfortable match, not least because slaves did not choose to be part of those localities themselves. In cases such as that of Deidamie, the enslaved Malay woman who lived in Colombo, we get closer to seeing slaves actively seeking to be part of a world – in this case spiritual – that transcended the master's household, Colombo and the island. To speak of cosmopolitanism in her case seems more appropriate than in others. Understanding the worlds the enslaved imagined themselves to be part of helps us understand the underclass that shaped Sri Lanka's coastal towns in the eighteenth century.

When we turn to the legal cosmopolis that slaves inhabited we see the diversity of experience exemplified in the Kandyan woman and Helena. While the Kandyan woman seemed to have been dominated by the system, Helena understood the wider institutional world of which she was a part and managed to navigate her way through it, requesting redress in the Supreme Court in Batavia to dispute her alleged slave status. Batavia was central to the legal order in VOC Sri Lanka as the Statutes of Batavia formed the foundation of Company law. The ordinances promulgated in the island were very clearly responsive, issued in an ad hoc manner and constantly amplifying the statutes in existence. The ordinances were, we have argued, an attempt to bring together legal traditions and experiences from various regions into one normative order. As noted, to what extent those rules and regulations were enforced in courts at all levels remains unclear. For its part, the Thesawalamai highlights the tension between local and imported conceptions of slavery and freedom. Untangling the relationship between slavery in the Roman legal sense, slave-castes and service labour is an avenue of research that needs to be pursued further and should incorporate the responses to such classification by the subjects involved. What this chapter has demonstrated is that through investigating VOC law-making, codification and legal practice, the interface between Dutch norms, local considerations and supra-local stakes comes into focus.

Along with the Dutch came a plurality of peoples, practices and norms with origins outside the island. We have seen instances where this prompted people to look outwards, such as Helena and Deidamie. At the same time, we signalled the process of localization of European concepts of slavery in Jaffna, a process that may have been detrimental to the interests of members of the Naḷavar and Paḷḷar castes. This in particular signals the downside to the workings of cosmopolitanism under coercive empires. Living with the Dutch implied living in a contradictory world: it is clear that human trafficking within the island was discouraged by law, although practised to some extent, and that the Dutch attempted to control the trade of humans to the island, but that there was a continuous import nonetheless.

The Dutch legal space across the Indian Ocean then could be seen as operating on both levels of cosmopolitanism suggested in the introduction to this volume. This chapter shows a Dutch legal cosmopolis at work, containing a world of plurality that was adaptable and locally responsive to some extent. At the same time, it allowed coastal Sri Lanka to participate in a much larger field of unity, insofar as the Dutch legal system did after all maintain its own integrity. While slavery was at one extreme end of the societal spectrum of Sri Lankan society and the Dutch Empire, it was central to the lived experience of many people on the island and central to colonial law-making. The lens of slavery has helped us to situate Sri Lanka more firmly in the eighteenth-century Indian Ocean World and move towards a more critical understanding of Dutch colonialism.

# 10

# Cosmopolitanism and indigeneity in four violent years: the fall of the kingdom of Kandy and the Great Rebellion revisited

*Sujit Sivasundaram*

The period 1815 to 1819 was tumultuous in the history of Sri Lanka as its politics swung between opposite poles.[1] The British accomplished what the Portuguese and Dutch had not achieved: the final subjugation of the kingdom of Kandy, marked by the deposition of the island's last king and his deportation to India together with his relatives. Buddha's Tooth Relic – the critical signifier of the right to rule – was appropriated by the British. Even the royal throne was sent to London. Two years after these indisputable marks of the advance of European colonization there occurred an extensive rebellion against foreign rule, which spread across the Kandyan territories. The rebellion picked up on the loss of the kingly line; the Tooth Relic was secretly stolen for the rebel cause and a pretender was enthroned. The British could contemplate the possibility of losing Kandy. This was a quick about-turn in politics. The twists and turns were accompanied at every point by the use of violence, the practice of plunder and burning was widespread, and famine was one result of these years.

These four years have not attracted sustained study as a stand-alone subject since P. E. Pieris' monumental and narrative *Sinhalé and the Patriots, 1815–1818*, which appeared two years after Ceylon's independence. For Pieris, the agenda was to honour the 'men and women and children who died for an ideal of a Community... as Patriots'.[2] Yet the nation was not founded so easily in resistance to colonialism. In 1815 to 1819, kingdom and nation, indigeneity and cosmopolitanism were repositioned and rebalanced, in accelerated fashion, in the various localities of the Kandyan periphery and ruling centres. They were redefined with respect to the memory of kingship and around the rise of the British. Such a non-teleological view of the 'end' of early modernity is essential in understanding the present Sri Lankan nation and its rich and violent contradictoriness.

It is a historiographical cliché that the 1817–18 rebellion was 'a real turning-point in the history of Sri Lanka'.[3] One of the burdens of this chapter is to return to the archive, beyond Pieris or even Vimalananda, the latter of whom published a set of primary sources from this period, to focus on the question of how early modern kingly and local conceptions of cosmopolitanism and indigeneity were restructured and absorbed by the arrival of the modern colonial state.[4] It is easy – especially following the important, ambitiously comparative and anthropologically inflected work of Alan Strathern – to see the parallels across time in the 'grammar of rebellion'.[5] Yet the impulse of this chapter and *Islanded* is slightly different.[6] The thrust of the argument comes from its engagement with a virulent debate in late eighteenth- and early nineteenth-century South Asian historiography, connected with how the British came to conquer South Asia, through a reliance on 'military-fiscalism', indigenous financiers and landowners, knowledge-brokers and 'subsidiary alliance' with princely states, followed by direct annexation at times.[7] In dismissing the dichotomy of continuity versus change, this chapter is challenging the terms of this specific literature. Such a dismissal does not deny the existence of either of these features, but insists on a more complex picture of reassembly. Past precedent *and* new innovation both featured. The British sought to connect themselves to the extant indigenous, even while recrafting it over and over again. This early nineteenth-century sense of the indigenous encompassed Kandyan tradition and also included Dutch and Portuguese practice, and descendants of both these colonizers who were sometimes termed 'native'.[8] Simultaneously, the British innovated with modes of state-making, surveillance, administrative and legislative reform and bureaucracy. It was the combination of these two contradictory impulses and the momentum with which they were pursued – on an island – that helps explain the violence of this moment.

In work elsewhere, I have utilized analytical terms that highlight that this reassembly was dynamic and yet incomplete: 'islanding', 'partitioning', 'recycling' and 'movement'. Its power and legacy for the twentieth century lay in these features. To stress long-term continuities over the early modern centuries is valuable. Such a view needs to contend with how the early modern ends in Lanka and what the links are between the early modern and the twentieth century, especially given later conceptions of territory, belonging and nationhood. In the account that follows, the entanglement of cosmopolitanism and indigeneity around the monarch or within specific locales in Kandy had a legacy for the period that follows. This counts as transition from the early modern, but not a dividing line, not a singular transition from one form to another, or a simple continuation of established patterns. In other words, the British had a lasting effect in ushering in late modernity, but the coming of that modernity in the late eighteenth and early nineteenth centuries was a rollercoaster, where the benchmarks of assessment cannot be taken for granted. Those benchmarks and their memory were redefined in the process. The early British islanding of Lanka narrowed prior pathways and was at an unprecedented scale; it was bequeathed unfinished to later colonial racialists and even later Lankan nationalists.

One further issue with following a narrative of continuity or change in discussing the British advent lies in how such explanations fall inevitably into colonial discourses that were circulating in the early nineteenth century. Take governor Robert Brownrigg, who went to war with Kandy in 1815 and crushed the ensuing rebellion. Towards the end of the period, he wrote that his troops were fatigued with warfare; the 'Constitution and Physical Powers' of both fighting European and 'natives' were exhausted. It was in this context that he envisaged the loss of Kandy: it would weaken 'the Force among the Nations of the Indian Continent of that Opinion of the invincible power of the British arms'.[9] Using the ascendant language of rule of the British imperial meridian in the late eighteenth and early nineteenth centuries, Brownrigg noted the need for 'the effectual maintenance of the Sovereignty of the United Kingdom, over the whole Island'. The eighteenth-century political unification of Britain on the one hand and the island on the other are brought together as processes that witness sovereignty exercised over the natural territory of the whole of these islands, taken as singular political units.[10]

Brownrigg also took the view that the Sinhalese were aware of the momentous changes: rebellion was an expected response. In Ūva, for instance, in the context of plunder and war, Brownrigg noted the 'abuses which it was not possible entirely to prevent' inflicted by his troops, and the need to appease the inhabitants of the 'new order of things'; and to deal with the 'fear of innovation upon established customs, powers and emoluments and that large part of confusion which necessarily takes place in great and sudden changes in publick affairs'.[11]

As the rebellion proceeded, further provinces fell: it spread from Ūva and Vellassa to Dumbara, Hēvahäta, the Seven Kōraḷēs and other Kandyan territories. As this occurred, there appeared a diametrically opposite account of this moment. Instead of it being characterized by Brownrigg as one of revolutionary or 'great and sudden' change, it was said to be a continuation of the timeless past. Brownrigg wrote to London:

> A greater facility also is afforded to factions and intriguing spirits, to raise disturbances in this Country at present, from Commotions having at all times been frequent in it. The little knowledge we have of Kandyan History, displays a continuation of rebellion on the part of the subjects and cruelties on the part of the Kings. That the former might be often the effect as well as the cause of the latter may be easily conceived, but the consequence on the minds of the Inhabitants has been that the moment any person of sufficient influence, to give them a command to revolt against the established Government directs it, they hide their Property and Families in the Woods, take up Arms with which every Man is provided, ostensibly for the defence of the Crops against Wild Beasts, being either Muskets or Bows and Arrows (more frequently the latter) and abandoning their dwellings follow their Leaders through the Country, hiding in Caves or

any other Places of concealment when closely pressed. The Manufacture of Gunpowder is general and of very ancient practise throughout the Country.[12]

In keeping with the claims marshalled in *Islanded*, what follows traces the rapidly changeable politics, ideology and state-making of this period around the themes of indigeneity and cosmopolitanism. Kandy was not a closed kingdom that was easily transformed by British takeover. Nor was British colonialism strong enough or confident enough to project its ideologies of sovereignty, governance and statehood, without reference to Kandyan norms (and indeed to past colonial practice). These years saw many people seeking to adopt the mantle of kingship: including Britons, ex-monks, Kandyan chiefs and supposed 'strangers' parading as Malabars. At the same time, a view of the nation was circulating in this period and it was turning increasingly ethnicized: such a discourse again was a compound result of the colonial as well as the indigenous, evident in both palm-leaf texts as well as the colonial archive. It has been described as associational and popular and it was a ratcheting up of ethnicization evident in prior centuries.[13] By the 1830s, as it became tied up with a bureaucratizing state, the nation came to overtake, if not wipe out, the memory of the kingdom. Now, British laws and regimes of paperwork dictated who the strangers and indigenes were, evident most potently in pronouncements about migrants. In these ways the shift from a king to a British governor is a story of the repeatedly changing relative placements of indigeneity and cosmopolitanism. The momentum of these changes together with their links to the past counted as a slow and less than total end to the early modern. This means that the beginning of modern Sri Lanka cannot be dated precisely to 1833, the supposed date of implementation of the Colebrooke-Cameron reforms.[14]

This chapter uses indigeneity and cosmopolitanism as an interlinked pair.[15] The fall of Kandy, the conduct of war, violence and plunder and then rebellion and the consolidation of a new British state can be approached as events that define and redefine the meanings of and links between indigeneity and cosmopolitanism. At the core of the idea of the Kandyan king was a notion of political Sinhalaness that was ethnicized. Yet it could not work without the services and symbolic capital connected to foreigners, such as Muslim doctors or Malabar traders, and even Malabar kings. The court and the body of the king may then be seen as a galactic field, where elements are drawn to the centre through the force of ritual, service or tribute.[16] This is why artefacts – such as the Tooth Relic or the golden sword of the king – were vital elements and even agents in determining the course of this story; for they linked the provinces to the centre in acts of adoration and obeisance. This notion of the kingdom was thus indigenous and cosmopolitan at the same time and lasted well into the period of British rule. Such a complex is also evident at the local level in Kandyan territories, for instance in the organization of villages in areas that witnessed rebellion. Yet such local and monarchic cosmopolitanism, resting around a sense of Sinhalaness, was resituated more than once by the British advance. In the new state, indigenes and 'strangers' were separated out as belonging in different places as legal advisers and bureaucrats specified new boundaries, for instance between the island and mainland. Later, free trade imperialism dictated the redefinition of the indigene yet again.

In other words, the Kandyan state or its people cannot be classed as a chronologically static terrain of otherness to the cosmopolitan colonial. Nor can the British advance be taken as a straightforward given in its invention of the indigenous. Rather the challenge of working on this short period is to tease apart the violent tussle over concepts that ensued on all sides, and to contextualize this in relation to the changing composition of the people in the Kandyan territories as fighters, traders, religious men and pilgrims felt the severity of invasion. By implication too, it is not the role of every historian to jump across centuries. Focusing on four years allows a deeper engagement with primary materials, and with the multiple dimensions, involving the imperial state as much as extra-colonial agents; the undoubted invasion of the British imperial state as much as its powerfully uneven borrowings, alliances and effects.

***

Cosmopolitanism and indigeneity were being repositioned not only at court but in the local provinces of the Kandyan territories, in areas where there were separate villages of predominantly Sinhala, Tamil or Muslim residents, and the discussion therefore begins at ground level to trace this tussle over concepts in such villages.

Some revealing observations, which are in manuscript and so understudied, come from travelling officers and representatives of the British government, in provinces taken by the British in 1815. Major Henry Hardy travelled out of Kandy on 8 May 1815, a couple of months after the kingdom's fall, and reached Badulla, journeying at first on the banks of the Mahaväli river and noting the features of the country and its agricultural potential. He called Ūva 'the Garden of Ceylon', and on the way from Passara to Attila collected a specimen of the bark and root of a cinnamon tree, which had 'attained an extraordinary growth'.[17] Yet in contrast to the abundant signs of natural life, he noted that every village on the route to Kataragama was 'entirely deserted' because they had been plundered of 'every thing they possessed, as well by our profligate coolies as by our disorderly Native troops'. His account strikes an uneasy balance between, on the one hand, an aestheticized description of the natural scenery and its potential for commercial improvement and, on the other, an unusually frank catalogue of crimes of war. This unique combination arose because the commentary was intended simply for the eyes of the governing elite: in fact Hardy would become Governor Brownrigg's aide de camp, a trusted confidential advisor, and he would be critical in the suppression of the rebellion of 1817–18.[18]

At Attila, the complaints of the villagers regarding plunder were directed against Malay soldiers who had quartered there: the villagers had 'been left with their Lives and nothing more'. In responding to these complaints, Hardy stressed the benevolence and justice of the British government. He alleged that the plunder had been undertaken by an unrepresentative minority. In Kataragama, which became a critical site for the rebellion that followed, Hardy noted that the scene was one of 'desolation' and depopulation. The temple only contained 'one inferior sort of Priest, an ignorant ill clothed creature & a more venerable looking Bramin'. The 'wealth of the Temple' had been taken by a British detachment and many of the houses had been 'unroofed for firewood'.[19] Indeed, a series of temples were plundered in the aftermath of the signing of the treaty ceding the kingdom to the British.[20]

After an annotation in the manuscript, 'From Boettle, 7th June', is an account of how the principal inhabitants of the Buttala met Hardy and Simon Sawers. Sawers took up the office of revenue commissioner in Kandy in 1816 and later became judicial commissioner in Kandy, and was now travelling with Hardy. The Buttala inhabitants met the party with tom toms, and there were soon 400 of them. There were many women who 'came to stare at [them] from a distance'.[21] Hardy wrote: 'The men came about us with the utmost confidence; they tell me that no act of oppression has been committed of late by our Soldiers'. Critically, in considering this observation, Hardy noted that Buttala had a 'great part' of Malabar residents ('Malabar' being a period term for the community who were later called Tamil), who had connections to Batticaloa on the coast, indicating perhaps an interest in trade. Hardy praised these people as 'frank and well disposed'. Revealingly, given the events of the rebellion to follow, which was led by Käppiṭipola, the Disāva of Ūva, 'they [the Malabars] labour under severe impositions from the Dessave of Ouva, who they tell me is now going about the Country laying contributions among them'.

It was after meeting these allegedly friendly Malabars that Hardy thought back to his earlier encounters in Ūva, noted above, writing: 'There is certainly to be observed a curious cold disposition on the part of the Chingalese [Sinhalese] and somehow they do not appear anxious to have us.' In an example of the contemporary theory of dramatic change witnessed in these years, he wrote that Ūva was in a 'state of anarchy', because the established headmen did not know whether they had the backing of the new English government. These episodes bear the signs of colonial ethnographic categorization, for instance pointing to the hard-pressed Malabars and their suspicion of the Sinhalese chief. Yet, this is a text which is formed *in situ*, and Hardy's views are forged through his conversations with local people and as he travelled from village to village and compared episodes. The view of ethnic rivalry which it presents was not wholly or easily a British colonial invention.

Straight after his time in Ūva, Hardy went on to Vellassa. This was another province that would become a central node of the later revolt. Hardy wanted to gather bullocks, to be used for the transportation of British supplies, from the Moor inhabitants ('Moor' being a term used to refer to the island's community of Muslims). Here too, like with the Malabars of Ūva, he noted that the Muslims were joyful and ready collaborators and supplied the government's need and were 'loud to testify their happiness at being placed under the British Government'.[22]

Yet again, their complaint was directed against the Sinhala disāva of Vellasṣa and his extortionate regime of taxes. It was alleged that the oppression of the disāva had led to their leaving their homes for the jungles. When the rātarāle, a deputy of the disāva, arrived to speak with Hardy, the British officer made a point of addressing the Muslims while in his company:

> I desired them to remember what I had told them before that they were now British Subjects, that no person on Earth, whether British officer or Soldier Dissave or Ratterale should injure them with impunity that I would remain among them some time, to defend them from such oppressions as they have complained of, and that they should be made to feel the advantage of the English Lives which they appeared so desirous to exchange their former slavery for. In return the Ratterale was now the person disconcerted. He was pierced during this harangue by the eyes of every man present.[23]

Straight after his time at this and another village that he denoted as inhabited entirely by Moors, Hardy entered a 'small Chingalese village'. Here he met with the disāva of Vellasṣa and spoke with him about the grievances of the Moor villagers. He noted that the answer he received was a 'bad one'. The disāva emphasized that the Moors were of a low caste. Hardy noted that the Moors would serve as a wedge with which to break down the oppressive chiefly system. Rather foolishly, given what followed, he also wrote that Vellasṣa was 'as fine a Country as any in Ceylon', and that a detachment did not need to be stationed there because there were so many Moors who would be loyal to the British, whatever the circumstances.

Hardy's diary in Ūva and Vellasṣa in 1815 provides a snapshot of the deterioration of ethnic relations and the local cosmopolitanism of the Kandyan provinces, denoted in the arrangement of different villages and the diversity of communities evident across them. Of course there were some long-term tensions in these areas between communities.[24] Yet the arrival of British rule recontextualized notions of indigenous affiliation. This was neither continuity nor change but rather continuity and change, the very forceful and violent restitution of a changing history of antecedents. In support of such an argument, one might note the British desire to find collaborators and trading partners, to take over the Kandyan kingdom and to initiate intrusive 'free trade'. There was also their insistence that ethnicities should be neatly demarcated and plotted on their map of new territories: note Hardy's view of the friendly 'Malabars' and helpful 'Moors' in contrast with the cold Sinhalese. Such ethnography may have had an effect on the self-conception of Muslims, Tamil and Sinhala communities and their local governors.[25] Another contributor to a worsening of relations at this specific point was the full force of invasion that the British unleashed through this territory. Despite the heterogeneity of the extant population, numerous new types of people entered these territories from 1815 to 1819 as soldiers, 'coolies' and interpreters, and their presence and actions set in train new patterns of violence and distrust between communities. The local cosmopolitanism of the area could not peacefully accommodate this many people.

In 1816 when Governor Brownrigg toured the interior, he found evidence for this, in being greeted by a large crowd of tenants in the vale of Badulla, 'who claimed protection for themselves, their Families and Premises from the Soldiers and Army Followers'.[26] Brownrigg sought to explain the pattern of plunder: it occurred when British detachments as well as 'Individual Travellers' resort to the houses of villagers in order to procure supplies, generating fear on the part of the inhabitants who flee their abodes, allowing them to be plundered by these visitors. Although Brownrigg minimized the aggressive intent of these supposed visitors, his comments reveal that the movement of so many people and the necessity for the supply of people as logistic help at a time of war, were part and parcel of this culture of plunder. It is useful here to remember one recent thesis about the significant militarization of the British imperial meridian – whereby extra-European polities could not keep up, by way of finance and organization, with the 'garrison state' the British marshalled by the end of the eighteenth century. This has been borne out too by recent work in Sri Lankan military history.[27]

The manuscript travel journal of Simon Sawers who travelled with Hardy provides further evidence of how plunder was undertaken.[28] For instance, alliances built up between Malay soldiers working for the British and Muslim communities resident in the provinces. In Vellassa, Sawers gave his particular explanation of why the Moor trading community spoke ill of their disāva while being keen on collaborating with the British: having travelled for trade to the maritime provinces governed by the English, they had seen 'the comparative mildness and Justice of [English] Government' and entertained 'more enlarged ideas of independence with a great share of hatred to the old instruments of their oppression'. Directly following this comment, Sawers documented how much of the plunder of 1815 in Vellassa had been undertaken by Malay troops working for the British, who had collaborated with Moor traders:

> [T]he people have suffered much in their property by the Company of Malays, that were lately Stationed here and I suspect that their depredations were not confined to Uvah, but were also extended into the Wellasey Country, and that the Tavelam Moors were their informers and conductors, and also participated in the plunder. It even appears that the Singalese acted in this capacity themselves, where they had old quarrels to revenge.[29]

Ethnic and cultural affiliations across the lines of colonial and local play a part here, for instance in explaining the collaboration between Malays and Moors, and yet they do not constitute the whole story. The uncertain politics of these years set the context for other kinds of crimes, beyond plunder, which also pitted communities against each other, while tying together new entrants into the Kandyan territories, who were working for the British and local people. For example, Governor Brownrigg was concerned by the severity of the disāva of Ūva's response when a Sinhala woman and her daughter, of some rank, were found within a British military cantonment, where the daughter had 'lived with one of the Native Malay Officers'. Once taken out of the camp at the demand of the disāva, the mother was said to have had 'her Leg broken and both her and her daughter much bruised and with other marks of severe treatment, supposed to have been inflicted by the Mother's own brother'. The headman of Kataragama was also found killed, and this murder apparently arose out of sexual intrigue. Yet another murder that was reported in the same letter involved 'a party of Traders from the Sea Coast [possibly Malabar or Moor], who were charged with robbing a House of the Village of Passere in the Province of Ouwa and shooting the Owners' Brother'.[30] These episodes document how the transition to British rule provided a context for crime and punishment that could be directed against traditional elites; at the same time, social relations and forms of intimacy and violence could develop between solders and local people.

In developing this argument about the compound result of British and local engagement, it is useful to attend to how the specific strategies of violence used by the British inspired the counter-techniques of the local inhabitants. Violence became cyclical and imitative. Towards the end of the rebellion, there was an account of the discovery of the head of an interpreter, who had served the British, 'upon a stake', 'and near it a Body hanging on a tree', taken to be the remains of the same man. This interpreter had worked for Mr Wilson, whose death at the hands of rebels was one of the first episodes of the rebellion. Wilson's head, in turn, it was alleged, had been given to the pretender to the throne who called for rebellion.[31] It is worth noting that execution was used by the British as a punishment in these years, and especially in the context of the rebellion.[32] With the interpreter's human remains, an ola was found wrapped in white cloth containing a proclamation from the rebellious leader calling for the death of every white man:

> Major MacDonald now thought an example of severity should be shown. The Houses all around were therefore burnt, and all the Property found, Cattle, Grain &c &c was either carried off or destroyed. The terrible sight appeared to dismay the Natives, they ceased to shout or skirmish at a distance, and only ventured upon the skirts of the Plain to gaze in silence upon the Flames which consumed their habitations. They seemed panic struck at the rapidity and undaunted courage with which our Troops had advanced upon them.[33]

The scorched-earth techniques utilized by the British through the course of these years were also at times matched by the local people. For instance, there was the case of one man who was 'scorched by a near relation on suspicion of theft'. 'He had lost the use of one Hand and was otherwise much injured and disfigured.'[34] Without noting any contradiction or connection to British use of fire, Brownrigg wrote that this was a crime that needed prompt and public investigation; he attempted to organize for the case to be tried in Kandy, while he was in the capital on tour.[35] Despite British attempts to stress their civility and to trumpet their difference by resort to colonial laws, in fact the violence of this moment was supercharged by the fact that it was undertaken on all sides, and in rather symmetrical fashion.

British ideology, ethnography and practical tactics were becoming entangled with local patterns of life and organization; local cosmopolitanism was being rebalanced into a culture of ethnic competition and differentiation, which in turn was as changeable as the British colonial state. The relation between cosmopolitanism and ethnicization was extant prior to this period of course – and yet because of how the British fell into past patterns, while launching an intensive project of surveillance and state-making, the pace of continuity and change gathered momentum in these years.

***

Moving on from local cosmopolitanism's fortunes in these years, it is important to stress that monarchic cosmopolitanism, consistent with Buddhist kingship and the last kings of Kandy, was also alive and well and at the heart of the rebellion of 1817–18. This kingly cosmopolitanism was remoulded and misunderstood by the British advance, in a similar way to how local cosmopolitanism fared in this period.

In 1816, Brownrigg had information of a plot to overthrow the English government, from Eknäligoḍa Nilame, a loyal disāva. Eknäligoḍa Nilame received an invitation from two Buddhist monks to join the plot.[36] According to him, invitations were issued to mudaliyārs, the headmen working under the British regime in the maritime provinces, and also to Malay troops via a muhandiram, one of another class of titled officers, to join the intended rebellion. The mudaliyārs of Colombo were said to have promised to send on for the rebel cause a 'number of Thieves and rogues'.[37] Eknäligoḍa Nilame reported his discussion with the priests in these terms:

> I asked the Priests, suppose you succeed in driving the English out, what will you do for a King – They answered we have already provided for that – That the late King's Son in Law; Mootal Samy Brother in Law, and a third, own Brother to Mootalsamy were now Prisoners in Slave Island at Colombo, that the Malays in their Interest would insure their escape. That a certain Day in the month would be fixed on, and be known through out when matters should burst out.

These relations of the ex-king, termed 'Malabar prisoners' in the translation, would thus combine with their Malay rescuers, Buddhist priests, lowland native heads and Kandyan chiefs to recreate a kingly and cosmopolitan polity.[38] Kandy would be struck and only its resident, John D'Oyly, would be spared for the information he possessed on the location of the king's treasure. The plot included elaborate instruction on the route through which the Malabars needed to march into Ūva, and also how the Malays were to use the pretext of a Muslim feast in order to undertake this resistance.[39] Although this was a plot orchestrated around a notion of kingship, with Buddhist priests as prime movers, it could encompass other communities around it, just as the Kandyan kings had done in the past.

Enrolled with this ideal of resistance were older transregional relations. For instance, at the very moment when Brownrigg reported the information gleaned from Eknäligoḍa Nilame, he wrote that a party of seven priests had departed to Ava in northern Burma with a long-term resident on the island, originating in Ava. He also noted that a delegation from Ava had made their way to Kandy without permission and without being much noticed and that he suspected devious motives. In addition D'Oyly discovered a plot at this moment to obtain a prince from Siam.[40] The idea of the Buddhist kingdom of Kandy as one that was set within a Buddhist ecumene stretching to Southeast Asia was a historic notion, which evidently returned to the scene even as the Kandyan line was evacuated. This prospect of kingly cosmopolitanism also reached out to Malay soldiers and even 'Black troops' or African-descent troops working for the British, in order to incorporate them into the progress of rebellion.[41] The kingly cosmopolitanism of this moment was thus able to rekindle longstanding traditions of association in addition to being responsive to the conditions of war and migration that marked the circumstances of British advance.

Regardless of this project of restoration, when the rebellion of 1817–18 formally began, Muslims and Malay troops mostly remained loyal to the British. In July 1818, it was reported, in keeping with Hardy's views above, that Muslim traders in Vellassa had provided critical support in conveying supplies.[42] In the same province, in the same period, a rebel leader was captured by Malay men under a native lieutenant, despite strenuous efforts and promises made by the rebels to try and effect a change of sides on the part of the Malays in question. These Malay soldiers and rebels 'marched together' for some miles until the native lieutenant gave 'the preconcerted signal to his men for seizing the rebel chief, which was instantly effected'. Despite the overwhelming number of rebels present on this occasion, the Malays killed thirty-three of them with bayonets and wounded several, while others dispersed or fled.[43] Other rebels were also captured by Moormen and Malays towards the end of the rebellion.[44] Yet, as always in the history of these four years, an interpretation of ethnic separation along the lines of the Sinhalese on one side and the British and their loyal supporters, the local minorities, on the other side, does not tell the whole story. For Eknäligoḍa Nilame's intelligence involved a Malay muhandiram who had agreed to organize support for the intended rebellion of 1816. This man had fled Kandy after its chief minister Pilima Talauvē had been executed by the king. In 1815 he had helped the British invade Kandy; now in 1816 he had offered his support to the rebels. He was one of the last king's fighters. Brownrigg decided to banish him from the island and 'to send him to Batavia, the Native place of his Family'.[45] Although he was placed on a ship at Galle, he managed to escape at Ambalangoḍa further up the coast, but was recaptured and placed under military guard at Galle awaiting the next means of deportation to the East Indies, together with his two grown sons and other family. It is pertinent here to note that the kings of Kandy utilized other foreign fighters, including men from Ava and Tanjore.[46]

This fragment of a life history is also revealing for how the British intervened in the notion of cosmopolitan kingship, and in the life of a man who had been at the heart of the late kingdom, with a product of the Age of Revolutions: the idea of the nation and its citizens. Increasingly in the aftermath of the French Revolution and Napoleonic Wars, during which Ceylon was taken for fear of its fall to the French, across the Indian Ocean the ideas of nationality and citizenship were circulating, set against arbitrary power and in some contexts kingship and imperialism. It was for this reason that the Malay muhandiram belonged in Batavia, his native place.[47] Although minorities could be employed effectively to support colonial expansion, in the end the British believed in a narrow idea of national indigeneity, as will be evident below.

***

British interaction with Ähälēpola, the chief minister of Kandy, who fled to British territories, is a good test case of how kingly cosmopolitanism is interlinked with a conception of indigeneity. In the early stages of the rebellion, the British could not imagine that Ähälēpola, the Disāva of Sabaragamuwa, would join the rebel cause: how could a man who wished to be king become subservient to a 'Malabar' pretender, from the race that had treated his family so cruelly? In accord with this view, the British circulated the account of how Ähälēpola's family was brutally murdered by the last king of Kandy. Yet this simple line of ethnicized and nationalized explanation did not last long as the British grew suspicious of the actions of Ähälēpola and charged him as a rebel, even though they had no precise information of his role in the rebellion.[48]

Moving beyond the colonial archive to the corpus of palm-leaf texts, it is possible to plot the attitudes of those connected with Ähälēpola around the taking of Kandy and the rebellion that followed. Two palm-leaf ballads in the genre of *hatan kavi* or war poems that emerged in this window of time were the *Vadiga Hatana* and the *Ähälēpola Hatana*, written in honour of Ähälēpola and arising in all probability from within his circle of admirers. The *Vadiga Hatana* begins as a panegyric of Ähälēpola, describing him as *yuvarāja* or second king.[49] It is thought that it may have been sung when he held court, beyond the purview of the British, as a king in waiting.[50] The ballads appear to have had successive additions, possibly in the context of the tumult of events that overtook these years. Criticism of the last king and praise of the English for getting rid of him gives way to critique of the English. Both the Tamils (*demala* or *vadiga*) who had dominated the court, and the English, personified by 'Gori', King George III, are cast as agents of violence and sacrilege against Buddhist and Sinhala sensibility. The ideological flux of these years, however, does not change the adoration of Ähälēpola as king.

The *Ähälēpola Hatana* begins by describing how the last king turned on Ähälēpola. Ähälēpola then received the devotion of the people of Sabaragamuwa: 'We shall sacrifice even our lives to the name of Ähälēpola.'[51]

Accordingly, he declared war upon the king. Finding himself in the midst of a conflict with Ähälēpola:

> That King Vickrama disregarding all humane feelings
> Went on killing men like a devil
> Causing fear of death to multitudes
> Continuing a rampage of executions every day.

The poem then recounts in gruesome detail how the king slayed Ähälēpola's family:

> Placing at once a pestle in the hand of the mother
> Told her to pound on the child's head.
> 'Woman, you must do this cruel deed.'
> Said the evil king happily, nodding his head.

When Ähälēpola responded by fleeing to the English, the English king, a reference to the governor of the British territories, is said to be attentive: 'The powerful British becoming angry, declaring war/Surrounded the great city from eight directions.' There is specific reference to the change of sovereignty; the Sinhala royal throne is evacuated and the English flag is hoisted in the city and George III becomes king of Kandy. Ähälēpola's disappointment at not being king sets the scene for the rebellion in the last section of the poem:

> The English troops, having chased away the enemy
> Spreading in ten directions, armed with bows, swords and guns
> Setting houses on fire and looting
> Went on a rampage, killing uncountable numbers of people.

The inhumanity of the English is comparable to the inhumanity of the last king, in his obsession with his own power. For now, while the rebellion is in progress, numerous people are 'living in jungles', 'not consuming sweet, soft food, but living on roots and leaves'. This may be a reference to the famine that gripped Ūva in the last stages of the rebellion and its aftermath, which according to at least one Briton was a strategy utilized by the colonists to quell the rebellion.[52] The *Ähälēpola Hatana* ends noting how the rebels, including Ähälēpola, were banished to the island of Mauritius.

The *Vadiga Hatana* bears out once again how there was an attempt to see Ähälēpola as a worthy and righteous king, set against the treachery of Śri Vickrama Rājasiṃha, the last king.[53] Väligala Kavisūndara, under whose name the poem appears, presents a picture of the kingdom taken over by Tamils. This is a vision of spiritual violation and natural pollution, as the king embarks on a programme of renovating his city: 'The great heal of soil was high as the sacred Bodhi/At night jackals and dogs roam and defecate on it.' The king also enjoys the pleasures of women in the shrine room of the Tooth Relic. A red sun, falling stars and comets and an earthquake announce that all is awry. The poem recounts the battle of 1815, naming the British officers, including Major Hardy. The troops are presented as a motley band of peoples:

> Kavisi, Habisi, Bengali, Vadiga [in this period, Tamil] and Dutch
> Malay, Javanese, Sepoy, Chetti, Muslim and mercenaries,
> With English soldiers in large numbers
> With [Christian] priests, to attend to the last rites when their time came.

In stressing his kingly role, Ähälēpola is said to act decisively in the battle, deploying his own army. He announces: 'I will catch the Tamil who destroys the country in eight days.' He is 'like Rāma, the hero, entering the city of Rāvana/He entered the city of Senkada [Kandy] by the power of the Buddha'. Meanwhile, he personally orchestrates the capture of the last king. Although there is no direct evidence for this, it is suggestive to keep in mind the British idea of the alienability of the Malabars in interpreting these productions. In the midst of Kandy's fall, the British took it to be dominated by tyrannical foreigners, and this is precisely the register taken by this poetry in portraying the last king and his relatives.

Turning to British sources, the view that Ähälēpola will not join the rebellion was offered up to those in higher authority several times on the basis of a racial argument too. For instance, in November 1817, Brownrigg wrote to London that although duplicity was very common among the Kandyan elite, Ähälēpola may be counted upon for his loyalty to the British, having confirmed by 'oath his unshaken fidelity to the British Government'. The governor carried on:

> the remembrance of the Cruelties which those most dear to him suffered from the deposed king, the animosity with which His own Rebellion and zealous assistance in the overthrow of the Malabar Royal Race, and His own Pride of sentiment present to my mind good grounds for believing that Eyheylapolle will never consent to undue homage to a Malabar King, or be instrumental in raising one to the Throne.[54]

In this belief of ethnic difference, the British sought to manage this man's expectations. Before the rebellion, Ähälēpola had complained to Brownrigg of his plight and asked for various honours to distinguish him from other chiefs.[55] For example, in late 1815, he insisted on being granted the honours of a king, by written document, and equivalent honours to those enjoyed on the part of the late 'Malabar' ruler. In response, the British explained the nature of sovereignty to Ähälēpola; two kings could not co-exist in the island. For the 'assumption of Kingly State was an infringement of the Royal Rights of His Majesty the King of England'. Ähälēpola was adamant that this was not the case and that he could still be king.[56] A rumour was also reported that if Ähälēpola was not to receive kingly honours he would retire to his village and 'raise the country'. In this context, Brownrigg awaited an overt act of disloyalty to arrest Ähälēpola, even if John D'Oyly had advised that an arrest was unnecessary. In seeking for kingship, Ähälēpola sought to project a sense of his rule as consistent with and incorporative of the rule of the British monarch. For instance, he attended Colombo for the birthday of the British king in 1816, and insisted on being supplied with a portrait of the British monarch that he could wear. The governor advised London that this request was worth meeting, as it would further link the name of Ähälēpola with British interests, thus making it difficult for him to become disloyal:

> With all his faults I am disposed to give him the credit of setting a just value on the honour of wearing the Royal Portrait, and as his ambition is deeply interested in preserving his Title to so flattering a decoration, that dangerous and alarming part of his character may thus be made subservient to the great object of attaching him to the British interests.[57]

This portrait may be interpreted as part of an exchange between Brownrigg and Ähälēpola, for the chief gave the governor the king's jewels, which had been brought to him in return for it. If so, was Ähälēpola trying to participate in a new set of symbols of kingship? During the birthday celebrations, he rode a black Arab horse, which had belonged to the late king's stud, but dismounted it for the ritual of the firing of guns.[58]

Despite the similarities in the portrayal of the aspirant king and court, within palm-leaf sources and British colonial documents, there is an important dissonance in the record of the late events of the rebellion, which gestures to the continuing life of monarchic cosmopolitanism and the failure of the British to grasp how it functioned. Although the Ähälēpola-related palm-leaves and British sources seem to separate true indigenes from vile and polluting outsiders, who inflict violence, in fact as the rebellion proceeded a 'stranger' became critical to its progress as a pretender. There was an assimilationist tendency – evident also in Ähälēpola's attempt to incorporate George III within his bid to be king – which did not conform to British expectations of kingly stateishness. One might note how Käppiṭipola, the disāva of Ūva and a relation of Ähälēpola's, organized a ceremony to enthrone a new king, a man he brought out of hiding from Kataragama. The ceremony took place in 'a large plan called Diabetme in lower Ouwa in which temporary buildings were erected, a solemn ceremony of inauguration took place before a crowd of about 3000 persons, assembled from nearly every part of the Kandyan provinces'. The ceremony thus arranged the provinces symbolically around the new king, and then deployed loyal adherents, who had witnessed the ritual, to all corners of the kingdom, with the instruction to be 'firm in opposition'.[59] In the aftermath, a spike was recorded in the number of attacks mounted on British troops and escorts. In another assembly at Hanguranketha, Käppiṭipola exhibited a casket said to contain the Tooth Relic, which 'he declared had been brought away from the Principal Temple in Kandy by Two Lascoreens who were on watch over it', as an indicator of the certain success of the rebel cause.[60] The Lascorins, in British uniform, also appeared alongside the displayed casket.[61] The word that recurred in colonial sources describing the so-called pretender was the word 'stranger', denoting both a lack of information and a lack of comprehension of the relationship between ethnicity and kingship. Note the words of Governor Brownrigg:

> When I was in Kandy in September last a Report was received that a Stranger of suspicious appearance had appeared in the South East part of Ouva (an unfrequented and wild Country) who occasionally dressed as a Malabar and sometimes as a Budhoo Priest by some of which Class he was accompanied... it was discovered that the Malabar was guarded by 100 armed Vedahs and the Native Headman who was sent to apprehend him was taken prisoner.[62]

He carried on that the chiefs had declared that this 'stranger was really connected with the Family of the deposed King', and that he was among the Malabars sent to India, who had returned to the island illegally. It was supposed at first that he was Doraisāmi, but inquiries in Madras revealed that Doraisāmi was still in the mainland. Brownrigg's theory was this: '[I]t is to my mind a probability nearly approaching a certainty that he is a Native Kandyan of good Family who had been much in the Galle and Matura Districts.' He had declared himself to be of royal stock at Kataragama temple.[63] In fact this pretender was Vilbavē, an ex-monk, who was posing as Doraisāmi in order to claim royal ancestry.[64] Ex-monks recur in the sources for this period: indeed they were among the spies deployed by John D'Oyly in the Kandyan territories in the period. Pilima Talauvē, another chief who was critical to the rebellion, intended to put forward another pretender as king. This second man was discovered to be 'a Malabar', 'who had resided in Poverty and Obscurity at Manar, not connected with the Kandyan Royal Family'.[65] Pilima Talauvē intended to display this 'phantom king' at Dambulla vihāra.[66] The dissonance amounts to this: in this project of restoration, non-Sinhaleseness still played a critical role, and this mystified the British and thwarted their policy of ethnic classificationism.

Both Käppiṭipola and Pilima Talauvē were arrested by Captain Fraser in October 1818; Ähälēpola was taken captive before this.[67] Soon followed the capture of Madugallē, another rebel leader and a Buddhist priest who had in his possession the Tooth Relic.[68] Yet it was not only the Kandyans who sought to resuscitate ideas of kingliness. In these years and after the rebellion, there was again an attempt on the part of the British to model their government as a replacement for Kandy. For instance, on entering Kandy, Brownrigg watched wild elephants set free in the centre of the city as Śri Vickrama Rājasiṃha had done in 1810.[69] When leaving the territories for the coast, he sought to take up 'ancient etiquette' by having as attendants 'all the chiefs in Kandy'.[70] Even offerings to Kataragama were made in order to appeal to popular sensibility.[71] This programme is in keeping with material I have discussed elsewhere on how British governors were enrolled as kings in palm-leaf narratives in the period after the taking of Kandy.[72]

***

Yet the play of concepts evident here – where Britons sought to be like Kandyan kings and where Kandyan elites sought to interact and assimilate themselves alongside and above British kings – still had to come to terms with the problem of strangers. Despite its turn to kingship, the British state of the early nineteenth century, when compared with the Kandyan one, was interested in quite distinct matters of free trade, liberalism, utilitarianism and the patronage of evangelical religion. These were the tools that had allowed it to reign supreme over its rivals in the Indian Ocean terrain and they were increasingly utilized in the Kandyan territories too. To support these ends required a bureaucratic and modernizing state; and the creation of such a state was premised on 'islanding', the unification of the whole island as a state set apart from the mainland.

Islanding required a rebalancing of cosmopolitanism and indigeneity, so that strangers and outsiders were not allowed in or were watched closely. When Kandy fell, Śri Vickrama Rājasiṃha and his relatives were taken to South India and to their 'native countries' under the East India Company. Elsewhere, I have explained in detail how the repatriation of so-called Malabars from Kandy was orchestrated in connection with an underpinning ideology of the foreignness of the Malabars and Moors of the island. This programme became connected with the dangers associated with strangers, a worry that recurred in the context of the rebellion, where the return of such Malabars was strictly policed, in fear of the emergence of yet further pretenders to the throne. In 1816, all those 'Malabars' who had resided in Kandy for one year as at 1 January 1815 and who were taken as prisoners of war were announced to be liable to imprisonment at hard labour if found in the Kandyan territories.[73] This regulation arose from Brownrigg's worry that 'communications are at least occasionally exchanged between persons in Kandy and the Nayaker family' in South India.[74] In India, the need to watch Kandyan prisoners and movement between the island and India gave rise to directives to magistrates and collectors across South India.[75]

Allegedly clandestine travellers were detected in this period: one named Vengutasāmi, for instance, taken in late 1816, was said to have announced himself as 'insane but is now well'.[76] In India in 1818, two men and a woman were detained on the way to Ceylon:

> They are strangers. Their names are said by themselves to be
> 1. Rammasawmy Naukin
> 2. Conareton, his wife
> 3. Swatheyan

Rāmaswāmi was said to have worked in the court of Kandy and had come to India, together with his wife, on pilgrimage, and now wished to return after performing a sacred vow. The third person noted above claimed to be a peon who worked for the British in Trincomalee, 'from whence he states he received a passport, about ten months ago to proceed to Tanjore, on a visit to his relatives'. There followed a detailed ethnographic report of these three, noting the colour of their hair and eyes and identifying marks. Rāmaswāmi for instance had a 'small pimple on the left cheek', three scars caused by a weapon on his right arms, three further scars on his right knee and a 'hairy breast and mark of a cut by a knife on his throat'.[77] This was the practical force of indigenism, being worked out within the regime of paper brought about by the newly bureaucratized British colonial state. For Malabars were seen as different to the Sinhalese, both physically and linguistically, and this now mattered in legal terms.[78]

In Lanka, John D'Oyly apprehended some Malabar travellers in this period and asked for a watch to be kept by British officers for 'any Malabar strangers of suspicious character'. Just like Rāmaswāmi, there were also pilgrims from India in the island who were apprehended under this regulation. Eleven mendicants were taken in 1816, who because of their 'appearance and manners', were said to be 'exactly the sort of men whom it is the desire of the Government to prevent penetrating into the interior'.[79] D'Oyly also took 'a young Malabar Priest of Buddhu'; this captive evidently troubled the neat delineations of nationality and belonging and had to be sent to Colombo for further questioning. In June 1819, D'Oyly provided Colombo with further advice, about this or another priest who was also classed in similar terms:

> As there are no grounds for believing that he is a person of high Rank & as he has given proofs of a peaceable & obedient Disposition, I perceive no objections to acquiescing in his wish to reside at some temple in the maritime Provs, provided it be at a distance from the limits... with some instruction not to wander far without leave for it seems desirable to provide that he shouldn't pass into the Kandyan country, where his Malabar extraction might possibly give rise to alarming Rumours.[80]

The arrest of travellers carried through into the 1820s. And the regime of bureaucracy, tied up with certificates and 'passports', a term that appears in these sources, was evident for instance at Jaffna, from which people were sent back to India:

> Persons are very frequently sent here to be removed to the coast [of India], but are immediately on their arrival put into a boat and sent off... the boats employed in taking them are almost always coast boats, passing through. Within the last fortnight no less than 7 persons were forwarded to me to be transported to the continent and were not detained more than 5 minutes after their arrival.[81]

Jumping ahead, by the 1830s the discourse of the stranger was reinvented once again. By this time, strangers were critical agents of free trade and their movements had to be watched and monitored in order to ensure that the colonial state's coffers benefited from their activities and that their trade did not bypass the system of duties and bonds that had been set in place. In 1831, a regulation was announced to the effect that 'All strangers arriving at Colombo either by sea or Land' had to report immediately to the office of the chief secretary of government; if they did not comply they were liable to be arrested. The relationship between the surveillance of migration and colonial trade was spelt out when Moors and Malabars were allowed to own houses in the fort and pettah of Colombo, annulling a Dutch law to the contrary. 'Foreigners' were said in this instance to be 'the most industrious and wealthy of the Inhabitants, the greater part of the trade of the Colony being carried on by them'.[82] Allowing such aliens to own houses was thus to the benefit of British goals.

The British colonial state of Ceylon and the notion of the nation that operated within that state as also its economic and legal rationale, intervened in the conception of the polity in Lanka, but not in a final or complete sense. Foreigners, aliens and strangers were cast as distinct from indigenes and this allowed a chain of restitutions of notions of belonging. Cosmopolitanism, of course, carried through the nineteenth century; yet its placement with respect to assertions of indigeneity was reforged as a result of this intervention. Nativeness was not encompassed within or arrayed around waves of migrants and strangers; rather the enumerative and bureaucratic functions of the new state cast belonging in exclusive terms. Indigenes were of one type. This was in keeping with the post-rebellion agenda of remodelling the government of the Kandyan provinces so that 'a great degree of Political liberty and the fullest security of Property' would be guaranteed.[83] Such liberty depended, it was thought, on indigenes and aliens being demarcated as distinct, so that foreign strangers, such as the Nāyakas, did not rule in Lanka; and it brought in train the added colonial benefit of the delineation of property, land and the law, which allowed the take-off of the plantation system and the expansion of an urban metropolis of 'free trade' such as Colombo. The British now commanded the bounds of cosmopolitanism and indigeneity and had the power to keep shifting them.

***

In interrogating cosmopolitanism, this chapter has insisted on treating it together with indigeneity. Without such a pairing it would be impossible to make sense of the terror of these years. A fundamental premise of the argument is that cosmopolitanism is always tied with its opposite and has the ability to mutate in form to support assertions of nativism. All forms of cosmopolitanism – ranging from the local to the royal and indeed the imperially sanctioned, depend on senses of self and other, the familiar and the foreign. Indigeneity feeds off, reacts against and informs cosmopolitanism. The realignment of these two terms was – and continues to be – the work of violence and war, rather than simply the effect of mobility, cultural hybridity and free association. In tracking cosmopolitanism and indigeneity in the period, the present chapter has sought to look from multiple points of view: the local village in as much as the urban centre; the imperial state in as much as the changing populace of the Kandyan periphery. Such an argument is critical in a literature that can romanticize the cosmopolitan as a precursor of the global self, and that tracks the cosmopolitan in the port rather than the hinterland and without a sense of the states and political forces within which it operates.[84] Simultaneously, this perspective eschews a romantic simplification of the indigenous.

Violent kings, chiefs and colonists were able to refashion these concepts in order to support their political visions of kingdoms, empires and nations. Such violence was motivated by material objects, such as relics of the Buddha and objects of royalty, and a culture of writing on palm-leaf and paper.[85] Tokens and signifiers of governance were resituated, and even plundered, in the cycle from kingdom to nation, and bureaucracy was key to the eventual triumph of the modern colonial state over its alternatives. Britons, Kandyans, Malabars, Moors, the priests of Ava and Siam, Batavian and Indian fighters and others were able to reassemble these objects and ideologies in order to suit their purposes and were able themselves, sometimes repeatedly, to switch sides. This is what made it possible for all comers to lay claim on the kingdom as well as the state and nation. Yet such reassembly cannot minimize the fact that Kandyan kingship and British statishness were in foundation different in the way they conceived of cosmopolitanism and indigeneity; this is undoubtedly why violence recurred into the nineteenth century and why the 1817–18 rebellion was not the last of the revolts. Although so many sought to rebuild the kingdom and a new state, a twinned and contradictory project like this was bound to fail in reaching fullness.

This chapter has traced the afterlife and fortunes of both local and monarchic cosmopolitanism. In both cases, the advent of the British added a new set of concerns for collaboration, trade and knowledge-gathering. Yet local and monarchic cosmopolitanism, despite at times being patronized or mimicked by the British, were misunderstood and eventually moulded into the form of a modern state. Cosmopolitanism in the Kandyan territories was not simply a practice that radiated out of the court; the local life of villages was bound up with their trade or pilgrimage. Similarly, British colonialism itself was predicated on alliances, for instance, between its Malay troops and local Muslims. The uncertainty and incompletion of this colonial transition was such that subalterns as well as chiefs and kings were participants in the tussle over concepts. It is important to point to both locales of belonging and political conception – at ground and centre – for otherwise the power of the court and colonialism is exaggerated. Indeed it is striking that Vilbavē, the pretender of 1817–18, came to prominence before having the patronage of a Kandyan chief. Käppiṭipola took charge of the man only at a later point. Local histories of cosmopolitanism and indigeneity, such as those from Ūva and Vellassa, or from a province at the peripheries of Kandy such as Nuvarakalāviya can converge and diverge with the story from the centre in revealing ways.[86] Thinking of the local can also counterbalance and problematize the all-island narrative of kingdoms made into a nation or a nation that has become a kingdom.

The theorization of nineteenth-century rebellion, and the Indian Rebellion of 1856–7 in particular, has been one of the most vigorously debated areas of South Asian scholarship, picking up Marxist and subalternist as well as politico-economic and intellectual historical approaches to the occurrence of rebellion.[87] It is welcome to see signs now that the topic of rebellion is opening up a range of analytical positions within Lankan historiography too. It is the consensus that rebellions in Lanka can be seen as long-running and 'perpetual'. This follows Kumari Jayawardena's conception of recurrent rebellion as a response to the 'hegemonic control' of elite colonists as well as monks and chiefs; she stresses the power of this politics without primitivizing it. This is in keeping with Ranajit Guha's subalternism rather than Eric Hobsbawm's Eurocentric Marxism. Meanwhile, Strathern sees rebellion as indigestion – the inability to domesticate the foreign – and Biedermann as part of a reflection of intra-elite tensions between rival noble factions. While Jayawardena draws a continuum from the Dutch to the British, Strathern moves from the Portuguese to the British. Yet in stressing longevity and continuity, is there a danger of falling into colonial views, especially for the point that Nira Wickramasinghe makes that colonists disseminated conspiracy to justify counter-rebellious offensive?[88] For this chapter, there is value in stressing continuity, and yet the particular circumstances of short periods of time – for their ideology, politics and forms of state-making – are critical too. Rebellion needs to be understood in the round as a process that picks up prior attachments while at the same time setting in sway the new. The violence that was enacted on all sides needs also to be kept securely in view and the increasingly invasive (although not always successful) power of the imperial should not be brushed aside. For Wickramasinghe, the rebellions between 1797 and 1800 were connected with 'a feeling of being exploited by a rapacious ruler and his representative, the renter'.[89] Accordingly, forms of government and misgovernment matter. The politics of identity and the economy need to be placed together alongside forms of imperialism.

Despite the array of terms and perspectives that come into play in this process of transition to British rule and to a colonial state and nation, it is striking that some concepts cut across and recur in the sources. 'Stranger' is a particularly interesting one. Whereas a stranger as king was critical to the coherence, power and standing of the Kandyan kingdom, with the British state the concept of the stranger was politically problematic.[90] By the early nineteenth century and in the context of the Napoleonic wars, strangers had to be watched and repatriated to their places of origin. So the concept history of the stranger, taken here as a period term, denotes a passage from integration into the core to repudiation across borders. Kingship itself recurs in this narrative; yet when a British governor occupied and took upon himself the space and ritual of a king, he nevertheless stood at the head of a centralizing bureaucracy that was answerable to a distant state and monarchy. He wasn't a king in the Kandyan sense. With respect to another concept, the 'nation' was evident in Kandy itself from the early modern period, but that sense of the 'nation', which is also a term that recurs in these sources, was becoming tied up with a newly colonial military-fiscal state, connected to weapons, taxation and plantation in a powerful combination that allowed it to diverge from its predecessors. In this sense, the play of concepts on all sides and the entanglement of the Kandyans and the British in utilizing the languages of kingdoms and nations, and the cosmopolitan and indigenous, nonetheless should not mask differences in kind. Mimicry and entanglement thus hid fundamental and at times small differences, which over the *longue durée* allowed the British moment to count as a slow and painful end to the story of early modern Lanka.

In avoiding the traditional alternatives in the literature on the late eighteenth and early nineteenth century in South Asia, namely continuity versus change, and adopting a more complex picture of the reassembly of concepts, it is possible to capture the dynamism of these years, without slipping into structural simplicities, so that Kandy is a terrain where rebellion recurs unendingly, or indeed post-colonial exaggerations, where British invasion sees a total rupture. Such a view is critical for Sri Lanka, for 1815–19 is still with us, especially in the context of postwar debates about what counts as a human rights violation and whether in fact the British are the perpetrators of such crimes. Curiously such a debate was afoot a few years ago in Sri Lanka: pitting contemporary events on the island alongside British responses to rebellion. The British monarch's representative, Prince Charles, and the British prime minister, David Cameron, were in Sri Lanka for a meeting of the heads of state of the Commonwealth in 2013. It was then that the island's former president Māhinda Rājapaksa gave this veiled critique of ex-colonial preaching: 'People who live in glass houses should not throw stones.' Indeed the re-enactment of anti-British rebellion has appeared recently on television screens in Sri Lanka in the form of a Sinhala teledrama on the Derana channel.[91] Rebellion's role in defining the nation – or perhaps the kingdom – carries on, drawing in long-term precedent.

# 11
# The digestion of the foreign in Lankan history, c. 500–1818

*Alan Strathern*

How is ethnic and patriotic sentiment manufactured in the face of the ceaseless absorption of the foreign? Historians have often reminded us of the latter in order to puncture the delusions that balloon around the former; an irresistible manoeuvre.[1] Following suit, we might start with the image of Kandy in the national consciousness of the Sinhalese, as the highland region where indigenous sovereignty held out for the longest time against European colonialism. To be 'KGB' (Kandyan Goyigama Buddhist) is still to signify a lofty purity in terms of ethnicity, caste and religion. But when Kandy was re-established in the 1590s it was under the leadership of a man by the name of Dom João de Áustria. He was a lascarin captain in the Portuguese army, his wife was a Portuguese orphan, and he was named after the great hero of the battle of Lepanto, a Catholic victory against Ottomans.[2] After he attained the throne, a Dutch visitor to his court noted the extent to which the aesthetic and domestic spheres were influenced by a taste for all things Portuguese.[3]

Yet it will not do to dwell for too long on this irony. It is no less important to note that in order for Dom João de Áustria to ascend the throne he had to become 'Vimaladharmasūriya I': he had to apostatize in a very conspicuous way, building a new Temple of the Tooth to house the Buddha's Tooth Relic, ejecting the Portuguese, forcing prisoners to apostatize, and patronizing the Sangha. This chapter is therefore as concerned with the limits to 'cosmopolitanism' – as a phenomenon and as a concept – as it is with its operation. If the potency of the foreign is sought after, it is usually domesticated in the process: this is the digestion of the foreign. In seeking to explain and underline this point, this chapter proceeds in the footsteps of Gananath Obeyesekere and Stanley Tambiah.[4] However, since their explorations of the processes of Sinhalacization and Buddhicization, historiography has undertaken a now discernible 'global turn'. This is reflected here not by establishing new historical connections, but by scrutinizing interpretations in the light of new historical comparisons.

A second organizing question for this chapter is therefore whether even to speak of 'ethnic and patriotic sentiment' outside of the West before the modern period is to lapse into parochialism. The first part answers this by examining how awkwardly Sri Lanka fits into Sheldon Pollock's theory of the contrasting developments of group identity in South Asia and Europe. Medieval Europe is thus the reference point here, implicitly or explicitly. The second part aims to deepen our appreciation of the complex and paradoxical ways in which societies view the identity of their ruling dynasties.[5] This involves considering how two different understandings of 'stranger-kingship' may be applied to Lankan history: a Sahlinsian model, and a political theory model. The final part is chronologically comparative, bringing together ways in which Lankan society responded to the imperial threat from the Portuguese and early British periods. In particular it focuses on a grammar of rebellion that seems to persist throughout. Readers should note that each of these three sections has a quite distinct focus. However, underlying them all is a common concern with the themes of Sinhalaness, the ambivalence of monarchical identity and the way that the sacred interacts with political projects and violence.

## A blot on the landscape? Sinhala group emotions and the Sanskrit cosmopolis

Sheldon Pollock's analysis of a millennium (c. 500–1500) of South and Southeast Asian history, in his *The Language of the Gods in the World of Men*, adopts the kind of genuinely panoramic comparative sensibility of world history at its best. Theoretical reflection on identity formation has usually focused on the modern period in which the influence of Western power and ideas bulks large; there have been few serious attempts to compare how different cultural regions may have construed group identity in the premodern world. Pollock's approach is particularly notable for the attempt to avoid the redeployment of concepts lifted semi-consciously from European history. It is only when a work such as this appears that we realize how much scholarship has lacked the conceptual rigour provided by the comparative method.

Pollock describes the Indic world in terms of a Sanskrit cosmopolis (a 'trans-regional culture-power sphere of Sanskrit') and then shows how, from the turn of the millennium, in region after region, this gave way to the development of vernacular literature.[6] These new literary cultures were deeply influenced by or even modelled on the Sanskrit inheritance, but they were now turned inwards to address a more local audience in its own language.[7] Pollock draws a striking parallel with the chronology of an equivalent process in Europe's turn from Latin to the vernacular. However, Pollock argues that vernacularization did not carry the same political and social implications in the Indic world: it did not represent the first steps in a journey towards nations, or even ethnic groups, but was rather the occasion for the development of 'vernacular polities'.[8]

It should be noted at the outset that there is some ambiguity in *The Language of the Gods* as to how far Sri Lanka is to be understood as a participant in the dynamics that shape the trajectory of the Sanskrit cosmopolis. Pollock recognizes that Sinhala has its deepest origins as a written language as far back as the centuries BCE,[9] and more importantly that Sri Lanka also participated in the Pāli ecumene, such that 'Sanskrit may never have occupied a dominant position in either aesthetic or political expression'.[10] We shall return to this point. Nevertheless, Pollock notes that the transformations in Sinhala literary culture from the end of the first millennium bear a strong resemblance to developments elsewhere. As a result, he refers to these developments a number of times, where they are depicted as an unusually early case of his central thesis – particularly exemplified in the ninth-century *Siyabaslakara*.[11] Moreover, presumably Pollock's many generalizations about the functioning of identity in 'South Asia' or the cosmopolis more widely are intended to include Sri Lanka.

One such insight is the way that the vernacular polity produces a distinctly bounded concept of its proper arena, so that we see in Lanka for the first time in the tenth and more strongly the twelfth centuries, 'the earliest literary representations... of a newly coherent geocultural space'.[12] The language of universal sovereignty appropriate for the old cosmopolis may still linger on in a symbolic form (so that a king is hailed as *cakravarti* with Jambudīpa-wide hegemony), but this is understood to refer in actuality to an identified territory.[13] Java presents an interesting comparison with Sri Lanka in this regard.[14] We need not thereby underplay the extent to which Lankan kings looked to extend their influence into South India and even Southeast Asia whenever they were strong enough. Yet Lankan kings rarely were strong enough to launch and sustain such projects; they never sought *lasting* dominion overseas.[15]

While this may indeed be comparable with developments in Europe, it is also true that in other ways the Lankan political imagination seems firmly branded with a certain 'cosmopolitan' quality found in societies across the wider Indic world. In terms of its religious self-fashioning, Lankan kingship could afford to be much more eclectic and flexible than its Christian counterparts, borrowing extensively from different Buddhist traditions as well as those now considered 'Hindu'. The latter included notions of divine kingship that rendered the king 'as a type of axis mundi cum avatar'.[16] Brahmans – as indeed across the Indic world – played the primary role in conducting the ritual life of the court. In this way, Sinhala kings could speak to their dynastic rivals across the seas and co-opt their claims to sacralized authority.

Indeed, if sovereignty was considered as geographically confined, it was not therefore culturally circumscribed, for the island itself was home to diverse groups. A claim to rule over Lanka entailed dominion over the Tamil-speaking parts of the north and the east, over the väddā of the interior, and over the mercantile and fishing groups of diverse origins strung along the coasts, as well as over the Sinhala-speaking population. Nor was such diversity simply an uncomfortable fact, but rather something that flattered the authority of the king or *cakravarti*. To that extent, a cosmopolitan or 'universalist' notion of kingship remained. In keeping with this general celebration of pluriformity, mastery over several languages remained an ideal for scholars – indeed for kings – well into the vernacular period and beyond.[17] By the time that the Portuguese arrived then in the first years of the sixteenth century, they found an elite culture that looked anything but monolithic. The kings of Kōṭṭe were dependent on quite recently arrived mercenaries from South India, and tried to tempt Karāvas to settle with land grants.[18] Bhuvanekabāhu VII (1521–51), the last king or 'emperor' of Kōṭṭe to resist Portuguese control, signed his letters with a phrase in Tamil. Nor was the 'digestion of the foreign' always a bargain premised on cultural assimilation: hence Muslims could be incorporated into the Kandyan socio-political order in a way that was both profound and tolerant of their faith.[19]

It is always salutary to remind ourselves of these facts, and careful analysis with Europe may indeed reveal some of these features to be rather distinctive of a South Asian or even Indic sensibility. Other features, however, may turn out to be applicable to premodern politics more generally, only acquiring any contrastive analytical relevance when set against some more modern visions of the nation-state.[20] For example, Britain in the period 1110–1400 CE would present an analogous example of an island populated by a number of distinct peoples according to their own self-understandings, and yet according to R. R. Davies, 'it was considered a sign of political maturity and power that a ruler governed several peoples rather than one', with rulers from Athelstan (r. 925–39) onwards granting themselves grandiloquent imperial titles as a result.[21]

But what might all this mean for the possibility of ethnicity or even politicized ethnicity?[22] Pollock's stance here is radically different to that of the modernization theorists for whom the basic conditions of life in the premodern period everywhere rendered national sentiments or even politicized ethnicity impossible or superficial. Rather than being held to be dependent on a certain stage in material and political development, Pollock holds the existence of such sentiments to depend essentially on a *cultural* matrix of remarkable longevity. Hence they may be a foundational element of European life from very early on and yet irrelevant to the Indic world. For, as he sees it, 'ethnic fictions' or origin stories simply found no foothold in the Sanskrit imagination.[23] Genealogy may have been a crucial element of dynastic aggrandizement, but we find no explicit discourses on the origins of peoples, they did not become the subject of chronicles as they did in Europe, and 'one is hard-pressed to identify a single instance of the propagation of shared group memories'.[24] Of the premodern Indian texts that have been read,

> nowhere is it possible to point to a discourse that links language, identity, and polity; in other words, nowhere does ethnicity – which for purposes of discussion we may define as the political salience of kin group sentiment – find even faint expression. It is equally impossible to locate evidence in South Asia for the linkage of blood and tongue so common in medieval Europe, or for cultures as associations restricted by so-called primordial ties.[25]

This definition of ethnicity places a lot of weight on 'fictive kinship', and in one sense this is productive for comparative purposes.[26] It serves to highlight what may well be a significant breach between the Indic and European. According to Davies, myths of biological descent were 'the veriest commonplaces of the historical mythology of the medieval world'.[27] In an emic sense, peoples were communities of common descent.[28] For John Watts, by the fourteenth century in Europe more generally, 'the hallmarks of nationhood were conventionally the ties of blood and language, though a common name, shared laws and customs, government and territory... were also often important'.[29] In the surviving source material from Sri Lanka, on the other hand, the dynasty greatly overshadows any role taken by 'the people', and the question of the blood descent of the linguistic group had much less salience.[30] In general, the *sandēśa* poems, and even the *haṭanas* (for example, the *Sītāvaka Haṭana*) seem more concerned with exalting royal lineages and the island itself rather than the Sinhala people in an explicit sense.[31] It is reasonable to suppose that the caste system, with its foundation in endogamy, presented an obstacle to larger group claims based on fictive kinship across South Asia – even if caste worked quite differently in Sri Lanka to many parts of India.[32]

In other ways, however, the definition obstructs comparative insight.[33] 'Peoplehood' may be imagined in a variety of ways: to make explicit claims about common descent a *necessary* feature of it is to foreclose too quickly on broadly comparable dynamics of group sentiment. For example, however much descent claims may feature in *emic* understandings of ethnicity in medieval Britain, Davies does not ultimately make it a necessary feature of his *etic* definition of peoplehood. Instead his definition is that of an imagined community – imagined by itself and/or by others.[34] This has much in common with Obeyesekere's richer notion of the 'ethnic moral community'.[35] Two other points emerge from Davies' analysis that will be helpful for us as we proceed: that the formation of ethnicity is not dependent on a single cohesive state structure; and that its subjective and often taken-for-granted qualities mean that it is not a phenomenon that implants itself in the historical record in a straightforward way.[36] It is 'alternatively a prominent and a strangely evanescent concept'.[37]

Nevertheless, over the course of Pollock's millennium, there is certainly evidence in the Lankan record for many of the features that are typically associated with ethnicity.[38] Notwithstanding the suggestion that blood had a rather weak salience in expressions of Sinhalaness, it may be that the famous origin story for the Sinhalas was in fact taken as such a descent claim for most or all of its very long history. The story of Sīhabāhu and Vijaya – itself probably an amalgamation of various such origin stories – is present in its extended form in the *Mahāvaṃsa* of the late fifth or early sixth century CE. It describes the fortunes of the miscreant Vijaya, descended from a lion, who pitched up in Lanka and overcame the *yakkhiṇī* Kuveṇī.[39] It was retold many times in both Pāli and Sinhala texts. It has, to be sure, been a source of much debate as to whether the Sinhalas of the *Mahāvaṃsa* narrative can be understood as a dynasty or a people. Yet, the likelihood is that these stories were already taken as describing the origin of a far broader group than a dynasty at the time the *Mahāvaṃsa* was composed. Vijaya arrives on the island, with 700 warriors, to find it uninhabited by humans but only by *yakkhas*: this is clearly a colonization myth.[40] Rather intriguingly, the logic deployed here follows that of many other 'stranger-king' stories across the world, which are usually taken to define the origin of both kingship and society *tout court*.[41]

The question as to whether and when Sinhalaness went from being an elite/dynastic category to one that encompassed all Sinhala-speakers stimulated an academic controversy in the 1980s and 1990s between K. N. O. Dharmadasa (who argued for an early emergence, by the tenth century at least) and R. A. L. H. Gunawardana (who argued for an initial emergence in the twelfth century but remaining muted until the nineteenth century). For our purposes, however, it is significant that both argue for an initial crystallization either before or within Pollock's vernacularization period.[42] One text that became the focus of debate is dated to the tenth century, the *Dhampiyā aṭuvā gäṭapadaya*, which was apparently written by the king Kassapa V (914–23) – and therefore has as great a claim as any to represent the 'public transcript' of communal origination.[43] Gunawardana gives the following translation of a critical excerpt (in which 'helu' is used as a synonym for Sinhala):

> How is (the term) in the *heḷu* language derived? That is derived on account of residents in the island being *heḷu*. How is it that (they) are (called) *heḷa*? Having killed a lion, King Sīhabāhu was called Sīhaḷa (as in the Pāli phrase), 'Sīhaḷa, on account of having cut (or killed) a (or the) lion.' On account of being his progeny (*ohu daru bävin*), Prince Vida (Vijaya) was called Sīhaḷa. Others came to be called Sīhaḷa on account of being their retinue (*ehuvu pirivara bävin*).[44]

Gunawardana notes that this is an inelegant translation because the exact meanings matter for his debate with Dharmadasa. Yet for all that Gunawardana wanted to push forward the salience of ethnic identity as late as possible, it seems clear that a significant group of residents of the island were known as Sinhalas by this time. Gunawardana argued that this group pertained to the 'kulīna' or ruling stratum, and that the lower classes were excluded from this group – but this element of the argument is not particularly compelling.[45]

Either way, this does not sit easily with Pollock's characterization of an Indic system in which 'the names for the vernaculars seem to abstract them from the domain of the group and locate them in what almost seem ecospheres… we must conclude it was far more often region that made a language (and a people) than the reverse'.[46] For what do we have in the *Dhampiyā aṭuvā gäṭapadaya* right at the beginnings of the vernacular turn? Yes, the name of the language derives from the land, but that in turn derives from residents of the land, who had taken their name from the lion-natured founding figures Sīhabāhu and Vijaya… The flow of causality in the development of identity described by this and later texts such as the twelfth-century *Dharmapradīpikā* are scholarly reflections and may or may not reflect what happened historically.[47] The more significant point is that by this time, the land, heroic founding figures, the residents of the land and the language were all profoundly identified with each other and grouped under the same name.[48] And that it was considered to be a matter of some significance to the highest elites how the name for the wider Sinhala group evolved and could be defined.

In fact, a lineage-based understanding may have been current much earlier than this (perhaps a century or so after the composition of the *Mahāvaṃsa*) to judge from the version of the Sīhabāhu story relayed by the Chinese traveller Xuanzang, which he must have heard from Lankan monks who had come to India.[49] It says that after the founder arrived to the island and tricked his way to power, he propagated and reproduced, and because his offspring became numerous they divided into classes and elected a king and ministers. The men of the 'Lion State' (*shizi guo*) are described in racial terms, possessing certain physical and psychological characteristics as a result of their ancestry from a lion. This may well reflect a strand of Chinese racial ethnology, but Xuanzang, at least, understood the Sinhala origin story as a descent claim – and for a whole society (note that all classes are held to be descended from the lion-fathered founder).[50] Indeed, there is surely an opportunity for drawing more on foreign deployments of the term 'Sinhala' from this period into our analysis.[51]

Furthermore, even Gunawardana saw the period of Cōḷa occupation in the tenth to eleventh centuries as providing the conditions for an 'archaic ethnicity' (that is, one sensed by sections of the elite and literati). In his view, the crucial shift to an inclusive definition of 'Sinhala' had happened by the reign of Parākramabāhu I's successor, Niśśankamalla (1187–96). The Cōḷas certainly provided the Sinhala kingdoms with more than enough alterity through which to fashion a contrasting image of themselves.[52] Sinhala texts of the thirteenth century, such as the Pūjāvaliya, show the lasting impact of these conflicts in inflaming identity politics. But the truth is that these texts were merely redeploying a discourse of alterity already formed in the Pāli *vaṃsas*.[53] This sense of opposition to a '*demaḷa*' foe has become a shared understanding, expressed and reinforced through more particular shared memories of particular wars and battles, as registered in a range of texts in different languages with different purposes.[54]

It is worth pausing here to underline that of course Tamils or *demaḷas* are not only demonized in the Pāli and Sinhala texts; they are present in them in a number of ways. This is to be expected: near 'outsiders' usually play several roles in the reproduction of domestic society; they are allies, marriage partners, ritual specialists and more.[55] This multivalency of the foreign is a theme that runs through Gananath Obeyesekere's work, and is also pursued in Marshall Sahlins' recent theories of the stranger-king: it is a key theme of this volume too.[56]

When the Portuguese and Dutch began to produce more ethnological material about Sri Lanka in the seventeenth century, what they report is not at all at odds with what we have gathered from these clues in the Sinhala and Pāli texts.[57] The European writers are quite clear that the Sīhabāhu-Vijaya narrative is an origin story for the whole people. Interestingly, this is not the only origin story they relate ('and as all nations seek to glorify their origin, and the heathen almost always imagine fabulous ones'), which indicates both that the *vaṃsa* narrative was not the only source of self-understanding and that there was a continuing need on the part of the Sinhalas and their neighbours to create stories to explain where they and their name came from.[58] Much more could be said in this vein – reflecting on the profound historical consciousness of the Sinhala texts for example – but we must move on.[59] Charles Hallisey has suggested that:

> the very period in which we see Sinhala fully realized as a literary language – that is, around the turn of the millennium – was also the time that use of the term 'Sinhala' was extended... to the general population and their language.[60]

If so, it would make sense to see this in the context of the first major unification of the island under the Okkākas in the tenth century.[61] Land, language, people and polity all seem to be subject to a project of conceptual solidification and reorganization. What about religion? Again, in Pollock's analysis this realm of life is afforded only a strangely attenuated connection to both political and aesthetic projects. Again, for Sri Lanka, this makes little sense.

That a certain religious cosmopolitanism should emerge as a major characteristic of the Indic world – and one that distinguishes it in enduring and profound ways from Europe – will be a surprise to no one. Ultimately its roots must lie not in a particular quality of Sanskrit or its literary development, but in the basic nature of the ideas developed in the formative period for South Asian religious and philosophical thought. Here the salvationist or transcendentalist urge was not initially expressed in a monotheistic devotion to a jealous god, and a given path to salvation could co-exist with all manner of projects of truth-seeking or attempts to access divine power for earthly purposes. Pollock goes further, however, to argue that there was nothing in India comparable to the Providential charter some poets and stoic thinkers provided for the Roman Empire, and he presumably has in mind the ubiquitous and long-lasting theme of Christian Providentialism too.[62] In India, by contrast the supreme deity was simply 'irrelevant as a source of royal authority. A talismanic or apotropaic force? Yes. But a granter of heavenly mandate, a justifier of rule, a transcendent real-estate agent awarding parcels of land? Never'.[63]

No one would claim that Sri Lanka presented an exact analogy to these late pagan and Christian ideas in the West. For one thing, the language of monotheistic agency is quite inappropriate in the Pāli Buddhist context. Insofar as 'Providence' implies the continuing interventions of an all-powerful deity, it has little relevance to Lanka. Moreover, it has long been a concern for scholars of Sri Lanka to object to modern nationalist-Buddhist readings of the past that have often assumed the timeless truth of very similar ideas. Yet the main dimension of Providentialism at issue here is the provision of a sacred mandate, and in this sense it does indeed become possible to discern an analogous logic as far back as the *Mahāvaṃsa*. Who can doubt that it is a major task of the *Mahāvaṃsa* to celebrate the special relationship between Buddha and the blessed realm of Lanka, to establish how deeply the Buddha impressed his *dhamma* on the land by his three visits, just as he physically sank his foot into the mountain of Sumanakūṭa (known today as Adam's Peak)?[64] Or that the kings of Lanka are thus charged with a cherished role in protecting his teachings against its enemies, which will in turn mean that they must flourish?[65]

We need not rehearse here well-known features of the *Mahāvaṃsa*'s account of Duṭugämaṇu's war against the *demaḷas* from South India, so bluntly framed as a sacred war.[66] As just one detail, consider the story of one of Duṭugämaṇu's ten preternaturally gifted warriors. Nandhimitta had grown up in Anurādhapura and witnessed the *demalas* of Elara's occupying force desecrating the *thüpas*, so he went among them tearing them apart and throwing their body parts over the walls.[67] Then he reasoned that such negative attrition against the enemy was not as good as positively serving the religion; if he waged such war on behalf of the (Sinhala) kings of the south then he could add lustre to the faith. When the post-vernacular *Thūpavaṃsa* of the thirteenth century relays this episode, it need only elaborate the same theme by adding a few pungent details – that the *demaḷas* had been defecating and urinating in the courtyard of the sacred Bodh tree, for example.[68] The line of alterity against the *demaḷas* from the *vaṃsas* to the most demotic war poems of the early modern period, is thus thickened with the sentiments of religious opposition.[69] To clarify: it is not that Pollock discounts the possibility of the mobilization of religious alterity elsewhere in South Asia. Indeed, in other publications he has made such a claim with regard to the Rāmāyaṇa's role in the face of aggression by Muslim powers.[70] It is rather that in the Lankan tradition a) this alterity may be expressed by a quasi-Providential connection between the fate of a religious project and the fate of a people and land, and b) was thus liable to become fused with other forms of group emotion.[71]

Naturally, the assertion of religious superiority also had an autonomous dynamic: it was never merely the waging of ethnic or dynastic warfare by other means. The *Mahāvaṃsa* – giving voice to the Mahāvihāra tradition that would eventually come to reign supreme from the twelfth century – tells us of monks and kings concerned to put down heretical doctrines, by burning books if necessary. It is notable that the chief 'heretical' threat the Mahāvihāra identified during the reign of Vohārika Tissa (214–36 CE) came from the Vaitulyas, who seem to have taught something rather close to monotheism, or at least theism.[72] But we know that elsewhere in the world such theological projects have often provided an irresistible ideological resource for political elites; nothing suggests Lanka was different in that regard.

If the quasi-Providentialist theme begins well before the shift to vernacular literature, once that shift was underway it was elaborated in more explicit terms. In a tenth-century inscription we have the first assertion that 'none but future Buddhas would become kings of prosperous Lanka'.[73] By this time, South Indian alterity was being provided by the Pāṇḍyas and then Cōḷas.[74] Now, Pollock does note in parentheses that the Cōḷa Empire, with its aggressive assertion of Saivism, stands as a rare exception to his remarks about the prevailing religious pluralism. By the ninth century, the Saiva canon was already shaping up against Jain and 'Theravāda' opponents.[75] It would seem, then, that along this southern periphery of the Sanskrit cosmopolis we have the sacred plunged into the dirty work of political competition and group struggle in a way that is all too familiar from other parts of the world (but is unmatched elsewhere in Pollockian India). This generated a pugnacious rhetoric about the sanctified morality of warfare that one could easily find parallels for in Europe.

It is always worth emphasizing that ideological strategies of boundary-hardening may work by co-opting or mimicking the discourse of those the boundary is hardened against. The following quotation, taken from Charles Hallisey's translation, is pertinent for many reasons. It is an inscription in Sinhala by Niśśankamalla (r. 1187–96):

> King Niśśanka Malla ensured the long stability of the state and the religion (*Lokaśāsanaya*). Moreover considering that the island of Lanka is a noble land because of the establishment of the *sāsana* there, that the living beings in it have lofty excellences and that, therefore, they should receive advice and protection, he out of compassion, proclaimed the following maxim of good counsel:
>
> Though kings appear in human form, they are human divinities (*naradēvatā*) and must, therefore, be regarded as gods. The appearance of an impartial king should be welcomed as the appearance of the Buddha... If the wishes of kings were not observed, the human world would be like hell, but if their wishes were respected it would be like heaven.[76]

Such a bald assertion of the divinity of the king is rare in a Lankan context and possibly due to a desire to assert the kind of authority that his Indian counterparts possessed: this is cosmopolitanism as a function of royal peer-to-peer relations. Yet the inscription also speaks of the creation of a moral community rooted in a space at once political and geographical, which has kingship at its core and the advancement of a specific tradition of religious teachings as its purpose. Hallisey must be right to connect this to Niśśankamalla's own origin in Kālinga and his unclear claims to the throne.[77] It is precisely because of the cosmopolitan origin of the king, and the cosmopolitan audience for his claims, that he must engage in a profound emphasis on localization. One would be hard-pressed to avoid interpreting these assertions as an unusually blatant exercise in 'legitimization'.

Nor can such immediate and contingent forms of legitimization simply be interpreted as evanescent strategies. Rather they streamed into and inflected a more enduring discourse that was picked up repeatedly in subsequent texts. The thirteenth-century *Pūjāvaliya* has been much-quoted for the way that it aggressively asserts that only Buddhist kings protecting the *sāsana* should – and indeed *would* – be able to rule over Lanka.[78] Any non-believers must simply fail just as the Buddha had banished the demons. This was written following the invasion of the Kalinga King Māgha (1215) who stimulated the ire of the vaṃsa-writers ever after with his book-burning brand of Saivism. The *Cūḷavaṃsa* accused him of forcing people to convert to 'wrong views': 'Thus the Damila warriors in imitation of the warriors of Māra, destroyed in the evil of their nature the laity and the order.'[79] In the midst of this 'Tamil conflagration', monks fled to a retreat in South India associated with a 'Cōḷaganga', and when Buddhism was restored under Parākramabāhu II (1236–70), *mahathēras* from India were brought over to assist.[80] The sense then of the wider Buddhist ecumene was still present, but there is little doubt that Māgha's unusually aggressive religious policy had stimulated another flash of electricity through the connection between religious community, sovereignty and land.[81]

Pollock argues that the connection between popularizing religious movements and vernacularization has been greatly exaggerated, that the original impetus for the vernacular came from the secular aesthetic concerns of courts and only later did a few regional vernacular movements emerge with some sort of religious purpose.[82] Whether this chronology fits Sri Lanka can be left to scholars with more expertise in this area.[83] But it may be artificial in the Lankan case to perceive two distinct vernacular flowerings, a cosmopolitan version divorced from religion and then a regional 'counterrevolution' closely linked with religious community. According to Jonathan Walters, the popularization of Buddhism can also be located in the tenth to twelfth centuries.[84] Certainly, whether they constitute a 'second wave' or not, various thirteenth- to fifteenth-century Sinhala texts could not be more explicit that their function was to make Buddhist teachings widely available to the non-learned.[85] The Sinhala *Thūpavaṃsa*, for example, reflects (or seeks to drive) the development of a cult of the relics in Lanka, and this is a major mechanism by which sacred power is concretized for a mass audience, or a population gathered into an imagined community of Buddhist devotees.[86] (Indeed, we shall see the continuing success of this project in the crucial role played by the Tooth Relic in political conflicts till the last days of the Kandyan kingdom.) It is likely that the identification between Buddhism and Lanka was further strengthened by the disappearance of Buddhist institutions in India from around this date.[87]

Notice that we have not yet broached modernity – or even what some scholars now refer to as 'early modernity'. When we come to the latter end of the premodern, Pollock does explore the possibility that the more northerly parts of South Asia may have experienced a form of alterity in the shape of the encroaching dominion of Muslim elites, and that in a few cases this might possibly have stimulated a vernacular response and a religious repudiation.[88] Ultimately, however, he is reluctant to assign this much causal weight.[89] A little later, Lanka had its own marauding monotheists to contend with, and these offered yet another manifestation of alterity. In general, no scholar has been willing to compare the Lankan experience of the introduction of European Christianity with the Indian experience of the introduction of West and Central Asian Islam further north. This is no doubt because the modern-day politics of the historiographies are so differently organized. Yet a range of practices – above all the controversial facts of temple-destruction – present points of comparison. Whatever current scholarship is prepared to concede for the northern case, it is easier to acknowledge that the aggressive exclusivism of Portuguese Catholicism stimulated intermittently more resistant and boundary-hardened forms of Buddhist sentiment.[90]

Pollock successfully isolates state formation and royal ambition as the main context for Sanskritization, yet the connection between the adoption of the whole Sanskrit imaginaire and the political will of kings is left ultimately mysterious. Underlying this is an initially laudable desire not to reduce cultural production to a matter of political instrumentality.[91] But so uncompromising is his theoretical antagonism to the notion of 'legitimization' that Indic culture ends up as divergent from the West even at the level of the most basic mechanism by which religion relates to politics. Hence 'ideology' may be a permissible concept for analysing Europe but not South Asia.[92] Elites did not 'need' religion, apparently, or 'use' it or even 'benefit' from it politically: in the Sanskrit mode of being, they simply lived and dreamed within its embrace.

In the case of Lanka, however, it seems that the celebration and imaginative evocation of the geography of the island of Lanka, the assertion of the moral supremacy of Buddhism, the elaboration of Pāli and Sinhala as literary languages, and the coalescence of Sinhalaness as an ethnic identity may all be related to the struggle to maintain a form of political unity and independence from foreign powers.[93]

It is not, after all, hugely surprising that Sri Lanka should sit uncomfortably within some of Pollock's generalizations: it is the fate of ambitious attempts at model building to be set upon by specialists agitated by the righteous indignation of the counterexample. It may serve to highlight a general problem with the method, however, which is to insist too much on the causal priority of cultural difference. This amounts to the exaltation of a different Indic 'ontology' from which various ogres of liberal academia have been gratifyingly banished: thus the Sanskrit world did not have 'empire' but cosmopolitics; it did not give rise to the nation-state but to 'vernacular polities'; it did not have 'race' or 'ethnicity' but entirely different kinds of groupings; and it was even free from 'ideology' itself insofar as its dealings with the sacred were simply sincere.

But let us assume, for the moment, that Pollock is right about the implications of vernacularization in the Sanskrit cosmopolis in general but Sri Lanka fails to fit the model in the ways addressed above. In that case, the more interesting question is *why* that should be so.[94] Unfortunately, it is also more difficult to answer. In his expressed reservations about Sri Lanka, Pollock refers to its participation in another cosmopolitan order, that of Pāli imaginaire. Indeed, the more that we privilege the foundational role of the Pāli worldview in Lanka, the more Lanka could even be seen as 'the exception that proves the rule' of Pollock's thesis. Does it show what happens when part of South Asia, so obviously part of the Indic world in so many ways, comes under the sway of a different literary or even cognitive regime? Steven Collins had already pointed out the difference between 'the Indic model of clerical-ideological power' in which Sanskrit was imposed as a medium of expression without seeking to impose a single belief system, and the Pāli Theravāda model in which there was 'an isomorphism between a single language and a unitary ideology'.[95] But given that what is at issue here is not Buddhism per se, which embedded itself in Asian societies in myriad ways, but the way that it was localized in the resurrected Pāli texts of the Lankan *vaṃsas*, to appeal to Pāli is therefore only to rephrase the question about Lanka.[96] If the 'Pāli cultural package' adopted by the Southeast Asian centres was first formed in Sri Lanka, we are pressed again to consider what may have made the history of identity formation in the island distinctive.[97]

Victor Lieberman's recent work of comparative history may provide us with the beginnings of an explanation framed in geopolitical terms.[98] He places great emphasis on variations in how 'protected' different parts of Eurasia were. In the first instance, this refers to whether they were vulnerable to conquest by Inner Asian warrior groups, but we could extend it more broadly to long-term openness to all kinds of conquest elites. The island of Lanka, as the Sanskrit poets were fond of pointing out, is surrounded by the ocean. However clichéd its island status has become and however much the global history of today tends to emphasize connectivity – yet those island boundaries mattered profoundly.[99] They presented a natural (although by no means implacable) limit to the political ambitions of Sinhala rulers from earliest times: there was really no need for any 'contraction to the vernacular polity' that Pollock discerns elsewhere. More significantly, the ocean meant that while Lanka was open to the extension of military and political might by South Indian powers from at least the mid-first millennium CE, these projects were never strong enough to sweep away rule by Sinhala-speaking Buddhist rulers for more than a few generations.[100]

Pollock refers to the 'veritable law of political entropy' in India such that few ruling lineages lasted more than two to three centuries.[101] Most significant for us is to note the relatively weak continuity of identity between the dynasties riding these cycles in the subcontinent, even if there were very long-running chains of imperial imitation and charter state referral. In Sri Lanka, the sense of the continuity between different instantiations of Sinhala kingship sustained by its relationship with the *sāsana* was presumably more profound. This may be partly because of its long gestation in Anurādhapura, which had its origins in the mid-first millennium BCE and was not abandoned until the very end of the first millennium CE and was the unrivalled centre of political life in the island for that time. It would be difficult to find an equivalent in India over the same vast stretch of time. After that, as Sri Lanka was drawn further into dynastic competition with South India, the life-cycle of political centres became shorter and shorter, but perhaps by that time extraordinary continuity had done its work. In short, Sri Lanka's geographical position may have provided it with enough 'protection' for profound sensations of continuity to develop, and enough 'exposure' or alterity for self-conscious identities to form around those continuities.[102]

This may seem like a very abstract analysis, but in one sense it does find an echo in the perceptions of historical Sinhala speakers themselves. As we saw, from the viewpoint of the courts in the Sinhala-dominated south, the island has long been a distinctive self-contained arena of political aspiration. That the 'reification' of Lanka has a considerable history before colonial powers ever started to imagine the land for themselves is worth emphasizing given a common tendency to emphasize British ideological manufacturing in particular. Nevertheless a certain puzzle remains. Was the rest of the Sanskrit cosmopolis really so divergent from the European trajectory as Pollock claims? If so, why should the Pāli landscape take on contours that look a little more 'European' in appearance – at least when viewed in a certain light? Was the Lankan crucible really so important?

## The function of the foreign in dynastic systems: a comparative perspective

Thus far we have touched upon ways in which rulers and subjects may be bound together as an imagined community tied to the land. But this tendency existed in tension with an equally common desire on the part of ruling elites to associate themselves with the world beyond the local. The purpose of this second part of the chapter is to develop an appreciation of the paradoxical manifestations of this tension, with the help of two brief comparative forays.

Rather than appeal to 'cosmopolitanism', we may do better to consider the drivers of premodern elite 'extraversion', by which the supra-local (its commercial fecundity, modes of civility, technology, potential allies and efficacious ritual) is seen as a source of local power. One of the most important of these was simply elite will to power – that is, their desire to conquer neighbouring realms and expand their hegemony: to create empires. Imperial rulership is almost by definition estranged from certain groups of subjects. But there is a less routinely observed process that works the other way, where elites sense their peripheral position in relation to imperial formations, and find themselves drawn to their glamorous, expansive and sophisticated civilizational traditions, their long-refined literary cultures and long-burnished imagery of rulership.[103] Local rulers are concerned with their position relative to their peers in the wider world, and these can only be addressed in a 'cosmopolitan' language of equivalent reach.[104]

But if local rulers suffer from status anxiety with relation to foreign rulers, their domestic status is hardly a matter of blithe assurance either. Another driver of elite extraversion then is lodged within the very process of erecting hierarchy, in the necessity for elites to distinguish themselves from the lower orders: to reign over the merely domestic by signalling their transcendence of it. In this way, kings find a way to lift themselves above the entanglements of local kinship claims, the pretensions of aristocrats and upstart chiefs.[105] In contrast to Pollock's vision of South Asian kingship as something simply accepted by the governed as an unquestionable fact of life, it is surely better to consider it as the site of constant symbolic labour, as new means of exaltation are gleaned and new audiences for its self-display are assembled. Just as ruling elites are driven to seize upon coercive powers from the outside (guns, mercenaries, alliances), and economic powers from the outside (trade revenues, commercial taxes), so they are prone to seek out means of symbolic distinction from the outside too.

In the inscription quoted above, Niśśankamalla may have emphasized the importance of Buddhist kingship in order to ward off any claims from other South Indian powers but he also sought to protect his position from local claimants by insisting that the kings of Lanka must be of *kṣatriya* caste, which appealed to a wider Indic normative tradition and a status that no one else on the island could claim.[106] This introduces a more specific aspect of this process of royal estrangement, which is a function of the biological reproduction of rarefied breeds. For such distinction to be maintained, it becomes desirable to find marriage partners boasting the best claims of royal blood, and where else could these be found but in foreign lands? The very claim of a dynasty to unique status within their realm drives the search for marital alliance without it. This is why in monarchical polities, foreign elites are rarely merely enemies; they are nearly always also affines.[107] To the extent that royal courts tend to participate in transregional kinship networks and elite cultures distinct from their subjects, and deny their subjects much meaningful participation in governance, all premodern dynastic states have a somewhat 'imperial' quality.[108]

The potency of the foreign is not simply a threat to local rulers then; it is also an opportunity. Another ubiquitous driver of elite extraversion is the way that internal factional conflicts within local centres lead rivals to appeal to foreign powers to support their cause: this is the key logic behind the phenomena of Lankan princes in exile explored in Biedermann's chapter in this volume (Chapter 7). But even on a symbolic level, declarations of vassalage or submission to external empires may be undertaken in order to strengthen claims to local sovereignty. This has been a theme in recent work on Lanka's sixteenth century, analysing both the initial accord with the Portuguese in 1506 and the subsequent proclamations of vassalage to the kings in Lisbon over the decades following 1518.[109] This is surely the context too in which to see Ähälēpola's willingness to advertise his acknowledgement of George III's suzerainty in 1816, and yet at the same time establish himself as a king in the full sense, which Sivasundaram mentions in this volume (Chapter 10).[110] This vision of hierarchical kingship was no longer acceptable to nineteenth-century British officials in the way that it had been to Portuguese kings of the sixteenth century, who had happily acted as liege to Lankan kings and *cakravartis*.[111]

In late eighteenth-century Hawaii, we see a similar movement on the part of local elites, but this also reflected a particularly powerful driver of elite extraversion: the tradition that their claims to superiority already depended on a conception of themselves as strangers or even as foreign aggressors to the native people. This phenomenon of stranger-kingship has been extensively analysed by Marshall Sahlins.[112] I have written on this analysis at length elsewhere, so this is not the place for a proper discussion, except to say that it alerts us to a globally prevalent means of understanding the ascension of kingship as a journey from the zones beyond – the wild, foreign, animal, supernatural, transgressive – to the heart of the domestic: it is the archetypal narrative of alien potency digested, and it appears over and again in the *Mahāvaṃsa*.[113] (Fundamentally, then, its initial emergence is not best seen as a legitimization of kingship so much as a collective means of understanding the origins of hierarchical society.)[114] Here we need only note that there seem to be at least two forms in which the logic of the stranger-king model may impress itself upon our sources: 1) as a structuring principle of origin myth for rulers and peoples, and 2) as a charter for a living mode of social organization. I have argued that the first is strongly present in the Pāli and Sinhala material, which thus bear striking analogies with other origin myths worldwide. Indeed, the Shamabala of Tanganyika have told a story about a lion king founder that is strikingly close to that of Sīhabāhu.[115] But it is worth taking this opportunity to note that the second was not, I think, present.[116]

To clarify: in the latter cases, Sahlins perceives a 'dual society' in which the foreign-born ruling dynasty must bow to the ritual primacy of the autochthonous people. The king may have overriding authority but by various means his dependency on the life-giving powers of the indigenous people is registered. There are a few indications that the symbolic relationship between the väddās and Sinhala kingship may have preserved some such understanding.[117] It is intriguing, for example, that the rebel king of 1815–18 should have been presented to the people surrounded by väddās.[118] But in general the väddās were symbolically as well as geographically on the margins of the Sinhala social order. This mirrors the manner in which the mythical indigenes, the yakkhas, are simply purged from the island in the vaṃsas (although note they return…), or that their descendants, the Pulindas (Vijaya's offspring with Kuveṇī) were banished. Whereas in the most typical 'dual society' the general name for the people is derived from the autochthons, in the case of Sri Lanka it derives, as we have seen, from the royal dynasty itself, which arrives to the island as foreign. In fact, in Lankan society, at times the most important court ritualists were Brahmans.

So the foreignness of the ruling stratum was not a predicate of Sinhala social and political life in quite the manner that it apparently was for the chiefly elites in parts of Oceania (such as the *ali'i* in Hawaii). This is not at all to deny that the dynasties ruling over Sinhala kingdoms often carried foreign blood or maintained foreign lifestyles as a matter of fact. We have already referred to the many reasons why that should be so in terms of the interests of the dynasty, chief among them the marital logic of dynastic systems and the political logic of hierarchical uniqueness. However, we can supplement this with a consideration of the interests of the noble class beneath it, which may in certain situations seek out stranger-kings in order to establish a relatively disinterested force of arbitration and maintain the balance of power among the various factions. In this way, they forgo the potential for immediate advantage for the long-term preservation of stability. This understanding of stranger-kingship – quite distinct from the

Sahlinsian model, and which rather recalls a Hobbesian vision of the development of the state – has been applied in Southeast Asian historiography and was introduced into a Lankan context by Alicia Schrikker.[119] To the extent that the ideology of kingship is thereby understood as a reflex of political calculation, however, it would imply a certain instability in the system. This is because the utility of the stranger-king to the nobility must be set against the bar it places to their highest pretensions, for a faction that finds itself suddenly out of favour that bar may seem disagreeably high.[120] We shall return to the implications of this below.

In what follows, we shall rather emphasize two vaguely paradoxical points: the first is that the foreignness of the king need not impede the coalescence of ethnic feeling beneath or around him, and the second is that his foreignness is usually subject to certain forms of domestication which renders it palatable. These two points have a certain relevance in the context of Lankan historiography. It is sometimes argued, for example, that the fact that the Nāyaka kings of Kandy (1739–1815) hailed from Madura and upheld a distinct identity and lifestyle distinguishing themselves from the Sinhala nobility must tell of the absence of Lankan patriotism or Sinhala group belonging.[121] Or that there must therefore be two distinct understandings of Sinhalaness at work, the 'political' and 'cultural', which were not equivalent.[122] This is the point at which the comparative method may provide some assistance, for our interpretation of any one case really depends on certain sociological or even psychological assumptions: how does group identity formation work in monarchical societies? What kind of logic does it tend to obey?

At this point, Britain may be appealed to for comparative purposes. From the late medieval period to the present day, England has had royal dynasties of foreign origin: the Welsh Tudors, Scottish Stuarts, followed by Germans of some description to the present day, with the Hanoverians and Windsors. George III (r. 1760–1820), for example, who claimed sovereignty over Sri Lanka in the 1810s, was the third Hanoverian king of Great Britain and Ireland but the first to use English as his first language, and was the result of a union between Frederick, Prince of Wales, and Princess Augusta of Saxe-Gotha.[123] This has been the way of things regardless of great transformations in the political structures over which the 'kings and queens of England' reigned from their medieval origins into their early modern expansions and then the era of the full-blooded nation-state and empire. Even the briefest consideration of early modern English history indicates then that the inherent 'extraversion' or rampant cosmopolitanism of premodern dynastic systems need not act as an indigestible obstacle to the emergence of ethnic and patriotic emotion.

## Indigestible Europeans

We should not then expect anything tidier about identity politics in Lanka. In the Kandyan kingdom, the kings may have been more visibly and emphatically foreign in certain ways than some of their counterparts in Britain, and they long retained the loyalty of most of their Sinhala subjects regardless.[124] But they too were made acceptable through certain limited forms of indigenization.[125] And there is nothing unexpected in comparative terms about the suggestion that their foreign status or Saivite inclinations could become a point of vulnerability to be probed by political opponents at specific moments. To follow Schrikker's reasoning, this might occur when the political attractions of the stranger-king began to pall for elements of the Kandyan aristocracy – when the Nāyakas became a more entrenched rival for resources.[126]

At this point, however, our notions about how Kandyan society functioned become confused by the possibility of European influence – on both our sources and local conceptions themselves. With regard to the former, could it be that Lankan society comes to seem comparable simply because the growing preponderance of Dutch and British source material has – deliberately or ignorantly – obscured cultural difference? As for the possibility that European assumptions had begun to infect the local political imagination, we could consider, in the first decade or two of the nineteenth century, the vituperative repudiation of the Nāyakas, in the *Vadiga Haṭana* and the *Kiraḷa Sandēśaya* of 1815. These disparage the last king of Kandy in the most blatantly ethnic manner as a 'demaḷa' eunuch who had displaced the Sinhalese. It has been suggested that this represents the fruits of Dutch and particularly British propaganda, as both had been trying to drive an ethnic wedge through the heart of the Kandyan kingdom for some time – with little success until this point.[127] Yet even if that hypothesis be granted, it involved the monarch's opponents in a redeployment of one of the oldest tropes in the Sinhala literature.[128]

The Portuguese, as far as we know, did not seek to found their rule on a principle of ethnic divide and rule. The distinct ethnicity, culture and political history of the Tamils of the north may have been one reason why relations with Jaffna were often managed separately from Mannar or South India before its conquest in 1619 – to that extent the Portuguese were involved in a project of 'de-islanding' – but the Portuguese made no attempt to incite or shape ethnic divisions for their own ends. Their intrigues worked through the manipulation of feelings of vassalage and royal authority that both sides understood, and through the insinuation of Christianity. What they were obsessed with was the management of religious difference rather than ethnic rivalry. Portuguese sources do occasionally speculate on the political consequences of ethnic emotion, however. Indeed, if the fall of Kandy in 1815 involved a play on xenophobia, it is intriguing that the collapse of Parākramabāhu VI's (1411–65) unification in the 1470s and the ultimate fall of Kōṭṭe in the 1590s also may have involved something similar.[129] When Rājasiṃha I of Sītāvaka died in 1593, the military was left in the hands of one of the old king's favourites, a Saivite immigrant by the name of Manamperuma Mohoṭṭāla. However, he was then forced to defect to the forces of Kōṭṭe and the Portuguese, who gave him a title and a Sinhala name invoking past Kandyan kings – Jayavīra Baṇḍāra. This was decisive: an exceptionally able commander, he played a vital role in the crushing of resistance in the lowlands and almost delivered the highlands to the Portuguese. The central point for us here is why he defected. Two Portuguese sources have it that he had been forced out of Sītāvaka because he was a foreigner and lacked the right dynastic genealogy. If we are inclined to read this as an early example of European ethno-thought, we must at least pause at the loose congruence with the *Rājāvaliya*'s assertion that he was driven out of Sītāvaka by popular mockery of his Saivism.[130]

The most significant way in which kings of foreign origin were domesticated, of course, was by establishing their status as protectors of Buddhism, as many scholars have emphasized.[131] Indeed, there seems something of a tendency for kings with the strongest foreign associations to be those who produce the strongest articulations of Lanka as a land of Buddhist truth and Buddhist kings.[132] If this is the case, could then European colonial rulers not also become appropriately domesticated to the extent that they were prepared to become patrons of Buddhism? The question hardly applies to the Portuguese, who repudiated Buddhism's place in the political order almost entirely. There is one partial exception: the strange and murky case of their first conquering captain-general, Jerónimo de Azevedo (1540–1625), who set up a court in Malvāna and who appears in a few reports as a Kurtz-like figure, being carried around on a palanquin and addressed as *deviyo*. But this was only ever a very partial accommodation. Azevedo was involved in some of the bloodiest campaigns of conquest, which involved the destruction of Buddhist and Hindu sacred structures too. Nevertheless, there is a potential analogy to be drawn between Azevedo and the first Briton in charge of Kandy after the conquest of 1815, John D'Oyly, who also seems to have partially indigenized in certain ways as resident. Both Azevedo and D'Oyly represent the high point in attempting to maintain continuity with Lankan traditions of government at the very start of imperial rule in the low country and Kandy respectively.[133] There is even a certain similarity between the Kandyan Convention of 1815 and the agreements in 1597 (once known as the 'Malvāna Convention'), which established Portuguese sovereignty over the lowlands.[134] But D'Oyly was far more sympathetic to Buddhism than any Portuguese officer could have been, and the Kandyan convention allowed the British to become more convincing patrons of Buddhism.[135] They deliberately cultivated this status in an attempt to defuse resistance – to garner, even in the crudest sense of the word, a modicum of legitimacy.

All this makes sense in terms of a very long-term structure of Buddhist authority on the island. And there are recurring patterns to be found in how authority was contested too. Now, such contestation of monarchical authority was rather routine in Lankan political life, for all kinds of structural reasons, but the questions here concern the symbolic repertoire that was mobilized when mounted against European rulers. In what follows, I shall suggest that the wars of 1815–18 – the subject of Sujit Sivasundaram's Chapter 10 in this volume – were conducted according to the same grammar of rebellion that we see in the period of Portuguese direct rule of the lowlands (1590s–1650s). In both cases, for all the efforts of Azevedo or D'Oyly and Brownrigg, a massive uprising followed shortly after direct rule was announced, such that it may be seen as a mutation in the leadership of the war of resistance as much as a rebellion. This timing indicates that the idea of the new imposition of direct rule by the European power was offensive and not only the playing out of exploitative policies.[136] In both cases, it is plausible that the failure of the new rulers to convincingly inhabit the ritual forms of Buddhist kingship was *partly* to blame.[137] As well as pointing to the pre-British propensity of Kandyan society for rebellion, Brownrigg also ascribes the cause of rebellion in 1815–18 to fears about the danger to Buddhism.[138] To that extent, it does indeed seem more restorationist than 'revolutionary'.[139] (The subsequent withdrawal of British support for Buddhism, thus reverting to more typical Christian stance, was one reason for the outbreak of rebellion in 1848.)[140]

In both periods, the attempt to crush the wave of resistance involved a ratcheting up of violence, displays of exemplary punishment and scorched earth tactics – no doubt the product of an essentially military logic at work.[141] Both reactions failed to produce lasting peace and were followed by several more uprisings.[142] More significant is that in both periods, the same symbolic repertoire of indigenous authority was deployed: resistance threw up pretenders with shadowy origins who claimed royal blood regardless, and these pretenders attempted to associate themselves with ancient sites and objects redolent of political unity. The British ended up chasing after the Tooth Relic in the manner of claimants to the throne of centuries long past.[143] During the course of the rebellion of 1817–18, there was an attempt to unveil a new pretender at Dambulla Vihāra and otherwise exploit the symbolic value of Anurādhapura.[144] This probably owed little to early British Orientalist interest in the Lankan past, to Dutch interpretations, nor even to specifically Kandyan developments, for the same pattern can be found in the rebellions of 1616–19. One of the leaders in the Seven Korales, Nikapiṭiya Baṇḍāra, claimed ancestry from Rājasiṃha of Sītāvaka, and announced his rebellion at Anurādhapura in the guise of a yogi (*jogue*) wearing animal skins.[145] If the British tried to manage the symbolic capital of the ancient capital, the Portuguese were also alarmed at the sheer antiquity of indigenous kingship as relayed in the popular memories surrounding Anurādhapura in the early seventeenth century.[146]

One point that emerges from this is that Buddhist patronage was not therefore the only traditional criterion by which kingship was imagined as legitimate. The manufacture of kingship involved appealing to the shared historical memory of the Sinhala group, its physical vestiges of ancient greatness, and its origin myths: letters from the Kandyan court in 1811 and 1812, for example, begin by placing the Nāyaka kings of Kandy in the line of kings reaching back to Vijaya.[147] As always and everywhere in monarchical societies, dynastic claims were crucial. The Nāyaka dynastic name long held its appeal, but if Gananath Obeyesekere is right, even this became a source of weakness in 1760 insofar as they could not claim the more exalted Buddhist lineage of the solar dynasty.[148] As for colonial elites, they may have been subject to a certain 'bottom-up' process of indigenization, particularly through the composition of praise poems in the style of *praśasti* – even marauding Portuguese governor-generals could become heroes in this way.[149] But as a matter of the top-down projection of rulership ideology, they could not and did not attempt to embody the traditional forms of kingship in the variety of ways that the Nāyakas strove to.[150] Their appeal (such as it was) had to rest on other grounds: on the material advantages that new power regimes may offer to collaborators, or eventually on rewriting the rules of legitimacy, among others.[151]

The continuities indicated above are only surprising if we imagine that the waves of Portuguese, Dutch and early British rule had had the power to reorganize the mental and emotional life of Sinhalese subjects in both conquered and unconquered areas in profound ways. It has been a continuing problem for Lankan historiography as to how to translate the great emphasis on the cognitive power of British colonialism in Indian historical writing to the Lankan case.[152] This is partly because Lanka had already endured more than 200 years of European rule before the British arrived. This means that ascribing apparently long-term patterns of Lankan agency to the misconceptions of 'colonial discourse' would involve stretching the latter term to include sixteenth- and late seventeenth-century Portuguese texts – but these operated according to a rather different logic to that of the nineteenth-century Orientalism that has invited so much academic attention. Sujit Sivasundaram has sought to move around the problem by refusing the conceptual dichotomies of indigenous/colonial or continuity/change and referring instead to continual 'recycling' and 'resituating'.[153] This comes at the price of leaving us unable to assess the extent to which any transition can be said to have occurred under the British or with the passage into the modern era. Ultimately, we have to establish some sort of interpretation of the pre-existing patterns of identity formation in order to have any chance of understanding the significance of subsequent developments.

Such transformations there surely were, and indeed there is still much opportunity for analysing the *changes* in identity politics over the whole period of imperial intrusion (1500–1950).[154] But any such analysis would have to begin by noticing the striking patterns of continuity we have discussed. One last such pattern can be found in the ideological expression of resistance to European powers, as we see in the genre of the *haṭana* poem, which displays a certain stability in imagery, tone and organizing ideas from the late sixteenth to the early nineteenth centuries, as Michael Roberts' work has shown.[155] The island of Lanka is exalted; its political unity under a cakravarti ruler conceived as a matter of natural perfection (although it uses an archaic political geography of the 'Trisiṃhala' to express this); the glory of its god-like kings are sung; present conflicts are described in terms of ancient ones; and enemies are disparaged in visceral manner, often as animals, demons, beef-eaters and depraved addicts.

In the climax to the first instance of the war-poem genre, the *Sītāvaka Haṭana* of 1585, King Māyādunnē, who is credited with keeping at bay the Portuguese and their local allies, hands over his throne to his son Rājasiṃha:

> To everyone who was in this island of Lanka called dhamma [*dahan namäti lakdiva*]
> I was like a lamp tree [*pahan ruka*], owning it.
> For the sake of dhamma in Sri Lanka in a noble way
> Noble lord, I hand over all of Trisiṃhale to you[156]

This is a very tricky verse to translate.[157] But it is difficult to avoid the sense that 'the island of the dhamma' concept is resonating rather loudly here rather than waiting for the nineteenth century to come round. However, the equation between the land and the Buddhist dispensation misses out the third point of a triad: kingship. Māyādunnē is made to compare himself to a great lit-up tree standing at the centre of the island and sheltering it with a canopy of Buddhist righteousness.[158] There also seems an echo here of the *kapruka*, the tree of bounty in Śakra's heaven.[159]

In the following verse, Māyādunnē compares his son and heir to Śakra, which returns us to Pollockian themes.[160] Indeed, it is perhaps ironic how much these profoundly vernacular poems register the continuing appeal of the Sanskrit cosmos as a means of glorifying Lankan personae and events. This must be partly because of the rich imagery of noble conflict in Sanskrit literature: the wars of Rāma and Rāvaṇa or the Suras and Asuras provided a means of expressing the heroism of the struggle against dreadful enemies.[161]

Royal prowess always has its cosmopolitan dimension – but as the subordination of alien potency. Thus the *Rājasiṃha Haṭana* of c. 1638 can celebrate Rājasiṃha's comprehensive mastery of languages – 'Demaḷa and Sinhala, Sanskrit, Pāli, and Nagara, Portugal, and many another lore he learnt'[162] – while comparing the Portuguese to ogres, demons and 'cruel demaḷas'.[163] The operation of the digestive principle should not be expected to look logically coherent. Lankan kings from before the sixteenth through to the early nineteenth century sought foreign troops of all kinds to have at their disposal – perhaps the most concrete image of outside strength appropriately harnessed. But this does not hinder the *haṭanas* from emphasizing the ethnic heterogeneity of enemy forces in a disparaging manner. If we find the *Vadiga Haṭana* listing the 'motley band' of groups fighting for the British in 1815, it is strikingly similar to the list of the foreign armies (*para senaga*) in the *Sītāvaka Haṭana* – with the qualification that the earlier poem is much more blatant in its xenophobic disgust.[164] Here again, analyses of local texts hunting for signs of British influence come up against the awkward fact of Lanka's earlier waves of engagement with European and earlier regional imperialisms. In one sense at least, the digestive principle gestures to a human universal: the *haṭanas* in this regard are no more contradictory than the

British who used Malay or Sinhalese Lascarins while developing an infamous form of ethnic and racial pride.

The concept of cosmopolitanism has its place as a quick means of referring to a disposition to esteem the non-local. But it does not get us very far in understanding the complex place of the foreign in the symbolic manufacture of monarchy or the drivers of royal 'extraversion' more widely. Sri Lanka participated vigorously in the Sanskrit imaginaire and digested it thoroughly in its vernacular literature; it also produced distinct modes of foreign incorporation that certainly diverged from the European experience. This does not equate, however, to the absence of either sensations of peoplehood or the elaboration of Providentialist-style legitimation. With regard to these phenomena, many useful comparisons with the long term of European history may be discerned. In more general terms still, premodern monarchs everywhere have had to find some balance between the imperatives of expressing the wider group identity of their subjects and setting themselves above and apart from them.[165] In Lanka, foreign potency always held a certain appeal, but if it appeared indigestible, the Lankan body politic knew well enough how to eject it.

# Notes

## Introduction: Querying the cosmopolitan in history

1 Ulf Hannerz, 'Cosmopolitanism,' in *A Companion to the Anthropology of Politics*, ed. David Nugent and Joan Vincent (Oxford: Blackwell, 2007), 70.

2 Nicholas Thomas, *Entangled Objects: Exchange, Material Culture, and Colonialism in the Pacific* (Cambridge, MA: Harvard University Press, 2009), 108.

3 See among the most helpful overviews, Gillian Brook, 'Cosmopolitanism,' in *The Oxford Handbook of World Philosophy*, ed. William Edelglass and Jay L. Garfield (Oxford: Oxford University Press, 2011), 582–95; J. Binnie, J. J. Holloway, S. Millington, and C. Young, 'Cosmopolitanism,' in *International Encyclopedia of Human Geography*, ed. R. Kitchin and N. Thrift (Oxford: Elsevier, 2009), 307–13, and Hannerz, 'Cosmpolitanism'.

4 See, for example Robert Fine, *Cosmopolitanism* (London: Routledge, 2007).

5 Indeed, the extent to which it is both normative and imprecise is summed up wonderfully by Carol Breckenridge, Sheldon Pollock, Homi K. Bhabha and Dipesh Chakrabarty in *Cosmopolitanism* (Durham, NC: Duke University Press, 2002), 1: 'specifying cosmopolitanism positively and definitely is an uncosmopolitan thing to do.'

6 As in 'human beings [should] have equal moral and political obligations to each other based solely on their humanity, without reference to state citizenship, national identity, religious affiliation, ethnicity, or place of birth'? Gareth Wallace Brown, 'Cosmopolitanism,' in *The Concise Oxford Dictionary of Politics*, 3rd edn, ed. Iain McMillan and Alistair McLean (Oxford: Oxford University Press, 2009).

7 Prasenjit Duara, *The Crisis of Global Modernity: Asian Traditions and a Sustainable Future* (Cambridge: Cambridge University Press, 2015), 20, emphasis in original.

8 See for example Akhil Gupta, 'Globalization and Difference: Cosmopolitanism before the Nation-State,' *Transforming Cultures e-Journal* 3, 2 (2008), 1–20.

9 Of course other forms – the rural, thc popular, the regional – have also played a role.

10 This is not quite to propose a catalogue of 'types' of cosmopolitanism, as we wish to safeguard the relational nature of the concept and refrain from essentializing it. Some types discussed in the literature include 'elite cosmopolitanism', 'aesthetic cosmopolitanism', 'everyday cosmopolitanism', as well as 'exclusionary' versus 'inclusionary cosmopolitanism', or even 'cosmopolitan communitarism'. See Steven Vertovec and Robin Cohen, eds., *Conceiving Cosmopolitanism: Theory, Context, Practice* (Oxford: Oxford University Press, 2002), 1–22.

11 Naturally, these types of cosmopolitanism often converge in practice: a great port city may be cosmopolitan both insofar as it is a teeming microcosm of the wider world, and insofar as it participates in a grander macrocosm.

12 Sheldon Pollock, *The Language of the Gods in the World of Men: Sanskrit, Culture, and Power in Premodern India* (Berkeley and Los Angeles: University of California Press, 2009), 10.

13 Pollock, *Language of the Gods*, 14.

14 Steven Collins, *Nirvana and other Buddhist Felicities: Utopias of the Pali imaginaire* (Cambridge University Press, 1998). Pollock, *Language of the Gods*, 387, also refers to this as 'a second cosmopolitan cultural formation'.

15 Kenneth R. Hall, 'Ports-of-Trade, Maritime Diasporas, and Networks of Trade and Cultural Integration in the Bay of Bengal Region of the Indian Ocean: c. 1300–1500,' *Journal of the Economic and Social History of the Orient* 53, 1–2 (2009), 109–45; Ronit Ricci, *Islam Translated: Literature, Conversion, and the Arabic Cosmopolis of South and Southeast Asia* (Chicago: University of Chicago Press, 2011).

16 Tilman Frasch, '1456: The Making of a Buddhist Ecumene in the Bay of Bengal,' in *Pelagic Passageways: The Northern Bay of Bengal World before Colonialism*, ed. Rila Mukherjee (Delhi: Primus, 2011), 383–405; Anne M. Blackburn, 'Buddhist Connections in the Indian Ocean: Changes in

Monastic Mobility, 1000–1500,' *Journal of the Economic and Social History of the Orient* 58, 3 (2015), 237–66.

17 O. W. Wolters, *Early Southeast Asia: Selected Essays*, ed. Craig J. Reynolds (Ithaca, NY: Cornell University Press, 2008). Hence we might consider that the local and the supra-local each functions as centric and peripheral at the same time.

18 O. W. Wolters, *History, Culture, and Region in Southeast Asian Perspectives*, revised edition (Ithaca, NY: Cornell University Press, 1999), 55. A number of mostly literary examples are given on pp. 58–67.

19 Sheldon Pollock, 'The Cosmopolitan Vernacular,' *Journal of Asian Studies* 57, 1 (1998), 33; Anthony Milner, *The Malays* (Oxford: Blackwell, 2008), 38.

20 Wang Gungwu, 'Introduction,' in *Southeast Asia in the 9th to 14th Centuries*, ed. David G. Marr and Anthony C. Milner (Singapore: Institute of Southeast Asian Studies, 1986), xv.

21 See Milner, *The Malays*, 38.

22 Wang, 'Introduction', xv.

23 Stanley Tambiah, *Buddhism Betrayed? Religion, Politics and Violence in Sri Lanka* (Chicago: University of Chicago Press, 1992), 145, refers to a 'standard South Asian mode of differentially incorporating into an existing society sectarian or alien minorities: inferiorize them and place them in a subordinate position in the hierarchy'. See also Gananath Obeyesekere, 'Buddhism, Nationhood and Cultural Identity: A Question of Fundamentals,' in *Fundamentalisms Comprehended*, ed. Martin E. Marty and R. Scott Appleby (Chicago: University of Chicago Press, 1995), 231–56 and 'On Buddhist Identity in Sri Lanka,' in *Ethnic Identity: Creation, Conflict and Accommodation*, ed. Lola Romanucci-Rossi and George A. de Vos (London: Mayfield, 1995), 222–41.

24 See Daud Ali, 'Connected Histories? Regional Historiography and Theories of Cultural Contact between Early South and Southeast Asia,' in *Islamic Connections: Muslim Societies in South and Southeast Asia*, ed. R. Michael Feener and Terenjit Sevea (Singapore: Institute of Southeast Asian Studies, 2009), 1–24 and 'The Early Inscriptions of Indonesia and the Problem of the Sanskrit Cosmopolis,' in *Early Interactions between South and Southeast Asia: Reflections on Cross-Cultural Exchange*, ed. Pierre-Yves Manguin, A. Mani and Geoff Wade (New Delhi and Singapore: Manohar and Institute of Southeast Asian Studies, 2011), 277–97. In this volume, also see the introduction by Manguin, and Peter Skilling, 'Buddhism and the Circulation of Ritual in Early Peninsular Southeast Asia,' 371–84.

25 Hall, 'Ports-of-Trade', 114, offers the following definition: 'A heterarchy is defined as including horizontally linked equitable urban centers that shared common goals, acknowledged the political independence of its "members," and included multiple networked power centers that had different levels of connectivity, and were based upon some degree of acknowledged cultural homogeneity.'

26 Anthony Reid uses 'cosmopolis' to refer to such relations where once a centre had achieved special authority (e.g. Malacca), but not yet configured an empire proper; see Hall, 'Ports-of-Trade', 115.

27 Marshall Sahlins, 'The Stranger-Kingship of the Mexica,' unpublished paper, 14. As he puts it, '[t]he peoples concerned have been well aware of these gradients of power and sophistication – can we not say, these differences of "civilization"?'

28 Mary W. Helms, *Ulysses' Sail: An Ethnographic Odyssey of Power, Knowledge, and Geographical Distance* (Princeton, NJ: Princeton University Press, 1988).

29 Alan Strathern, *Kingship and Conversion in Sixteenth-Century Sri Lanka. Portuguese Imperialism in a Buddhist Land* (Cambridge: Cambridge University Press, 2007) and Zoltán Biedermann, 'The *Matrioshka* Principle and How it was Overcome: Portuguese and Habsburg Attitudes toward Imperial Authority in Sri Lanka and the Responses of the Rulers of Kotte (1506–1656),' *Journal of Early Modern History* 13, 4 (2009), 265–310.

30 Sheldon Pollock, 'Cosmopolitan and Vernacular in History,' *Public Culture* 12, 3 (2000), 26, has it that the Sanskrit cosmopolis was formed by the 'circulation of traders, literati, religious professionals, and freelance adventurers. Coercion, cooptation, juridical control, and even persuasion are nowhere in evidence'.

31 Pollock, *Language of the Gods*, 572.

32 Indeed the Sanskrit cosmopolis even had an Indian Summer in the modern (late colonial) period, as discussed in Mark Ravinder Frost, 'Cosmopolitan Fragments from a Splintered Isle: "Ceylonese" Nationalism in Late-Colonial Sri Lanka,' in *Ethnicities, Diasporas and Grounded Cosmopolitanisms in Asia. Proceedings of the Asia Research Institute Workshop* (Singapore: Asia Research Institute, 2004), 59–69.

33 Victor Lieberman, *Strange Parallels. Southeast Asia in Global Context, c. 800–1830*, Vol. 2, *Mainland Mirrors: Europe, Japan, China, South Asia, and the Islands* (Cambridge: Cambridge University Press, 2009).

34 Charles Hallisey, 'Works and Persons in Sinhala Literary Culture,' in *Literary Cultures in History: Reconstructions from South Asia*, ed. Sheldon Pollock (Berkeley and Los Angeles: California University Press, 2003), 695–96.

35 According to R. A. L. H. Gunawardana, *Historiography in a Time of Ethnic Conflict: Construction of the Past in Contemporary Sri Lanka* (Colombo: Social Scientists' Association, 1995), 14, Sinhala arrives as 'a clearly distinguishable linguistic form' in the eighth and ninth centuries. Pollock, 'Cosmopolitan and Vernacular in History', places the arrival of Sinhala vernacular culture in the ninth century.

36 Hallisey, 'Works and Persons', 691.

37 Jonathan S. Walters, 'Lovely Lady Lanka: A Tenth-Century Depiction,' *Sri Lanka Journal of the Humanities* 39 (1993), 45–56; Sheldon Pollock, 'India in the Vernacular Millennium: Literary Culture and Polity, 1000–1500,' *Daedalus* 127 (1998), 41–74.

38 See Daud Ali, 'Royal Eulogy as World History: Re-thinking Copper-plate Inscriptions in Cōḻa India,' in *Querying the Medieval: Texts and the History of Practices in South* Asia, ed. Ronald Inden, Jonathan Walters and Daud Ali (New York: Oxford University Press, 2000), 210–12.

39 Stephen C. Berkwitz, *Buddhist Poetry and Colonialism. Alagiyavanna and the Portuguese in Sri Lanka* (New York: Oxford University Press, 2013), 34; W. R. McAlpine and M. B. Ariyapala, *The Crest-Gem of Poetry* (Dehiwala: Tisara Prakasakayo, 1990).

40 Hallisey, 'Works and Persons', 697. According to Hallisey, Sinhalese authors 'combined a profound appreciation for the vision of the literary found in Sanskrit literary culture with a resolute resistance to the encroachment of Sanskrit language on the forms of Sinhala used for poetry' (*ibid.*, 694).

41 Alan Strathern, 'Sri Lanka in the Long Early Modern Period: Its Place in a Comparative Theory of Second Millennium Eurasian History,' *Modern Asian Studies* 43 (2009), 809–64.

42 See Lieberman, *Strange Parallels*, Vol. 2 for more on the importance of external force in defining ethnicity.

43 Alan Strathern, 'Treachery and Ethnicity in Portuguese Representations of Sri Lanka,' in *Engaging Colonial Knowledge: Reading European Archives in World History*, ed. Ricardo Roque and Kim Wagner (New York: Palgrave, 2012), 217–34.

44 On the title 'Kālinga Wheel-Turning Monarch (*cakravartin*)' see Jonathan Walters, 'Buddhist History: The Sri Lankan Pali *Vaṃsas* and their Commentary,' in *Querying the Medieval. Texts and the History of Practices in South Asia*, ed. Ronald Inden, Jonathan Walters and Daud Ali (Oxford: Oxford University Press, 2000), 145. Also see John C. Holt, *The Buddhist Visnu: Religious Transformation, Politics, and Culture* (New York: Columbia University Press, 2004), 41–42, and S. Pathmanathan, 'South India and Sri Lanka, AD 1450–1650: Political, Commercial and Cultural Relations,' *Journal of Tamil Studies* 21 (1982), 36–57.

45 See K. W. Goonewardena, 'Kingship in XVIIth Century Sri Lanka: Some Concepts, Ceremonies and Other Practices,' *Sri Lanka Journal of the Humanities* 3 (1977), 1–32. This seems to be consonant with Pollock's account of the shift to the cosmopolitan vernacular (*Language of the Gods*, 386–90).

46 Goonewardena, 'Kingship in XVIIth Century Sri Lanka', 13.

47 Holt, *Buddhist Visnu*, 35.

48 Ricci, *Islam Translated*. Also see Lorna Dewaraja, 'Muslim Merchants and Pilgrims in Sarandib c.900–1500 AD,' in *Sri Lanka and the Silk Road of the Sea*, ed. S. Bandaranayake, L. Dewaraja, R. Silva and K. D. G. Wimalratne (Colombo: The Sri Lanka National Fund for UNESCO and Central Cultural Fund, 1990), 191–8.

49 See Sebastian Prange, 'Like Banners on the Sea: Muslim Trade Networks and Islamization in Malabar and Maritime Southeast Asia,' in *Islamic Connections: Muslim Societies in South and Southeast Asia*, ed. R. Michael Feener and Terenjit Sevea (Singapore: Institute of Southeast Asian Studies, 2009), 25–47, for a comparison of Malabar and Southeast Asia.

50 C. R. de Silva, 'Sri Lanka in the Early Sixteenth Century: Political Conditions,' in *University of Peradeniya History of Sri Lanka*, Vol. 2, ed. K. M. De Silva (Peradeniya: University of Peradeniya, 1995), 12–13. Also see Hall, 'Ports-of-Trade', 134 on Ibn Battuta.

51 De Silva, 'Sri Lanka in the Early Sixteenth Century', 13.

52 On the Māppiḷa-Portuguese wars, see Jorge M. Flores, *Os Portugueses e o Mar de Ceilão. Trato, diplomacia e guerra, 1498–1543* (Lisbon: Cosmos, 1998).

53 They included Arabs, Berbers, Persians and then increasingly South Asian Muslims such as Gujaratis and Tamil groups, and also Malays. R. A. L. H. Gunawardana, 'Seaways to Sielediba: Changing patterns of Navigation in the Indian Ocean and their impact on precolonial Sri Lanka,' in *Sri Lanka and the Silk Road of the Sea*, 32; Sirima Kiribamune, 'Muslims and Trade of the Arabian Sea with Special Reference to Sri Lanka from the Birth of Islam to the Fifteenth century,' *ibid.*, 180; Dewaraja, 'Muslim Merchants'; Hall, 'Ports-of-Trade', 133.

54 On the 'shadow empire' see Sanjay Subrahmanyam, *The Political Economy of Commerce: Southern India, 1500–1650* (Cambridge: Cambridge University Press, 1990). It could be that it only appears

as a unit of analysis for us because it has produced sources in a written Western language that – however scarce and scattered – made it into European archives. The definition of the Portuguese Empire as a network, now commonplace, goes back to Luís Filipe Thomaz, *De Ceuta a Timor*, 2nd edn (Lisbon: Difel, 1994), 210.

55 Serge Gruzinski, *Les quatre parties du monde. Histoire d'une mondialisation* (Paris: La Martinière, 2004).

56 The most comprehensive study to date is Ângela Barreto Xavier, *A Invenção de Goa. Poder Imperial e Conversões Culturais, Séculos XVI e XVII* (Lisbon: Imprensa de Ciências Sociais, 2008).

57 Zoltan Biedermann, 'Colombo versus Cannanore: Contrasting Structures of Two Early Colonial Port Cities in South Asia,' *Journal of the Economic and Social History of the Orient* 53, 2 (2009), 413–59; Charles R. Boxer, *Portuguese Society in the Tropics: The Municipal Councils of Goa, Macao, Bahia and Luanda* (Madison, WI: University of Wisconsin Press, 1965).

58 On the political, administrative and religious framework established in Sri Lanka after 1594, see Tikiri Abeyasinghe, *Portuguese Rule in Ceylon 1594–1612* (Colombo: Lake House, 1966) and C. R. de Silva, *The Portuguese in Ceylon 1617–1638* (Colombo: H.W. Cave, 1972).

59 Walter D. Mignolo, 'The Many Faces of Cosmo-Polis: Border Thinking and Critical Cosmopolitanism,' *Public Culture* 12, 3 (2000), 721.

60 *Sri Lanka and the Silk Road of the Sea* brings together some useful articles exploring such interactions. Walters, 'Buddhist History' is an important text for the earlier period that always places Lankan phenomena within a wider South Asian field. See also the essays of Tilman Frasch, 'Buddha's Tooth Relic: Contesting Rituals and the Early State in Sri Lanka', in *Ritual Dynamics and the Science of Ritual*, ed. Axel Michaels, Vol. 3, *State, Power and Violence*, ed. Marko Kitts et al. (Wiesbaden: Harrassowitz, 2010), 647–64 and '1456: The Making of a Buddhist Ecumene'. Among the many examples of postwar scholarship, two may be mentioned here: Senake Bandaranayake, 'Approaches to the External Factor in Sri Lanka's Historical Formation,' in *Continuities and Transformations: Studies in Sri Lankan Archaeology and History* (Colombo: Social Scientists' Association, 2012), 91–120 (originally published in 1974), and Amaradasa Liyanagamage, *State, Society and Religion in Premodern Sri Lanka* (Colombo: Social Scientists' Association, 2008).

61 Previous to this the only major influx of foreign troops was when King Abhayanaga brought over an army from India in the third century CE.

62 Jonathan Spencer, ed., *Sri Lanka: History and the Roots of Conflict* (London: Routledge, 1990). See Alan Strathern, 'Theoretical Approaches to Sri Lankan History and the Early Portuguese Period,' *Modern Asian Studies* 38 (2004), 189–226, on the opposition between 'traditionalist' and 'historicist' approaches.

63 See the discussion of the debate between R. A. L. H Gunawardana and K. N. O Dharmadasa as discussed in Strathern's Chapter 11 in this volume.

64 See Michael Roberts, 'Ethnicity after Said: Post-Orientalist Failures in Comprehending the Kandyan Period of Lankan History,' *Ethnic Studies Report* 19 (2001), 69–98.

65 Michael Roberts, *Sinhala Consciousness in the Kandyan period, 1590s–1815* (Colombo: Vijitha Yapa, 2004); Strathern, 'Treachery and Ethnicity'.

66 For recent reflections on the political salience of history, see Nira Wickramasinghe, *Producing the Present: History and Heritage in Post-War Patriotic Sri Lanka*, ICES Research Paper 2 (Colombo: International Centre for Ethnic Studies, 2012), and Nirmal Ranjith Dewasiri, *'History' after the War: Historical Consciousness in the Collective Sinhala-Buddhist Psyche in Post-War Sri Lanka*, ICES Research Paper 9 (Colombo: International Centre for Ethnic Studies, 2013).

67 As just one example, we could take a recent book published on the Portuguese mission of the sixteenth and seventeenth centuries by Gaston Perera, *The Portuguese Missionary in 16th and 17th Century Ceylon. The Spiritual Conquest* (Colombo: Vijitha Yapa, 2009). The tone adopted is akin to a document investigating a war crime. The Portuguese are presented as simply impelled by an 'innate right to exterminate other nations' (3); they have launched a psycho-spiritual attack on the cultural fabric of Lanka every bit as devastating to the vulnerable Buddhist nation as their malign political projections. See reviews by Biedermann in *eJournal of Portuguese History* 8, 1 (2010) and Strathern in *The Journal of Asian Studies* 70 (2011), 287–89.

68 A few examples are: Richard F. Gombrich and Gananath Obeyesekere, *Buddhism Transformed: Religious Change in Sri Lanka* (Princeton: Princeton University Press, 1988); Gananath Obeyesekere, *The Work of Culture: Symbolic Transformation in Psychoanalysis and Anthropology* (Chicago: University of Chicago Press, 1990); Gananath Obeyesekere, *The Apotheosis of Captain Cook: European Mythmaking in the Pacific* (Princeton, NJ: Princeton University Press, 1992);

Gananath Obeyesekere, 'On Buddhist Identity', in *Identity, Consciousness and the Past: Forging of Caste and Community in India and Sri Lanka*, ed. H. L. Seneviratne (Oxford: Oxford University Press, 1997).

69 This is most obvious in Gananath Obeyesekere, *Imagining Karma. Ethical Transformation in Amerindian, Buddhist, and Greek Rebirth* (Berkeley and Los Angeles: University of California Press, 2002) and *The Awakened Ones: Phenomenology of Visionary Experience* (New York: Columbia University Press, 2012).

## Chapter 1: Archaeology and cosmopolitanism

1 Margarita Diaz Andreu, Sam Lucy, Stasa Babić and David Edwards, eds., *The Archaeology of Identity: Approaches to Gender, Age, Status, Ethnicity and Religion* (London: Routledge, 2005); Lynn Meskell, *Cosmopolitan Archaeologies* (Durham: Duke University Press, 2009).

2 Meskell, Cosmopolitan Archaeologies.

3 Bruce Trigger, *A History of Archaeological Thought* (Cambridge: Cambridge University Press, 1989), 165.

4 Vere Gordon Childe, *The Dawn of European Civilization* (London: Kegan Paul, 1925); Stuart Piggott, *Prehistoric India* (London: Penguin, 1950).

5 Dilip Chakrabarti, *India: An Archaeological History: Palaeolithic Beginnings to Early Historic Foundations* (Delhi: Oxford University Press, 1999); Robin Coningham and Nick Lewer, 'The Vijayan Colonization and the Archaeology of Identity in Sri Lanka,' *Antiquity* 74 (2000), 707–12; George Erdosy, 'Language, Material Culture and Ethnicity: Theoretical Perspectives,' in *The Indo-Aryans of Ancient South Asia*, ed. George Erdosy (Berlin: Walter de Gruyter, 1995), 1–32; Edmund Leach, 'Aryan Invasions Over Four Millennia,' in *Culture Through Time: Anthropological Approaches*, ed. Emiko Ohnuki-Tierney (Stanford: Stanford University Press, 1995), 227–45.

6 Coningham and Lewer, 'Vijayan Colonization'.

7 Siân Jones, *The Archaeology of Ethnicity* (London: Routledge, 1997), 13.

8 Margarita Diaz Andreu and Sam Lucy, 'Introduction,' in *The Archaeology of Identity*, 1–2.

9 Robin Coningham, 'The Archaeology of Buddhism,' in *Archaeology and World Religion*, ed. Tim Insoll (London: Routledge, 2001), 61–95.

10 Robin Coningham, Prishanta Gunawardhana, Christopher Davis, Gamini Adikari, Ian Simpson, Keir Strickland and Mark Manuel, 'Contextualising the Tabbova-Maradanmaduva "Culture": Excavations at Nikawewa, Tirappane Division, Anurādhapura District, Sri Lanka', *South Asian Studies* 28, 1 (2012), 1–14.

11 *The Mahāvaṃsa: Or, The Great Chronicle of Ceylon*, trans. Wilhelm Geiger (1912; reprinted New Delhi: Asian Educational Series, 1993), x.

12 Geiger, *Mahāvaṃsa*, x–xi.

13 Geiger, *Mahāvaṃsa*, xi.

14 Coningham and Lewer, 'Vijayan Colonization', 707; Alan Strathern, 'The Vijaya Origin Myth of Sri Lanka and the Strangeness of Kingship,' *Past and Present* 203 (2009), 3–28.

15 *Cūḷavaṃsa: Being the More Recent Part of the Mahāvaṃsa*, trans. Wilhelm Geiger (London: Pali Text Society, 1929).

16 *The Mahawanso*, ed. George Turnour (1837; reprint Colombo: Central Cultural Fund, 2016).

17 James Tennent, *Ceylon: An Account of the Island, Physical, Historical, and Topographical with Notices of its Natural History, Antiquities and Productions* (London: Spottiswoode and Co., 1859), 315.

18 Don Titus Devendra, 'Seventy Years of Ceylon Archaeology,' *Artibus Asiae* 22, 1–2 (1959), 24.

19 Ananda Guruge, *From the Living Fountains of Buddhism: Sri Lankan Support to Pioneering Western Orientalists* (Colombo: Ministry of Cultural Affairs, 1984), xiv, xvii.

20 Heralivala Seneviratne, 'Identity and the Conflation of Past and Present,' in *Identity, Consciousness and the Past: Forging of Caste and Community in India and Sri Lanka*, ed. H. L. Seneviratne (Delhi: Oxford University Press, 1997), 6.

21 Errol Valentine Daniel, 'Three Dispositions Towards the Past: One Sinhala, Two Tamil,' in *Identity, Consciousness and the Past*, 49.

22 Sudharshan Seneviratne, 'Situating World Heritage Sites in a Multi-Cultural Island Society: The Ideology of Presenting the Sacred City of Anurādhapura, Sri Lanka,' paper originally presented in 2005 at the Conference of the European Association of Archaeologists, 4–8 July, British Museum,

London, www.archaeology.lk/monthly-theme/prof-sudharshan-seneviratne/situating-world-heritage-sites-in-a-multi-cultural-island-society-the-ideology-of-presenting-the-sacred-city-of-Anurādhapura-sri-lanka, accessed 5 November 2013.

23 Coningham and Lewer, 'Vijayan Colonization', 707.

24 Anne Monius, *Imagining a Place for Buddhism: Literary Culture and Religious Community in Tamil-Speaking South India* (Oxford: Oxford University Press, 2001).

25 Monius, *Imagining a Place for Buddhism*.

26 Strathern, 'Vijaya Origin Myth', 3.

27 Tennent, *Ceylon*, 340; Coningham and Lewer, 'Vijayan Colonization', 708.

28 Ponnampalam Ragupathy, *Early Settlements in Jaffna: An Archaeological Survey* (Madras: Thillimalar Ragupathy, 1987), 180.

29 Antonio Bertolacci, *A View of the Agricultural, Commercial, and Financial Interests of Ceylon* (London: Black, Parbury and Allen, 1817), 13.

30 Henry Parker, *Ancient Ceylon: An Account of the Aborigines and of Part of the Early Civilization* (London: Luzac and Co.,1909), 709.

31 Chakrabarti, *India*, 3.

32 Coningham and Lewer, 'Vijayan Colonization', 711.

33 Humphrey William Codrington, *A Short History of Ceylon* (London: Macmillan and Co., 1939), 172.

34 *Cūḷavaṃsa*, 55.19.22.

35 Coningham and Lewer, 'Vijayan Colonization', 709.

36 Keir Strickland, 'The Jungle Tide: "Collapse" in Early Medieval Sri Lanka,' PhD dissertation, Durham University, 2011.

37 Harry Charles Purvis Bell, *Archaeological Survey of Ceylon, Annual Report 1892* (Colombo: Ceylon Government Press, 1904), 7.

38 Paul Edward Pieris, 'Nagadipa and Buddhist Remains in Jaffna,' *Journal of the Royal Asiatic Society (Ceylon Branch)* 28 (1925), 41.

39 Chandra Wikramagamage, Siri Hettiarachchi, Jan Bouzek, Jiri Bren, and Petr Charvat, 'Excavations at Abhayagiri Vihara (Anurādhapura, Sri Lanka) in 1982,' *Archiv Orientalni* 51 (1983), 48; Strickland, 'Jungle Tide'.

40 Robin Coningham and Nick Lewer, 'Paradise Lost: The Bombing of the Temple of the Tooth – a UNESCO World Heritage Site in South Asia,' *Antiquity* 73 (1999), 865.

41 Stanley Tambiah, *Sri Lanka: Ethnic Fratricide and the Dismantling of Democracy* (Chicago: University of Chicago Press, 1986), 126.

42 Coningham and Lewer, 'Vijayan Colonization'.

43 Seneviratne, 'Situating World Heritage Sites'.

44 Central Cultural Fund Act of Sri Lanka, No. 57 of 1980 (certified on 18 December 1980), Chapter 388, 220–24.

45 Kingsley de Silva, *A History of Sri Lanka* (Colombo: Vijitha Yapa Publications, 2005), 197.

46 Coningham and Lewer, 'Vijayan Colonization', 709; Robin Coningham and Frank Christopher Hardman, 'Review of Dilip Chakrabati, *Archaeology in the Third World: A History of Indian Archaeology since 1947*,' *Cambridge Archaeological Journal* 14, 1 (2004), 158.

47 Don Martin de Zilva Wickremasinghe, *Epigraphia Zeylanica*, Vol. 2 (Colombo: Archaeological Department, 1927), 242–55; Karthigesu Indrapala, *The Evolution of an Ethnic Identity: The Tamils in Sri Lanka c. 300* BCE *to c. 1200* CE (Sydney: MV Publications, 2005).

48 Robin Coningham, 'The Excavations at ASW2,' in *Anurādhapura: The British-Sri Lankan Excavations at Anurādhapura Salgaha Watta 2*, Vol. 1, *The Site*, BAR International Series 824, ed. Robin Coningham (Oxford: Archaeopress, 1999).

49 Robin Coningham, Frank Raymond Allchin, Cathy Batt and David Lucy, 'Passage to India? Anurādhapura and the Early Use of the Brahmi Script,' *Cambridge Archaeological Journal* 6, 1 (1996), 73–97.

50 Siran Deraniyagala, 'The Citadel of Anurādhapura 1965: Excavations in the Gedige Area,' *Ancient Ceylon* 2 (1972), 48–170.

51 Mortimer Wheeler, *Rome Beyond the Imperial Frontiers* (London: Penguin Books, 1955).

52 Mortimer Wheeler, 'Arikamedu: An Indo-Roman Trading Station on the East Coast of India', *Ancient India* 2 (1946), 18.

53 Vimala Begley, *Ancient Port of Arikamedu: New Excavations and Researches 1989–1992* (Paris: École Française D'Extrême-Orient, 1996).

54 Robin Coningham, 'Beyond and before the Imperial Frontiers: Early Historic Sri Lanka and the Origins of Indian Ocean Trade,' *Man and Environment* 27 (2002) and Robin Coningham, ed.,

*Anurādhapura: The British-Sri Lankan Excavations at Anurādhapura Salgaha Watta 2*, Vol. 2, *The Artefacts*, BAR International Series 1508 (Oxford: Archaeopress, 2006).

55 Alessandra Avanzini, *A Port in Arabia between Rome and the Indian Ocean (3rd c. BC–5th c. AD): Khor Rori report 2* (Rome: Arabia Antica, 2008). Also see Heidrun Schenk, 'The Dating and Historical Value of Rouletted Ware,' *Zeitschrift für Archäologie Außereuropäischer Kulturen* 1 (2006), 123–52 and Heidrun Schenk, 'Parthian Glazed Pottery from Sri Lanka and the Indian Ocean Trade,' *Zeitschrift für Archäologie Außereuropäischer Kulturen* 2 (2007), 57–90.

56 Roberta Tomber, 'Rome and Mesopotamia – Importers into India in the First Millennium AD,' *Antiquity* 81 (2007), 972–88.

57 Ben Stern, Jacques Connan, Eleanor Blakelock, Rupert Jackman, Robin Coningham and Carl Heron. 'From Susa to Anurādhapura Reconstructing Aspects of Trade and Exchange in Bitumen-Coated Ceramic Vessels between Iran and Sri Lanka from the Third to the Ninth Centuries AD,' *Archaeometry* 50, 3 (2008), 409–28.

58 Tomber, 'Rome and Mesopotamia', 976.

59 J. Carswell, S. U. Deraniyagala and A. Graham, eds., *Mantai: City by the Sea* (Aichwald: Linden Soft, 2013).

60 Stern et al., 'Susa to Anurādhapura', 426.

61 Tomber, 'Rome and Mesopotamia', 980.

62 Frank Raymond Allchin, 'The Inscriptions and Graffiti,' in *Anurādhapura*, Vol. 2, 456.

63 Coningham et al., 'Passage to India?'

64 Robin Coningham and Prishanta Gunawardhana, eds., *Anurādhapura*, Vol. 3, *The Hinterland*, BAR International Series 2568 (Oxford: Archaeopress, 2013).

65 Robin Coningham and Paul Cheetham. 'The Fortifications,' in *Anuradhapura: The British-Sri Lankan Excavations at Anuradhapura Salgaha Watta 2*, Vol. 1: *The Site*, BAR International Series 824, ed. R. A. E Coningham. Oxford: Archaeopress, 1999.

66 Carswell et al., *Mantai*.

67 Deborah Carlson and Ken Trethewey, 'Exploring the Oldest Shipwreck in the Indian Ocean,' *The Institute of Nautical Archaeology Quarterly* 40 (2013), 8–14.

68 Samuel Beal, *Travels of Fah-Hian and Sung-Yun: Buddhist Pilgrims to India 400 AD to 518 AD* (London: Trubner and Co.,1869), 154.

69 Arthur Maurice Hocart, *Memoirs of the Archaeological Survey of Ceylon*, Vol. 1 (Colombo: A.C. Richards, Acting Government Printer, Ceylon, 1924).

70 Prabo Mihindukulasuriya, 'Persian Christians in the Anurādhapura Period,' in *A Cultured Faith: Essays in Honour of Prof. G. P. V. Somaratna*, ed. Prabo Mihindukulasuriya (Colombo: CTS Publishing, 2011).

71 The Tamil inscriptions of the *Aiññūṟṟuvar*, mercantile communities of South Indian origin in the medieval period certainly attest to their presence later in Polonnaruva. Sivasubramaniam Pathmanathan, *Facets of Sri Lankan History and Culture* (Colombo: Kumaran Book House, 2015), 199.

72 Robin Coningham and Ruth Young, *The Archaeology of South Asia: From the Indus to Aśōka* (Cambridge: Cambridge University Press, 2015).

73 *Mahāvaṃsa*, 7.

74 *Mahāvaṃsa*, 14.59–64.

75 *Mahāvaṃsa*, 18.

76 *Mahāvaṃsa*, 17.

77 Siran Deraniyagala, 'Excavations in the Citadel of Anurādhapura Gedige 1984: A Preliminary Report,' *Ancient Ceylon* 6 (1986), 47.

78 James Legge, *A Record of Buddhistic Kingdoms: Being an Account by the Chinese Monk Fa-Hien of his Travels in India and Ceylon (AD 399-414) in Search of the Buddhist Books of Discipline* (Oxford: Clarendon Press, 1886), 102, 107.

79 Beal, *Travels*.

80 Vincent Panditha, 'Buddhism During the Polonnaruva Period,' in *The Polonnaruva Period* (Colombo: Tisara Prakasakayo, 1955), 133.

81 Hematilaka Bandara Mangala Ilangasinha, *Buddhism in Medieval Sri Lanka* (Delhi: Sri Satguru Publications, 1992), 173–7.

82 Tilman Frasch, 'Buddha's Tooth Relic: Contesting Rituals and the Early State in Sri Lanka', in *Ritual Dynamics and the Science of Ritual*, ed. Axel Michaels, Vol. 3, *State, Power and Violence*, ed. Marko Kitts et al. (Wiesbaden: Harrassowitz, 2010), 647–64.

83 Shobhana Gokhale, 'Sri Lanka in Early Indian Inscriptions,' *Annals of the Bhandarkar Oriental Research Institute*, 85 (2004), 136–7.

84 Alexander Cunningham, *Mahabodhi or the Great Buddhist Temple under the Bodhi Tree at Buddha-Gaya* (London: W. H. Allen, 1892), 16.
85 T. N. Ramachandran, *Memoirs of the Archaeological Survey of India, No. 71: Nagarjunakonda, 1938* (Calcutta: Government of India Press, 1953), 5.
86 Ramachandran, *Memoirs*, 13.
87 Leslie Gunawardana, *Robe and Plough: Monasticism and Economic Interest in Early Medieval Sri Lanka* (Tuscon: University of Arizona Press, 1979), 17; Jeffrey Sundberg, 'The Wilderness Monks of the AbhayagiriVihāra and the Origins of Sino-Javanese Esoteric Buddhism,' *Bijdragen tot de Taal-, Land- en Volkenkunde* 160, 1 (2004), 96.
88 Robin Coningham, 'Monks, Caves and Kings: A Reassessment of the Nature of Early Buddhism in Sri Lanka (Ceylon),' *World Archaeology* 27 (1995), 235.
89 Coningham, 'Monks, Caves and Kings', 235.
90 Sundberg, 'Wilderness Monks', 100.
91 Wickremasinghe, *Epigraphia Zeylanica*, Vol. 2, 148–52.
92 Wickremasinghe, *Epigraphia Zeylanica*, Vol. 2, 165–78.
93 Ulrich Von Schroeder, *Buddhist Sculptures of Sri Lanka* (Hong Kong: Visual Dharma Publications, 1990), 206.
94 Alan Strathern and Zoltán Biedermann, introduction in this volume; W. M. Sirisena, *Sri Lanka and South-East Asia* (Leiden: E. J. Brill, 1978), 59–60.
95 Senerath Paranavitana, 'Sigiri – the Abode of a God-King,' *Journal of the Ceylon Branch of the Royal Asiatic Society*, New Series 1 (1950), 129–62.
96 Senerath Paranavitana, *Sigiriya Graffiti* (London: Oxford University Press, 1959), 17.
97 Paranavitana, 'Sigiri,' 137.
98 James Duncan, *The City as Text: The Politics of Landscape Interpretation in the Kandyan Kingdom* (Cambridge: Cambridge University Press, 1990), 54.
99 Ananda Wickremeratne, 'Shifting Metaphors of Sacrality: The Mythic Dimensions of Anurādhapura,' in *The City as Sacred Centre: Essays on Six Asian Contexts*, ed. Bardwell Smith and Holly Reynolds (Leiden: E. J. Brill, 1987).
100 Duncan, *The City as Text*.
101 Paranavitana, *Sigiriya Graffiti*.
102 Raja Henapala de Silva, *Sigiriya and its Significance: A Mahayana-Theravāda Monastery* (Nawala: Bibliotheque, 2002).
103 De Silva, *Sigiriya*.
104 Coningham and Gunawardhana, *Anurādhapura*, Vol. 3.
105 Robin Coningham, Prishanta Gunawardhana, Gamini Adikari, Mangala Katugampola, Ian Simpson and Ruth Young, 'The Anurādhapura (Sri Lanka) Project: The Hinterland (Phase II), Preliminary Report of the First Season 2005,' *South Asian Studies* 22 (2006), 53–64; Robin Coningham, Prishanta Gunawardhana, Mark Manuel, Gamini Adikari, Mangala Katugampola, Ruth Young, Armin Schmidt, Krishnan Krishnan, Ian Simpson, Gerry McDonnell and Cathy Batt, 'The State of Theocracy: Defining an Early Medieval Hinterland in Sri Lanka,' *Antiquity*, 81 (2007), 1–21; Robin Coningham, Prishanta Gunawardhana, Gamini Adikari, Mark Manuel, Christopher Davis and Ian Simpson, 'Discussion,' in *Anurādhapura*, Vol. 3.
106 Senake Bandaranayake, 'Traversing an Archaeological Landscape,' in *Further Studies in the Settlement Archaeology of the Sigiriya-Dambulla Region*, ed. Senake Bandaranayake and Mats Mogren (Colombo: Post Graduate Institute of Archaeology, University of Kelaniya, 1994); Prishanta Gunawardhana, *Buddhist Monasteries towards Urbanism in Southern Sri Lanka* (Battaramulla: Neptune Publications, 2009).
107 Julia Shaw, *Buddhist Landscapes in Central India: Sanchi Hill and Archaeologies of Religious and Social Change, c. Third Century BC to Fifth Century AD* (London: British Association of South Asian Studies, 2007); Jason Hawkes, 'The Wider Archaeological Contexts of the Buddhist Stupa site of Bharhut,' *Buddhist Stupas in South Asia*, eds. Jason Hawkes and Akira Shimada (Oxford: Oxford University Press, 2009).
108 Coningham et al., 'Discussion'.
109 Christopher Davis, Robin Coningham, Prishanta Gunawardhana and Mark Manuel, 'Epigraphy in the Hinterland,' in *Anurādhapura*, Vol. 3.
110 Gunawardana, *Robe and Plough*, 97.
111 Coningham, 'Archaeology of Buddhism' (2001).
112 Coningham et al., 'Tabbova-Maradanmaduva "Culture"'.
113 *Mahāvaṃsa*, 15.

114 *Mahāvaṃsa*, 33.83.
115 *Mahāvaṃsa*, 37.4.
116 *Mahāvaṃsa*, 37.7–8.
117 *Cūḷavaṃsa*, 37.53–66.
118 Coningham 'Monks, Caves and Kings', 228–9; Mālinī Dias, *The Growth of Buddhist Monastic Institutions in Sri Lanka from Brahmi Inscriptions* (Colombo: Department of Archaeological Survey, Government of Sri Lanka, 2001), 12.
119 Senake Bandaranyake, *Sinhalese Monastic Architecture: The Viharas of Anurādhapura*. (Leiden: Brill, 1974), 33.
120 Bandaranyake, *Sinhalese Monastic Architecture*, 48.
121 Ian Bailiff, Harriet Lacey, Robin Coningham, Prishanta Gunawardhana, Gamini Adikari, Christopher Davis, Mark Manuel and Keir Strickland, 'Luminescence Dating of Brick Stupas: An Application to the Hinterland of Anurādhapura, Sri Lanka,' *Antiquity* 87 (2013), 189–201.
122 William McAlpine and David Robson, *A Guide to Ritigala* (Colombo: Central Cultural Fund, 1983), 29.
123 Coningham, 'Archaeology of Buddhism' (2001), 87.
124 Bandaranyake, *Sinhalese Monastic Architecture*, 81.
125 Bandaranyake, *Sinhalese Monastic Architecture*; Gamini Wijesuriya, *Buddhist Meditation Monasteries of Ancient Sri Lanka* (Colombo: Department of Archaeology, Government of Sri Lanka, 1998).
126 M. H. F. Jayasuriya, Leelananda Prematilleke and Roland Silva, *Manjusri Vastuvidyasastra* (Colombo: The Archaeological Survey of Sri Lanka and Central Cultural Fund, 1995).
127 Harry Charles Purvis Bell, *Archaeological Survey of Ceylon. Anurādhapura. Fifth Progress Report, April to June, 1891* (Colombo: Ceylon Government Press, 1893).
128 Lakshman Perera, *The Institutions of Ancient Ceylon from Inscriptions (from 831 to 1016 AD)*, Vol. 2, Part 2, *Economic and Religious Institutions* (Kandy: International Centre for Ethnic Studies, 2005), 298.
129 Dias, *Growth of Buddhist Monastic Institutions*, 108.
130 Leelananda Prematilleke and Roland Silva, 'A Buddhist Monastery Type of Ancient Ceylon Showing Mahayanist Influence,' *Artibus Asiae* 30, 1 (1968), 61–84.
131 *Mahāvaṃsa*, 37.102.
132 *Cūḷavaṃsa*, 41.37; Prematilleke and Silva, 'A Buddhist Monastery Type of Ancient Ceylon', 62; Dias, *Growth of Buddhist Monastic Institutions*, 95.
133 Perera, *Institutions of Ancient Ceylon*, 260–1.
134 *Cūḷavaṃsa*, 49.24.
135 Coningham and Lewer, 'Paradise Lost'.
136 Robin Coningham, Prishanta Gunawardhana, Gamini Adikari, Christopher Davis, Mark Manuel, Ian Bailiff, Cathy Batt, Harendralal Namalgamuwa, Jayampath Senanayake and Umanga Rammungoda, 'Phasing the Hinterland,' in *Anurādhapura*, Vol. 3.
137 Bailiff et al., 'Luminescence Dating of Brick Stupas'; Coningham et al., 'Phasing the Hinterland'; Coningham, et al., 'Discussion'.
138 Arjuna Thantilage, 'Anurādhapura period bronzes of Sri Lanka: Schools and Resource-Utilization,' www.archaeology.lk/articles/Anurādhapura-period-bronzes-of-sri-lanka-schools-and-resource-utilization, accessed 5 November, 2013.
139 Robin Coningham, 'The Archaeology of Buddhism,' in *The Oxford Handbook of the Archaeology of Ritual and Religion*, ed. Tim Insoll. Oxford: Oxford University Press, 2011, 937.
140 Ragupathy, *Early Settlements in Jaffna*; Paramu Pushparatnam, *Tourism and Monuments of Archaeological Heritage in Northern Sri Lanka* (Jaffna: Department of History, University of Jaffna, 2014).
141 Even more diversity is illustrated from among the ancient Buddhist communities of the Maldives, Harry Charles Purvis Bell, *The Maldive Islands: Monograph on the History, Archaeology and Epigraphy* (Colombo: Ceylon Government Press, 1940).
142 Senerath Paranavitana, *Inscriptions of Ceylon*, Vol. 1, *Early Brahmi Inscriptions* (Colombo: Archaeological Survey of Ceylon, 1970); Coningham, 'Monks, Caves and Kings'; Davis et al., 'Epigraphy in the Hinterland'.
143 Davis et al., 'Epigraphy in the Hinterland'. Translations and discussions on the social rank of these donor categories is provided by Paranavitana, *Inscriptions of Ceylon*, Vol. 1.
144 Coningham, 'Monks, Caves and Kings'.
145 Coningham, 'Monks, Caves and Kings', 231.

146 Munugoda Sirisoma, 'Brahmi Inscriptions of Sri Lanka from 3rd Century BC to 65 AD,' in *Archaeological Department Centenary (1890–1990) Commemorative Series*, Vol. 2, *Inscriptions*, ed. Nandadeva Wijesekera (Colombo: State Printing Corporation, 1990), 30–1.
147 Paranavitana, *Inscriptions of Ceylon*, Vol. 1.
148 Coningham, 'Monks, Caves and Kings', 231.
149 *Mahāvaṃsa*, 6, 7.
150 *Mahāvaṃsa*, 10.84.
151 *Mahāvaṃsa*, 10.95–102.
152 *Mahāvaṃsa*, 10.101–2.
153 *Mahāvaṃsa*, 9.1–2.
154 Paranavitana, *Inscriptions of Ceylon*, Vol. 1.
155 *Mahāvaṃsa*, 37.41.
156 *Cūḷavaṃsa*, 48.143–4.
157 *Cūḷavaṃsa*, 55.65.
158 Pathmanathan, *Facets of Sri Lankan History and Culture*, 153.
159 Indrapala, *The Evolution of an Ethnic Identity*, 251.
160 Indrapala, *The Evolution of an Ethnic Identity*, 208.
161 *Cūḷavaṃsa*, 79.81; Pathmanathan, *Facets of Sri Lankan History and Culture*, 165.
162 Senerath Paranavitana, 'The Art and Architecture of the Polonnaruva Period,' in *The Polonnaruva Period*, ed. Sumana Saparamadu (Colombo: Tisara Prakasakayo, 1955), 79, 82.
163 Don Martin de Zilva Wickremasinghe, *Epigraphia Zeylanica*, Vol. 1 (Oxford: Oxford University Press, 1912), 121–35.
164 Bell, *Annual Report 1892*; Harry Charles Purvis Bell, *Archaeological Survey of Ceylon, Annual Report 1893* (Colombo: Ceylon Government Press, 1904).
165 Strickland, 'Jungle Tide', 230.
166 Robin Coningham, Prishanta Gunawardhana, Christopher Davis, Mark Manuel, Keir Strickland, Harendralal Namalgamuwa, and Jayampath Senanayake, 'Terracotta Objects,' in *Anurādhapura*, Vol. 3; Coningham et al. 'Tabbova-Maradanmaduva "Culture"'.
167 Coningham et al., 'Tabbova-Maradanmaduva "Culture"', 10; W. H. Wijayapala, 'Excavations at Randenigama, Rajangane,' *Administrative Report of the Director-General of Archaeology for the Year 1997* (1997), 34.
168 Coningham et al., 'Tabbova-Maradanmaduva "Culture"', 12.
169 Coningham et al., 'Tabbova-Maradanmaduva "Culture"', 12.
170 Coningham et al., 'Discussion'.
171 Coningham, *Anurādhapura*, Vol. 1 and Vol. 2.
172 *Kautilya, the Arthasastra*, trans. L.N. Rangarajan (New Delhi: Penguin, 1992), 2.3.4–6.
173 *Kautilya, the Arthasastra*, 2.4.1–2.
174 *Kautilya, the Arthasastra* 2.4.7–23.
175 *Mahāvaṃsa*, 10.88–9.
176 Arthur Maurice Hocart, 'The Four Quarters,' *Ceylon Journal of Science*, section G.1 (1928), 105–11.
177 Wickremeratne, 'Shifting Metaphors', 45.
178 Hocart, 'The Four Quarters', 156.
179 Robin Coningham, 'Contestatory Urban Texts or Were Cities in South Asia Built as Images?' *Cambridge Archaeological Journal* 10 (2000), 348–54; Duncan, *The City as Text*.
180 Robin Coningham and Ruth Young, 'The Archaeological Visibility of Caste,' in *Case Studies in Archaeology and World Religion*, ed. Tim Insoll (Oxford: Archaeopress, 1999), 84–93.
181 Coningham and Young, 'Archaeological Visibility'.
182 Nicholas Dirks, 'The Invention of Caste: Civil Society in Colonial India,' in *Identity, Consciousness and the Past: Forging of Caste and Community in India and Sri Lanka*, ed. Heralivala Seneviratne (Delhi: Oxford University Press, 1997), 120–35; Nicholas Dirks, *Castes of Mind: Colonialism and the Making of Modern India* (Princeton, NJ: Princeton University Press, 2001); Ursula Sharma, *Caste* (Buckingham: Open University Press, 1999).
183 Coningham and Young, 'Archaeological Visibility', 92.
184 Gunawardana, *Robe and Plough*, 190.
185 Dias, *Growth of Buddhist Monastic Institutions*, 115.
186 Coningham et al., 'The Anurādhapura (Sri Lanka) Project'; Coningham et al., 'The State of Theocracy'; Robin Coningham, Prishanta Gunawardhana, Mark Manuel, Gamini Adikari, Ruth Young, Armin Schmidt, Krishnan Krishnan, Ian Simpson, Christopher Davis and Cathy Batt,

'Response to Goonatilake,' *Antiquity* 85 (2011), 1065–67; Coningham and Gunawardhana, *Anurādhapura*, Vol. 3.

187 Coningham et al., 'The State of Theocracy'.

188 Coningham, 'Archaeology of Buddhism' (2011), 940; Coningham et al., 'Discussion'.

189 Indrapala, *The Evolution of an Ethnic Identity*.

190 Pawuludevage Leelananda Prematilleke, *Alahana Parivena, Polonaruva: First Archaeological Excavation Report* (Colombo: Ministry of Cultural Affairs, 1982); *Alahana Parivena, Polonaruva: Second Archaeological Excavation Report*. (Colombo: Ministry of Cultural Affairs, 1982); *Alahana Parivena, Polonaruva: Fourth Archaeological Excavation Report* (Colombo: Ministry of Cultural Affairs, 1985); *Alahana Parivena, Polonaruva: Sixth Archaeological Excavation Report* (Colombo: Ministry of Cultural Affairs, 1988).

191 Paranavitana, 'Art and Architecture', 79; H. Ratnayake, 'Hindu Bronzes from Jetavanaramaya, Anurādhapura: Bronzes from Jetavana 1984 – Circumstances of the Discovery,' in *Essays in Archaeology: Sirinimal Lakdusinghe Felicitation Volume*, eds. P. Gunawardhana, G. Adikari and R. A. E. Coningham (Battaramulla: Neptune Publication, 2010), 265; Thantilage, 'Anurādhapura Period Bronzes of Sri Lanka'.

192 Ratnayake, 'Hindu Bronzes'.

193 Coningham, 'The Excavations at ASW2'.

194 Harry Charles Purvis Bell, *Plans and Plates for Annual Report, 1893 (Eleventh and Twelfth Reports)* (Colombo: Ceylon Government Press, 1914), Plate XII.

195 Krista Gilliland, Ian Simpson, Paul Adderley, Christopher Burbidge, Alan Cresswell, David Sanderson, Robin Coningham, Mark Manuel, Keir Strickland, Prishanta Gunawardhana and Gamini Adikari. 'The Dry Tank: Development and Disuse of Water Management Infrastructure in the Anurādhapura Hinterland, Sri Lanka,' *Journal of Archaeological Sciences* 40 (2013), 1012–28.

196 Robin Coningham and Prishanta Gunawardhana. 'Looting or Rededication? Buddhism and the Expropriation of Relics,' in *Appropriating the Past: Philosophical Perspectives on the Practice of Archaeology*, ed. Geoffrey Scarre and Robin Coningham (Cambridge: Cambridge University Press, 2012), 293.

197 Debala Mitra, *Buddhist Monuments* (Calcutta: Samsad, 1971), 52; Himanshu Prabhu Ray, 'The Apsidal Shrine in Early Hinduism: Origins, Cultic Affiliation, Patronage,' *World Archaeology* 36 (2004), 343–59.

198 Beal, *Travels*.

199 Paranavitana, *Inscriptions of Ceylon*, Vol. 1.

200 Ramachandran, *Memoirs*, 71.

201 Tessa Bartholomeusz, *Women under the Bo Tree: Buddhist Nuns in Sri Lanka* (Cambridge: Cambridge University Press, 1994).

202 Strathern and Biedermann, introduction in this volume.

203 We are grateful to the British Academy and Central Cultural Fund for their generous financial support for our recent fieldwork in Polonnaruva, and to the Arts and Humanities Research Council for sponsoring our previous fieldwork at Anuradhapura. We are also extremely grateful to the Central Cultural Fund and Durham University for further institutional support. Thanks also to Dr Zoltan Biedermann, Dr Alan Strathern, UCL Press, Professor S. Pathmanathan, Professor Jagath Weerasinghe, Professor Gamini Adikari, Professor P. Pushparatnam, Dr Arjuna Thantilage, Dr Mangala Katugampola and Professor K. Krishnan for their advice and comments on earlier draft of this chapter.

## Chapter 2: 'Implicit cosmopolitanism'

1 Thanks for financial support while writing this chapter to the Arts and Humanities Research Council UK, Dumbarton Oaks Research Library and Collection, and the Warburg Institute – 'Bilderfahrzeuge' Project, supported by the Max Weber Siftung. During fieldwork in Sri Lanka, thanks go to the American Institute of Sri Lankan Studies (Colombo) and its local representatives, Mrs Ira Unamboowe and Mr Weerasooriya, Dr Senarath Wickramasinghe and Professor Osmund Bopearachchi for the opportunity to examine imitation Roman coins found on the island. For information on the collection of the Barber Institute of Fine Arts, I thank Maria Vrij, Curator of Coins, Barber Institute of Fine Arts, University of Birmingham. For support, discussion and invaluable critique: my doctoral supervisors Professor Leslie Brubaker and Dr Archie Dunn; Dr Reinhold Walburg and Professor H.-J. Weisshaar; Dr Daniel Reynolds and Dr Jonathan Jarrett; Dr Sujit Sivasundaram and the editors, Dr Alan Strathern and Dr Zoltán Biedermann. Naturally, all views expressed and any errors present remain entirely my responsibility.

2 O. Bopearachchi, 'Foreword,' in *Taprobanê: Ancient Sri Lanka as Known to Greeks and Romans*, ed. D. P. M. Weerakkody (Turnhout: Brepols, 1997), xxi.

3 Throughout this study 'Sri Lanka' is used to refer to the modern nation-state. 'Lanka' refers to the geographical area of the island prior to modern nationhood.

4 For specific application: Weerakkody, *Taprobanê*, 14. For wider themes: O. Bopearachchi, 'New Archaeological Evidence on Cultural and Commercial Relationships between Ancient Sri Lanka and Tamil Nadu,' *Journal of Interdisciplinary Studies in History and Archaeology* 1 (2004), 67; O. Bopearachchi, 'Archaeological Evidence on Shipping Communities of Sri Lanka' in *Ships and the Development of Maritime Technology in the Indian Ocean*, ed. D. Parkin and R. Barnes (London: Routledge Curzon, 2002), 92.

5 While often implicit, for explicit reference to Lankan agency see: Bopearachchi, 'Foreword,' xx; H. Roth, 'Excavation at the Port of Godavaya, Hambantota District, Sri Lanka,' in *Sri Lanka, Past and Present: Archaeology, Geography, Economics*, ed. M. Domroes and H. Roth (Weikersheim: Margraf Verlag, 1998), 11.

6 Romila Thapar, 'Early Mediterranean Contacts with India: An Overview,' in *Crossings: Early Mediterranean Contacts with India*, ed. F. de Romanis and A. Tchernia (New Delhi: Manohar, 1997), 11, provides comparison between the colonized experience of South Asia from the seventeenth century and an ancient period of greater local connectivity and autonomy while pp. 18–19 situates intensification of trade between India and Lanka alongside increased trade with the Roman Empire as equal potential drivers towards greater mobility.

7 S. Kemper, *The Presence of the Past: Chronicles, Politics and Culture in Sinhala Life* (Ithaca, NY, and London: Cornell University Press, 1991), 2.

8 S. Seneviratne, 'Situating World Heritage Sites in a Multicultural Society: The Ideology of Presentation at the Sacred City of Anuradhapura, Sri Lanka,' in *Archaeology and the Post-Colonial Critique*, ed. M. Liebmann and U. Z. Rizvi (New York: Altamira Press, 2008), 182–7.

9 Kemper, *The Presence of the Past*, 2–3.

10 For example: P. Francis, 'Western Geographic Knowledge of Sri Lanka and Mantai ca 325 BC to 1170 AD,' in *Mantai: City by the Sea*, ed. J. Carswell, S. U. Deraniyagala and A. Graham (Stuttgart: Linden Soft Verlag, 2013), especially 56–60; J. I. Miller, *The Spice Trade of the Roman Empire, 29 BC to AD 641* (Oxford: Clarendon Press, 1969), 258–9; Weerakkody, *Taprobanê*, 161; G. Young, *Rome's Eastern Trade: International Commerce and Imperial Policy, 31 BC–AD 305* (London: Routledge, 2001), 87.

11 For example: M. Hendy, *Studies in the Byzantine Monetary Economy* (Cambridge: Cambridge University Press, 1985), 277; O. Bopearachchi, 'Archaeological Evidence on Changing Patterns of International Trade Relations of Ancient Sri Lanka,' in *Origin, Evolution and Circulation of Foreign Coins in the Indian Ocean*, ed. O. Bopearachchi and D. P. M. Weerakkody (New Delhi: Manohar, 1998), 158; J. K. Choksy, 'Sailors, Soldiers, Priests and Merchants: Reappraising Iran's Early Connections to Ceylon,' *Iranica Antiqua* 48 (2013), 380.

12 L. Boulnois, *Silk Road: Monks, Warriors and Merchants on the Silk Road*, 2nd edn (London: Odyssey Books, 2005), 137.

13 F. Thierry, 'Maritime Silk Routes and Chinese Coin Hoards,' in *Origin, Evolution and Circulation*; J. Cribb, 'Chinese Coin Finds from South India and Sri Lanka,' in *Numismatic Panorama: Essays in the Memory of Late Shri S. M. Shukula*, ed. K. K. Maheshwari and B. Rath (New Delhi: Harman Publishing House, 1996); R. Walburg, *Coins and Tokens from Ancient Ceylon* (Wiesbaden: Reichert Verlag, 2008), 284–5.

14 V. Porter, 'Islamic Coins found in Sri Lanka,' in *Origin, Evolution and Circulation*.

15 J. Kennedy, 'The Secret of Kanishka,' *Journal of the Royal Asiatic Society of Great Britain and Ireland* (1912), 672.

16 Walburg records six individual finds of *denarii* (one doubtful), and a hoard possibly discovered in 1904/5, of which six subsequently entered a private collection (Walburg, *Coins and Tokens*, catalogue numbers 28, 74, 127, 143, 193 and 221). The hoard certainly consisted of six specimens and may have contained more. Walburg's figures therefore yield a minimum figure of 12 specimens. Bopearachchi, 'Changing Patterns of International Trade,' 158 likewise laments the loss of some finds and data about them and in total records fourteen *denarii* finds.

17 Bopearachchi, 'Changing Patterns of International Trade', 155, records '[a] certain number of coins belonging to these dynasties [Indo-Scythian, Indo-Parthian and Kushan]' found in Sri Lanka and lists 'about ten' coins of the *Soter Megas* type... seen by the author in private collections', a coin of Kanishka II discovered in excavations at Jetavanarama, and '[w]e have seen at least ten more coins of the same kings in two private collections'. This yields an approximate total of twenty-one Kushan coins found on the island. O. M. R. Sirisena, *Medieval Gold Coins of Sri Lanka, 700–1100* (Colombo: Unigraphics Ltd., 2002), 18 and 20, also lists three possible finds of Kushan gold coins on the island, which would take the total to around twenty-four. By contrast, Walburg lists only the coin from Jetavaranama as an uncontested Sri Lankan find and questions sharply the finds listed by Sirisena (Walburg, *Coins and Tokens*, 182) and Bopearachchi (pp. 200–3) as having an island provenance.

18 H. W. Codrington, *Ceylon Coins and Currency* (Ceylon: A. C. Richards, 1924), 32.

19 Walburg, *Coins and Tokens*, catalogue numbers 122, 139, 145.

20 Walburg, *Coins and Tokens*: Biddell collection (catalogue number 239): eleven coins, including silver and copper; Leslie de Saram collection (catalogue number 240): nine Byzantine coins from total of eighteen gold coins, all now lost. On their doubtful island provenance, 218 and 221.

21 For example (excluding numismatic publications): R. Gyselen, ed., *Circulation des Monnaies, des Marchandises et des Biens* (Leuwen: Peeters, 1993), 77; Weerakkody, *Taprobanê*, 161.

22 Codrington, *Coins and Currency*, 32.

23 Codrington, *Coins and Currency*, 157–65; Bopearachchi, 'Changing Patterns of International Trade', 161–2; O. Bopearachchi, 'Recent Discoveries of Ancient Foreign Coins, hitherto Unknown in Sri Lankan Context' *Sesquicentennial Commemorative Volume, Royal Asiatic Society of Sri Lanka, 1845–1995* (1995), 127–39, plates 1 and 2, images 15–17.

24 Bopearachchi, 'Archaeological Evidence on Shipping Communities', 110.

25 Walburg, *Coins and Tokens*, catalogue numbers 29, 115, 160, 161, 178 and 195.

26 Codrington, *Coins and Currency*, 45, 157–65; Porter, 'Islamic Coins Found in Sri Lanka'; Walburg, *Coins and Tokens*, catalogue number 142; T. Goodwin, *Arab-Byzantine Coinage* (London: The Nour Foundation, 2005).

27 In comparison, the total number of precious metal Roman coins from India comfortably exceeds 6,000 (R. Darley, 'Indo-Byzantine Exchange, 4th–7th Centuries: A Global History,' PhD dissertation, University of Birmingham, 2014, 184, taken primarily from P. Turner, *Roman Coins from India* (London: Royal Numismatic Society, 1989). A search of the Portable Antiquities Scheme database for 'Byzantine' and 'Coins' in January 2014 revealed more than sixty-five individual finds of fourth- to seventh-century Byzantine coins reported to British museums since 2011 (Portable Antiquities Scheme, http://finds.org.uk, accessed 26 January 2014). For published references: Richard Abdy and Gareth Williams, 'A Catalogue of Hoards and Single finds from the British Isles, c. 410–675,' in *Coinage and History in the North Sea World, c. AD 500–1250*, ed. B. Cook and G. Williams (Leiden: Brill, 2006) 11–74. Britain, however, is not represented as a cash-register for long-distance early medieval trade and arguments about its ties to wider economic networks tend towards caution. A. Harris, *Byzantium, Britain and the West: The Archaeology of Cultural Identity, AD 400–650* (Stroud: Tempus Publishing, 2003), 191.

28 Noteworthy for this tendency, not least because of the enormous volume of his publications is O. Bopearachchi. Examples include, on ancient Lankan coinage and maritime trade: 'Circulation of Roman and Byzantine Gold Coins in Sri Lanka: Fact or Fiction?,' in *Dal* Denarius *al* Dinar: *L'oriente e la Moneta Romana*, ed. F. de Romanis and S. Sorda (Rome: Instituto Italiano di Numismatica, 2006); 'Coins,' in *Anurādhapura: The British-Sri Lankan Excavations at Anuradhapura Salgaha Watta*, Vol. 2: *The Artefacts*, ed. R. A. E Coningham (Oxford: Archaeopress, 2006), 7–26. On cultural and commercial relationships between ancient Sri Lanka and Tamil Nadu: 'Inde du Sud et Sri Lanka,' in *A Survey of Numismatic Research, 1996–2000*, ed. C. Alfaro and A. Burnett (Madrid: International Association of Professional Numismatists, 2003); 'Archaeological Evidence on Cultural and Commercial Relationships between Ancient Sri Lanka and South India,' in *Honouring Martin Quéré OMI*, ed. Gérard Robuchon and Philippe Fabry (Negombo: Viator Publications, 2002). On archaeological evidence for shipping: 'Routes Maritime et Port de L'ancien Sri Lanka,' in *Aller et Venir: Faits et Perspectives*, ed. by F. Blanchon, Vol. 2 (Paris: Asies, 2002); 'Sites portuaires et emporia de l'ancien Sri Lanka. Nouvelles données archéologiques,' *Arts Asiatiques* 54 (1999), 5–23. On changing patterns of international trade: 'The Maritime Silk Road: Trade Relations between Central Asia and Sri Lanka from the Evidence of Recent Excavations,' *Silk Road Art and Archaeology* 5 (1997/8), 269–95; 'Ancient Coins in Sri Lanka,' *Economic Review* 23 (1997), 21–26; 'Seafaring in the Indian Ocean: Archaeological Evidence from Sri Lanka,' in *Tradition and Archaeology: Early Maritime Contacts in the Indian Ocean*, ed. H. P. Ray and J.-F. Salles (New Delhi: Manohar, 1996); 'Le commerce maritime entre Rome et Sri Lanka d'après les données numismatiques,' *Revue des Études Anciennes* 94 (1992), 107–21; O. Bopearachchi and R. M. Wickremesinhe, *Ruhuna: An Ancient Civilization Re-visited. Numismatic and Archaeological Evidence on Inland and Maritime Trade* (Colombo: Tharanjee Prints, 1999). Specific examples of 'soundbite' conclusions concerning Arab, Byzantine and Sasanian coinage include: Bopearachchi, 'Foreword', xx; Bopearachchi, 'Sites portuaires et emporia', 16, 18; Bopearachchi, 'Circulation of Roman and Byzantine Gold Coins', 197–8.

29 Sirisena, *Medieval Gold Coins of Sri Lanka*, 2.

30 Bopearachchi, 'Circulation of Roman and Byzantine Gold Coins', 197–8.

31 The terms 'bronze' and 'copper' are used interchangeably for late Roman base metal coins in numismatic literature. Since, however, these coins were made neither of pure copper or of a carefully regulated bronze alloy, this chapter uses the term 'copper-alloy' throughout.

32 Bopearachchi, 'Foreword', xiv–xv, xix–xx; 'Recent Discoveries,' 131 for further examples.

33 For example, Bopearachchi, 'Le commerce maritime entre Rome', 113; 'Foreword,' xix–xx; Walburg, *Coins and Tokens*, 57–84.

34 R. Krishnamurthy, *Late Roman Copper Coins from South India: Karur, Madurai and Tirukkoilur* (Chennai: Garnet Publishers, 2007); Walburg, *Coins and Tokens*, 81–4.

35 For imitations being included in a total count of 'Roman' coinage and presented as evidence for volume or significance of trade, Bopearachchi, 'Circulation of Roman and Byzantine Gold Coins', 193, repeated almost verbatim from Bopearachchi, 'Foreword', xix–xx. For a critique and analysis of this, see Walburg, *Coins and Tokens*, 54–5. For publications that cite Bopearachchi's work on Roman coinage and imitations found in Sri Lanka, the main source for vague and ambiguous but impressive-sounding tallies of such coinage: Bopearachchi, 'Seafaring in the Indian Ocean'; Young, *Rome's Eastern Trade*; J. Hinnells and A. Williams, *Parsis in India and the Diaspora* (London: Routledge, 2007); G. Parker, *The Making of Roman India* (Cambridge: Cambridge University Press, 2011); M. P. Canepa, *The Two Eyes of the Earth* (Berkeley: University of California Press, 2009); P. Brancaccio, *The Buddhist Caves at Aurangabad* (Leiden: Brill, 2010); S. E. Sidebotham, *Berenike and the Ancient Maritime Spice Route* (Berkeley: University of California Press, 2011); Choksy, 'Sailors, Soldiers, Priests'.

36 Bopearachchi, 'Circulation of Roman and Byzantine Gold Coins', 193, cites more than 200,000 Roman coins found in Sri Lanka.

37 Walburg, *Coins and Tokens*, 52–5.

38 Walburg, *Coins and Tokens*, catalogue numbers 35, 132, 144, 148, 149, 151, 152, 157, 158. For this estimate: hoard 144 = sum of three lots recorded by the British Museum; hoard 149 is taken at upper estimate of 350 items, 151 as 723 (listed as the minimum number of specimens but no information survives about how many more pieces may have been included) and 152, recorded at the time as 'a large hoard' is counted as 300 specimens, the approximate size of most documented 'large' hoards of Naimana.

39 Walburg, *Coins and Tokens*, 59.

40 Walburg, *Coins and Tokens*, 57–80.

41 Walburg, *Coins and Tokens*, 312–14.

42 As yet no wholly convincing explanation for the arrival of these coins or their use in India exists. That they arrived, however, is certain, and questions about their movement before they reached Lanka do not invalidate the thesis that they arrived on the island via South India; on the beginning of imitations, see Walburg, *Coins and Tokens*, 343.

43 For example, W. J. M. Lokubandara, 'Sri Lanka's Role in the Maritime Silk Route,' in *Sri Lanka and the Silk Road of the Sea*, 2nd edn, ed. S. Bandaranayake (Colombo: Sri Lanka Institute of International Relations, 2003), 14.

44 As a practical guide for the non-numismatist seeking to use coin finds alongside archaeological or literary sources, there are a number of details that any publication of a coin should include or explain the absence of:

1. Description of metal and design, or link to a catalogued type providing this information.
2. Weight.
3. Location (either of discovery or current storage or both).
4. Ideally, an image or drawing.
5. Unique identifying number within either the publication or (preferably) its host collection.

Publication of a coin hoard (two or more coins found together with evidence for intentional combined deposition) should include or explain the absence of the following details:

1. Total number of coins.
2. Description of any other items in the hoard.
3. Number of coins by design/type.
4. Circumstances, date and location of discovery.
5. Current location, including if in a museum and separately catalogued, the unique identifying numbers of the items.

A plethora of other information may be included, depending on the length, purpose and style of the publication. This may include referencing coin types to other published catalogues or detailed analysis of size and metallurgic composition. While presentations of numismatic material may vary, however, any publication that lacks the information listed above should be approached cautiously by a scholar seeking to synthesize the published coins into their own work.

45 D. Carlson, 'INA in Sri Lanka, Pearl of the Indian Ocean,' *The Institute of Nautical Archaeology Annual* (2010), 94.

46 P. Grierson, *Byzantine Coinage* (Washington, DC: Dumbarton Oaks Library and Collection, 1999), 3.

47 I would like to thank the Curator of Coins at the Barber Institute, Maria Vrij, for pointing these finds out to me during her work on the collection records and her assistance accessing them and examining those records myself. All images used with the permission of the Barber Institute of Fine Arts. For a brief history of Baldwin's auction house, see www.baldwin.co.uk, accessed 15 December 2015.

48 F. J. and G. de Saram, *F. J. & G. de Saram, 1841–2001: 160 Year Practice of a Law Firm in its Historical Setting* (Colombo: Vijitha Yapa Publications, 2001).

49 *Leslie de Saram Collection: A Classified List* (Peradeniya: Peradeniya University, 1981). The list mentions some coins, but not the five examples published here, which had clearly left de Saram's collection earlier.

50 I am grateful to Professor Ted Buttrey at the Fitzwilliam Museum, who very kindly checked the records of Baldwin sales for notice of a de Saram collection and confirmed that the coins could not in 1955 have been sold at auction (and thus could not have been recorded in an auction catalogue). It is therefore most likely that de Saram sold a lot of coins directly to Baldwin, who then sold them on piece-by-piece or as a job lot. It is not possible to verify whether the five coins bought by Whitting constituted all of the de Saram stock available at the time.

51 Whitting's collection, as donated to the Barber Institute, includes Byzantine, Arab-Byzantine, Sasanian and Arab-Sasanian, Hephthalite and Kushan coins, among others.

52 Walburg, *Coins and Tokens*, 20.

53 Codrington's 1921 acknowledgements in *Coins and Currency* record de Saram as among those whose collection had been consulted; Walburg, *Coins and Tokens*, 19–21.

54 Codrington, *Coins and Currency*, 252–5.

55 Walburg, *Coins and Tokens*, 20.

56 R. A. G. Carson, J. P. C. Kent and A. M. Burnett *The Roman Imperial Coinage*, Vol. 10, *The Empire Divided and the Fall of the Western Parts, AD 395–491* (London: Spink, 1994).

57 In Sri Lanka, Walburg, *Coins and Tokens*, catalogue number 146; in India, Darley, 'Indo-Byzantine Exchange', Appendix 1, catalogue numbers 1–14.

58 Parallels in the Akki Alur hoard, Darley, 'Indo-Byzantine Exchange', Appendix 1, catalogue numbers 7 and 9, though both have different *officina* letters (the final letter at the end of the reverse inscription).

59 On the discovery and recording of the Akki Alur hoard, R. Day, 'A Tale of "Four" Hoards (or Unpicking Akki Alur)', *Journal of the Oriental Numismatic Society* 211 (2012), 5–13. For full-weight Indian imitations of *solidi*, Darley, 'Indo-Byzantine Exchange', Appendix 1, catalogue numbers 1–3, 10, 30, 35, 55, 59.

60 R. Ratto, *Collection privée. Monnaies Byzantines et d'autres pays contemporains à l'epoque Byzantine* (Auction catalogue of 9 December 1930; reprint Amsterdam, 1959), 9. Translation: 'Of reduced size… Very rare. Very beautiful.'

61 W. Hahn, *Moneta Imperii Byzantini*, 3 vols. (Vienna: Veröffentlichungen der Österreichischen Akademie der Wissenschaften, 1973).

62 On the meaning and use of CONOB, see C. Morrisson, 'Byzantine Money: Its Production and Circulation,' in *The Economic History of Byzantium: From the Seventh through the Fifteenth Century*, ed. A. Laiou (Washington, DC: Dumbarton Oaks Research Library and Collection, 2001), 911; on the COMOB variety, see Hahn, *Moneta Imperii Byzantini*, Vol. 1, 48.

63 Darley, 'Indo-Byzantine Exchange', catalogue numbers 35–51.

64 Hahn, *Moneta Imperii Byzantini*.

65 Walburg, *Coins and Tokens*, 333.

66 Carson et al., *Roman Imperial Coinage*.

67 Hendy, *Byzantine Monetary Economy*, 250.

68 R. Krishnamurthy, 'Roman Gold Coins from Southern Tamil Nadu, India: some 5th cent. A.D. Solidi and their Imitations,' in *Dal Denarius al Dinar*, 176.

69 Darley, 'Indo-Byzantine Exchange', catalogue number 11.

70 Carson et al., *Roman Imperial Coinage*.

71 While it is not possible to reconstruct de Saram's personal library or the books in it that he personally read, the following works were either well-known among collectors of South Asian coins or new, widely available and considered to advance the field of Indian Ocean history: M. P. Charlesworth, *Trade Routes and Commerce of the Roman Empire* (Cambridge: Cambridge University Press, 1926);

E. Thurston, *Madras Government Museum: Coins Catalogue No. 2, Roman, Indo-Portuguese and Ceylon* (Madras: Government Press, 1888); M. Wheeler, *Rome Beyond the Imperial Frontiers* (London: G. Bell and Sons Ltd., 1954).

72 *Mahāvaṃsa: Great Chronicle of Ceylon*, trans. Wilhelm Geiger, assisted by Mabel Haynes Bode (London: Pali Text Society, 1912); *Cūḷavaṃsa: Being the More Recent Part of the Mahāvaṃsa*, trans. Wilhelm Geiger (London: Pali Text Society, 1930); B. C. Law, *The Chronicle of the Island of Ceylon, of the Dipavamsa, a Historical Poem of the 4th Century AD* (Colombo: Ceylon Historical Journal, 1957–58).

73 Most significantly, S. Paranavitana et al., eds., *Inscriptions of Ceylon*, 5 vols. (Colombo: Archaeological Survey of Ceylon, 1970) and D. M. de Zilva Wickremasinghe et al., eds., *Epigraphica Zeylanica*, 7 vols. (London: Published for the Government of Ceylon by Henry Milford, 1904).

74 S. Beal, *The Life of Hiuen Tsiang, translated from the Chinese of Shaman (monk) Hwui Li* (1911; reprint New Delhi: Munshiram Manoharlal, 1973) and J. Legge, *A Record of Buddhistic Kingdoms, Being an Account of the Chinese Monk Fa-Hien of his Travels in India and Ceylon (AD 399–414) in Search of the Buddhist Books of Discipline* (Oxford: Clarendon Press, 1886).

75 Bopearachchi, 'Circulation of Roman and Byzantine Gold Coins', 193.

76 *Cosmas Indicopleustes: Topographie Chrétienne*, trans. W. Wolska-Conus, Sources Chrétiennes 141 (Paris: Les éditions du Cerf, 1968), tome I, 15–16 cites evidence of two eclipses mentioned in the work, which she dates to 547 and 549. G. L. Huxley, 'On the Greek Martyrium of the Negranites,' *Proceedings of the Royal Irish Academy, Section C: Archaeology, Celtic Studies, History, Linguistics, Literature* 80 (1980), argues for the earlier date of 518–19 but this has not been widely accepted.

77 M. Kominko, *The World of Kosmas: Illustrated Byzantine Codices of the Christian Topography* (Cambridge: Cambridge University Press, 2013).

78 For example M. V. Anastos, 'The Alexandrian Origin of the "Christian Topography" of Cosmas Indicopleustes,' *Dumbarton Oaks Papers* 3 (1946), 77; T. L. Clark, 'Imaging the Cosmos: The *Christian Topography* by Kosmas Indikopleustes,' PhD dissertation, Temple University, Philadelphia, 2008, 10 §11; D. Peacock, E. Peacock and L. Blue, ed., *The Ancient Red Sea Port of Adulis, Eritrea Report of the Etrito-British Expedition 2004–5* (Oxford: Oxbow Books, 2007), 4; D. Whitehouse, *Siraf: History, Topography and Environment* (Oxford: Oxbow Books, 2009), 99.

79 Rome, Biblioteca Apostolica Vaticana, Cod. Gr., hereafter referred to as recension V.

80 Sinai, Monastery of St Katherine, Cod. Gr. 1186, hereafter recension S and Florence, Biblioteca Laurenziana, Cod. Plut. 9.28, hereafter recension L.

81 Photius, *Bibliotheke*, 3.36 in *Bibliothèque Photius; Texte établi et traduit*, ed. R. Henry, Vol. 1 (Paris: Les Belles Lettres, 1959). In English N. G. Wilson, *The Bibliotheca: A Selection. Photius, Translated with Notes* (London: Duckworth, 1994).

82 Including: Bopearachchi, 'Archaeological Evidence on Shipping Communities', 92; Bopearachchi, 'Circulation of Roman and Byzantine Gold Coins,' 190; R. T. J. Cappers, *Roman Food-Prints at Berenike: Archaeological Evidence of Trade and Subsistence in the Eastern Desert of Egypt* (Los Angeles: Cotsen Institute of Archaeology, 2006), 78; J. Carswell, 'The Port of Mantai, Sri Lanka,' in *Rome and India: The Ancient Sea Trade*, ed. V. Begley and R. D. de Puma (Madison, WI: University of Wisconsin Press, 1991), 199; F. A. Chami, 'Graeco-Roman Trade Link and the Bantu Migration Theory,' *Anthropos* 94 (1999), 211; F. de Romanis, 'Romanukharaṭṭha and Taprobane: Relations between Rome and Sri Lanka in the First Century AD,' in *Crossings*, 187–8; S. Devendra, 'Pre-Modern Sri Lankan Ships and Shipping,' in *Ships and the Development of Maritime Technology*, 168; G. Hudson, *Europe and China: A Survey of their Relations from the Earliest Times to 1800* (London: Edward Arnold and Co., 1931), 110; Miller, *The Spice Trade,* 159; S. T. Parker, 'The Roman Port of Aila: Economic Connections with the Red Sea Littoral,' in *Connected Hinterlands: Proceedings of Red Sea Project IV*, held at the University of Southampton (September 2008), ed. L. Blue et al. (Oxford: Archaeopress, 2009), 89; Peacock and Blue, *Adulis,* 4; I. Puskás, 'Trade Contacts between India and the Roman Empire,' in *India and the Ancient World: History, Trade and Culture before AD 650*, ed. G. Pollet (Leuven: Department Oriëntalisteik, 1987), 143; K. A. Sastri, *A History of South India from Prehistoric Times to the Fall of Vijayanagar*, 2nd edn (Oxford: Oxford University Press, 1958), 26; J. W. Sedlar, *India and the Greek World: A Study in the Transmission of Culture* (Totaw, NJ: Rowman and Littlefield, 1980), 85; E. H. Seland, 'Trade and Christianity in the Indian Ocean during Late Antiquity,' *Journal of Late Antiquity* 5, 1 (2012), 81; R. Tomber, *Indo-Roman Trade: from Pots to Pepper* (London: Duckworth, 2009), 168–9; Z. Wendrich et al., 'Berenike Crossroads: The Integration of Information,' *Journal of the Economic and Social History of the Orient* 46, 1 (2003), 71; D. Whitehouse, 'Epilogue: Roman Trade in Perspective,' in *Rome and India*, 218.

83 The author here glosses the term for the Persian silver coin, the *drachm* with the name of a late Roman silver denomination, the *miliaresion*, which would have been familiar to a sixth-century Roman reader.

84 Book 11.17–20, translation by Weerakkody, *Taprbanê*, 245–6.

85 Bopearachchi, 'Circulation of Roman and Byzantine Gold Coins', 193; De Romanis, 'Romanukharaṭṭha and Taprobane', 187–8.

86 Pliny, *Natural History*, trans. H. Rackham, Vol. 2 (Cambridge, MA: Harvard University Press, 1942), book 6, chapter 24.84–5.

87 J. E. Tennent, *Ceylon: An Account of the Island Physical, Historical and Topographical*, Vol. 1 (1860; reprint Project Gutenberg, 2004, www.gutenberg.org/files/13552), 563; De Romanis, 'Romanukharaṭṭha and Taprobane', 180–3, 187–8.

88 M. Kominko, 'New Perspectives on Paradise – The Levels of Reality in Byzantine and Latin Medieval Maps,' in *Cartography in Antiquity and the Middle Ages: Fresh Perspectives, New Methods*, ed. R. J. A. Talbert and R. W. Unger (Leiden: Brill, 2008), 141; *Cosmas Indicopleustes*, tome I, 38–43.

89 Pliny, *Natural History*, book 6.22(24).88; *Cosmas Indicopleustes*, tome I, book 2.52.1-9.

90 I. Carradice, 'Flavian Coinage,' in *The Oxford Handbook of Greek and Roman Coinage*, ed. W. Metcalf (Oxford: Oxford University Press, 2012), 375–90.

91 *Cosmas Indicopleustes*, tome I, book 2.77.

92 Whitehouse, 'Epilogue,' 218.

93 Weekakkoddy, *Taprobanê*, 218–44.

94 *Cosmas Indicopleustes*, tome III, book 12.15. Translation from Weerakkody, *Taprobanê*, 245.

95 Various sources confirm that among inhabitants of the Roman Empire involved in eastern trade, Greek-speakers from the eastern Mediterranean region were dominant, including the first-century CE *Periplous of the Erythreian Sea*, trans. L. Casson (Princeton, NJ: Princeton University Press, 1989); the so-called 'Muziris papyrus', a second-century contract dealing with shipping from South India, see L. Casson, 'New Light on Maritime Loans: P. Vindob. G 40822,' *Zeitschrift für Papyrologie und Epigraphik* 84 (1990), 195–206; and graffiti inscriptions on the island of Soqotra, see I. Strauch, *Foreign Sailors on Socotra: The Inscriptions and Drawings from the Cave Hoq* (Bremen: Ute Hempen Verlag, 2013).

96 For example: Seland, 'Trade and Christianity', 81; S. Kiribamune, 'The Role of the Port City of Mahatittha (Matota) in the Trade Networks of the Indian Ocean,' in Carswell, *Mantai*, 49.

97 Darley, 'Indo-Byzantine Exchange', 266–7.

98 Particularly R. Coningham, ed., Anurādhapura: *The British-Sri Lankan Excavations at Anuradhapura Salgaha Watta*, Vol. 2, *The Artefacts* (Oxford: Archaeopress, 2006); R. Coningham et al., 'The Anuradhapura (Sri Lanka) Project: The Hinterland (Phase II), Preliminary Report on the First Season 2005,' *South Asian Studies* 22, 1 (2006), 53–64; H.-J. H. Weisshaar et al., eds., *Ancient Ruhuna: Sri Lankan-German Archaeological Project in the Southern Province* (Mainz and Wiesbaden: Verlag Philipp von Zabern and Reichert Verlag, 2001).

99 Carlson, 'INA in Sri Lanka', 90; M. Gannon, 'Indian Ocean's Oldest Shipwreck Set for Excavation,' LiveScience Blog, 4 February 2014, www.livescience.com/42901-indian-ocean-oldest-shipwreck.html; R. Muthucumarana, 'Ancient Port City of Godawaya and the Recent Discovery of the Unknown Wooden Wreck with Black and Red Ware,' Maritime Archaeology Unit Blog, 2011, www.mausrilanka.lk/sub%20pages/Godawaya.html.

100 W. I. Siriweera, 'Godavaya: Ancient Port Near Modern Magamtota,' in *The Island* (Colombo), 10 January 2014, www.island.lk/index.php?page_cat=article-details&page=article-details&code_title=95650. P. Francis, 'The Beads,' in *Mantai*, 353–5.

101 P. Francis, *Asia's Maritime Bead Trade, 300 BC to the Present* (Hawai'i: University of Hawai'i Press, 2002), 136–40.

102 R. Muthucumarana, 'Ancient Port City of Godawaya'.

103 Trethewey, K. 'The Oldest Known Ship in the Indian Ocean: Logistics for an Upcoming INA Excavation,' *Institute of Nautical Archaeology Quarterly* 39, 1–2 (2012), 28–9.

104 Trethewey, 'The Oldest Known Ship', 29.

105 D. Carlson and K. Threthewey, 'Exploring the Oldest Shipwreck in the Indian Ocean,' *The Institute of Nautical Archaeology Quarterly* 40 (2013), 8–14.

106 M. Gannon, 'Indian Ocean's Oldest Shipwreck.'

107 Whitehouse, 'Epilogue', 218. The port of Anuradhapura: Bopearachchi, 'Archaeological Evidence on Shipping Communities', 95; T. Frasch, 'Religious and Economic Development of Ancient Anuradhapura,' in *Sri Lanka, Past and Present*, 67; D. N. Ghosh, *Business and Polity: Dynamics of a Changing Relationship* (London: Sage, 2011), 44–5.

108 A. Graham, 'Excavations 1887–1976 and the Condition of the Site in 1980,' in *Mantai*, 98–104.
109 A. Graham, 'The Limitation of the Evidence,' in J. Carswell, S. Deraniyagala and G. Campbell eds. *Mantai: City by the Sea* (Stuttgart: Linden Soft Verlag, 2013), 132–141.
110 Kiribamune, 'The Role of the Port City', 40–8.
111 Francis, 'Western Geographic Knowledge', 57–8.
112 Carswell, *Mantai*, 189–269 (ceramics), 271–507 (artefacts).
113 Kiribamune, 'The Role of the Port City', 46–7.
114 All are short notifications: J. Carswell and M. Prickett, 'Mantai 1980: A Preliminary Investigation,' *Ancient Ceylon* 5 (1984), 11–37; P. K. Chanmugam and F. L. W. Jayawardene, 'Skeletal Remains from Tirukketiswaram,' *Ceylon Journal of Science*, Section G V, 11 (1954), 65–6; R. Silva and J. Bouzek, 'Mantai – a Second Arikamedu?,' *Antiquity* 59 (1985), 46–7.
115 Francis, 'The Beads', 352–3.
116 R. Walburg and A. Graham, 'The Coins' in *Mantai*, appendix 3, 1–3.
117 A. Graham, 'The Primary Development of the Mound,' in, *Mantai*, 144–54.
118 A. Graham, 'Pottery from the Excavated Sequence in Trenches H and G,' and R. Mohanty, 'Indian Imported Pottery' in, *Mantai*, 191–212 and 213–27.
119 Bopearachchi, 'Changing Patterns of International Trade', 142–3; R. Gurukkal *Rethinking Classical Indo-Roman Trade. Political Economy of Eastern Mediterranean Exchange Relations* (New Delhi: Oxford University Press, 2016), 181.
120 O. Kessler, 'The Discovery of an Ancient Sea Port at the Silk Road of the Sea – Archaeological Relics of the Godavaya Harbor,' in *Sri Lanka: Past and Present; Archaeology, Geography, Economics, Selected Papers on German Research*, ed. M. Domroes and H. Roth (Würzburg: Margraf Verlag, 1998), 12–37.
121 The precise meaning of this inscription has recently been disputed. It was originally translated by Paranavitana as 'Success! The customs duties of the port of Goḍapavata, King Gāmanī Abhaya granted to the vihāra' (*Inscriptions of Ceylon*, Vol. 2, plate 67), but has been retranslated on the basis of new images and a re-examination by H. Falk, 'Three Epigraphs from Godawaya, Sri Lanka', in *Ancient Ruhuna: Sri Lankan-German Archaeological Project in the Southern Province*, Vol. 1, ed. H.-J. H. Weisshaar et al. (Mainz and Wiesbaden: Verlag Philipp von Zabern and Reichert Verlag, 2001), 328, as '*siddham*. Regular [*suka*] and minor [*sukiya*] duties [due] in the emporium of Goḍapavvata are given to the (Buddhist) monastery (by) king Gāmani Abhaya.' Nevertheless, for the purposes of an argument at the granularity currently possible with respect to ancient Lankan trade connections, both translations coincide in agreeing that a king granted revenues from an emporium to a third party with a religious status.
122 *Cosmas Indicopleustes*, trans. Wolska-Conus, tome III, book XI, 17.
123 Bopearachchi, 'Changing Patterns of International Trade', 138.
124 Bopearachchi, 'Changing Patterns of International Trade', 138.
125 Bopearachchi, 'Foreword', xix–xx.
126 Possible use of Roman copper coins as a local circulating currency either alongside or instead of an indigenous coinage has been more widely discussed with respect to India, e.g. P. L. Gupta, 'Coins in Rome's Indian Trade,' in *Coinage, Trade and Economy*, ed. A. K. Jha (Nasik: Indian Institute of Research in Numismatic Studies, 1991), 125. It remains as valid a hypothesis as that coins represent long-distance trade.
127 For example: Bopearachchi, 'Changing Patterns of International Trade', 149. The effect of this circularity is most clear from the map provided by Bopearachchi, which pinpoints 'Location of coin finds and ancient ports' without clarifying whether these two features should be interpreted as synonymous, or if not, how they are being distinguished (Bopearachchi, 'New Archaeological Evidence', 63).
128 Weerakkody, *Taprobanê*, 14.
129 Tomber, *Indo-Roman trade*.
130 T. Sen, 'Buddhism and the Maritime Crossings,' *China and Beyond in the Medieval Period: Cultural Crossings and Inter-Regional Connections*, ed. D. Wong and G. Heldt (Amherst and Delhi: Cambria and Manohar Press, 2014), 44–5.
131 Sen, 'Buddhism and the Maritime Crossings', 53.
132 I. Glover, 'The Archaeological Evidence for Early Trade between India and Southeast Asia,' in *The Indian Ocean in Antiquity*, ed. J. Reade (London: Kegan Paul International, 1996); K. D. Morrison, 'Commerce and Culture in South Asia: Perspectives from Archaeology and History,' *Annual Review of Anthropology* 26 (1997), 87–108; H. P. Ray, *The Winds of Change: Buddhism and the Maritime Links of Early South Asia* (Oxford: Oxford University Press, 1994).
133 For example Bopearachchi, 'Circulation of Roman and Byzantine Gold Coins', 192, attributes the change to the shift of western trade routes from the Red Sea towards the Arabian peninsular;

E. Seland, 'Trade and Christianity' posits a link between the expansion of monotheist, especially Christian and Jewish, religious groups into the western Indian Ocean and an increase in trade and diplomacy; Whitehouse, *Siraf*, 98–100, argues that the change derived in large part from a new drive by the Sasanian Empire in the sixth century to monopolize eastward trade into the Indian Ocean, a thesis that is desperately lacking in either physical or textual evidence.

134 Walburg, *Coins and Tokens*, 333–4.

135 Darley, 'Indo-Byzantine Exchange', 178, 336, 378.

## Chapter 3: A Pāli cosmopolis?

1 Research into such transnational (and global) relationships has meanwhile become a well-established field, being conducted at centres such as the Heidelberg Centre for Asian Transcultural Studies (www.asia-europe.uni-heidelberg.de), the American-based research group on Theravāda Civilizations (www.theravadaciv.org) or the 'Empires' project at the Austrian Academy of Science (www.oeaw.ac.at/empires), to name but a few.

2 Daud Ali, 'The Early Inscriptions of Indonesia and the Problem of the Sanskrit Cosmopolis,' in *Early Interactions between South and Southeast Asia: Reflections on Cross-Cultural Exchange*, ed. P.-Y. Manguin and A. Mani (New Delhi and Singapore: Manohar and Institute of Southeast Asian Studies, 2011), 277–95; Johannes Bronkhorst, 'The Spread of Sanskrit in Southeast Asia,' in *Early Interactions between South and Southeast Asia*, 263–76.

3 This terminology equates to a degree Collins' notion of a 'Pāli imaginaire', which is defined as a shared mental world, held together by Pāli texts and language: Steven Collins, *Nirvana and other Buddhist Felicities* (Cambridge: Cambridge University Press, 1998). Undeniably, of course, Sri Lankan culture was from the earliest time exposed to and considerably influenced by Sanskrit culture, stemming from the island's continuing demographic, political and military exchanges especially with South India. These influences have been amply documented by scholars such as Wilhelm Geiger (e.g. in the footnotes to his translation of the *Mahāvaṃsa* and *Cūḷavaṃsa*) or Heinz Bechert, for example in *Eine regionale hochsprachliche Tradition in Südasien: Sanskrit-Literatur bei den buddhistischen Singhalesen*, Sitzungsberichte der Österreichischen Akademie der Wissenschaften, Philiosophisch-Historische Klasse 718 (Vienna: Österreichische Akademie der Wissenschaften, 2005). Emphasis here rests on the notion of Pāli providing an alternative cultural system.

4 Examples to be mentioned here are the Mahābodhi Society formed at the end of the nineteenth century and the activities surrounding the Sixth Buddhist Council including the World Fellowship of Buddhists.

5 *The Irrawaddy*, 1 October 2014, www.irrawaddy.com/news/burma/burmas-wirathu-sri-lankan-nationalist-monks-sign-agreement.html, accessed 9 September 2016.

6 For this term, see Tilman Frasch, 'Der Buddhismus im Jahr 1000,' *Periplus. Jahrbuch für Außereuropäische Geschichte* 10 (2000), 56–72.

7 As Oskar von Hinüber has shown, the Burmese and Northern Thai textual traditions of the scriptures are often distinct from the Sri Lankan one and occasionally surpass the latter, see his *Die Sprachgeschichte des Pali im Spiegel der südostasiatischen Handschriftenüberlieferung*, Abhandlungen der geistes- und sozialwissenschaftlichen Klasse 8 (Mainz: Akademie der Wissenschaften und der Literatur, 1988).

8 This view is widespread in writings on Theravāda Buddhism by Sri Lankan and Western scholars alike.

9 Steven Collins, 'On the Very Idea of the Pāli Canon,' *Journal of the Pāli Text Society* 15 (1981), 89–126.

10 Collins, 'On the Very Idea'. For the economic background to these events see Tilman Frasch, 'Religious and Economic Development in Ancient Anuradhapura,' in *Sri Lanka Past and Present*, ed. Manfred Domrös and Helmut Roth (Weikersheim: Marggraf, 1998), 68–72.

11 *The Mahāvaṃsa*, ed. Wilhelm Geiger (London: Pali Text Society, 1909), 37.5. This seems to have been a real threat, as the king issued a specific type of coins or tokens, showing a maneless lion, which could have served in lieu of money donated to the monks. See Reinhold Walburg, *Coins and Tokens from Ancient Ceylon* (Wiesbaden: Reichert Verlag, 2008), 99.

12 *Mahāvaṃsa*, 37.11–12 and 37.34–8.

13 Tilman Frasch, 'Buddha's Tooth Relic: Contesting Rituals and the early State in Sri Lanka,' in *Ritual Dynamics and the Science of the Ritual*, ed. Axel Michaels, Vol. 3, *State, Power and Violence*, ed. Marko Kitts et al. (Wiesbaden: Harrassowitz, 2010) 647–64.

14 *A Record of the Buddhistic Kingdoms, Being an Account by the Chinese Monk Fâ-hien of his Travels in India and Ceylon*, trans. James Legge (1886; reprint New York: Paragon and Dover Publications, 1965), 104.

15 *Mahāvaṃsa*, 37.4–5.

16 For nunneries inside the Mahāvihāra complex, see R. A. L. H. Gunawardana, *Robe and Plough: Monasticism and Economic Interest in Early Medieval Sri Lanka* (Tucson: University of Arizona Press, 1979), 37–9, and (more elaborately) R. A. L. H. Gunawardana, 'Subtle Silks of Ferrous Firmness: Buddhist Nuns in Ancient and Early Medieval Sri Lanka and their Role in the Propagation of Buddhism,' *The Sri Lankan Journal of the Humanities* 14 (1988), 1–59.

17 Nuns were often associated with duties pertaining to the Bōdhi tree, see S. B. Hettiaratchi, *Social and Cultural History of Ancient Sri Lanka* (Delhi: Sri Satguru, 1988), 99–102. A further indication of their status in existence is provided by the *Dīpavaṃsa*, which contains one chapter recording the names of eminent nuns of Anurādhapura: *The Dīpavaṃsa*, ed. and trans. Hermann Oldenberg (London: Williams and Norgate, 1879), 18.7–44. For their missionary work in China see now Ann Heirman, 'Chinese Nuns and their Ordination in 5th Century China,' *Journal of the International Association of Buddhist Studies* 24, 2 (2001), 275–305.

18 Collins, 'On the Very Idea'.

19 Kate Crosby, 'The Origin of Pali as a Language Name in Medieval Theravada Literature,' *Journal of the Centre for Buddhist Studies of Sri Lanka* 2 (2004), 70–116. Although the origins of Pāli are still debated, it seems clear that the language is very specific and systematic in its adaption and transformation of Sanskrit vocabulary and grammar. The language does not fit into a chronological sequence from Sanskrit to Sinhala (for which Elu/Helu was an intermediate) nor any other middle-Indic dialect. If the language of the oldest datable Pāli text, the *Dīpavaṃsa*, is more than coincidental, its rather 'poor' or 'unrefined' form would suggest that Pāli was still in the making around the end of the fourth century CE.

20 See Collins, 'On the Very Idea', who does, however, avoid the term 'fundamentalism' despite working at Chicago when the 'Fundamentalism Project' there was underway. The definition of 'Buddhist fundamentalism' given here differs principally from the examples found in the volumes resulting from the project, for example in Scott Appleby and Martin Marty, eds., *Fundamentalisms Comprehended* (Chicago, University of Chicago Press, 1995).

21 Keyes even notes a certain 'aggressiveness of Sinhalese monks promoting their religion': Charles F. Keyes, *The Golden Peninsula: Culture and Adaptation in Mainland Southeast Asia* (London: Macmillan, 1977), 82.

22 Janice Stargardt, 'The Oldest Known Pāli Texts, 5th–6th Century,' *Journal of the Pāli Text* Society 21 (1995), 199–213; Harry Falk, 'Die Goldblätter aus Śrī Kṣetra,' *Wiener Zeitschrift für die Kunde Südasiens* 41 (1997), 53–92.

23 Peter Skilling, 'New Pāli Inscriptions from Southeast Asia,' *Journal of the Pāli Text Society* 23 (1997), 123–57, and Mendis Rohanadeera, 'The Noen Sa Bua Inscription of Dong Si Mahabo, Prachinburi,' *Journal of the Siam Society* (1988), 89–98. For general surveys of this early spread of Theravāda, see Prapod Assavavirulhakarn, *The Ascendancy of Theravāda Buddhism in Southeast Asia* (Chiang Mai: Silkworm, 2010), 71–112, and Peter Skilling, 'The Advent of Theravada Buddhism to Mainland Southeast Asia,' in *Buddhism and Buddhist Literature of Southeast Asia* (Bangkok and Lumbini: Fragile Palm Leaves Foundation, 2009), 104–19.

24 Peter Schalk, *Buddhism among Tamils in Tamil Ilam and Tamilakam*, 2 vols. (Uppsala: Uppsala University Press, 2004).

25 This association is obviously not without difficulties, as not all monks at the Abhayagiri monastery appear to have been Mahāyānists, and the Mahāyāna movement (if there ever was one) consisted of more groups and fraternities than the Abhayagirivāsins alone. For a discussion of this, see for example Stephen C. Berkwitz, *South Asian Buddhism: A Survey* (London: Routledge, 2010), 71–103.

26 An inscription from Lopburi (Thailand) states that Buddhist monks of both traditions as well as Brahmins lived there in the early eleventh century: Assavavirulhakarn, *Ascendancy*, 88.

27 As Verardi has shown, this was by no means a peaceful process: Giovanni Verardi, *Hardships and Downfall of Buddhism in India* (Singapore: Institute of Southeast Asian Studies, 2011).

28 Frasch, 'Buddhismus im Jahr 1000', 62–3.

29 Frasch, 'Buddha's Tooth Relic', 655–6. But see H. B. Ilangasinha, *Buddhism in Medieval Sri Lanka* (Delhi: Sri Satguru, 1992), 55ff., who claims that after Parākramabāhu's I unification all monks on the island would trace their origins to the Mahāvihāra.

30 *Cūḷavaṃsa*, 57.

31 The two major sources are the Kalyāṇī Inscriptions from Pegu (late fifteenth century) and the earliest Burmese chronicle to have survived, U Kala's 'Great Chronicle' (*Mahārājavaṅ-krī:*), finished around 1720, which depends on the report of that inscription. So far, scholarly studies have been content with highlighting Anawrahta's role as a champion of Theravāda to explain the rise of Theravāda in eleventh-century Burma (and, by extension, for its rise elsewhere in Southeast Asia), see for example Goh Geok-yian, *The Wheel-Turner and his House: Kingship in a Buddhist Ecumene* (DeKalb, IL: Northern Illinois University Press, 2015). But in his study of the 'Pāli imaginaire', Collins has argued that Theravāda as an ideology could pacify people and make them accept rulers and taxation. Steven Collins, 'What is Literature in Pāli?,' in *Literary Cultures in History*, ed. Sheldon Pollock (Berkeley and Los Angeles: University of California Press, 2003), 680–1.

32 The Aris (*araññ*) were portrayed as a counter-model to the true Buddhist monk, consuming alcohol, having intercourse with women and practising black magic. In reality, the Aris (if derived from *araññavāsi* or 'forest-dwellers') were a group within the *saṅgha* who took upon themselves a higher degree of asceticism by dwelling at a certain distance from the settlements of the laymen. See Tilman Frasch, *Pagan. Stadt und Staat* (Stuttgart: Steiner, 1996), 288.

33 *Cūḷavaṃsa*, 60.4–8.

34 For more details, see Tilman Frasch, 'A Buddhist Network in the Bay of Bengal: Relations between Bodhgaya, Burma and Sri Lanka, c. 300–1300,' in *From the Mediterranean to the China Sea. Miscellaneous Notes*, ed. Claude Guillot et al. (Wiesbaden: Harrassowitz, 1998), 69–93.

35 These include the struggle for the throne among members of the Sinhalese royal family after the death of both Vijaya Bāhu I and Parākramabāhu I and again in the early thirteenth century, when the island was twice invaded by Māgha and Candrabhānu. *Cūḷavaṃsa*, 80. 51–89 and 83.36–51.

36 Amaradasa Liyanagamage, *The Decline of Polonnaruwa and the Rise of Dambadeniya* (Colombo: Department of Cultural Affairs and Government Press, 1968).

37 For this, see G. P. Malalasekera, *The Pāli Literature of Ceylon* (Kandy: Buddhist Publication Society, 1994).

38 Reforms are mentioned for example in *Cūḷavaṃsa*, 81.40–52 and 84.7–8. For the royal orders, see *The Katikāvatas*, ed. and trans. Nandasena Ratnapala (Munich: Kitzinger, 1971).

39 Tilman Frasch, 'Kontakte, Konzile, Kontroversen: Begegnungen in der Theravada-Kosmopolis, ca. 1000–1300 CE', in *Begegnungen in den Religionen Asiens*, ed. Oliver Freiberger et al. (Göttingen: Vandenhoeck & Ruprecht, forthcoming).

40 E. Hultzsch, 'A Vaishnava Inscription from Pagan,' *Epigraphia Indica* 7 (1902–3), 197–8.

41 U Than Tun, *Hnaung-dwe Kyauksa-mya* (Yangon: Myanmar Historical Commission, 2005), no. 10, 26.

42 Close-ups of the image and its hands are shown in Pierre Pichard, *Inventory of the Monuments at Pagan*, Vol. 4 (Paris: UNESCO, 1994), 396, catalogue number 1133 (figures e and f).

43 Frasch, 'Kontakte, Konzile, Kontroversen'.

44 The inscription *in situ* (Pl. IV 373c) states that it had been endowed with three sets of articles of daily use such as cups and bed-stands. For the monastery, which has meanwhile been restored, see Pichard, *Inventory*, Vol. 4, 374–97, catalogue numbers 1115–18.

45 Pichard, *Inventory*, Vol. 4, 206–9, catalogue number 987. Another example of a stupa on an elephant-born platform is the Mahakassapa stupa (Pierre Pichard, *Inventory of the Monuments at Pagan*, Vol. 2 (Paris: UNESCO, 1993), catalogue number 545). Mahākassapa is said to have travelled to Lanka and was very likely the recipient of the Manavulu Sandesa, a Pāli letter from the thirteenth century sent from Poḷonnaruva to Bagan: Lionel D. Barnett, 'The Manavulu Sandesaya,' *Journal of the Royal Asiatic Society* (1905), 265–83.

46 Gordon H. Luce, *Old Burma – Early Pagan*, Vol. 2 (Locust Valley, NY: Augustine, 1969).

47 Gordon H. Luce and U Pe Maung Tin, 'Inscriptions of Burma, Edited and Translated,' *Bulletin of the Burma Historical Commission* 1 (1960), 1–28; *The Myazedi Inscription in Four Languages*, ed. Cultural Institute (Rangoon: Government Press, 1960); Luce, *Old Burma*, Vol. 1, 46.

48 *Inscriptions of Burma*, comp. G. H. Luce and U Pe Maung Tin, Vol. 3 (Oxford: University Press, 1939), pl. 302.

49 This inscription is still unedited. For a summary, see Frasch, 'Kontakte, Konzile, Kontroversen'.

50 *Inscriptions of Burma*, Vol. 3, pl. 226.

51 Luce, *Old Burma*, Vol. 2, 208–9, figure 449d.

52 *Cūḷavaṃsa*, 81.43–5 and 84.7–10.

53 G. P. Malalasekera, *The Pāli Literature of Ceylon* (London: Royal Asiatic Society, 1928), 221–37.

54 The most famous example of a grammar is the *Saddanīti*, which was allegedly composed in the mid-twelfth century. Other examples include the *Saddbindu*, which is ascribed to king Kyazwa

(r. 1235–48): Friedgard Lottermoser, 'Minor Pāli Grammar Texts: The *Saddabindu* and its "New" Commentary,' *Journal of the Pali Text Society* 11 (1987), 79–109. For an attempt to identify some of the Pāli scholars from Bagan see Frasch, *Pagan*, 328–32.

55 U Than Tun, 'History of Buddhism in Burma, AD 1000–1300,' *Journal of the Burma Research Society* 51 (1978), 77–87, and U Tin Htway, 'A Preliminary Note on the Vinayadharas of Pagan Period in Burma,' in *Festschrift für Prof. Manuel Sarkisyanz*, ed. Barbara Diehl-Eli et al. (Frankfurt: Peter Lang, 1987), 411–58.

56 U Than Tun, 'An Original Inscription Dated 10 September 1223, that King Badon Copied on 27 October 1785,' in *Études birmanes en hommage à Denise Bernot*, ed. Pierre Pichard and François Robinne (Paris: École Française d'Extrême-Orient, 1998), 37–42. Also see Mabel Bode, *The Pāli Literature of Burma* (London: Royal Asiatic Society, 1909).

57 Besides Senarat Paranavitana (passim), W. M. Sirisena, *Sri Lanka and Southeast Asia* (Leiden: Brill, 1978), and now Hema Goonatilake, 'Sri Lanka – Myanmar Historical Relations in Religion, Culture and Polity,' *Journal of the Royal Asiatic Society of Sri Lanka* 55 (2009), 80–104, these include (curiously enough) Gunawardena, *Robe and Plough*, who would otherwise not appear to fit any kind of 'nationalist' bill.

58 Another example for this is the spread of the position of a 'primate' or chief monk of the *saṅgha* (*saṅgharāja, mahāsāmi*). This office was the outcome of the unification of the Sri Lankan *saṅgha* by King Parākramabāhu I in 1165 CE, but was never copied at Bagan, see Frasch, 'Kontakte, Konzile, Kontroversen'.

59 Frasch, *Pagan*, 343–4.

60 This connection is represented by the monk Mahākassapa, who possibly hailed from the Lower Chindwin region and became the leader of a large forest monastery in mid-thirteenth-century Bagan. A local chronicle also attributes to him a visit to Ceylon. See Than Tun, 'History of the Buddhism in Burma', 120–5, and Frasch, *Pagan*, 296–98.

61 Michael Charney, *Powerful Learning: Buddhist Literati and the Throne in Burma's Last Dynasty* (Ann Arbor: University of Michigan Press, 2006).

62 G. H. Luce and U Ba Shin, 'A Chiang Mai Mahāthera visits Pagan (1368 AD),' *Artibus Asiae* 24, 3 (1961), 330–7; *The Chiang Mai Chronicle*, trans. David Wyatt and Aroonrut Wichienkeeo (Chiang Mai: Silkworm, 1998), 39–40.

63 *Inscriptions of Burma*, Vol. 3, pl. 345b, and Vol. 5, pl. 548a. Both are fragmentary. Kusumi/Bassein was allegedly the port of embarkation and arrival for the monks Uttarajiva and Chapada, who went to Lanka in the late twelfth century. Taw Sein Ko, *The Kalyani Inscriptions Erected by King Dhammaceti at Pegu in 1476 AD* (Rangoon, Government Printing, 1892).

64 Sirisena, *Sri Lanka and Southeast Asia*, 91–9.

65 Peter Skilling, 'New Pāli Inscriptions from Southeast Asia', and Anne Blackburn, 'Buddhist Connections in the Indian Ocean: Changes in Monastic Mobility, 1000–1500,' *Journal of the Social and Economic History of the Orient* 58, 3 (2015), 244–7. The earliest Pāli inscription from Cambodia dates from the year 1309, see Sirisena, *Sri Lanka and Southeast Asia*, 106.

66 Sirisena, *Sri Lanka and Southeast Asia*, 102–4; Blackburn, 'Buddhist Connections', 248–52.

67 I have dealt with this theme in greater detail already in Tilman Frasch, 'The Theravada Buddhist Ecumene in the 15th Century: Intellectual Foundations and Material Representations,' in *Buddhism across Asia: Networks of Material, Intellectual and Cultural Exchange*, Vol. 1, ed. Tansen Sen (Singapore and Delhi: Institute of Southeast Asian Studies and Manohar, 2014), 347–67. In agreeing on a common composition and wording of the canon accompanied by a re-ordination ceremony of all monks who accepted this version, the convention at Kōṭṭe bore the crucial hallmarks of a true (albeit forgotten) Buddhist World Council, see Tilman Frasch, 'Buddhist Councils in a Time of Transition: Globalism, Modernity and the Preservation of Textual Traditions,' in *Contemporary Buddhist Studies* 14, 1 (2013), 38–51.

68 Frasch, 'Theravada Buddhist Ecumene', 361. I am aware that the Pāli canon is not exactly the same for all Theravāda communities in South and Southeast Asia.

## Chapter 4: Beautifully moral

1 We are grateful to Zoltán Biedermann, Alan Strathern and the reviewers at UCL Press for their useful feedback on earlier drafts of this chapter. We also thank Whitney Cox, Tara Dankel, Paolo di Leo, Samson Lim, Gabriel Tusinski and Paolo Visigalli for their helpful comments on particular sections of this chapter.

2 Sheldon Pollock, *The Language of the Gods in the World of Men: Sanskrit, Culture, and Power in Premodern India* (Berkeley and Los Angeles: University of California Press, 2006), 11f.

3 Pollock, *Language of the Gods*, 524. See in particular chapter 4.

4 In this 'social aesthetic', as Pollock calls it, fortunately composed poetry and drama should portray behaviours and emotions appropriate for its characters, with respect to their social status, occupation, gender, moral constitution, etc. *Rasa*, emotion invoked while reading or hearing the text, arises only in its plenary, authentic form when characters are appropriately portrayed in this way. For instance, the erotic mood (*sṛṅgāra rasa*) does not arise if the desire of a character portrayed in a literary work does not have a proper object (as in the case of the pupil's desire for his teacher's wife, or that of a common man for a queen). Literary acumen – including the ability to experience *rasa* – is intimately associated with *social literacy*: an apprehension of different social classes and the behaviour, speech and emotional dispositions suitable for those who belong to them in the real world. This kind of social understanding goes hand-in-hand with a properly attuned *moral outlook*: when one experiences the proper emotion while confronted with a certain evocative situation; anger in the face of injustice, pity in the face of unavoidable tragedy. The emotions experienced by the skilled reader, then, are isomorphic to emotions experienced by that person in the everyday world. See especially Sheldon Pollock, 'The Social Aesthetic and Sanskrit Literary Theory,' *The Journal of Indian Philosophy* 29 (2001), 215, and *The Ends of Man at the End of Premodernity* (Amsterdam: Royal Netherlands Academy of Arts and Sciences, 2005), 28. Just as a high degree of literacy develops *phronēsis* for Aristotle, Sanskrit theorists argue that becoming an effective *rasika* enables the fulfillment of four 'life-goals' (*puruṣārtha*-s) (see Pollock, *The Ends of Man*, 10).

5 Pollock, *Language of the Gods*, 386. Regarding the late medieval period see Steven Collins, 'What is Literature in Pali?,' in *Literary Cultures in History: Reconstructions from South Asia*, ed. Sheldon Pollock (Berkeley: University of California Press, 2003), 649–88 and Charles Hallisey, 'Works and Persons in Sinhala Literary Culture,' in *Literary Cultures in History*, 689–746.

6 It was quite common for instance for medieval scholars to justify writing in Pāli on the basis that their works were to be read by monks in other lands. For more on literary exchange between Sri Lanka and Southeast Asia during this period, see Anne Blackburn, 'Buddhist Connections in the Indian Ocean: Changes in Monastic Mobility, 1000–1500,' *Journal of the Economic and Social History of the Orient* 68 (2015), 237–66.

7 On the development of Pāli as an 'ecclesiastical koiné', see Oskar von Hinüber, 'Pali as an Artificial Language,' *Indologica Taurinensia* 10 (1982), 133–40 and Steven Collins, 'On the Very Idea of a Pali Canon,' *Journal of the Pali Text Society* 15 (1990), 89–126. We intentionally avoid the term 'Theravāda', since the notion of a single monastic consortium or ordination lineage self-identifying as 'Theravādin' is largely anachronistic. See T. L. Perriera, 'Whence Theravāda? The Modern Genealogy of an Ancient Term,' in *How Theravāda is Theravāda? Exploring Buddhist Identities*, ed. Peter Skilling et al. (Chiang Mai: Silkworm Books, 2012), 443–571, and other contributions in the same volume.

8 See M. B. Ariyapala, *Society in Mediaeval Ceylon: The State of Society in Ceylon as Depicted in the Saddarma-ratnāvaliya and other Literature of the Thirteenth Century* (1956; reprint Colombo: Department of Cultural Affairs, 1968), 270, and O. H. de A. Wijesekera, 'Pali and Sanskrit in the Polonnaruva Period,' *Ceylon Historical Journal*, 4 (1954–5), 102–5.

9 Along with his infrastructural and civil works projects, King Parākramabāhu I (r. 1153–86) is remembered as having been a great promoter of higher learning. The *Cūḷavaṃsa* (84.27) records Parākramabāhu II's importation of many books from India, subsequently 'having many bhikkhus educated in religious texts as well as all [other scholastic disciplines], such as logic and grammar, and so sharpening their intellect' (*āgamesu tathā sabbatakkavyākaraṇādisu sikkhāpetvā bahū bhikkhū kārāpesi vicakkhaṇe*). *Cūḷavaṃsa: Being the More Recent Part of the Mahāvaṃsa*, ed. and trans. Wilhelm Geiger, 2 vols. (1925–29; reprint London: Pali Text Society, 1980). Geiger translates *kārāpesi vicakkhaṇe* as '[King Parākramabāhu] made of them cultivated people'. Parākramabāhu II is also credited with restoring a great many lands to the Saṅgha which had been lost in the intervening centuries of disorder and warfare, as well as with establishing three great *pariveṇas* in the Kurunegala area (*Cūḷavaṃsa*, 84.1–5, 85.56–63).

10 Collins, 'What is Literature in Pali?', 655.

11 K. R. Norman, *Pali Literature: A History of Indian Literature VII.2* (Wiesbaden: Otto Harrassowitz, 1983) – following Wilhelm Geiger, *The Dīpavaṃsa and Mahāvaṃsa and their Historical Development in Ceylon*, transl. E. M. Coomaraswamy (Colombo: H.C. Cottle, Government Printer, 1908) – and Collins, 'What is Literature in Pali?' characterize the *Mahāvaṃsa* as *kāvya*. Citing the first four verses of the work as testament, Geiger declares that in contrast to the more clumsy *Dīpavaṃsa*, the

*Mahāvaṃsa* 'is a work of art, a *kāvya*, according to the standard of Indian poetry' (*The Dīpavaṃsa and Mahāvaṃsa*, 16).

12 Including extended descriptions of the majesty of cities (*nagara vivaraṇa*), natural locations and the beauty of women.

13 The last quarter of the tenth century has been suggested as the date of the Pāli *Mahābodhivaṃsa* (Collins, 'What is Literature in Pali?', 655).

14 Dragomir Dimitrov, *The Legacy of the Jewel Mind: On the Sanskrit, Pali, and Sinhalese Works by Ratnamati* (Habilitationsschrift, Philipps-Universität Marburg, 2014), 99–101; *Subodhālaṅkāra, Porāṇa-ṭīkā (Mahāsāmi-ṭīkā) by Saṅgharakkhita Mahāsāmi, Abhinava-ṭīkā (Nissaya) (Anonymous)*, ed. Padhmanabh S. Jaini (Oxford: The Pali Text Society, 2000), xvi–xvii. Challenging the traditional authorities on the matter, J. C. Wright questions the joint authorship of the *kārikās* and the so-called '*porāṇa-ṭīkā*', claiming that the *kārikās* were written before the twelfth century and that only the *porāṇa-ṭīkā* was composed by Saṅgharakkhita: J. C. Wright, 'The Pali *Subodhālaṅkāra* and Daṇḍin's *Kāvyadarśa*,' *Bulletin of the School of Oriental and African Studies* 65, 2 (2002), 323–41. While it is not within the scope of this chapter to refute Wright's argument in detail, it will suffice to point out that Saṅgharakkhita quotes the *kārikās* of the *Subodhālaṅkāra* in his *Moggallāna-pañcikā-ṭīkā* using the phrase '*amhehi vuttaṃ*' ('I have said…'). Cf. *Moggallāna-pañcikā-ṭīkā*, ed. Aggadhammābhivaṃsathera (Rangoon: Zabu Meit Swe Press, 1955), B[e] 69.

15 Sheldon Pollock, 'The Cosmopolitan Vernacular,' *Journal of Asian Studies* 57, 1 (1998), 14.

16 For Tamil, see Anne. E. Monius, 'The Many Lives of Daṇḍin: The *Kāvyādarśa* in Sanskrit and Tamil,' *International Journal of Hindu Studies* 4, 1 (2000), 1–37. For Kannada, see Nagaraj, D. R. 'Critical Tensions in the History of Kannada Literary Culture,' in *Literary Cultures in History*, ed. S. Pollock (Berkeley and Los Angeles: University of California Press, 2003), 323–83, and Pollock, 'The Cosmopolitan Vernacular'. For Tibetan, see Dragomir Dimitrov, *Mārgavibhāga – Die Unterscheidung der Stilarten. Kritische Ausgabe des ersten Kapitels von Daṇḍins Poetik Kāvyādarśa und der tibetischen Übertragung Sñan ṅag me loṅ nebst einer deutschen Übersetzung des Sanskrittextes* (Marburg: Indica et Tibetica Verlag, 2002), 40, and *Śabdālaṃkāradoṣavibhāga – Die Unterscheidung der Lautfiguren und der Fehler. Kritische Ausgabe des dritten Kapitels von Daṇḍins Poetik Kāvyādarśa und der tibetischen Übertragung Sñan ṅag me loṅ samt dem Sanskrit-Kommentar des Dpaṅ Blo gros brtan pa und einer deutschen Übersetzung des Sanskrit-Grundtextes* (Wiesbaden: Harrassowitz Verlag, 2011).

17 G.D. Wijayawardhana, 'Siya-Bas-Lakara and a Theory of Suggestion,' *University of Ceylon Review* 12, 1–2 (1964), 21–8. See, for instance, G. D. Wijayawardhana, 'The Influence of Sanskrit Alankāra Śāstra on Early Sinhalese Poetry', PhD dissertation, University of Ceylon, Peradeniya, 1963; Hallisey, 'Works and Persons in Sinhala Literary Culture'; Dimitrov, *Legacy of the Jewel Mind*.

18 At around the same time, two Sinhala pedagogical translations or *sannayas* were composed for both the *Kāvyādarśa* and *Siyabaslakara*, possibly again by Ratnaśrījñāna. See *Siyabas Lakara or Sinhalese Rhetoric by King Siláméghavarṇa, Paraphrased by Ratnamadhvácárya Mahá Théra*, ed. Hendrick Jayatilaka (Colombo: Lakrivikiraṇa Press, 1892). For an overview of the debate on the date of the *Siyabaslakara*, see Dimitrov, *Legacy of the Jewel Mind*, 105–20.

19 *Kāvyādarśaya*, ed. Dharmakīrti Dharmārāma (Peliyagoda: Satyasamuccaya Press, 1925), v. 3. Translations are our own unless specified.

20 *Kāvyādarśa*, v. 4.

21 *Kāvyādarśa*, v. 5.

22 *Kāvyādarśa*, v. 6.

23 *Kāvyādarśa*, v. 7.

24 *Kāvyādarśa*, v. 8.

25 *Kāvyādarśa*, v. 9.

26 Ratnaśrījñāna states in the work's colophon that he is a Sinhalese monk and that he wrote the commentary under the patronage of a Rāṣṭrakūṭa ruler called Tuṅga in the twenty-third regnal year of King Rājyapāla. This date has been variously posited as 931 CE, 955 CE or, more recently, 952 CE: *Kāvyalakṣaṇa, also known as Kāvyādarśa: with commentary called Ratnaśrī of Ratnaśrījñāna*, ed. Anantalal Thakur and Upendra Jha (Darbhanga: Mithila Institute of Post-graduate Studies and Research in Sanskrit Learning, 1957), 20; S. Pollock, 'Ratnaśrījñāna,' *Encyclopedia of Indian Wisdom: Dr. Satya Vrat Shastri Felicitation Volume*, ed. R. K. Sharma (Delhi: Bharatiya Vidya Prakashan, 2005), 638; Dimitrov, *Legacy of the Jewel Mind*, 74. Both Dimitrov (p. 70) and Thakur and Jha (*Kāvyalakṣaṇa*, 18) identify Tuṅga Dharmavaloka as a Rāṣṭrakūṭa feudatory of King Rājyapāla. Pollock has argued instead that Tuṅga can be identified with the Rāṣṭrakūṭa monarch Kṛṣṇa III (r. 936–67), and that Ratnaśrījñāna attended his court in the Deccan.

27 Dimitrov, *Legacy of the Jewel Mind*, 19–94.

28 *Ratnaśrīṭīkā*, ad v. 2, p. 2, l. 22: *kāvyaṃ cedaṃ caturvargalakṣaṇam*. The relationship of connoisseurship to the accomplishment of the life-goals was a preoccupation among Sanskrit poetic theorists, and Pollock notes that *artha*, *kāma* and *dharma* 'had taken on the character of common sense' by the late premodern period (*The Ends of Man*, 10).

29 *Ratnaśrīṭīkā*, ad v. 6, p. 5, l. 6–7: *tataś cāśāstrajño 'yaṃ puruṣākṛtiḥ paśur iti viduṣāṃ heyaḥ syād ity anarthe patitaḥ*.

30 *Ratnaśrīṭīkā*, ad v. 6, p. 5, l. 8–12: *[manuṣyatvā]viśeṣe 'pi śāstrajño deva iva pūjyate guṇānurāgibhir itaras tu paśur iva dṛṣyata iti, yata evaṃ sarvatra guṇadoṣavivekaḥ śāstrād eva. guṇaś ca puruṣārthena yojayati doṣaś ca [itareṇa. ataḥ] śāstrānusāreṇa guṇavat [kāvyam ekāntataḥ] puruṣārthasādhanam. dośas tu svalpo 'pi śāstraprabhāvād evāpaneyaḥ*.

31 *Ratnaśrīṭīkā*, ad v. 9, p. 6, l. 23–4: *tatra sarvatra guṇāś ca doṣāś ca jñātavyāḥ. tatra guṇā vastutaḥ puruṣārthamayā eva*.

32 *Subodhālaṅkāra*, v. 4.

33 *Subodhālaṅkāra*, v. 5. In his discussion of these verses, Saṅgharakkhita includes a Pāli quotation of verse eight of the *Kāvyādarśa* (*Subodhālaṅkāra*, p. 11, l. 21–2) and a Pāli rendering (*sabbattha satthato yeva guṇadosavivecanaṃ* ı *yaṃ karoti vinā satthaṃ sāhasaṃ kim ato 'dhikan* ıı) of a verse quoted by Ratnaśrījñāna in his commentary on verse four of the *Kāvyādarśa* (*Subodhālaṅkāra*, p. 11, l. 17–18). In Thakur and Jha's edition (*Kāvyādarśa*, p. 3, l. 24–25) of the *Ratnaśrīṭīkā*, the fourth *pāda* of this verse has been lost, although using the verse quoted in the *Subodhālaṅkāra* it is possible to suggest a reconstruction: *śāstrād eva hi sarvatra guṇadoṣa[vicāra]ṇam* ı *vinā śāstreṇa yat* (*kṛtaṃ sāhasaṃ kiṃ ato'dhikam*) ıı.

34 *Subodhālaṅkāra*, ad vv. 4–5, p. 11, l. 19–20: *tasmā guṇadosavibhāgavicāraṇaṃ nāma tabbidūnaṃ yeva, nāsatthaññūnaṃ purisapasūnaṃ*.

35 See *Ratnaśrīṭīkā*, ad v. 6, p. 5, l. 6: *puruṣākṛtiḥ paśuḥ*.

36 *Subodhālaṅkāra*, ad vv. 4–5, p. 12, l. 24–5: *tato etādiso paññavā yev' ettha guṇadosavibhāgavivecane adhikārī. n' añño tabbiparīto purisapasū ti ayam etthādhippāyo*.

37 *The Nyāyabindu of Śrī Dharmakīrti with a Sanskrit Commentary by Śrī Dharmottarācārya*, ed. Candraśekhara Śāstrī (Banares: Chowkhamba Sanskrit Series Office, 1954), v. 6, l. 11–17.

38 *Subodhālaṅkāra*, ad vv. 4–5, p. 12, l. 6–9: *kā sā? paññā heyyopādeyyavivekarūpā. kīdisī ti āha anekasatthantarocitā ti. anekasmiṃ tipiṭakatakkabyākaraṇālaṅkārasatthādike satthantare ucitā savaṇadhāraṇādivasena paricitā sāyaṃ paññā yesaṃ na sañcitā ti pakataṃ*.

39 That Pāli literary theorists should count śāstric knowledge proper as a desideratum for a learned person is entirely natural within the South Asian Buddhist literary framework. The Pāli Jātakas refer often to the Bōdhisattva's mastery of the *śāstras* and *kalās* in former births. The Bōdhisattva masters the 'eighteen branches of knowledge' (*aṭṭhārasam vijjaṭṭhānam*) and three Vedas in the Dummedha Jātaka: *The Jātaka*, Vol. 1, ed. V. Fausbøll (Oxford: The Pali Text Society, 2000), no. 50, i. 256 and elsewhere. Twelfth- and thirteenth-century Sinhala Buddhist literature emphasizes competence in such traditionally pan-South Asian higher subjects as well as the Vedas (numbering variously three or four).

40 *Subodhālaṅkāra*, ad vv. 4–5, p. 12, l. 12–15: *tasmā pi kiñci pi heyyopādeyyarūpaṃ yaṃ kiñci-d-eva aṭṭhānāniyojakatādisagurupādasussūsānissayapaṭiladdhavivekapaññātisayālābhena nāvabujjhati, na jānantī ty attho*.

41 *Subodhālaṅkāra*, ad vv. 4–5, p. 14, l. 10–15.

42 AN B[e] 2.421 [E[e] 4.32]: *piyo garu bhāvanīyo vattā ca vacanakkhamo* ı *gambhīrañ ca kathaṃ kattā no cāṭṭhāne niyojako* ıı.

43 *Subodhālaṅkāra*, ad vv. 4–5, p. 13, l. 3–8: *ye...tappādarajehi tesaṃ gurūnaṃ pādadhūlīhi okiṇṇā onaddhā gavacchitā, te...sajjanā eva vivekino heyyopādeyyaguṇadosavibhāganiyamanapaññāsampattisamaṅgino honti. te yev' ettha guṇadosavivecane adhigatā ti adhippāyo*.

44 *Subodhālaṅkāra*, ad vv. 4–5, p. 12, l. 19–22: *nihīyati puriso nihīnasevī na ca hāyetha kadāci tulyasevī* ı *seṭṭham upanamam udeti dhīro tasmāttano uttaritaraṃ bhajethā* ıı *ti*.

45 Bhikkhu Bodhi, *The Numerical Discourses of the Buddha: A Translation of the Aṅguttara Nikāya* (Boston: Wisdom Publications Bodhi, 2012), 1125f.

46 G. P. Malalasekera, *The Pali Literature of Ceylon* (1928; reprint Colombo: M. D. Gunasena, 1958), 185; *Sāsanavaṃsa*, ed. Mabel Bode (London: H. Frowde, 1897), 74.

47 *Saddanīti: La Grammaire Palie D'Aggavaṃsa, I Padamālā (Pariccheda 1–XIV), II Dhātumālā (Pariccheda XV–XIX), III Suttamālā (Pariccheda XX–XXVIII)*, ed. Helmer Smith (Lund: C.W.K. Gleerup, 1928–30), III, 843, l. 30–844, l. 25. This is a much revised translation based on A. K. Warder's in *Pali Metre: A Contribution to the History of Indian Literature* (London: Pali Text Society, 1967), 67–8. Warder (pp. 66–7) also cites a second passage of a similar nature (*Saddanīti*, III, 843) in which it

is explicit that the potential criticism the Buddha might have feared was the criticism of 'the wise' (*paṇḍita*).

48 *Khuddaka-Pāṭha: A Pali Text*, ed. R. C. Childers (London: Trübner, 1869), 329, quotes his manuscript of the *Saddanīti* as follows: *imasmiṃ pakaraṇe ākulakkharatāyaṃ pāḷipakaraṇāgatanayena likhitaṃ. na tatthāmhākaṃ doso āropetabbo*.

49 It is possible that the shared terminology of '*doṣa*' (fault) and '*guṇa*' (merit) to describe moral behaviour in the *tipiṭaka* and literary qualities in *kāvyaśāstra* also assisted a convergence of the two moral systems. As noted by Margaret Cone in the *Dictionary of Pali*, the term '*guṇa*' in the Pāli canon is often used in the general sense of 'quality', though nearly always denotes some positive attribute or virtue (e.g. D III 153,18* *anavamatena guṇena yāti saggaṃ*). Likewise, the term '*dosa*' refers broadly speaking to 'faults,' though these often refer to a moral failure (e.g. J II 194,15: *surāpāne dosaṃ disvā*). That one's moral condition also determines one's social status is also a prominent theme in the Pāli canon. Perhaps the most famous example of this is the Buddha's reconceptualization of Brahminhood in chapter 26 of the *Dhammapada* as being obtained by virtue rather than by birth. In his *Papañcasudanī*, Buddhaghosa echoes these sentiments using the term '*guṇa*' (virtue) and states that 'a Brahmin is not a Brahmin by birth but by means of his virtues (*guṇa*)' (III 436–7: *na jātiyā brāhmaṇo guṇehi pana brāhmaṇo hoti*).

50 *Subodhālaṅkāra*, v. 11.

51 *Daiwagnakâmadhênu*, ed. C. A. Seelakkhanda (Benares: Vidyâ Vilâs Press, 1906), v. 3.

52 The *Dīgha Nikāya* refers to poetry as a 'bestial form of knowledge' and a 'wrong livelihood' (*tiracchānavijjā, micchājīvo*, DN 1:11, 69, in Collins, 'What is Literature in Pali?', 670).

53 *gṛhasthayanṭa solō āditya bäňda no-kiyä-yutu* (*Daṁbadeṇi Katikāvata*, §49, from N. Ratnapala's critical edition of the text in *The Katikāvatas: Laws of the Buddhist Order of Ceylon from the 12th Century to the 18th Century*, trans. Nandasena Ratnapala (Munich: Münchener Studien zur Sprachwissenschaft, 1971)). Sinhala *solō* derives from Sanskrit *śloka*.

54 *kāvya nāṭakādi garhita-vidyā tamā nū–gata-yutu; anunut nū-gän-viyä-yutu* (*Daṁbadeṇi Katikāvata*, §50, Ratnapala's translation).

55 This admonition concerning the composition of poetry was extended to lay readers in a Sinhala Buddhist devotional work a few decades later: the *Saddharma Ratnāvaliya* (written by a monk) advises its audience to 'give up such useless studies as poetry and drama' (Ariyapala, *Society in Mediaeval Ceylon*, 278).

56 J. L. Masson and M. V. Patwardhan, *Aesthetic Rapture: The Rasadhyaya of the Natyasastra* (Poona: Deccan College Postgraduate and Research Institute, 1970), 37.

57 Pollock, 'The Social Aesthetic', 220.

58 See *The Book of Discipline (Vinaya-Piṭaka)*, Vol. I: Sutta-vibhaṅga, ed. I. B. Horner (London: Luzac for Pali Text Society, 1949), I. 33.

59 'Awareness of the foul', *asubhasaññā*.

60 Johannes Bronkhorst, *Buddhism in the Shadow of Brahmanism*, Handbuch der Orientalistik 24 (Leiden: Brill, 2011), 168.

61 Later commentators identify Aśvaghoṣa as the earliest author and perhaps inventor of the epic poem (*mahākāvya*) (Pollock, *Language of the Gods*, 70). Aśvaghoṣa himself declares Vālmīki's *Rāmāyaṇa* to be the first verse-poem (*vālmīkir ādau ca sasarja padyam*): *Life of the Buddha*, trans. Patrick Olivelle (New York: New York University Press, 2008), 1.43.

62 The Buddha explains to Nanda, 'Hold your restless mind from the sense-pleasures common to all, which are dream-like and insubstantial. For sensual pleasures are no more satisfying for people than oblations are to a wind-blown fire.' *Handsome Nanda*, trans. Linda Covill (New York: New York University Press, 2007), 101, 5.20.

63 See Wright, 'The Pali *Subodhālaṅkāra*', 337.

64 See Wijayawardhana, 'The Influence of Sanskrit Alankāra Śāstra', 146.

65 Adapted from *Jinacarita, or, 'The Career of the Conqueror,'* trans. Charles Duroiselle (Ahmedabad: Parimal Publications, 1982), v. 70.

66 Steven Collins, *Nirvana and Other Buddhist Felicities: Utopias of the Pali Imaginaire* (Cambridge: Cambridge University Press, 1998), 315.

67 A monk is to refuse money to buy robes from a king or royal official, returning to them the message that they will only accept the cloth itself (*Pātimokkha*, no. 10). There are furthermore prohibitions against sleeping more than two or three nights with an army, going to see a battlefield or military roll call, and watching a battle formation or military parades (*Pātimokkha*, no. 48–50).

68 See Collins' discussion on Buddhist ideology both rejecting and depending on the production of food and human reproduction in *Nirvana and Other Buddhist Felicities*, 39–40.

69 Collins, *Nirvana and Other Buddhist Felicities*, 425–34.

70 In the *Mahāvaṃsa*, King Duṭṭhagāmaṇi accrues almost no karmic demerit in reclaiming Sri Lanka from the Tamils (since they have not taken the Three Refuges nor the Five Precepts). *The Mahāvaṃsa, or, The Great Chronicle of Ceylon*, trans. Wilhelm Geiger (1912; reprint Colombo: The Ceylon Government Information Department, 1950), 25.108–11. Throughout his entire campaign, Duṭṭhagāmaṇi accrued the demerit of killing only one and a half people: one who had taken the three refuges of the Buddha, Dhamma and Saṅgha, and one who had taken the five precepts. 'Unbelievers and men of evil life were the rest, not more to be esteemed than beasts.'

71 *ummādappattā viya manussā ahosi.*

72 Adapted from *A Chronicle of the Thūpa and the Thūpavaṃsa*, trans. N. A. Jayawickrama (London: Luzac for Pali Text Society, 1971), 86. The language style is straightforward Pāli prose, although the text is embellished throughout with verse quotations from the *Mahāvaṃsa*, and contains numerous literary devices, the example in this paragraph being the simile likening the sound of the conch to thunder. We might read into this text an attempt to honour its sponsor by way of proxy. King Parākramabāhu II had recently restored the island to Sinhalese rule after the exploitative reign of Māgha.

73 *A Chronicle of the Thupa*, xxxiv.

74 Or 'following on the path of statecraft' (*nītipathānuvattinaṃ*).

75 That is, the island of Sri Lanka made up of its three traditional geographical divisions: *rāja* (or *pihiṭi*, the northern portion of the island), *māyā* (the central highlands) and *rohaṇa* (*ruhuṇu*, the south).

76 *Dāṭhāvaṃsa*, v. 4–8: *vibhūsayaṃ kāḷakanāgaranvayaṃ parakkamo kāruṇiko camūpati gavesamāno jinasāsanassa yo virūḷhiṃ atthañ ca janassa patthayaṃ* (4); *sudhāmayūkhāmalapaṇḍuvaṃsajaṃ virūḷhasaddhaṃ munirājasāsane piyaṃvadaṃ nītipathānuvattinaṃ sadā pajānaṃ janikaṃ va mātaraṃ* (5); *piyaṃ parakkantibhujassa rājino mahesim accunnatabuddhisampadaṃ vidhāya līlāvatim icchitatthadaṃ asesalaṅkātalarajjalakkhiyaṃ* (6); *kumāram ārādhita-sādhumantinaṃ mahādayaṃ paṇḍunarindavaṃsajaṃ vidhāya saddhaṃ madhurindanāmakaṃ susikkhitaṃ pāvacane kalāsu ca* (7); *narindasuññaṃ suciraṃ tisīhaḷaṃ itippatītaṃ ayasaṃ apānudi ciraṃ paṇītena ca cīvarādinā susaññate saṃyamino atappayi* (8).

77 See §73, the account of the rebuilding of Pulatthinagara by Parākramabāhu, as well as the subsequent sections detailing his military conquests. This and later extensions of the chronicle (which records to the reign of Kīrti Śrī Rājasiṃha, 1747–80) contain lengthy descriptions of the beauty of royally maintained cities, kings' consorts, fierce battles, as well as similes drawn from Sanskrit poetry and explicit references to the *Rāmāyaṇa*.

78 *Daṁbadeṇi Katikāvata*, §9 in *The Katikāvatas: Laws of the Buddhist Order*. The passage contains long compounds in unmodified Sanskrit. The text continues: 'The king, while enjoying the glories of kingship, [§10] built dwellings for the Saṃgha, complete with image houses, mansions, terraces, ramparts, gates etc. in various places such as Śrīvardhanapura. (He then) accumulated heaps of merit (*aparimita puṇya-rāśi*) for himself and for a great number (of the members) of the laity and the bhikkhus by presenting many a bhikkhu with robes, food, dwellings and medicaments.'

79 Collins, 'What is Literature in Pali?', 682f. Collins clarifies that this is different from what Pāli literature *in general* does, which is to naturalize inequalities between social classes.

80 C. E. Godakumbura, *Sinhalese Literature* (Colombo: Colombo Apothecaries, 1955), 20; *Visuddhimagga: The Path of Purification*, trans. Bhikku Ñāṇamoli (1959; reprint Kandy: Buddhist Publication Society, 2010).

81 See Alastair Gornall, 'How Many Sounds are in Pāli?: Schism, Identity and Ritual in the Theravāda Saṅgha,' *Journal of Indian Philosophy* 42, 5 (2014), 511–50, and Anne Blackburn, 'Magic in the Monastery: Textual Practice and Monastic Identity in Sri Lanka,' *History of Religions* 38, 4 (1999), 354–72.

82 See Mahinda Deegalle, 'Buddhist Preaching and Sinhala Religious Rhetoric: Medieval Buddhist Methods to Popularize Theravāda,' *Numen* 44, 2 (1997), 180–210, and *Popularizing Buddhism: Preaching and Performance in Sri Lanka* (Albany, NY: State University of New York Press, 2006). Preaching texts were intended to be read all at once, with two monks taking turns throughout the course of a night as an audience of lay men and women listened. The *Pūjāvaliya*, a thirteenth-century *baṇa pota*, enjoins noble men and women, deputy kings and ministers to read the work privately on their own (Deegalle, 'Buddhist Preaching', 189–90).

83 An inscription at the Mahāthūpa in Anurādhapura dating to the year 1203 commemorates a royal minister's sponsorship of a public reading of a *Thūpavaṃsa* (almost certainly a Sinhala antecedent to Vācissara's Pali *Thūpavaṃsa*, and Vidyācakravarti's surviving Sinhala version). S. Paranavitana

and H. W. Codrington, eds., *Epigraphia Zeylanica*, Vol. IV, (Colombo: Archaeological Department, 1943), 252ff. Although it is not traditionally considered a preaching text, the surviving thirteenth-century *Sinhala Thūpavaṃsaya* resembles works of the *baṇa pot* genre stylistically in a number of respects, addressing its audience of 'virtuous persons' (*satpuruṣayo*) at the outset and punctuated with moralizing quips.

84 This may have been the case from the inauguration of the Pāli historiographic tradition in Sri Lanka. See Malalasekara's discussion of orality and the *Dīpavaṃsa* in *Pali Literature*, 135.

85 The *Mahābodhivaṃsa*'s remark in its opening verse is representative: 'Dispelling all calamities by the power of [the Buddha's] merit [earned by venerating the Bōdhi tree], I will show in the language of the Teacher (i.e. Pāli) the *Mahābodhivaṃsa*, which existed formerly in Sinhala, following in the manner of the ancients' (*puññaṃ tassānubhāvena bhetvā sabbe upaddave, dassayissam mahābodhivaṃsam bhāsāya satthuno pubbe sīhalabhāsāya ṭhitaṃ vuddhajanānugo*). *Mahābodhivaṃsa*, ed. S. A. Strong (London: Pali Text Society, 1891), 2. See also 'Dāṭhāvaṃsa,' T. W. Rhys Davids, ed., *Journal of the Pali Text Society* 1 (1884), 109–50, v. 10.

86 See Godakumbura, *Sinhalese Literature*, 106–21. Prior to these adaptations are the *Dharmapradīpikāva*, a Sinhala commentary on portions of the *Bodhivaṃsa* attributed to Guruḷugōmi (author of the *Amāvatura*), and the twelfth-century *Bodhivaṃsa Gäṭa Padaya* (Wasantha Amarakeerthi Liyanage, 'Narrative Methods of Sinhala Prose: A Historical and Theoretical Study of Sinhala Prose from Twelfth Century Narratives to Post-Realist Fiction,' PhD dissertation, University of Wisconsin-Madison, 2004, 23–7). These two works are commentarial in nature, not reworkings of their Pāli source material in the manner of later Sinhala adaptations.

87 See Berkwitz's discussion in his introduction to *History of the Buddha's Relic Shrine: A Translation of the Sinhala Thūpavaṃsa* (Oxford: Oxford University Press, 2007). The colophon of the Pāli *Thūpavaṃsa* says that its author, Vācissara, held a position in the religious library (*dhammāgāra*) of the mighty Parakkamabāhu (who, from the balance of evidence, was probably King Parakramabahu II, r. 1236–70), and is identified in one manuscript as *tamkālasāsanānusāsako mahāgaṇī yativaro*, 'the chief religious leader of the period, one with a great following, and best of sages' (*A Chronicle of the Thūpa*, xxiii).

88 See Daniel Veidlinger, *Spreading the Dhamma: Writing, Orality, and Textual Transmission in Buddhist Northern Thailand* (Honolulu: University of Hawai'i Press, 2006).

89 On the abundance of Sanskrit learning in Sri Lanka during the medieval period, see Dehigaspe Pannasara, *Sanskrit Literature Extant among the Sinhalese and the Influence of Sanskrit on Sinhalese* (Colombo: Wimala Dharma Hewavitarane Esqr, 1958).

90 *Daṁbadeṇi Asna*, ed. D. D. Ranasinha (Colombo: J. D. Pranandu, 1928), 1. The *Butsaraṇa*, a twelfth- or thirteenth-century Sinhala preaching text, also describes the manner in which the Buddha preached in eloquent Tamil along with Malaysian, Chinese and the languages of fish, bears, elephants, horses and cows. *Butsaraṇa of Vidyacakravarti*, ed. Bambarendē Siri Sīvalī Thera (Colombo: A. Gunaratne, 1968), 45.

91 S. Pathmanathan, *The Kingdom of Jaffna, Part I* (Colombo: Arul M. Rajendran, 1978), 229, n. 28.

92 Pollock, *Language of the Gods*, 571.

93 Pollock, *Language of the Gods*, 139–40, 146.

## Chapter 5: Sinhala *sandēśa* poetry

1 Sheldon Pollock, *The Language of the Gods in the World of Men: Sanskrit, Culture, and Power in Premodern India* (Berkeley: University of California Press, 2006), 12.

2 Edmund Jayasuriya, *Sälaḷihini Sandeśa of Toṭagamuve Srī Rāhula Thera* (Colombo: Postgraduate Institute of Archaeology and Central Cultural Fund, 2002), 4–5. Note also that poetic treatises like *Siyabaslakara* (*Treatise of Our Own Language*) – a Sinhala adaptation of Daṇḍin's *Kāvyadarśa* – begin to appear as early as the ninth century,

3 Pollock has argued against asserting that premodern Southern Asian kings required ways to legitimate their own power. Among his reasons for discounting an idea that he views as anachronistic, he notes that legitimation theory assumes that rulers possess knowledge about the condition of their rules that ordinary people fail to notice. He further argues that there is no evidence for premodern kings caring or even needing to secure the assent of their subjects, who would have never doubted the inevitability of kingship. See Pollock, *Language of the Gods*, 522–3. The Sinhala materials under

analysis here do not present any contrary evidence to what Pollock has argued. At the same time, however, it would be a mistake to downplay the political interests at play in the poetic praise for rulers.

4 Daud Ali, *Courtly Culture and Political Life in Early Medieval India* (Cambridge: Cambridge University Press, 2004), 70.

5 Chintaharan Chakravarti, 'The Origin and Development of Dūtakāvya Literature in Sanskrit,' *Indian Historical Quarterly* 3, 1 (1927), 290–1. See also C. E. Godakumbura, *Sinhalese Literature* (Colombo: The Colombo Apothecaries, 1955), 183.

6 David Shulman, *The Wisdom of the Poets: Studies in Tamil, Telugu, and Sanskrit* (Oxford: Oxford University Press, 2001), 245–6.

7 Steven P. Hopkins, trans., *The Flight of Love: A Messenger Poem of Medieval South India by Veṅkaṭanātha* (New York: Oxford University Press, 2016), 9–10.

8 Charles Hallisey, 'Works and Persons in Sinhala Literary Culture,' in *Literary Cultures in History: Reconstructions from South Asia*, ed. Sheldon Pollock (Berkeley: University of California Press, 2003), 699.

9 Steven P. Hopkins, 'Lovers, Messengers, and Beloved Landscapes: *Sandeśakāvya* in Comparative Perspective,' *International Journal of Hindu Studies* 8, 1–3 (2004), 33.

10 Jayasuriya, *Sälaḷihiṇi Sandeśa*, 18. See also Hopkins, 'Lovers, Messengers, and Beloved Landscapes', 33. See also *The Jātaka or Stories of the Buddha's Former Births*, ed. E. B. Cowell, Vol. 2, trans. W. H. D. Rouse (1895; reprint Delhi: Motilal Banarsidass, 1994), 302–3.

11 Hopkins, 'Lovers, Messengers, and Beloved Landscapes', 33–4. An earlier scholar likewise called the use of inanimate objects or 'irrational creatures' to carry a message of love 'the most important characteristics of *dūtakāvyas* in general'. See Chakravarti, 'Origin and Development of Dūtakāvya Literature', 286–7.

12 Shulman, *The Wisdom of Poets*, 245–6.

13 Chakravarti, 'Origin and Development of Dūtakāvya Literature', 275–8.

14 Yigal Bronner, 'Birds of a Feather: Vāmana Bhaṭṭa Bāṇa's *Haṃsasandeśa* and its Intertexts,' *Journal of the American Oriental Society* 133, 3 (2013), 500–1, 515–16.

15 Hopkins, 'Lovers, Messengers, and Beloved Landscapes', 34. See also Hopkins, *Flight of Love*, 25.

16 Anoma Pieris, 'Avian Geographies: An Inquiry into Nationalist Consciousness in Medieval Lanka,' *South Asia: Journal of South Asian Studies* 33, 13 (2010), 343.

17 Bronner, 'Birds of a Feather,' 522–24.

18 Pieris cites the work of Puñcibandara Sannasgala to arrive at this number. See Pieris, 'Avian Geographies', 345–6. Of these texts, only about a dozen have been judged worthy of sustained scholarly analysis, while the majority remain obscure.

19 Hallisey's 'Works and Persons in Sinhala Literary Culture' represents an authoritative account of the vernacularization of Sinhala poetry. It should be noted that prose adaptations of historical writings (*vaṃsas*) in Sinhala appear even earlier. On the use of Sinhala in historical prose, see Stephen C. Berkwitz, *Buddhist History in the Vernacular: The Power of the Past in Late Medieval Sri Lanka* (Leiden: Brill, 2004), 107–12.

20 Pollock, *Language of the Gods*, 25–27.

21 Hallisey, 'Works and Persons in Sinhala Literary Culture', 694–5.

22 The Pāli *sandesa* works are less numerous than the Sinhala works and tend to differ in terms of their content and scope. The oldest extant Pāli messenger poem, the *Mānāvulusandesa* from the twelfth or thirteenth century, contains a message composed in Sri Lanka by a monk on behalf of his teacher Nāgasena to be sent to another monk in the city of Arimaddanapura, or Pagan, in Myanmar. It has no avian messenger nor describes a specific route of travel, but nonetheless offers eulogistic verses about the monks and their cities of residence. See Lionel D. Barnett, 'The Manavulu-Sandesaya: Text and Translation,' *The Journal of the Royal Asiatic Society of Great Britain and Ireland* (1905), 265–83. A fifteenth-century Pāli *sandesa* called *Vuttamālāsataka* carries slightly more resemblance with the Sinhala *sandēśas*, as the message exchanged between monks calls for a petition to be made to the god Vibhīṣaṇa to secure blessings for the king. It also eulogizes leading monks, but lacks a bird that carries the message as well as some other descriptive features shared by Sinhala and Sanskrit messenger poems. See Polwatte Śri Buddhadatta, *Pālisāhityaya* (Colombo: Svabhasha Prakasakayo, 1966), 551–2. See also Hatarabage Sugatavamsa, *Pāli Sandēsa Sāhityaya* (Colombo: S. Godage and Brothers, 2015), 76. Based on this evidence, there is little reason to conclude that the authors of the Sinhala *sandēśas* were measurably inspired by Pāli messenger poems.

23 Hallisey, 'Works and Persons', 694–5.

24 Steven P. Hopkins, 'Sanskrit in a Tamil Imaginary: Sandeśakāvya and the *Haṃsasandeśa* of Veṅkaṭanātha,' in *Passages: Relationships between Tamil and Sanskrit*, ed. Kannan M. and Jennifer Clare (Pondicherry, India: Institut français de Pondichéry, 2009), 283.
25 K. T. W. Sumanasuriya, 'Sandēśa,' in *Sinhala Sāhityalatā*, ed. Kotmale Amaravansa (Colombo: S. Godae and Brothers, 2000), 270. See also Bandusena Gunasekara, *Kōṭṭē Yugayē Sandēśa Kāvya* (Colombo: Department of Cultural Affairs, 1997), 43.
26 Godakumbura, *Sinhalese Literature*, 198.
27 Stephen C. Berkwitz, *Buddhist Poetry and Colonialism: Alagiyavanna and the Portuguese in Sri Lanka* (New York: Oxford University Press, 2013), 62.
28 See, for example, select verses in Kālidāsa's *Meghadūta* and Dhoyī's *Pavanadūta*, in *Messenger Poems: By Kālidāsa, Dhoyī & Rūpa Gosvāmin*, trans. Sir James Mallinson (New York: New York University Press and JJC Foundation, 2006), 44–45, 110–15.
29 Godakumbura, *Sinhalese Literature*, 198–9.
30 *Sāradīpikā Kōkila Sandeśa Varṇanāva*, ed. Häḍigallē Paññātissa (Borella, Sri Lanka: Lankabhinava Vishruta Yantralaya, 1945), vv. 48–58.
31 Hopkins, 'Sanskrit in a Tamil Imaginary', 282, 285–6. See also Satyavrat Śastrī, *Essays on Indology* (Delhi: Meharchand Lachhmandass, 1963), 135–8, for some routes recounted in several renowned messenger poems.
32 Sumanasuriya, 'Sandēśa', 270–1.
33 See also Pieris, 'Avian Geographies', 347. Elsewhere, this feature has been described as 'regional efforts to envision and create local maps – political, cultural, linguistic, religious, and sectarian'. See Bronner, 'Birds of a Feather', 522.
34 Stephen Greenblatt, 'The Touch of the Real,' *Representations* 59 (1997), 21. See also Stephen Greenblatt, *Marvelous Possessions: The Wonder of the New World* (Chicago: University of Chicago Press, 1991), 12.
35 *Kōkila Sandeśa*, vv. 46, 60.
36 *Kōkila Sandeśa*, vv. 82, 120.
37 Berkwitz, *Buddhist Poetry and Colonialism*, 58.
38 Godakumbura, *Sinhalese Literature*, 201. An important exception here is the *Haṃsasandēśaya*, which is addressed to a leading monk rather than a god.
39 *Kōkila Sandeśa*, v. 32.
40 *Kōkila Sandeśa*, v. 26.
41 *Kōkila Sandeśa*, vv. 29–30.
42 *Kōkila Sandeśa*, v. 288.
43 Berkwitz, *Buddhist Poetry and Colonialism*, 59. On the worship of Saman in contemporary Sri Lanka, see Premakumara De Silva, 'God of Compassion and the Divine Protector of "Śrī Pāda": Trends in Popular Buddhism in Sri Lanka,' *Sri Lanka Journal of the Humanities* 34, 1–2 (2008), 105–6.
44 *Sävul Sandēśaya*, ed. Rä. Tennekoon (Colombo: M. D. Gunasena, 1955), v. 195.
45 *Sävul Sandēśaya*, v. 195.
46 *Sävul Sandēśaya*, vv. 189, 191, 195.
47 Pollock, *Language of the Gods*, 357.
48 *Sävul Sandēśaya*, v. 43.
49 *Sävul Sandēśaya*, vv. 66, 68.
50 *Kōkila Sandeśa*, vv. 266–7.
51 *Kōkila Sandeśa*, v. 57.
52 *Kōkila Sandeśa*, vv. 11–12, 14, 16. By comparison, the royal capital of Jayavaddanapura is compared to a heavenly city in *Sälaḷihiṇisandēśaya*, with a city-wall like a jewelled girdle, resonating with the sounds of bells, horses' hooves, and conch shells, with mansions upon which banners flutter and balconies hold women that appear like goddesses. See Jayasuriya, *Sälaḷihiṇi Sandeśa*, vv. 7–13.
53 *Sävul Sandēśaya*, vv. 11–12, 16, 19.
54 Jayasuriya, *Sälaḷihiṇi Sandeśa*, 30.
55 C. W. Nicholas and S. Paranavitana, *A Concise History of Ceylon: From the Earliest Times to the Arrival of the Portuguese in 1505* (Colombo: Ceylon University Press, 1961), 307–10.
56 *Kōkila Sandeśa*, v. 136.
57 *Kōkila Sandeśa*, v. 142.
58 Berkwitz, *Buddhist Poetry and the Portuguese*, 36.
59 Pollock, *Language of the Gods*, 142–43.
60 *Sävul Sandēśaya*, v. 56.
61 Berkwitz, *Buddhist Poetry and Colonialism*, 37.

62 *Sävul Sandēśaya*, v. 51.
63 Chakravarti, 'Origin and Development of Dūtakāvya Literature', 292–3. Dhoyī's *Pavanadūta*, for instance, contains numerous verses that describe women in an erotically charged manner. See Mallinson *Messenger Poems*, 107–21.
64 Sumanasuriya, 'Sandēśa', 271.
65 *Kōkila Sandeśa*, v. 127.
66 *Kōkila Sandeśa*, v. 272.
67 *Sävul Sandēśaya*, v. 22.
68 *Sävul Sandēśaya*, v. 160.
69 Dehigaspe Pannasara, *Sanskrit Literature: Extant among the Sinhalese and the Influence of Sanskrit on Sinhalese* (Colombo: Wimala David Hewavitarane, 1958), 111, 118–19.
70 See also Pollock, *Language of the Gods*, 357.
71 Ananda Kulasuriya, *Sinhala Sāhityaya 4* (Boralesgamuwa, Sri Lanka: C. S. Visidunu Prakasakayo, 1997), 384–90.
72 A similar ideology of the 'enjoyment' of kings appeared in the court poetry of South India also around the fifteenth century. See also Velcheru Narayana Rao, David Shulman and Sanjay Subrahmanyam, *Symbols of Substance: Court and State in Nāyaka Period Tamilnadu* (Delhi: Oxford University Press, 1992), 67.
73 Puñci Bandara Sannasgala, *Siṅhala Sāhitya Vaṁśaya* (Colombo: S. Godage and Brothers, 2009), 286. The South Indian preference for the term '*sandeśa*' over '*dūta*' in messenger poems is yet another sign of cultural exchange between Sri Lanka and South India. See also Sumanasuriya, 'Sandēśa', 268.
74 Hallisey, 'Works and Persons in Sinhala Literary Culture', 698–9.
75 Gunasekara, *Kōṭṭē Yugayē Sandēśa Kāvya*, 43.
76 Pollock, *Language of the Gods*, 338. For more on signs of ambivalence in cultural borrowings, see Stephen C. Berkwitz, 'Sinhala Buddhist Appropriations of Indic Cultural Forms: Literary Imitations and Conquests,' *Religions of South Asia* 10, 1 (2016), 31–53.
77 Pieris, 'Avian Geographies', 361.
78 *Kōkila Sandeśa*, v. 142.
79 *Sävul Sandēśaya*, vv. 30, 58.
80 *Kōkila Sandeśa*, v. 291.
81 *Sävul Sandēśaya*, v. 207.
82 Zoltán Biedermann, 'The *Matrioshka* Principle and How It was Overcome: Portuguese and Habsburg Imperial Attitudes in Sri Lanka and the Responses of the Rulers of Kotte (1506–1598),' *Journal of Early Modern History* 13 (2009), 269–71.
83 *Kōkila Sandeśa*, v. 150.
84 *Kōkila Sandeśa*, v. 151.
85 *Sävul Sandēśaya*, v. 38.
86 *Sävul Sandēśaya*, v. 80.

## Chapter 6: The local and the global

The research for this chapter was made possible by a generous start-up grant from Nanyang Technological University in Singapore that enabled me to study first-hand Sri Lankan ivories in Munich, Vienna, London and Peradeniya in 2013. I thank Dr. Konrad Schlegel of the Kunsthistorisches Museum in Vienna, Dr. Senerath Dissanayake of the Department of Archaeology in Sri Lanka, and Professor Sudharshan Seneviratne of the University of Peradeniya in Sri Lanka for all their assistance. I thank Dr Konrad Schlegel of the Kunsthistorisches Museum in Vienna and Professor Sudharshan Seneviratne of the University of Peradeniya for all their assistance during my visits. I also thank the editors for giving me the opportunity to write about Sri Lankan ivories. I am grateful to Zoltán Biedermann in particular for his careful reading of various drafts and for sharing his own forthcoming article 'Diplomatic Ivories: Sri Lankan Caskets and the Portuguese-Asian Exchange in the Sixteenth Century,' in *Global Gifts: The Material Culture of Diplomacy in Early Modern Eurasia*, ed. Zoltán Biedermann, Anne Gerritsen and Giorgio Riello (New York: Cambridge University Press, forthcoming). I am solely responsible for any errors or shortcomings.

1 'Baldassare degli Embriachi: Altarpiece' (17.190.489), in *Heilbrunn Timeline of Art History* (New York: The Metropolitan Museum of Art, 2000–17), www.metmuseum.org/toah/works-of-art/17.190.489 (May 2010), accessed 14 October 2014. A number of ivories made by Pfaff, the imperial court ivory carver for Emperor Rudolf II, are in the Kunsthistorisches Museum in Vienna (see 'The

Emperor's Ivories Masterpieces from the Habsburg Kunstkammer Collections,' www.khm.at/fileadmin/_migrated/downloads/wichtigste_Objekte_engl.pdf, accessed 16 November 2014).

2 In the 1970s, there were still living ivory carvers in the Kandyan region such as the carver named Rajaguru Otunu Pandita Swarnatilaka Sakya Seneviratna Moolacharige Appu Swarnatilaka. The long string of names and titles points to a lengthy tradition of royal patronage. See Jayadeva Tilakasiri, 'Ivory Carving of Sri Lanka,' *Arts of Asia* (1974), 45. I thank Sudharshana Bandara of the University of Peradeniya for bringing my attention to this article, and for all his help during my first visit to Peradeniya to study ivories at the university's museum.

3 Tilakasiri lists a variety of ivories: 'small panels for decorating doorways, palanquin railings, boxes large and small (for various purposes), relic caskets, statuettes, fan handles, manuscript covers, combs, bracelets, necklaces, hairpins, knife handles, styluses, toy-drums and flutes' ('Ivory Carving of Sri Lanka', 43).

4 Alan Strathern, *Kingship and Conversion in Sixteenth-Century Sri Lanka. Portuguese Imperialism in a Buddhist Land* (Cambridge: Cambridge University Press, 2007), 197.

5 Senake Bandaranayake, 'The Periodisation of Sri Lankan History and Some Related Historical and Archaeological Problems,' reprinted in *Continuities and Transformations Studies in Sri Lankan Archaeology and History* (Colombo: Social Scientists' Association, 2012), 146–7. Bandaranayke also points to another challenge in understanding the built landscape of this time period: the reuse of building materials by subsequent colonial authorities.

6 These ivory caskets are also often seen as objects made only in Kōṭṭe, Sri Lanka, the main kingdom with which the Portuguese had diplomatic relations. However, as Alan Strathern's book has emphasized, the Portuguese were in communication with numerous political factions in sixteenth-century Sri Lanka (Strathern, *Kingship and Conversion*, 24). Scholars have suggested that Dom João de Castro, governor of Portuguese India, did receive ivory caskets from non-Kōṭṭe rulers, including the king of the Sītāvaka Kingdom. See Amin Jaffer and Melanie Anne Schwabe, 'A Group of Sixteenth-Century Ivory Caskets from Ceylon,' *Apollo* 149 (1999), 8; Nuno Vasallo e Silva, 'An Art for Export: Sinhalese Ivory and Crystal in the Sixteenth and Seventeenth Centuries,' in *Re-exploring Links History and Constructed Histories between Portugal and Sri Lanka*, ed. Jorge Flores (Wiesbaden: Harrassowitz, 2007), 282; Annemarie Jordan Gschwend and Johannes Beltz, *Elfenbeine aus Ceylon. Luxusgüter für Katharina von Habsburg (1507–1578)* (Zurich: Museum Rietberg, 2010), 70. Martha Chaiklin, 'Ivory in Early Modern Ceylon: A Case Study in What Documents Don't Reveal,' *International Journal of Asian Studies* 6, 1 (2009), 42, also notes that Kandyan kings gifted ivory to other kingdoms, referring to C. R. de Silva, who cites a *tombo* from 1599. Colonial sources from the Dutch and British period also indicate that ivory was carved in various regions in Sri Lanka apart from Kōṭṭe: Jaffna, Kandy, Matara and Galle were centres of ivory carving ('Ivory in Early Modern Ceylon', 42–3). Recently, Ebeltje Hartkamp-Jonxis has argued for Matara as a centre of ivory carving ('Coveted by Princes and Citizens: Sri Lankan Ivory Carvings for the European Market 1550–1700,' Public lecture, Asian Civilizations Museum, Singapore, 11 June 2014).

7 Jaffer and Schwabe first reported on eight ivory caskets ('A Group of Sixteenth-Century Ivory Caskets', 3–14). In a later exhibition catalogue, Jaffer referred to nine ivory caskets. Amin Jaffer, *Luxury Goods from India: The Art of the Indian Cabinet-Maker* (London: V&A Publications, 2002), 14. Pedro Moura Carvalho expanded the corpus to ten caskets in *Luxury for Export: Artistic Exchange between India and Portugal Around 1600* (Boston: Isabella Stewart Gardner Museum, 2008), 25. Nuno Vasallo e Silva writes about twelve caskets ('An Art for Export', 281). I would further add the ivory casket at the University of Peradeniya's Senerat Paranavitana Teaching and Research Museum, bringing the total number of Sri Lankan ivory caskets produced in the sixteenth century for local and global consumption to thirteen.

8 Senake Bandaranayake has previously pointed to the idea of recovering the visual world of this time period by examining the 'manuscript-cover illustrations, the relief sculptures of the fourteenth century, and the ivory carvings of Kōṭṭe and its successors in the fifteenth–eighteenth century period' (*The Rock and Wall Paintings of Sri Lanka*, revised edition (Pannipitiya: Stamford Lake, 2006), 16).

9 Annemarie Jordan Gschwend, 'The Marvels of the East: Renaissance Curiosity Collections in Portugal,' in *The Heritage of Rauluchantim*, ed. Nuno Vassallo e Silva (Lisbon: Museu de São Roque, 1996), 100–07; Jaffer and Schwabe, 'A Group of Sixteenth-Century Ivory Caskets', 3; Silva, 'An Art for Export', 281–3.

10 Silva, 'An Art for Export', 279. Two leather caskets from the sixteenth century, currently in the collection of the Museu Nacional de Arte Antiga, in Lisbon (inv. 45 Cx) and Museu Nacional Machado de Castro, in Coimbra (inv. 1737; M247), clearly share a similar shape with this group of Sri Lankan

ivory caskets. Apart from the elaborate lock, there is hardly any ornamentation on the seven surfaces; however, each face is further divided into separate spaces by metal strips, similar to the way in which the Sri Lankan ivory caskets are divided by pillars or ornamented borders. The form and the division of space may have been borrowed from Portuguese travelling leather caskets. I thank Alexandre Morais of Jorge Welsh Oriental Porcelain and Works of Art for bringing my attention to these caskets in Portugal (personal communication, 2 January 2014).

11 John Holt, *The Buddhist Visnu: Religious Transformation, Politics, and Culture* (New York: Columbia University Press, 2005), 132–45. Also see Alan Strathern, 'Towards the Source-Criticism of Sitavaka Period Heroic Literature, Part Two: The Sitavaka Hatana: Notes on a Grounded Text,' *The Sri Lanka Journal of the Humanities* 34, 1–2 (2008), 64–5.

12 Jaffer and Schwabe, 'A Group of Sixteenth-Century Ivory Caskets', 3.

13 Apart from Lisbon, Renaissance curiosity collections existed at various European royal courts such as Madrid, Brussels, Vienna, Innsbruck and Prague (Gschwend, 'The Marvels of the East', 83).

14 Although Silva frames these ivories as export art, he himself points out that they could only be afforded by European royalty and aristocracy, in contrast to the more widely available export items such as porcelain (Silva, 'Art for Export', 288). Gaston Perera questions the assumption that these caskets were export products, due to the paucity in numbers and the lack of local literature suggesting any type of ivory industry (Gaston Perera, 'Ivory Caskets,' unpublished working paper, 2010).

15 Two ivory caskets are mentioned in the inventories of Catherine of Austria's (1507–78) *Kunstkammer* (Gschwend, 'The Marvels of the East', 104–8). Such collections were filled with *naturalia* and *artificialia* such as coconut shells, bezoar stones, jewels, textiles and porcelain. Annemarie Jordan Gschwend, 'Rarities and Novelties,' in *Encounters: The Meeting of Asia and Europe 1500–1800*, ed. Anna Jackson and Amin Jaffer (London: Victoria and Albert Museum, 2004), 32.

16 On Catherine of Austria, regent from 1557 to 1562, see Annemarie Jordan Gschwend, 'Catherine of Austria: A Portuguese Queen in the Shadow of the Habsburg court?,' *Portuguese Studies Review* 13, 1–2 (2005), 173–94. As the Queen of Portugal and wife of King John III (r. 1521–57), Catherine was a recipient of diplomatic gifts, but she also had privileged access to curiosities from Asia through various agents working for her in Goa, Cochin, and Malacca (Gschwend, 'The Marvels of the East', 183–5).

17 The earliest article in English about the topic of European influence on Sri Lankan ivories is by K. de B. Codrington, 'Western Influences in India and Ceylon: A Group of Sinhalese Ivories,' *Burlington Magazine* LIX (1934), 239–46.

18 Silva, 'An Art for Export', 287, emphasis added.

19 Gschwend and Beltz, *Elfenbeine aus Ceylon*.

20 Jaffer and Schwabe, 'A Group of Sixteenth-Century Ivory Caskets', 3.

21 Umberto Eco rightly points out this misconception regarding premodern visual traditions beyond Europe: 'We know very well that in certain examples of non-Western art, where we always see the same thing, the natives recognize the infinitesimal variations and feel the shiver of innovation.' Umberto Eco, 'Innovation and Repetition: Between Modern and Postmodern Aesthetics,' *Daedalus* 134, 4 (2005), 201. Although I appreciate Eco's observation, I believe we need to go beyond only the 'natives,' ability to identify degrees of difference and ask for a wider appreciation of non-Western visual traditions.

22 Although this still leaves an impression of *reaction* rather than *action*, a response implies an active decision rather than the passive action associated with terms such as 'copy'.

23 I thank Marie-Therese Barrett, my first professor in art history at Temple University Tokyo, for encouraging me to look at Afro-Portuguese objects during a research trip to London in June 2013.

24 Jay A. Levenson, ed., *Encompassing the Globe: Portugal and the World in the 16th and 17th Centuries* (Washington, DC: Arthur M. Sackler Gallery, Smithsonian Institution, 2007), 150.

25 Nicole N. Bridges, 'Kongo Ivories,' in *Heilbrunn Timeline of Art History*. New York: The Metropolitan Museum of Art, 2000, www.metmuseum.org/toah/hd/kong/hd_kong.htm, accessed 23 October 2016. More recently, Peter Mark has suggested the use of the term 'Luso-African ivories' because it reflects more accurately the origins of these objects. Peter Mark, 'Towards a Reassessment of the Dating and the Geographical Origins of the Luso-African Ivories, Fifteenth to Seventeenth Centuries,' *History in Africa* 34 (2007), 189–90. While Mark notes that 'this situation contrasts with the case of Indo-Portuguese art of the sixteenth century, some of which was produced by Indian or Ceylonese artists living and working in Lisbon' (p. 190) there is no evidence to suggest that the sixteenth-century ivory caskets from Sri Lanka were produced by Sri Lankan ivory carvers living outside of Sri Lanka.

26 Mark has recently questioned this chronology because of the lack of historical evidence that indicates Portuguese trading relationships with Benin. Instead, he suggests that these ivories also reflect the concerns of trading communities in the Guinea-Cape Verde region (Mark, 'Towards a Reassessment', 201–9).

27 Emma George Ross, 'Afro-Portuguese Ivories,' In *Heilbrunn Timeline of Art History*. New York: The Metropolitan Museum of Art, 2000, www.metmuseum.org/toah/hd/apiv/hd_apiv.htm, accessed 20 November 2014.

28 Bridges, 'Kongo Ivories'.

29 Bridges, 'Kongo Ivories'.

30 Levenson, *Encompassing the Globe*, 150; George Ross, 'Afro-Portuguese Ivories'.

31 William Fagg and Ezio Bassani, *Africa and the Renaissance: Art in Ivory* (New York: The Center for African Art, 1988), 61–2.

32 Bridges, 'Kongo Ivories'.

33 Comparable caskets inspired by Portuguese travelling boxes were made in a variety of materials in India, too. Amin Jaffer notes that this type was created in tortoiseshell, gold, ivory and mother-of-pearl (Jaffer, *Luxury Goods from India*, 17).

34 There are exceptions – the casket in Berlin has four panels, while some others have no divisions on the rectangular faces, indicating perhaps different workshops or time periods.

35 Jaffer and Schwabe, 'A Group of Sixteenth-Century Ivory Caskets', 3.

36 Jaffer and Schwabe, 'A Group of Sixteenth-Century Ivory Caskets', 3.

37 Some ivory caskets have been further adorned with mounts that raise their bottom surface. Once curiosities reached collectors, they received further enhancement as a way of displaying them and treasuring them.

38 I have not examined this ivory casket in person, but the casket sits on top of a feature that may be an ovolo or the S-shaped *cyma reversa*, which in turn is supported by a plinth. For a reproduction, see Jaffer and Schwabe, 'A Group of Sixteenth-Century Ivory Caskets'.

39 There are exceptions to these patterns: the bottom-most row of the second ivory casket in Munich is decorated by a row of jewels. However, such ornamentation is similar to the idea of adorning the bottom-most layer of the casket with lotus petals.

40 Senaka Bandaranayake, *Sinhalese Monastic Architecture*, Studies in South Asian Culture 4 (Leiden: Brill, 1974), 313–17.

41 Michael W. Meister, ed., *Encyclopaedia of Indian Temple Architecture: South India – Lower Dravidadesa 200 BC–AD 1324* (New Delhi: American Institute of Indian Studies and University of Pennsylvania Press, 1983).

42 Ananda Coomaraswamy, 'An Ivory Casket from Southern India,' *The Art Bulletin* 23, 3 (1941), 206.

43 For a recent reproduction, see Gschwend and Beltz, *Elfenbeine aus Ceylon*, 119, Figure 50.

44 See especially, chapters 1 and 2 in Sujatha Arundathi Meegama, 'From *Kovils* to *Devales*: Patronage and "Influence" at Buddhist and Hindu Temples in Sri Lanka,' PhD dissertation, University of California, Berkeley, 2011.

45 See note 78. In fact, the lion motif appears on a piece of furniture associated with King Rājasiṃha I of the Sītāvaka Kingdom (r. 1521–93) (see Ananda K. Coomaraswamy, *Medieval Sinhalese Art* (New York: Pantheon, 1956), 137)).

46 The ivory carvers from Sri Lanka were not alone in using motifs found in temple architecture. Amin Jaffer compares a possible ivory throne leg, in the shape of a rearing *yali* or a mythical leonine creature, to those adorning temple pillars of the Vijayanagara period in South India (Jaffer, *Luxury Goods from India*, 67).

47 This casket was acquired by Sir John Charles Robinson in Lisbon for the Victoria and Albert Museum in the 1880s. 'The Robinson Casket,' http://collections.vam.ac.uk/item/O18316/the-robinson-casket-casket-unknown, accessed 31 August 2014.

48 Silva, 'An Art for Export', 283 (emphasis added).

49 Jaffer and Schwabe, 'A Group of Sixteenth-Century Ivory Caskets', 9.

50 Jaffer and Schwabe, 'A Group of Sixteenth-Century Ivory Caskets', 9.

51 For more on Dharmapāla's conversion to Christianity, see Strathern, *Kingship and Conversion*, 171–3.

52 Silva, 'An Art for Export', 284. After examining a series of Books of Hours, I too am inclined to agree with Silva that the left niche contains a depiction of the Visitation. In depictions of the Visitation in Books of Hours from the late fifteenth and early sixteenth century, Mary and her cousin Elizabeth hold hands in the same manner that the two figures do in this carved version. Moreover, the depiction of Joseph in the right niche shows him as a man with a beard dressed in trousers and wearing a hat

and holding a staff. He is depicted very differently from the two figures with long hair and in flowing robes in the left niche.

53 Jaffer and Schwabe, 'A Group of Sixteenth-Century Ivory Caskets', 9. Although Jaffer and Schwabe have identified the source of the Tree of Jesse to the *Horae Beatae Mariae Virginis* printed by Thielman Kerver in Paris in 1499, the surroundings of the Tree of Jesse seem to differ in each Book of Hours published by Thielman Kerver. Moreover, it would be important to see whether the Books of Hours produced between 1499 and 1546 by Kerver contain the combination of scenes found in this ivory casket and depict these scenes in this exact manner, to further understand the ivory carver's choices.

54 First, in the niche to the right of the handle, two similar female heads are placed on top of each other: Jaffer and Schwabe suggest that the upper figure is wearing local clothing, while the bottom figure is in European dress; this, they argue, may be read as a dual representation of Dharmapāla's wife, who converted to Christianity along with him. Second, in the niche to the left of the handle, a cherub head is supported by two putti – again, a motif that would have been appropriated from ornament prints of the period. Jaffer and Schwabe, 'A Group of Sixteenth-Century Ivory Caskets', 9.

55 Jaffer and Schwabe, 'A Group of Sixteenth-Century Ivory Caskets', 8–9.

56 Jaffer and Schwabe, 'A Group of Sixteenth-Century Ivory Caskets', 10.

57 Jaffer and Schwabe, 'A Group of Sixteenth-Century Ivory Caskets', 10.

58 Gifts were given by Jesuit missionaries to the Mughal emperor Akbar and to the daimyos or warlords in Japan. Gauvin Bailey, *Art on the Jesuit Missions in Asia and Latin America 1542–1773* (Toronto, Buffalo and London: University of Toronto Press, 1999), 59–60, 116.

59 A pyx in a private collection that includes the Tree of Jesse also includes the Visitation and the Nativity along with three other scenes from the Life of the Virgin. Fagg and Bassani, *Africa and the Renaissance*, 83.

60 The European source for the Tree of Jesse in the pyx from Sierra Leone is believed to be the *Horae Beatae Mariae Virginis* printed in 1498 by Philippe Pigouchet in Paris for Simon Vostre. Sixteenth-century printed Books of Hours contained illustrations of the Life of the Virgin or the Life of Christ either as central images or as marginalia. The woodblocks for these illustrations were reused by various European publishers and hence similar images appeared in different books. Fagg and Bassani, *Africa and the Renaissance*, 111. Therefore, the Tree of Jesse appears in different forms in different publications. Sometimes it appears only in the margins, while at other times it appears as a central image.

61 Robert S. Nelson, 'Appropriation,' in *Critical Terms for Art History*, ed. Robert S. Nelson and Richard Shiff, 2nd edn (Chicago and London: University of Chicago Press, 2003), 161.

62 Nelson, 'Appropriation', 162. Within art history, Michael Baxandall was one of the first to criticize the term 'influence' because of the lack of agency and cause that it implies on the receiving side (Michael Baxandall, *Patterns of Intention: On the Historical Explanation of Pictures* (New Haven and London: Yale University Press, 1985), 59). Within Sri Lankan art history, Senake Bandaranayake has critiqued the term 'cultural diffusion' and pointed to its colonial character (Senake Bandaranayake, 'Sri Lanka and Monsoon Asia: Patterns of Local and Regional Architectural Development and the Problem of the Traditional Sri Lankan Roof,' in *Senerat Paranavitana Commemorative Volume*, ed. Leelananda Prematilleke et. al., Studies in South Asian Culture 7 (Leiden: Brill, 1978), 22–44).

63 Nelson, 'Appropriation', 162.

64 Nelson, 'Appropriation', 170–1.

65 Elsewhere I argue that the ivory carver appropriated Dürer's Bagpiper because he understood it as an auspicious motif to be placed on either side of the lock or 'entrance' to the casket. See Sujatha Arundathi Meegama, 'Albrecht Dürer in Sri Lanka: An Ivory Carver's Response to a European Print,' in *Sri Lanka: Connected Art Histories*, ed. Sujatha Arundathi Meegama (Mumbai: Marg, 2017).

66 It may have first appeared in the eleventh century. Arthur Watson, *The Early Iconography of the Tree of Jesse* (London: Oxford University Press, 1934), 2.

67 Fagg and Bassani, *Africa and the Renaissance*, 114.

68 Angelica J. Afanador-Pujol cites a 1498 version created by the Master of Anne de Bretagne, from the Book of Hours printed by Philippe Pigouchet for Simon Vostre,as the source for the family tree of the Uanacaze from the 'Relación de Michoacan'. Angelica J. Afanador-Pujol, 'The Tree of Jesse and the "Relación de Michoacan": Mimicry in Colonial Mexico,' *The Art Bulletin* 92, 4 (2010), 295.

69 Susan Lowndes Marques, *Portuguese Expansion Overseas and the Art of Ivory* (Lisbon: Comissão Nacional para as Comemorações dos Descobrimentos Portugueses, 1991), 41–2.

70 In addition, the pillars on either side of the tree are transformed into less ornamented pillars in the ivory. The carver also has taken the liberty not to include the two large flowers at the two top corners of the print.

71 'Floating flowers' also adorn the wooden covers of palm leaf manuscripts and temple wall painting in Sri Lanka. Bilinda Devage Nandadeva, 'Flowers for the Dhamma Painted Buddhist Palm Leaf Manuscript Covers (Kamba) of Sri Lanka,' in *Buddhist Manuscript Cultures: Knowledge, Ritual, and Art. Routledge Critical Studies in Buddhism*, ed. Stephen C. Berkwitz, Juliane Schober and Claudia Brown (London: Routledge, 2008), 159–60.

72 The version from the Book of Hours printed by Philippe Pigouchet for Simon Vostre, included in Afanador-Pujol, 'The Tree of Jesse', does not present cartouches with text.

73 However, to be fair to Jaffer and Schwabe, they do comment on all the local motifs found in this casket. Jaffer and Schwabe, 'A Group of Sixteenth-Century Ivory Caskets from Sri Lanka', 10. I agree with their understanding of the role of kingship through the presence of the lions. But, rather than seeing the motifs as only Christian notions of creation being conveyed through the combination of local and foreign motifs, I wish to highlight local notions of creation, auspiciousness and prosperity as well.

74 My ideas about continuity rather than rupture are inspired by Afanador-Pujol, 'The Tree of Jesse', 295.

75 As recorded in the fifth-century chronicle, the *Mahāvaṃsa*.

76 Coomaraswamy, *Medieval Sinhalese Art*, 86. Aśokan pillars, the earliest form of art related to Buddhism, also deployed the lion motif. Frederick Asher notes that 'the lion at the summit of the pillar simultaneously symbolizes royal authority, as lions did in ancient India, and also the Buddha, whose words were said to be like the lion's roar'. Frederick Asher, 'On Maurya Art,' in *A Companion to Asian Art and Architecture*, ed. Rebecca M. Brown and Deborah S. Hutton (Oxford: Wiley-Blackwell, 2011), 432. The pedestals of some of the earliest seated Buddha images from India are embellished with lions as well, while others are embellished with deer in reference to the first sermon at the Saranath deer park. See John C. Huntington, *The Art of Ancient India Buddhist, Hindu, and Jain* (New York and Tokyo: Weatherhill, 1999), 152 and 144. This motif is also seen again in the thrones of the Bōdhisattva-like kings depicted on three of these caskets (Figure 6.7).

77 The elephant is an auspicious animal associated with fertility, the Buddha and with kingship. During the annual temple processions in Sri Lanka, the tooth-relic of the Buddha, and the weapons or ornaments of deities are carried on the backs of elephants. Citing C. E. Godakumbura's study on the rainmaking symbolisms of such processions, John Holt points to the cloud-like nature of elephants. John Clifford Holt, *The Buddha in the Crown: Avalokitesvara in the Buddhist Traditions of Sri Lanka* (Oxford: Oxford University Press, 1991), 189. This group of caskets also shows that the Sri Lankan king rode an elephant in processions.

78 The *Mahāvaṃsa* and *Cūḷavaṃsa* are the two main chronicles in Sri Lanka that recount the histories of kings. The *Rājāvaliya*, which was written around this time period also recounts the stories of kings.

79 See Ulrich von Schroeder, *Buddhist Sculptures of Sri Lanka* (Hong Kong: Visual Dharma Publications, 1990), 83, 85, 89 and 93.

80 Jaffer and Schwabe, 'A Group of Sixteenth-Century Ivory Caskets', 9–10, do bring attention to what they call the cord of life iconography, but their emphasis is on the depictions of *kinnaras*, cords of life and *makaras* and their associated notions of creation, rebirth and renewal of life, while my emphasis lies in the act of response by the carver to the Tree of Jesse, because of his familiarity with a wish-fulfilling tree or a vine that envelopes living beings.

81 Although the depiction of the Visitation, which is about birth, does not include a wish-fulfilling tree or vine, the niche is populated by animals: birds, a deer, a mouse or lamb, a fish and a mongoose.

82 Ananda K. Coomaraswamy, 'The Tree of Jesse and Indian Parallels or Sources,' The Art Bulletin 11, 2 (1929), 217–220, examines the various textual sources that carry this image of Viṣṇu giving birth to Brahma, and also points to depictions in Southeast Asia. It is surprising that the Sri Lankan ivory carver did not turn to this tradition for his visual response to the Tree of Jesse; after all, the sixteenth century is a period in Sri Lankan temple and court culture when the *Rāmāyaṇa* had gained popularity, indicating perhaps a renewed interest in and contact with the subcontinent. Apart from the depiction of the *avatārs* of Viṣṇu, Rama and Krishna, Viṣṇu himself is depicted on a sixteenth-century ivory casket currently in Peradeniya, being carried by Garuda. But the ivory carver of the Robinson Casket chooses to respond through a standard motif of the wish-fulfilling creeper that he is perhaps more familiar with.

83 Coomaraswamy, 'The Tree of Jesse', 219.

84 Coomaraswamy also points to another motif connected to the wish-fulfilling tree: trees that bear divine girls. Called the *narilata* or woman-vine, this motif is popular in Sri Lankan art. The Arabic Waqwaq tree also bears fruit with human faces (Coomaraswamy, 'The Tree of Jesse', 219).

85 The typology of this casket in a private collection perhaps indicates a slightly different period, patron and workshop. Unlike the eight caskets in London, Munich, Vienna, Boston, Paris and Peradeniya, the body of this casket is not divided into frames. Moreover, the ivory casket in Berlin does not contain a single wish-fulfilling creeper, casting doubt as to whether this was really made by a Sri Lankan carver.

86 The Tree of Jesse was also appropriated in South India and carved in ivory in the form of ivory plaques, an ivory frame and even as a three-dimensional version. The latter is similar to the trees found in the ivory sculptures called the Good Shepherd. Marques, *Portuguese Expansion Overseas*, 41–2.

87 This pyx is reproduced in Fagg and Bassani, *Africa and the Renaissance*, 84, 114, and 232; see also Levenson, *Encompassing the Globe*, 158.

88 Fagg and Bassani, *Africa and the Renaissance*, 83.

89 These devotional books of the laity contained illustrations from the Life of the Virgin and were printed and widely available in Europe. This is certainly not the first instance of adorning an ivory pyx with narrative scenes from the Bible. Ivory pyxes made much earlier also carry important scenes connected to the Life of the Virgin. See the sixth-century Byzantine pyx with women at the Christ's Tomb, Metropolitan Museum of Art, www.metmuseum.org/toah/works-of-art/17.190.57, accessed 8 July 2014.

90 Fagg and Bassani, *Africa and the Renaissance*, 83, and 111–15.

91 Philippe Pigouchet, *Book of Hours*, for Simon Vostre, 1498. Incunable 1498, C25 Rosenwald Collection, Washington, Library of Congress.

92 In the Tree of Jesse from the Book of Hours printed by Philippe Pigouchet, Jesse raises the opposite hand. Therefore, the Tree of Jesse in the pyx may have been inspired by the Tree of Jesse in the Book of Hours printed by Thielman Kerver. Or the carver may have made this change for a particular reason.

93 In a silver pyx from sixteenth-century Portugal that has a similar shape and, held up by lions, Mary stands grandly on the lid wearing a crown. See the reproduction in Fagg and Bassani, *Africa and the Renaissance*, 84, Figure 76.

94 Another pyx from Sierra Leone contains a broken three-dimensional figure on top of its lid; most likely, it too represented a seated Mother Mary holding Jesus. Fagg and Bassani, *Africa and the Renaissance*, 84, 78. A similar three-dimensional motif of the Madonna and Child appears on the top of the lids of saltcellars (pp. 74).

95 Afanador-Pujol, 'The Tree of Jesse', 296.

96 Afanador-Pujol, 'The Tree of Jesse', 296.

97 For a reproduction, see Afanador-Pujol, 'The Tree of Jesse', 294.

98 Afanador-Pujol points out that the use of this motif around 1539–41 indicates the 'artist's Franciscan training' (Afanador-Pujol, 'The Tree of Jesse', 296). But it is difficult to ascertain whether the Sri Lankan ivory carver was a convert and was aware of Catholicism and its iconography. After all, unlike with the Jesuits in Japan, there was no art school set up in Sri Lanka by missionaries to train local artists in the Christian arts.

99 Afanador-Pujol, 'The Tree of Jesse', 293.

100 Although the European print that Afanador-Pujol compares this to does not contain the cartouches, the version printed by Thielman Kerver from 1499 and 1507 do include the cartouches. See 'The Tree of Jesse', 295.

101 Afanador-Pujol, 'The Tree of Jesse', 293.

102 Afanador-Pujol, 'The Tree of Jesse', 297.

103 Afanador-Pujol, 'The Tree of Jesse', 295. Afanador-Pujol notes that the indigenous artist in colonial Mexico was not the first to deploy this motif for the benefit of a royal house. European artists from the medieval to the early modern periods used this motif to bolster the image/pedigree of certain ruling houses in Europe (Afanador-Pujol, 'The Tree of Jesse', 296).

104 Afanador-Pujol, 'The Tree of Jesse', 299.

105 The local term for lineage is analogous to a tree (Afanador-Pujol, 'The Tree of Jesse', 302). In contrast to the European versions that depict rosebushes, a grapevine or a fruit tree, the artist of the

Uanacaze family tree uses an oak tree. The little stools on which the descendants sit are crowns of little acorns. Like the oak called *tocuz*, which grows in this region of Michoacan, the Uanacaze family tree also has many branches. Oaks are important trees in the religious traditions of this region: they are used to build fires at temples, as a form of protection, and as a site that hosts the communication between humans and gods (Afanador-Pujol, 'The Tree of Jesse', 303).

106 Most recently, Stephen Berkwitz has brought our attention to the literary works of the poet Alagiyavanna Mukevati, who wrote Sinhala poetry for both a Sri Lankan king and for the Portuguese. Stephen C. Berkwitz, *Buddhist Poetry and Colonialism: Alagiyavanna and the Portuguese in Sri Lanka* (New York: Oxford University Press, 2013). Such scholarship shows the diverse responses of individuals during the earliest encounter between European colonialists and colonial subjects in Asia.

107 Claire Farago, 'On the Peripatetic Life of Objects in the Era of Globalization,' in *Cultural Contact and the Making of European Art since the Age of Exploration*, ed. Mary D. Sheriff (Chapel Hill: University of North Carolina Press, 2012), 18.

108 Farago advocates for 'an approach that considers different cultural traditions, representational systems, worldviews, and contexts of use on equal footing' (Farago, 'On the Peripatetic Life', 18).

# Chapter 7: Cosmopolitan converts

1 My thanks to Alan Strathern and the two external readers for their comments on this piece, and to Pedro Pinto for his support with the archival research in Lisbon.

2 See Ronit Ricci, ed., *Exile in Colonial Asia: Kings, Convicts, Commemoration* (Honolulu: University of Hawai'i Press, 2016). The main conceptual contribution of this volume is to challenge the long-standing association between exile and (mostly unfree) labour, and highlight the forced migration of elites.

3 L. S. Perera, 'The Period of Dynastic Instability,' in *University of Ceylon History of Ceylon* [hereafter UCHC] (Colombo: Ceylon University Press, 1959–60), Vol. I, Part 1, 300–1.

4 Perera, 'The Period of Dynastic Instability', 308–9.

5 Perera, 'The Period of Dynastic Instability', 306.

6 L. S. Perera, 'Dynasty of Manavamma,' in *UCHC*, Vol. I, Part 1, 334.

7 C. W. Thomas, 'Civil Wars and the Emergence of Parakramabahu the Great,' in *UCHC*, Vol. I, Part 2, 441–2.

8 Sirima Wickremasinghe, 'Successors of Parākramabāhu I: Downfall of the Polonnaru Kingdom,' in *UCHC*, Vol. I, Part 2, 519–21.

9 Senarat Paranavitana, 'The Dambadeni Dynasty,' in *UCHC*, Vol. I, Part 2, 632–3.

10 Senarat Paranavitana, 'Gampala and Rayigama,' in *UCHC*, Vol. I, Part 2, 644.

11 Paranavitana, 'Gampala and Rayigama', 647–8. For a discussion of the clan's status see S. Paranavitana, 'The Pedigree of the Alagakesvaras,' in *UCHC*, Vol. I, Part 2, 653–9.

12 Senarat Paranavitana, 'The Kōṭṭe Kingdom up to 1505,' in *UCHC*, Vol. I, Part 2, 663–83; G. P. V. Somaratne, 'Grand Eunuch Ho and Ceylon,' *Journal of the Ceylon Branch of the Royal Asiatic Society*, New Series 15 (1971), 36–47; K. M. M. Werake, 'A Re-examination of Chinese Relations with Sri Lanka during the 15th Century AD,' *Modern Sri Lanka Studies* 2, 1–2 (1987), 89–102.

13 For overviews see Alan Strathern, *Kingship and Conversion in Sixteenth-Century Sri Lanka: Portuguese Imperialism in a Buddhist Land* (Cambridge: Cambridge University Press, 2007) and Zoltán Biedermann, 'The *Matrioshka* Principle and How it was Overcome: Portuguese and Habsburg Attitudes toward Imperial Authority in Sri Lanka and the Responses of the Rulers of Kotte (1506–1656),' *Journal of Early Modern History* 13, 4 (2009), 265–310.

14 Although there is no direct proof of a connection, it is worth mentioning that in the same year John III passed a decree granting rights to Goan converts equalling those of Portuguese colonists. Ângela Barreto Xavier, '*Conversos* and *Novamente Convertidos*: Law, Religion, and Identity in the Portuguese Kingdom and Empire,' *Journal of Early Modern History*, 15 (2011), 255–87.

15 See for example Śrī Rāmarakṣa to Catherine, Cochin, 28 January 1551, published in Georg Schurhammer and Ernst August Voretzsch, *Ceylon zur Zeit des Königs Bhuvaneka Bahu und Franz Xavers 1539–1552. Quellen zur Geschichte der Portugiesen, sowie der Franziskaner- und Jesuitenmission auf Ceylon, im Urtext herausgegeben und erklärt*, 2 vols. (Leipzig: Verlag der Asia Major, 1928), 564.

16 On the ivories see Sujatha Meegama in this volume (Chapter 6). Also see Annemarie Jordan Gschwend and Johannes Beltz, *Elfenbeine aus Ceylon: Luxusgüter für Katherine von Habsburg (1507–1578)* (Zurich: Museum Rietberg, 2010), and Zoltán Biedermann, 'Diplomatic Ivories: Sri Lankan Caskets and the Portuguese-Asian Exchange in the Sixteenth Century,' in *Global Gifts: The Material Culture of Diplomacy in Early Modern Eurasia*, ed. Zoltán Biedermann, Anne Gerritsen and Giorgio Riello (New York: Cambridge University Press, forthcoming).
17 Schurhammer and Voretzsch, *Ceylon*, 559.
18 Schurhammer and Voretzsch, *Ceylon*, 553.
19 Schurhammer and Voretzsch, *Ceylon*, 598. See also Diogo do Couto, *Da Asia de Diogo do Couto Dos Feitos, que os Portuguezes fizeram na Conquista, e Descubrimento das Terras, e Mares do Oriente* (Lisbon: Livraria de São Carlos, 1973–75), Vol. 6, 350.
20 Schurhammer and Voretzsch, *Ceylon*, 599.
21 See Vito Perniola, *The Catholic Church in Sri Lanka: The Portuguese Period. Original Documents translated into English* (Dehiwala: Tisara Prakasakayo, 1989–91), Vol. I, 350.
22 António Dias to his fellow Jesuits residing in Coimbra, Colombo, 15 December 1552, in Schurhammer and Voretzsch, *Ceylon*, 642.
23 Fernão de Queiroz, *Conquista Temporal e Espiritual de Ceilão* (Colombo: The Government Press, 1916), 262.
24 See C. R. de Silva and S. Pathmanathan, 'The Kingdom of Jaffna up to 1620,' in *University of Peradeniya History of Sri Lanka* (Peradeniya: The University of Peradeniya, 1995), Vol. 2, 106.
25 On the assassination of Pararajasekaran, see de Silva and Pathamanathan, 'The Kingdom of Jaffna', 107.
26 On this individual see Schurhammer and Voretzsch, *Ceylon*, 142, n. 6, and then Miguel Ferreira to Dom João de Castro, Meliapore, 28 March 1546, in Schurhammer and Voretzsch, *Ceylon*, 347. Also see Queiroz, *Conquista*, 144.
27 Ferreira to Castro; Schurhammer and Voretzsch, *Ceylon*, 347.
28 Gaspar Correia, *Lendas da Índia*, ed. M. Lopes de Almeida, 4 vols. (Porto: Lello & Irmão, 1975), Vol. 4, 325.
29 The massacre of about 600 recently converted fishing folk at Mannar is described in detail, although with considerable exaggeration, in A. J. B. Antoninus, *The Martyrs of Mannar: From Authentic Documents*, 2nd edn (Colombo, St. Joseph's Press, 1945). See also Georg Schurhammer, *Francis Xavier, His Life, His Times*, 4 vols. (Rome: Institutum Historicum Societatis Iesu, 1973–82), Vol. 2, 470–1.
30 Xavier to the Company, Cochin, 27 January 1545, in Schurhammer and Voretzsch, *Ceylon*, 143.
31 Xavier to Diogo de Borba and Misser Paulo, Meliapore, 8 May 1545, in Schurhammer and Voretzsch, *Ceylon*, 146–7.
32 Ferreira to Castro, Meliapore, 28 March 1546, in Schurhammer and Voretzsch, *Ceylon*, 347–8.
33 André de Sousa to Prince Henry, Goa, 15 November 1545, in Schurhammer and Voretzsch, *Ceylon*, 203.
34 Xavier to the Company, Cochin, 27 January 1545, in Schurhammer and Voretzsch, *Ceylon*, 143; Sousa to Prince Henry, in Schurhammer and Voretzsch, *Ceylon*, 203.
35 Schurhammer and Voretzsch, *Ceylon*, 143.
36 Sousa to Henry, 15 November 1545, in Schurhammer and Voretzsch, *Ceylon*, 203.
37 Dom João to Catarina, 15 October 1545, in Schurhammer and Voretzsch, *Ceylon*, 185; Sousa to Henry, in Schurhammer and Voretzsch, *Ceylon*, 202; Dom João to John III, Goa, November 1545, in Schurhammer and Voretzsch, *Ceylon*, 216.
38 Xavier to Rome, Cochin, 27 January 1545, in Schurhammer and Voretzsch, *Ceylon*, 144.
39 Dom João to Catherine, Goa, 15 October 1545, in Schurhammer and Voretzsch, *Ceylon*, 187.
40 Dom João to John III, Goa, 15 November 1545, in Schurhammer and Voretzsch, *Ceylon*, 217.
41 André de Sousa to John III, Goa, 15 November 1545, in Schurhammer and Voretzsch, *Ceylon*, 213.
42 Dom João to John III, Goa, 15 November 1545, in Schurhammer and Voretzsch, *Ceylon*, 217.
43 Dom João to Catherine, Goa, 15 October 1545, in Schurhammer and Voretzsch, *Ceylon*, 186.
44 Noronha to John III, Cochin, 27 January 1552, in Schurhammer and Voretzsch, *Ceylon*, 603–4.
45 Couto, *Da Asia de Diogo do Couto Dos Feitos*, Vol. 6, 354.
46 On the Kandyan context at this moment, see Strathern, *Kingship and Conversion*, 212.
47 Queiroz, *Conquista*, 356; see also *The Rājāvaliya or a Historical Narrative of the Sinhalese Kings from Vijaya to Vimala Dharmasuriya II*, ed. B. Gunasekara (Colombo: Ceylon Government, 1926), 82.
48 Philip II to Dom Duarte de Meneses, Lisbon, 6 February 1589, in *Archivo Portuguez-Oriental*, ed. J. H. da Cunha Rivara, 6 vols. (Nova Goa: Imprensa Nacional, 1855–76), Vol. 3, 187.

49 The original request is lost, but indirect evidence suggests that it was first made at the beginning of 1586 or even the end of 1585: Philip II to Dom Duarte de Meneses, Lisbon, 28 January 1588, *Archivo Portuguez-Oriental*, Vol. 3, 126.
50 Frei Paulo da Trindade, *Conquista Espiritual do Oriente*, ed. F. Lopes, 3 vols. (Lisbon: Centro de Estudos Históricos Ultramarinos, 1962–7), Vol. 3, 70. On this prince's religious behaviour see Strathern, *Kingship and Conversion*, 212.
51 Queiroz, *Conquista*, 361–2.
52 On Vimaladharmasūriya, see Strathern, *Kingship and Conversion*, 214–21. On Kandy, see Gananath Obeyesekere, Chapter 8 in this volume.
53 Dom João Dharmapala to Philipp II, Colombo, 29 November 1589, Archivo General de Simancas, Secretarías Pronvinciales, Portugal, Cod. 1551, fols. 796–796v.
54 Dom Antão to Philip II, Colombo, 29 November 1589, Archivo General de Simancas, Secretarías Pronvinciales, Codex 1551, fols. 799-799v.
55 This complex policy transition is explored in detail in Zoltán Biedermann, *Island Empire: Renaissance Portugal, Sri Lanka, and the Beginnings of Habsburg Colonialism in Asia* (forthcoming).
56 Royal letter to Dom Jerónimo de Azevedo, Lisbon, 20 December 1613, in *Documentos Remettidos da India ou Livros das Monções*, ed. R. A. Bulhão Pato and A. Silva Rego, 10 vols. (Lisbon: Academia Real das Sciencias/Imprensa Nacional, 1880–1982), Vol. 1, 465–6.
57 Queiroz, *Conquista*, 361, 577. Dom João was born around 1578.
58 On 'Mica Pita Adacym' (Nikaepiṭiya Baṇḍāra) see Queiroz, *Conquista*, 386.
59 Summary of a letter by viceroy Matias de Albuquerque in a royal letter to viceroy Dom Francisco da Gama, Lisbon, 15 January 1598, in *Archivo Portuguez-Oriental*, fasc. 3, 817–18.
60 *Archivo Portuguez-Oriental*, fasc. 3, 817.
61 Queiroz, *Conquista*, 578, refers that the orders came from the *Consejo de Portugal* in Madrid.
62 King to Martim Afonso de Castro, Lisbon, 18 January 1607, in *Documentos Remettidos*, Vol. 1, 106.
63 See Tikiri Abeyasinghe, *Portuguese Rule in Ceylon 1594–1612* (Colombo: Lake House, 1966), 52.
64 Sheldon Pollock, *The Language of the Gods in the World of Men. Sanskrit, Culture, and Power in Premodern India* (Berkeley and Los Angeles: University of California Press, 2006).
65 See Vito Perniola, *The Catholic Church in Sri Lanka*, Vol. 2, 149.
66 The life of Dom João is described in Sousa Viterbo, 'Relações de Portugal com alguns potentados africanos e asiáticos,' *Archivo Historico Portuguez* 2 (1904), 458–62 and 'D. João, Principe de Candia,' *Archivo Historico Portuguez* 3 (1905), 354–64, 441–59. Two recent publications reiterate much of what was written by Viterbo, but also add substantial new documentation, much of which is not directly relevant to this study but deserves further exploration: Maria Celeste Pereira, Fernando A. A. Lemos and Rosa Trindade Ferreira, *Documentos Inéditos para a História de Telheiras e do seu Convento* (Lisbon: Centro Cultural de Telheiras, 2007) and 'O Convento de Nossa Senhora da Porta do Céu,' *Cadernos de Telheiras*, 2ª série, 1 (2008), 29–57, online at https://issuu.com/gruvless/docs/cadernos_de_telheiras, accessed 28 October 2016. The latter piece is wrongly attributed to Madalena Larcher, whom I wish to thank for clarifying the matter and for putting me in touch with Father Rui Rosas of the Telheiras parish, who generously provided a copy of *Documentos Inéditos*.
67 Queiroz, *Conquista*, 578.
68 Queiroz, *Conquista*, 579, and Friar Manuel da Esperança, *Historia Serafica da Ordem dos Frades Menores de S. Francisco na Provincia de Portugal. Primeira parte, que contem seu principio, & augmentos no estado primeiro de Custodia* (Lisbon: Officina Craesbeeckiana, 1656–1721), Vol. 3, 609. Note that the exact chronology of events remains difficult to establish. If a first visit to Madrid occurred indeed around 1611, this might help explain the appearance, in Cervantes' *Quixote* (Second Part, chapter 38), printed in 1615, of a family of royal exiles from 'Candaya' near Taprobane. The decree, passed on 26 November 1611, is in the papers of the *Chancelaria de D. Filipe II, Doações*, livro 21, fol. 228v, Lisbon, Arquivo Nacional Torre do Tombo.
69 The second grant of 4,000 *cruzados*, to be paid from the revenues of the bishoprics of Porto and Lamego, was issued in Madrid in 1626. Whether the prince really went to Madrid twice is, however, not entirely clear.
70 Esperança, *Historia Serafica*, Vol. 5, 611. The full inventory of the prince's possessions, an impressive list of buildings and lands, is transcribed in Pereira et al., *Documentos Inéditos*, 28–47.
71 Esperança, *Historia Serafica*, Vol. 5, 612. She was given a dowry but also expected to renounce it again after her death in favour of the Franciscans. The entire testament, written on 31 March 1642 at Dom João's deathbed in the Mouraria palace, is transcribed in Viterbo, 'D. João, Principe', 449–51, and again in Pereira et al., *Documentos Inéditos*, 23–6.
72 It has been argued that this woman may have had a New Christian background. The hypothesis is based solely on her name, Abreu, and especially Susana pointing to the universe of Jewish converts.

73 Intriguingly, the testament also asks for the legitimate daughter to renounce some properties to the benefit of the illegitimate daughter. Viterbo, 'D. João, Principe', 451; Pereira et al., *Documentos Inéditos*, 25.

74 Esperança, *Historia Serafica*, Vol. 3, 612

75 Four were described as American Indians, and three of no specified origin: Viterbo, 'D. João, Principe', 441.

76 Record of the death of Jorge Henriques, *trombeta* of the prince, on 26 August 1640, in the parish register of Lumiar, Lisbon, Arquivo Nacional Torre do Tombo, fol. 53v.

77 Viterbo, 'D. João, Principe', 451; Pereira et al., *Documentos Inéditos*, 26.

78 Record of the entry of Dom João into the Brotherhood as its first member, Telheiras, 2 February 1625, Arquivo Histórico Militar, Lisbon, Codex 'Livro dos Irmãos,' Div. 1/1/2/2, fol. 1. A full description of the architecture of this church is now available in the beautifully produced book of Sagara Jayasinghe, *The Black Prince's Chapel: The Church Built by a Sinhalese Prince in Portugal* (Colombo: Vijitha Yapa, 2015). There is evidence suggesting that the authorities in Madrid were unhappy about the foundation and attempted to block it, for example in a letter dated 20 April 1633, Biblioteca da Ajuda, Lisbon, Codex 51-X-5, fol. 74v. Details of the negotiations are likely to be found in the Spanish state archive at Simancas, namely in the collection of the *Secretaría de Portugal*.

79 Esperança, *Historia Serafica*, Vol. 3, 612. An old photograph of the portrait can be seen online in Pereira et al., 'O Convento de Nossa Senhora da Porta do Céu', 40.

80 Viterbo, 'D. João, Principe', 443.

81 There is some uncertainty about the latter as the tomb disappeared in the 1755 earthquake; Viterbo, 'D. João, Principe', 443–4.

82 A reproduction is in Viterbo, 'Relações', 460.

83 Purity of blood was not imposed in Portugal through a monolithic legislation but mostly discussed on a case-by-case basis. Moreover, noble and especially royal blood had from early on prompted exemptions to the rules on blood purity even in Castile. See João Figuerôa-Rego, '"A honra alheia por um fio": os estatutos de limpeza de sangue no espaço de expressão Ibérica (sécs. XVI–XVIII),' PhD dissertation, Braga, Universidade do Minho, 2009. On the remarkable case of Afonso Álvares, a playwright of African ancestry claiming social superiority over the poet António Chiado, see: T. F. Earle, 'Black Africans versus Jews: Religious and Racial Tension in a Portuguese Saint's Play,' in *Black Africans in Renaissance Europe*, ed. T. F. Earle and K. J. P. Lowe (Cambridge: Cambridge University Press, 2005), 345–60.

84 This is on a casket at the Museum für Asiatische Kunst, Berlin, Inventory no. MIK I 9928. See Amin Jaffer and Melanie Anne Schwabe, 'A Group of Sixteenth-Century Ivory Caskets from Ceylon,' *Apollo*, 445 (1999), 10.

85 He could also in theory have had his origins elsewhere, though it would make sense to assume that a Lankan prince would gather other Lankans around himself in the first place.

86 Transcript of the accusation, Lisbon, 30 March 1645, published in Viterbo, 'D. João, Principe', 458–9.

87 See – with some caution – Stuart Schwartz, *All Can Be Saved: Religious Tolerance and Salvation in the Iberian Atlantic World* (New Haven: Yale University Press, 2008).

88 Transcript of the accusation, Lisbon, 30 March 1645, published in Viterbo, 'D. João, Principe', 458.

89 Ângela Barreto Xavier, 'Dissolver a Diferença – Conversão e Mestiçagem no Império Português,' in *Itinerários: A Investigação nos 25 Anos do ICS*, ed. Manuel Villaverde et al. (Lisbon: Imprensa de Ciências Sociais, 2008), 709–27.

90 Jaffer and Schwabe, 'A Group of Sixteenth-Century Ivory Caskets', 8–10; Sujatha Arundathi Meegama, Chapter 6 in this volume.

91 Record of the entry of Dom João into the Brotherhood as its first member, Telheiras, 2 February 1625, Arquivo Histórico Militar, Lisbon, Codex 'Livro dos Irmãos,' Div. 1/1/2/2, fol. 1.

92 *Missale Romanum ex decreto sacrosancti, Concilii tridentini restitutum, S. Pii V. Pont. max. jussu editum, Clementis VIII, & Urbani VIII* (Venetiis: ex Typographia Balleoniana, 1736, p. xxv of the section "Commune Sanctorum").

93 See Zacharias P. Thundy, *Buddha and Christ. Nativity Stories and Indian Traditions* (Leiden: Brill, 1993).

94 Genesis 28:13–14. Also note how the ladder is interpreted as a sign of the coming exiles of Israel in the Talmudic tradition, with which Dom João may well have been acquainted if the theory of his wife's Jewish origins is correct.

95 'And he called the name of that place Bethel: but the name of that city was called Luz at the first' (Genesis 28:19).

96 The following paragraphs are based on P. E. Pieris, *The Prince Vijaya Pala of Ceylon, 1634–1654: From the Original Documents at Lisbon* (Colombo, C. A. C. Press, 1927), 1–8.

97 Pieris, *Prince Vijaya Pala*, 8.
98 Pieris, *Prince Vijaya Pala*, 10.
99 Pieris, *Prince Vijaya Pala*, 16.
100 Pieris, *Prince Vijaya Pala*, 11 (original seventeenth-century quote from João Ribeiro).
101 Pieris, *Prince Vijaya Pala*, 12.
102 Pieris, *Prince Vijaya Pala*, 12–13.
103 Pieris, *Prince Vijaya Pala*, 14.
104 Sanjay Subrahmanyam, *Courtly Encounters. Translating Courtliness and Violence in Early Modern Eurasia* (Cambridge, MA: Harvard University Press, 2012).
105 As outlined above; see Couto, *Da Asia de Diogo do Couto Dos Feitos*, Vol. 6, 354.
106 Pieris, *Prince Vijaya Pala*, 51.
107 Pieris, *Prince Vijaya Pala*, 58.
108 Pieris, *Prince Vijaya Pala*, 59.
109 Pieris, *Prince Vijaya Pala*, 12.
110 Friar Simão de Coimbra to John III, Goa, 25 December 1546, in Schurhammer and Voretzsch, *Ceylon*, 431–3.
111 Alan Strathern, Chapter 11 in this volume.
112 In addition, it needs to be noted that while so far we have only found stories of elite exile and acculturation, it is legitimate to ask how many other experiences of movement, displacement and engagement with the wider world occurred that involved peasants, merchants or fishing folk. Sources on these may still be awaiting discovery in Iberian archives.

## Chapter 8: Between the Portuguese and the Nāyakas

1 This chapter is based on a lecture given at the South Asia Policy Research Institute (SAPRI) in Colombo in April 2013. I am greatly indebted in this work to my friends and colleagues, especially H. L. Seneviratne, Kitsiri Malalgoda, H. G. Dayasisira and the many scholars quoted – in particular Lorna Dewaraja, to whom all of us who work on the Kandy period are deeply indebted. It is therefore with sadness that we have to record the death of Lorna Dewaraja on 28 November 2014. Her work documented here and elsewhere is a monument to her scholarship.
2 See Tikiri Abeyasinghe, 'The Politics of Survival: Aspects of Kandyan External Relations in the Mid-Sixteenth Century,' *Journal of the Royal Asiatic Society of Sri Lanka*, New Series XVII (1973), 11–21 and 'The Kingdom of Kandy: Foundations and Foreign Relations to 1638,' in *University of Peradeniya History of Sri Lanka*, Vol. 2, ed. K.M. de Silva (Peradeniya: University of Peradeniya, 1995), 139–61; C. R. de Silva, 'The rise and fall of the kingdom of Sītāvaka,' in University of Peradeniya History of Sri Lanka, Vol. 2, 61–104; Zoltán Biedermann, *Island Empire: Renaissance Portugal, Sri Lanka, and the Beginnings of Habsburg Colonialism in Asia* (forthcoming).
3 On Vimaladharmasūriya see most recently Alan Strathern, *Kingship and Conversion in Sixteenth-Century Sri Lanka: Portuguese Imperialism in a Buddhist Land* (Cambridge: Cambridge University Press, 2007), 214–21.
4 *Cūḷavaṃsa*, trans. Wilhelm Geiger (Colombo: Government Press, 1953), 94.14. Unless otherwise specified I shall employ this version of the *Cūḷavaṃsa*.
5 *Cūḷavaṃsa*, 94.18–19.
6 Donald Ferguson, *The Earliest Dutch Visits to Ceylon* (1927–30; reprint New Delhi: Asian Educational Services, 1998), 44.
7 Kitsiri Malalgoda, *Buddhism in Sinhalese Society, 1750–1900* (Berkeley: University of California Press, 1976), 30–3.
8 Both Sinhala editions of the *Rājāvaliya* say of Konappu Banḍāra: 'Tammittarālagē doniyan kasāda bäňdalā kulavädī kolamba unnāha.' *The Rājāvaliya or a Historical Narrative of Sinhalese Kings*, trans. B. Gunasekara (Colombo: Information Department, 1953), 66. Here *kulavädī* has been translated by both Gunasekara and Suraweera as 'baptized', see *The Rājāvaliya: A Comprehensive Account of the Kings of Sri Lanka*, trans. A. V Suraweera (Rathmalana: Vishva Lekha, 2000), 86; Soratha Thero, *Sri Sumangalasabdakosaya*, Vol. 1 (Colombo: Maligatenne, 1952), 264, interprets *kula vadina* as joining another caste (*kula*) or another faith or religion.
9 Phillipus Baldaeus, *A True and Exact Description of the Great Island of Ceylon*, trans. Pieter Brohier (Maharagama: Saman Press, 1960), 38–40. This was originally published as Vol. 8, nos. 1–4 of the *Ceylon Historical Journal* (1958–9).
10 In Ferguson, *Earliest Dutch Visits*, 44.

11 Joris Van Spilbergen, *Journal of Spilbergen, the First Dutch Envoy to Ceylon*, trans. K.D. Paranavitana (Dehiwela: Sridevi Press, 1997), 32.
12 Van Spilbergen, *Journal of Spilbergen*, 32.
13 Paul E. Pieris, *Ceylon: The Portuguese Era Being a History of the Island for the Period 1505–1658*, 2 vols. (1913–14; reprint Dehiwala: Tisara Prakasakayo, 1992), Vol. 1, 365.
14 Paul E. Pieris, *Sinhale and the Patriots, 1815–1818* (Colombo: The Colombo Apothecaries, 1950), 115–16. For a modern view of this whole issue of clothes see Nira Wickramasinghe, *Dressing the Colonized Body: Politics, Clothing and Identity in Colonial Sri Lanka* (Hyderabad: Orient Longman, 2003).
15 *The Pybus Embassy to Kandy, 1762*, ed. R. Raven-Hart (Colombo: National Museums, 1958).
16 Ferguson, *Earliest Dutch Visits*, 61 (emphasis added).
17 R.K. de Silva and W.G.M. Beumer, *Illustrations and Views of Dutch Ceylon, 1602–1796* (London: Serendib Publications, 1988), 34.
18 Ferguson, *Earliest Dutch Visits*, 65.
19 Paul E. Pieris, *The Dutch Power in Ceylon, Some Documents Relating to the Rise of the Dutch Power in Ceylon, 1602–1670* (1929; reprint London: Curzon Press, 1973), 32.
20 Baldaeus, *Ceylon*, 38–40.
21 Van Spilbergen, *Journal of Spilbergen*, 39–42.
22 Robert Knox, *An Historical Relation of the Island of Ceylon* (1681), ed. J. H. O. Paulusz (Dehiwala: Tisara Prakasakayo, 1989). Knox was nineteen when he, his father and sixteen sailors were captured in 1660. The senior Knox died a year later but Knox made his escape in 1679. For a contemporary critique and rereading of Knox, see Sarojini Jayawickrama, *Writing that Conquers: Re-reading Knox's An Historical Relation of the Island Ceylon* (Colombo: Social Scientists' Association, 2004).
23 Ferguson, *Earliest Dutch Visits*, 42. Note that kings also did not eat beef but enjoyed 'meat from the hunt', generally provided by Veddah hunters.
24 Valentijn says of Bintänna-Alutnuvara that 'here the old Emperors used to hold court as it is a beautiful city where there are many large streets, beautiful buildings and wonderful pagodas or heathen temples [...] It has also a beautiful and large palace of the Emperor full of beautiful buildings within. Here the best galleys and *sampans* of the Emperors are made. Here are also many shops but no market, stone monasteries and a great many bamboo houses which stretch for a mile or two in distance along the river'. *Francois Valentijn's Description of Ceylon*, ed. and trans. Sinnappah Arasaratnam (London: Hakluyt Society, 1978), 153.
25 Lorna S. Dewaraja in *The Kandyan Kingdom, 1707–1760* (Colombo: Lake House Investments, 1972), 17, states that Senerat married Dona Catarina's daughters from two marriages and these would be in Sinhala kinship his own daughters – but this evidence comes from a footnote in Fernão De Queyroz, *The Temporal and Spiritual Conquest of Ceylon*, trans. Father S. G. Perera, 3 vols. (Colombo: Government Printer, 1930), Vol. 2, 788, which is not entirely reliable on this matter. See also Baldaeus, *Ceylon*, 80. Sinhala sources simply say that Senarat married Dona Catarina.
26 It is unfortunate that there are no full and rounded studies of these important monarchs, in particular Rājasiṃha II, who reigned for more than half a century.
27 Chandra Richard de Silva, *The Portuguese in Ceylon, 1617–1638* (Colombo: H. W. Cave, 1972), 85.
28 Sinnappah Arasaratnam, 'Oratorians and Predicants: The Catholic Church in Ceylon under Dutch Rule,' in *Ceylon and the Dutch, 1600–1800: External Influences and Internal Change in Early Modern Sri Lanka* (Aldershot, New Hampshire: Variorum, 1996), 219–21. W. L. A. Don Peter, *Francis Xavier, Teacher of Nations* (Colombo: Evangel Press, 1987), 81. One of their most prominent settlements is Vahakōṭṭe; other settlements are mentioned in Don Peter, Francis Xavier, 78.
29 Dewaraja, *The Kandyan Kingdom*, 183. Additionally, I think we can trust the panegyric (*praśasti*) on the king known as Rājasiṃha *Haṭana* ('Rājasiṃha's war' written in 449 four-line stanzas) when it mentions the education of the king, including training in arms, swordsmanship and the like. Stanza 52 refers to his education in Tamil, Sinhala, Sanskrit, Magadha, Nagara and Portuguese 'letters' (*akuru*). While this may be a panegyric trope and not signify actual competence in all these idioms, the fact that multilingualism is given as an ideal is in itself significant. See Allepola H.M. Somaratna, ed. *Rajasiha Haṭana* (Kandy: Godamune Brothers, 1966), 8.
30 Donald Ferguson, *Earliest Dutch Visits*, 41. The newer translation by Paranavitana rightly states that these were Brahmins, not monks as Ferguson thought (Van Spilbergen, *Journal of Spilbergen*, 62, n. 121).
31 Van Spilbergen, *Journal of Spilbergen*, 29, translator's parentheses.
32 Knox, *Historical Relation*, 324–5 and passim. The term 'prisoner' is somewhat of a misnomer and has no relation to that term in contemporary usage everywhere because Kandyan 'prisoners' were free

to wander in a demarcated region containing many villages, some even living in the city of Kandy. However, villagers were held responsible if 'prisoners' moved out of a permitted zone. Prisoners could practise crafts and sell their products and many of them were permitted, even encouraged, to marry Sinhala women, thus domesticating them.

33 Ryckloff Van Goens Jr, a Dutch governor (1675–79) who generally wished Rājasiṃha dead, put it thus: 'However, as long as Rajia Singa is alive, it would be well to often send His Majesty presents, such as hawks, horses, and curiosities from Socratta [Socotra], Persia, and other places, with which he would be more pleased than if we evacuated ten Provinces.' *Memoir of Ryclof Van Goens, Jun. Governor of Ceylon, 1675–1679, to his successor Laurens Pyl*, trans. Sophia Pieters (Colombo: Government Printer, 1910), 14.

34 H. W. Codrington, *A Short History of Ceylon* (1929; reprint New Delhi: Asian Educational Services, 1994), 136.

35 For a good discussion of the Dutch in Asia and their relations with the Portuguese see Markus Vink, 'Introduction,' in *Mission to Madurai: Dutch Embassies to the Nayaka Court of Madurai in the Seventeenth Century* (Delhi: Manohar, 2012), in particular 86–106.

36 Sinnappa Arasaratnam, 'Oratorians and Predicants', 221.

37 Father S. G. Perera rightly points out that 'Vimaladharmasūriya was one of the chief benefactors of the Church in Ceylon, for it is his tolerance and benevolence that enabled Father Joseph Vaz to effect the revival of the faith in the island'. S. G. Perera, *Life of the Venerable Father Joseph Vaz, Apostle of Ceylon* (Galle: Loyola Press, 1953), 173.

38 Perera, *Life of Joseph Vaz*, 174. In fairness to Rājasiṃha, he himself seems to have ignored some of the articles of that treaty, including no. 17 requiring the expelling of Catholic priests from his domain. See Valentijn's Description of Ceylon, 322–4 for details.

39 Perera, *Life of Joseph Vaz*, 165.

40 Dewaraja, *The Kandyan Kingdom*, 83.

41 Perera, *Life of Joseph Vaz*, 216.

42 Perera, *Life of Joseph Vaz*, 216–22. The few references to Vimaladharmasūriya II are in chapter XIV (173–87) and the detailed account of Narēndrasinha in chapter XVII (214–25). Both the ups and downs of the relationships with the Catholic Church are also well documented in the classic nine-volume work of Father V. Perniola, The Catholic Church in Sri Lanka, especially *The Catholic Church in Sri Lanka: The Dutch Period*, Vol. 1, *1658–1711* (Dehiwala: Tisara Prakasakayo, 1983). About Narēndrasinha a missionary report says: 'In the reign of that King our religions had every liberty and many churches were built and feasts were held [in the kingdom] with processions and other ceremonies without the least opposition but rather with all permission and favour' (Perniola, *The Catholic Church*, Vol. 3, 24). On Gonçalvez, another Konkani Brahmin, see W.A. Don Peter, *Studies in Ceylon Church History* (Colombo: The Catholic Press, 1963), 53–60.

43 *Cūḷavaṃsa*, 97.35–6.

44 *Cūḷavaṃsa*, 97.37–44.

45 *Cūḷavaṃsa*, 97.30.

46 *Cūḷavaṃsa*, 97.31–2.

47 For a discussion of the Viṣṇu shrine endowment see John Clifford Holt, *The Buddhist Viṣṇu: Religious Transformation, Politics, and Culture* (New York: Columbia University Press, 2004), 165–6; and *Cūḷavaṃsa*, 97.46–7.

48 Codrington, *A Short History*, 138.

49 The main Nāyaka territories were in Singi in the northern Tamil country, in Tanjavur (Tanjore) south of Senji, and further south in Madurai. There were other Nāyaka regimes, the most prominent among these lesser regimes being Ikkeri. See K. D. Swaminathan, *The Nāyakas of Ikkeri* (Madras: P. Varadachary and Co., 1957). The kings of Vijayanagara known as *rāyas* employed Nāyaka warrior chiefs as 'governors' to rule their extensive southern kingdoms. These gradually became independent in a process completed after the fall of the Vijayanagara Empire in 1565. The Madurai Nāyakas effectively controlled the southernmost part of India known as the Ramnad through their own district representatives known as the *pālaiyakkārār* (aka *poligar*). During most of the Madurai period the local chiefs of the Ramnad were known as *sētupatis* (*cetupatis*) or lords of Rama's bridge, and they in turn owed allegiance to Madurai until that kingdom split up and disintegrated with the Muslim onslaughts from the late seventeenth century.

50 Lorna S. Dewaraja, *The Kandyan Kingdom of Sri Lanka: 1707–1782*, 2nd edn (Colombo: Stamford Lake Publication, 2008), 26 (emphasis added).

51 Lorna S. Dewaraja, 'The Kandyan Kingdom and the Nāyakkars, 1739–1796,' in *University of Peradeniya, History of Sri L anka*, Vol. 2, ed. K. M. de Silva. Peradeniya: University of Peradeniya, 1995, 281.

52 Abeyasinghe, 'The Kingdom of Kandy', 150. See also Knox, *Historical Relation*, 183, and Dewaraja, 'The Kandyan Kingdom 1638–1739: A Survey of its Political History,' in *University of Peradeniya, History of Sri Lanka*, Vol. 2, 183–209.
53 Biedermann, *Island Empire* and Chapter 7 in this volume.
54 Dewaraja, 'The Kandyan Kingdom 1638–1739', 200.
55 *Cūḷavaṃsa,* 96.41–2 as given in *The Mahāvaṃsa*, trans. L. C. Wijesinha (1889; reprint New Delhi: Asian Educational Services, 1996). Geiger's better-known translation has 'king's daughters', but this usage might not be the best rendering of *kaññā*, which means 'young women' or 'maidens' or 'unmarried women'.
56 *Mahāvaṃsa*, 97.3.
57 Dewaraja, *The Kandyan Kingdom* (1972), 33–6.
58 *Cūḷavaṃsa,* 97.24.
59 *Cūḷavaṃsa,* 97.10–11
60 *Cūḷavaṃsa*, 97.13–15. These were also of high social extraction – in line with an unfortunate tradition of social exclusiveness that continued throughout Kandyan times.
61 Malalgoda, *Buddhism in Sinhalese Society*, 50. The name Ganebanḍāra indicates he was a *ganinnsānse* (*gane*) and an aristocrat. Arasaratnam affirms that he was appointed chief priest, suggesting that some *ganinnsānses* were held in high regard as monks even if not fully ordained. See Arasaratnam, *Ceylon and the Dutch*, 63.
62 *Cūḷavaṃsa*, 97.26.
63 Sinnappah Arasaratnam, 'Introduction: The Dutch in Ceylon and South India, 1700–1750,' *Memoir of Julius Stein Van Gollenesse, Governor of Ceylon, 1743–1751* trans. and ed. S. Arasaratnam (Colombo: Department of National Archives, 1974), 13.
64 *Cūḷavaṃsa,* 98. 5–20.
65 For succinct accounts of these two events, see Arasaratnam, 'The Dutch in Ceylon', 14–15, and Dewaraja, *The Kandyan Kingdom* (1972), 89–90.
66 Sri Vijaya's hostile attitude to Catholicism is described in the *Cūḷavaṃsa*, 98.80–3.
67 For a brief account of Gonçalvez, see Don Peter, *Ceylon Church History*, 53–60. I refer the reader to Don Peter's work but shall employ Father S. G. Perera's chapter on Gonçalvez in *Historical Sketches* (Colombo: Catholic Book Depot, 1962), 110–20, that deals with Gonçalvez because its polemics help us understand the conflicts between Buddhists, Catholics and Dutch Calvinists during Gonçalvez's dispensation. For a more detailed account see S. G. Perera, *Life of Father Jacome Gonsalves* (Madurai: De Nobili Press, 1942).
68 Perera, *Historical Sketches*, 116.
69 Perera, *Historical Sketches*, 115.
70 Perera, *Historical Sketches*, 117. The date for the presentation of Budumula is from Perniola, *The Catholic Church*, Vol. 3, 24, n. 1.
71 'Report of the Mission of Ceylon, 1746,' in Perniola, *The Catholic Church*, Vol. 2, 491–511.
72 Perniola, *The Catholic Church*, Vol. 2, 492.
73 Perniola, *The Catholic Church*, Vol. 2, 492.
74 Perniola, *The Catholic Church*, Vol. 2, 493.
75 Perniola, *The Catholic Church*, Vol. 2, 493. The date is my inference.
76 Perniola, *The Catholic Church*, Vol. 2, 497.
77 Perniola, *The Catholic Church*, Vol. 2, 24. Perniola gives the accepted version of what transpired when he says that all the councillors except Ähälepola, the first Adigar in Kandy, favoured the expulsion.
78 See 'The Triumph of the Catholic Faith,' in Perniola, *The Catholic Church*, Vol. 2, 422–38, especially 436.
79 Perhaps early British censuses might be able to supply demographic data on the spread and presence of Catholic populations in the Kandyan kingdom. It should be remembered, however, that owing to the power and prestige of British rule, many Catholics would have switched to the Church of England – a transition facilitated by the many resemblances between Catholicism and Anglicanism.
80 Gananath Obeyesekere, *The Doomed King: A Requiem for Śri Vikrama Rājasinha* (forthcoming).
81 Lewis de Saram, 'The Dutch Embassy to Kandy in 1731–32: Diary of Wijesiriwardhana Maha Mudiyanse, Otherwise Called Lewis de Saram, Maha Mudaliyar,' trans. Paul E. Pieris, *Journal of the Royal Asiatic Society, Ceylon Branch* 21, 62 (1909), 1–34.
82 De Saram, 'The Dutch Embassy to Kandy', 19–20.
83 Arasaratnam, 'The Dutch in Ceylon', 9.
84 John Holt points out that Kīrti Śri was brother in law of Śri Vijaya's chief queen. He was selected to be king at age sixteen and formally consecrated four years later. Holt considers him to be a Tamil, but

more likely he was a Telugu speaker, the label *vaḍuga* meaning 'northerner', that is from the Telugu speaking north, in Andhra Pradesh. John Clifford Holt, *The Religious World of Kīrti Śri: Buddhism, Art and Politics in Late Mediaeval Sri Lanka* (New York: Oxford University Press, 1996), 11.

85 Holt, *Religious World of Kīrti Śri*, 10.

86 The only place I found reference to Kīrti Śri's addiction to sacred ash is *Śasanāvatīrnavarṇaṇāva*, ed. C. E. Godakumbura (Moratuva: Dodangoda and Company, 1956), 22.

87 A good account of this work is in P. B. Sannasgala, *Sinhala Sāhityavaṅśaya* (Colombo: Cultural Affairs Department, 1994), 507.

88 J. H. Nelson, *The Political History of the Madura Country, Ancient and Modern* (1868; reprint New Delhi: Asian Educational Services, 1989), 211.

89 The Pybus Embassy to Kandy.

90 J. P. Lewis, 'Andrew's Journal of a Tour to Candia in the Year 1796,' *Journal of the Royal Asiatic Society, Ceylon Branch* 26, 70 (1917), 95. The peculiar language use is that of Andrew's.

91 Dewaraja, *The Kandyan Kingdom* (1972), 218.

92 A custom recorded by the Portuguese in South India from the early sixteenth century: see Dewaraja, *The Kandyan Kingdom* (1972), 215, and Zoltán Biedermann, 'Imagining Asia from the Margins: Early Portuguese Mappings of the Continent's Architecture and Space,' in *Architecturalized Asia. Mapping the Continent through Architecture and Geography*, ed. V. Rujivacharakul, H. H. Hahn, K. T. Oshima and P. Christensen (Hong Kong: Hong Kong University Press, 2013), 40.

93 Dewaraja, *The Kandyan Kingdom* (1972), 215.

94 Dewaraja, 'The Kandyan Kingdom and the Nayākkars', 310.

95 Tri Sinhala refers to the classic division of the Island into three regions: Rajaraṭa, in the north, Maya Raṭa in the west, and Ruhuna in the south. After the thirteenth century, owing to the decline of the Rajaraṭa, that region was renamed as Pihiṭi Raṭa, or the established country. The union of the three divisions was the ideal aspiration of kings.

96 *Cūḷavaṃsa*, 85.109–12.

97 The only exception might have been Kīrti Śri, about whose large palace based on Madurai models we know too little to make clear assertions.

## Chapter 9: Through the lens of slavery

1 This contribution draws from previous research published by Alicia F. Schrikker, 'Conflict Resolution, Social Control and Law-Making in Eighteenth-Century Dutch Sri Lanka,' in *Exploring the Dutch Empire: Agents, Networks and Institutions, 1600–2000*, eds. Catia Antunes and Jos Gommans (London: Bloomsbury, 2015), and Kate J. Ekama, 'Slavery in Dutch Colombo' (ResMA dissertation, Leiden University, 2012). Where sections carry considerable overlap with these texts, this is clearly indicated in the annotation. Both the approach and central argument in this chapter are new and stand apart from the two mentioned works.

2 For analyses of the size and composition of the enslaved population of Colombo, see Gerrit Knaap, 'Europeans, Mestizos and Slaves: The Population of Colombo at the End of the Seventeenth Century,' trans. Robert Ross, *Itinerario* 5, 2 (1981), 84–101; Remco Raben, 'Batavia and Colombo: The Ethnic and Spatial Order of Two Colonial Cities, 1600–1800,' PhD dissertation, Leiden University, 1996; Ekama, 'Slavery in Dutch Colombo,' 8–12.

3 Important exceptions are found in the work of S. Arasaratnam and Remco Raben.

4 Lodewijk Wagenaar, *Galle, VOC-vestiging in Ceylon: beschrijving van een koloniale samenleving aan de vooravond van de Singalese opstand tegen het Nederlandse gezag, 1760* (Amsterdam: Bataafsche Leeuw, 1994).

5 Nadeera Rupesinghe, 'Negotiating Custom: Colonial Lawmaking in the Galle Landraad,' PhD dissertation, Leiden University, 2016.

6 Kerry Ward, *Networks of Empire: Forced Migration in the Dutch East India Company* (New York: Cambridge University Press, 2009); Ronit Ricci, *Islam Translated: Literature, Conversion, and the Arabic Cosmopolis of South and Southeast Asia* (Chicago: University of Chicago Press, 2011). For more specific work on Sri Lanka, see Ronit Ricci, 'From Java to Jaffna: Exile and Return in Dutch Asia in the 18th Century,' in *Exile in Colonial Asia: Kings, Convicts, Commemoration*, ed. R. Ricci (Honolulu: University of Hawai'i Press, 2016), 94–116.

7 Nirmal Dewasiri, *The Adaptable Peasant: Agrarian Society in Western Sri Lanka under Dutch rule, 1740–1800* (Leiden: Brill, 2008).

8 John D'Oyly, *A Sketch of the Constitution of the Kandyan Kingdom* (Dehiwala: Tisara Prakasakayo, 1974). The texts by Sawers are found among the papers of the commissioners of enquiry, and are published as an addition to the collection of D'Oyly in this volume.

9 Indrani Chatterjee and Richard Eaton, 'Introduction,' in *Slavery in South Asian History*, ed. Indrani Chatterjee and Richard Eaton (Bloomington: Indiana Universtity Press, 2006).

10 Michael Banks, 'Caste in Jaffna,' in *Aspects of Caste in South India, Ceylon and North-West Pakistan*, ed. E. R. Leach (Cambridge: Cambridge University Press, 1960), 61–77.

11 Sinnappah Arasaratnam, *Ceylon and the Dutch, 1600–1800: External Influences and Internal Change in Early Modern Sri Lanka* (Aldershot: Variorum, 1996).

12 Jim Warren, *The Sulu Zone, 1768–1898: The Dynamics of External Trade, Slavery, and Ethnicity in the Transformation of a Southeast Asian Maritime State* (Singapore: Singapore University Press, 1981).

13 Sanjay Subrahmanyam, 'Slaves and Tyrants: Dutch Tribulations in Seventeenth-Century Mrauk-u,' *Journal of Early Modern History* 1, 3 (1997), 201–53.

14 Markus Vink, '"The World's Oldest Trade": Dutch Slavery and Slave Trade in the Indian Ocean in the Seventeenth Century,' *Journal of World History* 24, 2 (2003), 131–77; Richard B. Allen, *European Slave Trading in the Indian Ocean, 1500–1850* (Athens: Ohio University Press, 2014), 16 (Table 1).

15 Allen, *European Slave Trading*.

16 Matthias van Rossum, *Kleurrijke Tragiek. De geschiedenis van slavernij in Azië onder de VOC* (Hilversum: Verloren, 2015) and Ward, *Networks of Empire*. Furthermore, slaves owned privately were rented out to the Company for manual labour. Knaap, 'Europeans, Mestizos and Slaves', 96. See also Raben, 'Batavia and Colombo', 110. This practice was followed in Batavia: Bondan Kanumoyoso, 'Beyond the City Wall: Society and Economic Development in the Ommelanden of Batavia, 1684–1740,' PhD dissertation, Leiden University, 2011, 113. And at the Cape: Nigel Worden, *Slavery in Dutch South Africa* (Cambridge: Cambridge University Press, 1985), 81, 88.

17 VOC official Dirk Willem van der Brugghen who lived in Colombo in the 1750s owned such an orchestra. Lex de Raat, *The Life of Governor Joan Gideon Loten, 1710–1789: A Personal History of a Dutch Virtuoso* (Hilversum: Verloren, 2012), 141, 144. This it seems was no exception, references to slave orchestras in the Dutch Empire being scattered. See for example Jean Gelman Taylor, *The Social World of Batavia, European and Euroasians in Colonial Indonesia*, 2nd edn (Madison, WI: University of Wisconsin Press, 2009), 100, 110, and D. R. M. Irving, 'Trading Tunes: Thomas Forrest, Malay Songs and Musical Exchange in the Malay Archipelago, 1774–1784,' in *Intercultural Exchange in Southeast Asia: History and Society in the Early Modern World*, ed. Tara Alberts and D. R. M. Irving (London: Tauris, 2013), 221, 229, n. 22.

18 Alicia Schrikker, 'Caught between Empires: VOC Families in Sri Lanka after the British Takeover, 1806–1808,' *Annales de démographie historique* 2 (2011), 127–47.

19 This section draws for the larger part on Ekama, 'Slavery in Dutch Colombo'.

20 For the Cape, see Robert Ross, *Cape of Torments: Slavery and Resistance in South Africa* (London: Routledge & Kegan Paul, 1983); Gerald Groenewald and Nigel Worden, eds. *Slavery in Dutch South Africa; Trials of Slavery: Selected documents concerning slaves from the criminal records of the Council of Justice at the Cape of Good Hope, 1705–1794* (Cape Town: Van Riebeeck Society, 2005). For Batavia, see Eric Jones, *Wives, Slaves and Concubines: A History of the Female Underclass of Dutch Asia* (DeKalb, Il: Northern Illinois University Press, 2010).

21 Tamar vs Laborde: Sri Lanka National Archive (SLNA) 1/4613, Criminal Roll (CR) 1791; Itam: SLNA 1/4673; Floris and Mannan Dias: SLNA 1/4607, CR 1759. For a detailed analysis of these cases and in particular of the concept of dishonour see Ekama, 'Slavery in Dutch Colombo'.

22 SLNA 1/4740. See Ekama, 'Slavery in Dutch Colombo', for an extensive analysis of the case.

23 SLNA 1/4146 for the particular examples mentioned.

24 The roots of this diversity went as far back as the Portuguese period, during which time Colombo 'became quite literally a melting pot'. Zoltán Biedermann, *The Portuguese in Sri Lanka and South India: Studies in the History of Diplomacy, Empire and Trade, 1500–1650* (Wiesbaden: Harrassowitz Verlag, 2014), chapter 10, esp. 142.

25 Linguistic transfer and adaptation is a particularly interesting dimension to explore in terms of the depth of interaction and effect. Lodewijk Wagenaar has found traces of the Dutch language in Sinhala, in the vocabulary around playing cards, among other areas. Lodewijk Wagenaar, 'The Cultural Dimension of the Dutch East India Company settlements in Dutch-Period Ceylon, 1700–1800,' in *Mediating Netherlandish Art and Material Culture in Asia*, ed. Thomas Da Costa Kauffmann and Michael North (Amsterdam: Amsterdam University Press, 2014), 172. Studies of the legacy of the languages spoken by slaves in Sri Lanka could yield useful insights. In South Africa, the Afrikaans language bears traces of Malay spoken by some of the imported slaves. For a brief note on

the development of the Afrikaans language see Nigel Worden, Elizabeth van Heyningen and Vivian Bickford-Smith, *Cape Town: The Making of a City* (Kenilworth: David Philip, 2004), 127.

26 SLNA 1/4692. All details of the case recounted here are from the court dossier. See Ekama, 'Slavery in Dutch Colombo' for narrative and analysis of this case and for other examples of such Sufi talismans in Cape Town and Batavia.

27 In Greek mythology, Deidamia was Achilles' lover. On the use of mythological, biblical and other categories of names for slaves, see Wagenaar, *Galle*, 51. On naming and the use of toponyms in Colombo and Cape Town see Ekama, 'Slavery in Dutch Colombo', 13–15.

28 Ronit Ricci, 'Asian and Islamic Crossings: Malay Writing in Nineteenth-Century Sri Lanka,' *South Asian History and Culture* 5, 2 (2014), 179–94. Also see Ricci, *Islam Translated*.

29 There is some overlap between this section and the previously published article by Schrikker, 'Conflict Resolution'.

30 Resolution Governor and Council of Colombo, 6 October 1780, National Archive, The Hague, Verenigde Oostindische Compagnie (VOC), access number 1.04.02, inventory number *3573*.

31 Letter from the governor general to Batavia, 28 January 1793, National Archive, The Hague, VOC, 1.04.02, inventory number *3878*, fol. 2188–89. The name of the Chetty involved is not given in the letter.

32 Lodewijk Hovy, *Ceylonees Plakkaatboek: Plakkaten en andere wetten uitgevaardigd door het Nederlandse bestuur op Ceylon, 1638–1796*, 2 vols. (Hilversum: Verloren, 1991), xcviii–cix. See also Tambyah Nadaraja, *The Legal System of Ceylon in its Historical Setting* (Leiden: Brill, 1972).

33 Carla van Wamelen, *Family life onder de VOC. Een handelscompanie in huwelijks- en gezinszaken* (Hilversum: Verloren, 2015).

34 Van Wamelen, *Family life onder de VOC*.

35 Hovy, *Ceylonees Plakkaatboek*, Vol. 1, 62, plakkaat 59.

36 Allen, *European Slave Trading*. Vink, 'The World's Oldest Trade'.

37 Hovy, *Ceylonees Plakkaatboek*, Vol. 1, 97, plakkaat 65 (20).

38 Hovy, *Ceylonees Plakkaatboek*, Vol. 1, 227, plakkaat 163.

39 *Memoir of Hendrick Zwaardecroon, commandeur of Jaffnapatam, (afterwards governor-general of Nederlands India), 1697, for the guidance of the council of Jaffnapatam, during his absence at the coast of Malabar Memoir*, trans. Sophia Pieters (Colombo: Cottle, 1911). This number is often reproduced in the literature. Zwaardecroon gives interesting context revealing that this should not be taken as simply 'Dutch slave trade'. Zwaardencroon quotes this number when he discusses whether this trade is beneficial to the Company. The trade yields import duties, so in that sense the company benefits, but he witnessed the larger part of these slaves traded to the Vanniyar chiefs, who potentially transported them into Kandy. Furthermore, he reasons, import of more people means more mouths to feed, while rice rather than labour was dear at the time. He explicitly states that he would have preferred it if traders had brought in rice rather than humans. The relationship between rice and slave markets in the Indian Ocean would be an interesting line of enquiry, but well beyond the scope of this paper.

40 Hovy, *Ceylonees Plakkaatboek*. For a more extensive analysis of themes and issues relating to slaves in the ordinances see Ekama, 'Slavery in Dutch Colombo', 30–42.

41 Governor general to Batavia, 28 January *1793*, National archive, The Hague, VOC, 1.04.02, inventory number *3878*, fol. 2188–2189.

42 Resolution in Council, 20 May 1780, National archive, The Hague, VOC, 1.04.02, inventory number *3571*. For a more extensive discussion of the case of Ali van Makassar and other examples of this cultural relativism in the practice of justice see Schrikker, 'Conflict Resolution'.

43 Hovy, *Ceylonees Plakkaatboek*, Vol. 2, 762, plakkaat 518.

44 SLNA 1/2711; NA CO 54/125. This a highly reflective and informative memorandum on the administration of Batticaloa, written up by Jacob Burnand in 1793. See also Alicia Schrikker, *Dutch and British Colonial Intervention in Sri Lanka, 1780–1815* (Leiden: Brill, 2007), 89–92.

45 The name Chandios is not used in Tamil. According to Arasaratnam it is probably a Dutch and Portuguese corruption of the word Shanar, a caste he suggests developed into the Naḷavar caste during the Jaffna kingdom. As the Theswalamai is of later date and clearly makes a distinction between the Chandios and the Naḷavar, we decided to use the colonial term Chandios here to avoid confusion. Arasaratnam, S. 'Social History of a Dominant Caste Society: The Vellalar of North Ceylon in the 18th Century,' *Indian Economic and Social History Review* 18, 3–4 (1982), 380–81.

46 Hovy, *Ceylonees Plakkaatboek*. M. Jurriaanse, 'The Compilation of the Customary Law of Jaffna,' *Bijdragen tot de Taal-, Land- en Volkenkunde / Journal of the Humanities and Social Sciences of Southeast Asia* (BKI) 110, 4 (1954), 293–304; see also Nadaraja, *The Legal System*. In short, by

around 1700 the *landraad* was malfunctioning: too many cases were brought forward in which the judges could not reach a verdict and this delayed the operation of the court to such an extent that the governor asked for a collection to be made of all ordinances regarding Jaffna that were published by the Company. In what came to be referred to as the Jaffna Compendium, the relationship between the Company and Jaffna subject stood central. It dealt with rights and duties, criminal offences, and some provisions were made regarding family law and property, but these did not suffice. It turned out that the majority of cases brought forward dealt with more complex civil disputes over material transactions and inheritance issues. This led the rural administrator, *dessave* Isaac Isaaksz, to embark upon the difficult task of composing an overview of the Jaffna customary laws.

47 Nadaraja, *The Legal System*.

48 Nadaraja, *The Legal System*.

49 Arasaratnam, 'Social History of a Dominant Caste Society'.

50 C. van Vollenhoven, ed., 'Ceilonsch volksrecht opgetekend in 1707. Met glossarium van P.S. van Ronkel,' *Bijdragen tot de Taal-, Land- en Volkenkunde/Journal of the Humanities and Social Sciences of Southeast Asia* (BKI) 75 (1919), 240–80.

51 Van Vollenhoven, 'Ceilonsch volksrecht'.

52 Van Vollenhoven, 'Ceilonsch volksrecht'.

53 Van Vollenhoven, 'Ceilonsch volksrecht'.

54 Jurriaanse, 'The Compilation of the Customary Law of Jaffna'; Arasaratnam, 'Social History of a Dominant Caste Society'.

55 How local people responded to the way they were classified would be a fruitful line of enquiry – civil and criminal court cases from Jaffna, Galle and Colombo kept in the Sri Lankan National Archives could be scrutinized to understand the practice of this negotiation.

56 Alicia Schrikker, '"Op de dijk gezet." Schuld, onrust en bestuurlijke onzekerheid in Jaffna in de achttiende eeuw,' in *Aan de overkant. Ontmoetingen in dienst van de VOC en WIC (1600–1800)*, ed. Lodewijk Wagenaar (Leiden: Sidestone Press, 2015), 145–65.

57 John D. Rogers, 'Post-Orientalism and the Interpretation of Premodern and Modern Political Identities: The Case of Sri Lanka,' *Journal of Asian Studies* 53, 1 (1994), 10–23; Arasaratnam, 'Social History of a Dominant Caste Society'.

## Chapter 10: Cosmopolitanism and indigeneity

1 I am very grateful to the editors and to Robert Aldrich at the University of Sydney for very close readings of this chapter.

2 P. E. Pieris, *Sinhalē and the Patriots, 1815–1818* (1950; reprint Delhi: Navrang, 1995), 422. This is a highly narrative volume, heavily based on primary materials. Sometimes the precise quotations are difficult to track because of the style of footnoting adopted by Pieris.

3 K. M. de Silva, *A History of Sri Lanka* (Chennai: Oxford University Press, 1981), 235.

4 Tennakoon Vimalananda, *The British Intrigue in the Kingdom of Ceylon* (Colombo: M. D. Gunasena, 1973); Tennakoon Vimalananda, *The Great Rebellion of 1818: The Story of the First War of Independence and the Betrayal of the Nation* (Colombo: M. D. Gunasena, 1970); and also Tennakoon Vimalananda, *Sri Wickrema, Brownrigg and Ehelapola: Being Letters Addressed to the Home Government from 1811–1815 by Major General John Wilson and Lieut-General Robert Brownrigg, Governor of Ceylon* (Colombo: M. D. Gunasena, 1984). Vimalananda provides a partial sample of sources and does not routinely reproduce enclosures to despatches, therefore showing a bias towards the highest level of correspondence between London and Colombo.

5 See Alan Strathern, Chapter 11 in this volume, for 'grammar of rebellion'. For his account of an earlier period of rebellion see, Alan Strathern, 'Treachery and Ethnicity in Portuguese Representations of Sri Lanka', in *Engaging Colonial Knowledge: Reading European Archives in World History*, ed. Ricardo Roque and Kim Wagner (Basingstoke: Palgrave Macmillan,2012), 217–34. For recent work on rebellion in the early British period, see Nira Wickramasinghe, 'Many Little Revolts or One Rebellion? The Maritime Provinces of Ceylon/Sri Lanka between 1796 and 1800,' *South Asia: Journal of South Asian Studies* 32 (2009), 170–88; James Wilson, 'Reappropriation, Resistance and British Autocracy in Sri Lanka, 1820–1850,' forthcoming in *The Historical Journal*; Kumari Jayawardena, *Perpetual Ferment: Popular Revolts in Sri Lanka in the Eighteenth and Nineteenth Centuries* (Colombo: Social Scientists' Association, 2010).

6 This chapter builds on Sujit Sivasundaram, *Islanded: Britain, Sri Lanka and the Bounds of an Indian Ocean Colony* (Chicago: University of Chicago Press, 2014).

7 For debates about this colonial transition from multiple perspectives see Seema Alavi, ed., *The Eighteenth Century in India* (Delhi: Oxford University Press, 1998); C. A. Bayly, *The Origins of Nationality in India: Patriotism and Ethical Government in the Making of Modern India* (Delhi: Oxford University Press, 1998); Partha Chatterjee, *The Nation and its Fragments: Colonial and Postcolonial Histories* (Princeton, NJ: Princeton University Press, 1993); Nicholas Dirks, *Castes of Mind: Colonialism and the Making of Modern India* (Princeton, NJ: Princeton University Press 2001); Peter Marshall, ed., *The Eighteenth Century in Indian History: Evolution or Revolution?* (Delhi: Oxford University Press, 2003); Jon Wilson, *The Domination of Strangers: Modern Governance in Eastern India 1780–1835* (Basingstoke: Palgrave Macmillan, 2008); Gyan Prakash, 'Writing Post-Orientalist Histories of the Third World: Perspectives from Indian Historiography,' *Comparative Studies in Society and History* 31 (1990), 383–408.

8 Sivasundaram, *Islanded*, for example 294–6. For the relationship between Dutch modes of governance and British ones, see Alicia Schrikker, *Dutch and British Colonial Intervention in Sri Lanka, 1780–1815* (Leiden: Brill, 2007) and Nadeera Rupesinghe, 'Negotiating Custom: Colonial Lawmaking in the Galle Landraad,' PhD dissertation, University of Leiden, 2015. For definitions of the 'native' in Lanka in a comparative lens see Sujit Sivasundaram, 'Appropriation to Supremacy: Ideas of the "Native" in the Rise of British Imperial Heritage,' in *From Plunder to Preservation: Britain and the Heritage of Empire, c.1800–1940*, ed. Peter Mandler and Astrid Swenson (Oxford: British Academy Publications, 2013), 149–70.

9 All quotations in this paragraph from letter dated Kandy, 28 April 1818, from Robert Brownrigg to His Excellency the Marquis of Hastings, CO 54/70, The National Archives, Kew, London (hereafter TNA).

10 For the nature of this period and the relationship between definitions of Britain at home and overseas see, C. A. Bayly, *Imperial Meridian: The British Empire and the World, 1780–1830* (London: Longman, 1989). For earlier relations between changing tides of European politics (in the Iberian union of Crowns) and Sri Lankan events see Zoltán Biedermann, 'The *Matrioshka* Principle and How it was Overcome: Portuguese and Habsburg Imperial Attitudes in Sri Lanka and the Response of the Rulers of Kotte,' *Journal of Early Modern History* 13, 4 (2009), 265–310.

11 Despatch dated 5 June 1816 from Robert Brownrigg to the Earl Bathurst, C0 54/60, TNA.

12 Despatch dated 19 February 1818, from Robert Brownrigg to the Earl Bathurst, CO 54/70, TNA.

13 This picks up on the argument of Michael Roberts, *Sinhala Consciousness in the Kandyan Period: 1590s to 1815* (Colombo: Vijitha Yapa Press, 2004). However, it builds on this argument to make the point that this kind of associational logic could cut in multiple ways, allowing Britons to cast themselves as Kandyan kings and allowing outsiders to take up the rhetoric and practice of Sinhalaness.

14 For more on this see, Sivasundaram, *Islanded*, chapter 8.

15 For how I use cosmopolitanism and indigeneity here please see, Sivasundaram, *Islanded*, 12–13. 'Indigeneity' is consistent with the looseness and 'inter-meshing' across local and Portuguese, which Strathern emphasizes with respect to indigenism. See Alan Strathern, *Kingship and Conversion in Sixteenth-Century Sri Lanka. Portuguese Imperialism in a Buddhist Land* (Cambridge: Cambridge University Press, 2007), 236ff.

16 This picks up on the notion of the galactic kingdom proposed by Stanley J. Tambiah, *World Conqueror and World Renouncer: A Study of Buddhism and Polity in Thailand Against a Historical Background* (Cambridge: Cambridge University Press, 1976).

17 Extracts of Letters from Major Hardy to His Excellency the Governor, CO 54/56, TNA. These 'extracts' together with those from Sawers used below are followed by 'extracts' from D'Oyly, and appear as an addendum to a despatch dated 20 July 1815; they range across fifty pages of manuscript copy.

18 'Obituary of Lieut. Col. Hardy,' *The Gentleman's Magazine* 4 (1835), 549.

19 Extracts of Letters from Major Hardy.

20 Pieris, *Sinhalē and the Patriots*, 61.

21 Extracts of Letters from Major Hardy.

22 Extracts of Letters from Major Hardy.

23 Extracts of Letters from Major Hardy.

24 For the role of Muslims for instance in the Kandyan territories see Lorna Dewaraja, *The Muslims of Sri Lanka* (Colombo: Lanka Islamic Foundation, 1994).

25 It is notable that Hardy had a map with him and took note of where the 1803 war took place.

26 Despatch dated 5 June 1816 from Brownrigg to Bathurst, CO 54/60.

27 C. A. Bayly, 'The First Age of Global Imperialism, c.1780–1830,' *The Journal of Imperial and Commonwealth History*, 26 (1998), 28–47; Bayly, *Imperial Meridian*. For rising numbers of troops and tactics of war by the eighteenth century, see Channa Wickremesekera, *Kandy at War: Indigenous Military Resistance to European Expansion in Sri Lanka, 1594–1818* (Vijitha Yapa: Colombo, 2004). One critical factor was British ability to bring to Lanka troops from India and to organize their troops in small detachments that scoured the entire territory, see Wickremesekera, *Kandy at War*, 208.

28 Extracts of Letters from Mr. Sawers to the Secretary of the Kandyan Provinces, CO 54/56, TNA.

29 Extracts of Letters from Mr Sawers.

30 These were all reported in despatch dated 26 September 1815 from Robert Brownrigg to the Earl Bathurst, CO 54/56, TNA.

31 Despatch dated Kandy, 7 November 1817, from Robert Brownrigg to the Earl Bathurst, CO 54/66, TNA.

32 For the punishments meted out to the rebels see, 'Return of Courts Martial held in the Kandyan Provinces under the several Proclamations declaring Martial Law,' CO 54/73, TNA.

33 Despatch dated Kandy, 7 November 1817, from Brownrigg to Bathurst, CO 54/66, TNA.

34 Despatch dated 5 June 1815, from Brownrigg to Bathurst, CO 54/60, TNA.

35 Despatch dated 5 June 1815.

36 Despatch dated Colombo, 5 November 1816, CO 54/61, TNA.

37 This quote and the one below arise from 'Narrative of Eknellegode Nilame,' dated Ratnapura, 20 July 1816, CO 54/61, TNA.

38 See Biedermann, Chapter 7 in this volume for the earlier history of throne pretenders moving across the straits with their retinues.

39 'Narrative of Eknellegode Nilame'.

40 Pieris, *Sinhalē and the Patriots*, 134.

41 Eknäligoḍa Nilame reported that 'Caffir' troops had allegedly been contacted by those plotting rebellion in 1816, in 'Narrative of Eknellegode Nilame'.

42 Despatch dated Kandy, 24 July 1818, from Robert Brownrigg to the Earl Bathurst, CO 54/71, TNA.

43 Letter from L. De Bussche, dated Kandy, 1 May 1818, CO 54/71, TNA.

44 Despatch dated Colombo, 8 January 1819, from Robert Brownrigg to the Earl Bathurst, CO 54/73, TNA, and dispatch dated Colombo, 1 April 1819, from Robert Brownrigg to the Earl Bathurst, CO 54/74, TNA.

45 Despatch dated Colombo, 5 November 1816, from Brownrigg to Bathurst.

46 Pieris, *Sinhalē and the Patriots*, 301.

47 This forms a central concern of my present research project and a book tentatively titled *Revolutionary Empire*.

48 Pieris labels Ähālēpola as a patriot and critiques the colonial literature for ignoring the fact that there was no evidence about his intrigues with the rebels; see Pieris, *Sinhalē and the Pariots*, 416–18

49 Brownrigg himself noted how Ähälēpola was referred to as second king in these years, see Pieris, *Sinhalē and the Patriots*, 82.

50 See C. E. Godakumbura, *Sinhalese Literature* (Colombo: The Colombo Apothecaries' Co., 1955), 241.

51 All quotations from the Ähälēpola Hatana arise from translation undertaken with Prof. Udaya Meddegama from K.F. Perera, *Ehalepola Hatanaya* (Colombo: Subhadraloka Press, 1911).

52 Despatch dated Colombo, 8 January 1819, from Brownrigg to Bathurst, CO 54/73. For famine as a tactic of the suppression of the rebellion, see, Pieris, *Sinhalē and the Patriots*, 343

53 All quotations from the *Vadiga Hatana* from translation undertaken with Prof. Udaya Meddegama from Kusuma Jayasuriya, *Waduga Hatana* (Colombo: Department of Cultural Affairs, 1966).

54 Despatch dated Kandy, 27 November 1817, from Brownrigg to Bathurst, Co 54/66, TNA.

55 See Pieris, *Sinhalē and the Patriots*, 33–6.

56 Despatch dated Colombo, 26 September 1815, from Robert Brownrigg to the Earl Bathurst, CO 54/56, TNA.

57 Despatch dated Colombo, 5 November 1816, from Brownrigg to Bathurst, CO 54/61, TNA.

58 Pieris, *Sinhalē and the Patriots*, 36, 79.

59 Despatch dated Kandy, 24 July 1818, from Robert Brownrigg to the Earl Bathurst, CO 54/71, TNA.

60 Quotation from *ibid*. Other artefacts connected with royal prerogative kept falling out of British hands in this period. In addition to the jewels given by Ähälēpola to the British, the ran kāduwa (gold sword) as well as oṭunna (crown) were removed to Ūva. See Pieris, *Sinhalē and the Patriots*, 154.

61 Pieris, *Sinhalē and the Patriots*, 322.

62 Letter dated Kandy, 23 February 1818, from Robert Brownrigg to the Marquis Hastings, CO 54/71, TNA.

63 Letter dated Kandy, 23 February 1818, from Brownrigg to the Marquis Hastings. For the inquiry of Doraisāmi's whereabouts see letter dated Colombo, 27 October 1817, from James Sutherland, Secretary of the Kandyan Provinces to the Chief Secretary of Government, Fort St. George, P/318/9, India Office Collections, British Library, London (hereafter IOC). See Biedermann, Chapter 7 in this volume for Lankan princes in South India and their migrations.
64 De Silva, *A History of Sri Lanka*, 232; and also see Pieris, *Sinhalē and the Patriots*, 248–9.
65 Despatch dated Kandy, 27 October 1818, from Robert Brownrigg to the Earl Bathurst, CO 54/71, TNA.
66 Cited from Sujit Sivasundaram, 'Buddhist Kingship, British Archaeology and Historical Narratives in Sri Lanka c. 1750–1850,' *Past & Present* 197 (2007), 130.
67 Despatch dated Kandy, 31 October 1818, from Robert Brownrigg to the Earl Bathurst, CO 54/71, TNA; for Ähälēpola see de Silva, *A History of Sri Lanka*, 234.
68 Despatch dated Colombo, 8 January 1819, from Robert Brownrigg to the Earl Bathurst, CO 54/73, TNA.
69 Pieris, *Sinhalē and the Patriots*, 116.
70 Despatch dated Colombo, 8 January 1819, from Brownrigg to Bathrust, CO 54/73.
71 Pieris, *Sinhalē and the Patriots*, 217.
72 See for this and also for the idea of 'islanding' as also the repatriation of Kandyan Malabars, which follow in the first two paragraphs in the next section, Sivasundaram, *Islanded*.
73 Regulation of Government No. 6 of 1816, P 318/1, IOC.
74 Letter dated Colombo, 29 July 1816, from Robert Brownrigg to Hugh Elliot, P 317/94, IOC.
75 See correspondence in P 318/12, IOC.
76 Letter dated 19 July 1816 from Robert Brownrigg to Hugh Elliot, P 317/94, IOC.
77 All of the above from the papers in P 318/17, IOC.
78 See Sivasundaram, *Islanded*, chapter 1 for more on this.
79 These cases are discussed and quotations appear in Sivasundaram, *Islanded*, 50–4.
80 For the 'young Malabar priest of Buddhu' see letter dated Kandy 26 February 1817 from John D'Oyly to James Sutherland, Lot 21 51/B and for this quotation, letter dated Kandy 19 June 1819 from John D'Oyly to James Sutherland, Lot 21 51/B, the National Archives of Sri Lanka, Kandy Branch.
81 Letter dated 31 August 1829 from J. W. Huskisson, Collector Manar Cutcherry to Advocate Fiscal, Jaffna. Lot 19/96, The National Archives of Sri Lanka, Colombo.
82 Regulations concerning strangers and new arrival in the colony, despatch dated 22 November 1831 from Robert Horton to Lord Viscount Goderich, CO 54/114, TNA.
83 For the detailed attempt to remodel the Kandyan territories in the aftermath of the rebellion see: Minute of his Excellency the Governor addressed to the Board of Commissioners in Kandy, dated Kandy, 25 September 1819, CO 54/73, TNA.
84 For more on this and the 'limits of cosmopolitanism' see the editors' introduction and also Strathern, Chapter 11 in this volume.
85 For the materiality of palm-leaf and paper see Sujit Sivasundaram, 'Materialities in the making of World History: South Asia and the South Pacific,' in *Oxford Handbook for History and Material Culture* (forthcoming).
86 Sivasundaram, 'Buddhist Kingship' seeks to do this for Nuvarakalāviya.
87 See for instance the classic work of Eric Stokes, *The Peasant Armed: The Indian Revolt of 1857* (Oxford: Clarendon, 1986); C. A. Bayly, *Empire and Information: Intelligence Gathering and Social Communication in India, 1780–1870* (Cambridge: University of Cambridge, 2000); T. R. Metcalf, *Ideologies of the Raj* (Cambridge: Cambridge University Press, 1994); Crispin Bates, *Mutiny on the Margins: New Perspectives on the Indian Rebellion of 1857*, 6 vols. (New Delhi: Sage, 2013); Ranajit Guha, ed., *Subalatern Studies IV* (Delhi: Oxford University Press, 1994); and other writings of the subaltern studies collective.
88 Wickramasinghe, 'Many Little Revolts'.
89 Wickramasinghe, 'Many Little Revolts', 187.
90 This is not an intervention in the debate about 'stranger-kings' in historical anthropology as much as a comment on how the period's sense of the 'stranger' shifted as the British start to deal with strangers. For the former see, Alan Strathern, 'The Vijaya Origin Myth of Sri Lanka and the Strangeness of Kingship,' *Past & Present* 203 (2013), 3–28.
91 For some basic details, see 'Great Battle Against British Rule', *The Sunday Times Magazine*, 9 February 2014, www.sundaytimes.lk/140209/magazine/great-battle-against-british-rule-84509.html, accessed 13 August 2014.

# Chapter 11: Digestion of the foreign in Lankan history

I would like to thank Peter Ditmanson for his assistance in translating a portion of a Chinese text, and Victor Lieberman, Justin Henry and Zoltán Biedermann for their comments.

1 As in E. Hobsbawm and T. Ranger, eds., *The Invention of Tradition* (Cambridge: Cambridge University Press, 1983). To judge by the papers at a recent large conference ('Identity, Ethnicity, and Nationhood before Modernity: Old Debates and New Perspectives,' at Oxford University, 24–26 April 2015), there is now, however, considerable appetite among premodern scholars to push ethnic and even national sentiments deep into the premodern era.

2 He was not related to the first Kandyan dynasty, but was the son of a nobleman, Vīrasundara Baṇḍāra, installed by Rājasiṃha I of Sītāvaka.

3 His new wife, Dona Catarina, may have been a member of the old ruling Baṇḍāra family of Kandy, but her Lusitanization was no more superficial: she remained an apparently sincere Catholic to the end. See Joris van Spilbergen, *Journal of Spilbergen: The First Dutch Envoy to Ceylon, 1602*, ed. and trans. K. D. Paranavitana. (Colombo: Sridevi Printers, 1997), 30–2, 39, 43; Alan Strathern, *Kingship and Conversion in Sixteenth-Century Sri Lanka* (Cambridge: Cambridge University Press, 2007), 217; and Gananath Obeyesekere's contribution to this volume (Chapter 8).

4 Gananath Obeyesekere, 'On Buddhist Identity in Sri Lanka,' in *Ethnic Identity: Creation, Conflict and Accommodation*, ed. Lola Romanucci-Rossi and George A. de Vos (London: Mayfield, 1995), 222–41; S. J. Tambiah, *Buddhism Betrayed? Religion, Politics and Violence in Sri Lanka* (Chicago: University of Chicago Press 1992), 129–77.

5 The focus of the chapter is therefore on the Sinhala-speaking elite groups of the island.

6 Sheldon Pollock, *The Language of the Gods in the World of Men: Sanskrit, Culture, and Power in Premodern India* (Berkeley and Los Angeles: University of California Press, 2009), 12.

7 Pollock, *Language of the Gods*, 26, on the 'cosmopolitan vernacular – that register of the emergent vernacular that aims to localize the full spectrum of literary qualities of the supposed cosmopolitan code'.

8 Pollock, *Language of the Gods*, 28.

9 Also see Charles Hallisey, 'Works and Persons in Sinhala Literary Culture,' in *Literary Cultures in History: Reconstructions from South Asia*, ed. Sheldon Pollock (Berkeley and Los Angeles: University of California Press, 2003), 721.

10 He goes on: 'though important *kāvya* in the language was produced there and power did sometimes express itself in Sanskrit as late as the mid-ninth century. Yet Sanskrit was a shaping force behind the scenes in Sri Lanka and elsewhere in the Pāli world.' Pollock, *Language of the Gods*, 386. See Gornall and Henry in this volume on the development of Pāli as literary language under Sanskritic influence (Chapter 4).

11 Pollock, *Language of the Gods*, 399.

12 Pollock, *Language of the Gods*, 387.

13 Pollock, *Language of the Gods*, 413. On Lankan understandings of the term *cakravarti* in this period see John Clifford Holt, *The Buddhist Viṣṇu: Religious Transformation, Politics and Culture* (New York: Columbia University Press, 2004), 41, and S. Pathmanathan, 'South India and Sri Lanka, AD 1450–1650: Political, Commercial and Cultural Relations,' *Journal of Tamil Studies* 21 (1982), 36–57.

14 Pollock, *Language of the Gods*, 390.

15 The most significant example being the expeditions sent to Southeast Asia by Parākramabāhu I (1153–86). Jonathan Walters, 'Buddhist History: The Sri Lankan Pāli Vaṃsas and their Community,' in *Querying the Medieval: Texts and the History of Practices in South Asia*, ed. Ronald Inden, Jonathan Walters and Daud Ali (New York, 2000), 141, argues that the Okkaka dynasty's claims to dominance over South Indian dynasties was a serious expression of the political imagination. See also Pollock, *Language of the Gods*, 420, and Berkwitz's discussion in this book of the geography of the fifteenth-century Sandēśa poems (Chapter 5).

16 Holt, *Buddhist Viṣṇu*, 42–3.

17 R. A. L. H. Gunawardana, 'The People of the Lion: The Sinhala Identity and Ideology in History and Historiography,' in *Sri Lanka: History and the Roots of Conflict*, ed. Jonathan Spencer (London and New York: Routledge, 1990), 61. Also see Hallisey, 'Works and Persons in Sinhala Literary Culture', 733.

18 Strathern, *Kingship and Conversion*, 127–28.

19 See Lorna Dewaraja, 'The Indigenisation of the Muslims of Sri Lanka,' in *Sesquicentennial Commemorative Volume of the Royal Asiatic Society of Sri Lanka, 1845–1995*, ed. G. P. S. H. de Silva and C. G. Uragoda (Colombo: Royal Asiatic Society of Sri Lanka, 1995), 427–39.

20 Also see Elizabeth Nissan and R. L. Stirrat, 'The Generation of Communal Identities,' in *Sri Lanka: History and the Roots of Conflict*, 19–44, which is influenced by Gellnerian modernization theory.

21 R. R. Davies, 'The People of Britain and Ireland 1100–1400. I. Identities,' *Transactions of the Royal Historical Society*, Sixth Series 4 (1994), 11. Indeed, premodern polities in general contained an 'imperial' propensity to rule over others. The distinction between imperial and vernacular polities cannot therefore be pushed too far.

22 See Gunawardana, 'People of the Lion', 69, and Michael Roberts, 'Ethnicity after Said: Post-Orientalist Failures in Comprehending the Kandyan Period of Lankan History,' *Ethnic Studies Report* 19 (2001), 69–98, for two contrasting views.

23 Pollock, *Language of the Gods*, 474, see also 505–10, and Sheldon Pollock, 'Cosmopolitan and Vernacular in History', in *Cosmopolitanism*, ed. Sheldon Pollock, Homi K. Bhabha, Carol Appadurai Breckenridge and Dipesh Chakrabarty (Durham, NC and London: Duke University Press, 2002), 36–7.

24 Pollock, *Language of the Gods*, 476, 510.

25 Pollock, *Language of the Gods*, 475. Although Pollock refers to 'Indian' texts here, in the same paragraph he refers to 'South Asian'.

26 Pollock, *Language of the Gods*, 276. Shared descent is emphasized in the list of features of ethnicity in Anthony D. Smith, *National Identity* (London: Penguin, 1991), 21–2.

27 Davies, 'People of Britain and Ireland', 4.

28 Davies, 'People of Britain and Ireland', 6.

29 John Watts, *The Making of Polities: Europe, 1300–1500* (Cambridge: Cambridge University Press, 2009), 141–3.

30 As Pollock, *Language of the Gods*, 511, says, the great Indian regional narratives are of kings and places – to which we must add in the Lankan case, monastic orders.

31 See Berkwitz, Chapter 5 in this volume and Alan Strathern, 'Towards the Source-Criticism of Sītāvakan Heroic Literature. Part 2: The *Sītāvaka Haṭana*: Notes on a Grounded Text,' *Sri Lanka Journal of the Humanities* 34 (2008), 45–72.

32 Pollock, *Language of the Gods*, 475–6, 510. See Gunawardana, 'People of the Lion', 63, for evidence of the rigidity of caste (*jāti*) distinctions in the eleventh century, for example. See also John D. Rogers, 'Caste as a Social Category and Identity in Colonial Lanka,' *The Indian and Economic Social History Review* 41 (2004), 51–77.

33 At one point Pollock, *Language of the Gods*, 511, indicates that this definition is only according to 'current scholarly opinion', and he shows little inclination elsewhere to tag along where current scholarly opinion leads. Yet alternative definitions of ethnicity or 'peoplehood' are not explored.

34 Davies, 'People of Britain and Ireland', 4.

35 Obeyesekere, 'On Buddhist Identity', 230.

36 Davies, 'People of Britain and Ireland', 9, on Ireland in particular, which had a much weaker all-island regnal tradition than Lanka. Otherwise it is a good comparator for Sri Lanka given that it is roughly the same size and also endowed with a form of hierarchical kingship and awkward relations with overbearing neighbours. Indeed, according to Patrick Wadden, 'Ethnic or National? Identity in early Medieval Ireland,' paper at the 'Identity, Ethnicity, and Nationhood before Modernity' conference (see footnote 1), Irish common identity persisted despite a far weaker record of actual political attainment of unity than we find in Lanka.

37 Davies, 'People of Britain and Ireland'.

38 Including features that Pollock identifies beyond fictive kinship, for example, 'a discourse that links language, identity, and polity'. Michael Roberts has published extensively on Sinhala ethnicity. His latest account is 'Sinhalaness and its Reproduction, 1232–1818,' in *The Sri Lankan Republic at Forty: Reflections on Constitutional History, Theory and Practice*, Vol. 1, ed. Asanga Welikala (Colombo: Centre for Policy Alternatives, 2012), 253–87.

39 *Mahāvaṃsa, The Great Chronicle of Sri Lanka*, trans. Ananda W. Guruge (Colombo: Associated Newspapers of Ceylon, 1989), chapters 6–7; *The Dīpavaṃsa*, trans. Hermann Oldenburg (1879; reprint New Delhi: Asian Educational Services, 2004), chapter 9.

40 See Alan Strathern, 'The Vijaya Origin Myth of Sri Lanka and the Strangeness of Kingship,' *Past and Present* 203 (2009), 3–28.

41 Strathern 'The Vijaya Origin Myth'. Since writing the latter I have come across Peter Schalk, 'Referents and Meanings of Siṃhala/Sīhaḷa/Ciṅkaḷam,' in *Kontinuitäten und Brüche in der Religionsgeschichte*, ed. Michael Stausberg (Berlin and Boston: De Gruyter, 2012), but it does not bear centrally on the main arguments here.

42 Gunawardana, 'People of the Lion', and later, *Historiography in a Time of Ethnic Conflict: Construction of the Past in Contemporary Sri Lanka* (Colombo: Social Scientists' Association, 1995); K. N. O. Dharmadasa, *Language, Religion and Ethnic Awareness: The Growth of Sinhalese Nationalism in Sri Lanka* (Michigan: University of Michigan Press, 1992).

43 Gunawardana, *Historiography*, 35–51. The phrase 'public transcript' is taken from James C. Scott, *Domination and the Arts of Resistance: Hidden Transcripts* (New Haven: Yale University Press, 1990).

44 Gunawardana, *Historiography*, 41; compare Dharmadasa, *Language, Religion*, 20.

45 Gunawardana argues that the text should be read as referring to (some) residents of the land; Dharmadasa to (the) residents of the land. Yet if one grants the former, this may simply refer to the fact that the Sinhalas shared the island with Tamil-speakers and *väddās* and others. The tenth-century *Vaṃsatthappakāsinī* says that the 700 followers and all their descendants 'up to the present day' are called Sinhala. Gunawardana argues that this implies the exclusion of the service castes whose arrival is also mentioned. But see Alan Strathern, 'Vijaya and Romulus: Interpreting the Origin Myths of Sri Lanka and Rome,' *Journal of the Royal Asiatic Society of Great Britain and Ireland* 24 (2013), 12–13, for a different interpretation of the significance of the arrival of the service castes in the Mahāvaṃsa. See Hallisey, 'Works and Persons in Sinhala Literary Culture', 730, for a tenth-century Sanskrit reference to the 'Island of the Sinhalas'.

46 Pollock, *Language of the Gods*, 474.

47 In the *Dharmapradīpikā*, the founding exploit of the dynasty gives the latter its name, this extends to the land itself, the land then gives its name to the people who reside in it. Gunawardana, 'People of the Lion', 64; Gunawardana, *Historiography*, 53, argues that this represents the shift to the more inclusive sense of Sinhala that he does not see in the *Dhampiyā Aṭuvā Gäṭapadaya* and even says (p. 58) that 'the process leading to this change would have very well started at an earlier time'.

48 Pollock, *Language of the Gods*, 387, concedes in an equivocal fashion: 'Some scholars also suggest that it was at this time that the term "Sinhala" first acquired more noticeable if still somewhat vague connotations of a wider political community, no longer referring, as it had earlier, merely to ruling lineages.'

49 As a testament to Lanka's participation in a cosmopolitan Buddhist order, Xuanzang seems to have picked up his information from Lankan monks who had come to stay in Kanchipura in Southern India, see Hui Li, *The Life of Hiuen-Tsiang* (1911; reprint Delhi: Munshiram Manoharlal, 1973), 139. Yet he may have digested this by means of a Chinese discourse of essentializing barbarian peoples. Xunazang's account differs in certain details from the Mahāvaṃsa account; indeed it belongs to what I identified as the 'Sinhala' strain in Strathern, 'Vijaya and Romulus', see the table on p. 9. It is odd that Peter Schalk, 'Referents and Meanings', 555, discusses Xunzang but not these details.

50 I am very grateful to Peter Ditmanson, of the Faculty of Oriental Studies at Oxford University, for translating this section of the text on my behalf. In 'Vijaya Origin Myth', 28, I referred briefly to this text and there relied on the translation in *Si-Yu-Ki: Buddhist Records of the Western World, Translated from the Chinese of Hiuen Tsiang (AD 629)*, trans. Samuel Beal (Delhi: Motilal Banarsidass: 1994), 240, which is not literal enough for our purposes here (the term 'race', for example, has no equivalent in the text).

51 My thanks to Jeffrey Sundberg for bringing to my attention its use in texts and inscriptions from Lanka, Java and Chinese travellers, particularly around the eighth century. See, for example, Jeffrey Sundberg in collaboration with Rolf Giebel, 'The Life of the Tang Court Monk Vajrabodhi as Chronicled by Lü Xiang: South Indian and Śrī Laṅkān Antecedents to the Arrival of the Buddhist Vajrayāna in Eighth-Century Java and China,' *Pacific World*, Third Series 13 (2011), 204, n. 135, and 207, n. 137; and Jeffrey Sundberg, 'The Abhayagirivihāra's Pāṃśukūlika Monks in Second Lambakaṇṇa Śrī Laṅkā and Śailendra Java: The Flowering and Fall of a Cardinal Center of Influence in Early Esoteric Buddhism,' *Pacific World*, Third Series 16 (2014), 119, n. 20; and H. Sarkar, 'The Kings of Sri Sailam and the foundation of the Sailendra Dynasty of Indonesia,' in *Bijdragen tot de Taal-, Land- en Volkenkunde* 141 (1985), 323–38.

52 See Hallisey, 'Works and Persons in Sinhala Literary Culture', 698, for an inscription by the eleventh-century king Mahinda IV.

53 Apart from the Pūjāvaliya, see Stephen C. Berkwitz, *The History of the Buddha's Relic Shrine: A Translation of the Sinhala Thūpavaṃsa* (New York: Oxford University Press, 2007), 187–91.

54 On war as the shaper *par excellence* of group self-identity, see Davies, 'People of Britain and Ireland', 10.

55 See Gananath Obeyesekere, 'Buddhism, Nationhood and Cultural Identity: A Question of Fundamentals,' in *Fundamentalisms Comprehended*, ed. Martin E. Marty and R. Scott Appleby (Chicago: University of Chicago Press, 1995), 239–44.

56 See also Marshall Sahlins, 'The Stranger-King: or, Elementary Forms of the Political Life,' in *Stranger-Kings in Indonesia and Beyond*, ed. Ian Caldwell and David Henley, special issue of *Indonesia and the Malay World* 36 (2008), 177–99.

57 They represent the Sinhalas as an ethnic group possessing particular natural characteristics; a certain religious system, literary tradition, script, set of customs and also ancestry. Naturally, we must always be alert to the imposition of European understandings on these stories, but see the discussion in Strathern, *Kingship and Conversion*, 236–40.

58 Fernão de Queyroz, *The Temporal and Spiritual Conquest of Ceylon*, trans. and with introduction by S. G. Perera, 3 vols. (1931; reprint New Delhi: Asian Educational Services, 1992), Vol. 1, 7. See also, for example Diogo do Couto in *The History of Ceylon from the Earliest Times to 1600 AD as Related by João de Barros and Diogo do Couto*, ed. and trans. D. Ferguson (New Delhi: Asian Educational Services, 1993), 65, 101.

59 See Alan Strathern, 'Treachery and Ethnicity in Portuguese Representations of Sri Lanka,' in *Engaging Colonial Knowledge: Reading European Archives in World History*, ed. Ricardo Roque and Kim Wagner (Basingstoke: Palgrave Macmillan, 2012), 217–34. Note that Pollock (e.g. *Language of the Gods*, 511, n. 21) is more prepared to see ethnicity emerging in some parts of India during the early modern period.

60 Hallisey, 'Works and Persons in Sinhala Literary Culture', 691.

61 Walters, 'Buddhist History', 135–6.

62 Pollock, *Language of the Gods*, 278–80. It is not always clear whether and when 'Sanskrit Cosmopolis' and 'India' are intended as synonyms – or if the latter was carefully chosen to avoid Lanka.

63 Pollock, *Language of the Gods*, 279.

64 *Mahāvaṃsa*, 1.84, on the three visits to Lanka of Buddha. Guruge's translation is 'the island, honoured by the pious, came to be resplendent as the righteous isle'. This has often been glossed as rendering Sri Lanka *dhammadīpa* (island of the *dhamma*). Steven Collins, *Nirvana and Other Buddhist Felicities. Utopias of the Pāli Imaginaire* (Cambridge: Cambridge University Press, 1998), 598–9 (whose translation is 'the island made radiant with the light of the Dhamma, became highly respected by all good people'), and Walters, 'Buddhist History', 147, argue that this gloss is recent and carries inappropriate connotations of exclusivity. But an explicit claim to exclusivity need not be an element of European Providentialism either. What is crucial and common to both is the idea of a territory/society/polity as an exemplary and leading force in the establishment of a religious dispensation, which will reap both earthly and salvific rewards as a result. Moreover, see below on an intriguing verse from the *Sītāvaka Haṭana* of 1585.

65 See for example Obeyesekere, 'On Buddhist Identity', 229. For an analysis of the functioning of national Providentialism in medieval England, see Andrea Ruddick, 'National Sentiment and Religious Vocabulary in Fourteenth-Century England,' *The Journal of Ecclesiastical History* 60 (2009), 1–18.

66 *Mahāvaṃsa*, 23.7–17. Berkwitz, *Thūpavaṃsa*, 179; and see Gornall and Henry in this volume (Chapter 4).

67 *Mahāvaṃsa*, 23.8–15.

68 Berkwitz, *Thūpavaṃsa*, 166. Note that at one point the Sangha is described as the family deity [*kuladēvatā*] of the royal family (p. 164).

69 The fourteenth-century *Saddharmalankaraya* has Duṭugāmaṇu announce 'it is time to rid the country of the Tamil scum and to purify the Dispensation of the Buddha' as translated in *An Anthology of Sinhalese Literature up to 1815*, ed. C. H. B. Reynolds (London: George Allen and Unwin, 1970), 245, and also see the account in the seventeenth-century *Rājāvaliya*, ed. and trans. A. V. Suraweera (Ratmalana: Vishva Lehka, 2000), 35, 41.

70 Sheldon Pollock, 'Rāmāyaṇa and Political Imagination in India,' *The Journal of Asian Studies* 52 (1993), 261–97.

71 See Victor Lieberman, *Strange Parallels: Southeast Asia in Global Context c.800–1830*, Vol. 2: *Mainland Mirrors: Europe, Japan, China, South Asia and the Islands* (Cambridge: Cambridge University Press, 2009), 43, on how universal religions such as Theravāda Buddhism may fuel ethnic particularism and disdain.

72 *Mahāvaṃsa*, 36.41, 36.110–11; Amaradasa Liyanagamage, *State, Society and Religion in Premodern Sri Lanka* (Colombo: Social Scientists,' Association, 2008), 121–33; John Clifford Holt and Sree

Padma, 'Buddhism in Andhra and its Influence on Buddhism in Sri Lanka,' in *Buddhism in the Krishna River Valley of Andhra*, ed. Sree Padma and A. W. Barber (Albany, NY: SUNY Press, 2008), 116.

73 Hallisey, 'Works and Persons in Sinhala Literary Culture', 702; R. A. L. H. Gunawardana, *Robe and Plough: Monasticism and Economic Interest in Early Medieval Sri Lanka* (Tucson: University of Arizona Press, 1979), 172.

74 Charles Hallisey, 'Devotion in the Buddhist Literature of Medieval Sri Lanka', PhD dissertation, University of Chicago, 1988.

75 Walters 'Buddhist History', 133. 'Theravāda' has been placed in quotation marks here because before the nineteenth century it carried rather different meanings, as discussed in Peter Skilling, 'Theravāda in History,' *Pacific World*, Third Series 11 (2009), 61–93. Nevertheless, whatever its changing emic contents, it remains a reasonable etic term to describe the particular form of Buddhism dominant in Lanka and Southeast Asia.

76 Hallisey, 'Works and Persons in Sinhala Literary Culture', 701.

77 See also Gunawardana, *Robe and Plough*, 177.

78 Obeyesekere, 'On Buddhist Identity', 234, has given us the following translation of an excerpt: 'Just as the demons could not find permanence here, neither can this land become a place of residence for non-believers (*mityādṛṣṭi gatavungē vāsaya*). If any non-believer becomes a king of Sri Lanka by force at any time, that dynasty will not last owing to the special influence of the Buddha. Because this Lanka is rightfully those of kings who have right views [Buddhists], their rightful dynastic tenure (kula pravēṇiya) will absolutely prevail. For these various reasons the kings of Sri Lanka are drawn by a natural love of mind to the Buddha and will establish the *sāsana* without delay or neglect and protect the wheel of the law and the wheel of doctrine and reign so that the rightful dynastic tenure will be preserved.'

79 *Cūḷavaṃsa: Being the More Recent Part of the Mahāvaṃsa*, ed. and trans. Wilhelm Geiger, 2 vols. (1925–9; reprint London: Pali Text Society, 1980), 80.54–70; Liyanagamage, *State, Society and Religion*, 24.

80 The phrase is from the *Upāsakajanālaṅkāra* (*The Adornment of the Buddhist Laity*), which Liyanagamage, *State, Society and Religion*, 19, dates to the thirteenth century.

81 Liyanagamage, *State, Society and Religion*, 255–65, places this in the context of some other lapses from the usual Indic pattern of religious tolerance in the twelfth century (Kashmir and South India).

82 Pollock, *Language of the Gods*, 430–2, 479, refers to Karnataka (twelfth and thirteenth centuries) and Gujarat (fifteenth century).

83 One might consider here the *Dahampiyā Aṭuvā Gāṭapadaya*, a Sinhala glossary of Pāli terms with an exegetical function, from the ninth century. However this may relate to scholarly activity with little popularizing purpose, Stephen Berkwitz, personal communication, 7 June 2013.

84 Alan Strathern, 'Sri Lanka in the Long Early Modern Period: Its Place in a Comparative Theory of Second Millennium Eurasian History,' *Modern Asian Studies* 43 (2009), 809–64, which cites Walters (personal communication, 21 June 2004) on these early vernacular centuries as pivotal for 'the deep integration of Buddhism into popular consciousness and practice', the establishment of 'domesticated Buddhism'. See also Gornall and Henry in this volume, on Sinhala texts with a lay audience in mind developing alongside the adoption of Sanskritic aesthetic norms from the twelfth century (Chapter 4).

85 Hallisey, 'Works and Persons in Sinhala Literary Culture', 707, 732–37.

86 Berkwitz, *Thūpavaṃsa*, 7–12, 17–20. Berkwitz (pp. 20–2), suggests that it introduces dramatic moments into its Pāli source in order to captivate its audience.

87 Stephen C. Berkwitz, 'The Expansion of Buddhism in South and Southeast Asia,' in *Dynamics in the History of Religions between Asia and Europe: Encounters, Notions, and Comparative Perspectives*, ed. Volkhard Krech (Leiden: Brill, 2011), 228.

88 Pollock, *Language of the Gods*, 490–4; Pollock, 'Rāmāyaṇa'.

89 Pollock is prevented from pursuing further such suggestions as 'war may have made vernacular polities' by an aversion to functionalism.

90 Strathern, *Kingship and Conversion*, 168–73, 196–7.

91 Of course, legitimation theory may be an inappropriate – and certainly an insufficient – prism through which to perceive a whole range of cultural artefacts. The logical misstep is to claim that it is irrelevant to all cultural production within a certain society or civilization. In short, if it would be perverse to read Shakespeare's Richard II (cited below) as merely an exercise in royal legitimation, it would hardly do to conceive of Ben Johnson and Inigo Jones' masques as artistic exercises unrelated to the projection of power. As the case of the masques well illustrates, however, such exercises rarely simply flatter power but also seek to shape, constrain and critique it.

92 Pollock, *Language of the Gods*, 18, 257–58, 511–31 on legitimation theory. A vast accumulation of insight from the social sciences (not just the old targets of Marx and Weber, but Bourdieu and Foucault to James Scott) is thereby set aside – but also misconceived. Pollock assumes that legitimation entails the deployment of conscious strategies and even deceptions by ruling elites. Although some innovations of sacred kingship imagery surely involved an element of calculation, such as Niśśankamalla's proclamation above, in general it is quite wrong to imagine that the production and reproduction of ideology depends on the insincerity of individual utterances or the adoption of some disenchanted locus of perspective above the society in question. In the end, Pollock fails to find a route between the Scylla of 'total state ideology' and the Charybdis of the 'theatre state' (p. 257) as he terms it. At one point he does finally make an analytical connection between culture and power by suggesting that literature worked towards the 'ennoblement of political life' (p. 524) – which is surely to invite a version of legitimation theory through the back door. It is worth noting, however, that the religious and literary embellishment of kingship is rarely only a production for *subject* consumption but is also aimed at establishing a certain status with regard to *other rulers*: as we have emphasized, much court culture is a function of peer rivalry.

93 It makes sense to connect the 'constant struggle for autonomy' in the literary material, as Hallisey, 'Works and Persons in Sinhala Literary Culture', 699, puts it, with the struggle for autonomy in political terms.

94 I am not in a position to judge the extent to which Pollock is right about the rest of the Indic world.

95 Collins, *Nirvana*, 72.

96 See Tilman Frasch, Chapter 3 in this volume.

97 In her recent and stimulating 'Wilde Lectures in Natural and Comparative Religion: Defining Buddhist Formations Across the Indian Ocean,' Oxford University, May–June, 2016, Anne Blackburn made the case for setting aside the term 'Theravāda' (as having a quite different emic resonance in this period) in favour of the term 'Pāli-oriented Buddhism', and also warned against assuming that there was any one-directional export of a coherent 'package' from Lanka to Southeast Asia. I have not sought to draw on her arguments properly here but note that they may help us in the future to reframe how we consider these and related issues explored in the introduction.

98 Lieberman, *Strange Parallels*.

99 Previous generations of historians have often stressed its island status, and not always with crudely nationalistic aims. See R. A. L. H. Gunawardana, *Periodization in Sri Lankan History: Some Reflections with Special Emphasis on the Development of the State* (Colombo: Social Scientists' Association, 2008), 20.

100 This point was also made in Strathern, 'Sri Lanka in the Long Early Modern Period'. Note, however, that the north of the island was ruled as a province of the Cōḷa empire for seventy-seven years after the fall of Anurādhapura, 993–1070 CE.

101 Pollock, *Language of the Gods*, 411.

102 See Jonathan S. Walters, 'Mahāsena at the Mahāvihāra: On the Interpretation and Politics of History in Pre-Colonial Sri Lanka,' in *Invoking the Past: The Uses of History in South Asia*, ed. Daud Ali (New Delhi: Oxford University Press, 1999), 338–41, for a strong emphasis on the consciousness of overbearing neighbours (sometimes lieges, sometimes conquerors) through the Anurādhapura period and beyond.

103 Pollock makes some such voluntarist urge central to his argument about the spread of Sanskrit, although he prefers a different terminology and seeks to detach it from empire per se in the Sanskrit case; it also has much in common with Marshall Sahlins' notion of 'galactic mimesis'.

104 Hence in Berkwitz in this volume, kings are consistently compared to deities with an Indic wide relevance (Chapter 5).

105 See, for example R. A. L. H. Gunawardana, 'Colonialism, Ethnicity and the Construction of the Past. The Changing Identity of the last Four Kings of the Kandyan Kingdom,' in *Pivot Politics: Changing Cultural Identities in Early State Formation Processes*, ed. M. van Bakel et. al. (Amsterdam: Het Spinhuls, 1994), 203, or Lorna Dewaraja, *The Kandyan Kingdom of Sri Lanka 1707–1782* (Colombo: Lake House Investments, 1988), 31–2.

106 Hallisey, 'Works and Persons in Sinhala Literary Culture', 697.

107 Obeyesekere, 'On Buddhist Identity', 226.

108 This is particularly clear when we make a contrast with the modern nation-state. On the paradoxes of cultural integration and elite distinction in imperial systems, see Alan Strathern, 'Religion and Empire,' in *The Encyclopedia of Empire*, ed. John M. MacKenzie (Oxford: Wiley-Blackwell, 2016).

109 Strathern, *Kingship and Conversion*, 41–6, and 22–4, and Zoltán Biedermann, 'Tribute, Vassalage and Warfare in Early Luso-Lankan Relations (1506–1545),' in *Indo-Portuguese History: Global Trends. Proceedings of the XIth International Seminar of Indo-Portuguese History*, ed. Fátima Gracias and Charles Borges (Goa: Maureen & Camvet Publishers, 2005), 185–206.

110 Compare the way that Ähälēpola wanted to wear a picture of King George with the way that Kamehameha flew the Union Jack from his house even before the 'cession' of the Hawaiian Islands. See Marshall Sahlins, 'Alterity and Autochthony: Austronesian Cosmographies of the Marvellous,' *Hau: Journal of Ethnographic Theory* 2 (2010), 143.

111 See also Zoltan Biedermann, 'The *Matrioshka* Principle and How it was Overcome: Portuguese and Habsburg Attitudes toward Imperial Authority in Sri Lanka and the Responses of the Rulers of Kōṭṭe (1506–1656),' *Journal of Early Modern History* 13 (2009), 265–310. The crystallization of the concept of sovereignty as indivisible power among European elites from the late sixteenth century was an important watershed here, see Paul Kléber Monod, *The Power of Kings: Monarchy and Religion in Europe 1589–1715* (New Haven: Yale, 1999), 73–9.

112 For example Sahlins, 'Alterity and Autochthony'.

113 Strathern, 'The Vijaya Origin Myth'; Strathern, 'Vijaya and Romulus'. In the latter paper, I explored the possibility that the Vijaya and Kuveṇī strand of the plot had a distant origin in stories about Odysseus and Circe issuing from the Graeco-Roman world. If so, it would have emerged in-between the writing of the *Dīpavaṃsa* (early fourth century CE) and *Mahāvaṃsa* (mid-fifth or sixth century CE). This is intriguingly coincident with the period in which Darley, Chapter 2 in this volume, sees as witnessing a shift in Lanka's connectivity towards the West, i.e. 'between the middle of the fifth and the middle of the sixth century'.

114 This, then, is an aspect of the textual tradition for which legitimization theory is insufficient. Note, for example, that it also allows the dark side of kingship to be kept in view, and that it is an origin story for a whole society rather than kingship per se. None of this impedes the possibility that in the hands of the *vaṃsa* authors it may have assisted in the glamorization of the ruling dynasty, however.

115 Edgar Vincent Winans, *Shambala: The Constitution of a Traditional State* (Berkeley and Los Angeles: University of California Press, 1962), 16, cited in Marshall Sahlins, 'The Atemporal Dimensions of History: In the Old Kongo Kingdom, For Example' (unpublished paper).

116 This was implied in Strathern, 'Vijaya Origin Myth', 23, but not explicitly argued. I have recently come across Nancy E. Falk, 'Wilderness and Kingship in Ancient South Asia,' *History of Religions* 13 (1973), 1–15, which argues, using the *Mahāvaṃsa* material as its main case, that 'It appears that a king had to have some kind of transaction with the wilderness and the beings that inhabited it to acquire or hold his kingship', and 'the pattern that we have been studying suggests that something of a chaotic nature also was made a foundation of the ordinary human community. It perhaps first had to be mastered, and we have seen several instances in which kings in particular managed to subdue it. But once it was subdued, it was available to its master'. This speaks very much to the interpretations developed in the two articles on Vijaya above.

117 A. M. Hocart did argue that the Tooth Relic originally derived its power from associations with the yakkhas, see Falk, 'Wilderness and Kingship', 8. Obeyesekere, 'On Buddhist Identity', 236, reads the Vijaya narrative as a 'myth of ethnic seperation and integration'.

118 Yatinuwere Sattamby of Haliyadde, Kandy, 30 June 1818 (CO 54/71), and Robert Brownrigg to Earl Bathurst, 23 Feb 1818 (CO 54/71), in T. Vimalananda, *The Great Rebellion of 1818* (Colombo: M. D. Gunasena, 1970), 189, 223, and see Sivasundaram, Chapter 10 in this volume.

119 Ian Caldwell and David Henley, eds., *Stranger-Kings in Indonesia and Beyond*, special issue of *Indonesia and the Malay World*, 36 (2008), and Alicia Schrikker, *Dutch and British Colonial Intervention in Sri Lanka, 1780–1815* (Leiden: Brill, 2007), 23, 207–8.

120 Schrikker, *Dutch and British Colonial Intervention*, 244, argues that such tensions were rising from the 1780s.

121 Gunawardana, 'People of the Lion', 68, and E. Nissan and R. L. Stirrat, 'Generation of Communal Identities', contra K. N. O. Dharmadasa, 'The Sinhala-Buddhist Identity and the Nayaka Dynasty in the Politics of the Kandyan Kingdom, 1739–1815,' in *Collective Identities, Nationalisms and Protests in Modern Sri Lanka*, ed. M. Roberts (Colombo: Marga, 1979), 79–104.

122 John Rogers, 'Early British Rule and Social Classification in Lanka,' *Modern Asian Studies* 38 (2004), 629; Sujit Sivasundaram, *Islanded: Britain, Sri Lanka and the Bounds of an Indian Ocean Colony* (Chicago and London: University of Chicago Press, 2013), 33.

123 His father, George II (r. 1727–60), was born in Hanover and retained the title of Duke of Brunswick-Lüneburg (Hanover). This monarch had to face down the Jacobite rebellion of 1745 to place the

Young Pretender, Bonnie Prince Charlie, on the throne of Great Britain and Ireland. The prince was of Scots (Stuart) and Polish descent, although born and raised in Italy, and had tried to raise a French fleet to retake the throne from the German Hanoverians. So when the British confronted the pseudo-Malabar 'Pretender' of Kandy in 1816 (see below) they did not have to look far back into their own history for analogies of rampant dynastic cosmopolitanism.

124 See the failure of Lord North to extend the subsidiary alliance system in 1800–3, in U. C. Wickremeratne, 'Lord North and the Kandyan Kingdom, 1798–1805,' *Journal of the Royal Asiatic Society of Great Britain and Ireland* 1 (1973), 31–42.

125 Gunawardana, 'Colonialism, Ethnicity', 199–205, emphasizes the flexibility of Sinhalaness, but also ends up thereby underlining its importance to kingship. Thus the *Iṅgrisi Haṭana* compares the last Nāyaka king with Duṭugämaṇu, while another text emphasizes his patronage of the Tooth Relic. This is eloquent on foreignness digested.

126 Schrikker, *Dutch and British Colonial Intervention*, 204–10, gives a compelling analysis of the Nāyaka's utility as stranger-kings, giving primacy to political and economic sentiments. If we identify factionalism as the primary motivating force, however, this need not be to discount the relevance of ethnic discourse in the playing out of that factionalism.

127 As Sivasundaram, *Islanded*, 9, 46 suggests, while noting the absence of evidence for the hypothesis, and also Sivasundaram, 'Ethnicity, Indigeneity, and Migration in the Advent of British Rule to Sri Lanka,' *American Historical Review* 115, 2 (2010), 442. We await also the argument of Obeyesekere on this in a work in progress. Gunawardana, 'Colonialism, Ethnicity', 205, gives a useful discussion of the shift in British discourse to the characterization of the Nāyakas as 'Malabar'.

128 The quasi-Sinhalacized and Buddhicized Telugu-speakers were therefore rendered as *demaḷa*.

129 On the possibility of the utilization of anti-Tamil feeling by elite factions that led to the break-up of Kōṭṭe in the 1470s see Alan Strathern, 'The Role of Sinhala Group Identity in the "Sinhala Rebellion" Against Bhuvanekabahu VI (1469–77),' in *The Portuguese in the Orient*, ed. Gaston Perera (Kandy: International Centre for Ethnic Studies, 2010), 13–27.

130 *Rājāvaliya*, 91–2. See the discussion in Strathern, *Kingship and Conversion*, 206–8. For denunciations of theistic foolishness in the medieval period, see Hallisey, 'Devotion in the Buddhist Literature', 181–4, and see the *Subhasitiya* of Alagiyavanna from c. 1611: Stephen C. Berkwitz, *Buddhist Poetry and Colonialism: Alagiyavanna and the Portuguese in Sri Lanka* (New York: Oxford University Press, 2013), 146. The Portuguese sources were written much closer in time than the *Rājāvaliya*, but it is a moot point as to whether here they have mistaken ethnic for religious conflict – or even the extent to which that distinction was clear-cut. On the way that Saivism and 'demaḷa-ness' may have been associated by the Sinhalese, see Michael Roberts, *Sinhala Consciousness in the Kandyan Period, 1590s–1815* (Colombo: Vijitha Yapa Publications, 2004), 50–1.

131 For example, Obeyesekere, 'On Buddhist Identity'; H. L. Seneviratne, ed., *Identity, Consciousness and the Past: Forging of Caste and Community in India and Sri Lanka* (Oxford: Oxford University Press 1997), 10; Roberts, *Sinhala Consciousness*, 48; James S. Duncan, *City as Text: The Politics of Landscape in the Kandyan Kingdom* (Cambridge: Cambridge University Press, 1990).

132 John Clifford Holt, *The Religious World of Kirti Sri: Buddhism, Art, and Politics of Late Medieval Sri Lanka* (New York: Oxford University Press, 1996), on Kīrti Śrī Rājasiṃha (1747–82). But compare with Bhuvanekabāhu VI (r. 1469–77) in Strathern, 'Role of Sinhala Group Identity'.

133 Sivasundaram, *Islanded*, 6, 128. Note that while Azevedo was carried in a palanquin, the British also moved to maintain the bearers of the Royal Palanquin for the person of the governor. See 'In the Board of Commissioners,' 1 November 1818 (CO 54/73), in Vimalananda, *Great Rebellion*, 381.

134 Strathern, *Kingship and Conversion*, 211. For a compelling argument contrary to earlier scepticism about the existence of some such agreement, see Zoltán Biedermann, 'The "Malwana Convention" Revisited: Notes on the Lankan Transition to Iberian Rule,' in *The Portuguese in the Orient*, ed. Gaston Perera (Kandy: International Centre for Ethnic Studies, 2010), 29–48.

135 See, for example, Robert Brownrigg to Earl Bathurst, 8 January 1819 (CO 54/73, no. 317), in Vimalananda, *Great Rebellion*, 315.

136 Note however the argument of Schrikker, *Dutch and British Colonial Intervention*, 208, that noble factions realized they had not gained from the installation of the British as the new stranger-kings after all. We do not need either to doubt that anti-colonial rebellions could be triggered by specific policy changes – as explored in Nira Wickramasinghe, 'Many Little Revolts or One Rebellion? The Maritime Provinces of Ceylon/Sri Lanka between 1796 and 1800,' *South Asia: Journal of South Asian Studies* 32, 2 (2009), 177–88.

137 See Kumari Jayawardena, *Perpetual Ferment: Popular Revolts in Sri Lanka in the Eighteenth and Nineteenth Centuries* (Colombo: Social Scientists' Association, 2010), 20–2, 113–15, for the consistent role of bhikkhus in revolts in 1816–48.

138 See Strathern, *Kingship and Conversion*, 222–9, for the Portuguese period, and Robert Brownrigg to Earl Bathurst, 24 July 1818 (CO 54/71, no. 298), in Vimalananda, *Great Rebellion*, 183; Robert Brownrigg to Marquis of Hastings, 28 April 1818 (CO 54/71), in Vimalananda, *Great Rebellion*, 197. Also K. M. de Silva, *A History of Sri Lanka* (Colombo: Vijitha Yapa Publications, 2005), 235.

139 Robert Brownrigg to Earl Bathurst, 19 February 1818 (CO 54/70, no. 267), in Vimalananda, *Great Rebellion*, 138.

140 De Silva, *A History of Sri Lanka*, 279; Vimalananda, *Great Rebellion*, lxxv.

141 Strathern, *Kingship and Conversion*, 197, for the Portuguese case.

142 Rebellions in 1820, 1823, 1824, 1830, 1835: see Gunawardana, 'Colonialism, Ethnicity', 208.

143 Robert Brownrigg to Earl Bathurst, 8 January 1819 (CO 54/73, no. 317), in Vimalananda, *Great Rebellion*, 311, notes that recovery of it from the rebel 'had a manifest effect on all classes'. See Robert Brownrigg to Earl Bathurst, 24 July, 1818 (CO 54/71, no. 298), in Vimalananda, *Great Rebellion*, 176, for a quite good understanding of the Tooth Relic's significance, 'on which it is considered the Government and Prosperity of the Country depended'.

144 Sivasundaram, *Islanded*, 147–8, see also 127, 324.

145 António Bocarro, *Década 13 da História da India*, ed. Rodrigo José de Lima Felner (Lisbon: Academia Real das Sciencias, 1876), 497, and see Strathern, *Kingship and Conversion*, 228. This also speaks of an intriguing association between religious charisma and kingship.

146 Jorge Manuel Flores, *Os Olhos do Rei: Desenhos e Descrições Portuguesas da Ilha de Ceilão (1624, 1638)* (Lisbon: Commissão Nacional para as Commemorações dos Descobrimentos Portugueses, 2001), 171. Queyroz, *Conquest of Ceylon*, 1155, relays advice that if Ceylon was to be reconquered, administrative measures were necessary to prevent visitors to Anurādhapura plotting rebellion there.

147 Gunawardana, 'Colonialism, Ethnicity', 201; Roberts, *Sinhala Consciousness*, 904, 132.

148 Gananath Obeyesekere, *Murder in the Cathedral* (manuscript in progress), but he cautions that some such claims may exist in popular texts.

149 On the *Kustantinu Haṭana* of 1619, see Berkwitz, *Buddhist Poetry*, chapter 6. We know very little as to how much these poems were received by the wider population.

150 These comments are subject to the qualification that the British managed to inhabit the role of Buddhist patrons in certain ways, as was suggested earlier.

151 As the Portuguese managed to do with some success among the Kōṭṭe elites through their conversion to Catholicism.

152 See Roberts, 'Ethnicity after Said'.

153 Sivasundaram, *Islanded*, 12, 17, 24, 59–60, 321. That ethnicity is always a relational phenomenon does not mean that it has no origins or no historical dimension to its waxing and waning.

154 If history is always a complex interweaving of continuity and change, it is the historian's task to illuminate the distinct threads. I pointed out that Roberts, *Sinhala Consciousness*, lacked a diachronic dimension in my review of it in *Modern Asian Studies*, but in fairness Roberts explicitly presented it as synchronic exposition: Alan Strathern, 'Sinhala Conciousness in the Kandyan Period 1590s to 1815 by Michael Roberts,' *Modern Asian Studies* 39 (2005), 1007–20.

155 Roberts, *Sinhala Consciousness*, chapter 7.

156 *Sītāvaka Haṭana*, ed. Rohini Paranavitana (Colombo: Madhyama Saṅskṛitika Aramudala, 1999), verse 998. I am very grateful to Nilmini Dissanayake for translating this verse for me and for subsequent discussions. My thanks to Gananath Obeyesekere for also sending me a translation of the *Sītāvaka Haṭana* he had independently commissioned, in which this verse is rendered: 'To all people living in this Lakdiva known as Dahan (diva) [*dhammadīpa*], I have been like a lamp-stand, occupying it. Thinking of Dharma throughout the country, Noble Lord, we entrust you the charge of the country of Tri-Sinhale.'

157 Particularly the strange key term 'dahan', which is probably a poetic version of 'dhamma', in the first line. Another possible meaning is *dhana*, i.e., alms-giving, but this makes less sense in the context.

158 See also verses 350–2, which bemoans how prosperous Sri Lanka was made sterile by Bhuvanakebahu VII's alleged disregard for the Buddhist *Sāsana* in his alliance with the Portuguese. The quasi-providential aspect is generally muted elsewhere in the poem, perhaps because of Rājasiṃha I's dealings with Saivism. However, we find an echo in the seventeenth-century *Rājasiṃha Haṭana*. It says that Senerat had an astrologer who prophesied Rājasiṃha with 'Lo a Chakravarti is born for our land; he will make the Three Sinhalas into one; he will protect the

Doctrine; and the foe shall quail before him'. See P. E. Pieris, *Ribeiro's History of Ceylon with notes from de Barros, de Couto and Antonio Bocarro* (Galle: Albion, 1909), 290, verse 48.

159 We can compare with the likening of Parākramabāhu VI to a heavenly tree in *Kōkilasandēśaya*: see Berkwitz, Chapter 5 in this volume.

160 Assuming that 'Amarapathi' is Śakra.

161 It is true that the *haṭanas*, like the earlier *sandēśa* poems, depart from the Sanskrit inheritance by reference to real geographic locations in the island, see Anoma Pieris, 'Avian Geographies: An Inquiry into Nationalist Consciousness in Medieval Lanka,' *South Asia: Journal of South Asian Studies* 33, 3 (2010), 336–62. However, as Berkwitz indicates in this volume (Chapter 5), they also re-impose the former on the latter. For example, the war between the asuras and dēvas is invoked in *Sītāvaka Haṭana*, verses 179, 270, 277, 323, 513, 631–80.

162 Thus the translation in Pieris, *Ribeiro's History of Ceylon*, 290, verse 57, which gives it the title *Parangi Haṭana*.

163 Pieris, *Ribeiro's History of Ceylon*, verse 297; a demon host (305); a beef-eating host (306).

164 Compare Sivasundaram in this volume (Chapter 10) with Strathern, *Kingship and Conversion*, 178. The analysis of the passage emphasizes the blatantly ethnic – even biological – logic at work here. The first verse (1107) quoted runs: 'Accompanied by Vadakkara, Mukkaru, Doluvara, Kavisi and Uruvusi/The Portuguese who fought having come with vast foreign armies [*para senaga*]/Were, without even a cloth at the waist, felled in the middle of the paddy fields and heads were cut and piled up/Half-castes [*tuppahin*] of this country [*meratē*] who had joined to swell their bellies were caught and tied up.' A similar derogation of groups of foreign mercenaries can be found in the *Rājasiṃha Haṭana*, See Pieris, *Ribeiro's History of Ceylon*, 300, verse 240, and Roberts, *Sinhala Consciousness*, 127. Incidentally, Vadakkara probably means here *vadugai*, the Tamil word for northerners. The Nāyaks of Madurai were vaddakaru and strictly speaking it is misleading to refer to them as 'Tamil'. The fact that these Telugu-speakers are nonetheless assimilated to the category of demaḷa, shows that the latter had taken on a broader significance than simply 'Tamil speaker'. See Roberts, *Sinhala Consciousness*, 51 (especially n. 46) on 'vadiga' and 'demaḷa'.The British term 'Malabar' also brought the two together, although D'Oyly recognized that the Nāyakas were 'Talingu' rather than Tamil, see D'Oyly, 'The Information of Kaykara Maduwe Mudiynase of Udunuwere' (CO 54/71), in Vimalananda, *Great Rebellion*, 220.

165 The more 'imperial' we consider a polity to be, the elite distinction is likely to matter than the creation of a moral community. But even empires from time to time attempt projects of cultural and emotional integration.

# Bibliography

## Introduction


Abeyasinghe, Tikiri. *Portuguese Rule in Ceylon 1594–1612*. Colombo: Lake House, 1966.

Ali, Daud. 'Royal Eulogy as World History: Re-thinking Copper-plate Inscriptions in Cōḻa India,' in *Querying the Medieval: Texts and the History of Practices in South* Asia, ed. Ronald Inden, Jonathan Walters and Daud Ali. New York: Oxford University Press, 2000, 165–229.

Ali, Daud. 'Connected Histories? Regional Historiography and Theories of Cultural Contact between Early South and Southeast Asia,' in *Islamic Connections: Muslim Societies in South and Southeast Asia*, ed. R. Michael Feener and Terenjit Sevea. Singapore: Institute of Southeast Asian Studies, 2009, 1–24.

Ali, Daud. 'The Early Inscriptions of Indonesia and the Problem of the Sanskrit Cosmopolis,' in *Early Interactions between South and Southeast Asia: Reflections on Cross-Cultural Exchange*, ed. Pierre-Yves Manguin, A. Mani and Geoff Wade. New Delhi and Singapore: Manohar and Institute of Southeast Asian Studies, 2011, 277–97.

Bandaranayake, Senake. 'Approaches to the External Factor in Sri Lanka's Historical Formation,' in *Continuities and Transformations: Studies in Sri Lankan Archaeology and History*. Colombo: Social Scientists' Association, 2012, 91–120.

Bandaranayake, Senake, Lorna Dewaraja, Roland Silva and K. D. G Wimalaratne, eds. *Sri Lanka and the Silk Road of the Sea*. Colombo: The Sri Lanka National Commission for UNESCO and the Central Cultural Fund, 1990.

Berkwitz, Stephen C. *Buddhist Poetry and Colonialism: Alagiyavanna and the Portuguese in Sri Lanka*. New York: Oxford University Press, 2013.

Biedermann, Zoltan. 'Colombo versus Cannanore: Contrasting Structures of Two Early Colonial Port Cities in South Asia,' *Journal of the Economic and Social History of the Orient* 53, 2 (2009), 413–59.

Binnie, J, J. J. Holloway, S. Millington and C. Young. 'Cosmopolitanism,' in *International Encyclopedia of Human Geography*, ed. R. Kitchin and N. Thrift. Oxford: Elsevier, 2009, 307–13.

Blackburn, Anne M. 'Buddhist Connections in the Indian Ocean: Changes in Monastic Mobility, 1000–1500,' *Journal of the Economic and Social History of the Orient* 58, 3 (2015), 237–66.

Boxer, Charles R. *Portuguese Society in the Tropics: The Municipal Councils of Goa, Macao, Bahia and Luanda*. Madison, WI: University of Wisconsin Press, 1965.

Breckenridge, Carol, Sheldon Pollock, Homi K. Bhabha and Dipesh Chakrabarty, eds. *Cosmopolitanism*. Durham, NC: Duke University Press, 2002.

Brook, Gillian. 'Cosmopolitanism,' in *The Oxford Handbook of World Philosophy*, ed. William Edelglass and Jay L. Garfield. Oxford: Oxford University Press, 2011, 582–95.

Brown, Gareth Wallace. 'Cosmopolitanism,' in *The Concise Oxford Dictionary of Politics*, 3rd edn, ed. Iain McMillan and Alistair McLean. Oxford: Oxford University Press, 2009.

Collins, Steven. *Nirvana and other Buddhist Felicities: Utopias of the Pali imaginaire*. Cambridge University Press, 1998.

De Silva, C. R. *The Portuguese in Ceylon 1617–1638*. Colombo: H. W. Cave, 1972.

De Silva, C. R. 'Sri Lanka in the Early Sixteenth Century: Political Conditions,' in *University of Peradeniya History of Sri Lanka*, Vol. 2, ed. K. M. De Silva, Peradeniya: University of Peradeniya, 1995, 37–60.

Dewaraja, Lorna. 'Muslim Merchants and Pilgrims in Sarandib c.900–1500 AD,' in *Sri Lanka and the Silk Road of the Sea*, ed. S. Bandaranayake, L. Dewaraja, R. Silva and K. D. G. Wimalratne. Colombo: The Sri Lanka National Fund for UNESCO and Central Cultural Fund, 1990, 191–8.

Dewasiri, Nirmal Ranjith. *'History' after the War: Historical Consciousness in the Collective Sinhala-Buddhist Psyche in Post-War Sri Lanka*, ICES Research Paper 9. Colombo: International Centre for Ethnic Studies, 2013.

Duara, Prasenjit. *The Crisis of Global Modernity: Asian Traditions and a Sustainable Future*. Cambridge: Cambridge University Press, 2015.

Fine, Robert. *Cosmopolitanism*. London: Routledge, 2007.

Flores, Jorge M. *Os Portugueses e o Mar de Ceilão: Trato, diplomacia e guerra, 1498–1543*. Lisbon: Cosmos, 1998.

Frasch, Tilman. 'Buddha's Tooth Relic: Contesting Rituals and the Early State in Sri Lanka', in *Ritual Dynamics and the Science of Ritual*, ed. Axel Michaels, Vol. 3, *State, Power and Violence*, ed. Marko Kitts et al. Wiesbaden: Harrassowitz, 2010, 647–64

Frasch, Tilman. '1456: The Making of a Buddhist Ecumene in the Bay of Bengal,' in *Pelagic Passageways: The Northern Bay of Bengal World before Colonialism*, ed. Rila Mukherjee. Delhi: Primus, 2011, 383–405.

Frost, Mark Ravinder. 'Cosmopolitan Fragments from a Splintered Isle: "Ceylonese" Nationalism in Late-Colonial Sri Lanka,' in *Ethnicities, Diasporas and Grounded Cosmopolitanisms in Asia. Proceedings of the Asia Research Institute Workshop*. Singapore: Asia Research Institute, 2004, 59–69.

Gombrich, Richard F. and Gananath Obeyesekere. *Buddhism Transformed: Religious Change in Sri Lanka*. Princeton, NJ: Princeton University Press, 1988.

Goonewardena, K. W. 'Kingship in XVIIth Century Sri Lanka: Some Concepts, Ceremonies and Other Practices,' *Sri Lanka Journal of the Humanities* 3 (1977), 1–32.

Gruzinski, Serge. *Les quatre parties du monde. Histoire d'une mondialisation*. Paris: La Martinière, 2004.

Gunawardana, R. A. L. H. 'Seaways to Sielediba: Changing Patterns of Navigation in the Indian Ocean and Their Impact on Precolonial Sri Lanka,' in *Sri Lanka and the Silk Road of the Sea*, ed. S. Bandaranayake, L. Dewaraja, R. Silva and K. D. G. Wimalratne. Colombo: The Sri Lanka National Fund for UNESCO and Central Cultural Fund, 1990, 25–44.

Gunawardana, R. A. L. H. *Historiography in a Time of Ethnic Conflict: Construction of the Past in Contemporary Sri Lanka*. Colombo: Social Scientists' Association, 1995.

Gupta, Akhil. 'Globalization and Difference: Cosmopolitanism before the Nation-State,' *Transforming Cultures e-Journal* 3, 2 (2008), 1–20.

Hall, Kenneth R. 'Ports-of-Trade, Maritime Diasporas, and Networks of Trade and Cultural Integration in the Bay of Bengal Region of the Indian Ocean: c. 1300–1500,' *Journal of the Economic and Social History of the Orient* 53, 1–2 (2009), 109–45.

Hallisey, Charles. 'Works and Persons in Sinhala Literary Culture,' in *Literary Cultures in History: Reconstructions from South Asia*, ed. Sheldon Pollock. Berkeley and Los Angeles: California University Press, 2003, 689–746.

Hannerz, Ulf. 'Cosmopolitanism,' in *A Companion to the Anthropology of Politics*, ed. David Nugent and Joan Vincent. Oxford: Blackwell, 2007, 69–85.

Helms, Mary W. *Ulysses' Sail: An Ethnographic Odyssey of Power, Knowledge, and Geographical Distance*. Princeton, NJ: Princeton University Press, 1988.

Holt, John Clifford. *The Buddhist Visnu: Religious Transformation, Politics, and Culture*. New York: Columbia University Press, 2004.

Kiribamune, Sirima. 'Muslims and Trade of the Arabian Sea with Special Reference to Sri Lanka from the Birth of Islam to the Fifteenth century,' in *Sri Lanka and the Silk Road of the Sea*, ed. S. Bandaranayake, L. Dewaraja, R. Silva and K. D. G. Wimalratne. Colombo: The Sri Lanka National Fund for UNESCO and Central Cultural Fund, 1990, 179–90.

Lieberman, Victor B. *Strange Parallels. Southeast Asia in Global Context, c. 800–1830*, Vol. 2, *Mainland Mirrors: Europe, Japan, China, South Asia, and the Islands*. Cambridge: Cambridge University Press, 2009.

Liyanagamage, Amaradasa. *State, Society and Religion in Premodern Sri Lanka*. Colombo: Social Scientists' Association, 2008.

Manguin, Pierre- Yves, A. Mani and Geoff Wade, eds. *Early Interactions between South and Southeast Asia: Reflections on Cross-Cultural Exchange*. New Delhi and Singapore: Manohar and Institute of Southeast Asian Studies, 2011.

McAlpine, W. R. and M. B. Ariyapala. *The Crest-Gem of Poetry*. Dehiwala: Tisara Prakasakayo, 1990.

Mignolo, Walter D. 'The Many Faces of Cosmo-Polis: Border Thinking and Critical Cosmopolitanism,' *Public Culture* 12, 3 (2000), 721–48.

Milner, Anthony. *The Malays*. Oxford: Blackwell, 2008.

Obeyesekere, Gananath. *The Work of Culture: Symbolic Transformation in Psychoanalysis and Anthropology*. Chicago: University of Chicago Press, 1990.

Obeyesekere, Gananath. *The Apotheosis of Captain Cook: European Mythmaking in the Pacific*. Princeton, NJ: Princeton University Press, 1992.

Obeyesekere, Gananath. 'Buddhism, Nationhood and Cultural Identity: A Question of Fundamentals,' in *Fundamentalisms Comprehended*, ed. Martin E. Marty and R. Scott Appleby. Chicago: University of Chicago Press, 1995, 231–56.

Obeyesekere, Gananath. 'On Buddhist Identity in Sri Lanka,' in *Ethnic Identity: Creation, Conflict and Accommodation*, ed. Lola Romanucci-Rossi and George A. de Vos. London: Mayfield, 1995, 222–41.

Obeyesekere, Gananath. 'On Buddhist Identity', in *Identity, Consciousness and the Past: Forging of Caste and Community in India and Sri Lanka*, ed. H. L. Seneviratne. Oxford: Oxford University Press, 1997.

Obeyesekere, Gananath. *Imagining Karma: Ethical Transformation in Amerindian, Buddhist, and Greek Rebirth*. Berkeley and Los Angeles: University of California Press, 2002.

Obeyesekere, Gananath. *The Awakened Ones: Phenomenology of Visionary Experience*. New York: Columbia University Press, 2012.

Pathmanathan, S. 'South India and Sri Lanka, AD 1450–1650: Political, Commercial and Cultural Relations,' *Journal of Tamil Studies* 21 (1982), 36–57.

Perera, Gaston. *The Portuguese Missionary in 16th and 17th Century Ceylon: The Spiritual Conquest*. Colombo: Vijitha Yapa, 2009.

Pollock, Sheldon. 'The Cosmopolitan Vernacular,' *Journal of Asian Studies* 57, 1 (1998), 6–37.

Pollock, Sheldon. 'India in the Vernacular Millennium: Literary Culture and Polity, 1000–1500,' *Daedalus* 127 (1998), 41–74.

Pollock, Sheldon. 'Cosmopolitan and Vernacular in History,' *Public Culture* 12, 3 (2000), 591–625.

Pollock, Sheldon. *The Language of the Gods in the World of Men: Sanskrit, Culture, and Power in Premodern India*, Berkeley and Los Angeles: University of California Press, 2009.

Prange, Sebastian. 'Like Banners on the Sea: Muslim Trade Networks and Islamization in Malabar and Maritime Southeast Asia,' in *Islamic Connections: Muslim Societies in South and Southeast Asia*, ed. R. Michael Feener and Terenjit Sevea. Singapore: Institute of Southeast Asian Studies, 2009, 25–47.

Ricci, Ronit. *Islam Translated: Literature, Conversion, and the Arabic Cosmopolis of South and Southeast Asia*. Chicago: University of Chicago Press, 2011.

Roberts, Michael. 'Ethnicity after Said: Post-Orientalist Failures in Comprehending the Kandyan Period of Lankan History,' *Ethnic Studies Report* 19 (2001), 69–98.

Roberts, Michael. *Sinhala Consciousness in the Kandyan period, 1590s–1815*. Colombo: Vijitha Yapa, 2004.

Sahlins, Marshall. 'The Stranger-Kingship of the Mexica,' unpublished paper.

Seneviratne, H. L., ed. *Identity, Consciousness and the Past: Forging of Caste and Community in India and Sri Lanka*. Delhi: Oxford University Press, 1997.

Skilling, Peter. 'Buddhism and the Circulation of Ritual in Early Peninsular Southeast Asia,' in *Early Interactions between South and Southeast Asia: Reflections on Cross-Cultural Exchange*, ed. Pierre-Yves Manguin, A. Mani and Geoff Wade. New Delhi and Singapore: Manohar and Institute of Southeast Asian Studies, 2011, 371–84.

Spencer, Jonathan, ed. *Sri Lanka: History and the Roots of Conflict*. London: Routledge, 1990.

Strathern, Alan. 'Theoretical Approaches to Sri Lankan History and the Early Portuguese Period,' *Modern Asian Studies* 38 (2004), 189–226.

Strathern, Alan. 'Sri Lanka in the Long Early Modern Period: Its Place in a Comparative Theory of Second Millennium Eurasian History,' *Modern Asian Studies* 43 (2009), 809–64.

Strathern, Alan. 'Treachery and Ethnicity in Portuguese Representations of Sri Lanka,' in *Engaging Colonial Knowledge: Reading European Archives in World History*, ed. Ricardo Roque and Kim Wagner. New York: Palgrave, 2012, 217–34.

Subrahmanyam, Sanjay. *The Political Economy of Commerce: Southern India, 1500–1650*. Cambridge: Cambridge University Press, 1990.

Tambiah, Stanley. *Buddhism Betrayed? Religion, Politics and Violence in Sri Lanka*. Chicago: University of Chicago Press, 1992.

Thomas, Nicholas. *Entangled Objects: Exchange, Material Culture, and Colonialism in the Pacific*. Cambridge, MA: Harvard University Press, 2009.

Thomaz, Luís Filipe. *De Ceuta a Timor*, 2nd edn. Lisbon: Difel, 1994.

Vertovec, Steven and Robin Cohen, eds. *Conceiving Cosmopolitanism: Theory, Context, Practice*. Oxford: Oxford University Press, 2002.

Walters, Jonathan. 'Lovely Lady Lanka: A Tenth-Century Depiction,' *Sri Lanka Journal of the Humanities* 39 (1993), 45–56.

Walters, Jonathan. 'Buddhist History: The Sri Lankan Pali *Vaṃsas* and their Commentary,' in *Querying the Medieval. Texts and the History of Practices in South Asia*, ed. Ronald Inden, Jonathan Walters and Daud Ali. Oxford: Oxford University Press, 2000, 99–164.

Wang Gungwu. 'Introduction,' in *Southeast Asia in the 9th to 14th Centuries*, ed. David G. Marr and Anthony C. Milner. Singapore: Institute of Southeast Asian Studies, 1986, xi–xvii.

Wickramasinghe, Nira. *Producing the Present: History and Heritage in Post-War Patriotic Sri Lanka*, ICES Research Paper 2. Colombo: International Centre for Ethnic Studies, 2012.

Wolters, O. W. *History, Culture, and Region in Southeast Asian Perspectives*, revised edition. Ithaca, NY: Cornell University Press, 1999.

Wolters, O. W. *Early Southeast Asia: Selected Essays*, ed. Craig J. Reynolds. Ithaca, NY: Cornell University Press, 2008.

Xavier, Ângela Barreto. *A Invenção de Goa. Poder Imperial e Conversões Culturais, Séculos XVI e XVII*. Lisbon: Imprensa de Ciências Sociais, 2008.

## Chapter 1

### Primary sources

Central Cultural Fund of Sri Lanka Act, No. 57 of 1980 (certified on 18 December 1980), Chapter 388, 220–4.

*Cūḷavaṃsa: Being the More Recent Part of the Mahāvaṃsa*, trans. Wilhelm Geiger. Colombo: Ceylon Government Information, 1929.

*Kautilya, the Arthasastra*, trans. L. N. Rangarajan. New Delhi: Penguin, 1992.

*The Mahāvaṃsa: Or, The Great Chronicle of Ceylon*, trans. Wilhelm Geiger. London, 1912; reprint New Delhi: Asian Educational Series, 1993.

*The Mahawanso*, ed. George Turnour, 1837; reprint Colombo: Central Cultural Fund, 2016.

### Secondary sources

Allchin, Frank Raymond. 'The Inscriptions and Graffiti,' in *Anurādhapura: The British-Sri Lankan Excavations at Anuradhapura Salgaha Watta*, Vol. 2, *The Artefacts*, ed. R. A. E. Coningham. Oxford: Archaeopress, 2006, 431–500.

Avanzini, Alessandra. *A Port in Arabia between Rome and the Indian Ocean (3rd c. BC–5th c. AD)*, Khor Rori report 2. Rome: Arabia Antica, 2008.

Bailiff, I. K., H. R. Lacey, R. A. E. Coningham, P. Gunawardhana, G. Adikari, C. E. Davis, M. J. Manuel and K. M. Strickland. 'Luminescence Dating of Brick Stupas: An Application to the Hinterland of Anuradhapura, Sri Lanka,' *Antiquity* 87 (2013), 189–201.

Bandaranyake, Senake. *Sinhalese Monastic Architecture: The Viharas of Anurādhapura*. Leiden: Brill, 1974.

Bandaranayake, Senake. 'Traversing an Archaeological Landscape,' in *Further Studies in the Settlement Archaeology of the Sigiriya-Dambulla Region*, ed. Senake Bandaranayake and Mats Mogren. Colombo: Post Graduate Institute of Archaeology, University of Kelaniya, 1994, 9–23.

Bartholomeusz, Tessa. *Women under the Bo Tree: Buddhist Nuns in Sri Lanka*. Cambridge: Cambridge University Press, 1994.

Beal, Samuel. *Travels of Fah-Hian and Sung-Yun: Buddhist Pilgrims to India 400 AD to 518 AD*. London: Trubner and Co, 1869.

Begley, Vimala. *Ancient Port of Arikamedu: New Excavations and Researches 1989–1992*. Paris: École Française D'Extrême-Orient, 1996.

Bell, Harry Charles Purvis. *Archaeological Survey of Ceylon. Anurādhapura. Fifth Progress Report, April to June, 1891*. Colombo: Ceylon Government Press, 1893.

Bell, Harry Charles Purvis. *Archaeological Survey of Ceylon, Annual Report 1892*. Colombo: Ceylon Government Press, 1904.

Bell, Harry Charles Purvis. *Archaeological Survey of Ceylon, Annual Report 1893*. Colombo: Ceylon Government Press, 1904.

Bell, Harry Charles Purvis. *Plans and Plates for Annual Report, 1893 (Eleventh and Twelfth Reports)*. Colombo: Ceylon Government Press, 1914.

Bell, Harry Charles Purvis. *The Maldive Islands: Monograph on the History, Archaeology and Epigraphy*. Colombo: Ceylon Government Press, 1940.

Bertolacci, Antonio. *A View of the Agricultural, Commercial, and Financial Interests of Ceylon*. London: Black, Parbury and Allen, 1817.

Carlson, Deborah and Ken Trethewey. 'Exploring the Oldest Shipwreck in the Indian Ocean,' *The Institute of Nautical Archaeology Quarterly* 40 (2013), 8–14.

Carswell, J., S. U. Deraniyagala and A. Graham, eds. *Mantai: City by the Sea*. Aichwald: Linden Soft, 2013.

Chakrabarti, Dilip. *India: An Archaeological History: Palaeolithic Beginnings to Early Historic Foundations*. Delhi: Oxford University Press, 1999.

Childe, Vere Gordon. *The Dawn of European Civilization*. London: Kegan Paul, 1925.

Codrington, Humphrey William. *A Short History of Ceylon*. London: Macmillan and Co., 1939.

Coningham, Robin. 'Monks, Caves and Kings: A Reassessment of the Nature of Early Buddhism in Sri Lanka (Ceylon),' *World Archaeology* 27 (1995), 222–42.

Coningham, Robin. 'The Excavations at ASW2,' in *Anurādhapura: The British-Sri Lankan Excavations at Anuradhapura Salgaha Watta 2*, Vol. 1, *The Site*, ed. R. A. E Coningham. Oxford: Archaeopress, 1999, 71–124.

Coningham, Robin. 'Contestatory Urban Texts or Were Cities in South Asia Built as Images?' *Cambridge Archaeological Journal* 10 (2000), 348–54.

Coningham, Robin. 'The Archaeology of Buddhism,' in *Archaeology and World Religion*, ed. Tim Insoll. London: Routledge, 2001, 61–95.

Coningham, Robin. 'Beyond and before the Imperial Frontiers: Early Historic Sri Lanka and the Origins of Indian Ocean Trade,' *Man and Environment* 27 (2002), 99–108.

Coningham, Robin, ed. *Anurādhapura: The British-Sri Lankan Excavations at Anurādhapura Salgaha Watta 2*, Vol. 2, *The Artefacts*, BAR International Series 1508. Oxford: Archaeopress, 2006.

Coningham, Robin. 'The Archaeology of Buddhism,' in *The Oxford Handbook of the Archaeology of Ritual and Religion*, ed. Tim Insoll. Oxford: Oxford University Press, 2011, 932–45.

Coningham, Robin and Paul Cheetham. 'The Fortifications,' in *Anurādhapura: The British-Sri Lankan Excavations at Anuradhapura Salgaha Watta*, Vol. 1: *The Site*, ed. R. A. E Coningham. Oxford: Archaeopress, 1999, 47–69.

Coningham, Robin and Prishanta Gunawardhana. 'Looting or Rededication? Buddhism and the Expropriation of Relics,' in *Appropriating the Past: Philosophical Perspectives on the Practice of Archaeology*, ed. Geoffrey Scarre and Robin Coningham. Cambridge: Cambridge University Press, 2012, 281–94.

Coningham, Robin and Prishanta Gunawardhana, eds. *Anuradhapura*, vol. 3: The Hinterland, BAR International Series 2568. Oxford: Archaeopress, 2013.

Coningham, Robin and Frank Christopher Hardman. 'Review of Dilip Chakrabati, *Archaeology in the Third World: A History of Indian Archaeology since 1947*,' *Cambridge Archaeological Journal* 14, 1 (2004), 156–8.

Coningham, Robin and Nick Lewer. 'Paradise Lost: The Bombing of the Temple of the Tooth – a UNESCO World Heritage Site in South Asia,' *Antiquity* 73 (1999), 857–66.

Coningham, Robin and Nick Lewer. 'The Vijayan Colonization and the Archaeology of Identity in Sri Lanka,' *Antiquity* 74 (2000), 707–12.

Coningham Robin and Ruth Young. 'The Archaeological Visibility of Caste,' in *Case Studies in Archaeology and World Religion*, ed. Tim Insoll. Oxford: Archaeopress, 1999, 84–93.

Coningham, Robin and Ruth Young. *The Archaeology of South Asia: From the Indus to Aśōka*. Cambridge: Cambridge University Press, 2015.

Coningham, Robin, Frank Raymond Allchin, Cathy Batt and David Lucy. 'Passage to India? Anurādhapura and the Early Use of the Brahmi Script,' *Cambridge Archaeological Journal* 6, 1 (1996), 73–97.

Coningham, Robin, Prishanta Gunawardhana, Gamini Adikari, Mangala Katugampola, Ian Simpson and Ruth Young. 'The Anurādhapura (Sri Lanka) Project: The Hinterland (Phase II), Preliminary Report of the First Season 2005,' *South Asian Studies* 22 (2006), 53–64.

Coningham, Robin, Prishanta Gunawardhana, Mark Manuel, Gamini Adikari, Mangala Katugampola, Ruth Young, Armin Schmidt, Krishnan Krishnan, Ian Simpson, Gerry McDonnell and Cathy Batt. 'The State of Theocracy: Defining an Early Medieval Hinterland in Sri Lanka,' *Antiquity* 81 (2007), 1–21.

Coningham, Robin, Prishanta Gunawardhana, Mark Manuel, Gamini Adikari, Ruth Young, Armin Schmidt, Krishnan Krishnan, Ian Simpson, Christopher Davis and Cathy Batt. 'Response to Goonatilake,' *Antiquity* 85 (2011), 1065–67.

Coningham, Robin, Prishanta Gunawardhana, Christopher Davis, Gamini Adikari, Ian Simpson, Keir Strickland and Mark Manuel. 'Contextualising the Tabbova-Maradanmaduva "Culture": Excavations at Nikawewa, Tirappane Division, Anurādhapura District, Sri Lanka,' *SouthAsian Studies* 28, 1 (2012), 1–14.
Coningham, Robin, Prishanta Gunawardhana, Gamini Adikari, Christopher Davis, Mark Manuel, Ian Bailiff, Cathy Batt, Harendralal Namalgamuwa, Jayampath Senanayake and Umanga Rammungoda. 'Phasing the Hinterland,' in *Anurādhapura*, Vol. 3, *The Hinterland*, BAR International Series 2568, ed. R. A. E. Coningham and P. Gunawardhana. Oxford: Archaeopress, 2013, 31–48.
Coningham, Robin, Prishanta Gunawardhana, Gamini Adikari, Mark Manuel, Christopher Davis and Ian Simpson. 'Discussion,' in *Anurādhapura*, Vol. 3, *The Hinterland*, BAR International Series 2568, ed. R. A. E. Coningham and P. Gunawardhana. Oxford: Archaeopress, 2013, 459–79.
Coningham, Robin, Prishanta Gunawardhana, Christopher Davis, Mark Manuel, Keir Strickland, Harendralal Namalgamuwa and Jayampath Senanayake. 'Terracotta Objects,' in *Anurādhapura*, Vol. 3, *The Hinterland*, BAR International Series 2568, ed. R. A. E. Coningham and P. Gunawardhana. Oxford: Archaeopress, 2013, 333–92.
Cunningham, Alexander. *Mahabodhi or the Great Buddhist Temple under the Bodhi Tree at Buddha-Gaya*. London: W. H. Allen, 1892.
Daniel, Errol Valentine. 'Three Dispositions Towards the Past: One Sinhala, Two Tamil,' in *Identity, Consciousness and the Past: Forging of Caste and Community in India and Sri Lanka*, ed. Heralivala Seneviratne. Delhi: Oxford University Press, 1997, 42–69.
Davis, Christopher, Robin Coningham, Prishanta Gunawardhana and Mark Manuel. 'Epigraphy in the Hinterland,' in *Anurādhapura*, Vol. 3, *The Hinterland*, BAR International Series 2568, ed. R. A. E. Coningham and P. Gunawardhana. Oxford: Archaeopress, 2013, 445–58.
De Silva, Kingsley. *A History of Sri Lanka*. Colombo: Vijitha Yapa Publications, 2005.
De Silva, Raja Henapala. *Sigiriya and its Significance: A Mahayana-Theravāda Monastery*. Nawala: Bibliotheque, 2002.
Deraniyagala, Siran. 'The Citadel of Anurādhapura 1965: Excavations in the Gedige Area,' *Ancient Ceylon* 2 (1972), 48–170.
Deraniyagala, Siran. 'Excavations in the Citadel of Anurādhapura Gedige 1984: A Preliminary Report,' *Ancient Ceylon* 6, 1986, 39–48.
Devendra, Don Titus. 'Seventy Years of Ceylon Archaeology,' *Artibus Asiae* 22, 1–2 (1959), 23–40.
Dias, Mālinī. *The Growth of Buddhist Monastic Institutions in Sri Lanka from Brahmi Inscriptions*. Colombo: Department of Archaeological Survey, Government of Sri Lanka, 2001.
Diaz Andreu, Margarita, Sam Lucy, Stasa Babić and David Edwards, eds. *The Archaeology of Identity: Approaches to Gender, Age, Status, Ethnicity and Religion*. London: Routledge, 2005.
Diaz Andreu, M., S. Lucy, S. Babić and D. N. Edwards. 'Introduction,' in *The Archaeology of Identity: Approaches to Gender, Age, Status, Ethnicity and Religion*, ed. M. Diaz Andreu et al. London: Routledge, 2005, 1–12.
Dirks, Nicholas. 'The Invention of Caste: Civil Society in Colonial India,' in *Identity, Consciousness and the Past: Forging of Caste and Community in India and Sri Lanka*, ed. Heralivala Seneviratne. Delhi: Oxford University Press, 1997, 120–35.
Dirks, Nicholas. *Castes of Mind: Colonialism and the Making of Modern India*. Princeton, NJ: Princeton, University Press, 2001.
Duncan, James. *The City as Text: The Politics of Landscape Interpretation in the Kandyan Kingdom*. Cambridge: Cambridge University Press, 1990.
Erdosy, George. 'Language, Material Culture and Ethnicity: Theoretical Perspectives,' in *The Indo-Aryans of Ancient South Asia*, ed. George Erdosy. Berlin: Walter de Gruyter, 1995, 1–32.
Frasch, Tilman. 'Buddha's Tooth Relic: Contesting Rituals and the Early State in Sri Lanka', in *Ritual Dynamics and the Science of Ritual*, ed. Axel Michaels, Vol. 3, *State, Power and Violence*, ed. Marko Kitts et al. Wiesbaden: Harrassowitz, 2010, 647–64.
Gilliland, Krista, Ian Simpson, Paul Adderley, Christopher Burbidge, Alan Cresswell, David Sanderson, Robin Coningham, Mark Manuel, Keir Strickland, Prishanta Gunawardhana and Gamini Adikari. 'The Dry Tank: Development and Disuse of Water Management Infrastructure in the Anurādhapura Hinterland, Sri Lanka,' *Journal of Archaeological Sciences* 40 (2013), 1012–28.
Gokhale, Shobhana. 'Sri Lanka in Early Indian Inscriptions,' *Annals of the Bhandarkar Oriental Research Institute*, 85 (2004), 135–9.
Gunawardana, Leslie. *Robe and Plough: Monasticism and Economic Interest in Early Medieval Sri Lanka*. Tuscon: University of Arizona Press, 1979.
Gunawardhana, Prishanta. *Buddhist Monasteries towards Urbanism in Southern Sri Lanka*. Battaramulla: Neptune Publications, 2009.

Guruge, Ananda. *From the Living Fountains of Buddhism: Sri Lankan Support to Pioneering Western Orientalists*. Colombo: Ministry of Cultural Affairs, 1984.

Hawkes, Jason. 'The Wider Archaeological Contexts of the Buddhist Stupa Site of Bharhut,' *Buddhist Stupas in South Asia*, ed. Jason Hawkes and Akira Shimada. Oxford: Oxford University Press, 2009, 146–74.

Hocart, Arthur Maurice. *Memoirs of the Archaeological Survey of Ceylon*, Vol. 1, Colombo: A. C. Richards, Acting Government Printer, Ceylon, 1924.

Hocart, Arthur Maurice, 'The Four Quarters,' *Ceylon Journal of Science*, section G.1 (1928), 105–11.

Ilangasinha, Hematilaka Bandara Mangala, *Buddhism in Medieval Sri Lanka*. Delhi: Sri Satguru Publications, 1992.

Indrapala, Karthigesu. *The Evolution of an Ethnic Identity: The Tamils in Sri Lanka c. 300 BCE to c. 1200 CE*. Sydney: MV Publications, 2005.

Jayasuriya, M. H. F., Leelananda Prematilleke and Roland Silva, *Manjusri Vastuvidyasastra*. Colombo: The Archaeological Survey of Sri Lanka and Central Cultural Fund, 1995.

Jones, Siân. *The Archaeology of Ethnicity*. London: Routledge, 1997.

Leach, Edmund. 'Aryan Invasions Over Four Millennia,' in *Culture Through Time: Anthropological Approaches*, ed. Emiko Ohnuki-Tierney. Stanford: Stanford University Press, 1995, 227–45.

Legge, James. *A Record of Buddhistic Kingdoms: Being an Account by the Chinese Monk Fa-Hien of his Travels in India and Ceylon (AD 399–414) in Search of the Buddhist Books of Discipline*. Oxford: Clarendon Press, 1886.

McAlpine, William and David Robson. *A Guide to Ritigala*. Colombo: Central Cultural Fund, 1983.

Meskell, Lynn. *Cosmopolitan Archaeologies*. Durham: Duke University Press, 2009.

Mihindukulasuriya, Prabo. 'Persian Christians in the Anurādhapura Period,' in *A Cultured Faith: Essays in Honour of Prof. G. P. V. Somaratna*, ed. Prabo Mihindukulasuriya. Colombo: CTS Publishing, 2011, 1–24.

Mitra, Debala. *Buddhist Monuments*. Calcutta: Samsad, 1971.

Monius, Anne. *Imagining a Place for Buddhism: Literary Culture and Religious Community in Tamil-Speaking South India*. Oxford: Oxford University Press, 2001.

Panditha, Vincent. 'Buddhism During the Polonnaruva Period,' in *The Polonnaruva Period*, ed. Sumana Saparamadu. Colombo: Tisara Prakasakayo, 1955, 127–45.

Paranavitana, Senerath. 'Sigiri – the Abode of a God-King,' *Journal of the Ceylon Branch of the Royal Asiatic Society*, New Series 1 (1950), 129–62.

Paranavitana, Senerath. 'The Art and Architecture of the Polonnaruva Period,' in *The Polonnaruva Period*, ed. Sumana Saparamadu. Colombo: Tisara Prakasakayo, 1955, 69–90.

Paranavitana, Senerath. *Sigiriya Graffiti*. London: Oxford University Press, 1959.

Paranavitana, Senerath. *Inscriptions of Ceylon*, Vol. 1, *Early Brahmi Inscriptions*. Colombo: Archaeological Survey of Ceylon, 1970.

Parker, Henry. *Ancient Ceylon: An Account of the Aborigines and of Part of the Early Civilization*. London: Luzac and Co, 1909.

Pathmanathan, Sivasubramaniam. *Facets of Sri Lankan History and Culture*. Colombo: Kumaran Book House, 2015.

Perera, Lakshman. *The Institutions of Ancient Ceylon from Inscriptions (from 831 to 1016 AD)*, Vol. 2, Part 2, *Economic and Religious Institutions*. Kandy: International Centre for Ethnic Studies, 2005.

Pieris, Paul Edward. 'Nagadipa and Buddhist Remains in Jaffna,' *Journal of the Royal Asiatic Society (Ceylon Branch)* 28 (1925), 40–67.

Piggott, Stuart. *Prehistoric India*. London: Penguin, 1950.

Prematilleke, Leelananda and Roland Silva. 'A Buddhist Monastery Type of Ancient Ceylon Showing Mahayanist Influence,' *Artibus Asiae* 30, 1 (1968), 61–84.

Prematilleke, Pawuludevage Leelananda. *Alahana Parivena, Polonaruva: First Archaeological Excavation Report*. Colombo: Ministry of Cultural Affairs, 1982.

Prematilleke, Pawuludevage Leelananda. *Alahana Parivena, Polonaruva: Second Archaeological Excavation Report*. Colombo: Ministry of Cultural Affairs, 1982.

Prematilleke, Pawuludevage Leelananda. *Alahana Parivena, Polonaruva: Fourth Archaeological Excavation Report*. Colombo: Ministry of Cultural Affairs, 1985.

Prematilleke, Pawuludevage Leelananda. *Alahana Parivena, Polonaruva: Sixth Archaeological Excavation Report*. Colombo: Ministry of Cultural Affairs, 1988.

Pushparatnam, Paramu. *Tourism and Monuments of Archaeological Heritage in Northern Sri Lanka*. Jaffna: Department of History, University of Jaffna, 2014.

Ragupathy, Ponnampalam. *Early Settlements in Jaffna: An Archaeological Survey*. Madras: Thillimalar Ragupathy, 1987.

Ramachandran, T. N. *Memoirs of the Archaeological Survey of India, No. 71: Nagarjunakonda, 1938*. Calcutta: Government of India Press, 1953.

Ratnayake, H. 'Hindu Bronzes from Jetavanaramaya, Anurādhapura: Bronzes from Jetavana 1984 – Circumstances of the Discovery,' in *Essays in Archaeology: Sirinimal Lakdusinghe Felicitation Volume*, ed. P. Gunawardhana, G. Adikari and R. A. E. Coningham. Battaramulla: Neptune Publication, 2010, 263–84.

Ray, Himanshu Prabhu. 'The Apsidal Shrine in Early Hinduism: Origins, Cultic Affiliation, Patronage,' *World Archaeology* 36 (2004), 343–59.

Schenk, Heidrun. 'The Dating and Historical Value of Rouletted Ware,' *Zeitschrift für Archäologie Außereuropäischer Kulturen* 1 (2006), 123–52.

Schenk, Heidrun. 'Parthian Glazed Pottery from Sri Lanka and the Indian Ocean Trade,' *Zeitschrift für Archäologie Außereuropäischer Kulturen* 2 (2007), 57–90.

Seneviratne, H. L. 'Identity and the Conflation of Past and Present,' in *Identity, Consciousness and the Past: Forging of Caste and Community in India and Sri Lanka*, ed. H. L. Seneviratne. Delhi: Oxford University Press, 1997, 3–22.

Seneviratne, Sudharshan. 'Situating World Heritage Sites in a Multi-Cultural Island Society: The Ideology of Presenting the Sacred City of Anurādhapura, Sri Lanka.' Paper presented at the Conference of the European Association of Archaeologists, British Museum, London, 4–8 July 2005.

Sharma, Ursula. *Caste*. Buckingham: Open University Press, 1999.

Shaw, Julia. *Buddhist Landscapes in Central India: Sanchi Hill and Archaeologies of Religious and Social Change, c. Third Century BC to Fifth Century AD*. London: British Association of South Asian Studies, 2007.

Sirisena, W. M. *Sri Lanka and South-East Asia*. Leiden: E. J. Brill, 1978.

Sirisoma, Munugoda. 'Brahmi Inscriptions of Sri Lanka from 3rd Century BC to 65 AD,' in *Archaeological Department Centenary (1890–1990) Commemorative Series*, Vol. 2, *Inscriptions*, ed. Nandadeva Wijesekera. Colombo: State Printing Corporation, 1990, 3–54.

Stern, Ben, Jacques Connan, Eleanor Blakelock, Rupert Jackman, Robin Coningham and Carl Heron. 'From Susa to Anurādhapura Reconstructing Aspects of Trade and Exchange in Bitumen-Coated Ceramic Vessels between Iran and Sri Lanka from the Third to the Ninth Centuries AD,' *Archaeometry* 50, 3 (2008), 409–28.

Strathern, Alan. 'The Vijaya Origin Myth of Sri Lanka and the Strangeness of Kingship,' *Past and Present* 203 (2009), 3–28.

Strickland, Keir. 'The Jungle Tide: "Collapse" in Early Medieval Sri Lanka,' PhD dissertation, Durham University, 2011.

Sundberg, Jeffrey. 'The Wilderness Monks of the AbhayagiriVihāra and the Origins of Sino-Javanese Esoteric Buddhism,' *Bijdragen tot de Taal-, Land- en Volkenkunde* 160, 1 (2004), 95–123.

Tambiah, Stanley. *Sri Lanka: Ethnic Fratricide and the Dismantling of Democracy*. Chicago: University of Chicago Press, 1986.

Tennent, James. *Ceylon: An Account of the Island, Physical, Historical, and Topographical with Notices of its Natural History, Antiquities and Productions*. London: Spottiswoode and Co., 1859.

Thantilage, Arjuna. 'Anurādhapura Period Bronzes of Sri Lanka: Schools and Resource-Utilization,' accessed 5 November 2013, www.archaeology.lk/articles/Anurādhapura-period-bronzes-of-sri-lanka-schools-and-resource-utilization.

Tomber, Roberta. 'Rome and Mesopotamia – Importers into India in the First Millennium AD,' *Antiquity* 81 (2007), 972–88.

Trigger, Bruce. *A History of Archaeological Thought*. Cambridge: Cambridge University Press, 1989.

Von Schroeder, Ulrich. *Buddhist Sculptures of Sri Lanka*. Hong Kong: Visual Dharma Publications, 1990.

Wheeler, Mortimer. 'Arikamedu: An Indo-Roman Trading Station on the East Coast of India', *Ancient India* 2 (1946), 17–124.

Wheeler, Mortimer. *Rome Beyond the Imperial Frontiers*. London: Penguin Books, 1955.

Wickremasinghe, Don Martin de Zilva. *Epigraphia Zeylanica*, Vol. 1. Oxford: Oxford University Press, 1912.

Wickremasinghe, Don Martin de Zilva. *Epigraphia Zeylanica*, Vol. 2. Colombo: Archaeological Department, 1927.

Wickremeratne, Ananda. 'Shifting Metaphors of Sacrality: The Mythic Dimensions of Anurādhapura,' in *The City as Sacred Centre: Essays on Six Asian Contexts*, ed. Bardwell Smith and Holly Reynolds. Leiden: E. J. Brill, 1987, 45–59.

Wijayapala, W. H. 'Excavations at Randenigama, Rajangane,' *Administrative Report of the Director-General of Archaeology for the Year 1997* (1997), 32–5.

Wijesuriya, Gamini. *Buddhist Meditation Monasteries of Ancient Sri Lanka*. Colombo: Department of Archaeology, Government of Sri Lanka, 1998.

Wikramagamage, Chandra, Siri Hettiarachchi, Jan Bouzek, Jiri Bren and Petr Charvat. 'Excavations at Abhayagiri Vihara (Anurādhapura, Sri Lanka) in 1982,' *Archiv Orientalni* 51 (1983), 337–71.

# Chapter 2

## Primary sources

*Cosmas Indicopleustes: Topographie Chrétienne*, trans. W. Wolska-Conus, Sources Chrétiennes 141. Paris: Les éditions du Cerf, 1968.

*Cūḷavaṃsa: Being the More Recent Part of the Mahāvaṃsa*, trans. Wilhelm Geiger, London: Pali Text Society, 1930.

*Mahāvaṃsa: Great Chronicle of Ceylon*, trans. Wilhelm Geiger assisted by Mabel Haynes Bode. London: Pali Text Society, 1912.

*Periplous of the Erythreian Sea*, trans. L. Casson. Princeton, NJ: Princeton University Press, 1989.

Photius, *Bibliothèque Photius*; Texte établi et traduit, ed. R. Henry, Vol. 1. Paris: Les Belles Lettres, 1959.

Pliny, *Natural History*, trans. H. Rackham, Vol. 2. Cambridge, MA: Harvard University Press, 1942.

## Secondary sources

Abdy, Richard and Gareth Williams. 'A Catalogue of Hoards and Single Finds from the British Isles, c. 410–675,' in *Coinage and History in the North Sea World, c. A.D. 500–1250*, ed. B. Cook and G. Williams. Leiden: Brill, 2006, 11–74.

Anastos, M. V. 'The Alexandrian Origin of the "Christian Topography" of Cosmas Indicopleustes,' *Dumbarton Oaks Papers* 3 (1946), 73–80.

Beal, S. *The Life of Hiuen Tsiang, translated from the Chinese of Shaman (Monk) Hwui Li*. 1911; reprint New Delhi: Munshiram Manoharlal, 1973.

Bopearachchi, O. 'Le commerce maritime entre Rome et Sri Lanka d'après les données numismatiques,' *Revue des Études Anciennes* 94 (1992) 107–21.

Bopearachchi, O. 'Recent Discoveries of Ancient Foreign Coins, hitherto Unknown in Sri Lankan Context,' *Sesquicentennial Commemorative Volume, Royal Asiatic Society of Sri Lanka, 1845–1995* (1995), 127–39.

Bopearachchi, O. 'Seafaring in the Indian Ocean: Archaeological Evidence from Sri Lanka,' in *Tradition and Archaeology: Early Maritime Contacts in the Indian Ocean*, ed. H. P. Ray and J.-F. Salles. New Delhi: Manohar, 1996, 59–78.

Bopearachchi, O. 'Ancient Coins in Sri Lanka,' *Economic Review* 23 (1997), 21–6.

Bopearachchi, O. 'Foreword,' in *Taprobanê: Ancient Sri Lanka as Known to Greeks and Romans*, ed. D. P. M. Weerakkody. Turnhout: Brepols, 1997, i–xv.

Bopearachchi, O. 'The Maritime Silk Road: Trade Relations between Central Asia and Sri Lanka from the Evidence of Recent Excavations,' *Silk Road Art and Archaeology* 5 (1997/8), 269–95.

Bopearachchi, O. 'Archaeological Evidence on Changing Patterns of International Trade Relations of Ancient Sri Lanka,' in *Origin, Evolution and Circulation of Foreign Coins in the Indian Ocean*, ed. O. Bopearachchi and D. P. M. Weerakkody. New Delhi: Manohar, 1998, 133–78.

Bopearachchi, O. 'Sites portuaires et emporia de l'ancien Sri Lanka: nouvelles données archéologiques,' *Arts Asiatiques* 54 (1999), 5–23.

Bopearachchi, O. 'Archaeological Evidence on Cultural and Commercial Relationships between Ancient Sri Lanka and South India,' in *Honouring Martin Quéré OMI*, ed. Gérard Robuchon and Philippe Fabry. Negombo: Viator Publications, 2002, 61–76.

Bopearachchi, O. 'Archaeological Evidence on Shipping Communities of Sri Lanka,' in *Ships and the Development of Maritime Technology in the Indian Ocean*, ed. D. Parkin and R. Barnes. London: Routledge Curzon, 2002, 92–128.

Bopearachchi, O. 'Routes Maritime et Port de L'ancien Sri Lanka,' in *Aller et Venir: Faits et Perspectives*, ed. F. Blanchon, Vol. 2. Paris: Asies, 2002, 27–43.

Bopearachchi, O. 'Inde du Sud et Sri Lanka,' in *A Survey of Numismatic Research, 1996–2000*, ed. C. Alfaro and A. Burnett. Madrid: International Association of Professional Numismatists, 2003, 685–8.

Bopearachchi, O. 'New Archaeological Evidence on Cultural and Commercial Relations between Ancient Sri Lanka and Tamil Nadu,' *Journal of Interdisciplinary Studies in History and Archaeology* 1 (2004), 60–72.

Bopearachchi, O. 'Circulation of Roman and Byzantine Gold Coins in Sri Lanka: Fact or Fiction?,' in *Dal Denarius al Dinar: L'Oriente e la Moneta Romana*, ed. F. de Romanis and S. Sorda. Rome: Instituto Italiano di Numismatica, 2006, 181–200.

Bopearachchi, O. 'Coins,' in *Anurādhapura: The British-Sri Lankan Excavations at Anuradhapura Salgaha Watta*, Vol. 2: *The Artefacts*, ed. R. A. E Coningham. Oxford: Archaeopress, 2006, 7–26.

Bopearachchi, O. and R. M. Wickremesinhe. *Ruhuna: An Ancient Civilization Re-visited. Numismatic and Archaeological Evidence on Inland and Maritime Trade*. Colombo: Tharanjee Prints, 1999.

Boulnois, L. *Silk Road: Monks, Warriors and Merchants on the Silk Road*, 2nd edn. London: Odyssey Books, 2005.

Brancaccio, P. *The Buddhist Caves at Aurangabad*. Leiden: Brill, 2010.

Canepa, M. P. *The Two Eyes of the Earth*. Berkeley: University of California Press, 2009.

Cappers, R. T. J. *Roman Food-Prints at Berenike: Archaeological Evidence of Trade and Subsistence in the Eastern Desert of Egypt*. Los Angeles: Cotsen Institute of Archaeology, 2006.

Carlson, D. 'INA in Sri Lanka, Pearl of the Indian Ocean,' *The Institute of Nautical Archaeology Annual* (2010), 89–95.

Carlson, D. and K. Threthewey. 'Exploring the Oldest Shipwreck in the Indian Ocean,' *The Institute of Nautical Archaeology Quarterly* 40 (2013), 8–14.

Carradice, I. 'Flavian Coinage,' in *The Oxford Handbook of Greek and Roman Coinage*, ed. W. Metcalf. Oxford: Oxford University Press, 2012, 375–90.

Carson, R. A. G., J. P. C. Kent and A. M. Burnett. *The Roman Imperial Coinage*, Vol. 10, *The Empire Divided and the Fall of the Western Parts, AD 395–491*. London: Spink, 1994.

Carswell, J. 'The Port of Mantai, Sri Lanka,' in *Rome and India: The Ancient Sea Trade*, ed. V. Begley and R. D. de Puma. Madison, WI: University of Wisconsin Press, 1991, 197–203.

Carswell, J. and M. Prickett. 'Mantai 1980: A Preliminary Investigation,' *Ancient Ceylon* 5 (1984), 11–37.

Carswell, J., S. U. Deraniyagala and A. Graham, eds. *Mantai: City by the Sea*. Stuttgart: Linden Soft Verlag, 2013.

Casson, L. 'New Light on Maritime Loans: P. Vindob. G 40822,' *Zeitschrift für Papyrologie und Epigraphik* 84 (1990) 195–206.

Chami, F. A. 'Graeco-Roman Trade Link and the Bantu Migration Theory,' *Anthropos* 94 (1999), 205–15.

Chanmugam P. K. and F. L. W. Jayawardene. 'Skeletal Remains from Tirukketiswaram,' *Ceylon Journal of Science*, Section G V, 11 (1954), 65–6.

Charlesworth, M. P. *Trade Routes and Commerce of the Roman Empire*. Cambridge: Cambridge University Press, 1926.

Choksy, J. K. 'Sailors, Soldiers, Priests and Merchants: Reappraising Iran's Early Connections to Ceylon,' *Iranica Antiqua* 48 (2013), 363–91.

Clark, T. L. 'Imaging the Cosmos: The *Christian Topography* by Kosmas Indikopleustes,' PhD dissertation, Temple University, Philadelphia, 2008.

Codrington, H. W. *Ceylon Coins and Currency*. Ceylon: A. C. Richards, 1924.

Coningham, R., ed. *Anurādhapura: The British-Sri Lankan Excavations at Anuradhapura Salgaha Watta*, Vol. 2, *The Artefacts*. Oxford: Archaeopress, 2006.

Coningham, R., P. Gunawardhana, G. Adikari, M. Katugampola, I. Simpson and R. Young. 'The Anuradhapura (Sri Lanka) Project: The Hinterland (Phase II), Preliminary Report on the First Season 2005,' *South Asian Studies* 22, 1 (2006), 53–64.

Cribb, J. 'Chinese Coin Finds from South India and Sri Lanka,' in *Numismatic Panorama: Essays in the Memory of Late Shri S. M. Shukula*, ed. K. K. Maheshwari and B. Rath. New Delhi: Harman Publishing House, 1996, 253–69.

Darley, R. 'Indo-Byzantine Exchange, 4th–7th Centuries: A Global History,' PhD dissertation, University of Birmingham, 2014.

Day, R. 'A Tale of "Four" Hoards (or Unpicking Akki Alur),' *Journal of the Oriental Numismatic Society* 211 (2012), 5–13.

De Romanis, F. 'Romanukharaṭṭha and Taprobane: Relations between Rome and Sri Lanka in the First Century AD,' in *Crossings: Early Mediterranean Contacts with India*, ed. F. de Romanis and A. Tchernia. Delhi: Manohar, 1997, 161–237.

De Saram, F. J. and G. *F. J. & G. de Saram, 1841–2001: 160 Year Practice of a Law Firm in its Historical Setting*. Colombo: Vijitha Yapa Publications, 2001.

Devendra, S. 'Pre-Modern Sri Lankan Ships and Shipping,' in *Ships and the Development of Maritime Technology across the Indian Ocean*, ed. D. Parkin and R. Barnes. New York: Routledge Curzon, 2002, 128–73.

Falk, H. 'Three Epigraphs from Godawaya, Sri Lanka', in *Ancient Ruhuna: Sri Lankan-German Archaeological Project in the Southern Province*, Vol. 1, ed. H.-J. H. Weisshaar et al. Mainz and Wiesbaden: Verlag Philipp von Zabern and Reichert Verlag, 2001, 327–34.

Francis, P. *Asia's Maritime Bead Trade, 300 BC to the Present*. Hawai'i: University of Hawai'i Press, 2002.

Francis, P. 'Western Geographic Knowledge of Sri Lanka and Mantai ca 325 BC to 1170 AD,' in *Mantai: City by the Sea*, ed. J. Carswell, S. U. Deraniyagala and A. Graham. Stuttgart: Linden Soft Verlag, 2013, 53–60.

Frasch, T. 'Religious and Economic Development of Ancient Anuradhapura,' in *Sri Lanka, Past and Present*, ed. M. Domroes and H. Roth, Weikersheim: Margraf, 1998, 61–81.

Gannon, M. 'Indian Ocean's Oldest Shipwreck Set for Excavation,' LiveScience Blog, 4 February 2014, www.livescience.com/42901-indian-ocean-oldest-shipwreck.html.

Ghosh, D. N. *Business and Polity: Dynamics of a Changing Relationship*. London: Sage, 2011.

Glover, I. C. 'The Archaeological Evidence for Early Trade between India and Southeast Asia,' in *The Indian Ocean in Antiquity*, ed. J. Reade. London: Kegan Paul International, 1996, 365–400.

Goodwin, T. *Arab-Byzantine Coinage*. London: The Nour Foundation, 2005.

Graham, A. 'Excavations 1887–1976 and the Condition of the Site in 1980,' in *Mantai: City by the Sea*, ed. J. Carswell, S. U. Deraniyagala and A. Graham. Stuttgart: Linden Soft Verlag, 2013, 98–101.

Graham, A. 'Pottery from the Excavated Sequence in Trenches H and G,' in *Mantai: City by the Sea*, ed. J. Carswell, S. U. Deraniyagala and A. Graham. Stuttgart: Linden Soft Verlag, 2013, 191–212.

Graham, A. 'The Primary Development of the Mound,' in *Mantai: City by the Sea*, ed. J. Carswell, S. U. Deraniyagala and A. Graham. Stuttgart: Linden Soft Verlag, 2013, 143–56.

Grierson, P. *Byzantine Coinage*. Washington, DC: Dumbarton Oaks Library and Collection, 1999.

Gupta, P. L. 'Coins in Rome's Indian Trade,' in *Coinage, Trade and Economy*, ed. A. K. Jha. Nasik: Indian Institute of Research in Numismatic Studies, 1991, 122–37.

Gurukkal, R. *Rethinking Classical Indo-Roman Trade. Political Economy of Eastern Mediterranean Exchange Relations*. New Delhi: Oxford University Press, 2016.

Gyselen, R. M. ed. *Circulation des Monnaies, des Marchandises et des Biens*. Leuven: Peeters, 1993.

Hahn, W. *Moneta Imperii Byzantini*, 3 vols. Vienna: Veröffentlichungen der Österreichischen Akademie der Wissenschaften, 1973.

Harris, A. *Byzantium, Britain and the West: The Archaeology of Cultural Identity, AD 400–650*. Stroud: Tempus Publishing, 2003.

Hendy, M. *Studies in the Byzantine Monetary Economy*. Cambridge: Cambridge University Press, 1985.

Hinnells J. and A. Williams, *Parsis in India and the Diaspora*. London: Routledge, 2007.

Hudson, G. *Europe and China: A Survey of their Relations from the Earliest Times to 1800*. London: Edward Arnold and Co., 1931.

Huxley, G. L. 'On the Greek Martyrium of the Negranites,' *Proceedings of the Royal Irish Academy, Section C: Archaeology, Celtic Studies, History, Linguistics, Literature* 80 (1980), 41–55.

Kemper, S. *The Presence of the Past: Chronicles, Politics and Culture in Sinhala Life*. Ithaca, NY, and London: Cornell University Press, 1991.

Kennedy, J. 'The Secret of Kanishka,' *Journal of the Royal Asiatic Society of Great Britain and Ireland* (1912), 665–88.

Kessler, O. 'The Discovery of an Ancient Sea Port at the Silk Road of the Sea – Archaeological Relics of the Godavaya Harbor,' in *Sri Lanka: Past and Present; Archaeology, Geography, Economics, Selected Papers on German Research*, ed. M. Domroes and H. Roth, Würzburg: Margraf Verlag, 1998, 12–37.

Kiribamune, S. 'The Role of the Port City of Mahatittha (Mantota) in the Trade Networks of the Indian Ocean,' in *Mantai: City by the Sea, ed.* J. Carswell , S. U. Deraniyagala and A. Graham. Stuttgart: Linden Soft Verlag, 2013, 40–52.

Kominko, M. 'New Perspectives on Paradise – The Levels of Reality in Byzantine and Latin Medieval Maps,' in *Cartography in Antiquity and the Middle Ages: Fresh Perspectives, New Methods*, ed. R. J. A. Talbert and R. W. Unger. Leiden: Brill, 2008, 139–53.

Kominko, M. *The World of Kosmas: Illustrated Byzantine Codices of the Christian Topography*. Cambridge: Cambridge University Press, 2013.

Krishnamurthy, R. 'Roman Gold Coins from Southern Tamil Nadu, India: some 5th cent. A.D. Solidi and their Imitations,' in *Dal Denarius al Dinar: L'Oriente e la Moneta Romana*, ed. F. de Romanis and S. Sorda. Rome: Instituto Italiano di Numismatica, 2006, 173–9.

Krishnamurthy, R. *Late Roman Copper Coins from South India: Karur, Madurai and Tirukkoilur* Chennai: Garnet Publishers, 2007.
Law, B. C. *The Chronicle of the Island of Ceylon, of the Dipavamsa, a Historical Poem of the 4th Century AD*. Colombo: Ceylon Historical Journal, 1957–8.
Legge, J. *A Record of Buddhistic Kingdoms, Being an Account of the Chinese Monk Fa-Hien of his Travels in India and Ceylon (AD 399–414) in Search of the Buddhist Books of Discipline*. Oxford: Clarendon Press, 1886.
*Leslie de Saram Collection: A Classified List*. Peradeniya: Peradeniya University, 1981.
Lokubandara, W. J. M. 'Sri Lanka's Role in the Maritime Silk Route,' in *Sri Lanka and the Silk Road of the Sea*, 2nd edn, ed. S. Bandaranayake. Colombo: Sri Lanka Institute of International Relations, 2003, 13–15.
Miller, J. I. *The Spice Trade of the Roman Empire, 29 BC to AD 641*. Oxford: Clarendon Press, 1969.
Mohanty, R. 'Indian Imported Pottery,' in *Mantai: City by the Sea*, ed. J. Carswell, S. U. Deraniyagala and A. Graham. Stuttgart: Linden Soft Verlag, 2013, 213–27.
Morrison, K. D. 'Commerce and Culture in South Asia: Perspectives from Archaeology and History,' *Annual Review of Anthropology* 26 (1997), 87–108.
Morrisson, C. 'Byzantine Money: Its Production and Circulation,' in *The Economic History of Byzantium: From the Seventh through the Fifteenth Century*, ed. A. Laiou. Washington, DC: Dumbarton Oaks Research Library and Collection, 2001, 906–66.
Muthucumarana, R. 'Ancient Port City of Godawaya and the Recent Discovery of the Unknown Wooden Wreck with Black and Red Ware,' Maritime Archaeology Unit Blog, 2011, www.mausrilanka.lk/sub%20pages/Godawaya.html.
Paranavitana, S., ed. *Inscriptions of Ceylon*, 5 vols. Colombo: Archaeological Survey of Ceylon, 1970.
Parker, G. *The Making of Roman India*. Cambridge: Cambridge University Press, 2011.
Parker, S. T. 'The Roman Port of Aila: Economic Connections with the Red Sea Littoral,' in *Connected Hinterlands: Proceedings of Red Sea Project IV*, held at the University of Southampton (September 2008), ed. L. Blue et al. Oxford: Archaeopress, 2009, 79–84.
Peacock, D. P. S, E. Peacock and L. Blue, *The Ancient Red Sea Port of Adulis: Eritrea Report of the Etritro-British Expedition 2004–5*. Oxford: Oxbow Books, 2007.
Porter, V. 'Islamic Coins found in Sri Lanka,' in *Origin, Evolution and Circulation*, ed. O Bopearachchi and D. P. M Weerakkody. New Delhi: Manohar, 1998, 225–72.
Puskás, I. 'Trade Contacts between India and the Roman Empire,' in *India and the Ancient World: History, Trade and Culture before AD 650*, ed. G. Pollet. Leuven: Department Oriëntalisteik, 1987, 141–56.
Ratto, R. *Collection privée. Monnaies Byzantines et d'autres pays contemporains à l'epoque Byzantine*. Auction catalogue of 9 December 1930; reprint Amsterdam, 1959.
Ray, H. P. *The Winds of Change: Buddhism and the Maritime Links of Early South Asia*. Oxford: Oxford University Press, 1994.
Roth, H. 'Excavation at the Port of Godavaya, Hambantota District, Sri Lanka,' in *Sri Lanka, Past and Present: Archaeology, Geography, Economics*, ed. M. Domroes and H. Roth. Weikersheim: Margraf Verlag, 1998, 1–11.
Sastri, K. A. *A History of South India from Prehistoric Times to the Fall of Vijayanagar*, 2nd edn. Oxford: Oxford University Press, 1958.
Sedlar, J. W. *India and the Greek World: A Study in the Transmission of Culture*. Totaw, NJ: Rowman and Littlefield, 1980.
Seland, E. 'Trade and Christianity in the Indian Ocean during Late Antiquity,' *Journal of Late Antiquity* 5, 1 (2012), 72–86.
Sen, T. 'Buddhism and the Maritime Crossings,' in *China and Beyond in the Medieval Period: Cultural Crossings and Inter-Regional Connections*, ed. D. Wong and G. Heldt. Amherst and Delhi: Cambria and Manohar Press, 2014, 39–62.
Seneviratne, S. 'Situating World Heritage Sites in a Multicultural Society: The Ideology of Presentation at the Sacred City of Anuradhapura, Sri Lanka,' in *Archaeology and the Post-Colonial Critique*, ed. M. Liebmann and U. Z. Rizvi. New York: Altamira Press, 2008, 177–95.
Sidebotham, S. E. *Berenike and the Ancient Maritime Spice Route*. Berkeley: University of California Press, 2011.
Silva, R. and J. Bouzek, 'Mantai – a Second Arikamedu?,' *Antiquity* 59 (1985), 46–7.
Sirisena, O. M. R. *Medieval Gold Coins of Sri Lanka, 700–1100*. Colombo: Unigraphics Ltd., 2002.
Siriweera, W. I. 'Godavaya: Ancient Port Near Modern Magamtota,' *The Island* (Colombo), 10 January 2014, www.island.lk/index.php?page_cat=article-details&page=article-details&code_title=95650.

Strauch, I. *Foreign Sailors on Socotra: The Inscriptions and Drawings from the Cave Hoq*. Bremen: Ute Hempen Verlag, 2013.

Tennent, J. E. *Ceylon: An Account of the Island Physical, Historical and Topographical*, Vol. 1. 1860; reprint Project Gutenberg, 2004, www.gutenberg.org/files/13552.

Thapar, R. 'Early Mediterranean Contacts with India: An Overview,' in *Crossings: Early Mediterranean Contacts with India*, ed. F. de Romanis and A. Tchernia. New Delhi: Manohar, 1997, 11–40.

Thierry, F. 'Maritime Silk Routes and Chinese Coin Hoards,' in *Origin, Evolution and Circulation of Foreign Coins in the Indian Ocean*, ed. O. Bopearachchi and D. P. M. Weerakkody. New Delhi: Manohar, 1998, 199–223.

Thurston, E. *Madras Government Museum: Coins Catalogue No. 2, Roman, Indo-Portuguese and Ceylon*. Madras: Government Press, 1888.

Tomber, R. *Indo-Roman Trade: From Pots to Pepper*. London: Duckworth, 2009.

Trethewey, K. 'The Oldest Known Ship in the Indian Ocean: Logistics for an Upcoming INA Excavation,' *Institute of Nautical Archaeology Quarterly* 39, 1–2 (2012), 28–9.

Turner, P. *Roman Coins from India*. London: Royal Numismatic Society, 1989.

Walburg, R. *Coins and Tokens from Ancient Ceylon*. Wiesbaden: Reichert Verlag, 2008.

Walburg, R. and A. Graham, 'The Coins,' in *Mantai: City by the Sea*, ed. J., Carswell, S. U. Deraniyagala and A. Graham. Stuttgart: Linden Soft Verlag, 2013, appendix 3, 1–3.

Weerakkody, P. M. *Taprobanê: Ancient Sri Lanka as Known by the Greeks and Romans*. Turnhout: Brepols, 1997.

Weisshaar, H.-J. H., H. Roth and W. Wijeyapala eds. *Ancient Ruhuna: Sri Lankan-German Archaeological Project in the Southern Province*, Mainz and Wiesbaden: Verlag Philipp von Zabern and Reichert Verlag, 2001.

Wendrich, Z. R., S. Tomber, S. E. Sidebotham, J. A. Harrell, R. T. J. Cappers and R. S. Bagnall. 'Berenike Crossroads: The Integration of Information,' *Journal of the Economic and Social History of the Orient* 46 (2003), 46–87.

Wheeler, M. *Rome Beyond the Imperial Frontiers*. London: G. Bell and Sons Ltd., 1954.

Whitehouse, D. 'Epilogue: Roman Trade in Perspective,' in *Rome and India: The Ancient Sea Trade*, ed. V. Begley and R. D. de Puma, 1991, 216–18.

Whitehouse, D. *Siraf: History, Topography and Environment*. Oxford: Oxbow Books, 2009.

Wickremasinghe, D. M. de Zilva et al., *Epigraphica Zeylanica*, 7 vols. London: Published for the Government of Ceylon by Henry Milford, 1904.

Wilson, N. G. *The Bibliotheca: A Selection. Photius, Translated with Notes*. London: Duckworth, 1994.

Young, G. *Rome's Eastern Trade: International Commerce and Imperial Policy, 31 BC–AD 305*. London: Routledge, 2001.

## Chapter 3

### Primary sources

*The Chiang Mai Chronicle*, trans. David Wyatt and Aroonrut Wichienkeeo. Chiang Mai: Silkworm, 1998.

*The Dīpavaṃsa*, ed. and trans. Hermann Oldenberg. London: Williams and Norgate, 1879.

*Inscriptions of Burma*, comp. G. H. Luce and U Pe Maung Tin, Vol. 3 Oxford: University Press, 1939.

*The Katikavatas. Laws of the Buddhist Order of Ceylon from the 12th Century to the 18th Century*, ed. and trans. Nandasena Ratnapala. Munich, Kitzinger, 1971.

*The Mahāvaṃsa*, ed. Wilhelm Geiger. London: Pali Text Society, 1909.

*The Myazedi Inscription in Four Languages*, ed. Cultural Institute. Rangoon: Government Press, 1960.

*A Record of the Buddhistic Kingdoms, Being an Account by the Chinese Monk Fâ-hien of his Travels in India and Ceylon*, trans. James Legge. 1886; reprint New York: Paragon and Dover Publications, 1965.

### Secondary sources

Ali, Daud. 'The Early Inscriptions of Indonesia and the Problem of the Sanskrit Cosmopolis,' in *Early Interactions between South and Southeast Asia: Reflections on Cross-Cultural Exchange*, ed. P.-Y. Manguin and A. Mani. New Delhi and Singapore: Manohar and Institute of Southeast Asian Studies, 2011, 277–95.

Appleby, Scott and Martin Marty, eds. *Fundamentalisms Comprehended*. Chicago: University of Chicago Press, 1995.
Assavavirulhakarn, Prapod. *The Ascendancy of Theravāda Buddhism in Southeast Asia*. Chiang Mai: Silkworm, 2010, 71–112.
Barnett, Lionel D. 'The Manavulu Sandesaya,' *Journal of the Royal Asiatic Society* (1905), 265–83.
Bechert, Heinz. *Eine regionale hochsprachliche Tradition in Südasien: Sanskrit-Literatur bei den buddhistischen Singhalesen*, Sitzungsberichte der Österreichischen Akademie der Wissenschaften, Philiosophisch-Historische Klasse 718. Vienna: Österreichische Akademie der Wissenschaften, 2005.
Berkwitz, Stephen C. *South Asian Buddhism: A Survey*. London: Routledge, 2010.
Blackburn, Anne. 'Buddhist Connections in the Indian Ocean: Changes in Monastic Mobility, 1000–1500', *Journal of the Social and Economic History of the Orient* 58, 3 (2015), 237–66.
Bode, Mabel. *The Pāli Literature of Burma*. London: Royal Asiatic Society, 1909.
Bronkhorst, Johannes. 'The Spread of Sanskrit in Southeast Asia,' in *Early Interactions between South and Southeast Asia: Reflections on Cross-Cultural Exchange*, ed. Pierre-Yves Manguin, A. Mani and Geoff Wade. Singapore: ISEAS, 2011, 263–76.
Charney, Michael. *Powerful Learning: Buddhist Literati and the Throne in Burma's Last Dynasty*. Ann Arbor: University of Michigan Press, 2006.
Collins, Steven. 'On the Very Idea of the Pāli Canon,' *Journal of the Pāli Text Society* 15 (1981), 89–126.
Collins, Steven. *Nirvana and other Buddhist Felicities*. Cambridge: Cambridge University Press, 1998.
Collins, Steven. 'What is Literature in Pāli?' in *Literary Cultures in History*, ed. Sheldon Pollock. Berkeley and Los Angeles: University of California Press, (2003), 680–1.
Crosby, Kate 'The Origin of Pali as a Language Name in Medieval Theravada Literature,' *Journal of the Centre for Buddhist Studies of Sri Lanka* 2 (2004), 70–116.
Falk, Harry. 'Die Goldblätter aus Śrī Kṣetra,' *Wiener Zeitschrift für die Kunde Südasiens* 41 (1997), 53–92.
Frasch, Tilman. *Pagan. Stadt und Staat*. Stuttgart: Steiner, 1996.
Frasch, Tilman. 'A Buddhist Network in the Bay of Bengal: Relations between Bodhgaya, Burma and Sri Lanka, c. 300–1300,' in *From the Mediterranean to the China Sea: Miscellaneous Notes*, ed. Claude Guillot et al. Wiesbaden: Harrassowitz, 1998, 69–93.
Frasch, Tilman. 'Religious and Economic Development in Ancient Anuradhapura,' in *Sri Lanka Past and Present*, ed. Manfred Domrös and Helmut Roth. Weikersheim: Marggraf, 1998, 68–72.
Frasch, Tilman. 'Der Buddhismus im Jahr 1000,' *Periplus. Jahrbuch für Außereuropäische Geschichte* 10 (2000), 56–72.
Frasch, Tilman. 'Buddha's Tooth Relic: Contesting Rituals and the Early State in Sri Lanka,' in *Ritual Dynamics and the Science of the Ritual*, ed. Axel Michaels, Vol. 3, *State, Power and Violence*, ed. Marko Kitts et al. Wiesbaden: Harrassowitz, 2010, 647–64.
Frasch, Tilman. 'Buddhist Councils in a Time of Transition: Globalism, Modernity and the Preservation of Textual Traditions,' in *Contemporary Buddhist Studies* 14, 1 (2013), 38–51.
Frasch, Tilman. 'The Theravada Buddhist Ecumene in the 15th Century: Intellectual Foundations and Material Representations', in *Buddhism across Asia: Networks of Material, Intellectual and Cultural Exchange*, Vol. 1, ed. Tansen Sen. Singapore/Delhi: ISEAS/Manohar, 2014, 347–67.
Frasch, Tilman 'Kontakte, Konzile, Kontroversen: Begegnungen in der Theravada-Kosmopolis, ca. 1000–1300 CE,' in *Begegnungen in den Religionen Asiens*, ed. Oliver Freiberger et al. Göttingen: Vandenhoeck & Ruprecht, forthcoming.
Goh Geok-yian. *The Wheel-Turner and His House: Kingship in a Buddhist Ecumene*. DeKalb, IL: Northern Illinois University Press, 2015.
Goonatilake, Hema. 'Sri Lanka – Myanmar Historical Relations in Religion, Culture and Polity,' *Journal of the Royal Asiatic Society of Sri Lanka* 55 (2009), 80–104.
Gunawardana R. A. L. H. *Robe and Plough: Monasticism and Economic Interest in Early Medieval Sri Lanka*. Tucson: University of Arizona Press, 1979.
Gunawardana R. A. L. H. 'Subtle Silks of Ferrous Firmness: Buddhist Nuns in Ancient and Early Medieval Sri Lanka and their Role in the Propagation of Buddhism,' *The Sri Lankan Journal of the Humanities* 14 (1988), 1–59.
Heirman, Ann. 'Chinese Nuns and their Ordination in 5th Century China,' *Journal of the International Association of Buddhist Studies* 24, 2 (2001), 275–305.
Hettiaratchi, S. B. *Social and Cultural History of Ancient Sri Lanka*. Delhi: Sri Satguru, 1988, 99–102.
Htway, U Tin. 'A Preliminary Note on the Vinayadharas of Pagan Period in Burma,' in *Festschrift für Prof. Manuel Sarkisyanz*, ed. Barbara Diehl-Eli et al. Frankfurt: Peter Lang, 1987, 411–58.
Hultzsch, E. 'A Vaishnava Inscription from Pagan,' *Epigraphia Indica* 7 (1902–3), 197–8.
Ilangasinha, H. B. *Buddhism in Medieval Sri Lanka* Delhi: Sri Satguru, 1992.

Keyes, Charles F. *The Golden Peninsula: Culture and Adaptation in Mainland Southeast Asia*. London: Macmillan, 1977.
Ko, Taw Sein. *The Kalyani Inscriptions Erected by King Dhammaceti at Pegu in 1476 AD*. Rangoon: Government Printing, 1892.
Liyanagamage, Amaradasa. *The Decline of Polonnaruwa and the Rise of Dambadeniya*. Colombo: Department of Cultural Affairs and Government Press, 1968.
Lottermoser, Friedgard. 'Minor Pāli Grammar Texts: The *Saddabindu* and its "New" Commentary,' *Journal of the Pali Text Society* 11 (1987), 79–109.
Luce, Gordon H. *Old Burma – Early Pagan*, Locust Valley, NY: Augustine, 1969.
Luce, Gordon H. and U. Ba Shin. 'A Chiang Mai Mahāthera Visits Pagan (1393 AD),' *Artibus Asiae* 24, 3 (1961), 330–7.
Luce, Gordon H. and U Pe Maung Tin. 'Inscriptions of Burma, Edited and Translated,' *Bulletin of the Burma Historical Commission* 1 (1960), 1–28.
Malalasekera, G. P. *The Pāli Literature of Ceylon*. London: Royal Asiatic Society, 1928.
Malalasekera, G. P. *The Pāli Literature of Ceylon*. Kandy: Buddhist Publication Society, 1994.
Pichard, Pierre. *Inventory of the Monuments at Pagan*, Vol. 2. Paris: UNESCO, 1993.
Pichard, Pierre. *Inventory of the Monuments at Pagan*, Vol. 4. Paris: UNESCO, 1994
Rohanadeera, Mendis. 'The Noen Sa Bua Inscription of Dong Si Mahabo, Prachinburi,' *Journal of the Siam Society* (1988), 89–98.
Schalk, Peter. *Buddhism among Tamils in Tamil Ilam and Tamilakam*, 2 vols. Uppsala: Uppsala University Press, 2004.
Sirisena, W. M. *Sri Lanka and Southeast Asia*. Leiden: Brill, 1978.
Skilling, Peter. 'New Pāli Inscriptions from Southeast Asia,' *Journal of the Pāli Text Society* 23 (1997), 123–57.
Skilling, Peter. 'The Advent of Theravada Buddhism to Mainland Southeast Asia,' in *Buddhism and Buddhist Literature of Southeast Asia*. Bangkok and Lumbini: Fragile Palm Leaves Foundation, 2009, 104–19.
Stargardt, Janice. 'The Oldest Known Pāli Texts, 5th–6th Century,' *Journal of the Pāli Text* Society 21 (1995), 199–213.
Tun, U Than. 'History of Buddhism in Burma, AD 1000–1300,' *Journal of the Burma Research Society* 51 (1978), 77–87.
Tun, U Than. 'An Original Inscription Dated 10 September 1223, that King Badon Copied on 27 October 1785,' in *Études birmanes en hommage à Denise Bernot*, ed. Pierre Pichard and François Robinne. Paris: École Française d'Extrême-Orient, 1998, 37–42.
Tun, U Than. *Hnaung-dwe Kyauksa-mya*. Yangon: Myanmar Historical Commission, 2005.
Verardi, Giovanni. *Hardships and Downfall of Buddhism in India*. Singapore: Institute of Southeast Asian Studies, 2011.
von Hinüber, Oskar. *Die Sprachgeschichte des Pali im Spiegel der südostasiatischen Handschriftenüberlieferung*, Abhandlungen der geistes- und sozialwissenschaftlichen Klasse 8. Mainz: Akademie der Wissenschaften und der Literatur, 1988.
Walburg, Reinhold. *Coins and Tokens from Ancient Ceylon*. Wiesbaden: Reichert Verlag, 2008.

# Chapter 4

## Primary sources

*The Book of Discipline (Vinaya-Piṭaka)*, Vol. 1, *Sutta-vibhaṅga*, ed. I. B. Horner. London: Luzac for Pali Text Society, 1949.
*Butsaraṇa of Vidyacakravarti*, ed. Bambarendē Siri Sīvalī Thera. Colombo: A. Gunaratne, 1968.
*A Chronicle of the Thūpa and the Thūpavaṃsa*, trans. N. A. Jayawickrama. London: Luzac for Pali Text Society, 1971.
*Cūḷavaṃsa: Being the More Recent Part of the Mahāvaṃsa*, ed. and trans. Wilhelm Geiger, 2 vols. 1925–9; reprint London: Pali Text Society, 1980.
*Daiwagnakâmadhênu*, ed. C. A. Seelakkhanda. Benares: Vidyâ Vilâs Press, 1906.
*Daṁbadeṇi Asna*, ed. D. D. Ranasinha. Colombo: J. D. Pranandu, 1928.
'Dāṭhāvaṃsa,' ed. T. W. Rhys Davids, *Journal of the Pali Text Society* 1 (1884), 109–50.
Dimitrov, Dragomir. *Mārgavibhāga – Die Unterscheidung der Stilarten. Kritische Ausgabe des ersten Kapitels von Daṇḍins Poetik Kāvyādarśa und der tibetischen Übertragung Sñan ṅag me loṅ nebst einer deutschen Übersetzung des Sanskrittextes*. Marburg: Indica et Tibetica Verlag, 2002.

Dimitrov, Dragomir. *Śabdālaṃkāradoṣavibhāga – Die Unterscheidung der Lautfiguren und der Fehler. Kritische Ausgabe des dritten Kapitels von Daṇḍins Poetik Kāvyādarśa und der tibetischen Übertragung Sñan ṅag me loṅ samt dem Sanskrit-Kommentar des Dpaṅ Blo gros brtan pa und einer deutschen Übersetzung des Sanskrit-Grundtextes*. Wiesbaden: Harrassowitz Verlag, 2011.

Geiger, Wilhelm. *The Dīpavaṃsa and Mahāvaṃsa and their Historical Development in Ceylon*, trans. E. M. Coomaraswamy. Colombo: H.C. Cottle, Government Printer, 1908.

*Handsome Nanda*, trans. Linda Covill. New York: New York University Press, 2007.

*The Jātaka*, Vol. 1, ed. V. Fausbøll. Oxford: The Pali Text Society, 2000.

*Jinacarita, or, 'The Career of the Conqueror,'* trans. Charles Duroiselle Ahmedabad: Parimal Publications, 1982.

*The Katikāvatas: Laws of the Buddhist Order of Ceylon from the 12th Century to the 18th Century*, trans. Nandasena Ratnapala. Munich: Münchener Studien zur Sprachwissenschaft, 1971.

*Kāvyādarśaya*, ed. Dharmakīrti Dharmārāma. Peliyagoda: Satyasamuccaya Press, 1925.

*Kāvyalakṣaṇa, also known as Kāvyādarśa: with commentary called Ratnaśrī of Ratnaśrījñāna*, ed. Anantalal Thakur and Upendra Jha. Darbhanga: Mithila Institute of Post-graduate Studies and Research in Sanskrit Learning, 1957.

*Khuddaka-Pāṭha: A Pali Text*, ed. R. C. Childers. London: Trübner, 1869.

*Life of the Buddha*, trans. Patrick Olivelle. New York: New York University Press, 2008.

*Mahābodhivaṃsa*, ed. S. A. Strong. London: Pali Text Society, 1891.

*The Mahāvaṃsa, or, The Great Chronicle of Ceylon*, trans. Wilhelm Geiger. 1912; reprint Colombo: The Ceylon Government Information Department, 1950.

*Moggallāna-pañcikā-ṭīkā*, ed. Aggadhammābhivaṃsathera. Rangoon: Zabu Meit Swe Press, 1955.

*The Nyāyabindu of Śrī Dharmakīrti with a Sanskrit Commentary by Śrī Dharmottarācārya*, ed. Candraśekhara Śāstrī. Banares: Chowkhamba Sanskrit Series Office, 1954.

Paranavitana, Senarat and H. W Codrington, eds. *Epigraphia Zeylanica*, Vol. IV, Colombo: Archaeological Department, 1943.

*Saddanīti: La Grammaire Palie D'Aggavaṃsa, I Padamālā (Pariccheda 1–XIV), II Dhātumālā (Pariccheda XV–XIX), III Suttamālā (Pariccheda XX–XXVIII)*, ed. Helmer Smith Lund: C. W. K. Gleerup, 1928–30.

*Sāsanavaṃsa*, ed. Mabel Bode. London: H. Frowde, 1897.

'Siya-Bas-Lakara and a Theory of Suggestion,' trans. N. P. Unni. *University of Ceylon Review* 12, 1–2 (1964), 21–8.

*Siyabas Lakara or Sinhalese Rhetoric by King Silámēghavarṇa, Paraphrased by Ratnamadhvácárya Mahá Théra*, ed. Jayatilaka, Hendrick. Colombo: Lakrivikiraṇa Press, 1892.

*Subodhālaṅkāra, Porāṇa-ṭīkā (Mahāsāmi-ṭīkā) by Saṅgharakkhita Mahāsāmi, Abhinava-ṭīkā (Nissaya)*, ed. Padhmanabh S. Jaini. Oxford: The Pali Text Society, 2000.

*Visuddhimagga: The Path of Purification*, trans. Bhikku Ñāṇamoli. 1959; reprint Kandy: Buddhist Publication Society, 2010.

## Secondary sources

Ariyapala, M. B. *Society in Mediaeval Ceylon: The State of Society in Ceylon as Depicted in the Saddarma-ratnāvaliya and other Literature of the Thirteenth Century*. 1956; reprint Colombo: Department of Cultural Affairs, 1968.

Berkwitz, S. *History of the Buddha's Relic Shrine: A Translation of the Sinhala Thūpavaṃsa*. Oxford: Oxford University Press, 2007.

Bhikkhu Bodhi. *The Numerical Discourses of the Buddha: A Translation of the Aṅguttara Nikāya*. Boston: Wisdom Publications, 2012.

Blackburn, Anne. 'Magic in the Monastery: Textual Practice and Monastic Identity in Sri Lanka,' *History of Religions* 38, 4 (1999), 354–72.

Blackburn, Anne. 'Buddhist Connections in the Indian Ocean: Changes in Monastic Mobility, 1000–1500,' *Journal of the Economic and Social History of the Orient* 68 (2015), 237–66.

Bronkhorst, Johannes. *Buddhism in the Shadow of Brahmanism*, Handbuch der Orientalistik 24. Leiden: Brill, 2011.

Collins, Steven. 'On the Very Idea of a Pali Canon,' *Journal of the Pali Text Society* 15 (1990), 89–126.

Collins, Steven. *Nirvana and Other Buddhist Felicities: Utopias of the Pali Imaginaire*. Cambridge: Cambridge University Press, 1998.

Collins, Steven. 'What is Literature in Pali?,' in *Literary Cultures in History: Reconstructions from South Asia*, ed. Sheldon Pollock. Berkeley: University of California Press, 2003, 649–88.

Cone, Margaret. *A Dictionary of Pali. Part 1, a-kh*. Oxford: Pali Text Society, 2001.

Deegalle, Mahinda. 'Buddhist Preaching and Sinhala Religious Rhetoric: Medieval Buddhist Methods to Popularize Theravāda,' *Numen* 44, 2 (1997), 180–210.
Deegalle, Mahinda. *Popularizing Buddhism: Preaching and Performance in Sri Lanka*. Albany, NY: State University of New York Press, 2006.
Dimitrov, Dragomir. 'The Legacy of the Jewel Mind: On the Sanskrit, Pali, and Sinhalese Works by Ratnamati,' Habilitationsschrift, Philipps-Universität Marburg, 2014.
Godakumbura, C. E. *Sinhalese Literature*. Colombo: Colombo Apothecaries, 1955.
Gornall, Alastair. 'How Many Sounds are in Pāli? Schism, Identity and Ritual in the Theravāda Saṅgha,' *Journal of Indian Philosophy* 42, 5 (2014), 511–50.
Hallisey Charles. 'Works and Persons in Sinhala Literary Culture,' *Literary Cultures in History: Reconstructions from South Asia*, ed. Sheldon Pollock. Berkeley and Los Angeles: University of California Press, 2003, 689–746.
Liyanage, Wasantha Amarakeerthi. 'Narrative Methods of Sinhala Prose: A Historical and Theoretical Study of Sinhala Prose from Twelfth Century Narratives to Post-Realist Fiction,' PhD dissertation, University of Wisconsin-Madison, 2004.
Malalasekera, G. P. *The Pali Literature of Ceylon*. 1928; reprint Colombo: M. D. Gunasena, 1958
Masson, J. L. and M. V. Patwardhan, *Aesthetic Rapture: The Rasadhyaya of the Natyasastra*. Poona: Deccan College Postgraduate and Research Institute, 1970.
Monius, Anne. E. 'The Many Lives of Daṇḍin: The *Kāvyādarśa* in Sanskrit and Tamil,' *International Journal of Hindu Studies* 4, 1 (2000), 1–37.
Nagaraj, D. R. 'Critical Tensions in the History of Kannada Literary Culture,' in *Literary Cultures in History*, ed. S. Pollock. Berkeley and Los Angeles: University of California Press, 2003, 323–83.
Norman, K. R. *Pali Literature: A History of Indian Literature VII.2*. Wiesbaden: Otto Harrassowitz, 1983.
Pannasara, Dehigaspe. *Sanskrit Literature Extant among the Sinhalese and the Influence of Sanskrit on Sinhalese*. Colombo: Wimaladharma Hewavitarane Esqr, 1958.
Pathmanathan, S. *The Kingdom of Jaffna, Part I*. Colombo: Arul M. Rajendran, 1978.
Perriera, T. L. 'Whence Theravāda? The Modern Genealogy of an Ancient Term,' in *How Theravāda is Theravāda? Exploring Buddhist Identities*, ed. Peter Skilling et al. Chiang Mai: Silkworm Books, 2012, 443–571.
Pollock, Sheldon. 'The Cosmopolitan Vernacular,' *Journal of Asian Studies* 57, 1 (1998), 6–37.
Pollock, Sheldon. 'The Social Aesthetic and Sanskrit Literary Theory,' *The Journal of Indian Philosophy* 29 (2001), 197–229.
Pollock, Sheldon. *The Ends of Man at the End of Premodernity*. Amsterdam: Royal Netherlands Academy of Arts and Sciences, 2005.
Pollock, Sheldon. 'Ratnaśrījñāna,' *Encyclopedia of Indian Wisdom: Dr. Satya Vrat Shastri Felicitation Volume*, ed. R. K. Sharma. Delhi: Bharatiya Vidya Prakashan, 2005, 637–43.
Pollock, Sheldon. *The Language of the Gods in the World of Men: Sanskrit, Culture, and Power in Premodern India*. Berkeley and Los Angeles: University of California Press, 2006.
Veidlinger, Daniel. *Spreading the Dhamma: Writing, Orality, and Textual Transmission in Buddhist Northern Thailand*. Honolulu: University of Hawai'i Press, 2006.
von Hinüber, Oskar. 'Pali as an Artificial Language,' *Indologica Taurinensia* 10 (1982), 133–40.
Warder, A. K. *Pali Metre: A Contribution to the History of Indian Literature*. London: Pali Text Society, 1967.
Wijayawardhana, G. D. 'The Influence of Sanskrit Alankāra Śāstra on Early Sinhalese Poetry,' PhD dissertation, University of Ceylon, Peradeniya, 1963.
Wijesekera, O. H. de A. 'Pali and Sanskrit in the Polonnaruva Period,' *Ceylon Historical Journal*, 4 (1954–5), 102–5.
Wright, J. C. 'The Pali *Subodhālaṅkāra* and Daṇḍin's *Kāvyadarśa*,' *Bulletin of the School of Oriental and African Studies* 65, 2 (2002), 323–41.

## Chapter 5

### Primary sources

*Messenger Poems: By Kālidāsa, Dhoyī & Rūpa Gosvāmin*, trans. Sir James Mallinson. New York: New York University Press and JJC Foundation, 2006.

*Sāradīpikā Kōkila Sandeśa Varṇanāva*, ed. Häḍigallē Paññātissa. Borella, Sri Lanka: Lankabhinava Vishruta Yantralaya, 1945.
*Sävul Sandēśaya*, ed. Rä Tennekoon. Colombo: M. D. Gunasena, 1955.

## Secondary sources

Ali, Daud. *Courtly Culture and Political Life in Early Medieval India*. Cambridge: Cambridge University Press, 2004.
Barnett, Lionel D. 'The Manavulu-Sandesaya: Text and Translation,' *The Journal of the Royal Asiatic Society of Great Britain and Ireland* (1905), 265–83.
Berkwitz, Stephen C. *Buddhist History in the Vernacular: The Power of the Past in Late Medieval Sri Lanka*. Leiden: Brill, 2004.
Berkwitz, Stephen C. *Buddhist Poetry and Colonialism: Alagiyavanna and the Portuguese in Sri Lanka*. New York: Oxford University Press, 2013.
Berkwitz, Stephen C. 'Sinhala Buddhist Appropriations of Indic Cultural Forms: Literary Imitations and Conquests,' *Religions of South Asia* (forthcoming).
Biedermann, Zoltán. 'The *Matrioshka* Principle and How It was Overcome: Portuguese and Habsburg Imperial Attitudes in Sri Lanka and the Responses of the Rulers of Kotte (1506–1598),' *Journal of Early Modern History* 13 (2009), 265–310.
Bronner, Yigal. 'Birds of a Feather: Vāmana Bhaṭṭa Bāṇa's *Haṃsasandeśa* and its Intertexts,' *Journal of the American Oriental Society* 133, 3 (2013), 495–526.
Buddhadatta, Polwatte Śri. *Pālisāhityaya*. Colombo: Svabhasha Prakasakayo, 1966.
Chakravarti, Chintaharan. 'The Origin and Development of Dūtakāvya Literature in Sanskrit,' *Indian Historical Quarterly* 3, 1 (1927), 273–97.
Cowell, E. B., ed. *The Jātaka or Stories of the Buddha's Former Births*, Vol. 2, trans. W. H. D. Rouse. 1895; reprint Delhi: Motilal Banarsidass, 1994.
De Silva, Premakumara. 'God of Compassion and the Divine Protector of "Śrī Pāda": Trends in Popular Buddhism in Sri Lanka,' *Sri Lanka Journal of the Humanities* 34, 1–2 (2008), 93–107.
Godakumbura, C. E. *Sinhalese Literature*. Colombo: The Colombo Apothecaries' Co., 1955.
Greenblatt, Stephen. *Marvelous Possessions: The Wonder of the New World*. Chicago: University of Chicago Press, 1991.
Greenblatt, Stephen. 'The Touch of the Real,' *Representations* 59 (1997), 14–29.
Gunasekara, Bandusena. *Kōṭṭē Yugayē Sandēśa Kāvya*. Colombo: Department of Cultural Affairs, 1997.
Hallisey, Charles. 'Works and Persons in Sinhala Literary Culture,' in *Literary Cultures in History: Reconstructions from South Asia*, ed. Sheldon Pollock. Berkeley and Los Angeles: University of California Press, 2003, 689–746.
Hopkins, Steven P. 'Lovers, Messengers, and Beloved Landscapes: *Sandeśakāvya* in Comparative Perspective,' *International Journal of Hindu Studies* 8, 1–3 (2004), 29–55.
Hopkins, Steven P. 'Sanskrit in a Tamil Imaginary: Sandeśakāvya and the *Haṃsasandeśa* of Veṅkaṭanātha,' in *Passages: Relationships between Tamil and Sanskrit*, ed. Kannan M. and Jennifer Clare. Pondicherry: Institut français de Pondichéry, 2009, 281–312.
Hopkins, Steven P., trans. *The Flight of Love: A Messenger Poem of Medieval South India by Veṅkaṭanātha*. New York: Oxford University Press, 2016.
Jayasuriya, Edmund. *Sälaḷihini Sandeśa of Toṭagamuve Srī Rāhula Thera*. Colombo: Postgraduate Institute of Archaeology and Central Cultural Fund, 2002.
Kulasuriya, Ananda. *Sinhala Sāhityaya 4*. Boralesgamuwa, Sri Lanka: C. S. Visidunu Prakasakayo, 1997.
Narayana Rao, Velcheru, David Shulman and Sanjay Subrahmanyam. *Symbols of Substance: Court and State in Nāyaka Period Tamilnadu*. Delhi: Oxford University Press, 1992.
Nicholas, C. W. and S. Paranavitana. *A Concise History of Ceylon: From the Earliest Times to the Arrival of the Portuguese in 1505*. Colombo: Ceylon University Press, 1961.
Pannasara, Dehigaspe. *Sanskrit Literature: Extant among the Sinhalese and the Influence of Sanskrit on Sinhalese*. Colombo: Wimala David Hewavitarane, 1958.
Pieris, Anoma. 'Avian Geographies: An Inquiry into Nationalist Consciousness in Medieval Lanka,' *South Asia: Journal of South Asian Studies* 33, 3 (2010), 336–62.
Pollock, Sheldon. *The Language of the Gods in the World of Men: Sanskrit, Culture, and Power in Premodern India*. Berkeley and Los Angeles: University of California Press, 2006.
Sannasgala, Puñci Bandara. *Siṅhala Sāhitya Vaṁśaya*. Colombo: S. Godage and Brothers, 2009.
Śastrī, Satyavrat. *Essays on Indology*. Delhi: Meharchand Lachhmandass, 1963.

Shulman, David. *The Wisdom of the Poets: Studies in Tamil, Telugu, and Sanskrit*. Oxford: Oxford University Press, 2001.
Sugatavamsa, Hatarabage. *Pāli Sandēsa Sāhityaya*. Colombo: S. Godage and Brothers, 2015.
Sumanasuriya, K. T. W. 'Sandēśa,' in *Sinhala Sāhityalatā*, ed. Kotamale Amaravansa. Colombo: S. Godage and Brothers, 2000, 262–73.

# Chapter 6

## Secondary sources

Afanador-Pujol, Angelica J. 'The Tree of Jesse and the "Relación de Michoacan": Mimicry in Colonial Mexico,' *The Art Bulletin* 92, 4 (2010), 293–307.
Asher, Frederick. 'On Maurya Art,' in *A Companion to Asian Art and Architecture*, ed. Rebecca M. Brown and Deborah S. Hutton. Oxford: Wiley-Blackwell, 2011, 421–43.
Bailey, Gauvin. *Art on the Jesuit Missions in Asia and Latin America 1542–1773*. Toronto, Buffalo and London: University of Toronto Press, 1999.
Bandaranayake, Senake. *Sinhalese Monastic Architecture*, Studies in South Asian Culture 4. Leiden: Brill, 1974.
Bandaranayake, Senake. 'Sri Lanka and Monsoon Asia: Patterns of Local and Regional Architectural Development and the Problem of the Traditional Sri Lankan Roof,' in *Senerat Paranavitana Commemorative Volume*, ed. Leelananda Prematilleke et al. Studies in South Asian Culture 7. Leiden: Brill, 1978, 22–44.
Bandaranayake, Senake. *The Rock and Wall Paintings of Sri Lanka*, revised edition. Pannipitiya: Stamford Lake, 2006.
Bandaranayake, Senake. 'The Periodisation of Sri Lankan History and Some Related Historical and Archaeological Problems,' reprinted in *Continuities and Transformations Studies in Sri Lankan Archaeology and History*. Colombo: Social Scientists' Association, 2012, 121–52.
Baxandall, Michael. *Patterns of Intention: On the Historical Explanation of Pictures*. New Haven and London: Yale University Press, 1985.
Berkwitz, Stephen C. *Buddhist Poetry and Colonialism: Alagiyavanne and the Portuguese in Sri Lanka*. New York: Oxford University Press, 2013.
Biedermann, Zoltan. 'Diplomatic Ivories: Sri Lankan Caskets and the Portuguese-Asian Exchange in the Sixteenth Century,' in *Global Gifts: The Material Culture of Diplomacy in Early Modern Eurasia*, ed. Zoltán Biedermann, Anne Gerritsen and Giorgio Riello. New York: Cambridge University Press, forthcoming.
Bridges, Nicole N. 'Kongo Ivories,' in *Heilbrunn Timeline of Art History*. New York: The Metropolitan Museum of Art, 2000, accessed 23 October 2016, www.metmuseum.org/toah/hd/kong/hd_kong.htm.
Carvalho, Pedro Moura. *Luxury for Export: Artistic Exchange between India and Portugal Around 1600*. Boston: Isabella Stewart Gardner Museum, 2008.
Chaiklin, Martha. 'Ivory in Early Modern Ceylon: A Case Study in What Documents Don't Reveal,' *International Journal of Asian Studies* 6, 1 (2009), 37–63.
Codrington, K. de B. 'Western Influences in India and Ceylon: A Group of Sinhalese Ivories,' *Burlington Magazine* LIX (1934), 239–46.
Coomaraswamy, Ananda K. 'The Tree of Jesse and Indian Parallels or Sources,' *The Art Bulletin* 11, 2 (1929), 217–20.
Coomaraswamy, Ananda K. 'An Ivory Casket from Southern India,' *The Art Bulletin* 23, 3 (1941), 207–12.
Coomaraswamy Ananda K. *Medieval Sinhalese Art, 1908*. New York: Pantheon, 1956.
Eco, Umberto. 'Innovation and Repetition: Between Modern and Postmodern Aesthetics,' *Daedalus* 134, 4 (2005), 191–207.
Fagg, William and Ezio Bassani, *Africa and the Renaissance: Art in Ivory*. New York: The Center for African Art, Munich: Prestel Verlag, 1988.
Farago, Claire. 'On the Peripatetic Life of Objects in the Era of Globalization,' in *Cultural Contact and the Making of European Art since the Age of Exploration*, ed. Mary D. Sheriff. Chapel Hill: University of North Carolina Press, 2012, 17–41.
Gschwend, Annmarie Jordan. 'The Marvels of the East: Renaissance Curiosity Collections in Portugal,' in *The Heritage of Rauluchantim*, ed. Nuno Vassallo e Silva. Lisbon: Museu de Sao Roque, 1996, 82–127.
Gschwend, Annemarie Jordan. 'Rarities and Novelties,' in *Encounters: The Meeting of Asia and Europe 1500–1800*, ed. Anna Jackson and Amin Jaffer. London: Victoria and Albert Museum, 2004, 32–41.

Gschwend, Annemarie Jordan, 'Catherine of Austria: A Portuguese Queen in the Shadow of the Habsburg Court?' *Portuguese Studies Review* 13, 1–2 (2005), 173–94.
Gschwend, Annemarie Jordan and Johannes Beltz, *Elfenbeine aus Ceylon. Luxusgüter für Katharina von Habsburg (1507–1578)*. Zurich: Museum Rietberg, 2010.
Hartkamp-Jonxis, Ebeltje. 'Coveted by Princes and Citizens: Sri Lankan Ivory Carvings for the European Market 1550–1700,' Public lecture, Asian Civilizations Museum, Singapore, 11 June 2014.
Holt, John Clifford. *The Buddha in the Crown: Avalokitesvara in the Buddhist Traditions of Sri Lanka*. Oxford: Oxford University Press, 1991.
Holt, John Clifford. *The Buddhist Visnu: Religious Transformation, Politics, and Culture*. New York: Columbia University Press, 2005.
Huntington, John C. *The Art of Ancient India Buddhist, Hindu, and Jain*. New York and Tokyo: Weatherhill, 1999.
Jaffer, Amin. *Luxury Goods from India: The Art of the Indian Cabinet-Maker*. London: V&A Publications, 2002.
Jaffer, Amin and Melanie Anne Schwabe, 'A Group of Sixteenth-Century Ivory Caskets from Ceylon,' *Apollo* 149 (1999), 3–14.
Levenson, Jay A., ed. *Encompassing the Globe: Portugal and the World in the 16th and 17th Centuries*. Washington, DC: Arthur M. Sackler Gallery, Smithsonian Institution, 2007.
Mark, Peter. 'Towards a Reassessment of the Dating and the Geographical Origins of the Luso-African Ivories, Fifteenth to Seventeenth Centuries,' *History in Africa* 34 (2007), 189–211.
Marques, Susan Lowndes. *Portuguese Expansion Overseas and the Art of Ivory*. Lisbon: Comissão Nacional para as Comemorações dos Descobrimentos Portugueses, 1991.
Meegama, Sujatha Arundathi. 'From *Kovils* to *Devales*: Patronage and "Influence" at Buddhist and Hindu Temples in Sri Lanka,' PhD dissertation, University of California, Berkeley, 2011.
Meegama, Sujatha Arundathi. 'Albrecht Dürer in Sri Lanka: An Ivory Carver's Response to a European Print,' in *Connected Cultures: Art Histories of Sri Lanka*, ed. Sujatha Arundathi Meegama. Mumbai: Marg, 2017.
Meister, Michael W., ed. *Encyclopaedia of Indian Temple Architecture: South India – Lower Dravidadesa 200 BC–AD 1324*, New Delhi: American Institute of Indian Studies and University of Pennsylvania Press, 1983.
Nandadeva, Bilinda Devage. 'Flowers for the Dhamma Painted Buddhist Palm Leaf Manuscript Covers (Kamba) of Sri Lanka,' in *Buddhist Manuscript Cultures: Knowledge, Ritual, and Art. Routledge Critical Studies in Buddhism*, ed. Stephen C. Berkwitz, Juliane Schober and Claudia Brown. London: Routledge, 2008, 159–71.
Nelson, Robert S. 'Appropriation,' in *Critical Terms for Art History*, ed. Robert S. Nelson and Richard Shiff, 2nd edn. Chicago and London: University of Chicago Press, 2003, 160–73.
Perera, Gaston. 'Ivory Caskets,' unpublished working paper, 2010.
Pigouchet, Philppe. *Book of Hours*, for Simon Vostre, 1498. Incunable 1498, C25 Rosenwald Collection, Washington, Library of Congress.
Ross, Emma George. 'Afro-Portuguese Ivories,' in *Heilbrunn Timeline of Art History*. New York: The Metropolitan Museum of Art, 2000, accessed 20 November 2014, www.metmuseum.org/toah/hd/apiv/hd_apiv.htm.
Schroeder, Ulrich von. *Buddhist Sculptures of Sri Lanka*. Hong Kong: Visual Dharma Publications, 1990.
Silva, Nuno Vasallo e. 'An Art for Export: Sinhalese Ivory and Crystal in the Sixteenth and Seventeenth Centuries,' in *Re-exploring the Links: History and Constructed Histories between Portugal and Sri Lanka*, ed. Jorge Flores. Wiesbaden: Harrassowitz, 2007, 279–96.
Strathern, Alan. *Kingship and Conversion in Sixteenth-Century Sri Lanka: Portuguese Imperialism in a Buddhist Land*. Cambridge: Cambridge University Press, 2007.
Strathern, Alan. 'Towards the Source-Criticism of Sitavaka Period Heroic Literature, Part Two: The Sitavaka Hatana: Notes on a Grounded Text,' *The Sri Lanka Journal of the Humanities* 34, 1–2 (2008), 45–72.
Tilakasiri, Jayadeva. 'Ivory Carving of Sri Lanka,' *Arts of Asia* (1974), 42–6.
Watson, Arthur. *The Early Iconography of the Tree of Jesse*. London: Oxford University Press, 1934.

# Chapter 7

## Primary sources

Archivo General de Simancas. Secretaría de Portugal, Codex 1551.
*Archivo Portuguez-Oriental*, ed. J. H. da Cunha Rivara, 6 vols. Nova Goa: Imprensa Nacional, 1855–76.

Arquivo Histórico Militar, Lisbon. Div. 1/ 1/ 2/ 2, Codex 'Livro dos Irmãos.'
Arquivo Nacional Torre do Tombo, Lisbon. Chancelaria de D. Filipe II, Doações, livro 21.
Arquivo Nacional Torre do Tombo, Lisbon. Registos paroquiais, Lumiar.
Biblioteca da Ajuda, Lisbon. Codex 51-X-5.
Cervantes, Don Miguel de, *Don Quixote*, trans. Edith Grossman. London: Vintage, 2005.
Correia, Gaspar. *Lendas da Índia*, ed. M. Lopes de Almeida, 4 vols. Porto: Lello & Irmão, 1975.
Couto, Diogo do. *Da Asia de Diogo do Couto Dos Feitos, que os Portuguezes fizeram na Conquista, e Descubrimento das Terras, e Mares do Oriente*, 15 vols. Lisbon: Livraria de São Carlos, 1973–5.
*Documentos Remettidos da India ou Livros das Monções*, ed. R. A. Bulhão Pato and A. Silva Rego, 10 vols. Lisbon: Academia Real das Sciencias/Imprensa Nacional, 1880–1982.
Esperança, Friar Manuel da. *Historia Serafica da Ordem dos Frades Menores de S. Francisco na Provincia de Portugal. Primeira parte, que contem seu principio, & augmentos no estado primeiro de Custodia*, 3 vols. Lisbon: Officina Craesbeeckiana, 1656–1721.
Pereira, Maria Celeste, Fernando A. A. Lemos and Rosa Trindade Ferreira, *Documentos Inéditos para a História de Telheiras e do seu Convento*. Lisbon: Centro Cultural de Telheiras, 2007.
Queiroz, Fernão de. *Conquista Temporal e Espiritual de Ceilão*. Colombo: The Government Press, 1916.
*Rājāvaliya or a Historical Narrative of the Sinhalese Kings from Vijaya to Vimala Dharmasuriya II*, ed. B. Gunasekara. Colombo: Ceylon Government, 1926.
Schurhammer, Georg. *Francis Xavier, His Life, His Times*, 4 vols. Rome: Institutum Historicum Societatis Iesu, 1973–82.
Schurhammer, Georg and Ernst August Voretzsch, *Ceylon zur Zeit des Königs Bhuvaneka Bahu und Franz Xavers 1539–1552. Quellen zur Geschichte der Portugiesen, sowie der Franziskaner- und Jesuitenmission auf Ceylon, im Urtext herausgegeben und erklärt*, 2 vols. Leipzig: Verlag der Asia Major, 1928.
Trindade, Frei Paulo da. *Conquista Espiritual do Oriente*, ed. F. Lopes, 3 vols. Lisbon: Centro de Estudos Históricos Ultramarinos, 1962–7.

## Secondary sources

Abeyasinghe, Tikiri. *Portuguese Rule in Ceylon 1594–1612*. Colombo: Lake House, 1966.
Antoninus, A. J. B. *The Martyrs of Mannar: From Authentic Documents*, 2nd edn. Colombo, St. Joseph's Press, 1945.
Biedermann, Zoltán. 'The *Matrioshka* Principle and How it was Overcome: Portuguese and Habsburg Attitudes toward Imperial Authority in Sri Lanka and the Responses of the Rulers of Kotte (1506–1656),' *Journal of Early Modern History* 13, 4 (2009), 265–310.
Biedermann, Zoltán. 'Diplomatic Ivories: Sri Lankan Caskets and the Portuguese-Asian Exchange in the Sixteenth Century,' in *Global Gifts: The Material Culture of Diplomacy in Early Modern Eurasia*, ed. Zoltán Biedermann, Anne Gerritsen and Giorgio Riello. New York: Cambridge University Press, forthcoming.
Biedermann, Zoltán. *Island Empire: Renaissance Portugal, Sri Lanka, and the Beginnings of Habsburg Colonialism in Asia*, forthcoming.
De Silva, C. R. and S. Pathmanathan, 'The Kingdom of Jaffna up to 1620,' in *University of Peradeniya History of Sri Lanka*, Vol. 2. Peradeniya: The University of Peradeniya, 1995.
Earle, T. F. 'Black Africans versus Jews: Religious and Racial Tension in a Portuguese Saint's Play,' in *Black Africans in Renaissance Europe*, ed. T. F. Earle and K. J. P. Lowe. Cambridge: Cambridge University Press, 2005, 345–60.
Figuerôa-Rego, João. '"A honra alheia por um fio": os estatutos de limpeza de sangue no espaço de expressão Ibérica (sécs. XVI– XVIII),' PhD dissertation, Braga, Universidade do Minho, 2009.
Gschwend, Annemarie Jordan and Johannes Beltz, *Elfenbeine aus Ceylon: Luxusgüter für Katherine von Habsburg (1507–1578)*. Zurich: Museum Rietberg, 2010.
Jaffer, Amin and Melanie Anne Schwabe, 'A Group of Sixteenth-Century Ivory Caskets from Ceylon,' *Apollo* 149 (1999), 3–14.
Jayasinghe, Sagara. *The Black Prince's Chapel: The Church Built by a Sinhalese Prince in Portugal*. Colombo: Vijitha Yapa, 2015.
Nicholas, C. W. 'Civil Wars and the Emergence of Parakramabahu the Great,' in *University of Ceylon History of Ceylon*, Vol. 1, Part 2. Colombo: Ceylon University Press, 1960, 438–60.
Paranavitana, Senarat. 'The Dambadeni Dynasty,' in *University of Ceylon History of Ceylon*, Vol. 1, Part 2. Colombo: Ceylon University Press, 1959, 613–35.
Paranavitana, Senarat. 'Gampala and Rayigama,' in *University of Ceylon History of Ceylon*, Vol. 1, Part 2. Colombo: Ceylon University Press, 1959, 636–52.

Paranavitana, Senarat. 'The Kōṭṭe Kingdom up to 1505,' in *University of Ceylon History of Ceylon*, Vol. 1, Part 2. Colombo: Ceylon University Press, 1959, 660–83.

Paranavitana, Senarat. 'The Pedigree of the Alagakesvaras,' in *University of Ceylon History of Ceylon*, Vol. 1, Part 2. Colombo: Ceylon University Press, 1959, 653–59.

Pereira, Maria Celeste, Fernando A. A. Lemos and Rosa Trindade Ferreira. 'O Convento de Nossa Senhora da Porta do Céu,' *Cadernos de Telheiras*, 2ª série, 1 (2008), 29–57, accessed 28 October 2016, https://issuu.com/gruvless/docs/cadernos_de_telheiras.

Perera, L. S. 'Dynasty of Manavamma,' in *University of Ceylon History of Ceylon* Vol. 1, Part 1. Colombo: Ceylon University Press, 1959, 315–43.

Perera, L. S. 'The Period of Dynastic Instability,' in *University of Ceylon History of Ceylon*, Vol. 1, Part 1. Colombo: Ceylon University Press, 1959–60, 300–14.

Perniola, Vito. *The Catholic Church in Sri Lanka: The Portuguese Period. Original Documents translated into English*, 3 vols. Dehiwala: Tisara Prakasakayo, 1989–91.

Pieris, P. E. *The Prince Vijaya Pala of Ceylon, 1634–1654: From the Original Documents at Lisbon*. Colombo: C. A. C. Press, 1927.

Pollock, Sheldon. *The Language of the Gods in the World of Men. Sanskrit, Culture, and Power in Premodern India*. Berkeley and Los Angeles: University of California Press, 2006.

Ricci, Ronit, ed. *Exile in Colonial Asia: Kings, Convicts, Commemoration*. Honolulu: University of Hawai'i Press, 2016.

Schwartz, Stuart. *All Can Be Saved: Religious Tolerance and Salvation in the Iberian Atlantic World*. New Haven: Yale University Press, 2008.

Somaratne, G. P. V. 'Grand Eunuch Ho and Ceylon,' *Journal of the Ceylon Branch of the Royal Asiatic Society*, New Series 15 (1971), 36–47.

Strathern, Alan. *Kingship and Conversion in Sixteenth-Century Sri Lanka: Portuguese Imperialism in a Buddhist Land*. Cambridge: Cambridge University Press, 2007.

Subrahmanyam, Sanjay. *Courtly Encounters: Translating Courtliness and Violence in Early Modern Eurasia*. Cambridge, MA: Harvard University Press, 2012.

Thundy, Zacharias P. *Buddha and Christ: Nativity Stories and Indian Traditions*. Leiden: Brill, 1993.

Viterbo, Sousa. 'Relações de Portugal com alguns potentados africanos e asiáticos,' *Archivo Historico Portuguez* 2 (1904), 443–62.

Viterbo, Sousa. 'D. João, Principe de Candia,' *Archivo Historico Portuguez* 3 (1905), 354–64, 441–59.

Werake, K. M. M. 'A Re-examination of Chinese Relations with Sri Lanka during the 15th Century AD,' *Modern Sri Lanka Studies* 2, 1–2 (1987), 89–102.

Wickremasinghe, Sirima. 'Successors of Parākramabāhu I: Downfall of the Polonnaru Kingdom,' in *University of Ceylon History of Ceylon*, Vol. 1, Part 2. Colombo: Ceylon University Press, 1959, 507–28.

Xavier, Ângela Barreto. 'Dissolver a Diferença – Conversão e Mestiçagem no Império Português,' in *Itinerários: A Investigação nos 25 Anos do ICS*, ed. Manuel Villaverde et al. Lisbon: Imprensa de Ciências Sociais, 2008, 709–27.

Xavier, Ângela Barreto. '*Conversos* and *Novamente Convertidos*: Law, Religion, and Identity in the Portuguese Kingdom and Empire,' *Journal of Early Modern History*, 15 (2011), 255–87.

## Chapter 8

### Primary sources

Baldaeus, Phillipus. *A True and Exact Description of the Great Island of Ceylon*, trans. Pieter Brohier. Maharagama: Saman Press, 1960.

*Cūḷavaṃsa*, trans. Wilhelm Geiger. Colombo: Government Press, 1953.

De Queyroz, Fernão. *The Temporal and Spiritual Conquest of Ceylon*, trans. Father S. G. Perera, 3 vols. Colombo: Government Printer, 1930.

De Saram, Lewis. 'The Dutch Embassy to Kandy in 1731–32: Diary of Wijesiriwardhana Maha Mudiyanse, Otherwise Called Lewis de Saram, Maha Mudaliyar,' trans. Paul E. Pieris, *Journal of the Royal Asiatic Society, Ceylon Branch* 21, 62 (1909), 1–34.

*Francois Valentijn's Description of Ceylon*, ed. and trans. Sinnappah Arasaratnam. London: Hakluyt Society, 1978.

Knox, Robert. *An Historical Relation of the Island of Ceylon* (1681), ed. J. H. O. Paulusz. Dehiwala: Tisara Prakasakayo, 1989.
Lewis J. P. 'Andrew's Journal of a Tour to Candia in the Year 1796,' *Journal of the Royal Asiatic Society, Ceylon Branch* 26, 70 (1917), 172–229.
*The Mahāvaṃsa*, trans. L. C. Wijesinha. 1889; reprint. New Delhi: Asian Educational Services, 1996.
*The Pybus Embassy to Kandy, 1762*, ed. R. Raven-Hart. Colombo: National Museums, 1958.
*The Rājāvaliya: A Comprehensive Account of the Kings of Sri Lanka*, trans. A. V Suraweera. Rathmalana: Vishva Lekha, 2000.
*The Rājāvaliya or a Historical Narrative of Sinhalese Kings*, trans. B. Gunasekara. Colombo: Information Department, 1953.
*Śasanāvatīrnavarṇaṇāva*, ed. C. E. Godakumbura. Moratuva: Dodangoda and Company, 1956.
Van Goens, Ryckloff. *Memoir of Ryclof Van Goens, Jun. Governor of Ceylon, 1675–1679, to his successor Laurens Pyl*, trans. Sophia Pieters. Colombo: Government Printer, 1910.
Van Spilbergen, Joris. *Journal of Spilbergen, the First Dutch Envoy to Ceylon*, trans. K. D. Paranavitana. Dehiwela: Sridevi Press, 1997.

## Secondary sources

Abeyasinghe, Tikiri. 'The Politics of Survival: Aspects of Kandyan External Relations in the Mid-Sixteenth Century,' *Journal of the Royal Asiatic Society of Sri Lanka*, New Series XVII (1973), 11–21.
Abeyasinghe, Tikiri. 'The Kingdom of Kandy: Foundations and Foreign Relations to 1638,' in *University of Peradeniya, History of Sri Lanka*, Vol. 2, ed. K. M. de Silva. Peradeniya: University of Peradeniya, 1995, 139–61.
Arasaratnam, Sinnappah. 'Introduction: The Dutch in Ceylon and South India, 1700–1750,' in *Memoir of Julius Stein Van Gollenesse, Governor of Ceylon, 1743–1751*, trans and ed. S. Arasaratnam. Colombo: Department of National Archives, 1974, i–vii.
Arasaratnam, Sinnappah. 'Oratorians and Predicants: The Catholic Church in Ceylon under Dutch Rule,' in *Ceylon and the Dutch, 1600–1800: External Influences and Internal Change in Early Modern Sri Lanka*. Aldershot, New Hampshire: Variorum, 1996, 216–22.
Biedermann, Zoltán. 'Imagining Asia from the Margins: Early Portuguese Mappings of the Continent's Architecture and Space,' in *Architecturalized Asia. Mapping the Continent through Architecture and Geography*, ed. V. Rujivacharakul, H. H. Hahn, K. T. Oshima and P. Christensen. Hong Kong: Hong Kong University Press, 2013, 35–52.
Biedermann, Zoltán. *Island Empire: Renaissance Portugal, Sri Lanka, and the Beginnings of Habsburg Colonialism in Asia*, forthcoming.
Codrington, H. W. *A Short History of Ceylon*. 1929; reprint New Delhi: Asian Educational Services, 1994.
De Silva, C. R. *The Portuguese in Ceylon, 1617–1638*. Colombo: H. W. Cave, 1972.
De Silva, C. R. 'The Rise and Fall of the Kingdom of Sītāvaka,' *in University of Peradeniya, History of Sri Lanka*, Vol. 2, ed. K. M. de Silva. Peradeniya: University of Peradeniya, 1995, 61–104.
De Silva, R. K. and W. G. M. Beumer. *Illustrations and Views of Dutch Ceylon, 1602–1796*. London: Serendib Publications, 1988.
Dewaraja, Lorna S. *The Kandyan Kingdom, 1707–1760*. Colombo: Lake House Investments, 1972.
Dewaraja, Lorna S. 'The Kandyan Kingdom 1638–1739: A Survey of its Political History,' in *University of Peradeniya, History of Sri Lanka*, Vol. 2, ed. K. M. de Silva. Peradeniya: University of Peradeniya, 1995, 183–209
Dewaraja, Lorna S. 'The Kandyan Kingdom and the Nāyakkars, 1739–1796,' in *University of Peradeniya, History of Sri Lanka*, Vol. 2, ed. K. M. de Silva. Peradeniya: University of Peradeniya, 1995, 281–320.
Dewaraja, Lorna S. *The Kandyan Kingdom of Sri Lanka: 1707–1782*, 2nd edn. Colombo: Stamford Lake Publication, 2008.
Don Peter, W. L. A. *Studies in Ceylon Church History*. Colombo: The Catholic Press, 1963.
Don Peter, W. L. A. *Francis Xavier, Teacher of Nations*. Colombo: Evangel Press, 1987.
Ferguson, Donald. *The Earliest Dutch Visits to Ceylon*. 1927–30; reprint New Delhi: Asian Educational Services, 1998.
Holt, John Clifford. *The Religious World of Kīrti Śrī: Buddhism, Art and Politics in Late Mediaeval Sri Lanka*. New York: Oxford University Press, 1996.
Holt, John Clifford. *The Buddhist Viṣṇu: Religious Transformation, Politics, and Culture*. New York: Columbia University Press, 2004.

Jayawickrama, Sarojini. *Writing that Conquers: Re-reading Knox's An Historical Relation of the Island Ceylon*. Colombo: Social Scientists' Association, 2004.
Malalgoda, Kitsiri. *Buddhism in Sinhalese Society, 1750–1900*. Berkeley: University of California Press, 1976.
Nelson J. H. *The Political History of the Madura Country, Ancient and Modern*. 1868; reprint New Delhi: Asian Educational Services, 1989.
Obeyesekere, Gananath. *The Doomed King: A Requiem for Śri Vikrama Rājasinha*, forthcoming.
Perera, S. G. *Life of Father Jacome Gonsalves*. Madurai: De Nobili Press, 1942.
Perera, S. G. *Life of the Venerable Father Joseph Vaz, Apostle of Ceylon*. Galle: Loyola Press, 1953.
Perera, S. G. *Historical Sketches*. Colombo: Catholic Book Depot, 1962.
Perniola, V. *The Catholic Church in Sri Lanka: The Dutch Period*, Vol. 1, *1658–1711*; reprint Dehiwala: Tisara Prakasakayo, 1983.
Pieris, Paul E. *Sinhale and the Patriots, 1815–1818*. Colombo: The Colombo Apothecaries, 1950.
Pieris, Paul E. *The Dutch Power in Ceylon, Some Documents Relating to the Rise of the Dutch Power in Ceylon, 1602–1670*. 1929; reprint London: Curzon Press, 1973.
Pieris, Paul E. *Ceylon: The Portuguese Era Being a History of the Island for the Period 1505–1658*, 2 vols. 1913–14; reprint Dehiwala: Tisara Prakasakayo, 1992.
Sannasgala, P. B. *Sinhala Sāhityavaṅśaya*. Colombo: Cultural Affairs Department, 1994.
Somaratna, Allepola H. M. ed. *Rajasiha Haṭana*. Kandy: Godamune Brothers, 1966.
Strathern, Alan. *Kingship and Conversion in Sixteenth-Century Sri Lanka: Portuguese Imperialism in a Buddhist Land*. Cambridge: Cambridge University Press, 2007.
Swaminathan, K. D. *The Nāyakas of Ikkeri*. Madras: P. Varadachary and Co., 1957.
Soratha Thero. *Sri Sumangalasabdakosaya*, Vol. 1. Colombo: Maligatenne, 1952.
Vink, Markus. *Mission to Madurai: Dutch Embassies to the Nayaka Court of Madurai in the Seventeenth Century*. Delhi: Manohar, 2012.
Wickramasinghe, Nira. *Dressing the Colonized Body: Politics, Clothing and Identity in Colonial Sri Lanka*. Hyderabad: Orient Longman, 2003.

## Chapter 9

### Primary sources

Hovy, Lodewijk. *Ceylonees Plakkaatboek: Plakkaten en andere wetten uitgevaardigd door het Nederlandse bestuur op Ceylon, 1638–1796*, 2 vols. Hilversum: Verloren, 1991.
*Memoir of Hendrick Zwaardecroon, Commandeur of Jaffnapatam, (afterwards Governor-General of Nederlands India), 1697, for the Guidance of the Council of Jaffnapatam, During his Absence at the Coast of Malabar Memoir*, trans. Sophia Pieters. Colombo: Cottle, 1911.
National Archive, The Hague. Verenigde Oostindische Compagnie (VOC), access number 1.04.02, inventory numbers 3571, 3573, 3878.
Sri Lanka National Archive, Colombo. SLNA 1/2711, 1/4146, 1/4607, 1/4613, 1/4673, 1/4692, 1/4740.

### Secondary sources

Allen, Richard B. *European Slave Trading in the Indian Ocean, 1500–1850*. Athens: Ohio University Press, 2014.
Arasaratnam, S. 'Social History of a Dominant Caste Society: The Vellalar of North Ceylon in the 18th Century,' *Indian Economic and Social History Review* 18, 3–4 (1982), 377–91.
Arasaratnam, S. *Ceylon and the Dutch, 1600–1800: External Influences and Internal Change in Early Modern Sri Lanka*. Aldershot: Variorum, 1996.
Banks, Michael. 'Caste in Jaffna,' in *Aspects of Caste in South India, Ceylon and North-West Pakistan*, ed. E. R. Leach. Cambridge: Cambridge University Press, 1960, 61–77.
Biedermann, Zoltán. *The Portuguese in Sri Lanka and South India: Studies in the History of Diplomacy, Empire and Trade, 1500–1650*. Wiesbaden: Harrassowitz Verlag, 2014.
Chatterjee, Indrani and Richard Eaton, 'Introduction,' in *Slavery in South Asian History*, ed. Indrani Chatterjee and Richard Eaton. Bloomington: Indiana Universtity Press, 2006, 1–16.

De Raat, Lex. *The Life of Governor Joan Gideon Loten, 1710–1789: A Personal History of a Dutch Virtuoso*. Hilversum: Verloren, 2012.

Dewasiri, Nirmal. *The Adaptable Peasant: Agrarian Society in Western Sri Lanka under Dutch rule, 1740–1800*. Leiden: Brill, 2008.

D'Oyly, Sir John. *A Sketch of the Constitution of the Kandyan Kingdom*. Dehiwala: Tisara Prakasakayo, 1974.

Ekama, Kate J. 'Slavery in Dutch Colombo.' ResMA dissertation, Leiden University, 2012.

Irving, D. R. M. 'Trading Tunes: Thomas Forrest, Malay Songs and Musical Exchange in the Malay Archipelago, 1774–1784,' in *Intercultural Exchange in Southeast Asia: History and Society in the Early Modern World*, ed. Tara Alberts and D. R. M. Irving. London: Tauris, 2013, 203–55.

Jones, Eric. *Wives, Slaves and Concubines: A History of the Female Underclass of Dutch Asia*. DeKalb, IL: Northern Illinois University Press, 2010.

Jurriaanse, M. 'The Compilation of the Customary Law of Jaffna,' *Bijdragen tot de Taal-, Land- en Volkenkunde/Journal of the Humanities and Social Sciences of Southeast Asia* (BKI) 110, 4 (1954), 293–304.

Kanumoyoso, Bondan. 'Beyond the City Wall: Society and Economic Development in the Ommelanden of Batavia, 1684–1740,' PhD dissertation, Leiden University, 2011.

Knaap, Gerrit. 'Europeans, Mestizos and Slaves: The Population of Colombo at the End of the Seventeenth Century,' trans. Robert Ross, *Itinerario* 5, 2 (1981), 84–101.

Nadaraja, Tambyah. *The Legal System of Ceylon in its Historical Setting*, Leiden: Brill, 1972.

Raben, Remco. 'Batavia and Colombo: The Ethnic and Spatial Order of Two Colonial Cities, 1600–1800,' PhD dissertation, Leiden University, 1996.

Ricci, Ronit. *Islam Translated: Literature, Conversion, and the Arabic Cosmopolis of South and Southeast Asia*. Chicago: University of Chicago Press, 2011.

Ricci, Ronit. 'Asian and Islamic Crossings: Malay Writing in Nineteenth-Century Sri Lanka,' *South Asian History and Culture* 5, 2 (2014), 179–94.

Ricci, Ronit. 'From Java to Jaffna: Exile and Return in Dutch Asia in the 18th Century,' in *Exile in Colonial Asia: Kings, Convicts, Commemoration*, ed. R. Ricci. Honolulu: University of Hawai'i Press, 2016, 94–116.

Rogers, John D. 'Post-Orientalism and the Interpretation of Premodern and Modern Political Identities: The Case of Sri Lanka,' *Journal of Asian Studies* 53, 1 (1994), 10–23.

Ross, Robert. *Cape of Torments: Slavery and Resistance in South Africa*. London: Routledge & Kegan Paul, 1983.

Rupesinghe, Nadeera. 'Negotiating Custom: Colonial Lawmaking in the Galle Landraad,' PhD dissertation, Leiden University, 2016.

Schrikker, Alicia. *Dutch and British Colonial Intervention in Sri Lanka, 1780–1815*, Leiden: Brill, 2007, 89–92.

Schrikker, Alicia. 'Caught between Empires: VOC Families in Sri Lanka after the British Takeover, 1806–1808,' *Annales de démographie historique* 2 (2011), 127–47.

Schrikker, Alicia F. 'Conflict Resolution, Social Control and Law-Making in Eighteenth-Century Dutch Sri Lanka,' in *Exploring the Dutch Empire: Agents, Networks and Institutions, 1600–2000*, eds. Catia Antunes and Jos Gommans. London: Bloomsbury, 2015, 227–44.

Schrikker, Alicia F. '"Op de dijk gezet." Schuld, onrust en bestuurlijke onzekerheid in Jaffna in de achttiende eeuw,' in *Aan de overkant. Ontmoetingen in dienst van de VOC en WIC (1600–1800)*, ed. Lodewijk Wagenaar. Leiden: Sidestone Press, 2015, 145–65.

Subrahmanyam, Sanjay. 'Slaves and Tyrants: Dutch Tribulations in Seventeenth-Century Mrauk-u,' *Journal of Early Modern History* 1, 3 (1997), 201–53.

Taylor, Jean Gelman. *The Social World of Batavia, European and Euroasians in Colonial Indonesia*, 2nd edn. Madison, WI: University of Wisconsin Press, 2009.

van Rossum, Matthias. *Kleurrijke Tragiek. De geschiedenis van slavernij in Azië onder de VOC*. Hilversum: Verloren, 2015.

van Vollenhoven, C. ed. 'Ceilonsch volksrecht opgetekend in 1707. Met glossarium van P.S. van Ronkel,' *Bijdragen tot de Taal-, Land- en Volkenkunde/Journal of the Humanities and Social Sciences of Southeast Asia* (BKI) 75 (1919), 240–80.

van Wamelen, Carla. *Family life onder de VOC. Een handelscompanie in huwelijks- en gezinszaken*. Hilversum: Verloren, 2015.

Vink, Markus. '"The World's Oldest Trade": Dutch Slavery and Slave Trade in the Indian Ocean in the Seventeenth Century,' *Journal of World History* 24, 2 (2003), 131–77.

Wagenaar, Lodewijk. *Galle, VOC-vestiging in Ceylon: beschrijving van een koloniale samenleving aan de vooravond van de Singalese opstand tegen het Nederlandse gezag, 1760*. Amsterdam: Bataafsche Leeuw, 1994.

Wagenaar, Lodewijk. 'The Cultural Dimension of the Dutch East India Company Settlements in Dutch-Period Ceylon, 1700–1800,' *Mediating Netherlandish Art and Material Culture in Asia*, ed. Thomas Da Costa Kauffmann and Michael North. Amsterdam: Amsterdam University Press, 2014.
Ward, Kerry. *Networks of Empire: Forced Migration in the Dutch East India Company*. New York: Cambridge University Press, 2009.
Warren, Jim. *The Sulu Zone, 1768–1898: The Dynamics of External Trade, Slavery, and Ethnicity in the Transformation of a Southeast Asian Maritime State*. Singapore: Singapore University Press, 1981.
Worden, Nigel. *Slavery in Dutch South Africa*. Cambridge: Cambridge University Press, 1985.
Worden, Nigel, and Gerald Groenewald, eds. *Trials of Slavery: Selected Documents Concerning Slaves from the Criminal Records of the Council of Justice at the Cape of Good Hope, 1705–1794*. Cape Town: Van Riebeeck Society, 2005.
Worden, Nigel, Elizabeth van Heyningen and Vivian Bickford-Smith, *Cape Town: The Making of a City*. Kenilworth: David Philip, 2004.

## Chapter 10

### Primary sources

British Library, London. India Office Collections, Correspondence in P 317/94, P 318/1, P 318/9, P 318/12, P 318/17.
'Great Battle Against British Rule', *The Sunday Times Magazine*, 9 February 2014, accessed 13 August 2014, www.sundaytimes.lk/140209/magazine/great-battle-against-british-rule-84509.html.
Jayasuriya, Kusuma. *Waduga Hatana*, trans. Udaya Meddegama. Colombo: Department of Cultural Affairs, 1966.
National Archives, Kew, London. CO 54/56, CO 54/60, CO 54/61, CO 54/66, CO 54/70, CO 54/71, CO 54/73, CO 54/74, CO 54/114
Perera, K. F. *Ehalepola Hatanaya*, trans. Udaya Meddegama. Colombo: Subhadraloka Press, 1911.
'Obituary of Lieut. Col. Hardy,' *The Gentleman's Magazine* 4 (1835).
Sri Lanka National Archive, Colombo. Lot 19/96.
Sri Lanka National Archive, Kandy Branch. Lot 21 51/B.
Vimalananda, Tennakoon. *Sri Wickrema, Brownrigg and Ehelapola: Being Letters Addressed to the Home Government from 1811–1815 by Major General John Wilson and Lieut-General Robert Brownrigg, Governor of Ceylon*. Colombo: M. D. Gunasena, 1984.

### Secondary sources

Alavi, Seema, ed. *The Eighteenth Century in India*. Delhi: Oxford University Press, 1998.
Bates, Crispin. *Mutiny on the Margins: New Perspectives on the Indian Rebellion of 1857*, 6 vols. New Delhi: Sage, 2013.
Bayly, C. A. *Imperial Meridian: The British Empire and the World, 1780–1830*. London: Longman, 1989.
Bayly, C. A. 'The First Age of Global Imperialism, c.1780–1830,' *The Journal of Imperial and Commonwealth History* 26 (1998), 28–47.
Bayly, C. A. *The Origins of Nationality in India: Patriotism and Ethical Government in the Making of Modern India*. Delhi: Oxford University Press, 1998.
Bayly, C. A. *Empire and Information: Intelligence Gathering and Social Communication in India, 1780–1870*, Cambridge: University of Cambridge, 2000.
Biedermann Zoltán, 'The *Matrioshka* Principle and How it was Overcome: Portuguese and Habsburg Imperial Attitudes in Sri Lanka and the Response of the Rulers of Kotte,' *Journal of Early Modern History* 13, 4 (2009), 265–310.
Chatterjee, Partha. *The Nation and its Fragments: Colonial and Postcolonial Histories*. Princeton, NJ: Princeton University Press, 1993.
De Silva, K. M. *A History of Sri Lanka*. Chennai: Oxford University Press, 1981.
Dewaraja, Lorna, *The Muslims of Sri Lanka*. Colombo: Lanka Islamic Foundation, 1994.

Dirks, Nicholas. *Castes of Mind: Colonialism and the Making of Modern India*. Princeton, NJ: Princeton University Press 2001.
Godakumbura, C. E. *Sinhalese Literature*. Colombo: The Colombo Apothecaries' Co., 1955.
Guha, Ranajit, ed. *Subalatern Studies IV*. Delhi: Oxford University Press, 1994.
Jayawardena, Kumari. *Perpetual Ferment: Popular Revolts in Sri Lanka in the Eighteenth and Nineteenth Centuries*. Colombo: Social Scientists' Association, 2010.
Marshall, Peter, ed. *The Eighteenth Century in Indian History: Evolution or Revolution?* Delhi: Oxford University Press, 2003.
Metcalf, T. R. *Ideologies of the Raj*. Cambridge: Cambridge University Press, 1994.
Pieris P. E. *Sinhalē and the Patriots, 1815–1818*. 1950; reprint Delhi: Navrang, 1995.
Prakash, Gyan. 'Writing Post-Orientalist Histories of the Third World: Perspectives from Indian Historiography,' *Comparative Studies in Society and History* 31 (1990), 383–408.
Roberts, Michael. *Sinhala Consciousness in the Kandyan Period: 1590s to 1815*. Colombo: Vijitha Yapa Press, 2004.
Rupesinghe, Nadeera. 'Negotiating Custom: Colonial Lawmaking in the Galle Landraad,' PhD dissertation, University of Leiden, 2015.
Schrikker, Alicia. *Dutch and British Colonial Intervention in Sri Lanka, 1780–1815*. Leiden: Brill, 2007.
Sivasundaram, Sujit. 'Buddhist Kingship, British Archaeology and Historical Narratives in Sri Lanka c. 1750–1850,' *Past & Present* 197, 2007.
Sivasundaram, Sujit. 'Appropriation to Supremacy: Ideas of the "Native" in the Rise of British Imperial Heritage,' in *From Plunder to Preservation: Britain and the Heritage of Empire, c.1800–1940*, ed. Peter Mandler and Astrid Swenson. Oxford: British Academy Publications, 2013, 149–70.
Sivasundaram, Sujit. *Islanded: Britain, Sri Lanka and the Bounds of an Indian Ocean Colony*. Chicago: University of Chicago Press, 2014.
Sivasundaram, Sujit. 'Materialities in the Making of World History: South Asia and the South Pacific,' in *Oxford Handbook for History and Material Culture*, forthcoming.
Stokes, Eric. *The Peasant Armed: The Indian Revolt of 1857*. Oxford: Clarendon, 1986.
Strathern, Alan. *Kingship and Conversion in Sixteenth-Century Sri Lanka. Portuguese Imperialism in a Buddhist Land*. Cambridge: Cambridge University Press, 2007.
Strathern, Alan. 'Treachery and Ethnicity in Portuguese Representations of Sri Lanka,' in *Engaging Colonial Knowledge: Reading European Archives in World History*, ed. Ricardo Roque and Kim Wagner. Basingstoke: Palgrave Macmillan, 2012, 217–34.
Strathern, Alan. 'The Vijaya Origin Myth of Sri Lanka and the Strangeness of Kingship,' *Past & Present* 203 (2013), 3–28.
Tambiah, Stanley J. *World Conqueror and World Renouncer: A Study of Buddhism and Polity in Thailand Against a Historical Background*. Cambridge: Cambridge University Press, 1976.
Vimalananda, Tennakoon. *The Great Rebellion of 1818: The Story of the First War of Independence and the Betrayal of the Nation*. Colombo: M. D. Gunasena, 1970.
Vimalananda, Tennakoon. *The British Intrigue in the Kingdom of Ceylon*. Colombo: M. D. Gunasena, 1973.
Wickramasinghe, Nira. 'Many Little Revolts or One Rebellion? The Maritime Provinces of Ceylon/Sri Lanka between 1796 and 1800,' *South Asia: Journal of South Asian Studies* 32 (2009), 170–88.
Wickremesekera, Channa. *Kandy at War: Indigenous Military Resistance to European Expansion in Sri Lanka, 1594–1818*. Vijitha Yapa: Colombo, 2004.
Wilson, James. 'Reappropriation, Resistance and British Autocracy in Sri Lanka, 1820–1850,' *The Historical Journal* (forthcoming).
Wilson, Jon. *The Domination of Strangers: Modern Governance in Eastern India 1780–1835*. Basingstoke: Palgrave Macmillan, 2008.

## Chapter 11

### Primary sources

Bocarro, António. *Década 13 da História da India*, ed. Rodrigo José de Lima Felner. Lisbon: Academia Real das Sciencias, 1876.
Couto, Diogo do. *The History of Ceylon from the Earliest Times to 1600 A.D. as Related by João de Barros and Diogo do Couto*, ed. and trans. D. Ferguson. New Delhi: Asian Educational Services, 1993.

*Cūḷavaṃsa: Being the More Recent Part of the Mahāvaṃsa*, ed. and trans. Wilhelm Geiger, 2 vols. 1925–9; reprint London: Pali Text Society, 1980.
Dharmakirti, Devarakshita Jayabahu. 'Saddharmalankaraya,' trans. V. and C. B Cooke, in *An Anthology of Sinhalese Literature up to 1815*, ed. C. H. B. Reynolds. London: George Allen and Unwin, 1970, 233–65.
*The Dīpavaṃsa*, trans. Hermann Oldenburg. 1879; reprint New Delhi: Asian Educational Services, 2004.
*Mahāvaṃsa, The Great Chronicle of Sri Lanka*, trans. Ananda W. Guruge. Colombo: Associated Newspapers of Ceylon, 1989.
Pieris, P. E. *Ribeiro's History of Ceylon with Notes from de Barros, de Couto and Antonio Bocarro*. Galle: Albion, 1909.
Queyroz, Fernão de. *The Temporal and Spiritual Conquest of Ceylon*, trans. and with introduction by S. G. Perera, 3 vols. 1931; reprint New Delhi: Asian Educational Services, 1992.
*Rājāvaliya*, ed. and trans. A. V. Suraweera. Ratmalana: Vishva Lehka, 2000.
*Sītāvaka Haṭana*, ed. Rohini Paranavitana. Colombo: Madhyama Sanskṛitika Aramudala, 1999.
*Si-Yu-Ki: Buddhist Records of the Western World, Translated from the Chinese of Hiuen Tsiang (AD 629)*, trans. Samuel Beal. Delhi: Motilal Banarsidass, 1994.
van Spilbergen, Joris. *Journal of Spilbergen: The First Dutch Envoy to Ceylon, 1602*, ed. and trans. K. D. Paranavitana. Colombo: Sridevi Printers, 1997.

## Secondary sources

Berkwitz, Stephen C. *The History of the Buddha's Relic Shrine: A Translation of the Sinhala Thūpavaṃsa*. New York: Oxford University Press, 2007.
Berkwitz, Stephen C. 'The Expansion of Buddhism in South and Southeast Asia,' in *Dynamics in the History of Religions between Asia and Europe: Encounters, Notions, and Comparative Perspectives*, ed. Volkhard Krech. Leiden: Brill, 2011, 223–34.
Berkwitz, Stephen C. *Buddhist Poetry and Colonialism: Alagiyavanna and the Portuguese in Sri Lanka*. New York: Oxford University Press, 2013.
Biedermann, Zoltán. 'Tribute, Vassalage and Warfare in Early Luso-Lankan Relations (1506–1545),' in *Indo-Portuguese History: Global Trends. Proceedings of the XIth International Seminar of Indo-Portuguese History*, ed. Fátima Gracias and Charles Borges. Goa: Maureen & Camvet Publishers, 2005, 185–206.
Biedermann, Zoltán. 'The *Matrioshka* Principle and How it was Overcome: Portuguese and Habsburg Attitudes toward Imperial Authority in Sri Lanka and the Responses of the Rulers of Kōṭṭe (1506–1656),' *Journal of Early Modern History* 13 (2009), 265–310.
Biedermann, Zoltán. 'The "Malwana Convention" Revisited: Notes on the Lankan Transition to Iberian Rule,' in *The Portuguese in the Orient*, ed. Gaston Perera. Kandy: International Centre for Ethnic Studies, 2010, 29–48.
Caldwell, Ian and David Henley, eds. *Stranger-Kings in Indonesia and Beyond*, special issue of *Indonesia and the Malay World* 36 (2008).
Collins, Steven. *Nirvana and Other Buddhist Felicities: Utopias of the Pāli Imaginaire*. Cambridge: Cambridge University Press, 1998.
Davies, R. R. 'The People of Britain and Ireland 1100–1400. I. Identities,' *Transactions of the Royal Historical Society*, Sixth Series 4 (1994), 1–20.
De Silva, K. M. *A History of Sri Lanka*. Colombo: Vijitha Yapa Publications, 2005.
Dewaraja, Lorna. *The Kandyan Kingdom of Sri Lanka 1707–1782*. Colombo: Lake House Investments, 1988.
Dewaraja, Lorna. 'The Indigenisation of the Muslims of Sri Lanka,' in *Sesquicentennial Commemorative Volume of the Royal Asiatic Society of Sri Lanka, 1845–1995*, ed. G. P. S. H. de Silva and C. G. Uragoda. Colombo, Royal Asiatic Society of Sri Lanka, 1995, 427–39.
Dharmadasa, K. N. O. 'The Sinhala-Buddhist Identity and the Nayaka Dynasty in the Politics of the Kandyan Kingdom, 1739–1815,' in *Collective Identities, Nationalisms and Protests in Modern Sri Lanka*, ed. M. Roberts. Colombo: Marga, 1979, 79–104.
Dharmadasa, K. N. O. *Language, Religion and Ethnic Awareness: The Growth of Sinhalese Nationalism in Sri Lanka*. Michigan: University of Michigan Press, 1992.
Duncan, James S. *City as Text: The Politics of Landscape in the Kandyan Kingdom*. Cambridge: Cambridge University Press, 1990.
Falk, Nancy E. 'Wilderness and Kingship in Ancient South Asia,' *History of Religions* 13 (1973), 1–15.

Flores, Jorge Manuel. *Os Olhos do Rei: Desenhos e Descrições Portuguesas da Ilha de Ceilão (1624, 1638)*. Lisbon: Commissão Nacional para as Commemorações dos Descobrimentos Portugueses, 2001.

Gunawardana, R. A. L. H. *Robe and Plough: Monasticism and Economic Interest in Early Medieval Sri Lanka*. Tucson: University of Arizona Press, 1979.

Gunawardana, R. A. L. H. 'The People of the Lion: The Sinhala Identity and Ideology in History and Historiography,' in *Sri Lanka: History and the Roots of Conflict*, ed. Jonathan Spencer. London and New York: Routledge, 1990, 45–86.

Gunawardana, R. A. L. H, 'Colonialism, Ethnicity and the Construction of the Past: The Changing Identity of the last Four Kings of the Kandyan Kingdom,' in *Pivot Politics: Changing Cultural Identities in Early State Formation Processes*, ed. M. van Bakel et al. Amsterdam: Het Spinhuls, 1994, 197–221.

Gunawardana, R. A. L. H, *Historiography in a Time of Ethnic Conflict: Construction of the Past in Contemporary Sri Lanka*. Colombo: Social Scientists' Association, 1995.

Gunawardana, R. A. L. H, *Periodization in Sri Lankan History: Some Reflections with Special Emphasis on the Development of the State*. Colombo: Social Scientists' Association, 2008.

Hallisey, Charles. 'Devotion in the Buddhist Literature of Medieval Sri Lanka,' PhD dissertation, University of Chicago, 1988.

Hallisey Charles, 'Works and Persons in Sinhala Literary Culture,' in *Literary Cultures in History: Reconstructions from South Asia*, ed. Sheldon Pollock. Berkeley and Los Angeles: University of California Press, 2003, 689–745.

Hobsbawm, E. and T. Ranger, eds. *The Invention of Tradition*. Cambridge: Cambridge University Press, 1983.

Holt, John Clifford. *The Religious World of Kirti Sri: Buddhism, Art, and Politics of Late Medieval Sri Lanka*. New York: Oxford University Press, 1996.

Holt, John Clifford. *The Buddhist Viṣṇu: Religious Transformation, Politics and Culture*. New York: Columbia University Press, 2004.

Holt, John Clifford and Sree Padma, 'Buddhism in Andhra and its Influence on Buddhism in Sri Lanka,' in *Buddhism in the Krishna River Valley of Andhra*, ed. Sree Padma and A. W. Barber. Albany, NY: SUNY Press, 2008, 105–26.

Jayawardena, Kumari. *Perpetual Ferment: Popular Revolts in Sri Lanka in the Eighteenth and Nineteenth Centuries*. Colombo: Social Scientists' Association, 2010.

Li, Hui. *The Life of Hiuen-Tsiang*. 1911; reprint Delhi: Munshiram Manoharlal, 1973.

Lieberman, Victor. *Strange Parallels: Southeast Asia in Global Context c.800–1830*, Vol. 2, *Mainland Mirrors: Europe, Japan, China, South Asia and the Islands*. Cambridge: Cambridge University Press, 2009.

Liyanagamage, Amaradasa. *State, Society and Religion in Premodern Sri Lanka*. Colombo: Social Scientists' Association, 2008.

Monod, Paul Kléber. *The Power of Kings: Monarchy and Religion in Europe 1589–1715*. New Haven: Yale University Press, 1999.

Nissan, Elizabeth and R. L. Stirrat, 'The Generation of Communal Identities,' in *Sri Lanka: History and the Roots of Conflict*, ed. Jonathan Spencer. London and New York: Routledge, 1990, 19–44.

Obeyesekere, Gananath. 'Buddhism, Nationhood and Cultural Identity: A Question of Fundamentals,' in *Fundamentalisms Comprehended*, ed. Martin E. Marty and R. Scott Appleby. Chicago: University of Chicago Press, 1995, 239–44.

Obeyesekere, Gananath. 'On Buddhist Identity in Sri Lanka,' in *Ethnic Identity: Creation, Conflict and Accommodation*, ed. Lola Romanucci-Rossi and George A. de Vos. London: Mayfield, 1995, 222–41.

Obeyesekere, Gananath. 'Murder in the Cathedral'. Unpublished manuscript.

Pathmanathan, S. 'South India and Sri Lanka, AD 1450–1650: Political, Commercial and Cultural Relations,' *Journal of Tamil Studies* 21 (1982), 36–57.

Pieris, Anoma. 'Avian Geographies: An Inquiry into Nationalist Consciousness in Medieval Lanka,' *South Asia: Journal of South Asian Studies* 33, 3 (2010), 336–62.

Pollock, Sheldon. 'Rāmāyaṇa and Political Imagination in India,' *The Journal of Asian Studies* 52 (1993), 261–97.

Pollock, Sheldon. 'Cosmopolitan and Vernacular in History,' in *Cosmopolitanism*, ed. Sheldon Pollock, Homi K. Bhabha, Carol Appadurai Breckenridge and Dipesh Chakrabarty. Durham, NC and London: Duke University Press, 2002, 15–53.

Pollock, Sheldon. *The Language of the Gods in the World of Men: Sanskrit, Culture, and Power in Premodern India*. Berkeley and Los Angeles: University of California Press, 2009.

Roberts, Michael. *Sinhala Consciousness in the Kandyan Period, 1590s–1815*. Colombo: Vijitha Yapa Publications, 2004.

Roberts, Michael. 'Ethnicity after Said: Post-Orientalist failures in Comprehending the Kandyan Period of Lankan History,' *Ethnic Studies Report* 19 (2001), 69–98.

Roberts, Michael. 'Sinhalaness and its Reproduction, 1232–1818,' in *The Sri Lankan Republic at Forty: Reflections on Constitutional History, Theory and Practice*, Vol. 1, ed. Asanga Welikala. Colombo: Centre for Policy Alternatives, 2012, 253–87.

Rogers, John D. 'Caste as a Social Category and Identity in Colonial Lanka,' *The Indian and Economic Social History Review* 41 (2004), 51–77.

Rogers, John D. 'Early British Rule and Social Classification in Lanka,' *Modern Asian Studies* 38 (2004), 625–47.

Ruddick, Andrea. 'National Sentiment and Religious Vocabulary in Fourteenth-Century England,' *The Journal of Ecclesiastical History* 60 (2009), 1–18.

Sahlins, Marshall. 'The Stranger-King: or, Elementary Forms of the Political Life,' in *Stranger-Kings in Indonesia and Beyond*, ed. Ian Caldwell and David Henley, special issue of *Indonesia and the Malay World* 36 (2008), 177–99.

Sahlins, Marshall. 'Alterity and Autochthony: Austronesian Cosmographies of the Marvellous,' *Hau: Journal of Ethnographic Theory* 2 (2010), 131–60.

Sahlins, Marshall. 'The Atemporal Dimensions of History: In the Old Kongo Kingdom, For Example,' unpublished paper.

Sarkar, H. 'The Kings of Sri Sailam and the foundation of the Sailendra Dynasty of Indonesia,' *Bijdragen tot de Taal-, Land- en Volkenkunde* 141 (1985), 323–38.

Schalk, Peter. 'Referents and Meanings of Siṃhala/Sīhaḷa/Ciṅkaḷam,' in *Kontinuitäten und Brüche in der Religionsgeschichte*, ed. Michael Stausberg. Berlin and Boston: De Gruyter, 2012, 549–56.

Schrikker Alicia, *Dutch and British Colonial Intervention in Sri Lanka, 1780–1815*. Leiden: Brill, 2007.

Scott, James C. *Domination and the Arts of Resistance: Hidden Transcripts*. New Haven: Yale University Press, 1990.

Seneviratne, H. L., ed. *Identity, Consciousness and the Past: Forging of Caste and Community in India and Sri Lanka*. Oxford: Oxford University Press 1997.

Sivasundaram, Sujit. 'Ethnicity, Indigeneity, and Migration in the Advent of British Rule to Sri Lanka, *American Historical Review* 115, 2 (2010), 428–52.

Sivasundaram, Sujit. *Islanded: Britain, Sri Lanka and the Bounds of an Indian Ocean Colony*. Chicago and London: University of Chicago Press, 2013.

Skilling, Peter. 'Theravāda in History,' *Pacific World*, Third Series 11 (2009), 61–93.

Smith, Anthony D. *National Identity*. London: Penguin, 1991.

Strathern, Alan. 'Sinhala Conciousness in the Kandyan Period 1590s to 1815 by Michael Roberts,' *Modern Asian Studies* 39 (2005), 1007–20.

Strathern, Alan. *Kingship and Conversion in Sixteenth-Century Sri Lanka*. Cambridge: Cambridge University Press, 2007.

Strathern, Alan. 'Towards the Source-Criticism of Sītāvakan Heroic Literature. Part 2: The *Sītāvaka Haṭana*: Notes on a Grounded Text,' *Sri Lanka Journal of the Humanities* 34 (2008), 45–72.

Strathern, Alan. 'Sri Lanka in the Long Early Modern Period: Its Place in a Comparative Theory of Second Millennium Eurasian History,' *Modern Asian Studies* 43 (2009), 815–64.

Strathern Alan, 'The Vijaya Origin Myth of Sri Lanka and the Strangeness of Kingship,' *Past and Present* 203 (2009), 3–28.

Strathern, Alan. 'The Role of Sinhala Group Identity in the "Sinhala Rebellion" Against Bhuvanekabahu VI (1469–77),' in *The Portuguese in the Orient*, ed. Gaston Perera. Kandy: International Centre for Ethnic Studies, 2010, 13–27.

Strathern, Alan. 'Treachery and Ethnicity in Portuguese Representations of Sri Lanka,' in *Engaging Colonial Knowledge: Reading European Archives in World History*, ed. Ricardo Roque and Kim Wagner. Basingstoke: Palgrave Macmillan, 2012, 217–34.

Strathern, Alan. 'Vijaya and Romulus: Interpreting the Origin Myths of Sri Lanka and Rome,' *Journal of the Royal Asiatic Society of Great Britain and Ireland* 24 (2013), 51–73.

Strathern, Alan. 'Religion and Empire,' in *The Encyclopedia of Empire*, ed. John M. MacKenzie. Oxford: Wiley-Blackwell, 2016.

Sundberg, Jeffrey. 'The Abhayagirivihāra's Pāṃśukūlika Monks in Second Lambakaṇṇa Śrī Laṅkā and Śailendra Java: The Flowering and Fall of a Cardinal Center of Influence in Early Esoteric Buddhism,' *Pacific World*, Third Series 16 (2014), 49–185.

Sundberg, Jeffrey and Rolf Giebel. 'The Life of the Tang Court Monk Vajrabodhi as Chronicled by Lü Xiang: South Indian and Śrī Laṅkān Antecedents to the Arrival of the Buddhist Vajrayāna in Eighth-Century Java and China,' *Pacific World*, Third Series 13 (2011), 129–222.

Tambiah S. J. *Buddhism Betrayed? Religion, Politics and Violence in Sri Lanka*. Chicago: University of Chicago Press, 1992.

Vimalananda, T. *The Great Rebellion of 1818*. Colombo: M. D. Gunasena, 1970.

Walters, Jonathan. 'Mahāsena at the Mahāvihāra: On the Interpretation and Politics of History in Pre-Colonial Sri Lanka,' in *Invoking the Past: The Uses of History in South Asia*, ed. Daud Ali. New Delhi: Oxford University Press, 1999, 322–66.

Walters, Jonathan. 'Buddhist History: The Sri Lankan Pāli Vaṃsas and their Community,' in *Querying the Medieval: Texts and the History of Practices in South Asia*, ed. Ronald Inden, Jonathan Walters and Daud Ali. New York: Oxford University Press, 2000, 99–164.

Watts, John. *The Making of Polities: Europe, 1300–1500*. Cambridge: Cambridge University Press, 2009.

Wickramasinghe, Nira. 'Many Little Revolts or One Rebellion? The Maritime Provinces of Ceylon/Sri Lanka between 1796 and 1800,' *South Asia: Journal of South Asian Studies* 32, 2 (2009), 177–88.

Wickremeratne, U. C. 'Lord North and the Kandyan Kingdom, 1798–1805,' *Journal of the Royal Asiatic Society of Great Britain and Ireland* 1 (1973), 31–42.

Winans, Edgar Vincent. *Shambala: The Constitution of a Traditional State*. Berkeley and Los Angeles: University of California Press, 1962.

# Index

CPSIA information can be obtained
at www.ICGtesting.com
Printed in the USA
BVOW11s0804080318
509887BV00022B/324/P

9 781911 307846